The Essential Guide to Flash Games

Building Interactive Entertainment with ActionScript 3.0

Jeff Fulton

Steve Fulton

DESIGNER TO DESIGNER™

an Apress® company

The Essential Guide to Flash Games
Building Interactive Entertainment with ActionScript
Copyright © 2010 by Jeff Fulton and Steve Fulton

ISBN-13 (pbk): 978-1-4302-2614-7

ISBN-13 (electronic): 978-1-4302-2615-4

Printed and bound in the United States of America 9 8 7 6 5 4 3 2 1

Trademarked names may appear in this book. Rather than use a trademark symbol with every occurrence of a trademarked name, we use the names only in an editorial fashion and to the benefit of the trademark owner, with no intention of infringement of the trademark.

Distributed to the book trade worldwide by Springer-Verlag New York, Inc., 233 Spring Street, 6th Floor, New York, NY 10013. Phone 1-800-SPRINGER, fax 201-348-4505, e-mail orders-ny@springer-sbm.com, or visit http://www.springeronline.com.

For information on translations, please e-mail info@apress.com, or visit http://www.apress.com.

Apress and friends of ED books may be purchased in bulk for academic, corporate, or promotional use. eBook versions and licenses are also available for most titles. For more information, reference our Special Bulk Sales–eBook Licensing web page at http://www.apress.com/info/bulksales.

The source code for this book is available to readers at http://www.apress.com. You will need to answer questions pertaining to this book in order to successfully download the code.

Credits

For Jeanne, Jacob, Ryan, and Justin

–Jeff Fulton

For Dawn, Rachel, Daphnie, and Kaitlyn

–Steve Fulton

Contents at a Glance

Contents

About the Authors

Jeff Fulton has been making and playing computer and video games as a hobby for over 30 years. In his early years, Jeff dreamed of programming games for a living, but he never considered a career as a professional game developer. Rather, he fashioned himself as a writer and filmmaker. After creating a handful of no-budget college films on video with friends, he discovered that he was just as drawn to the technical side of the process as he was to the creative side. The Atari ST computer that he and his brother Steve had used to create animations and title sequences for these films turned out to be the inspiration that pushed him toward professional game development. In 1991, Jeff read a series of game development articles by the great Llamasoft game developer Jeff Minter, in the back of ST Action magazine. This series of articles planted the seed of his future career. He was drawn to the colorful language, the exciting stories, and the wonderfully post-retro games that Minter described and created. With the understanding that game development was not just a creative pursuit, Jeff dropped all of his film classes at the university and took as many technical and business classes as he could find. After college, Jeff dove into game coding and development in his spare time while working during the day coding systems in Perl and C++ for a variety of business applications. When the web boom hit in the late 1990s, Jeff jumped at the chance to parley his skills into a job making kids' web sites and games for a large multinational corporation. In 2006, with over 200 games and sites under his belt, he and his brother Steve (also a game and site developer) started their own web site, www.8bitrocket.com. The goals of the site are to celebrate web and retro style games and to teach others the methods they had gathered from their considerable experience in game design, coding, and development.

Jeff's all time favorite games include Super Breakout (Atari 2600), River Raid (Atari 2600), Dragon Stomper (Atari 2600), Rally Speedway (Atari 800), Fort Apocalypse (Atari 800), Mule (Atari 800), Asteroids (Arcade), Ms. Pac-man (Arcade), Star Castle (Arcade), Phantasie (Atari ST), Megaroids (Atari ST), Oids (Atari ST), Anco Player Manager (Atari ST), Galaga (Arcade), Food Fight (Atari 7800), Tempest 2000 (Jaguar), Wolfenstein 3D (DOS), Medal Of Honor (PS1), Point Blank 2 (PS1), Duke Nuke 'Em 3D (DOS), System Shock 2 (PC), Tony Hawk Pro Skater (PS1), Half Life (PC), New Star Soccer (PC / Mac), and Baldur's Gate: Dark Alliance (PS2).

 A self-professed Atari nerd, **Steve Fulton** has wanted to make games as long as he can remember. While dabbling in both film school and rock journalism, Steve found his footing as a C++/Assembly language programmer in the early 1990s. However, after working several the client-server software companies that were crushed under the weight of the burgeoning World Wide Web, Steve saw the light in 1995 and started developing in HTML/Java and Perl/CGI. This shift led to very early (before the Web explosion) jobs creating web sites and interactive applications like chat, word searches, and simple games that utilized only HTML and server-side scripts. After developing web sites for small clients and large corporations alike for most of the 1990s, Steve's path led to developing customer-facing web sites for one of the world's largest entertainment companies. For the past ten years, he has worked on web based games and entertainment using a variety of technologies including Flash. Along with dozens of high-profile, high-traffic web sites, and web-based communities, Steve has designed, developed, or programmed hundreds of Flash applications and web sites, including dozens of single-player and multiplayer web-based games played over 1 billion times. Along with his brother Jeff, Steve runs the popular and influential Flash and retro game development and news site *www.8bitrocket.com*. The site is updated frequently with news, tutorials, demonstration games, experiments, and musing about Flash and the viral web game world.

Steve's favorite games of all-time are Breakout (Atari 2600), Asteroids (coin operated), Star Castle (coin operated) River Raid (Atari 2600), Castle Wolfenstein (Apple IIe), Galaga (coin operated), Time Pilot (coin operated), Star Wars (coin operated), MULE (Atari 800), Ultima IV (Atari 800), Temple Of Apshai (Atari 800), Dungeom Master (Atari ST), Oids (Atari ST), Food Fight (Atari 7800), Wizards's Crown (Atari ST), Anco Player Manager (Atari ST), Machine Bride of Pinbot (pinball coin operated) Dune 2 (PC), Fallout (PC), Desert Strike (Genesis), Tempest 2000 (Jaguar), Zolar Mercenary (Lynx), Roller Coaster Tycoon (PC), Baldur's Gate: Dark Alliance (PS2), Knights Of The Old Republic (PC), Final Fantasy 1 and 2(GBA), Wii Sports Resort (Wii), Mario And Luigi: Partners In Time (DS), Pinball Hall Of Fame: Williams Collection (Wii), Pac-Man Championship Edition (Xbox Live Arcade), Puzzle Quest (DS), Bookworm Adventures(PC), and Dragon Age (PC).

About the Technical Reviewer

Iain Lobb is a freelance Flash games developer and designer, and a nine-year veteran of London's hectic digital agency scene. Until early 2009, Iain was head of interactive at the award-winning studio Bloc, where he cocreated some of the best-loved games on the web, including ZW0K!, Stackopolis, Pop Pirates, and Meta4orce. Along the way, his work has picked up awards and nominations from the likes of BAFTA, the FWA, Cannes Lions, and NewGrounds, with Stackopolis winning the 2006 Webby award for best game.

Iain now runs his own game company, Dull Dude, where he develops games for clients, as well as creating original game ideas and characters.

Acknowledgments

Writing a book, especially a technical one, requires a team much larger than the author, or authors, in this case.

First, thanks to the incredible team at Apress / friends of ED: Ben who gave us the chance to prove ourselves; Kelly for putting up with the temperamental twins; Heather for making it read much better than it should; Iain Lobb for helping us to standardize and improve every aspect of our code. You guys rock!

We'd also like thank the teachers and mentors that helped us find our way including Mr. Hughes and Ms. Brown from Foster A. Begg Middle School; Mr. Scott, Mr. Lang, Mr Fredricks, Mr. Holland, Mr. Sumpter, and Ms. Staich from Mira Costa High School; Dr. Gessford and Dr. Godfrey from Long Beach State; Dave Robinson, Laurie Shammel, Myron Bowman, Tim Cashin, and Shel Klee from TXS; Mike Gitchel and Joe Loo from Investors Business Daily; and John Watson, Bruce Williams, and Tim Locke from the wild corporate world.

We want to thank the game developers, game journalists, and authors who have instructed and inspired us over the years including Nolan Bushnell, Al Alcorn, David Crane, Alan Miller, Ed Logg, Dan(i) Bunten, Ihor Wolosenko, David Heller, Chris Crawford, Bill Budge, Rob Fulop, Lord British, Winston Douglas Wood, all the guys from FTL, the Bitmap Brothers, Jeff Minter, Jeffery Stanton, Chris Sawyer, Katz/Kunkel/Worley, Steve Levy, Steven L. Kent, Tom Chick, Jeff Green, Johnny L. Wilson, Andrew Bub, Simon Carless, Ari Feldman, Jobe Makar, Gary Rosenzweig, Keith Peters, and Colin Moock. Plus, we thank all at Flash Game License, Mochi Media, Adobe, and Macromedia (R.I.P.)—especially Jonathan Gay, the inventor of Flash.

We also like to acknowledge the fellow game heads who have contributed to our love of video games including Carrie Lennihan, Alex Mortensen, Eric Barth, John and Richard Campi, Kenny Brown, Mike Jackson, Greg Dyer, Scott Johnson, Mike Foti, Evan Pershing, Jonas Sills, Wesley Crews, Brandon Crist, James Ku, Ian Legler, John Little, Dan Cady, Chris Cutler, Scott Delamater, Scott Jeppesen, Alan Donnelly, Mark "Icky Dime" Grossnickl, Richard "Mr. Atari ST" Davey, Richard "Squize" Myles, Oliver "nGfx" Sons, Dave "Retro Shoot" Munsie, Julian "LongAnimals" Scott, Tony "The Symbol" Pa, and everyone else on The Board, plus Ace the Super Villian and all of our friends at www.8bitrocket.com.

We'd also like to thank the rock bands without which we would not have made it through high school, college, and beyond: The Alarm & Mike Peters, Slade, Stiff Little Fingers, The Damned, The Business, Icicle Works, The Smithereens, The Hoodoo Gurus, Soul Asylum, Cactus World News, Minor Threat, Midnight Oil, CH3, Fugazi, The Gear Daddies, The Dead Milkmen, The Mr. T Experience, Naked Raygun, The Nils, All, The Descendents, TSOL, The Long Ryders, Drivin' N Cryin', Green Day, Big Drill Car, U2, Big Country, The Who, Social Distrotion, The Wonderstuff, The Sweet, The Equals, Love, The Replacements, Husker Du, The Shoes, Grant Hart, The Goo Goo Dolls, Pete Droge, Tom Petty, Material Issue, Weezer, Pearl Jam, The White Stripes, Daft Punk, LCD Soundsystem, 8 Bit Weapon, The Mooney Suzuki, the Gas Light Anthem, The Brady 6, Pain, Snow Pink, and many more. We'd also like to thank the filmmakers who have enlightened us, including John Hughes, Wes Anderson, Allen Moyle, Paul Feig, Judd Apatow, Mike White, Amy Heckerling, and Jason Reitman, plus Sid and Marty Croft. As well, we'd like to mention the authors who have written the books we love the most, including Donald J. Sobol, Robert A.

Arthur, Sue Townsend, Edward Packard, R.A. Montgomery, Paul Zindel, Judy Blume, Frank Portman, Nick Hornby, D.B. Weiss, Doug Stumpf, Steve Almond, Joe Meno, Mark Haddon, Sara Gruen, Chuck Klosterman, Dr. Seuss, Richard Scarry, and Bill Pete.

Finally, we'd like to thank our sister, Carol, for trying to teach us math on her chalkboard when we were just four years old, and our other sister Mari who was instrumental in helping us acquire our own Atari 2600 for Christmas in 1981. Thanks to Dad for purchasing the Atari 800 as a 1983 Christmas present, without which today we can only imagine that Steve would be the guitarist and I would be the bass player in a struggling retro punk band making terrible movies. Thanks to Mom for tolerating us reading the book Dr. C. Wacko's Miracle Guide to Designing and Programming Your Own Atari Computer Arcade Games before, during, and after church and for waiting long hours in the car as we copied public domain libraries from SBACE user group software library. Finally, love and thanks go to our wives, Dawn and Jeanne, for putting up with this process and supporting us unconditionally along the way and to our children, Rachel, Daphnie, Ryan, Kaitlyn, and Justin, for being the reason we work as hard as we do.

Preface

We are twin brothers who were born right at the beginning of the 1970s just about the same time the first video games were being created and marketed by people like Nolan Bushnell at Atari and Ralph Baer for Magnavox. While we did not know of these video game advances at the time, something exciting was obviously in the air in those years. As far back as we can remember, we have wanted to make our own games. We grew up just like most suburban kids of the 1970s—riding bikes, playing guns and ditch 'em at the school yard, and staying out all day only to come home when the street lights came on. There was never a lot of extra money in the household, so that meant we had to find creative ways to entertain ourselves. At a very early age, we started designing games to help fill the days.

First came sports contests. We spent many days conceiving two-player versions of nearly every sport imaginable on the 100-foot driveway that adorned our 1950s tract house. Not too long after, we graduated to experimenting with our dad's surplus batteries, wires, lights, motors, and potentiometers; we were trying to make anything electronic. Through trial and error, we made electric gadgets with blinking lights, switches, and running motors, and even crude pinball machines. Soon, almost any household item had the potential to become an interactive toy or game. We spent many days creating animated flip-books out of every paperback we could find. There was one full summer in the Fulton household during which you could not read any soft-cover book without being distracted by cartoons of exploding Tie-Fighters, flying arrows and text rearranging itself running up the side of every page. Toys did not escape this frenzy either. For example, an Etch-A-Sketch became our first "hand-held game development platform." By using scotch tape to create tracks and a digital watch, we created our own simple racing games and other activities.

These uber-analog game designs might have gone on ad infinitum, but something else was on the horizon. It seemed that just as soon as we had discovered a way to create new games out of our old toys, new experiences many times more interesting suddenly arrived on the scene. First came Star Wars in 1977, which basically made everything else irrelevant. All we wanted to do after seeing that movie was re-create Star Wars, think Star Wars, and be Star Wars. Then, a year or so later, the Space Invaders coin-operated game arrived in the arcades, and we were able to actually play Star Wars—or at least a reasonable facsimile.

By 1980, if we were not in an arcade playing Asteroids or Missile Command, we were designing our own pixelated arcade games on graph paper our dad brought home from Hughes Aircraft. Soon after, we taught ourselves BASIC and, in stolen minutes on a borrowed Apple IIe computer, starting writing our own primitive text-based games. By 1984, we had our own second-hand Atari 800 computer and had taught ourselves enough BASIC programming skills to try and create more elaborate games. We made sentence generators, game show simulations, a poker game, a horse racing contest, and even a small role-playing game. By the age of 14, we had both simultaneously discovered what we wanted do when we grew up— program computer games. We felt like we were naturals at programming and nothing could stop us.

However, things do not always turn out the way you plan them. In fact, those early successes led to more difficult times ahead. It was one thing to make a little game in BASIC, but it was another thing entirely to try to create a fast-action arcade game that was fun to play. As we moved from an 8-bit Atari 800 to a 16-bit Atari ST, programming only became more difficult. Balancing success in high school and college classes with learning lower level computer languages became a very time-intensive process. We managed to finish a game in 1989 with the STOS game creator for the ST. We made our first finished, compiled game—Zamboozal Poker Dice, complete with animated sprites and digitized sound. But the joy was short-lived. STOS, while powerful, was a shortcut that could not replace the solid programming skills we had not yet developed. As college got underway in earnest, our hobby programming projects fell by the wayside and soon were mostly forgotten. We never made a second game with STOS.

Eleven years later, after many false starts making games that rarely saw the light of day, plus detours dabbling in both indie filmmaking and music, we found ourselves in a completely different situation. In that time, we had both paid some dues in the development world, working for many years developing software in Perl, C, C++, and Assembly language. At that moment, in the year 2000, we were working together at a major corporation that manufactured products for kids, developing marketing web sites in HTML and ASP. With the need to create web-based games and activities growing daily, we were introduced to Flash 5 and its new programming language named ActionScript. With ActionScript, Flash had gone from a simple animation tool with some embedded timeline events into a real client application development platform. At first, though, we had a bit of consternation about the coding of ActionScript. Most of Flash 5 was based on timeline interactions with MovieClips. To us, this felt like STOS all over again. It was a quick way to create simple games but still a shortcut around a solid grounding in software development. Still, without a better answer, we dove into Flash 5 and set off to help define the next generation of interactive games on the World Wide Web.

The games we helped make in Flash 5 were pretty crude by today's standards, but cool for the time. We made puzzle games, click-fests, dress-up games, customization activities, and even a few action contests. With the advent of Flash MX, we moved to building entire web sites using the technology. Games now included streaming audio, loadable assets, and backend integration to save customizations beyond a single user session.

However, it was with Flash MX 2004 that things really started to take-off. ActionScript 2 provided a better programming language that was only hinted at in previous versions of Flash. Flash games could be designed like real software, using design patterns and object-oriented methodologies. The games we designed and built became ever more sophisticated with features like particle effects, parallax scrolling, and customizable levels. By the time Flash 8 was released, we were using raw bitmap data, tile sheets, and more complex physics and creating multiplayer games with technologies like Electrotanks' Electrosever 3.

Even though we were able to create some really nice games, things did not get really cool until Flash CS3 was released in 2007. CS3 included a completely rewritten programming language named ActionScript 3.0, which ran many times faster than ActionScript 2. All of a sudden, things like 3D effects and true fast-action arcade games (just like the ones we wanted to make as kids) were finally within our grasp. With ActionScript 3.0, we were able to bury our concerns about Flash being a shortcut. By carefully using ActionScript 3.0, not only could we create solid products based on sound development techniques, but we could write code that was portable to other platforms if need be.

Ten years, and hundreds of Flash games and projects later, we look back and wonder how things would have turned out if we had ActionScript 3.0 available to us back in 1989. Would we have made the same choices we made to get where we are today? How many more games would we have made?

Flash is a great tool, but you only get out what you put into it. In this book, we show how we make games in ActionScript 3.0 using techniques that we believe strike a supportable balance between Flash technology and sound coding practices. We love Flash and the freedom it has given us to exercise our creativity. If we seem overly enthusiastic about Flash and ActionScript 3.0, it is because it helped us make our childhood dreams of making video games come true. Our hope is that we can do the same for you.

Steve Fulton and Jeff Fulton

Layout Conventions

To keep this book as clear and easy to follow as possible, the following text conventions are used throughout.

Important words or concepts are normally highlighted on the first appearance in **bold type**.

Code is presented in `fixed-width font`.

New or changed code is normally presented in **`bold fixed-width font`**.

Pseudo-code and variable input are written in *`italic fixed-width font`*.

Menu commands are written in the form `Menu ➤ Submenu ➤ Submenu`.

Where I want to draw your attention to something, I've highlighted it like this:

Ahem, don't say I didn't warn you.

Sometimes code won't fit on a single line in a book. Where this happens, I use an arrow like this: ➡.

This is a very, very long section of code that should be written all on the same ➡

line without a break.

Part 1

The Basic Game Framework

In Part 1, you will learn how to create an optimized game framework.

Chapter 1

The Second Game Theory

Second game—what about the first game? Well, of course, you need to make your first game, but inevitably your first game will not be all that you hoped it to be. It just happens. Don't blame yourself. You will cut features for time, get frustrated, and sometimes not even finish. However, this is the most important thing we want you to do: finish your game, and move onto the next. It is the only way you will get better at making games. This is the **second game theory**.

This book is set up in a way that we believe will help you finish a game and move onto your *second* game. It is important to us, as developers and teachers of Flash and Flex as well as game design and programming, that developers actually finish their games. We love to play great Flash games online. Every time you finish a game, no matter how good it is, you get little bit better at your craft. When you get better, we get better games to play. We get more innovative games to play. The craft of making online Flash games advances a little bit more. Your job is to finish something, learn from it, and move onto the next project. Move onto your *second* game, and when you've done that, move onto your third, then your fourth, then your fifth until Flash games are in your blood, and the whole Internet is buzzing in anticipation of your next masterpiece.

However, your *first* game should not be considered a prototype, a beta, or an alpha version. It should be considered a finished product. If not, you may always be stuck on your *first* game, and that can lead to *development hell*: a place where games are tortured to the brink of life but never born.

Making games is an iterative process

We believe that making games in an *iterative* process on two levels. First, the process of making each individual game is iterative. You code your game, refine it, code it, and refine it, over and over until you mold something that you finally finish. Many times, when you start a game project, you only have a general idea of where you are going. After each development iteration, the destination gets clearer until you finally reach something that is playable.

Making games is different to making most other types of software for one main reason: the initial requirements do not always equate into a successful product. In other words, the initial thoughts that went into designing a game do not always produce something worth playing.

For example, if you planned to make a piece of software that burned files to CD, you can be fairly certain what your destination will be when you are finished. Once files actually get on the CD, and those files can then be read again by a CD-ROM drive, your job is pretty much complete. You may add other features, but the requirements you set out to accomplish with your program have been met.

This clear endpoint is not always true with a game. The best and most intricate requirements laid out for a game might not equal a product that anyone wants to play. For example, simply wanting a game to be playable is not enough, and it's rare that you will get it right the first time through. That is where the iterations come in. Small changes and updates and tweaks and brainstorms within the development cycle help to turn a pile of programming into a game worth playing.

However, these iterations can all be taken to higher level. Besides the process of making individual games, the actual craft of making games as a whole is also iterative. With each game you finish, you improve your code, processes, libraries, object models, game ideas, game designs, and so on. That is why it is so important to get to your *second* game. Writing your *second* game means you will improve on your first, which can then be improved by your third.

Figures 1-1 and 1-2 are examples of the second game theory. Zeno Fighter (Figure 1-1) was a first attempt at a rock shooter style game. Retro Blaster (Figure 1-2) was a further iteration, extending the basic game idea. However, without completing Zeno Fighter, there would have never been a Retro Blaster. Zeno Fighter was not a prototype, an alpha, or a beta version; it was a finished game. The entire game development cycle was utilized in its creation. When it was finished, the code base and lessons learned were synthesized into Retro Blaster, a second game.

Just to be clear, though, a second game does not have to be in the same type of genre as the first game. In fact, in this book, we will create many different genres of games, all using the second game theory of iteration and improvement.

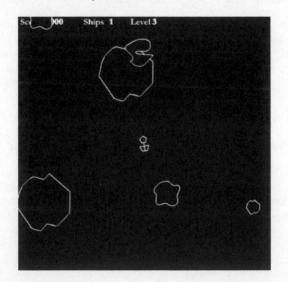

Figure 1-1. A Zeno Fighter screen shot

Figure 1-2. A Retro Blaster screen shot

Understanding why you want to make games

Now, take a step back for minute and think about this question: *Why do you want to make games?*

You just bought a book about making games in Flash, so you probably have thought about this question in the past. Even if you have not, think about it now. It is important to know why you are doing this. You are about to embark on a great adventure, but it's an adventure that has an endpoint. There is a finish line for you to cross. To get there, you need to know why you started the race.

- Do you want to learn some advanced ActionScript 3.0?
- Do you need to make a game for work?
- Do you need to make a game for school?
- Was it because you want to impress your friends with your ninja-like programming skills?
- Was it because you have always had the burning desire to create a game and never had the chance?
- Are you an experienced programmer or game programmer who wants to learn how to make games in ActionScript 3.0?

Understanding why you want to make games is important, because it is the only way you will be able to succeed. Starting the process of making a game can be fairly easy. A would-be game developer can spend a couple of hours reading a chapter in a book and typing in some code, and then feel like good headway has been made. However, the difficult part is getting beyond that point and devoting time to finishing the game. We want to help you get beyond this stumbling block by making the process of finishing your first game, and moving onto your second, third, and so on as painless as possible.

5

There is no time like the present to program a game and see it come to life. In fact, there has never been a time with better tools, more mature delivery mechanisms, or even a wider audience for games than there is today. Since some fairly easy avenues now exist to both distribute and get feedback on your work, there is no reason to let a half-finished first game sit on your hard drive any longer, and there is no reason not to move on from there and make your second game.

Who this book is for

Anyone!

OK, well, anyone who wants to make games. Actually, anyone who wants to make games and has some programming experience, preferably with an objected-oriented language like ActionScript 2 or 3.0 (AS2 or AS3), C++, C#, Java, or JavaScript. Since we want to dive right into making some games, we are not going to spend much time trying to teach you the basics of programming. Intuitive learners (like yourself, of course) should be able to pick up most of the major programming concepts by following the code and descriptions, but we can't slow down to dwell on them too much. We want to make some games, and to make games, we need to write some AS3 code.

So we're not starting at the beginning?

Sure, we are. We start at the beginning of programming games in AS3. Other sources can teach you the basics of programming in AS3, such as *Foundation ActionScript 3.0 for Flash and Flex* (ISBN: 978-1-4302-1918-7) and *Foundation Game Design with Flash* (ISBN: 978-1-4302-1821-0), both from friends of ED. In this book, we want to teach you the basic concepts behind writing some reusable game code to make some enjoyable games that can be built on, modified, and improved.

Having said that, we will need to teach you some basic AS3 concepts as we go along. Again, intuitive readers should be able to pick up the concepts with ease, so we will move quickly over them.

Comparing AS3 and AS2

"AS3" is short for ActionScript 3.0, and it is the core programming language for Flash and Flex games and applications. It is a complete rewrite of ActionScript 2, so if you only know AS2, you will have to bring yourself up to speed on AS 3.0 programming basics before starting this book.

Flash has included a simple programming language since Flash 4 was released in the late 1990s. Macromedia introduced ActionScript with Flash 5, and the language evolved through several minor iterations to the final version of ActionScript 2 with Flash 8. ActionScript 2 was a good language. You could develop with object-oriented methodologies, use event models, access bitmaps, and so on. However, it was a rewrite of a rewrite, and performance suffered because of all the legacy functions that it had to support and because the code was interpreted rather than compiled. As you can imagine, this backward compatibility, while a great advantage for application support, also limited the performance of the Flash Player running in the web browser.

At that point, the Flash development team went back the drawing board to rewrite ActionScript as a brand new language. They rebuilt it from the ground up, attempting to fix many of the problems that AS2 (and its associated baggage) carried with it. When they were finished, they had created a language in AS3 that had significant advantages over AS2.

You can't stick with AS2 because it's dead

There's no getting away from the fact that AS3 can be more complicated than AS2. Many tutorials online that are still written with AS2 code; you'll find many game functions and engines that are written in AS2; and many developers are still very comfortable with AS2. So why change? The main problem with AS2 is that it is *dead*. Adobe does not want to support it any longer and has been working very hard to convince Flash developers to move up to AS3. In fact, AS3 has many big advantages over AS2 for game developers; here are a few of them:

- **Speed**: AS3 simply executes much faster than AS2. A brand new Flash virtual machine was created to run AS3 applications, and it has been optimized for their execution with a just-in-time compiler. The most limiting factor for the performance of many games is the speed of the machine they are running on. With AS3, execution speed is two to five times faster than AS2 (depending on who you ask and what tests they have performed).

- **Error handling/debugging**: With AS2, error handing and debugging was a trial-and-error process that involved many trace statements and much frustration. AS3 adds a more powerful compiler that looks for errors in logic as well as syntax and a runtime error system to help diagnose problems with code that compiles perfectly but does not work when executed.

- **Advanced event model**: Since many games are not simple procedural programs that sit and wait for user input, but instead create a world where events occur that need to be handled within your program, a solid event model is essential. While AS2 used events, its event model was not very mature. With AS3, events are built into the system, making their use seem natural and, at the same time, helping developers design software that more logically and is easier to maintain.

There are many other differences too, but these are some of the ones that will affect you the most when developing games in AS3. For more information, check the Adobe AS3 migration reference located at http://help.adobe.com/en_US/AS3LCR/Flash_10.0/index.html?migration.html&all-classes.html.

What you need to use this book

You need to own a copy of Flash CS3 or above or of Flex or Flash Builder, or you can download the Flex SDK and a programming editor (i.e., Flash Develop). Internet access is also required to download software and to implement some of the viral strategies near the end of this book.

We will make every attempt to describe how the code in this book will work in various development tools, but at some point, you will have to translate a bit of the included code to suit your development tastes.

The craft of making games in the AS3 game framework

In this book, we will create a **game framework** and then proceed to create a set of games that use it. However, this framework is not a **game engine**. A game engine is more like a finished piece of code that you would use as a black box to make a game; it's more about instantiation and configuration than software engineering. An engine has functions that you use, so you don't have to write the code yourself.

A game framework, on the other hand, is used to help you organize your code and game functions. It can start out fairly simple but can be expanded and changed as your games get more complicated. However, the basic pieces of the framework stay the same.

You can use engines with a game framework, but the framework itself is used as way to hang everything else on. However, our framework does a bit more. It is going to make your games run efficiently so they can really shine!

While we will be presenting our own game framework in this book, you should only consider it a starting point for your own work. Once you get good at making games, you will be able to customize this framework to suit your own needs (or even make your own framework from scratch). The purpose of this book is *not* to evangelize our own framework, but instead, to give you the tools and understanding to create your own games, at the same time illustrating that a reusable framework can help you create that all important second game, third game, and so on.

Object-oriented methodology

Much of recent modern programming development involves both object-oriented. Since the game framework is based on some these concepts, we will offer a short explanation them and why we think they are necessary. While these concepts require a bit of preplanning to use them effectively, they are also flexible enough that you can alter your design as you develop your game and discover problems and features you did not consider when you started.

Object-oriented (OO) methodology is a software development concept that gives developers a way to organize their software into logical parts that both act as their own entities and relate to other objects through clearly defined interfaces. There are many features of OO design, but we will mostly only use encapsulation and inheritance.

Encapsulation

Encapsulation is the idea you can break down your program into component parts (**objects**) that in turn can contain properties (**variables**) and methods (**functions**) that can be concealed or revealed to other objects. We will use this extensively within our game framework. Many game framework services (e.g., the Sound Manager) will be updated throughout this book, but because they keep a common interface, newer versions will be compatible with games that were built with older framework objects. Encapsulation makes this possible.

We will be using the concept of **packages** with encapsulation. A package is finite grouping of classes that are used for a similar purpose. The game framework itself will be package, and each game will have a package of its own. Classes in a package have the benefit of "knowing" about the other classes in the same package, so they do not have to be explicitly imported.

Inheritance

Inheritance is the idea that a more specialized subclass can be created from another object by extending the first object, and only defining new and altered properties and methods. For example, creating a basic Screen class might work most of the time (e.g., **Title Screen** or **Instructions Screen**). However, you might need some different methods and properties to support a Between Levels screen. We use inheritance in the game framework to effectively reuse objects and simplify game development.

You will see that by using inheritance we will significantly reduce the amount of cut-and-paste code that needs to be created when you start a new game project. We have found (on our own projects) that using inheritance has reduced our development time for new projects by 10–30 percent depending on the scope of the work. That means that not only is inheritance a good idea, it will actually save you money if it is used effectively.

Using object-oriented design to make games

Using OO design with game development involves breaking your game idea down to component parts and defining how those parts interact. For a game, you might sit down for a short time and consider the objects you will need when developing.

Let's pretend we are making a space rocks style space shooter. For that type of game, you might think about the following parts:

- Player ship
- Player shots
- Asteroids (3 sizes)
- UFO (2 sizes)
- UFO shots
- Scoreboard

In a very basic sense, you have just created your object model. It's not code, but you could quickly mock up these objects to organize your thoughts. However, you can do more to help design your game before you write any code. Objects in objected-oriented methodology contain both properties (variables) and methods (functions). You can organize your design further by thinking of variables and methods that your objects might contain.

The player ship might contain

- Properties

  - Speed
  - Angle
  - Rotation

- Functions

  - turn()
  - thrust()
  - fire()

Player shots might contain

- Properties
    - Speed
    - Angle
    - Life

- Functions
    - `move()`

Asteroids might contain

- Properties

    - Size
    - Speed
    - Angle
    - Rotation

- Functions

    - `move()`
    - `explode()`

UFOs might contain

- Properties

    - Size
    - Speed
    - Angle
    - Firing rate
    - Functions
    - `shoot(0)`
    - `move()`

UFO shots might contain

- Properties

    - Speed
    - Angle
    - Life

- Functions

    - `move()`

The scoreboard might contain

- Properties

  - Score
  - Ships left
  - Level

- Functions

  - updateScore()
  - updateShips()
  - updateLevel()

You can see that type of planning can illuminate most of the parts that will be necessary to make a working game. Beyond that, you can take this design and use it to create actual working parts for your game. While this process may seem a bit complicated now, as we start to create games, you will see how this type of planning and design can help immensely when you build games in AS3. You will also notice that games can be very tricky to develop. When a game needs to be high performance or needs to fit into a particular file size, many of these rules and ideas can go out the window. We will try to keep as close as possible to these principles, but where we diverge, there will be good reasons for it that we'll explain.

Creating the basic game framework

Now, we are going to create a very basic version of our game framework to illustrate how games will be created in the rest of this book. This framework will be updated, altered, improved, and changed as the games get more intricate, but we need to start someplace, and this is it. We will create the code for a very simple game. The game itself is not really consequential, but the structure of the code is very important. However, don't worry if you don't get this right away, as we will be covering these topics over and over as we progress. Here are the basic elements of the simple game.

This game is no more than a simple program to test to see if the mouse button has been clicked. However, this very simple game will be used to illustrate the major parts of the game framework. The first of these is the **state loop**. Our game can be in one of three states: an initialization state, a play state, and a game over state. The game decides what it needs to do by testing to see which state it is currently running within. This constant testing is the state loop. For example, in the play state, the game waits for the user to click the mouse button, and when the button is clicked, the state is changed to game over. The state loop is constantly checking which state the game's in, so when it sees this change it takes the appropriate action and runs the game over code. This iterative checking of the state loop is controlled by a **game timer**, the second of the core parts of our framework. Finally, when the mouse button is clicked, a function is called that will process the click. This is the **event model**, and forms the last core part of our framework. Let's look over those three parts in more detail.

State loop

The state loop is the traffic cop that will direct the game program into a set of actions. A very basic version of this can be created using some constants and a switch statement. Constants are values that never change. They are declared just like variables, but without the var keyword. The following code demonstrates an example of this. The var keyword is for variables, which, by definition, can change value when your program is executing.

The following code sets up the states the class will use. These states will control the flow of the game. We make them const variables, so they will be considered static and can be accessed from other classes without creating an instance of this class.

```
public static const STATE_INIT:int = 10;
public static const STATE_PLAY:int = 20;
public static const STATE_GAME_OVER:int  = 30;
public var gameState:int = 0;
```

The first three statements represent the possible states that our game could execute. We set them as constant values, because our game will depend on these values never changing since the game will use these states to control the on-screen action. Again, this example is very simple; your game could have many more states and, in fact, have multiple states within a single state (see Chapters 8 and 9 for examples of these kinds of nested states).

The last statement, public var gameState:int = 0;, creates a variable to hold the current game state that will be tested in the state loop.

The following function, gameLoop(), acts as the main game loop. It will be called repeatedly by the game timer (see the following code). The switch statement decides what the game should do based on the current state (held in the gameState variable).

```
public function gameLoop(e:Event):void {
    switch(gameState) {
        case STATE_INIT :
            initGame();
            break
        case STATE_PLAY:
            playGame();
            break;
        case STATE_GAME_OVER:
            gameOver();
            break;
    }
}
```

This state loop was developed for a very specific reason. Without a state loop, you might have to keep track of the program flow with multiple Boolean (true or false) variables. This can work for a simple game, but for something more complex, it can become a nightmare. If just one Boolean is not set correctly, the whole system falls apart. The state solves this problem by limiting the game to one single state (with possible nested states) that can be executing at any one moment.

Game timer

The Game timer calls the state loop at regular intervals to check the state of the game. Notice that the previous code has a function named gameLoop(). By its name, you'd be right in thinking that it needs to be called iteratively to execute the game logic. The game timer provides this functionality by calling gameLoop() every time an ENTER_FRAME event occurs. The code looks like this:

```
public function Game() {
addEventListener(Event.ENTER_FRAME, gameLoop);
gameState = STATE_INIT;
}
```

This code will call the gameLoop function every time the EnterFrame event is fired in Flash. This is the most basic game timer we will introduce in this book. It's a legitimate game timer, but as you will see later, there are ways to make it work much more efficiently. However, this simple event illustrates perfectly how a game timer works. The game timer repeatedly calls the gameLoop function on a regular basis to run the game. We have also set the gameState to STATE_INIT, which will have our gameLoop() function call initGame() the next time it is called.

Event model

Events tell the game that something interesting has happened so it can perform an action because of them. AS3 contains many built-in events, and you can create your own, which we will do later in this book. For this simple example, we are going to listen for (or more accurately, observe) the event that is created when someone clicks the mouse button. While this event might not be very exciting, this basic example will be reused and modified for most other events that we use, either internal to AS3 or custom ones that we create. We'll now look at the code for setting up a listener for an event.

The initGame() function defines the event model for this game. The following line of code states that our class will listen for the mouse button click:

```
stage.addEventListener(MouseEvent.CLICK, onMouseClickEvent);
```

The first parameter (MouseEvent.CLICK) is the name of the event, and the second parameter (onMouseClickEvent) is the function to call when the event is observed. We also set the clicks variable to 0 and the gameState to STATE_PLAY so the gameLoop() function will know that to do the next time it is called.

```
public function initGame():void {
    stage.addEventListener(MouseEvent.CLICK, onMouseClickEvent);
    clicks = 0;
    gameState = STATE_PLAY;
}
```

The playGame() function is called by gameLoop() if gameState is equal to STATE_PLAY. This function simply checks the clicks variable to see if it is greater than 10. If so it sets the gameState to STATE_GAME_OVER.

```
public function playGame() {
    if (clicks >=10) {
        gameState = STATE_GAME_OVER;
    }
}
```

The following function is called when the mouse click event occurs. It increases the clicks variable every time the function is called.

```
public function onMouseClickEvent(e:MouseEvent):void {
  clicks++;
  trace("mouse click number:" + clicks);
}
```

Finally, the endgame() function is called by the gameLoop() when the gameState is set to STATE_GAME_OVER by playGame(). Just to get use to the process, we call removeEventListener() for the MouseEvent.CLICK event. We do this because event listeners should be cleaned up when a game is finished. We then set the gameState to STATE_INIT, so the game will automatically start over, and we trace out the text game over just to tell the player what is happening.

```
public function gameOver():void  {
    stage.removeEventListener(MouseEvent.CLICK, onMouseClickEvent);
    gameState = STATE_INIT;
    trace("game over");
}
```

Now, we will put all of this code together to make the very simple game. The code we have just described will all be collected into a class named Game. This code can be compiled with Flex or dropped directly into the Flash IDE as the document class (the main class that will be executed when a program is run) for an empty AS3 application.

Here is simple model of how this program will flow:

1. The Game class is instantiated.

2. The game constructor is called.

3. The game constructor sets up the game timer to be called every frame.

4. The game constructor sets the gameState to STATE_INIT to set up the game.

5. The game timer calls gameLoop() after the next frame is fired in Flash or Flex.

6. gameLoop() decides which function to call based on the gameState variable.

7. initGame() is called to set up the game. The event listener for the mouse is created, and variables are reset.

8. initGame() sets the gameState to STATE_PLAY.

9. The game timer calls gameLoop() after the next frame is fired in Flash or Flex.

10. gameLoop() decides which function to call based on the gameState variable.

11. playGame() called to check the game over condition (clicks >= 10).

These steps will go on forever unless the MouseEvent.Click event is observed from (you guessed it) someone clicking the mouse. Once that happens, this is the flow:

12. If clicks is greater than 10, playGame() changes gameState to STATE_GAME_OVER.

13. The game constructor sets the gameState to STATE_INIT to set up the game.

14. The game timer calls gameLoop() after the next frame is fired in Flash or Flex.

15. gameLoop() decides which function to call based on the gameState variable.

16. gameOver() is called to clean up the game and start over.

In short, when the game is executed, it simply counts the number of times the left mouse button is clicked. The new playGame() function keeps count of the mouse clicks and changes the gameState variable when the number reaches 10.

Believe it or not, we are now ready to present the entire code listing for the game. This is the most basic game possible. All the player has to do is click the mouse button 10 times to win!

Here are some things to notice about the AS3 code listing.

- package {}: Unlike AS2 classes, all AS3 classes need to be part of a package. If you don't specify a package name, AS3 will simply use a default package. We will create a package later in the book, but for now leave this as-is.
- import: In AS3, you must import all necessary classes that are not in the same package as your class. This is different from AS2 where some classes were included by default.
- public class Game extends flash.display.MovieClip{}: A document class needs to inherit from the full class path to MovieClip. This is different from AS2 where you could just extend from MovieClip

And that's all you need to know! Here is the full code of this very first game:

```
package {
import flash.display.MovieClip;
import flash.events.Event;
import flash.events.MouseEvent;
import flash.display.*;
import flash.events.*;
import flash.net.*;

public class Game extends  flash.display.MovieClip{


    public static const STATE_INIT:int = 10;
    public static const STATE_PLAY:int = 20;
    public static const STATE_GAME_OVER:int = 30;

    public var gameState:int = 0;
    public var clicks:int = 0;

    public function Game():void {
        addEventListener(Event.ENTER_FRAME, gameLoop);
        gameState = STATE_INIT;
    }

    public function gameLoop(e:Event):void {
        switch(gameState) {
            case STATE_INIT :
                initGame();
                break
            case STATE_PLAY:
                playGame();
                break
            case STATE_GAME_OVER:
                gameOver();
                break;
```

```
        }
    }

    public function initGame():void {
        stage.addEventListener(MouseEvent.CLICK, onMouseClickEvent);
        clicks = 0;
        gameState = STATE_PLAY;
    }

    public function playGame() {
        if (clicks >=10) {
            gameState = STATE_GAME_OVER;
        }
    }

    public function onMouseClickEvent(e:MouseEvent) {
        clicks++;
        trace("mouse click number:" + clicks);
    }

    public function gameOver():void  {
        stage.removeEventListener(MouseEvent.CLICK, onMouseClickEvent);
        gameState = STATE_INIT;
        trace("game over");
    }
    }
}
```

Testing the game

Why not go ahead and test the game?

This might be a good time to download the code for the book from the web address printed on the back cover.

If you are new to AS3 and you are using the Flash IDE, you can test this game as follows:

1. Save the code as Game.as.

2. Create a new Flash AS3 .fla document named clickgame.fla in the IDE, and save it in the same directory as Game.as.

3. Set the **Document** property in the Flash IDE for your new .fla document to **Game**.

4. In the **Modify ➤ Document** menu, set the dimensions for the game to 550×400.

5. Test the game by pressing Ctrl/Cmd+Enter or using the **Control ➤ Test Movie** menu option.

6. You can find the code for this game in /source/projects/ch1_clickgame in the downloaded source.

Note that if you are interested in making games without the Flash IDE, we will start that process in Chapter 2. Also, we will reuse this method for nearly every game in this book, so if you forget, refer to this chapter to review.

Exciting, huh? OK, so this game is not going to win any awards, but it's the basis of much bigger things. It includes the three core parts of our game framework that we discussed earlier and a couple more gems that might not be obvious at first. For example, notice, in the gameOver function, that we remove the mouse click event listener. It is good practice to always clean up your event listeners. A very common source of memory leaks in AS3 is event listeners that are not removed. If you don't remove listeners, you will find that your games run slower the longer they are played. If you build those basics correctly at the beginning, you'll find your life will be much easier later on when your games get more complex.

Your Second Game: Balloon Saw

So now that you have completed a very simple first game, let's use those ideas to create an actual game: your *second game*. Balloon Saw is a game in which the player controls a spinning blade and tries to pop as many balloons as possible. If the player misses 5 balloons, the game is over. We will expand the previous game framework for this project.

Assets for this game

We will discuss ideas on creating your own assets for your games later in this book, so for now, we will just describe what we will be using to create Balloon Saw. This might be a good time to download the code for the book from the web address printed on the back cover. You can find these assets in /source/projects/ch1_balloons/ballons.fla.

Graphics

We need only three graphical assets for this game, and all are MovieClips in the .swf library:

- enemy: The "enemies" in this game are balloons. This MovieClip contains five frames, each with a differently colored balloon on a keyframe. The colors are red, blue, green, yellow, and purple. Figure 1-3 shows this asset.

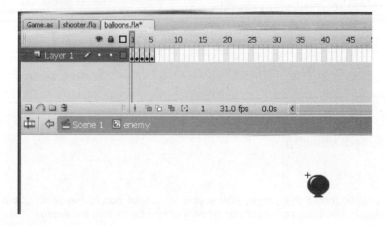

Figure 1-3. The enemy MovieClip

- `player`: The player is saw blade looking object (see Figure 1-4). It is a static asset, but we will rotate it in code to make it look like it is spinning. We have centered the graphic for the player inside the `MovieClip` so that it when it rotates it will look like it is spinning from the center.

Figure 1-4. The player MovieClip

- `back()`: We will supply a 550 × 400 vector background to the screen as a background (see Figure 1-5). We use a background image for two reasons: First, the background color you set in the Flash IDE can be altered by the Flash `<embed>`, which in some cases can mess up your game, especially on viral web sites that are not careful with how they post your game. Second, a background image is more flexible and can be used for ambient animations and other special effects.

Figure 1-5. The back MovieClip

Sounds

We use only one sound in this game. The sound is named pop in the library, and it makes a standard popping noise. Users will hear this when the saw blade hits a balloon.

Settings

This game requires following setting for your AS3 project:

- **Dimensions**: 550 × 400
- **Frames per second**: 30

The Code

With the graphics and sound assets in your library, you are now ready to create the Balloon Saw game.

For this example, we need only a single Game.as class that will be the document for our Flash movie, as we did previously. Since the code for this game is fairly limited, we will start by showing you all of its code, highlighting the differences from the first example in bold. We will then describe what is happening.

```
package {
    import flash.display.MovieClip;
    import flash.events.Event;
    import flash.events.MouseEvent;
    import flash.display.*;
    import flash.events.*;
    import flash.geom.Rectangle;
    import flash.media.Sound;
    import flash.text.*;

    public class Game extends  flash.display.MovieClip{

    public static const STATE_INIT:int = 10;
    public static const STATE_PLAY:int = 20;
    public static const STATE_END_GAME:int = 30;

    public var gameState:int = 0;
    public var score:int - 0;
    public var chances:int = 0;

    public var bg:MovieClip;
    public var enemies:Array;
    public var player:MovieClip;
    public var level:Number = 0;

    public var scoreLabel:TextField = new TextField();
    public var levelLabel:TextField = new TextField();
    public var chancesLabel:TextField = new TextField();
    public var scoreText:TextField = new TextField();
    public var levelText:TextField = new TextField();
    public var chancesText:TextField = new TextField();

    public const SCOREBOARD_Y:Number =380;

    public function Game() {
        addEventListener(Event.ENTER_FRAME, gameLoop);
```

```
        bg = new BackImage();
        addChild(bg);

        scoreLabel.text = "Score:";
        levelLabel.text = "Level:";
        chancesLabel.text ="Misses:"
        scoreText.text ="0";
        levelText.text ="1";
        chancesText.text ="0";

        scoreLabel.y = SCOREBOARD_Y;
        levelLabel.y = SCOREBOARD_Y;
        chancesLabel.y = SCOREBOARD_Y;
        scoreText.y = SCOREBOARD_Y;
        levelText.y = SCOREBOARD_Y;
        chancesText.y = SCOREBOARD_Y;
        scoreLabel.x = 5;
        scoreText.x  = 50;
        chancesLabel.x = 105;
        chancesText.x = 155;
        levelLabel.x = 205;
        levelText.x = 260;

        addChild(scoreLabel);
        addChild(levelLabel);
        addChild(chancesLabel);
        addChild(scoreText);
        addChild(levelText);
        addChild(chancesText);

        gameState = STATE_INIT;
    }

    public function gameLoop(e:Event):void {
        switch(gameState) {
            case STATE_INIT :
            initGame();
            break;
        case STATE_PLAY:
            playGame();
            break;
        case STATE_END_GAME:
            endGame();
            break;
        }
    }

    public function initGame():void {

        score = 0;
        chances = 0;
        player = new PlayerImage();
        enemies = new Array();
```

```
            level = 1;
            levelText.text = level.toString();
            addChild(player);
            player.startDrag(true,new Rectangle(0,0,550,400));
            gameState = STATE_PLAY;
    }

        public function playGame():void {
            player.rotation += 15;
            makeEnemies();
            moveEnemies();
            testCollisions();
            testForEnd();
        }

        public function makeEnemies():void {
            var chance:Number = Math.floor(Math.random() *100);
            var tempEnemy:MovieClip;
            if (chance < 2 + level) {
                tempEnemy = new EnemyImage()
                tempEnemy.speed = 3 + level;
                tempEnemy.gotoAndStop(Math.floor(Math.random()*5) + 1);
                tempEnemy.y = 435;
                tempEnemy.x = Math.floor(Math.random() * 515)
                addChild(tempEnemy);
                enemies.push(tempEnemy);
            }
        }

        public function moveEnemies():void {
            var tempEnemy:MovieClip;
            for (var i:int = enemies.length -1;i >= 0;i--) {
                tempEnemy = enemies[i];
                tempEnemy.y -= tempEnemy.speed;
                if (tempEnemy.y < -35) {
                    chances++;
                    chancesText.text = chances.toString();
                    enemies.splice(i,1);
                    removeChild(tempEnemy);
                }
            }
        }

        public function testCollisions():void {
            var sound:Sound = new Pop();
            var tempEnemy:MovieClip;
            for (var i:int = enemies.length -1;i >= 0;i--) {
                tempEnemy = enemies[i];
                if (tempEnemy.hitTestObject(player)) {
                    score++;
                    scoreText.text = score.toString();
```

```
            sound.play();
            enemies.splice(i,1);
            removeChild(tempEnemy);
        }
    }
}

public function testForEnd():void {
    if (chances>= 5) {
        gameState = STATE_END_GAME;
    } else if(score > level*20) {
        level++;
        levelText.text = level.toString();
    }
}

public function endGame():void {
    for(var i:int = 0; i < enemies.length; i++) {
        removeChild(enemies[i]);
    }
    enemies =[];
    player.stopDrag();
    }
  }
}
```

OK, we fibbed a bit. There is *a lot* of new code. You didn't think an AS3 game would be *that* easy, did you? In reality, this example is not much more complicated than the first. We are still calling a game loop on a timer and waiting for user input. We have just added a few more elements to make it into a *bona fide* Flash game.

Balloon Saw gameplay

Why don't you take this code and compile it in your chosen development tool to see what it looks like before we continue? If you are using the Flash IDE, recall that you can test this game as follows:

1. Save the code as Game.as.

2. Create a new Flash AS3 .fla document in the IDE, and save it in the same directory as Game.as.

3. Set the **Document** property in the Flash IDE for your new .fla document to **Game**.

4. In the **Modify ➤ Document** menu, set the dimensions for the game to **550 × 400**.

5. Test the game with Ctrl/Cmd+Enter or by using the **Control ➤ Test Movie** menu option. Figure 1-6 shows the game screen as you should see it.

Note, if you interested in making games without the Flash IDE, that we will start that process in Chapter 2.

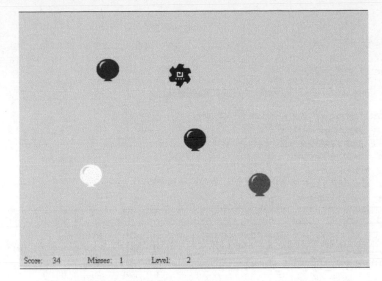

Figure 1-6. Balloon Saw game screen

In this game, the player controls the spinning blade with the mouse. Balloons fly up from the bottom of the screen. The player must move the spinning saw blade into the balloons to pop them and make them disappear from the screen. As the player continues to pop balloons, the level increases, and the balloons start to move faster. If the player misses five balloons, the game is over. There is no end game sequence, so restarting means quitting the game and running it again.

Breaking down the Balloon Saw code

We'll now take apart the code one section at a time and explain what is happening in detail. We have left the unchanged code in these code segments so you can view it in context, but we won't describe much of this code as it was just covered in the last section.

Imports

First, we must import the necessary classes into our Game class. The flash.geom.Rectangle class is used to create a bounding box for the mouse; flash.media.Sound is used to play the pop() sound, and flash.text will be used to create TextField objects for our scoreboard.

```
package {
    import flash.display.MovieClip;
    import flash.events.Event;
    import flash.events.MouseEvent;
    import flash.display.*;
    import flash.events.*;
    import flash.geom.Rectangle;
    import flash.media.Sound;
    import flash.text.*;
```

Variables

Now, we move to the code inside our Game class. The first thing we do is define variables to hold the player's score (the renamed clicks variable from the first game), chances (the number of missed balloons), and level.

```
public class Game extends  flash.display.MovieClip{

    const STATE_INIT:int = 10;
    const STATE_PLAY:int = 20;
    const STATE_END_GAME:int = 30;
    public var gameState:int = 0;
    public var score:int = 0;
    public var chances:int = 0;
    public var level:Number = 0;
```

Next, we need to create some variables to hold the objects that we will create while the game is being played. bg will hold the background image—BackImage()—from the library. enemies is an array that will hold all the instances of EnemyImage() (the balloons) that we create for the player to pop. The player is an instance of PlayerImage() from the library.

```
    public var bg:MovieClip;
    public var enemies:Array;
    public var player:MovieClip;
```

Next, we will create TextField objects for displaying the score, level, and chances (misses). We will now refer to this as the scoreboard, even though it is only logically a scoreboard with all the elements defined individually. We will need two TextField objects for each item we want to display, a label and place to display the value:

```
    public var scoreLabel:TextField = new TextField();
    public var levelLabel:TextField = new TextField();
    public var chancesLabel:TextField = new TextField();
    public var scoreText:TextField = new TextField();
    public var levelText:TextField = new TextField();
    public var chancesText:TextField = new TextField();
```

Finally, we need to create one other new variable; we need to define a y position on the screen for the scoreboard TextField objects, and we want this to be at the bottom of the screen. Since the height of the screen is 400, we will set this to 380 so that they will appear just at the bottom of the screen.

```
    public const SCOREBOARD_Y:Number = 380;
```

We created this variable because when the y value of the scoreboard changes, all of the elements move. Using y will save us from editing each line of code that contains the y values for the scoreboard. The x value always changes per item, so we leave that one alone.

Game constructor

Now, we move onto the constructor for Game. The first thing we do is create an instance of BackImage and add it to the screen using addChild(). We need not set the (x,y) location, because it will automatically be placed at (0,0), exactly where we want it.

```
public function Game() {
    addEventListener(Event.ENTER_FRAME, gameLoop);
    bg = new BackImage();
    addChild(bg);
```

Next, we move on to the scoreboard. Unfortunately, adding text to the screen programmatically in AS3 takes a few more lines of code than we would like. This seemingly daunting set of code that follows really only sets the initial values for the scoreboard (**Score: 0**, **Level: 1**, and **Misses: 0**) and places those items on the screen. We set all the x values individually across the screen, while the y value for each item's location is the SCOREBOARD_Y we created a earlier. After we set all the values for the TextFields, we add them to the display list using addChild(TextField) for each one. Since we are using the Flash IDE, we could simply drag these items to the stage, but instantiating them in code makes this easily portable to Flex or even other languages.

```
scoreLabel.text = "Score:";
levelLabel.text = "Level:";
chancesLabel.text ="Misses:"
scoreText.text ="0";
levelText.text ="1";
chancesText.text ="0";

scoreLabel.y = SCOREBOARD_Y;
levelLabel.y = SCOREBOARD_Y;
chancesLabel.y = SCOREBOARD_Y;
scoreText.y = SCOREBOARD_Y;
levelText.y = SCOREBOARD_Y;
chancesText.y = SCOREBOARD_Y;
scoreLabel.x = 5;
scoreText.x  = 50;
chancesLabel.x = 105;
chancesText.x = 155;
levelLabel.x = 205;
levelText.x = 260;

addChild(scoreLabel);
addChild(levelLabel);
addChild(chancesLabel);
addChild(scoreText);
addChild(levelText);
addChild(chancesText);

gameState = STATE_INIT;
}
```

Initializing the game loop

Since we set the state to STATE_INIT at the end of the constructor, we know that initGame() will be called the next time the gameLoop() is called. initGame() simply resets all the values to what they need to be to start playing. We initialize score, level, and chances and update the levelText.text property to the value of level.toString() (because levelText.text requires a String).

Next, we create an instance of `PlayerImage()` from the library (this is the saw blade graphic), and add it to the screen using `addChild(player)`. Since the saw blade will be controlled with the mouse, we will do this the simplest way possible: having the mouse drag the saw around the screen by attaching player to the mouse. We do this with the `player.startDrag()` function, which accepts two parameters:

- `lockCenter`: This object is locked to center of the mouse cursor. We want this, so we set it to `true`.
- `bounds`: This defines a `Rectangle` (the `flash.geom.Rectangle` class) that specifies where the mouse can go on the screen. This parameter is not required. However, we have added it, but we have set it to the full bounds for the screen. Why? Because it might be interesting to tweak the bounds in this game to make it work more like a traditional catch game where the player is restricted to x movement only. You could do this by setting the bounds to `0,0,550,0`.

Last, we create the `enemies` array that will hold the balloons (`EnemyImage`) objects that the saw will try to pop.

```
public function initGame() {
    score = 0;
    chances = 0;
    level = 1;
    levelText.text = level.toString();
    player = new PlayerImage();
    addChild(player);
    player.startDrag(true,new Rectangle(0,0,550,400));
    enemies = new Array();
    gameState = STATE_PLAY;
}
```

The playGame() function

The `playGame()` function is called from the `gameLoop()`.It is the workhorse `gameState` for Balloon Saw. The first thing this function does is update the `rotation` of player 15 degrees. This makes the player's saw look like it is rotating—just like a real saw blade. Setting the `rotation` property of a `MovieClip` is very handy way to make objects appear to spin in AS3. `rotation` is set in degrees. A positive number rotates clockwise, a negative number, counter-clockwise.

The next call to `makeEnemies()` checks to see if an enemy should be created, and if so, put it on the screen. `moveEnemies()` updates the y location for the balloons and removes them if they have left the screen. The `testCollisions()` functions checks to see if the player's saw is touching any objects in the `enemies` array and, if so, handles that event. Finally, `testForEnd()` tests to see if the `level` needs to be increased or the game needs to end. All of these functions will be described in detail after the code.

```
public function playGame() {
    player.rotation += 15;
    makeEnemies();
    moveEnemies();
    testCollisions();
    testForEnd();
}
```

Making the Balloons

In many games, you will need to have some kind of logic that makes things happen without user interaction. In an action game like Balloon Saw, this logic usually centers around creating enemies that they player must fight. The timing, number, and placement of these enemies are the main ingredients in adding both challenge and difficulty to the game. As you might imagine, there are many ways to tackle the job of creating these objects. These methods range from completely random to exactly the same every time the game is played. For Balloon Saw, we are using a completely random method. However, throughout this book, we will introduce many different ways to accomplish this task, each suited to a particular game.

The makeEnemies() function performs a simple test to see if a balloon needs to be created on a frame. The frequency of balloons is controlled by a random value and the current game level. First, we retrieve a random number between 0 and 99 by calling Math.floor(Math.random() *100) and put that into the chance variable. Next, we test chance to see if it is less than 2 + level (e.g., 3 on level 1, 4 on level 2, or 5 on level 3). As the level increases, the chance for an enemy balloon to be created increases as well.

When we drop into the if statement, it is time to create a balloon to put on the screen. We do this by creating a temporary variable named tempEnemy that we will configure. First, we create a new instance of EnemyImage() and set tempEnemy to its value. Next, we set the speed, which we create as a dynamic variable. Flash MovieClip objects can be assigned new variables at runtime, and that is a very flexible feature. However, the trade-off is that they take more system memory then a regular class property. We are using one here because doing so is easy for this example and we don't have to create a separate Enemy class (something we will do later in this book). We set the speed dynamic variable to 3 + level, which means that as the level increases, the balloons will move up the screen faster, thus making the game a bit harder.

Our EnemyImage MovieClip has five frames, each with a different colored balloon. We randomly choose one of these colors and jump to it using tempEnemy.gotoAndStop (Math.floor(Math.random()*5)+1);. These colors are is just for effect, but in a more elaborate game, different colored balloons could be used for things such as bonuses or extra chances.

Next, we set the x and y values for the initial placement of the balloon. The y value is always 435, which means it will start just off the bottom of the screen. The x value is a random number between 0 and 514. The balloon graphic in EnemyImage() is 35 pixels across, and the registration point is set to 0,0. This will allow the balloons to appear at a random x location but still remain fully on the screen. If we used a random value up to 550 (the width of the Flash movie), some balloons could appear partly or completely off the screen. For a game that tracks how many objects a player has missed, this would be unfair. Finally, we use addChild() to put the new balloon into the display list and push it into the enemies array so we can track it during the game.

```
public function makeEnemies() {
    var chance:Number = Math.floor(Math.random() *100);
    if (chance < 2 + level) {
        var tempEnemy:MovieClip;
        tempEnemy = new EnemyImage()
        tempEnemy.speed = 3 + level;
        tempEnemy.gotoAndStop(Math.floor(Math.random()*5)+1);
        tempEnemy.y = 435;
        tempEnemy.x = Math.floor(Math.random()*515)
        addChild(tempEnemy);
```

```
        enemies.push(tempEnemy);
    }
}
```

Moving balloons

Another core function of an action game is to move objects on the screen. We will create a function that controls the movement of all of the objects in the game (except the player, which is attached to the mouse). While this game only has one set of objects to move (the balloons), this structure can be (and later, will be) used for multiple types of objects in a single game.

The moveEnemies() function loops through the enemies array, updating each balloon's y position. Since the balloons are moving up the screen, we subtract the speed from each balloon's y property. If a balloon has reached a y position of –35, we remove it from the enemies array and from the screen using removeChild(). Notice that the for loop we use counts backward (from enemies.length-1 to 0). You will see this logic many times in this book. Iterating backward through arrays is a very useful tool in games, especially when you are looping through an array and possibly removing items from it. If you looped forward and removed items, errors will be created because the length of the array would change as items are removed from it.

```
public function moveEnemies() {
    var tempEnemy:MovieClip;
    for (var i:int = enemies.length-1;i >= 0;i--) {
        tempEnemy = enemies[i];
        tempEnemy.y -= tempEnemy.speed;
        if (tempEnemy.y < -35) {
            chances++;
            chanceText.text = chances.toString();
            enemies.splice(i,1);
            removeChild(tempEnemy);
        }
    }
}
```

Testing collisions between the saw and balloons

Now, we get to the heart of this game—testing to see if any of the objects are touching each other. A core function of many games is **collision detection**. Collision detection is the process of testing to see if objects are touching each other and, if so, processing the changes to those objects. Collision detection is not a single algorithm; it is a whole class of algorithms that are suitable for different circumstances. For this game, we will be using a very simple version of collision detection built into AS3.

Here, we get to the good news and the bad news. The good news is that AS3 has the same functionality of older versions of ActionScript: the hitTest() method of MovieClip for testing collisions. It's called MovieClip.hitTestObject() now, but it works pretty much the same as the old hitTest(). You pass a reference to another MovieClip object to see if there is a collision. In our game, we test a balloon (represented by tempEnemy) to see if it has hit the player: tempEnemy.hitTestObject(player). Like its predecessor, hitTestObject() is both a blessing and a curse. It's blessing because it's really easy to implement. It's curse because it doesn't really work that well for games. hitTestObject() uses **bounding box collision detection**, which means that it detects objects touching based on an invisible box that represents the extreme bounds of any pixel in the image. See Figure 1-7.

Figure 1-7. Bounding boxes colliding (boxes shown for illustration only)

For square objects, bounding box collision works fine, but for objects that have curves, spikes, and so on, it doesn't really work at all. We used bounding box collision detection for this game because it is quick, but later in this book, we will show you multiple other ways to detect in a more precise manner collisions (including using pixel-perfect collision detection, which would be more appropriate for this game). By the way, there is also a MovieClip.hitTestPoint() method that tests if an object has reach a particular (x,y) coordinate on the screen, but we will leave that one for your own personal explorations.

This function iterates backward through the enemies array, testing each one to see if they have collided with player. If they do collide, we update the score by 1 point, and increase the text value in the TextField by one, and then remove the balloon from the enemies array with enemies.splice(i,1) and from the screen using removeChild(tempEnemy).

The other interesting thing we do in this function is play a sound. We create an instance of the Pop sound from the library as sound and then call sound.play() every time a balloon is popped. This is the simplest way to play a sound. It works, but this method lacks any way to control the volume and other properties of the sound that is played. We will discuss other ways to manage sounds as you progress through this book.

```
public function testCollisions() {
    var sound:Sound = new Pop();
    var tempEnemy:MovieClip;
    for (var i:int=enemies.length-1;i>=0;i--) {
        tempEnemy = enemies[i];
        if (tempEnemy.hitTestObject(player)) {
            score++;
            scoreText.text = score.toString();
            sound.play();
            enemies.splice(i,1);
            removeChild(tempEnemy);
        }
    }
}
```

Ending the game

We have gone through most of code now, and only a couple things are left to talk about. The first is the function testForEnd(). This function is called by the gameLoop() to test for the level or game end. First, it tests to see if the game has ended. We do this by checking chances to see if it is great than 5. If so, we set gameState to STATE_END_GAME, which will then call endgame() (described later in this section) the next time gameLoop() is called. If the game is not over, we test to see if the level should be increased (thus making the game harder). We do this by testing the score to see if it is greater than 20 * level. Since we give the player only one point per balloon, it is easy to test when a level ends and another begins. If a player needs to pop 20 balloons per level, we know to increase the level (level++) when that player has popped 20 balloons multiplied by the number of the level (e.g., 20 equals level 2, and 40 equals level 3).

```
public function testForEnd() {
if (chances >= 5) {
   gameState = STATE_END_GAME;
} else if(score > level * 20) {
   level ++;
   levelText.text = level.toString();
}
}
```

Finally, endGame() is called when the gameSate is set to STATE_END_GAME. All this function does is remove all the enemies from the screen and then stay static. You will need to relaunch the game to play again. We will discuss ways to easily start games, end games, and transition levels as this book progresses.

```
public function endGame() {
   for(var i:int = 0; i < enemies.length; i++) {
      removeChild(enemies[i]);
      enemies = [];
   }
   player.stopDrag();
}
```

So that's it. Balloon Saw is a pretty simple game. However, as an illustration of game loop, state machine, and handler of multiple objects and user input, it's a pretty good starting point for your further explorations into AS3 games.

Creating your third game: Pixel Shooter

Before we move on to creating a more efficient and complex game framework in Chapter 2, why don't we try to create another type game based on Balloon Saw. We won't discuss this one in quite the same detail as Balloon Saw; instead, we'll highlight the major differences and let you explore the rest. This game changes up the Balloon Saw code just enough to create something very different, but it's based on the same ideas. Because of that, it is a perfect illustration of second game theory and the iterative process of making games.

Pixel Shooter game design

Pixel Shooter is very basic shoot 'em up. Alien ships enter the screen from the top, and the player's job is to shoot them with missiles. The player controls a ship with the mouse, and fires missiles with the mouse button. The speed of the alien ships move increases as the game progresses. If an alien touches the player's ship, it is destroyed. The player loses when his/her ships have been depleted.

Pixel Shooter graphics

We will have four MovieClips in this game, each one stored in the .swf library.

This might be a good time to download the code for the book from the web address printed on the back cover. You can find these assets in /source/projects/ch1_shooter/shooter.fla.

The first is exported as a class named ExplodeImage. It has three frames, each created a single .gif image. The MovieClip is structured so that each animation graphical image takes two frames. The last frame is blank, with a stop() action. This means the MovieClip will play and then stop on the seventh frame, which is blank. We will test for this frame in our code to see when the explosion is finished and can be removed from the screen. See Figure 1-8.

Figure 1-8. Explosion frames (top) and the explosion MovieClip (bottom)

The other three graphics we will need in this game follow and are shown in Figure 1-9:

- PlayerImage: The ship the player controls
- EnemyImage: The alien ships the player is trying to shoot
- MissileImage: The missiles the player fires

Figure 1-9. PlayerImage, EnemyImage, MissileImage

Pixel Shooter sounds

We will use two sounds for the game, and both will go into the `.swf` library and will be exported as the following classes:

- Explode: An explosion sound for when the aliens are destroyed
- Shoot: The sound of the pixel ship's cannon

Pixel Shooter code

The entire code listing for Pixel Shooter follows. Since we used Balloon Saw as the basis for Pixel Shooter, we have highlighted the code that is different from that game.

```
package {
    import flash.display.MovieClip;
    import flash.events.Event;
    import flash.events.MouseEvent;
    import flash.display.*;
    import flash.events.*;
    import flash.geom.Rectangle;
    import flash.media.Sound;
    import flash.text.*;

    public class Game extends  flash.display.MovieClip{

        public static const STATE_INIT:int = 10;
        public static const STATE_START_PLAYER:int = 20;
        public static const STATE_PLAY_GAME:int = 30;
        public static const STATE_REMOVE_PLAYER:int = 40;
        public static const STATE_END_GAME:int = 50;

        public var gameState:int = 0;
        public var score:int = 0;
        public var chances:int = 0;

        public var bg:MovieClip;
        public var enemies:Array;
        public var missiles:Array;
        public var explosions:Array;
        public var player:MovieClip;
        public var level:Number = 0;

        public var scoreLabel:TextField = new TextField();
        public var levelLabel:TextField = new TextField();
        public var chancesLabel:TextField = new TextField();
        public var scoreText:TextField = new TextField();
```

```
public var levelText:TextField = new TextField();
public var chancesText:TextField = new TextField();

public const SCOREBOARD_Y:Number = 5;

public function Game() {
    addEventListener(Event.ENTER_FRAME, gameLoop);
    bg = new BackImage();
    addChild(bg);
    scoreLabel.text = "Score:";
    levelLabel.text = "Level:";
    chancesLabel.text ="Ships:";
    scoreText.text ="0";
    levelText.text ="1";
    chancesText.text ="0";

    scoreLabel.y = SCOREBOARD_Y;
    levelLabel.y = SCOREBOARD_Y;
    chancesLabel.y = SCOREBOARD_Y;
    scoreText.y = SCOREBOARD_Y;
    levelText.y = SCOREBOARD_Y;
    chancesText.y = SCOREBOARD_Y;
    scoreLabel.x = 5;
    scoreText.x  = 50;
    chancesLabel.x = 105;
    chancesText.x = 155;
    levelLabel.x = 205;
    levelText.x = 260;

    scoreLabel.textColor =0xFF0000;
    scoreText.textColor = 0xFFFFFF;
    levelLabel.textColor =0xFF0000 ;
    levelText.textColor = 0xFFFFFF;
    chancesLabel.textColor = 0xFF0000;
    chancesText.textColor= 0xFFFFFF;

    addChild(scoreLabel);
    addChild(levelLabel);
    addChild(chancesLabel);
    addChild(scoreText);
    addChild(levelText);
    addChild(chancesText);


    gameState = STATE_INIT;
}

public function gameLoop(e:Event) {
    switch(gameState) {
        case STATE_INIT :
            initGame();
            break
        case STATE_START_PLAYER:
            startPlayer();
```

33

```
         break;
      case STATE_PLAY_GAME:
         playGame();
         break;
      case STATE_REMOVE_PLAYER:
         removePlayer();
         break;
      case STATE_END_GAME:
         break;
      }
   }

public function initGame() {
      stage.addEventListener(MouseEvent.MOUSE_DOWN, onMouseDownEvent);
      score = 0;
      chances = 3;
      enemies = new Array();
      missiles = new Array();
      explosions = new Array();
      level = 1;
      levelText.text = level.toString();
      player = new PlayerImage();
      gameState = STATE_START_PLAYER;
}

public function startPlayer() {
      addChild(player);
      player.startDrag(true,new Rectangle(0,365 ,550,365));
      gameState = STATE_PLAY_GAME;
}

   public function removePlayer() {
      for(var i:int = enemies.length-1; i >= 0; i--) {
         removeEnemy(i);
      }
      for(i = missiles.length-1; i >= 0; i--) {
         removeMissile(i);
      }
      removeChild(player);
      gameState = STATE_START_PLAYER;
   }

   public function playGame() {
      makeEnemies();
      moveEnemies();
      testCollisions();
      testForEnd();
   }

   public function makeEnemies() {
      var chance:int = Math.floor(Math.random() *100);
      var tempEnemy:MovieClip;
      if (chance < 2 + level) {
```

```
                tempEnemy = new EnemyImage()
                tempEnemy.speed = 1 + level;
                tempEnemy.y = -25;
                tempEnemy.x = Math.floor(Math.random()*515)
                addChild(tempEnemy);
                enemies.push(tempEnemy);
            }
        }

        public function moveEnemies() {
            var tempEnemy:MovieClip;
            for (var i:int = enemies.length-1;i>=0;i--) {
                tempEnemy = enemies[i];
                tempEnemy.y+=tempEnemy.speed;
                if (tempEnemy.y > 435) {
                    removeEnemy(i);
                }
            }
            var tempMissile:MovieClip;
            for (i=missiles.length-1;i>=0;i--) {
                tempMissile = missiles[i];
                tempMissile.y-=tempMissile.speed;
                if (tempMissile.y < -35) {
                    removeMissile(i);
                }
            }

            var tempExplosion:MovieClip;
            for (i=explosions.length-1;i>=0;i--) {
                tempExplosion = explosions[i];
                if (tempExplosion.currentFrame >= tempExplosion.totalFrames) {
                    removeExplosion(i);
                }
            }
        }

        public function testCollisions() {
            var tempEnemy:MovieClip;
            var tempMissile:MovieClip;
            enemy: for (var i:int=enemies.length-1;i>=0;i--) {
                tempEnemy = enemies[i];
                for (var j:int = missiles.length-1;j>=0;j--) {
                    tempMissile = missiles[j];
                    if (tempEnemy.hitTestObject(tempMissile)) {
                        score++;
                        scoreText.text = score.toString();
                        makeExplosion(tempEnemy.x, tempEnemy.y);
                        removeEnemy(i);
                        removeMissile(j);
                        break enemy;
                    }
                }
            }

            for (i=enemies.length-1;i>=0;i--) {
```

```
                tempEnemy = enemies[i];
                if (tempEnemy.hitTestObject(player)) {
                    chances--;
                    chancesText.text = chances.toString();
                    makeExplosion(tempEnemy.x, tempEnemy.y);
                    gameState = STATE_REMOVE_PLAYER;
                }
            }
        }

        public function makeExplosion(ex:Number, ey:Number) {
            var tempExplosion:MovieClip;
            tempExplosion = new ExplosionImage();
            tempExplosion.x = ex;
            tempExplosion.y = ey;
            addChild(tempExplosion);
            explosions.push(tempExplosion);
            var sound:Sound = new Explode();
            sound.play();
        }

        public function testForEnd() {
            if (chances <= 0) {
                removePlayer();
                gameState = STATE_END_GAME;
            } else if(score > level*30) {
                level++;
                levelText.text = level.toString();
            }
        }

        public function removeEnemy(idx:int) {
            removeChild(enemies[idx]);
            enemies.splice(idx,1);
        }

        public function removeMissile(idx:int) {
            removeChild(missiles[idx]);
            missiles.splice(idx,1);
        }

        public function removeExplosion(idx:int) {
            removeChild(explosions[idx]);
            explosions.splice(idx,1);
        }


        public function onMouseDownEvent(e:MouseEvent) {
            if (gameState == STATE_PLAY_GAME) {
                var tempMissile:MovieClip = new MissileImage();
                tempMissile.x = player.x + (player.width/2);
                tempMissile.y = player.y;
                tempMissile.speed = 5;
                missiles.push(tempMissile);
                addChild(tempMissile);
                var sound:Sound = new Shoot();
```

```
        sound.play();
    }
  }
 }
}
```

Just like you did with Balloon Saw, why don't you take this code and create a .swf with your preferred development tools that you can test?

Again, if you are using the Flash IDE, you can test this game as follows:

1. Save the code as Game.as.

2. Create a new Flash AS3 .fla document in the IDE, and save in the same directory as Game.as.

3. Set the Document property in the Flash IDE for your new .fla document to Game.

4. In the Modify ➤ Document menu, set the dimensions for the game to 550 × 400.

5. Test the game by pressing Ctrl/Cmd+Enter or using the Control ➤ Test Movie menu option.

And again, if you are interested in making games without the Flash IDE, we will start that process in Chapter 2.

When you do this, you should see a game screen something like Figure 1-10.

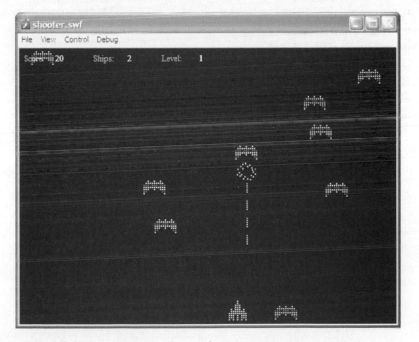

Figure 1-10. A Pixel Shooter screen shot

Pixel Shooter is a simple arcade game where waves of faster and faster aliens fly down toward the player's ship. The player's ship is controlled with the mouse, and missiles are fired with the left button. When a missile hits an enemy ship, instead of having the ship just disappear as enemies did in Balloon Saw, we will display an explosion on the screen.

For a game of this type, we will need to track a few more things than Balloon Saw. Besides enemies, we must also keep track of and move missiles and explosions. In addition to testing collisions between the player's ship and the enemies, we will need to test collision between the missiles and the enemies. This time, a collision between an enemy and the player's ship results in the player losing a chance, not gaining points. Points are scored when missiles hit enemies. We will also be counting down the player's ships as they are destroyed, not counting up misses.

Pixel Shooter code highlights

We are not going to cover every line of Pixel Shooter, but we will discuss the major changes we have made to the code to iterate a catch style game like Balloon Saw into a shoot 'em up.

New variables

We do not need many new variables to turn Balloon Saw into Pixel Shooter, and the ones we do need are variations on variables that already existed.

The first two new variables are game states. We need both of these to help us start and restart the player's ship on the screen. In Balloon Saw, the player's ship was never destroyed, so we never had to restart it. However, in Pixel Shooter the player's ship can be destroyed, so we need to handle that situation. With do that with STATE_START_PLAYER and STATE_REMOVE_PLAYER.

```
const STATE_START_PLAYER:int = 20;
const STATE_REMOVE_PLAYER:int = 40;
```

The next two variables are arrays that will hold the new objects types that we need to account for in this game: missiles (fired by the player) and explosions (when an alien ship is hit with a missile).

```
public var missiles:Array;
public var explosions:Array;
```

Starting and restarting the player

Since we need to start and restart the player's ship, we also need to handle these states in our game loop. For STATE_START_PLAYER, we call a newly created function named startPlayer(). For STATE_REMOVE_PLAYER, we call removePlayer().

```
        public function gameLoop(e:Event) {
            switch(gameState) {
                case STATE_INIT :
                    initGame();
                    break
                case STATE_START_PLAYER:
                    startPlayer();
                    break;
                case STATE_PLAY_GAME:
                    playGame();
                    break;
                case STATE_REMOVE_PLAYER:
```

```
            removePlayer();
            break;
        case STATE_END_GAME:
            break;
        }
    }
```

The startPlayer() function adds the player object to the screen with addChild() and then attaches it to the mouse using startDrag(). The main difference here is that the box that the player must stay within is at the bottom of the screen, like a traditional top-down shooter.

```
    public function startPlayer() {
        addChild(player);
        player.startDrag(true,new Rectangle(0,365 ,550,365));
        gameState = STATE_PLAY_GAME;
    }
```

The removePlayer() function actually does a bit more than you might think. Since we will be calling removePlayer() when the player's ship has been hit by an alien or when the game is over, we can also remove all the enemies, missiles, and explosions on the screen. This will make it appear like the level is resetting. One drawback to this is that while we remove the player from the screen, we then call startPlayer() (by setting the gameState to STATE_START_PLAYER) immediately, which will put the player back on the screen. We don't have time to show an explosion or make it look like the player has left the playing field. While this limitation is OK for this little game, it's really not an elegant way to show the player the intended result. Later in this book, we will discuss strategies around creating these nuances that will make your games seem much more like polished products.

```
    public function removePlayer() {
        for(var i:int = enemies.length-1; i >= 0; i--) {
            removeEnemy(i);
        }
        for(i = missiles.length-1; i >= 0; i--) {
            removeMissile(i);
        }
        removeChild(player);
        gameState = STATE_START_PLAYER;
    }
```

Tracking multiple objects

In Balloon Saw, we only had to move one type of object, the enemy balloons. In Pixel Shooter, we need to move three. Other than that, the code should look pretty familiar. The enemies now move down, so we update each y value by adding the value of speed to it, and we remove the enemy when it reaches the bottom of the screen. Missiles on the other hand, move almost exactly like the balloons from Balloon Saw: they move up the screen and are removed when they reach the top.

The explosions though, work a bit differently. Recall that the explosion_image MovieClip from the library has seven frames in it, with a stop(); in the last frame. Since explosions don't move, the only way we know when to remove them is when they have reached their last frame. Since every MovieClip has a property of currentFrame and totalFrames (the last frame) that you can test, we can do this with this line of code:

```
if (tempExplosion.currentFrame >= tempExplosion.totalFrames{}
```

Here's the complete object-tracking code:

```
public function moveEnemies() {
    var tempEnemy:MovieClip;
    for (var i:int = enemies.length-1;i>=0;i--) {
        tempEnemy = enemies[i];
        tempEnemy.y+=tempEnemy.speed;
        if (tempEnemy.y > 435) {
            removeEnemy(i);
        }
    }
    var tempMissile:MovieClip;
    for (i=missiles.length-1;i>=0;i--) {
        tempMissile = missiles[i];
        tempMissile.y-=tempMissile.speed;
        if (tempMissile.y < -35) {
            removeMissile(i);
        }
    }

    var tempExplosion:MovieClip;
    for (i=explosions.length-1;i>=0;i--) {
        tempExplosion = explosions[i];
        if (tempExplosion.currentFrame >= tempExplosion.totalFrames) {
            removeExplosion(i);
        }
    }
}
```

Firing missiles

Firing missiles is the one entirely new function of Pixel Shooter that we did not evolve from Balloon Saw. Since the player will fire missiles with the mouse button, we need to add an EventListener to the Game class so that it will receive mouse event messages. We do this in the initGame() function. When the mouse is clicked, we call a function named onMouseDownEvent().

```
public function initGame() {
    stage.addEventListener(MouseEvent.MOUSE_DOWN,onMouseDownEvent);
    …
}
```

The onMouseDownEvent() function is where we will create missiles that are fired by the player. The first thing we do is check to see if the gameState is STATE_PLAY_GAME. That is the only state in which missiles can be fired. If the gameState is STATE_PLAY_GAME, we create a missile object in much the same way we created objects and pushed them into the enemies array, except this time, they go into the missiles array. We also play the Shoot() sound, to give the player feedback that their button press worked and a missile will appear very soon.

```
public function onMouseDownEvent(e:MouseEvent) {
    if (gameState == STATE_PLAY_GAME) {
        var tempMissile:MovieClip = new MissileImage();
        tempMissile.x = player.x + (player.width/2);
```

```
            tempMissile.y = player.y;
            tempMissile.speed = 5;
            missiles.push(tempMissile);
            addChild(tempMissile);
            var sound:Sound = new Shoot();
            sound.play();
        }
    }
```

Detecting collisions on multiple types of objects

For Balloon Saw, we had to check to see only if the player touched any of the objects in the enemies array. For Pixel Shooter, we need to check two types of collisions:

- Enemies and missiles
- Enemies and the player

We need to do this in two different loops. The first loop tests the enemies array against each missile by nesting two for loops inside each other. First, we create a for loop that iterates through all the enemies (backward) and tests each enemy against all the missiles in the missiles array, iterating those backward as well.

For the collision test, we use the now familiar function hitTestObject() with

if (tempEnemy.hitTestObject(tempMissile)) { }

If we detect a hit, we call createExplosion() (passing the x,y location of the enemy so we know where to put the explosion on the screen), update the score, and remove the missile and enemy objects from the screen. The last line, break enemy;, is very important. It sends the execution back to the enemy: for (var i=enemies.length-1;i>=0;i--) for loop. This enemy: code is called a **label**. We use this functionality often to break out of nested loops during collision detection, but it might be confusing. The basic idea is that this label (or break) methodology allows you to get out of a loop when necessary. We need to do this because both the tempEnemy and tempMissile have been removed from the screen and from the enemies and missiles arrays. If we continue in the nested loop, we will test against values that don't exist any longer, and AS3 will throw an error. This construct might appear to be like a "go to" statement, but it really is not. It's more like saying "break out of this nested loop AND get me the next item from the main loop."

```
public function testCollisions() {
    var tempEnemy:MovieClip;
    var tempMissile:MovieClip;
    enemy: for (var i:int=enemies.length-1;i>=0;i--) {
        tempEnemy = enemies[i];
        for (var j:int = missiles.length-1;j>=0;j--) {
            tempMissile = missiles[j];
            if (tempEnemy.hitTestObject(tempMissile)) {
                score++;
                scoreText.text = score.toString();
                makeExplosion(tempEnemy.x, tempEnemy.y);
                removeEnemy(i);
                removeMissile(j);
            break away;
            }
        }
    }
}
```

We also need to test the player against the enemies. This test is much like the test we made in Balloon Saw with balloons against the player. The difference is that in Balloon Saw, the player scored points in this loop. In Pixel Shooter, the player's ship is destroyed. We need to handle that event by decrementing the chances variable and setting the gameState to STATE_REMOVE_PLAYER.

```
        for (i=enemies.length-1;i>=0;i--) {
    tempEnemy = enemies[i];
    if (tempEnemy.hitTestObject(player)) {
        chances--;
        chancesText.text = chances.toString();
        makeExplosion(tempEnemy.x, tempEnemy.y);
        gameState = STATE_REMOVE_PLAYER;
    }
  }
}
```

Creating explosions

The last bit of interesting code we will look at in Pixel Shooter is the makeExplosions() function. makeExplosions() takes x and y positions as its two parameters and creates an instance of ExplosionImage. It also plays the Explode sound by creating an instance of that object from the library and calling its play() method. Other than those two things, creating an explosion is much like putting any other object on the screen. The main difference is that we do not set a speed variable, because explosions don't move. However, the explosion will animate (recall, it has seven frames to run through). The MovieClip will play automatically when it is created, so all we have to do is put it on the screen using addChild() and push it into the explosions array so we can manage it later.

```
    public function makeExplosion(ex:Number, ey:Number) {
        var tempExplosion:MovieClip;
        tempExplosion = new ExplosionImage();
        tempExplosion.x = ex;
        tempExplosion.y = ey;
        addChild(tempExplosion);
        explosions.push(tempExplosion);
        var sound:Sound = new Explode();
        sound.play();
    }
```

There is a bit more code that we have changed to iterate Balloon Saw into Pixel Shooter, but you should get the idea. The point we trying to illustrate is this: by using the code from a completed game as the starting point, you can get a jump start on your development of another game. We took the code from the click game and added functionality to create Balloon Saw. We then added more functionality and changes to morph it into Pixel Shooter. In theory, you could easily take the code from Pixel Shooter and make an even more elaborate game, using the same iterative concepts.

Summary

The basic ideas we have described in this chapter will get you started on the path to making games in AS3. You could, in effect, continue evolving these game concepts into dozens of different games and never read another page of this book. However, throughout these simple projects, we pointed out some glaring issues have been raised that need to be resolved if you want your games to be successful. Here are just a few of them:

- There is no simple way to start and restart the games or change levels.
- Adding text to scoreboard is a cumbersome process.
- Handling sounds is simple but inefficient, because you need to create them each time you use them.
- The use of MovieClips makes developing games without the Flash IDE a bit of challenge. Many organizations use a combination of the Flash IDE and other IDEs to be successful.
- The performance of the games is poor, and they stutter and slow down as they continue to run.
- Bounding box collision detection does not work very well for intricate shapes.

The rest of this book is dedicated to creating a game framework that solves all of these problems (and more), while showing you how to take the lessons learned here and make a multitude of different types of games.

So, there you have It, you've created your first games using a game frame work in AS3. We covered a lot of ground so far, and this was just Chapter 1! You have learned the basic parts of a game framework (state loop, game timer, event model), as well as a little bit about the philosophy behind using one (second game theory). As you can see, we will move fast, but stay with us, because it will be worth the effort.

Let's be honest though; while this chapter's code contains the core concepts, it is not optimized in any way whatsoever. Therefore, in the following chapters, we will create an advanced game framework and then a succession of games that improve on this design, while supplying real-world game examples that are 100 percent ready for you to compile, run, and modify. Now, if you are ready, let's start writing a game framework that will get you on the path to building more games!

Chapter 2

Creating an AS3 Game Framework

In the previous chapter, we created a sufficient framework to start making a game. However, our job here is not to be sufficient. You did not buy this book because it was sufficient. If you wanted sufficient, you would have purchased *Sufficient Flash Games* by Sufficiently Boring Textbook Programmer and his brother. However, you did not. You bought *The Essential Guide to Flash Games* because you wanted *the goods*. We will not let you down. This chapter takes the ideas from Chapter 1 and starts to turn them into a reusable framework for making games. We will iterate and reuse this framework for most of the rest of this book.

The game framework is the foundation for making the *second* game. It is an expanded version of the first chapter's framework with an emphasis on organization and reuse. Since this book is also *not* called *Proper Object-Oriented Design Patterns and Principles for Games*, you will see little theory here and mostly practice. Many of these techniques have been hard won and developed over many years of ActionScript programming. We have fought the wars through AS1, AS2, and now AS3, so you don't have to do it yourself.

While our framework borrows from some design patterns, we feel that games are a very expressive medium. We want you, the reader of this book, to think outside that proverbial, over-used box. While design pattern ideas lend them selves to all manner of application development, we don't want you to feel hemmed in to using any one set of ideas for creating their games. Our framework gives structure to the overall flow of a game but does *not* dictate how to code the actual game logic.

Exploring the Framework

The game framework is housed in a reusable package structure. A package structure at its very basic is an organized set of folders that will contain reusable classes. All of the standard class files for using the framwork will be in this package structure. We will update and extend this structure as we proceed through this book. Let's start by giving you an idea of what classes we will be creating for the framework.

The GameFrameWork.as class

The GameFrameWork.as class is the foundation of the framework. It contains a simple state machine and a basic game loop timer. Our state machine is a simple construct containing a set of state constants to switch the framework between states. States are handled by state functions inside the GameFrameWork.as file. We will employ a variable to reference the current state function. The game timer will use this refernce to call the current state function on each frame tick. We will create states for such things as the title screen, instructions screen, game play, game over, and more.

When we create a new game our document class will be an instance of GameFrameWork called Main.as. This Main.as will have an init (short for "initialization") function that will set up the framework for use. This Main.as class will also act as a sort of message gateway between the game and the framework classes. If you are confused, don't worry; we'll be explaining this in greater detail soon.

The FrameWorkStates.as class

This FrameWorkStates.as class will simply contain a set of constant integer values representing the state machine states. When we first create the framework we will have 10 different state constants. All will begin with the STATE_SYSTEM designation. For example, we will have a state that displays the title screen. The state constant for this will be STATE_SYSTEM_TITLE. More states will be added as we progress through the chapters in this book.

The BasicScreen class and SimpleBlitButton helper class

The BasicScreen class will be used to display very simple game state screens. These screens can have a basic background color with transparency (if needed), as well as some text centered on the screen. Each screen can also have a button that needs to be clicked to move to a new state in the state machine. This class is so simple that it will probably never be used without major modification in your own commercial games. We present it here, in its very simple form, for utility purposes.

The SimpleBlitButton helper class is used to create a clickable button with rollover and off states. The button is created completely in code with a simple color background for the over and off states to be sed in the BasicScreen class. We do this for simplicity and to demonstrate some Sprite blitting techniques (much more on these later in the book) using a set of BitmapData instances for the background color change of the button on rollover.

The ScoreBoard class and SideBySideScoreElement helper class

The ScoreBoard class displays information for the user during game play. Data such as the current game score, time remaining, and other useful information can be displayed to the user with a very basic look and feel by using this class. It can be used as is, but when you start to make your own commercial games, you might find it useful to extend this class with more functionality. This very basic class is used inside the framework to demonstrate how to use events from a Game instance to update a game score board.

The SideBySideScoreElement helper class is used to display a text label and corresponding dynamic text field as a pair side by side on the screen. For example, it can be implemented by the ScoreBoard class to display the word Score followed by the user's current score.

The Game class

The Game class is a stub style class that all games in the framework will inherit from. It contains the basic variables and functions needed to work with the GameFrameWork class.

The Custom event classes

The framework makes use of events to communicate between classes. The instances of the Game class will use events to communicate with the ScoreBoard and the Main classes. We will create a custom Main.as class for each game. This Main class will be a sub-class (or child) of the GameFrameWork class. Some of the events we will use will be simple events. These are instances of the standard Flash Event class used for basic communication. By this, we mean events that don't need to send any data along with them. For example, instances of the Game.as framework class will have a constant variable called GAME_OVER. This constant will be used as the name of a simple Event instance that is fired off with the standard dispatchEvent function call. This example GAME_OVER event wil be used to tell the Main.as to move to the game over (STATE_SYSTEM_GAME_OVER) state in the main state loop when the current game has completed.

We will also be creating three distinct custom event classes as part of the framework. These will be used to send specific data from the Game class instance to the Main.as (GameFrameWork.as instance) class. The Main.as will act on the data sent and if needed, pass the data to other framework classes. By doing this, we are using Main.as as a sort of message gateway.

The CustomEventButtonId.as class

This custom event will have the ability to pass an identification integer value to the listening function. It is used for cases where multiple buttons share the same listener function. It will be used in the framework (specifically in the GameFrameWork instance, Main.as) to allow BasicScreen instances to each share the same listener functions if they employ a SimpleBlitButton. You will see this when we examine the GameFrameWork class file. It can also be used for any game or application that needs to send a basic integer id along with an Event instance.

The CustomEventLevelScreenUpdate.as class

This custom event will be used by the Game.as class instance to send data to a BasicScreen instance we will create called levelInScreen. The levelInScreen will have the ability to display custom text between each level. The event listnener for this event will change this text with a value passed when the event is fired off. The Main.as (GameFrameWork.as sub-class) will listen for this event and pass the data to the levelInScreen.

The CustomEventScoreBoardUpdate.as class

This custom event will be used by the the Game.as class instance to update the values on the ScoreBoard class instance. The Main.as class will listen to for this event and pass the data on to the ScoreBoard.as class instance.

The framework package structure

We will be organizing all of the code we will create into a package structure. The reusable framework classes will be in one package, and the games we will create will be in a separate package. Let's to create these two package structures now.

The source folder

Choose a spot on your disk drive of choice, and create a folder called source. This will be the root or base level for all of the code and games we will create in this book.

The classes package

The reusable framework classes will be in a package called classes. Create a folder called classes inside the source folder from the previous step. You should now have a folder structure that looks a little like this:

```
[source]
      [classes]
```

Next, we will create the actual package that will contain all of the source code for the reusable framework classes. We will name this package com.efg.framework. To create this, you must first create a folder inside the classes folder called com, then a folder called efg inside the com folder, and finally a framework folder inside the efg folder. By the way, the "efg" is an abbreviation for the book title, *Essential Flash Games*. You should now have a folder structure that looks like this:

```
[source]
      [classes]
            [com]
                  [efg]
                        [framework]
```

When we start to create all of the class files necessary for the framework, they will all go into the framework folder. You will see that when we create these classes, the package name will look like this:

```
package  com.efg.framework {
```

The projects package

The second package we will create is called the projects package. You can start this right away by creating a folder inside the root source folder called projects. The projects folder is not going to be a straight package structure like the classes folder. It is organized in a manner to allow individual custom game development using the framework.

Inside this projects folder, we are going to create a unique folder for each game in the book. The first game we are going to create is called stubgame. A stub is usually a function or class that contains very little (if any) usable code but is instead a simple placeholder. Our game will be slightly more than a placeholder but not much more. It will be used to demonstrate the basic functionality of the framework. Go ahead and create a folder called stubgame in the projects folder. You should have a projects set of folders that look like this:

```
[source]
     [classes]
          ...
     [projects]
          [stubgame]
```

Next, we are going to create two folders, each to hold a different version of our game. Why are we going to do this? This book is meant to support Flash game development with a variety of tools. There are many popular methods to create Flash games with an assortment of tools and code integrated development environments (IDEs). We are going to focus on two such tools in this book: the Flash IDE (the one with the library, timelines, drawing tools, and so on all combined into a single tool) and Flash Develop (a very popular, free IDE made specifically for ActionScript development). You can use any tool with this book, but you will need to follow the documentation specific to your own tool when setting up projects.

You will need to pay careful attention to linking the reusable code package structure to your games, because linking may vary depending on the Flash code editor environment you are using. Linking the package to a game is actually a very simple process, but it differs between the various code IDE versions. Jeff does most of his Flash game development Flash Develop using the free Flex SDK that Adobe provides. Steve, on the other-hand, uses the Flash IDE almost exclusively. We have combined our efforts on all of the chapter games to bring you code that will work with both a Flex SDK project and a Flash IDE project.

On that note, the next two folders you will create inside the stubgame folder are called flashIDE and flexSDK. You don't have to create both for any project. You just need to create the one that works with the tools you are going to use to create Flash games. Each is set up differently, so pay attention to the specifics of the one you will be using the most.

You should now have a projects folder that looks like this:

```
[projects]
     [stubgame]
          [flashIDE]
          [flexSDK]
```

The Flash IDE package structure

The Flash IDE package structure begins right inside the flashIDE folder. The package name is very similar to the classes package you saw in the last section. The package structure will be com.efg.games.[game name]. For instance, with the stub game we are going to create in this chapter, the package name will be com.efg.games.stubgame. Go ahead and create those folders now. You should have this package structure when you are complete:

```
[projects]
     [stubgame]
          [flashIDE]
               [com]
                    [efg]
                         [games]
                              [stubgame]
          [flexSDK]
```

The Flex SDK package structure

The Flex SDK package structure is very similar to the Flash IDE package structure with one small difference. Flash Develop and other Flex tools use a specific set of folders for organizing their own project structures. To accommodate these and still have a common package structure for our games, we must add the Flash Develop created `src` folder to the `flexSDK` folder. You will not have to create the `src` folder or the package structure by hand, as Flash Develop will create it automatically for you when you start a new project. In the section called "Setting up the game in Flash Develop," we will go into the details. For now, here is the way the structure will be laid out (including the Flash Develop specific folders such as `bin`, `obj`, and `lib`. If you have used Flash Develop to create a Flex SDK project, you will recognize the following structure:

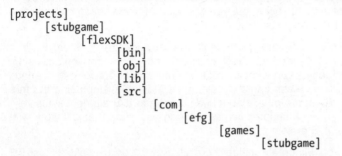

```
[projects]
    [stubgame]
        [flexSDK]
            [bin]
            [obj]
            [lib]
            [src]
                [com]
                    [efg]
                        [games]
                            [stubgame]
```

Notice that we have created the exact same package structure inside the `src` folder as we will use with the Flash IDE. The package name for our game will be `com.efg.games.stubgame`.

The package name in the code for classes in both the Flash IDE and Flex SDK will be the same:

```
package com.efg.games.stubgame
{
```

The Main.as and StubGame.as files

When we start to add files to the `subgame` package we will be creating two subclasses (or children) of framework classes that will be unique to our game. The `Main.as` will be created as a subclass (or child) of `GameFrameWork.as` framework class. The `StubGame.as` class will be a subclass (or child) of the `Game.as` framework class.

Starting a project using the framework packages

You have just seen the basic package structure for both the framework reusable classes and the projects we are going to create. Let's make use of this right away by creating a project for the stub game. The stub game will be very similar to the Chapter 1 game where the player is tasked with clicking the mouse ten times.

Creating the stub game project in the Flash IDE

Follow these steps to set up stub game using the Flash IDE:

1. Start up your version of Flash. I am using CS3, but this will work exactly the same in CS4 and CS5.

2. Create a .fla file in the /source/projects/stubgame/flashIDE/ folder called stubgame.

3. In the /source/projects/stubgame/flashIDE/ folder, create the following package structure for your game: /com/efg/games/stubgame/

4. Set the frame rate of the Flash movie to 30 FPS. Set the width and height both to 400.

5. Set the document class to com.efg.games.stubgame.Main

6. We have not yet created the Main.as class so you will see a warning. We are going to create this later in this chapter.

7. Add the framework reusable class package to the class path for the .fla file

   - In the publish settings, select [Flash] ➤ [ActionScript 3 Setting].
   - Click the **Browse to Path** button and find the /source folder we created earlier for the package structure. Select the classes folder, and click the **choose** button. Now the com.efg.framework package will be available for use when we begin to create our game. We have not created the framework class files yet, but we will be doing this very shortly.

Creating the stub game project in Flash Develop

And these are the steps to create the same project using Flash Develop:

1. Create a folder inside the [source][projects][stubgame] folder called [flexSDK] (if you have not already done so).

2. Start Flash Develop, and create a new project:

   - Select **Flex 3 Project**.
   - Give the project the name stubgame.
   - The location should be the /source/projects/stubgame/flexSDK folder.
   - The package should be com.efg.games.stubgame.
   - *Do not* have Flash Develop create a project folder automatically. Make sure the **Create Folder For Project** box is *unchecked*.
   - Click the OK button to create the project.

3. Add the class path to the framework to the project:

   - Go to the [project] ➤ [properties] ➤ [classpaths] menu item.
   - Click the **add class path** button.
   - Find the /source folder we created earlier, and select the classes subfolder.
   - Click the **ok** button and then the **apply** button.

You now have the basic structure to start creating projects inside the framework. We are now going to discuss a few topics concerning the structure of the framework classes and then move into building the reusable framework code.

> *Here are a couple of things to note:*
>
> *For Flex Builder, Flash Builder, or other IDEs, please refer to the documentation provided for that product to create a new project and set the default compile class.*
>
> *A common method of Flash development is to use the Flash IDE for assets and organization and Flash Develop for code editing. If this is your workflow of choice, you will want to follow the Flash IDE folder and package structure rather than the Flex SDK folder structure.*

Creating game timers

There are two basic methods that most Flash developers implement when creating a frame-based game timer. By "frame-based," we mean a timer that uses the idea of a segment of time broken up into logical slices (or frames) to manage game logic. There are other types of methods for timing game updates, but we will make extensive use of time-slice or frame-based timers in this book. The basic game timer we will use most of the games will attempt to squeeze all processing and screen updates into each segment or frame. We will also explore a time-step timer and a sleep-based timer in chapter 11.

The first timer method is the `Event.ENTER_FRAME` event timer. The standard `Event.ENTER_FRAME` event handler will attempt to run the game loop at the `.swf` file's set frame rate. This very handy game loop timer has been in use for a number of years. The second standard game loop timer method makes use of the `Timer` class. The `Timer` class is used to call the game loop at millisecond intervals specified by a delay interval. For example, if the millisecond delay interval is set to 100, the `Timer` instance would run ten times a second (there are 1,000 milliseconds in a single second). Our framework will begin by using this `Timer` instance game loop timer. We will do this so we can make use of the `TimerEvent.TIMER` updateAfterEvent function. As you will see, this function will help smooth out screen updates.

Defining "frame timer tick"

You will see the phrases "frame timer tick," "timer tick," and "frame tick" used in this book. When we refer to a "tick" or a "frame tick," we simply mean one frame's worth of processing. When we run a game at 30 frames per second, we have 30 ticks or 30 frame ticks. This also means that we only have 33.33 milliseconds (or 1,000/30) inside each tick to do all of our processing.

State Machines

A traditional state machine at its very basic is a mechanism that controls the state, or current actions a system can perform. Sometimes this is called a finite state machine. Finite state machines have traditionally been used to model complex mathematical computations and more recently artificial intelligence. The "finite" in the name refers to the fact that the system can only be in a single state at any one time. Our game framework is built on a simple state machine pattern that employs a separate code function or method for each state. There are many other styles of state machines; some use entire classes for each individual state (sometimes called an object-oriented state machine) and some use a simple `switch:case` statement block called on each frame tick to control state. We will use a third type that borrows from these two.

We call our state machine pattern a function reference pattern. Unlike the object-oriented state machine, our machine will contain a separate method or function for each state inside a single framework class. Each of these state functions will control elements in the framework such as instances of the BasicScreen and Game classes. We will use a switch:case statement to move between states. Unlike the afore mentioned very simple switch/case state machine structures that call this switch/state control structure on each frame tick, we only need to call it when we are switching states. The switch:case we call will simply change the function reference we call on each frame tick. The GameFrameWork.as will contain the state machine that controls overall game flow. This will move our game system between states defined in the FrameWorkStates.as file.

Each individual game package we create will contain a Main.as (in the game's own package structure) that will extend GameFrameWork.as. We will also create a unique Game.as child class for each game. The Game class children that we create can also employ their own internal state machines based on the function reference pattern when needed.

Richard (Squize) Myles of www.gamingyourway.com was one of the first to offer the idea of a function reference state machine for ActionScript 3 on his well-respected blog.

The FrameWorkStates.as class file

This class file is a simple collection of constants that will define the states for the game framework. They will be consumed by the GameFrameWork.as class file. The following code listing shows the entire code for this file; you will want to create this file according to the package structure in the previous section:

```
package  com.efg.framework
{
    /**
    * ...
    * @author Jeff and Steve Fulton
    *
    */
    public class FrameWorkStates {
        public static const STATE_SYSTEM_WAIT_FOR_CLOSE:int = 0;
        public static const STATE_SYSTEM_TITLE:int = 1;
        public static const STATE_SYSTEM_INSTRUCTIONS:int = 2;
        public static const STATE_SYSTEM_NEW_GAME:int = 3;
        public static const STATE_SYSTEM_GAME_OVER:int = 4;
        public static const STATE_SYSTEM_NEW_LEVEL:int = 5;
        public static const STATE_SYSTEM_LEVEL_IN:int = 6;
        public static const STATE_SYSTEM_GAME_PLAY:int = 7;
        public static const STATE_SYSTEM_LEVEL_OUT:int = 8;
        public static const STATE_SYSTEM_WAIT:int = 9;
    }

}
```

The first thing you should notice about this class is the package name in the first line. It conforms to the file system structure we created earlier. No matter if you are using a version of Flash, Flex Builder, Flash Builder, Flash Develop, TextMate, or even plain old Notepad, this package name will be the same. The package name is not depended on the code development environment but the chosen file structure for organizing the code. Save this file in the location we created previously.

/source/classes/com/efg/framework/FrameWorkStates.as

The state variables

The state variables are constants that the game loop state machine will use to move between game states. We have set up the most common basic states in this sample file, but you will be able to create as many as you need. As we progress through the chapters, more will be added as necessary.

- STATE_SYSTEM_TITLE: This state is used to display a basic title screen with an OK button for the user to click to move on. Once the instructions are on the screen, the state will change to the next state.
- STATE_SYSTEM_WAIT_FOR_CLOSE: This one waits until the OK button is clicked for any instance of the BasicScreen class.
- STATE_SYSTEM_INSTRUCTIONS: This state is used to display basic instructions with the same OK button as in the SYSTEM_TITLE state. It also changes to the STATE_SYSTEM_WAIT_FOR_CLOSE state until the OK button is clicked.
- STATE_SYSTEM_NEW_GAME: This state will call the game logic class and fire off its game.newGame() function. It does not wait but moves on to the NEW_LEVEL state right away.
- STATE_SYSTEM_NEW_LEVEL: With this state, we can call the game.newLevel() function to set up a new level for the given game.
- STATE_SYSTEM_LEVEL_IN: This state is used to display some basic information, if needed, for the beginning of a level. In this basic game, we simply display the level screen and wait a few seconds before moving on. The wait is accomplished by changing state to the STATE_SYSTEM_WAIT state for the specified number of frame ticks.
- STATE_SYSTEM_GAME_PLAY: This one simply calls the game logic class's runGame function repeatedly and lets the game take care of its own logic and states.
- STATE_SYSTEM_GAME_OVER: The game over state displays the basic game over screen and waits for the OK button to be clicked before moving back to the instructions screen. It quickly changes state to the STATE_SYSTEM_WAIT_FOR_CLOSE until the OK button is clicked.
- STATE_SYSTEM_WAIT: This state waits for a specified number of frames and then fires off a simple custom event constant called WAIT_COMPLETE.

The GameFrameWork.as class file

The GameFrameWork.as will be that parent of our game's document class. Main.as (the game's document class) for our games will extend this class and call functions to modify the framework for each unique game. The entire code listing is provided at the end of this section. We will explore it in detail once your have had a chance to type in the code. The location for this file in the package structure is

/source/classes/com/efg/framework/GameFrameWork.as

The GameFrameWork.as will be the parent class to the Main.as class we will use for our games, and it's shown in the following listing. In later chapters, we will add some functions to this file and even create one that uses a completely different timer. The Main.as will subclass this class with the extends syntax and override the blank stub init function we are about to create. This class will also contain all of the state functions that coincide with the state variables in the FrameWorkStates class. All of the functions in the GameFrameWork.as are public so all can be overridden by the Main.as if needed. In this way, we can customize the behavior of the state functions if we need to.

For example, in later chapters, we will want to play music on the title screen. The function call to play the music will need to be added to the systemTitle state function. Not all games will need this though, so we will not add it to the GameFrameWork.as file's systemTitleFunction. Instead, we will create a new version of the function in Main.as to override the one in GameFrameWork.as. The new one will play the sound needed and then call the systemTitle function inside GameFrameWork.as with the super.systemTitle() function call.

```
package com.efg.framework
{
    import flash.display.Bitmap;
    import flash.display.BitmapData;
    import flash.display.MovieClip;
    import flash.events.Event;
    import flash.geom.Point;
    import flash.text.TextFormat;
    import flash.utils.Timer;
    import flash.events.TimerEvent;

    public class GameFrameWork extends MovieClip {

        public static const EVENT_WAIT_COMPLETE:String = "wait complete";

        public var systemFunction:Function;
        public var currentSystemState:int;
        public var nextSystemState:int;
        public var lastSystemState:int;

        public var appBackBitmapData:BitmapData;
        public var appBackBitmap:Bitmap; ;

        public var frameRate:int;
        public var timerPeriod:Number;
        public var gameTimer:Timer;

        public var titleScreen:BasicScreen;
        public var gameOverScreen:BasicScreen;
        public var instructionsScreen:BasicScreen;
        public var levelInScreen:BasicScreen;
        public var screenTextFormat:TextFormat;
        public var screenButtonFormat:TextFormat;

        public var levelInText:String;

        public var scoreBoard:ScoreBoard;
        public var scoreBoardTextFormat:TextFormat;

        //Game is our custom class to hold all logic for the game.
        public var game:Game;

        //waitTime is used in conjunction with the
        //STATE_SYSTEM_WAIT state
```

```
// it suspends the game and allows animation or other
//processing to finish

public var waitTime:int;
public var waitCount:int=0;

public function GameFrameWork() {

}

public function init():void {
    //stub to override
}

public function setApplicationBackGround(width:Number,⏎
 height:Number,isTransparent:Boolean = false, ⏎
 color:uint = 0x000000):void {

  appBackBitmapData = new BitmapData(width, height, ⏎
  isTransparent, color);

  appBackBitmap = new Bitmap(appBackBitmapData);
  addChild(appBackBitmap);
}

public function startTimer():void {
    timerPeriod = 1000 / frameRate;
    gameTimer=new Timer(timerPeriod);
    gameTimer.addEventListener(TimerEvent.TIMER, runGame);
    gameTimer.start();
}

public function runGame(e:TimerEvent):void {
    systemFunction();
    e.updateAfterEvent();
}

//switchSystem state is called only when the
//state is to be changed
//(not every frame like in some switch/case
//based simple state machines

public function switchSystemState(stateval:int):void {
    lastSystemState = currentSystemState;
    currentSystemState = stateval;

    switch(stateval) {
       case FrameWorkStates.STATE_SYSTEM_WAIT:
          systemFunction = systemWait;
          break;

       case FrameWorkStates.STATE_SYSTEM_WAIT_FOR_CLOSE:
          systemFunction = systemWaitForClose;
          break;
```

```
        case FrameWorkStates.STATE_SYSTEM_TITLE:
            systemFunction = systemTitle;
            break;

        case FrameWorkStates.STATE_SYSTEM_INSTRUCTIONS:
            systemFunction = systemInstructions;
            break;

        case FrameWorkStates.STATE_SYSTEM_NEW_GAME:
            systemFunction = systemNewGame;
            break;

        case FrameWorkStates.STATE_SYSTEM_NEW_LEVEL:
            systemFunction = systemNewLevel;
            break;

        case FrameWorkStates.STATE_SYSTEM_LEVEL_IN:
            systemFunction = systemLevelIn;
            break;

        case FrameWorkStates.STATE_SYSTEM_GAME_PLAY:
            systemFunction = systemGamePlay;
            break

        case FrameWorkStates.STATE_SYSTEM_GAME_OVER:
            systemFunction = systemGameOver;
            break;
    }
}

public function systemTitle():void {
    addChild(titleScreen);
    titleScreen.addEventListener(CustomEventButtonId.BUTTON_ID,↵
     okButtonClickListener, false, 0, true);

    switchSystemState(FrameWorkStates.↵
     STATE_SYSTEM_WAIT_FOR_CLOSE);
    nextSystemState = FrameWorkStates.STATE_SYSTEM_INSTRUCTIONS;
}

public function systemInstructions():void {

    addChild(instructionsScreen);

    instructionsScreen.addEventListener(CustomEventButtonId.↵
     BUTTON_ID,okButtonClickListener, false, 0, true);

    switchSystemState(FrameWorkStates.↵
     STATE_SYSTEM_WAIT_FOR_CLOSE);

    nextSystemState = FrameWorkStates.STATE_SYSTEM_NEW_GAME;
}

public function systemNewGame():void {
    addChild(game);
```

```
    game.addEventListener(CustomEventScoreBoardUpdate.↵
     UPDATE_TEXT,scoreBoardUpdateListener,false, 0, true);

    game.addEventListener(CustomEventLevelScreenUpdate.↵
     UPDATE_TEXT,levelScreenUpdateListener,false, 0, true);

    game.addEventListener(Game.GAME_OVER, gameOverListener,↵
     false, 0, true);

    game.addEventListener(Game.NEW_LEVEL, newLevelListener,↵
     false, 0, true);

    game.newGame();
    switchSystemState(FrameWorkStates.STATE_SYSTEM_NEW_LEVEL);
}
public function systemNewLevel():void {
    game.newLevel();
    switchSystemState(FrameWorkStates.STATE_SYSTEM_LEVEL_IN);
}

public function systemLevelIn():void {
    addChild(levelInScreen);
    waitTime = 30;
    switchSystemState(FrameWorkStates.STATE_SYSTEM_WAIT);
    nextSystemState = FrameWorkStates.STATE_SYSTEM_GAME_PLAY;
    addEventListener(EVENT_WAIT_COMPLETE, ↵
     waitCompleteListener, false, 0, true);
}

public function systemGameOver():void {
    removeChild(game);
    addChild(gameOverScreen);
    gameOverScreen.addEventListener(CustomEventButtonId.↵
     BUTTON_ID,okButtonClickListener, false, 0, true);

    switchSystemState(FrameWorkStates.↵
     STATE_SYSTEM_WAIT_FOR_CLOSE);

    nextSystemState = FrameWorkStates.STATE_SYSTEM_TITLE;
}


public function systemGamePlay():void {
    game.runGame();
}

public function systemWaitForClose():void {
    //do nothing
}

public function systemWait():void {
    waitCount++;
    if (waitCount > waitTime) {
        waitCount = 0;
```

```
                dispatchEvent(new Event(EVENT_WAIT_COMPLETE));
            }
        }

        public function okButtonClickListener(e:CustomEventButtonId):void {
            switch(e.id) {
                case FrameWorkStates.STATE_SYSTEM_TITLE:
                    removeChild(titleScreen);
                    titleScreen.removeEventListener(CustomEventButtonId.↵
                     BUTTON_ID,okButtonClickListener);
                    break;

                case FrameWorkStates.STATE_SYSTEM_INSTRUCTIONS:
                    removeChild(instructionsScreen);

                    instructionsScreen.removeEventListener(↵
                     CustomEventButtonId.BUTTON_ID,okButtonClickListener);
                    break;

                case FrameWorkStates.STATE_SYSTEM_GAME_OVER:
                    removeChild(gameOverScreen);

                    gameOverScreen.removeEventListener(↵
                     CustomEventButtonId.BUTTON_ID,okButtonClickListener);
                    break;
            }
            switchSystemState(nextSystemState);
        }
        public function scoreBoardUpdateListener(e:↵
         CustomEventScoreBoardUpdate):void {

         scoreBoard.update(e.element, e.value);
        }

        public function levelScreenUpdateListener(e:↵
         CustomEventLevelScreenUpdate):void {
            levelInScreen.setDisplayText(levelInText + e.text);
        }

        //gameOverListener listens for Game.GAMEOVER simple
        //custom events calls and changes state accordingly

        public function gameOverListener(e:Event):void {
            switchSystemState(FrameWorkStates.STATE_SYSTEM_GAME_OVER);

            game.removeEventListener(CustomEventScoreBoardUpdate.↵
             UPDATE_TEXT,scoreBoardUpdateListener);

            game.removeEventListener(CustomEventLevelScreenUpdate.↵
             UPDATE_TEXT, levelScreenUpdateListener);

            game.removeEventListener(Game.GAME_OVER, gameOverListener);
            game.removeEventListener(Game.NEW_LEVEL, newLevelListener);
        }
```

59

```
    //newLevelListener listens for Game.NEWLEVEL
    //simple custom events calls and changes state accordingly

    public function newLevelListener(e:Event):void {
        switchSystemState(FrameWorkStates.STATE_SYSTEM_NEW_LEVEL);
    }

    public function waitCompleteListener(e:Event):void {
        switch(lastSystemState) {
            case FrameWorkStates.STATE_SYSTEM_LEVEL_IN:
                removeChild(levelInScreen);
                break
        }
        removeEventListener(EVENT_WAIT_COMPLETE,waitCompleteListener);
        switchSystemState(nextSystemState);
    }
  }
}
```

The class imports

The class import section contains the necessary Flash core classes needed for the Main class. Notice the package name coincides with the package structure we created earlier in the chapter for the framework:

```
package com.efg.framework
{
```

We also must import all of the classes needed for the framework to run. You will see this put to use shortly.

The variable definitions

The variable definition section defines all of the global scope variables for the class. These include all of the variables needed for the state machine, screens, and the game timer.

We will make use of constants to define the current state and a set of variables to hold the state information. These have been be defined on the FrameWorkStates.as file we created in the last section. More states can be added to the basic ones, but these will be sufficient for many games that we will create in this book. There are two special states that are used for the system and wait for button clicks or things like animations to complete. These are the STATE_SYSTEM_WAIT_FOR_CLOSE and STATE_SYSTEM_WAIT respectively. We will also make use of a generic function called systemFunction that will hold the current state function to call in our game loop. Combined with this, we use a set of integer variables to hold the value of the current state (currentSystemState), the last state (lastSystemState) and the next state (nextSystemState) for processing purposes. These states should not be confused with an actual game pause function. This will be handled in a different manner and added to the framework in Chapter 11.

> If you are using the Flash IDE and have any assets in the library that need to be exported in the first frame, you must extend MovieClip and not Sprite even if you don't plan to use the main time line for anything else. We have extended MovieClip for the GameFrameWork so it will work with both Flex SDK and Flash IDE projects.

The state control variables

The control variables keep the system functioning within the context of the current state. The main control variable is an instance of the Function class called systemFunction. This function holds a reference to the current function that will be repeatedly called on each frame tick. This saves us from having to evaluate a switch:case statement on each frame to decide which function to call. The function is changed to a new reference by called the switchSystemState() function and passing a new constant that represents the new state.

> *Optimization! switchSystemState() is the first of many optimizations we will make to the game framework. All of these optimizations will make the Flash games run much more efficiently. These efficiencies in the game framework will allow the actual game code to perform more complex operations and still run with a reasonable frame rate.*

The currentSystemState integer variable holds a number representing the constant of the current state the system is running. The nextSystemState contains the constant integer value for the state to transition to after this state is complete. The lastSystemState variable holds the integer constant of the previous system state. This is used in the rare occurrence that the game loop needs to return to the previous system state.

The lastSystemState variable will become useful when we use a shared state such as STATE_SYSTEM_WAIT. The STATE_SYSTEM_LEVEL_IN state will implement a 30-millisecond delay before moving on to the STATE_SYSTEM_GAME_PLAY state. The nextSystemState will be STATE_SYSTEM_WAIT and the lastSystemState will be STATE_SYSTEM_LEVEL_IN. When the 30-millisecond wait time has expired, the waitCompleteListener function will be called. It will use the lastSystemState to determine where the processing was before the wait was started. You'll see this in detail later in this chapter when we examine the waitCompleteListener function.

The background fill variables

All Flash applications have a background color of some type. No matter what game we are going to be creating, the framework can control this background color. You should never rely on the background color setting in HTML for your Flash application's background color. This leaves the HTML embed code with control over major aspect of your application. If you are creating a viral game to be placed on game portals, you will lose control of your game's background color, and it will default to what ever the game portal operators have selected as the standard background color in their embed code. The framework allows you to override the HTML settings here by placing a simple colored Bitmap behind the entire application. We will simply define a BitmapData object called appBackBitmapData and a Bitmap object called appBackBitmap that will be used to place the BitmapData onto the displayList.

We will not define the background in the GameFrameWork.as file, but rather the Main.as subclass of the GameFrameWork will set the background if needed in its init function override.

The timer variables

The timer will control the frame rate of the game and help smooth out the display by employing the TimerEvent.updateAfterEvent method. The frameRate variable will be defined in Main.as as the number of frame ticks per second we want our game timer to run.

The most important thing to note is that we are making use of the built-in Timer class (gameTimer). We are not using the standard EnterFrame event. This allows us to create our own frame rate for the game and specify it in the frameRate variable. By doing this, we can control game timer tick rate independent of the `.swf` file's frame rate (FPS). The `.swf` file can have a frame rate setting of 25 (for example), but the game can run at a 30 frame ticks a second. To do this, we first set the `frameRate` to the desired number of frame update ticks we want per second (30). When `Main.as` calls the `startTimer` function (described in detail when we get to the section on the `init` function), the `gameTimer` is put into action. First, we will calculate the `timerPeriod` value as `1000 / frameRate`. With the `updateAfterEvent` function call (in the `runGame` function), we help to smooth out the render of the screen by asking the Flash display engine to update at the rate of the `Timer`, not the frame rate set in the `.swf`. So, going back to our example, if the game SWF is set to run at 25 FPS, and the `frameRate` is set to 30 ticks, the `updateAfterEvent` will help to smooth out the rendering of the screen by asking the Flash display engine to update at the timer tick rate (30), not the `.swf` file's FPS setting (25).

The `timerPeriod` will be passed into the `Timer` instance and the game will attempt to run at this rate. We say "attempt" because if the game includes too many on screen moving objects or more logic than can be computed inside the `timerPeriod` number of milliseconds (or a combination of both), then there will be a noticable slowdown in the game screen updates. In later chapters, we will add functionality to the `runGame` function to mitigate some of these issues.

The screen definition variables

The screen definition variables create instances of our `BasicScreen` class. This is a rather simple class that allows a single positional text box and an **OK** button on the screen. We will use this simple screen for the title, instructions, level, and game over screens. We will customize each screen when we create the `init` function override in our game's `Main.as` class. Note that the `levelInText` is a special variable. Setting this string to a default value will allow the `leveInScreen` to display some default text along on each new level. This text can be combined with dynamic text to create a screen that says something like **Level 1** with the word "Level" being the default text and the number "1" being the dynamic text.

```
public var titleScreen:BasicScreen;
public var gameOverScreen:BasicScreen;
public var instructionsScreen:BasicScreen;
public var levelInScreen:BasicScreen;
public var levelInText:String;
public var screenTextFormat:TextFormat;
public var screenButtonFormat:TextFormat;
```

We also create two `TextFormat` objects that will be used for defining the format of the text on the screens and the format of the button text.

The ScoreBoard variables

The `scoreBoard` instance of the `ScoreBoard` class will handle a simple heads up display (HUD) for the user with information such as the current score. It is a simple framework class that will be customized in the `init` function override in each game's `Main.as` class. The changes will depend on the game that is to be created. We also define a `TextFormatObject` for the basic look of the text for our scoreboard text: `scoreBoardTextFormat`.

The Game object variable

The `Game` object, represented by the variable simply named `game`, is an instance of the `Game` class. The `Main.as` class's `init` function override will inistantiate this. For example, the `StubGame.as` we will create for the game in this chapter will be a child of the Game.as base class. It will override some of the Game.as base classes and hold the custom logic for the game.

```
//Game is our custom class to hold all logic for the game.
private var game:Game;
```

The wait variables

These variables are used for the simple wait period in the STATE_SYSTEM_WAIT state. waitTime can be set to a different value each time it is used. 30 is the default. We have set the frame rate for our application framework to 30 frames per second, so this would be a one second wait time. 30 frame ticks equals 1 second of time in our game timer if the frame rate is set to 30. waitCount is incremented each frame when a wait is occurring. When waitCount==waitTime, the control moves to the next state.

```
//waitTime is used in conjunction with the STATE_SYSTEM_WAIT state
// it suspends the game and allows animation or other processing to
//finish
private var waitTime:int = 30;
private var waitCount:int=0;
```

The constructor function definition

The constructor for GameFrameWork.as does not contain any code. It is simply a placeholder. We will subclass GameFrameWork.as to create the unique Main.as for each game. The Main.as constructor will contain code to call the init function override.

```
public function GameFrameWork() {
}
```

The init function definition

The init() function is simply a stub to be overridden by the Main.as subclass of GameFrameWork.as.

The setApplicationBackGround function definition

This function accepts in parameters to create a basic back ground for the game. The width, height, transparency Boolean, and color values for the back ground are passed and used to instantiate the appBackBitmapData and place it on to the display list.

The startTimer function definition

This function will be called by the Main.as subclass inside its init function. It will use the frameRate variable to create the timerPeriod. Since the timerPeriod must be expressed in milliseconds (1,000/1 of a second equals a timerPeriod of 1000 or a single second), we simply divide the frameRate into 1,000 to get the number of times per second that the timer must run. In the case of a frameRate that is set to 30 ticks for example, the timerPeriod would be 33.33.

The runGame function definition

The `runGame` function is the core of the state machine. Once the `systemFunction` has been set with the `switchSystemState` (discussed next) function call, the `runGame` function will call it repeatedly at the set `timerPeriod` rate every 33 milliseconds (or so) for or frame rate of 30.

```
public function runGame(e:TimerEvent):void {
    systemFunction();
        e.updateAfterEvent();
}
```

The `e.updateAfterEvent()` function call tells the Flash player to make an extra screen update after the frame tick is over, rather than waiting for the next system frame update to occur. System frame update events happen based on the SWF's stage frame rate. If we don't call `e.updateAfterEvent` here, the screen would not be updated until an actual system frame update event occurs. By using this, we smooth out the look of the screen updates to coincide with out selected `gameTimer` delay value.

The switchSystemState function definition

While the `runGame` function is the core of the timer, the `switchSystemState()` function is the core of the simplified state machine. It is passed a constant value for the state. Using that value, it switches the `systemFunction` reference accordingly.

The `switchSystemState` function is used to change the current `systemFunction` of the timer for the next frame timer tick. A reference to one of the state constants is passed into the function, and it acts on it to change the `systemState` variable. It also changes the `lastSystemState` and `nextSystemState` variables. As a refresher, here are the constants from the variable definition section of this `FrameWorkStates.as` class:

```
public static const STATE_SYSTEM_WAIT_FOR_CLOSE:int = 0;
public static const STATE_SYSTEM_TITLE:int = 1;
public static const STATE_SYSTEM_INSTRUCTIONS:int = 2;
public static const STATE_SYSTEM_NEW_GAME:int = 3;
public static const STATE_SYSTEM_GAME_OVER:int = 4;
public static const STATE_SYSTEM_NEW_LEVEL:int = 5;
public static const STATE_SYSTEM_LEVEL_IN:int = 6;
public static const STATE_SYSTEM_GAME_PLAY:int = 7;
public static const STATE_SYSTEM_LEVEL_OUT:int = 8;
public static const STATE_SYSTEM_WAIT:int = 9;
```

We first set `lastSystemState = currentSystemState`, so we can have a reference if needed to switch back to previous state. This might occur in circumstances where we need to jump to the `STATE_SYSTEM_WAIT` state for a period of time and then jump back to the state we were in before the wait. The `systemLevelIn` function is a good example of this. Once we get to the `systemLevelIn` function, we want to wait a specified number of milliseconds before removing the `levelInScreen` from the display. Once the wait is over, the `WAIT_COMPLETE` event is fired off. The `waitCompleteListener` function will need to know what the previous `systemState` was before the wait so it can determine what to do next.

We then set `currentSystemState = stateval`. The `stateval` was passed when we called the `switchSytemState` function. This forces the switch/case statement to set the current `systemFunction` to the function we want to repeatedly call in our loop. We will now start with the first function state the loop calls, the `systemTitle` function.

The systemTitle function definition

The systemTitle function sets up the display of the title screen and then jumps to a common state used for all button clicks that close the BasicScreen windows (STATE_SYSTEM_WAIT_FOR_CLOSE).

We have not looked at the set of functions that control the STATE_SYSTEM_TITLE, STATE_SYSTEM_INSTRUCTIONS, SYSTEM_LEVEL_IN, and STATE_SYSTEM_GAME_OVER states in detail yet, so let's do that now. There are two basic screen types represented:

- Those that wait for a click of the OK button: titleScreen, instructionsScreen, and gameOverScreen
- Those that wait a predefined time to display the screen before moving on: levenInScreen

First, we add an event listener to listen for the OK button clicked event to call the okButtonClickListener function that is shared among all of the screens. After that, we switch the systemState to the constant STATE_SYSTEM_WAIT_FOR_CLOSE. We then set the nextSystemState to be called after okButtonClickListener is fired off.

This the first use for one of the three custom event classes we will create:

```
titleScreen.addEventListener(CustomEventButtonId.BUTTON_ID,
okButtonClickListener,false, 0, true);
```

All of the BasicScreen instances share the same okButtonClickListener function. The custom event passes the id value of the BasicScreen instance to this listening function. The id value is used to determine which screen the button was on and then moves the state machine to a new state based on this evaluation.

The systemTitle, systemInstructions, and systemGameOver functions all look very similar. We'll take a look at those in a bit. First, let's examine the waitForclose and okButtonClickListener functions.

The systemWaitForClose function definition

The systemWaitForClose() function is associated with the STATE_SYSTEM_WAIT_FOR_CLOSE state. It simply does nothing until the OK button on a screen is clicked.

This is the simplest function that you will encounter in this book. It does absolutely nothing! It is just a placeholder that the game loop can call while waiting for the OK button to be clicked.

The okButtonClickListener function definition

The okButtonClickListener function is used to determine what to do when an OK button on one of the various BasicScreen instances is clicked. It switches to the nextSystemState when complete.

This "listener" function is only fired off when it receives a CustomEventButtonId.BUTTON_ID event.

No matter which OK button was clicked (on any of the three screens that we will define with them), we remove the event listener before we change state. Even though the same listener is used for both the title and the instructions screens (for example), and we remove it from the title screen before adding it again in the systemInstructions function. We do this to be sure we never have extra listeners hanging around. Unused listeners waste memory and can slow down processing.

This function shows how we can share a single listener for the OK button click on three different screens (title, instructions, and game over). We switch on the id value passed from CUSTOMEVENT_OK_CLICKED.

No matter which screen we were on, the last line of the function calls the switchSystemState function and passes in the nextSystemState variable.

The systemInstructions function definition

The systemInstructions function is used to display the instructions screen to the user. It is associated with the STATE_SYSTEM_INSTRUCTIONS state. It is called a single time and then processing is passed to the STATE_SYSYEM_WAIT_FOR_CLOSE state.

The systemInstructions function is very similar to the systemTitle function. In fact, they are almost identical with a few minor changes. We first add the systemInstructionsScreen to the displayList with an addChild call.

We also setup a listener for the same CustomEvent that the titleScreen used and we switch to the STATE_SYSTEM_WAIT_FOR_CLOSE state. Again, this state does nothing but let the system wait for the CustomEventButtonId.BUTTON_ID on an instance of the BasicScreen class. Finally, we switch to the STATE_SYSYEM_WAIT_FOR_CLOSE on to wait for the OK button to be clicked. We also set the nextSystemState to be evaluated and used once the OK button is clicked.

The systemGameOver function definition

The systemGameOver function displays the gameOverScreen. It is associated with the STATE_SYSTEM_GAMEOVER state and waits for the OK button click shared with the other BasicScreen instances.

We take a look at the systemGameover function now, because it uses the BasicScreen instance gameOverScreen in a similar manner as the titleScreen and instructionsScreen instances. The systemGameOver state is set in Main when the Game class instance sends out the simple custom event called GAME_OVER. In the next section, we will see the Main class set up to listen for this event from the Game class.

The sytemGameOver function follows the exact same format as the systemTitle and systemInstructions functions. There is one difference though: it takes care of removing the Game class instance, game, from the display list with a call to the removeChild function.

The systemNewGame function definition

The systemNewGame function is associated with the STATE_SYSTEM_NEW_GAME state. It is called one time and then moves on to the STATE_SYSTEM_NEW_LEVEL state. Its purpose is to add all of the event listeners for communication between the Game class and some other framework classes (such as the ScoreBoard class). It also calls the game.newGame function to allow the Game instance to do its own internal new game related processing.

When setting up a new game, we first add our Game class instance (game) to the display list with the addChild function call. This will display the Game.as Sprite (or MovieClip) on the screen. Next, we set up some basic communication between the Game.as and the Main.as classes. We do this by creating four event lsteners. The first two we set up are custom event class instances (classes we will discuss in detail later in the chapter).

The CustomeEventLevelScreenUpdate class allows the passing of a text String instance with the event. The String is used in the Game class to pass the level number (or any text) back to the Main.as class. The Main.as class updates the levelInString variable with the passed in text. We will see this listener function shortly.

The CustomEventScoreBoardUpdate class is used to update the ScoreBoard (another class we will discuss later in this chapter). This event passes data back to the scoreBoadUpdateListener indicating which field on the ScoreBoard to update and what the new value will be. For example: If we wanted to update the player's score, we would pass back the name of the score field (probably "score") and the value of the player's score (example, 5000).

We also create two simple event constants called GAME_OVER and NEW_LEVEL. These will not pass any data back to the listening functions so they will be fired by passing the GAME_OVER or NEW_LEVEL constant into the dispatchEvent function. We do not need custom classes for these types of events.

The systemNewLevel function definition

The systemNewLevel function is associated with the STATE_SYSTEM_NEW_LEVEL state. Its purpose is to call the game.newLevel function and allow the game to start its own internal new level processing.

The systemNewLevel function doesn't do much inside Main. It is merely there to call the Game classes' newLevel function. This function will be demonstrated when we get to the simple stub game example. It is used to initialize variables and difficulty for the new level. When it is complete, it switches the system state to STATE_SYSTEM_LEVEL_IN.

The systemLevelIn function definition

The systemLevelIn() function is associated with the STATE_SYSTEM_LEVEL_IN state. It displays a new level message for 30 frame ticks and then moves processing on to the STATE_SYSTEM_GAME_PLAY state.

Using systemLevelIn is by no means the only method of forcing the state machine to wait. There are a number of third party custom classes and tools such as TweenMax that can be used for the synchronization of clips and tweens between screens and states. We have added this simple wait state to the state machine for it to be complete framework. The state machine is designed to be easily updated with new states and system functions. Feel free to implement any custom or third-party library or tools that will make your job easier.

The systemLevelIn function is used to allow the developer to display some sort of special text or animation as a precursor to each game level. It employs the use of the STATE_SYSTEM_WAIT state. It is set right after the levelInScreen is added to the display list. The levelInScreen is a BasicScreen instance that does not use the OK button. Instead, it simply waits for the specified waitTime (30 frame ticks in this example) and then fires off the WAIT_COMPLETE simple custom event. The Main class listens for this event and calls the associated listener function. The text on this screen is a combination of the levelInText variable we created in the variable definition section and text passed through the CustomeEventLevelScreenUpdate event. The levelIntext can be set in the init function override of the Main.as (GameFrameWork.as child class). It will be combined with the text passed from the event to create the text on the levelInScreen. We will examine the listener function that does this shortly.

The systemWait function definition

The levelInscreen is very similar to the instructionsScreen, but instead of using the STATE_SYSTEM_WAIT_FOR_CLOSE state, it uses the STATE_SYSTEM_WAIT state. What's the difference? The STATE_SYSTEM_WAIT state calls a function that counts for a specified number of frame ticks before moving on to the nextSystemFunction rather than waiting for the click of the OK button.

When the systemState is switched to the STATE_SYSTEM_WAIT state, it calls the systemWait function repeatedly (on each frame tick) until the waitCount is greater than the waitTime set in the systemLevelIn function. When the waitCount is reached, we dispatch a WAIT_COMPLETE event that calls the waitCompleteListener (see the next section). Currently, there is only one systemState that uses the systemWait function, so there is only one item in the case statement. We could add many states that use this systemWait function though, so we have it set up for later expansion.

The waitCompleteListener function definition

The waitCompleteListener function is triggered when the WAIT_COMPLETE event is fired off from the levelInScreen. It can be used for more screens by updating the switch:case statement.

Once the waitCompleteListener fires off, it switches on the lastSystemState because the currentSystemState is now the STATE_SYSTEM_WAIT. This allows us to share a single listener function for all uses of the WAIT_COMPLETE event. It then switches state to the nextSystemState when it calls switchSystemState(nextSystemState). In this example, the nextSystemState is systemGameplay.

The systemGameplay() function definition

The systemGameplay function is the heart of the gameTimer. It is associated with the STATE_SYSTEM_GAME_PLAY state. The game.runGame function is called on each frame tick when systemGamePlay is the systemFunction reference. The Game class instance (game) will handle all of the game's processing within the game.runGame function.

```
private function systemGameplay():void {
  game.runGame();
}
```

The custom event listener functions

The last four functions inside GameFrameWork.as are listener functions for simple and complex custom events that are needed by the Game instance class to communicate with Main class, as well as the levelInScreen and scoreBoard class instances. We'll briefly explain each here so you have a complete version of all the Main.as code in one place. Their use inside those classes will be examined later as we go through the Game, ScoreBoard, and CustomEvent classes.

The scoreBoardUpdateListener function definition for Main.as

The scoreBoardUpdateListener receives updates from the Game class instance that are passed to the ScoreBoard through a CustomEventScoreBoardUpdate instance.

The scoreBoardUpdateListener passes data, represented by a simple key/value pair of String object class instances to the ScoreBoard class instance. The element variable will contain a string value representing a constant that we will define in the Main.as (GameFrameWork.as child class). The constant will be the id string name of the element on the scoreBoard to update. The value variable passed will be a string representing the value to show on the scoreBoard for the corresponding TextField. It's constructed to allow the Game class instance and its associated classes to update the ScoreBoard class instance without having to maintain a reference to it. This allows the Game and its associated classes to remain decoupled from the Main.as and the basic framework classes. We will see the same thing with the levelInScreen a little later. Why is the ScoreBoard part of the framework and not part of the Game class? We wanted to have the ScoreBoard be part of the Main class game framework because the Game class instance is not the only object that might interact with the ScoreBoard. We do not implement it in this simple example, but the Main might have other data such as a system-held high score, links out, or even a frame counter in the ScoreBoard.

Why decouple the scoreboard from the game class instance? It is true that we could make calls directly to the ScoreBoard from Game by using the root or parent attribute of the Game class. While this is certainly possible, if we decouple the Game class from the ScoreBoard class, then the Game class will be reusable across multiple frameworks (even your own) with no need to use our framework. The new framework would just need its own ScoreBoard or the Game would need to implement its own.

The levelScreenUpdateListener function definition for Main.as

The levelScreenUpdateListener allows the Game class to update the text on the levelInScreen.

Like the scoreBoardUpdateListener, the levelScreenUpdateListener function is used to pass data from the Game class instance to the levelInScreen. When the Game class updates the level value using its own newLevel function, the levelInScreen must also update its text so the correct level number will be shown on the screen during the systemLevelIn function. The predefined default String variable, levelIntext will be combined with the passed in value:

levelInScreen.setDisplayText(levelInText + e.text);

The gameOverListener function definition for Main.as

The gameOverListener listens for the Game.GAME_OVER simple custom event and then changes the framework state accordingly.

When the Game class instance fires off the GAME_OVER simple custom event, the Main listens for it and runs this function. It cleans up all of the game-related listeners by removing them and then changes state to the STATE_SYSTEM_GAME_OVER state which was discussed earlier

The newLevelListener function definition for Main.as

The newLevelListener listens for the Game.NEW_LEVEL simple custom event and changes the state accordingly.

The newLevelListener listens for the Game class instance to fire off the simple custom event, NEW_LEVEL. It then changes the systemState to the STATE_SYSTEM_NEW_LEVEL state.

Framework classes beyond Main

The framework does not rely on `FrameWorkStates` and the `GameFrameWork` classes alone. We are now going to define and explain the classes that make up the `BasicScreen` (and its helper classes), `ScoreBoard`, and the custom event classes. We have discussed all each of these briefly in the `GameFrameWork.as` class description. Now, we take a look at each in greater detail.

The BasicScreen class

All of the simple screens in this basic game framework are created using a very simplified `BasicScreen` class. The `BasicScreen` class can become a parent class for more elaborate screens, but in the basic framework, it is very simple. Each screen contains some text positioned on the screen, an **OK** button if needed and a background color. That is all. If the **OK** button is needed, there is an event inside the `BasicScreen` class that is fired off, and it, in turn, fires off its own event to tell `GameFrameWork` class that it has been clicked. This makes use of a custom event class instance (`okButtonClickListener`) that we will create in the next section.

You should save this class file in the folder structure we created earlier in the chapter to correspond to the framework package.

/source/classes/com/efg/framework/BasicScreen.as

Here is entire code listing for this class.

```
package  com.efg.framework
{
    // Import necessary classes from the flash library
    import flash.display.Bitmap;
    import flash.display.BitmapData;
    import flash.display.Sprite;
    import flash.events.Event;
    import flash.geom.Point;
    import flash.text.TextField;
    import flash.text.TextFormat;
    import flash.events.Event;
    import flash.events.MouseEvent;
    import flash.text.TextFormatAlign;


    /**
    * ...
    * @author Jeff Fulton, Steve Fulton
    */

    public class BasicScreen extends Sprite {
    private var displayText:TextField = new TextField();
    private var backgroundBitmapData:BitmapData;
    private var backgroundBitmap:Bitmap;
    private var okButton:SimpleBlitButton;

    //ID is passed into the constructor. When the OK button is
    //clicked,a custom event sends this id back to Main

    private var id:int;
```

```
public function BasicScreen(id:int,width:Number, ↵
 height:Number,isTransparent:Boolean, color:uint) {

   this.id = id;
   backgroundBitmapData = new BitmapData(width, height, ↵
    isTransparent, color);

   backgroundBitmap = new Bitmap(backgroundBitmapData);
   addChild(backgroundBitmap);
}


public function createDisplayText(text:String, ↵
 width:Number, location:Point,textFormat:TextFormat):void {

   displayText.y = location.y;
   displayText.x = location.x;
   displayText.width = width;
   displayText.defaultTextFormat=textFormat;
   displayText.text = text;
   addChild(displayText);
}

public function createOkButton(text:String,location:↵
 Point, width:Number,height:Number, textFormat:↵
 TextFormat, offColor:uint=0x000000, overColor:uint=↵
 0xff0000, positionOffset:Number=0):void{

   okButton = new SimpleBlitButton(location.x, location.y, ↵
    width, height, text, 0xffffff, 0xff0000, textFormat,↵
    positionOffset);

   addChild(okButton);
   okButton.addEventListener(MouseEvent.MOUSE_OVER,↵
    okButtonOverListener, false,0, true);

   okButton.addEventListener(MouseEvent.MOUSE_OUT,↵
    okButtonOffListener, false, 0, true);

   okButton.addEventListener(MouseEvent.CLICK,↵
    okButtonClickListener, false, 0, true);
}

public function setDisplayText(text:String):void {
   displayText.text = text;
}

//Listener functions
//okButtonClicked fires off a custom event and sends the
//"id" to the listener.

private function okButtonClickListener(e:MouseEvent):void {
   dispatchEvent(new CustomEventButtonId↵
    (CustomEventButtonId.BUTTON_ID,id));
}
```

```
        private function okButtonOverListener(e:MouseEvent):void {
            okButton.changeBackGroundColor(SimpleBlitButton.OVER);
        }

        private function okButtonOffListener(e:MouseEvent):void {
            okButton.changeBackGroundColor(SimpleBlitButton.OFF);
        }
    }
}
```

Class import and variable definition section for BasicScreen

The class import section imports the necessary core Flash classes we will see in action shortly.

The one custom class the BasicScreen class makes use of is the CustomEventButtonId class. We will dissect this class in detail later in the chapter, but for now, know that we dispatch an instance of it if the OK button is clicked on any of the instances of this BasicScreen.

The variable definition section of the BasicScreen class creates variables to hold data for the three optional pieces of the BasicScreen:

- The background color BackGroundBitmapData, which is associated BackGroundBimap
- The text to display on the screen, displayText
- The button that will fire off the CustomEventButtonId when clicked, which is an instance of another framework custom class we will create called SimpleBlitButton

All three of these optional items are set with public functions inside the BasicScreen class. The Main.as class we create for each unique game will customize the BasicScreen instances by passing values to these public functions inside its init function override of the GameFrameWork's init function.

One of the most interesting things about this BasicScreen class is the way we are creating this background for the OK button. We decided not to import or embed any external assets for this first game, because it would necessitate explaining how to do it in both the Flash IDE and Flash Develop (with the open source Flex SDK), and it's too early in this book for that discussion. Instead, we have created a very simple custom button class called SimpleBlitButton. The instance name for this button is okButton. We will discuss this class in detail in the SimpleBlitButton class deinition.

The final variable we need is the id integer. This is passed into the BasicScreen instance from Main. It is used in the switch:case inside the GameFrameWork classes' okButtonClickListener function to change state based on the screen whose OK button was clicked.

Class constructor function definition

The constructor for the BasicScreen class accepts in the basic information needed to set up a screen for display. A screen needs an id value passed in as an integer, as well as the information needed to create the background color for the screen. This is done by passing values needed to customize the backGroundBitmapData variable that was created in the variable definition section. A BitmapData instance needs these four pieces of data passed:

- A width
- A height

- A Boolean (true/false) value to indicate whether or not the BitmapData will use transparency
- A color represented as an unsigned integer (uint).

A completely transparent background can be set for a screen by passing in true for the isTransparent parameter and a 32-bit color value with an alpha channel set to 00. Colors are represented as AARRBBGG where the alpha (AA) values ranging from 0x00 (0) (completely transparent) to 0xFF (255) (completely opaque) can be passed in.

The init function is used to set up the field for the display text (displayText) and the OK button (okButtonSprite). The OK button is added only if the passed in okNeeded is set to true.

The first actual line of code might be a little cryptic:

```
textformat1.align = flash.text.textFormayAlign.CENTER
```

When we set up the textFormat1 variable, we didn't set the alignment to center because not all uses of it will be centered. We can change the alignment on the fly, and we do so here before we apply it to the displayText field as its defaultTextFormat. Then, we simply add the text to the screen. In the first init call, there is no text to actually add to the screen. It is added with the setDisplytext function described next. The setDisplayText function is public and is called by the Main class when the BasicScreen instances (title, instruction, game over, and so on) are placed on the display list. This allows the text for the screen to be customized for each showing.

The createDisplayText function definition

By calling the createDisplayText function on a BasicScreen instance, we can turn on and set the default location and text value for the text that displays on the BasicScreen instance. The function adds the defaultText to the displayList with the addChild function call. The game screen is shown in Figure 2-1.

The parameters passed into this function follow:

- text: The actual text to put in the .text attribute of the defaultText TextField
- location: A Point class instance that will be used to define the x and y values of the upper left-hand corner for the defaultText TextField
- width: The width in pixels of the defaultText TextField
- textFormat: A TextFormat instance used to format the text in the defaultText TextField

Figure 2-1. The Super Click screenTitle with the OK button

The createOkButton function definition

If the BasicScreen instance is to have a button used to move the state machine on to the next systemState, it can be added with the public createOkButton function. This function actually does quite a bit. First, it creates an instance of the SimpleBlitButton framework class (we will dig into this class next). The SimpleBlitButton class takes some parameters into its constructor and then uses them to create a button with OVER and OFF states. OVER occurs when the mouse is placed over the button, and OFF is the default state when the cursor is not on the button. For our simple basic screens, we are going to have a single, reusable OK button. It will have black text on a white background in the OFF state and the same black text but on a red background for the OVER state. The function then adds event listeners for the mouse events on the okButton SimpleBlitButton instance.

The parameters passed into this function follow:

- text: The actual text to put on to the button
- location: A Point class instance that will be used to define the x and y values for the upper left-hand corner for the okButton SimpleBlitButton
- width: The width of the button
- height: The height of the button
- textFormat: The TextFormat of the button text

- offColor: The background color of the button when the mouse is not hovering over it
- overColor: The background color of the button when the mouse is hovering over it
- positionOffset: The movement buffer to bump the text from the left side of the button after it is drawn, which is useful with some fonts when positioning the text properly.

The setDisplayText function definition

This function is used to reset the displayText.text to a new value if needed. It accepts in a single string parameter, text, and changes out displayText.text with the new value. This is useful for setting the levelInScreen text to display the game level number on each new level.

The button listener function definitions

The BasicScreen class needs to respond to the click, over, and off events created in the createOkButton function of the BasicScreen class. We do this by creating this set of three listener functions:

- OkButtonClickListener: This event dispatches a CustomEventButtonId instance and passes the id variable value back to the listeners. In the GameFrameWork class, we have set up a listener for this event.
- okButtonOverListener: This event calls the changeBackGroundColor function of the SimpleBlitButton and passes in the constant OVER. The SimpleBlitButton will respond by changing the color of the button to the OVER color.
- okButtonOffListener: This event calls the changeBackGroundColor function of the SimpleBlitButton and passes in the constant OFF. The SimpleBlitButton will respond by changing the color of the button to the OFF color.

The SimpleBlitButton class

The SimpleBlitButton class is used to create very simple UI buttons that have only a background color (two actually, one for OFF and one for OVER states), and a text label. It uses BitmapData to create the background and a Bitmap instance holder for this BitmapData instance. It is called a blit button because we use a simple blitting technique of swapping out the BitmapData reference on the bitmap when we want to change the color of the button. Also, we draw the text for the button into a BitmapData to demonstrate the use of BitmapData for dynamically created display object.

> The terms "blitting" or "to blit" come from the classic game development method of moving bits of data around in memory very fast. In some cases, the bits moved with this technique were referred to as sprites, player missile graphics, blobs, or any other number of machine-specific terms. We use "blitting" to mean painting the screen or the contents of a Bitmap instance with BitmapData in various ways.

Create the SimpleBlitButton.as file in the framework package structure we created earlier:

/source/classes/com/efg/framework/SimpleBlitButton.as

Here is entire code listing for this class:

```
package  com.efg.framework
{
   import flash.display.Bitmap;
```

```
import flash.display.BitmapData;
import flash.display.Sprite;
import flash.text.TextFormat;
import flash.text.TextField;

/**
 * ...
 * @author Jeff Fulton and Steve Fulton
 */
public class SimpleBlitButton extends Sprite {
    public static const OFF:int = 1;
    public static const OVER:int = 2;

    private var offBackGroundBD:BitmapData;
    private var overBackGroundBD:BitmapData;

    private var positionOffset:Number;

    private var buttonBackGroundBitmap:Bitmap;
    private var buttonTextBitmapData:BitmapData;
    private var buttonTextBitmap:Bitmap;

    public function SimpleBlitButton(x:Number,y:Number,width:↵
     Number,height:Number,text:String, offColor:uint, ↵
     overColor:uint, textformat:TextFormat,positionOffset:Number=0) {

        this.positionOffset = positionOffset;
        this.x = x;
        this.y = y;

        //background
        offBackGroundBD = new BitmapData(width, height, ↵
         false, offColor);

        overBackGroundBD = new BitmapData(width, height,↵
         false, overColor);

        buttonBackGroundBitmap = new Bitmap(offBackGroundBD);

        //text
        var tempText:TextField = new TextField();
        tempText.text = text;
        tempText.setTextFormat(textformat);

        buttonTextBitmapData  = new BitmapData↵
         (tempText.textWidth+positionOffset, tempText.↵
         textHeight+positionOffset, true, 0x00000000);

        buttonTextBitmapData.draw(tempText);
        buttonTextBitmap = new Bitmap(buttonTextBitmapData);
        buttonTextBitmap.x = ((buttonBackGroundBitmap.width -↵
         int(tempText.textWidth))/2)-positionOffset;

        buttonTextBitmap.y = ((buttonBackGroundBitmap.height - ↵
         int(tempText.textHeight))/2)-positionOffset;
```

```
        addChild(buttonBackGroundBitmap);
        addChild(buttonTextBitmap);
        this.buttonMode = true;
        this.useHandCursor = true;

    }

    public function changeBackGroundColor(typeval:int):void {

        if (typeval == SimpleBlitButton.OFF) {
            buttonBackGroundBitmap.bitmapData = offBackGroundBD;
        }else {
            buttonBackGroundBitmap.bitmapData = overBackGroundBD;
        }
    }
  }

}
```

The class import and variable definition for the SimpleBlitButton class

The button we create is actually a Sprite container instance with two Bitmap layers. The bottom layer is the buttonBackGroundBitmap. The bitmapData property of the buttonBackGroundBitmap can be easily swapped between our offBackGroundBD and overBackGroundBD BitmapData rectangles on rollover and rollout. The text portion of the button is the top Bitmap layer. It will contain the buttonTextBitmapData BitmapData instance. We create two constants to define these two basic states for the button:

- public static const OFF:int = 1;
- public static const OVER:int = 2;

We will create this button text in the constructor of the class. The buttonTextBitmapData text is drawn into a BitmapData instance for display. While we could simply use TextField directly in the Sprite button, we are focusing on games in this book. Because of this, we want to show an early use of Bitmaps and BitmapData for animation. We will focus on this simple blit technique, because we want to introduce a use of bitting animation early in this section. The more you are familiar with the various uses of BitmapData, the more comfortable you will be as we progress through the rest of the chapters.

We have one other variable to define in this section. It is used to "bump" the text position back to the upper left-hand corner of the button if needed. With some fonts you might find that the text on the button has been truncated to the right. The positionOffset variable can be set in the constructor to help mitigate this issue.

The constructor definition for the SimpleBlitButton class

The constructor function for the SimpleBlitButton class accepts in the parameters necessary for creating the correct size, colors and text for the Button and its two states: OFF and OVER.

This constructor for the SimpleBlitButton accepts these parameters:

- x value screen placement
- y value screen placement
- width of the button

- height of the button
- text String for the button's label
- Color for the OFF background (as a uint)
- Color for the OVER background (as a uint)
- TextFormat object we pass into the button for styling the text.
- positionOffset value representing a value that will be used to bump the button text back toward the upper-left if needed

After setting the x and y values for the button, we move on to creating backgrounds for the OFF and OVER states with simple BitmapData objects. The width, height, and colors (offColor and overColor) passed in are used to create simple opaque BitmapData rectangles in the appropriate size. The buttonBackGroundBitmap, which is the on screen display holder for the background, is set to use the OFF bitmapData by default.

```
buttonBackGroundBitmap = new Bitmap(offBackGroundBD);
```

After the background, we move on to the text. The goal is to place the text in its own BitmapData instance and center it (if possible) on the button. We create the tempText TextField that will be used to set up and format the BitmapData text.

In this simple button, we don't check to see if the text will fit on the button, so if the width and height are not sufficient to house the width and height of the text, it will simply be truncated. The BitmapData instance that holds the text will not let the text run off the sides, as BitmapData does not have any space outside of its viewable area (unlike the Stage or Sprites and MovieClips). The final thing we do to the tempText field is to set its textFormat property to the passed in textformat.

Now, we move on to placing the text on the button and centering it. This takes a little extra measuring, as we will find that in some cases there is a little 2-pixel margin in TextField objects that we have to compensate for when we create the BitmapData holder for our tempText field. We used the passed in positionOffset for this. We will use the passed in actual width and height of the tempText field (the textWidth and textHeight values), a transparent background (true) and no background color (0x00000000):

```
buttonTextBD  = new BitmapData(tempText.textWidth,↵
 tempText.textHeight, true, 0x00000000);
```

The 0x00000000 is a 32-bit integer that represents the AARRBBGG color values. The AA is the transparency value. By setting it to 00, we effectively create an invisible background, no matter the color (black in this instance).

To get the tempText.text value into the buttonTextBitmapData BitmapData instance, we simply call the draw method of the buttonTextBitmapData and pass in the tempText variable:

```
buttonTextBitmapData.draw(tempText);
```

The draw method takes the contents of any display object and paints the current set of pixels into the BitmapData object. The draw method can be used to take pretty much any vector (or bitmap contents) of a display object and effectively cache them for use later. This method is notoriously slow, but we won't use it often in actual game play. We use it to set up our objects for later use.

The final thing we must do with our text for the button is to add it to an actual display object. We have created a Bitmap instance holder for the text and have called it buttonTextBitmap. This is the display object that will be layered on top of the buttonBackGroundBitmap to create the illusion of a clickable button with OFF and OVER states. The line of code that creates the buttonTextBitmap follows; note that we will pass in the instance of the `buttonTextBitmapData`. This becomes the `bitmapData` property of the `buttonTextBitmap`:

```
buttonTextBitmap = new Bitmap(buttonTextBD);
```

When centering the text on the button we have to compensate for an unchangeable, invisible 2-pixel buffer around at the top and left of the `tempText` (`TextField object`) when it is drawn into `buttonTextBitmapData`. We could use a matrix operation to translate the position of the text when it is drawn, but for simplicity, we will simply subtract two pixels from the x and y position to compensate for this buffer. We calculate the center x and y positions like this:

```
//X: (the background width - the text width)/2 minus the 2pixel buffer
//Y: (the background height - the text height)/2 minus
//the 2pixel buffer
buttonTextBitmap.x = ((buttonBackGroundBitmap.width - int(tempText.textWidth))/2)-2;
buttonTextBitmap.y = ((buttonBackGroundBitmap.height - ↵
 int(tempText.textHeight))/2)-2;
```

The second-to-last thing we do to the button is to add both the `buttonBackGroundBitmap` and then the `buttonTextBitmap` to the `Sprite`'s display list in that order. The last thing we do is to set the `handCursor` and `buttonMode` for this `Sprite` to true. This will allow the hand cursor to show up rather than the arrow when the mouse is over our buttons.

The changeBackGroundColor function definition

The `changeBackGroundColor` function is used to swap out the color under the text of the button when moving between the OFF and OVER states and to swap out the background on rollover. A constant is passed in; either OFF or OVER is used in the `if` clause to set the `bitmapData` property of the `buttonBackGroundBitmap` to the corresponding `BitmpData` instance for the background that we created in the constructor.

The CustomEventButtonId class

The `CustomEventButtonId` class is used to pass data to an event listener when an event occurs. It is a relatively simple class that extends the built-in `Event` class. Its primary function is to allow the passing of a simple integer value along with the dispatched `Event` instance.

Create the `CustomEventButtonId.as` file in the framework package structure we created earlier:

/source/classes/com/efg/framework/CustoEventButtonId.as

Here is entire code listing for this class:

```
package com.efg.framework
{
    import flash.events.*;
    /**
    * ...
    * @author Jeff Fulton
    */
    public class CustomEventButtonId extends Event {

        public static const BUTTON_ID:String = "button id";
        public var id:int;
```

```
public function CustomEventButtonId(type:String,⏎
 id:int, bubbles:Boolean=false, cancelable:Boolean=false){

    super(type, bubbles,cancelable);
    this.id = id;
}

public override function clone():Event {
    return new CustomEventButtonId(type,id, bubbles,cancelable)
}

}

}
```

Class import and variable definition for the CustomEventButtonId class

In this section, we set up all of the variables necessary for the class. We will create a single constant that will be used for the button ID event.

BUTTON_ID:String = "button id"

The id String variable is used to pass data between the event and the listener.

We pass the id value of the instance of the BasicScreen class where the OK button was clicked. If the button was on an instance of the BasicScreen class, the id (set in Main when we instantiate the BasicScreen instance) is passed to all objects listening to the event. In the framework, Main listens for this event and changes state based on the screen where the OK button was clicked.

The constructor definition for the CustomEventButtonId class

The first String in the constructor should be the BUTTON_ID constant defined previously. You can also create CustomEventButtonId instances on the fly by passing a String value for the type, rather than one of the preset string constants, into the constructor. It is better organizationally to use the preset constants (you can always add more) than to pass in an arbitrary String value. It also helps eliminate runtime errors associated with an unknown or unhandled type value being passed in. If your listener function is set to listen for an event called GAME_OVER but you mistype the type as GAMR_OVER, you might have a difficult time debugging the fact that your game never handles that event properly.

Let's look at the BasicScreen's use of the CustomEvent class again:

dispatchEvent(new CustomEvent(CustomEventButtonId.BUTTON_ID,id));

When the Event is created, we pass in the CustomEventButtonId.BUTTON_ID constant to define what event we are going to fire off, and we pass a newly created int representing the id of the BasicScreen instance.

How does GameFrameWork.as listen for a custom Event? Main needs to add a listener for each of the three screens that have OK buttons. These are added when needed and deleted when not needed. You have already seen the full text of the functions for each screen state in GameFrameWork here is a reminder example from the title screen:

titleScreen.addEventListener(CustomEventButtonId.BUTTON_ID,⏎
 okButtonClickListener, false, 0, true);

Here, we are adding a listener to *any* instance of a `CustomEventButtonId` called `CustomEventButtonId.BUTTON_ID`. In this way, all of the screens can share the same event and the same listener in the `Main` class. We have already taken a quick look at the `okButtonClickedListener` function. It uses the `id` value of the `Event` object passed from the `CustomEventButtonId` instance in a switch/case statement to change to the next state after the button click.

The constructor must also call the constructor of its parent class, `Event`, by making the call to `super` and passing in the parameters from its own constructor:

```
super(type, bubbles,cancelable);
```

The `this.id` variable is set by taking the passed in id and assigning it:

```
this.id = id;
```

The clone function definition for the CustomEventButtonId class

The clone function is a part of the preexisting `Event` class. It must be declared with override, because the `type` and `attributes` properties of out `CustomEvent` must be added to the clone function.

```
public override function clone():Event {
    return new CustomEvent(type,id, bubbles,cancelable)
}
```

The clone function is standard in the `Event` class, but we have to override it to make sure we pass the attributes into the call to create a new version of the `CustomEvent`. The `attributes` object is our own creation, so we must make sure that we change the original clone function and include it.

The CustomLevelScreenUpdate class

The `CustomLevelScreenUpdate Event` class is very similar to to `CustomEventButtonId` class. It is used to pass a new text value back to the listening function. Specifically, it is used by the `GameFrameWork.as` to add text to the `leveininScreen` on each new level.

Create the `CustomEventLevelScreenUpdate.as` file in the framework package structure we created earlier:

```
/source/classes/com/efg/framework/CustoEventLevelScreenUpdate.as
```

Here is the entire code listing for this class:

```
package com.efg.framework
{
    import flash.events.Event;
    /**
     * ...
     * @author Jeff Fulton
     */
    public class CustomEventLevelScreenUpdate extends Event {
        public static const UPDATE_TEXT:String = "update level text";
        public var text:String;

        public function CustomEventLevelScreenUpdate(type:String,↵
          text:String,bubbles:Boolean=false,cancelable:Boolean=false) {
```

```
            super(type, bubbles,cancelable);
            this.text = text;
        }

    public override function clone():Event {
        return new CustomEventLevelScreenUpdate(type,text,↵
         bubbles,cancelable)
        }
    }
}
```

The only real differences in all three of the custom `Event` classes we will create are the constant values used to create an instance of the event and the data that is passed along with the event:

```
public static const UPDATE_TEXT:String = "update level text";
public var text:String;
```

We also need to modify the constructor and the clone functions for the new data passed.

The CustomEventScoreBoardUpdate class

This custom `Event` class is very similar to to `CustomEventButtonId` and `CustomEventLevelScreenUpdate` classes. It is used to pass two `String` values back to the listening function. Specifically, it is used by the `GameFrameWork.as` to add text to update elements on the `ScoreBoard` class instance.

Create the `CustomEventScoreBoardUpdate.as` file in the framework package structure we created earlier:

/source/classes/com/efg/framework/CustoEventScoreBoardUpdate.as

Here is entire code listing for this class:

```
package com.efg.framework
{
    import flash.events.Event;
    /**
    * ...
    * @author Jeff Fulton
    */

    public class CustomEventScoreBoardUpdate extends Event {

        public static const UPDATE_TEXT:String = ↵
         "update scoreboard text";

        public var element:String;
        public var value:String;

        public function CustomEventScoreBoardUpdate(type:↵
         String,element:String, value:String, ↵
         bubbles:Boolean=false,cancelable:Boolean=false) {

            super(type, bubbles,cancelable);
            this.element = element;
            this.value = value;
        }
```

```
    public override function clone():Event {
        return new CustomEventScoreBoardUpdate(type,element,↵
         value, bubbles,cancelable)
    }
  }
}
```

The only real differences in all three of the custom `Event` classes we will create are the constant values used to create an instance of the event and the data that is passed along with the event:

```
    public static const UPDATE_TEXT:String = ↵
     "update scoreboard text";

    public var element:String;
    public var value:String;
```

The `element` variable represents a constant value in the `Main.as` (`GameFrameWork.as` child class) representing the element on the score board to update. The `value` variable is the actual value to change the element to. Let's jump into a discussion of the `ScoreBoard` framework class now to help solidify this topic.

The ScoreBoard class

Most likely, the `ScoreBoard` class will be custom for each game you create. Like the `BasicScreen` class, the `ScoreBoard` class in the framework is as very simple and will probably need some modification or enhancements if you were to use it in a full commercial game. There are some basic things that all scoreboards will need though, such as events and communication between itself and the `Game` class instance. The `ScoreBoard` allows the `Main.as` to create and position as many instances of the `SideBySideScoreElement` framework class (to be discussed next) as needed. These are set up each with a name value that corresponds to constants set up in the `Main.as` class. Let's take a look at the code for this class now, and you will see the `Main.as` customizations to create elements on the `ScoreBoard` when we get to the final section on creating the stub game.

Create the `ScoreBoard.as` file in the framework package structure we created earlier:

`/source/classes/com/efg/framework/ScoreBoard.as`

Here is entire code listing for this class:

```
package  com.efg.framework
{
    // Import necessary classes from the flash libraries
    import flash.text.TextField;
    import flash.text.TextFormat;
    import flash.display.Sprite;
    /**
    * ...
    * @author Jeff Fulton and Steve Fulton
    */

    public class ScoreBoard extends Sprite {

        private var textElements:Object;

        //Constructor calls init() only
```

```
    public function ScoreBoard() {
        init();
    }

    private function init():void {
        textElements = {};
    }

    public function createTextElement(key:String, ↵
     obj:SideBySideScoreElement):void {

        textElements[key] = obj;
        addChild(obj);
    }

    public function update(key:String, value:String):void {
        var tempElement:SideBySideScoreElement = textElements[key];
        tempElement.setContentText(value);
    }
  }

}
```

Class import and variable definition for the ScoreBoard class

This version of the ScoreBoard class places text labels and their corresponding values next to one another horizontally on the screen. Just as we created the SimpleBlitButton class to help create simple sprite-like buttons to use on any instance of the BasicScreen class, we will also create a UI element called SideBySideScoreElement as a helper class for the ScoreBoard.

The textElements object will hold an array of instances of the SideBySideScoreElement class. Next, we define SideBySideScoreElement instances to hold our scoreboard UI objects.

The ScoreBoard is an attribute the GameFrameWork class, not of the Game class. In fact, we are going to get a "design pattern" oriented here and say that the ScoreBoard class and the Game class cannot even communicate with one another except through the GameFrameWork class. We do this to keep our classes very clean and free of extraneous references that will make future reuse difficult. In the case of the framework, the GameFrameWork class could be said to be a type of controller class. The Game class will stay independent from Main as much as possible. We are decoupling the game logic completely from the other classes in the framework. We do this essentially to be able to pull the game from the framework and use it in another framework (if needed).

The constructor and init follow the structure that we will use for almost all custom classes (with the exception of some helper classes). If nothing is passed into the constructor, we usually simply call an init function to set up the custom class.

The init function simply initializes the textElements object that will hold instances of the SideBySideScoreElement class. We will discuss the SideBySideScoreElement class in the next section. When we get to the section of this chapter on customizing the GameFrameWork.as class (as a file called Main.as in our game project), we call a public function in this class named createTextElement. This creates an associative array of the textElement object instances that we can access by the key. The key will be the String name we pass into the constructor of the SideBySideScoreElement. For example, the String score will be used to access the SideBySideScoreElement instance that represents the score for the user.

The elements needed in a call to the createTextElement function follow:

- A String representing the key for the element, which is very much like the id in the BasicScreenClass and will be used to determine what element to update
- An instance of the SideBySideScoreElement class

There are eight elements needed to create an instance of the SideBySideScoreElement class. The class creates an instance of Sprite with a field for a static label and a field for changeable content text. The SideBySideScoreElement class will be discussed in detail in the next section. For now, you just need to understand that it creates a visual screen element on the ScoreBoard that shows a String label and then a String content next to the label. They are separated by a buffer space. For instance, we need a SideBySideScoreElement instance for the score. The label will be the word **Score** and the content will be the player's score.

- The x location for the Sprite holding the label and the text
- The y location for the Sprite holding the label and the text
- The buffer space, in pixels, between the label and the text
- The String of text for the label, for example **Score**
- The TextFormat of the label
- The width in pixels for the label
- The initialization text for the context text, for example, **0** for a new game's beginning score
- The TextFormat for the content

The createTextElement function definition

The createTextElement function stores the passed key value into the associative array and the newly created instance of the SideBySideScoreElement as the value of the key/value pair. These will be used in the update function that is called by Main to update score elements.

```
public function createTextElement(key:String, ↵
 obj:SideBySideScoreElement):void {

 textElements[key] - obj;
 addChild(obj);
}
```

The update function definition

The update function is a public function that allows the updating of a SideBySideScoreElement instance on the ScoreBoard. In the framework, the Main class calls this function after receiving events from the Game class instance.

```
//update() is called by Main after receiving a custom event
//from the Game class

 tempElement.setContentText(value);
```

When we get to th we will see a CustomEventSCoreBoardUpdate that fires off when the score needs to be updated.

```
dispatchEvent(new CustomEventScoreBoardUpdate↩
(CustomEventScoreBoardUpdate.UPDATE_TEXT, ↩
 Main.SCORE_BOARD_CLICKS,String(clicks)));
```

The GameFrameWork(listens for ScoreBoard class updates from this CustomEventScoreBoardUpdate:

```
game.addEventListener(CustomEventScoreBoardUpdate.↩
 UPDATE_TEXT, scoreBoardUpdateListener, false, 0, true);
```

The GameFrameWork class acts on those events with the scoreBoardUpdateListener function and passes the values needed to the ScoreBoard.update method. The function takes the passed in key as a parameter and calls the setContentText function of the corresponding SidebySideScoreElement to set the new value for the content field. A detailed description of the SideBySideSoreElement class is next.

The SideBySideScoreElement class

SideBySideScoreElement is what we like to call a helper class. It probably could exist on its own and be used by other game elements, but its primary goal is to simplify the ScoreBoard class structure and code. As we were writing this framework, we found a few places where we were creating a lot of duplicated code in a class. This was and usually is a red flag that signifies a class is trying to do too much and needs to by modified and or split into some helper classes. The other helper class we created was the CustomBlitButton for the BasicScreen class.

Create the SieBySideScoreElement.as file in the framework package structure we created earlier:

/source/classes/com/efg/framework/SideBySideScoreElement.as

Here is entire code listing for this class:

```
package   com.efg.framework
{
    import flash.display.Sprite;
    import flash.text.TextField;
    import flash.text.TextFormat;

    /**
     * ...
     * @author Jeff Fulton
     */

        public class SideBySideScoreElement extends Sprite {
        private var label:TextField = new TextField();
        private var content:TextField = new TextField();
        private var bufferWidth:Number;

        public function SideBySideScoreElement(x:Number, y:Number,↩
         bufferWidth:Number, labelText:String,labelTextFormat:↩
         TextFormat, labelWidth:Number, contentText:String,↩
         contentTextFormat:TextFormat) {

            this.x = x;
            this.y = y;

            this.bufferWidth= bufferWidth;
```

```
            label.autoSize;
            label.defaultTextFormat = labelTextFormat;
            label.text = labelText;

            content.autoSize;
            content.defaultTextFormat = contentTextFormat;
            content.text = contentText;

            label.x = 0;
            content.x = labelWidth + bufferWidth;

            addChild(label);
            addChild(content);

        }

        public function setLabelText(str:String):void {
            label.text = str;
        }

        public function setContentText(str:String):void {
            content.text = str;
        }
    }
}
```

What exactly is a score board element? The player's score, for example, is something that we want to display to the user. So, we have a label of Score followed by the actual score value. On the screen it would look something like this: Score   850.

There is nothing spectacular here really, but it's adequate for the simple display needed in this book.

The variable definition section for this class is very simple. We need to define variables to hold the label and content values as well as the buffer value for the number of pixels to separate these two text elements.

This class extends Sprite and contains two text fields, separated by a buffer set of pixels defined by the bufferWidth variable. The label variable holds the text that represents the left-side static label for the display. The content variable represents the content to the right of the label. So, for the previous example, the word Score is the label and the value 8500 is the content.

The constructor definition

The constructor does most of the heavy lifting in this class. Here are definitions of the passed-in parameters:

- x is the x axis screen location for the starting point to draw the label and the content on the ScoreBoard.
- y is the y axis screen location for the starting point to draw the label and the content on the ScoreBoard.
- bufferWidth is the buffer space, in pixels, between the label and the content.
- labelText is the String of text for the label.

- ■ labelTextFormat is the TextFormat of the label.
- ■ labelWidth is the width in pixels for the label.
- ■ contentText is the initialization text for the context.
- ■ contentTextFormat is the TextFormat for the content.

The constructor sets the label TextField instance and the content TextField instance to the appropriate passed in values. The content.x is set to the width of the label field plus the bufferWidth value. This will act as a way to make sure that the label and content elements float together nicely on the screen. Other than that, all of the other attribute assignments are pretty straightforward.

The final thing we do is add the content and label TextField instances to the display list of the SideBySideScoreElement instance.

The setLabelText and setContentText definition functions

These two functions are public, and they allow the label and content text to be changed externally by the ScoreBoard class. We described the label text as static previously, but since there is no real way to create a static text field from a dynamically created TextField instance, we decided to allow the label to be changed just in case there was a need for it down the road.

```
public function setLabelText(str:String):void {
  label.text = str;
}

public function setContentText(str:String):void {
  content.text = str;
}
```

The Game class

The Game.as framework class is the parent class for all games we will make that use the framework. It contains the bare minimum information needed to communicate with the GameFrameWork.as sub-class Main that we will create for our game.

Create the Game.as file in the framework package structure we created earlier:

/source/classes/com/efg/framework]Game.as

Here is entire code listing for this class:

```
package  com.efg.framework
{
   // Import necessary classes from the flash libraries
   import flash.display.MovieClip;
   import com.efg.framework.CustomEventScoreBoardUpdate;
   import com.efg.framework.CustomEventLevelScreenUpdate;

   /**
   * ...
   * @author Jeff Fulton
   */
   public class Game extends MovieClip {
      //Create constants for simple custom events
      public static const GAME_OVER:String = "game over";
```

```
        public static const NEW_LEVEL:String = "new level";

        //Constructor calls init() only
        public function Game() {}

        public function newGame():void {}

        public function newLevel():void {}

        public function runGame():void {}

    }

}
```

The Game.as class is a shell that contains only the necessary functions and constants necessary for a child of it to work with and communicate with the GameFrameWork.as class and its child class, Main.as, which will be customized for each game.

The two constants, GAME_OVER and NEW_LEVEL, are used to communicate state changes to the GameFrameWork class. The GameFrameWork class has listeners for these two events that we have seen previously.

We also set up the newGame, newLevel, and runGame functions that the GameFrameWork will call when it reaches the systemNewGame, systemNewLevel, and systemGamePlay functions respectively.

Let's create the stub game now to demonstrate how to create the Main.as sub class of GameFrameWork.as and the StubGame.as sub class of this Game.as class.

A stub game class

We are about to embark on the first game of this book using the set of framework classes that we have covered in this chapter. This is not an ambitious game but is helpful in getting your feet wet testing the framework code. This will be a good way for you to make sure the entire framework set of classes are working before we start on the Super Click game in Chapter 3.

Game objective

Click the mouse ten times. That's it. We made the same game in Chapter 1.

Game state screen flow

We are going to need four instances of the BasicScreen class for our game. Three of these screens with contain an instance the SimpleBlitButton to move between game states. These screens will be called titleScreen, instructionsScreen, and gameOverScreen. We will make use of one other screen called levelInScreen. This screen will not make use of a SimpleBlitButton to move to a new game state. All four of these BasicScreen instances have already been created as part of the GameFrameWork class. We will create a Main.as class unique to our game that will extend GameFrameWork.as and customize these screens for our stub game.

Game ScoreBoard constants

We will need to create a single element on our `scoreBoard` object to hold the number of times the player has clicked the mouse. We will always create constants in the `Main.as` class to handle the `scoreBoard` elements. The constant for this element will be called `SCORE_BOARD_CLICKS`.

Creating the Main.as class

Let's get to the goods now. After the next few pages, you will have created your first game within the framework and will be ready to create the rest of the games in this book. We covered creating a project for two different development environments earlier in this chapter. If you have not created the `Main.as` class file yet, it is time to do so. You will need to create a `Main.as` class and save it in the project folder for your chosen development environment:

In the Flash IDE, your folder structure will look something like the following:

```
[source]
    [projects]
        [stubgame]
            [flashIDE]
                [com]
                    [efg]
                        [games]

                            [stubgame]
                                Main.as
```

Using the Flex SDK (that is, Flash Develop), your structure will look like this:

```
[source]
    [projects]
        [stubgame]
            [flexSDK]
                [bin]
                [obj]
                [lib]
                [src]
                    [com]
                        [efg]
                            [games]
                                [stubgame]
                                    Main.as
```

Here is entire code listing for this class:

```
package com.efg.games.stubgame
{
    import flash.text.TextFormat;
    import flash.text.TextFormatAlign;
    import flash.geom.Point;

    import com.efg.framework.FrameWorkStates;
    import com.efg.framework.GameFrameWork;
    import com.efg.framework.BasicScreen;
    import com.efg.framework.ScoreBoard;
    import com.efg.framework.SideBySideScoreElement;
```

```
public class Main extends GameFrameWork {

    //custom sccore board elements
    public static const SCORE_BOARD_CLICKS:String = "clicked";

    public function Main() {
        init();
    }


    override public function init():void {
        game = new StubGame();
        setApplicationBackGround(400, 400, false, 0x000000);

        //add score board to the screen as the seconf layer
        scoreBoard = new ScoreBoard();
        addChild(scoreBoard);

        scoreBoardTextFormat= new TextFormat
        ("_sans", "11", "0xffffff", "true");

        scoreBoard.createTextElement(SCORE_BOARD_CLICKS,
         new SideBySideScoreElement(25, 5, 15, "Clicks",
         scoreBoardTextFormat, 25, "0",scoreBoardTextFormat));

        //screen text initializations
        screenTextFormat = new TextFormat("_sans", "16",
        "0xffffff", "false");

        screenTextFormat.align = flash.text.TextFormatAlign.
         CENTER;
        screenButtonFormat = new TextFormat("_sans", "12",
         "0x000000", "false");

        titleScreen = new BasicScreen(FrameWorkStates.
         STATE_SYSTEM_TITLE,400,400,false,0x0000dd );

        titleScreen.createOkButton("OK", new Point(170, 250),
         40, 20, screenButtonFormat, 0x000000, 0xff0000,2);

        titleScreen.createDisplayText("Stub Game", 100,new
         Point(145,150),screenTextFormat);

        instructionsScreen = new BasicScreen(FrameWorkStates.
         STATE_SYSTEM_INSTRUCTIONS,400,400, false,0x0000dd);

        instructionsScreen.createOkButton("Play", new Point
        (150, 250), 80, 20,screenButtonFormat, 0x000000, 0xff0000,2);

        instructionsScreen.createDisplayText(
        "Click the mouse\n10 times",150,new Point(120,150),
         screenTextFormat);

        gameOverScreen = new BasicScreen(FrameWorkStates.
         STATE_SYSTEM_GAME_OVER,400,400,false,0x0000dd);
```

```
gameOverScreen.createOkButton("OK", new Point(170, 250),↵
40, 20,screenButtonFormat, 0x000000, 0xff0000,2);

gameOverScreen.createDisplayText("Game Over",100,new↵
 Point(140,150),screenTextFormat);

levelInScreen = new BasicScreen(FrameWorkStates.↵
 STATE_SYSTEM_LEVEL_IN, 400, 400, true, 0xaaff0000);

levelInText = "Level ";
levelInScreen.createDisplayText(levelInText,100,new ↵
 Point(150,150),screenTextFormat);

//Set standard wait time between levels
waitTime= 30;

//set initial game state
switchSystemState(FrameWorkStates.STATE_SYSTEM_TITLE);


//create timer and run it one time
frameRate = 30;
startTimer();
    }
  }
}
```

Class import and variable definitions for the Main class

Along with the Flash library classes we need for text and formatting, we also import in the Point class, so we can pass Point instances that contain the location values for the BasicScreen and SimpleBlitButton instances we will instantiate in the init function. The only variables we need to define are the constants for the ScoreBoard. We have only a single element on the ScoreBoard for our stub game, so we only create a single constant:

```
public static const SCORE_BOARD_CLICKS:String = "clicked";
```

Notice that Main.as extends the GameFramework class. This gives it access to all of the public methods and properties of GameFrameWork to use as if they were its own. We will need to override the init function of GameFrameWork.as to instantiate customize the screens and score board for each unique game.

Applying the constructor and init function definitions

The constructor of our Main.as class simply calls the init function. In Chapter 12, we will create preloaders for both the Flash IDE and the Flex SDK. The preloaders will require us to add code to our game that waits for the Stage object to be available. We do not need that code for this game, so we simply call the init function.

The heart of this Main.as class is the init function override of the GameFrameWork.as file's init function. Here, we will modify the framework for each particular game. It is very important that you completely understand what is going on in this function, as it will be modified and used in every game we will create throughout this book.

Creating our game instance

The game variable is defined in the GameFrameWork.as file, but instantiated in Main.as. We will create the Game subclass called instance StubGame.as in the next section.

```
game = new StubGame();
```

Setting the application back ground

The appBackGroundBitmapData variable is defined in the GameFrameWork.as file but set up in Main.as by calling the setApplicationBackGround public function in the Main.as parent class, GameFrameWork. For our stub game, we are creating a 400, 400 opaque black background.

```
setApplicationBackGround(400, 400, false, 0x000000);
```

Creating the score board

The scoreBoard variable is defined in the GameFrameWork.as file and instantiated in Main.as. To set up scoreBoard, we need to create a TextFormat for the look of the scoreBoard text (scoreBoardTextFormat) and then create each text element we will need on the scoreBoard. We only have a single element on the scoreBoard in this stub game. We pass in the constant, SCORE_BOARD_CLICKS, which was defined in the variable definition section of this Main.as class file, into the public scoreBoard.createTextElement function along with the definition of the SideBySideScoreElement class instance for this scoreBoard element.

```
scoreBoard = new ScoreBoard();
addChild(scoreBoard);
scoreBoardTextFormat= new TextFormat("_sans", "11", "0xffffff", ↵
 "true");

scoreBoard.createTextElement(SCORE_BOARD_CLICKS, new ↵
 SideBySideScoreElement(25, 5, 15, "Clicks", scoreBoardTextFormat,↵
 25, "0", scoreBoardTextFormat));
```

In this definition, we are setting the "Clicks" string label to reside at the 25, 5 location on the scoreBoard. We have also set a 15 pixel buffer between the "Clicks" label text and the value that will be displayed and have given the label a width of 25 pixels. We have set the TextFormat for both the label and the content to the scoreBoardTextFormat we defined earlier.

Creating the title screen

All of the BasicScreen instances will be set up in a similar manner. All are defined in the GameFrameWork.as file and instantiated in the Main.as init function. The first thing we do is set up a separate TextFormat object (screenTextFormat) to be shared between all of the screens. We could actually use a different TextFormat for each screen, but for simplicity, we are using one in this example game. We also create a TextFormat for SimpleBlitButton instances that can be added to each BasicScreen instance.

```
screenTextFormat = new TextFormat("_sans", "16", "0xffffff", "false");
screenTextFormat.align = flash.text.TextFormatAlign.CENTER;

screenButtonFormat = new TextFormat("_sans", "12", "0x000000", ↵
 "false");
```

```
titleScreen = new BasicScreen(FrameWorkStates.STATE_SYSTEM_TITLE,↵
400,400,false,0x0000dd );

titleScreen.createOkButton("OK", new Point(170, 250), 40, 20, ↵
screenButtonFormat, 0x000000, 0xff0000,2);

titleScreen.createDisplayText("Stub Game", 100,new Point↵
(145,150), screenTextFormat);
```

The `titleScreen` object is created by passing in a constant for the `id` value of the `BasicScreen` instance. We are using the `FrameWorkStates` constants for the `BasisScreen` `id` values. The `titleScreen` also accepts in the `width` (400), `height` (400), `isTransparent` (false), and color value for the background of the screen (0x0000dd).

The next task we must complete when creating an instance of the `BasicScreen` class is decide if we want any text or **OK** button on the screen. Those are set up by calling the associated public functions in the `BasicScreen` class. The `titleScreen.createOkButton` function all in the stub game creates a `SimpleBlitButton` instance with `OK` as the text of the button, 170,250 as the location, and 20 as the width of the button. We also pass in the `screenButtonFormat` as the `TextFormat` for the **OK** text, the off color as black, and the over color and red. The final number we pass in, 2, is a buffer amount used for positioning the text on the button.

The `createDisplayText` function takes in the text to put on to the `titleScreen`, Stub Game, as well as the `width` (100), location for the text box (145,150), and the `TextFormat` (screenTextFromat) for the text on the screen.

Creating the instructions screen

The `instructionsScreen` is instantiated exactly like the `titleScreen` only with parameter values passed in specific to the instructions. Some of the differences you will notice are the use of the `FrameWorkStates.STATE_SYSTEM_INSTRUCTIONS` for the `id` value of the `BasicScreen` instance, the new text for the button Play, and the new text for the screen, Click the mouse\n10 times. You will also notice that some sizes and locations have been customized for these new text values. The "\n" character is an "escape sequence". When placed in a String, it will force the TextField to start a "new line" and place the text following it on this new line.

```
instructionsScreen = new BasicScreen(FrameWorkStates.↵
STATE_SYSTEM_INSTRUCTIONS,400,400, false,0x0000dd);

instructionsScreen.createOkButton("Play", new Point↵
(150, 250), 80, 20,screenButtonFormat, 0x000000, 0xff0000,2);

instructionsScreen.createDisplayText(↵
"Click the mouse\n10 times",150,new Point(120,150), screenTextFormat);
```

Creating the game over screen

The `gameOverScreen` is instantiated exactly like the `instructionsScreen` only with parameter values passed in specific to the game over state. Some of the differences you will notice are the use of the `FrameWorkStates.STATE_SYSTEM_GAME_OVER` for the `id` value of the `BasicScreen` instance, the new text for the button **OK**, and the new text for the screen, Game Over You will also notice that some sizes and locations have been customized for these new text values.

```
gameOverScreen = new↵
 BasicScreen(FrameWorkStates.STATE_SYSTEM_GAME_OVER,400,400,↵
 false,0x0000dd);

gameOverScreen.createOkButton("OK", new Point(170, 250), 40, ↵
 20,screenButtonFormat, 0x000000, 0xff0000,2);

gameOverScreen.createDisplayText("Game Over",100,new ↵
 Point(140,150),screenTextFormat);
```

Creating the level in screen

The levelInScreen is different than the other three screens because it doesn't make use of BasicScreen classes' okButton. It does make use of custom Main.as variable called levelInText. This variable will hold the default prefix that will be added to the levelInScreen object's text box on each new level.

```
levelInScreen = new BasicScreen(FrameWorkStates.↵
 STATE_SYSTEM_LEVEL_IN, 400, 400, true, 0xaaff0000);

levelInText = "Level ";
levelInScreen.createDisplayText(levelInText,100,new Point(150,150),↵
 screenTextFormat);

//Set standard wait time between levels
waitTime= 30;
```

We also set the waitTime variable to be 30 frames (or the equivalent of 1 second if our frame rate is set to 30). This will be used by the STATE_SYSTEM_WAIT as the default wait time. The levelInScreen uses this state for a transition time delay before the game level starts.

Setting the initial state machine's state

The starting state for our Main.as to run is set by calling the GameFrameWork classes' switchSystemState function and passing in the state constant we would like to start the game in. For this game, we are going to state at the title screen

```
switchSystemState(FrameWorkStates.STATE_SYSTEM_TITLE);
```

Starting the game timer

By setting the frameRate variable and then calling the GameFrameWork classes' startTimer function the framework will begin processing.

```
//create timer and run it one time
frameRate = 30;
startTimer();
```

The stub Game.as class

The stub Game class is a very simple game that just waits for the player to click the mouse ten times before the game ends. It is used to demonstrate the basics of Game.as communication with Main.as using events. You will need to create a StubGame.as class and save it in the project folder for your chosen development environment.

The Flash IDE's file structure looks like this:

```
[source]
      [projects]
            [stubgame]
                  [flashIDE]
                        [com]
                              [efg]
                                    [games]

                                          [stubgame]
                                                StubGame.as
```

And the structure for the Flex SDK (using Flash Develop) looks like this:

```
[source]
      [projects]
            [stubgame]
                  [flexSDK]
                        [bin]
                        [obj]
                        [lib]
                        [src]
                              [com]
                                    [efg]
                                          [games]
                                                [stubgame]
                                                      StubGame.as
```

Here is entire code listing for this class:

```
package  com.efg.games.stubgame
{
   // Import necessary classes from the flash libraries
   import flash.display.Sprite;
   import flash.events.MouseEvent;
   import flash.events.Event;

   import com.efg.framework.Game;
   import com.efg.framework.CustomEventLevelScreenUpdate;
   import com.efg.framework.CustomEventScoreBoardUpdate;

      /**
       * ...
       * @author Jeff Fulton
       */
   public class StubGame extends  Game {
      //Create constants for simple custom events
      public static const GAME_OVER:String = "game over";
      public static const NEW_LEVEL:String = "new level";

      private var clicks:int = 0;
      private var gameLevel:int = 1;
      private var gameOver:Boolean = false;

      public function StubGame() {}
```

```
override public function newGame():void {
   clicks = 0;
   gameOver = false;
   stage.addEventListener(MouseEvent.↵
   MOUSE_DOWN, onMouseDownEvent);

   dispatchEvent(new CustomEventScoreBoardUpdate(↵
     CustomEventScoreBoardUpdate.UPDATE_TEXT, ↵

   Main.SCORE_BOARD_CLICKS,String(clicks)));
}


override public function newLevel():void {

   dispatchEvent(new CustomEventLevelScreenUpdate↵
   (CustomEventLevelScreenUpdate.UPDATE_TEXT, ↵
   String(gameLevel)));
}
```

```
override public function runGame():void {
   if (clicks >= 10) {
      gameOver = true;
   }
   checkforEndGame();
}

public function onMouseDownEvent(e:MouseEvent):void {
   clicks++;
   dispatchEvent(new CustomEventScoreBoardUpdate↵
   (CustomEventScoreBoardUpdate.UPDATE_TEXT, ↵
   Main.SCORE_BOARD_CLICKS,String(clicks)));

   trace("mouse click number:" + clicks);
}

private function checkforEndGame():void {
   if (gameOver) {
      dispatchEvent(new Event(GAME_OVER));
   }
  }
 }
}
```

What we are doing in this class

This will be one of the most simple games you will ever create. When the user clicks the mouse button, we set up a MOUSE_DOWN event listener to increase the clicks variable and dispatch a CustomEventScoreBoardUpdate event to Main to update the scoreBoard. The runGame function is called on each frame tick. If the clicks variable is equal to 10, the gameOver variable is set to true. The runGame function also calls the checkForEndGame function on each frame tick. If the gameOver variable is set to true, then the GAME_OVER event is dispatched to Main.as.

Test it!

Make sure all of the package classes are in the correct folders for developmenment environment you have chosen as described earlier in this chapter. Select to **Build the project**, **Export the movie**, **Publish**, or the similar option in your development envrionment.

If the game doesn't work properly, the most common problem will be class path errors. If you are having problems with the build process, start by rechecking the path to the framework package structure.

Summary

In this chapter, we covered a lot of ground that will be the basis for all of the games throughout the rest of this book. We created the basic framework and package structures that all the games in this book will use. We also created a very simple game to demonstrate the basic interaction between the various classes in the framework.

In the next chapter, we are going to make the first full-blown game with the framework. Super Click is a relatively simple game, but going though the design and the code necessary to hook it into the framework will help solidify the concepts we have covered in this chapter.

Chapter 3

Creating Super Click

We have spent a good portion of this book creating a game framework, but so far, we don't have much to show for it. We will now create a simple game that makes use of the framework as a demonstration.

Let's take a deep dive into our first example game, Super Click. It is a simple game that is similar to many early Flash viral games. It is not original by any means, but the main point we want to demonstrate here is how the Game and Main classes interact. To do this, we'll first discuss the elements we need for the game in a simple technical design specification. Next, we will discuss how we tie all of this together into a set of functions to actually create a game. Before we start with the code, we will lay out a very simple technical design document for our game. This document will be used to modify create a Main.as class for Super Click that extends the GameFrameWork.as class. It will also be used to create the SuperClick.as class file that will extend the Game.as framework class.

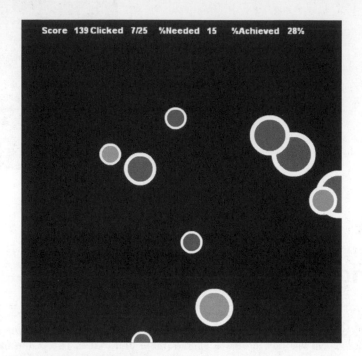

Score 139 Clicked 7/25   %Needed 15   %Achieved 28%

Figure 3-1. The Super Click game screen

Creating a Super Click game design specification

We are going to create a simple game technical specification document. It will describe basic game play, but more importantly it will describe how we are going to plan on implementing the game logic. There is nothing wrong with just jumping in and starting to code a game for fun. Experimentation can bring you great rewards, but when you start to design a game that you want to sell or especially one that might be for a client, you will want to plan out the game logic at least to some degree before you jump in and start coding.

Defining the game basics

The game basics will describe the idea behind the game and the general game play fundamentals.

- **Game name**: Super Click
- **Game objective**: Click the good circles, and avoid clicking the bad circles.
- **Game play description**: Blue and red circles will start to appear on the screen. They start small and get bigger, finally disappearing when they have reached a certain size. The player must avoid the red circles and click the blue circles. The quicker the player clicks a blue circle, the more points are awarded. If the player does not click enough circles on a level, the game will be over. It the player clicks a red circle that game will also be over.

Calculating level progression

The level progression calculations describe how the difficulty will increase on each game level. We are going to make the game play more difficult by increasing the number of circles that need to be clicked and the growth speed of the circles. We will also decrease the maximum size of the circles and the increase the percentage of good (blue) circles that have to be clicked before the game moves to the next level.

- **Number of blue circles per level**: 25 times the level number
- **Percent chance for a bad circle**: Level number plus 9 (After level 25 the percentage is 40, which keeps the game from becoming impossible.)
- **Circle growth speed**: .01 times the level number
- **Maximum circle size**: 5 minus the level number, with a minimum of 1
- **Percent successful clicks needed to move to next level**: 5 times the level number, plus 10
- **Maximum number of circles on the screen**: 10 times level number

Defining the basic screens needed

The basic screens will all be instances of the BasicScreen class introduced in Chapter 2. As you might recall, this BasicScreen class allows for a button (an instance of the BasicBlitButton class) to be displayed, which is referred to as the OK button. The screen that displays before a new level starts (levelInScreen) does not need a button. It will wait for a small amount of time before starting the next level. No button click is necessary. The basic screens follow:

- **Title**: Contains an OK button and the text Super Click
- **Instructions**: Contains an OK button and the text Quickly Click Blue Circles
- **Game over**: Contains an OK button and the text Game Over
- **Level**: Contains the text Level and the level variable (does not include an OK button)

Defining the game play variables

The game play variables are used to control the game logic and level difficulty. These are broken up into variables that control game logic and variables needed to set the difficulty level.

The following variables pertain to the *game logic*:

- circles: This array holds all of the current on-screen circle class instances. We will create a custom class called Circle that will be used to create the objects in this array.
- gameOver: This Boolean is set to true if the player clicks a red circle or does not click enough circles (percentNeeded) on a level.
- level: This variable holds the current game level.
- numClicks: This one holds number of blue circles clicked by the user.
- numCreated: This is the number of circles created so far this level. Circles are created until maxCirclesOnScreen is reached.

- `maxScore`: This is the maximum score for a blue circle. The maximum score decreases as the circles' size increases. They have an inverse relationship. The smaller the circle, the more points the player will score by clicking on it.
- `percent`: This variable holds the current percentage of blue circles clicked. It's calculated as `100 * (clicked / numCircles)`.
- `score`: This holds the player's score.
- `tempCircle`: Holding a reference to a `Circle` object, this variable is used in loops through the circles array.
- `scoreTexts`: This variable holds an array of current on-screen score text messages. We will create a custom class called `ScoreTextField` that will be used to create the objects in this array.
- `tempScoreText`: This one holds a reference to a `ScoreTextField` class instance that will be used in loops through the `scoreTexts` array.
- `textFormat`: The final game logic variable holds an instance of the Flash `TextFormat` class that will be used to format the text for the `ScoreTextField` instances.

These variables control the *game difficulty*:

- `circleGrowSpeed`: The amount a circle should grow in `scaleX` and `scaleY` on each frame tick
- `circleMaxSize`: The maximum size for a circle on a level, which starts at 5 and goes down to a minimum of 1
- `maxCirclesOnscreen`: The maximum number of circles on the screen at one time (so they don't all get blasted on the screen in the first few frames)
- `numCircles`: The number of blue circles for this level
- `percentNeeded`: The percentage of blue circles clicks needed for the level
- `percentBadCircles`: The percent chance that a bad circle will show up on a frame tick when trying to create a new circle

Defining the custom ScoreBoard elements

The `ScoreBoard` class was created in Chapter 2. It is a very simple class that allows for the developer to place instances of the `SideBySideScoreElement` (also created in chapter 2) on to its display list. You'll need to add the following custom elements to `ScoreBoard`:

- `SCORE_BOARD_SCORE`: The `scoreBoard` name constant in `Main.as` for the score display
- `scoreLabel`: Holds the label **Score**
- `scoreText`: Displays the current score
- `SCORE_BOARD_CLICKED`: The `scoreBoard` name constant in `Main.as` for the clicked display
- `clickedText`: Displays the `clicked` value followed by a slash (/) and the `numCircles` values, to indicate how many of the circles available in this level have already been clicked
- `SCORE_BOARD_PERCENT_NEEDED`: The `scoreBoard` name constant in `Main.as` for the percent needed display

- percentNeededLabel: Displays **% needed**
- percentNeededText: Displays the percent of blue circles needed per level value
- SCORE_BOARD_PERCENT_ACHIEVED: The scoreBoard name constant in Main.as for the percent achieved display
- percentAchievedLabel: Displays **% achieved**
- percentAchievedText: Displays the value representing the percent of blue circles clicked

Describing the game play and flow

The game is split into a series of levels with ever increasing difficulty. A level will start by randomly placing circles on to the game screen until circle.length == maxCirclesOnscreen. As circles are created, the percentBadCircles variable will be used to determine whether to create a good (blue) or bad (red) circle. Circles will grow at the circleGrowSpeed rate. This will increase the scaleX and scaleY values for the Circle instance on each frame tick.

The player must click as many blue circles as possible before the circles reach circleMaxSize. The smaller a Circle, the more points the player will receive for clicking it. If the player does not click a Circle before it reaches circleMaxSize, it will leave the screen.

When a Circle is clicked or leaves the screen because it reached circleMaxSize, a new circle will be created to replace it if the numCreated variable is less than the numCircles variable.

When a good Circle instance is clicked, the Circle will fade out, and a text field containing the score the player received will be displayed close to the Circle.

Evaluating the end of a level

A game level is over when all of the circles (numCircles) have been displayed on the screen. The logic will also need to make sure that there are no Circle instances in the circles array before the level can be considered over.

If the circle array length is 0 and number of circles created so far is equal to the number of circles required for the level, the level is complete. (aCircle.length == 0 && numCreated == numCircles).

Evaluating the end of a game

The game is over when the player clicks a red circle at any time or completes a level without clicking enough blue circles (that is, if the percentage clicked is not greater than or equal to percentNeeded).

Defining the necessary events

Events are used throughout the framework to signify changes to the state of the game and to update the scoreboard instance and the levelInScreen. We split events into two different categories. The first are **simple custom events**. These are simply String constants that will be passed to the standard dispatchEvent function call. They are not used to pass any data to the listening function. The second type of events we will use are called **complex custom events**. These make use of the customized Event classes created in Chapter 2 and have the ability to pass data to the listening functions.

These are the simple custom event constants:

- GAME_OVER: Dispatched to Main to change state to STATE_SYSYEM_GAME_OVER
- NEW_LEVEL: Dispatched to Main to change state to STATE_SYSTM_NEW_LEVEL

The complex custom events needed for this game are few. We will need some basic events for Main to update the ScoreBoard class that we will create for this game. These CustomEventScoreBoardUpdate.UPDATE_TEXT events pass two variables in the custom events object: Key and Value. We also have to pass CustomEventLevelScreenUpdate.UPDATE_TEXT to Main (CUSTOMEVENT_SCORE_BOARD_UPDATE). This simply passes the new level value in the custom event object. The custom events, along with the key/value pairs they pass, that we will be using are as follows:

- Updating the score on the scoreboard:

    - **Event**: CustomEventScoreBoardUpdate.UPDATE_TEXT
    - **Key**: Main.SCORE_BOARD_SCORE
    - **Value**: 0 for a new game or the current score during game play

- Updating the clicked text on the scoreboard:

    - **Event**: CustomEventScoreBoardUpdate.UPDATE_TEXT
    - **Key**: Main.SCORE_BOARD_CLICKED
    - **Value**: 0/0 for new game and level or clicked + "/" + numCircles during game play

- Updating the percent needed on the scoreBoard

    - **Event**: CustomEventScoreBoardUpdate.UPDATE_TEXT
    - **Key**: Main.SCORE_BOARD_PERCENT_NEEDED
    - **Value**: 0% for new game or percentNeeded during game play for new level

- Updating the percent achieved on the scoreBoard

    - **Event**: CustomEventScoreBoardUpdate.UPDATE_TEXT
    - **Key**: Main.SCORE_BOARD_PERCENT_ACHIEVED
    - **Value**: 0% for a new game or percentAchieved during game play for new level

- Updating the level number on the levelInScreen

    - **Event**: CustomEventLevelScreenUpdate.UPDATE_TEXT
    - **Key**: "level" + level variable

Defining the game-specific custom classes

When we need more than one instance of an object and if those objects will each need to store unique data about themselves, we usually create a custom class for the object. We will create the following custom classes for the circles that need to be clicked and also for displaying the score the player received for clicking on a circle:

- Circle instances will contain data for a type (GOOD or BAD) and whether or not they have been clicked.

■ ScoreTextField instances will contain data for the life span they will stay on the screen before being removed.

Creating Super Click

We are now going to take the game design specification and apply it to the game framework from Chapter 2 to create our game. We will start by creating a new Game.as class.

The Super Click game requires you to create a new Game.as file for the Game class and a new Circle.as file for the Circle class.

Starting the project

Like in the stub game in Chapter 2, we will be creating Super Click as part of the overall framework package structure. In this chapter, we will discuss how to add a new game to the existing framework and package structure. Please refer to Chapter 2's detailed discussion on the framework and package structure if you have not done so previously.

Creating the Super Click game project in the Flash IDE

Here are the steps to create this project in the Flash IDE:

1. Start up your version of Flash. I am using CS3, but this process should work exactly the same in CS4 and CS5.

2. Create a .fla file in the [source][projects][superclick][flashIDE] folder called superclick.

3. In the [source]projects][superclick][flashIDE] folder, create the package structure for your game: [com][efg][games][superclick].

4. Set the frame rate of the Flash movie to 30 FPS. Set the width and height both to **400**.

5. Set the document class to com.efg.games.superclick.Main

6. We have not yet created the Main.as class so you will see a warning. We are going to create this later in this chapter.

7. Now, add the framework reusable class package to the class path for the .fla file. In the **Publish Settings**, select **Flash ➤ Actionscript 3 Setting**.

8. Click the **Browse to Path** button, and find the /source folder we created in Chapter 2 for the package structure.

9. Select the classes folder and click the **Choose** button. Now the com.efg.framework package will be available for use when we begin to create our game.

Creating the Super Click game project in the Flash Develop

Here are the steps we will go through to create the project in Flash Develop:

1. Create a folder inside the [source][projects][superclick] folder called flexSDK (if you have not already done so).

2. Start Flash Develop, and create a new project. Select **Flex 3 Project**, and give the project the name **superclick**. The location should be the /source/projects/superclick/flexSDK folder, and the package should be com.efg.games.superclick.

   Do not have Flash Develop create a project folder automatically. Make sure **Create Folder For Project** is *unchecked*.

3. Click the **OK** button to create the project.

4. To add the class path to the framework to the project, go to the **Project ➤ Properties ➤ Classpaths** menu item.

5. Click the **Add Classpath** button. Find the /source folder we created earlier, and select the classes subfolder.

6. Click the **OK** button and then the **Apply** button.

You now have the basic structure to start creating projects inside the framework. We are now going to discuss a few topics concerning the structure of the framework classes and then move into building the reusable framework code.

> *For Flex Builder, Flash Builder, or another IDE, please refer to the documentation provided for that product to create a new project and set the default compile class.*
>
> *Here's a note on the Flash Develop and Flash IDE workflow: A common method of Flash development is to use the Flash IDE for assets and organization and Flash Develop for code editing. If this is your workflow of choice, you will want to follow the Flash IDE folder and package structure rather than the Flex SDK folder structure.*

The Class file list

The class file list is a list of all the classes that that we will need to create to successfully compile and run the Super Click game. All of these will reside in the com.efg.games.superclick package:

- Main.as (will extend the GameFrameWork.as framework class)
- SuperClick.as (will extend the Game.as framework class)
- Circle.as
- ScoreTextField.as

Creating the Main.as class

Let's get to the goods now. After the next few pages, you will have created your first game within the framework and will be ready to create the rest of the games in this book. We covered creating a project for two different development environments earlier in this chapter. If you have not done this yet, it is time to do so. You will need to create a `Main.as` class and save it in the project folder for your chosen development environment:

This is the folder structure for the Flash IDE:

```
[source]
     [projects]
          [superclick]
               [flashIDE]
                    [com]
                         [efg]
                              [games]

                                   [superclick]
                                        Main.as
```

And this is the file structure for the Flex SDK (using Flash Develop):

```
[source]
     [projects]
          [superclick]
               [flexSDK]
                    [bin]
                    [obj]
                    [lib]
                    [src]
                         [com]
                              [efg]
                                   [games]
                                        [superclick]
                                             Main.as
```

Here is entire code listing for this class.

```
package com.efg.games.superclick
{

    import flash.text.TextFormat;
    import flash.text.TextFormatAlign;
    import flash.geom.Point;

    import com.efg.framework.FrameWorkStates;
    import com.efg.framework.GameFrameWork;
    import com.efg.framework.BasicScreen;
    import com.efg.framework.ScoreBoard;
    import com.efg.framework.SideBySideScoreElement;

    public class Main extends GameFrameWork {

        //custom sccore board elements
        public static const SCORE_BOARD_SCORE:String = "score";
        public static const SCORE_BOARD_CLICKED:String = "clicked";
        public static const SCORE_BOARD_PERCENT_NEEDED:String ↵
         = "percent needed";
        public static const SCORE_BOARD_PERCENT_ACHIEVED:String ↵
         = "percent achieved";
```

```
public function Main() {
    init();
}

// init() is used to set up all of the things that
//we should only need to do one time

override public function init():void {
    game = new SuperClick();
    setApplicationBackGround(400, 400, false, 0x000000);

    //add score board to the screen as the seconf layer
    scoreBoard = new ScoreBoard();
    addChild(scoreBoard);
    scoreBoardTextFormat= new TextFormat("_sans", "11",↵
    "0xffffff", "true");

    scoreBoard.createTextElement(SCORE_BOARD_SCORE, new ↵
    SideBySideScoreElement (25, 5, 15, "Score",↵
    scoreBoardTextFormat, 25, "0",scoreBoardTextFormat));

    scoreBoard.createTextElement(SCORE_BOARD_CLICKED, new ↵
    SideBySideScoreElement(85, 5, 10, "Clicked", ↵
    scoreBoardTextFormat, 40, "0/0",scoreBoardTextFormat));

    scoreBoard.createTextElement(SCORE_BOARD_PERCENT_NEEDED,↵
    new SideBySideScoreElement(170,5, 10, "%Needed", ↵
    scoreBoardTextFormat, 50, "0%",scoreBoardTextFormat));

    scoreBoard.createTextElement(SCORE_BOARD_PERCENT_ACHIEVED,↵
    new SideBySideScoreElement(260, 5, 10, "%Achieved", ↵
    scoreBoardTextFormat, 60, "0%",scoreBoardTextFormat));

    //screen text initializations
    screenTextFormat = new TextFormat("_sans", "16", ↵
    "0xffffff", "false");

    screenTextFormat.align = flash.text.TextFormatAlign.CENTER;

    screenButtonFormat = new TextFormat("_sans", "12", ↵
    "0x000000", "false");

    titleScreen = newBasicScreen(FrameWorkStates.↵
    STATE_SYSTEM_TITLE, 400,400,false, 0x0000dd );

    titleScreen.createOkButton("OK", new Point(170, 250), ↵
    40, 20, screenButtonFormat, 0x000000, 0xff0000,2);

    titleScreen.createDisplayText("Super Click", 100,new↵
    Point(145,150),screenTextFormat);
```

```
instructionsScreen = new BasicScreen(FrameWorkStates.↵
 STATE_SYSTEM_INSTRUCTIONS,400,400, false,0x0000dd);

instructionsScreen.createOkButton("Play", new Point↵
 (150, 250), 80, 20, screenButtonFormat, 0x000000, ↵
 0xff0000,2);

instructionsScreen.createDisplayText(↵
 "Click the blue\ncircles",150, new Point(120,150),↵
 screenTextFormat);

gameOverScreen = new BasicScreen (FrameWorkStates.↵
 STATE_SYSTEM_GAME_OVER,400,400,false,0x0000dd);

gameOverScreen.createOkButton("OK", new Point(170, 250),↵
 40, 20,screenButtonFormat, 0x000000, 0xff0000,2);

gameOverScreen.createDisplayText("Game Over",100,new↵
 Point(140,150),screenTextFormat);

levelInScreen = new BasicScreen(FrameWorkStates.↵
 STATE_SYSTEM_LEVEL_IN, 400, 400, true, 0xaaff0000);

levelInText = "Level ";

levelInScreen.createDisplayText(levelInText,100,new ↵
 Point(150,150),screenTextFormat);

//set initial game state
switchSystemState(FrameWorkStates.STATE_SYSTEM_TITLE);

waitTime= 40;

//create timer and run it one time
frameRate = 30;
startTimer();
    }
   }
 }
```

In Chapter 2, we discussed in detail each of these changes to the Main.as init function necessary to customize it for the stub game. There is very little new introduced in this version of Main for Super Click, but in case you need a refresher read through the next section. If not, you can skip to "The Game class for Super Click" section.

Importing classes and defining variables for Main.as

Along with the Flash library classes we need for text and formatting, we also import in the Point class, so we can pass Point instances that contain the location values for the BasicScreen and SimpleBlitButton instances we will instantiate in the init function. The only variables we need to define are the constants for the ScoreBoard. We have four elements on the ScoreBoard for our stub game, so we have created a constant name for each.

```
public static const SCORE_BOARD_SCORE:String = "score";
public static const SCORE_BOARD_CLICKED:String = "clicked";
public static const SCORE_BOARD_PERCENT_NEEDED:String = ↵
 "percent needed";

public static const SCORE_BOARD_PERCENT_ACHIEVED:String = ↵
 "percent achieved";
```

Notice that Main.as extends the GameFramework class, which gives it access to all of the public methods and properties of GameFrameWork to use as if they were its own. We will need to override the init function of GameFrameWork.as to instantiate customize the screens and score board for each unique game.

Defining the constructor and init function the constructor of our Main.as class simply calls the init function. In Chapter 12, we will create preloaders for both the Flash IDE and the Flex SDK. The preloaders will require us to add code to out game that waits for the Stage object to be available. We do not need that code for this game, so we simply call the init function.

The heart of this Main.as class is the init function override of the GameFrameWork.as file's init function. Here, we will modify the framework for each particular game. It is very important that you completely understand what is going on in this function, because it will be modified and used in every game we will create throughout this book.

Creating our game instance

The game variable is defined on the GameFrameWork.as file but instantiated in Main.as. We will create the Game subclass called instance SuperClick.as in the next section.

```
game = new SuperClick();
```

Setting the application background

The appBackGroundBitmapData variable is defined in the GameFrameWork.as file but set up in Main.as by calling the setApplicationBackGround public function in the Main.as parent class, GameFrameWork. For Super Click, we are creating a 400 × 400–pixel opaque black background.

```
setApplicationBackGround(400, 400, false, 0x000000);
```

Creating the Scoreboard

The scoreBoard variable is defined in the GameFrameWork.as file and instantiated in Main.as. To set up scoreBoard, we need to create a TextFormat instance for the look of the scoreBoard text (scoreBoardTextFormat) and then create each text element we will need on the scoreboard. We have the following four sets of text elements our scoreBoard instance:

```
scoreBoard = new ScoreBoard();
addChild(scoreBoard);
scoreBoardTextFormat= new TextFormat("_sans", "11", "0xffffff", ↵
 "true");

scoreBoard.createTextElement(SCORE_BOARD_SCORE, new ↵
 SideBySideScoreElement(25, 5, 15, "Score", scoreBoardTextFormat,↵
 25,"0", scoreBoardTextFormat));
```

```
scoreBoard.createTextElement(SCORE_BOARD_CLICKED, new ↵
 SideBySideScoreElement(85, 5, 10, "Clicked", scoreBoardTextFormat,↵
  40, "0/0", scoreBoardTextFormat));

scoreBoard.createTextElement(SCORE_BOARD_PERCENT_NEEDED, new ↵
 SideBySideScoreElement(170, 5, 10, "%Needed",scoreBoardTextFormat,↵
 50, "0%", scoreBoardTextFormat));

scoreBoard.createTextElement(SCORE_BOARD_PERCENT_ACHIEVED, new ↵
 SideBySideScoreElement(260, 5, 10, "%Achieved", ↵
 scoreBoardTextFormat, 60, "0%", scoreBoardTextFormat));
```

Creating the title screen

All of the BasicScreen instances will be set up in a similar manner. All are defined in the GameFrameWork.as file and instantiated in the Main.as init function. The first thing we do is set up a separate TextFormat object (screenTextFormat) to be shared among all of the screens. We could actually use a different TextFormat for each screen if we like, but for simplicity, we are using one in this example game. We also create a TextFormat for SimpleBlitButton instances that can be added to each BasicScreen instance.

```
screenTextFormat = new TextFormat("_sans", "16", "0xffffff", "false");
screenTextFormat.align = flash.text.TextFormatAlign.CENTER;
screenButtonFormat = new TextFormat("_sans", "12", "0x000000", ↵
 "false");

titleScreen = new BasicScreen(FrameWorkStates.↵
 STATE_SYSTEM_TITLE,400,400,false,0x0000dd );
titleScreen.createOkButton("OK", new Point(170, 250), 40, 20, ↵
 screenButtonFormat, 0x000000, 0xff0000,2);

titleScreen.createDisplayText("Super Click", 100,new ↵
 Point(145,150),screenTextFormat);
```

The titleScreen object is created by passing in a constant for the id value of the BasicScreen instance. We are using the FrameWorkStates constants for the BasicScreen id values. The titleScreen also accepts in the width (400), height (400), isTransparent (false), and color values for the background of the screen (0x0000dd).

The next task we must do when creating an instance of the BasicScreen class is decide if we want any text or an **OK** button on the screen. Either of those is set up by calling the associated public functions in the BasicScreen class. The titleScreen.createOkButton function all in Super Click creates a SimpleBlitButton instance with "OK" as the text of the button, 170,250 as the location, and 20 as the width of the button. We also pass in the screenButtonFormat as the TextFormat for the **OK** text, and two color values. One for OFF color of the button text and one for the OVER color. We will use black for the OFF color and red for the OVER color. The final number we pass in, 2, is a buffer amount used for positioning the text on the button.

The createDisplayText function takes in the text to put on to the titleScreen, **Super Click**, as well as the width (100), location for the text box (145,150), and the TextFormat (screenTextFromat) for the text on the screen.

111

Creating the instructions screen

The instructionsScreen is instantiated exactly like the titleScreen only with parameter values passed in specific to the instructions. Some of the differences you will notice are the use of the FrameWorkStates.STATE_SYSTEM_INSTRUCTIONS for the id value of the BasicScreen instance, the new text for the button **Play**, and the new text for the screen, "Click the blue\nCircles". You will also notice that some sizes and locations have been customized for these new text values.

```
instructionsScreen = new BasicScreen(FrameWorkStates.↵
 STATE_SYSTEM_INSTRUCTIONS,400,400, false,0x0000dd);

instructionsScreen.createOkButton("Play", new Point(150, 250),↵
  80, 20,screenButtonFormat, 0x000000, 0xff0000,2);

instructionsScreen.createDisplayText("Click the blue\ncircles",150,↵
 new Point(120,150), screenTextFormat);
```

Creating the game over screen

The gameOverScreen is instantiated exactly like the instructionsScreen only with parameter values passed in specific to the game over state. Some of the differences you will notice are the use of the FrameWorkStates.STATE_SYSTEM_GAME_OVER for the id value of the BasicScreen instance, the new text for the button "OK", and the new text for the screen, **GAME OVER**. You will also notice that some sizes and locations have been customized for these new text values.

```
gameOverScreen = new BasicScreen↵
 (FrameWorkStates.STATE_SYSTEM_GAME_OVER,400,400,false,0x0000dd);

gameOverScreen.createOkButton("OK", new Point(170, 250), 40,↵
  20,screenButtonFormat, 0x000000, 0xff0000,2);

gameOverScreen.createDisplayText("Game Over",100,new ↵
 Point(140,150),screenTextFormat);
```

Creating the Level In screen

The levelInScreen is different than the other three screens, because it doesn't make use of BasicScreen classes' okButton. It does make use of a custom Main.as variable called levelInText.. This variable will hold the default prefix that will be added to the levelInScreen object's text box on each new level.

```
levelInScreen = new BasicScreen(FrameWorkStates.↵
 STATE_SYSTEM_LEVEL_IN, 400, 400, true, 0xaaff0000);

levelInText = "Level ";
levelInScreen.createDisplayText(levelInText,100,new Point(150,150),screenTextFormat);
//Set standard wait time between levels
waitTime= 30;
```

We also set the waitTime variable to be 30 frames (or the equivalent of 1 second if our frame rate is set to 30). This variable will be used by the STATE_SYSTEM_WAIT as the default wait time. The levelInScreen uses this state for a transition time delay before the game level starts.

Setting up the initial state machine

The starting state for our Main.as to run is set by calling the GameFrameWork classes' switchSystemState function and passing in the state constant we would like to start the game in. For this game we are going to start at the title screen.

```
switchSystemState(FrameWorkStates.STATE_SYSTEM_TITLE);
```

Starting the game timer

Once we set the frameRate variable and then call the GameFrameWork classes' startTimer function, the framework will begin processing.

```
//create timer and run it one time
frameRate = 30;
startTimer();
```

Creating the Game class for Super Click

The Game class for Super Click follows the same basic structure as the stub game from the previous chapter and is used to demonstrate the basics of Game.as communication with Main.as using events. You will need to create a SuperClick.as class and save it in the project folder for your chosen development environment.

This is the folder structure for the Flash IDE:

```
[source]
    [projects]
        [superclick]
            [flashIDE]
                [com]
                    [efg]
                        [games]
                            [superclick]
                                SuperClick.as
```

And this one is for the Flex SDK (using Flash Develop):

```
[source]
    [projects]
        [superclick]
            [flexSDK]
                [bin]
                [obj]
                [lib]
                [src]
                    [com]
                        [efg]
                            [games]
                                [superclick]
                                    SuperClick.as
```

The SuperClick.as class is the largest piece of code in the first three chapters. Let's take is step by step to go through the details of the code.

Importing the classes and defining the variables for SuperClick.as

The class import and variable definition section sets up the class with the all needed framework and Flash library classes needed as well as creates all of the necessary class level variables for the game to run.

```
package com.efg.games.superclick
{
    // Import necessary classes from the flash libraries
    import flash.display.Sprite;
    import flash.events.*;
    import flash.text.TextField;
    import flash.text.TextFormat;

    import com.efg.framework.Game;
    import com.efg.framework.CustomEventLevelScreenUpdate;
    import com.efg.framework.CustomEventScoreBoardUpdate;


    /**
     * ...
     * @author Jeff Fulton
     */

    public class SuperClick extends com.efg.framework.Game {

        //game logic and flow
        private var score:int;
        private var level:int;
        private var percent:Number;
        private var clicked:int;
        private var gameOver:Boolean;
        private var circles:Array;
        private var tempCircle:Circle;
        private var numCreated:int;

        //messaging
        private var scoreTexts:Array;
        private var tempScoreText:ScoreTextField;
        private var textFormat:TextFormat = new TextFormat(↵
          "_sans", 12, "0xffffff", "true");

        //game level difficulty
        private var maxScore:int = 50;
        private var numCircles:int;
        private var circleGrowSpeed:Number;
        private var circleMaxSize:Number;
        private var percentNeeded:Number;
        private var maxCirclesOnscreen:int;
        private var percentBadCircles:Number;
```

Notice that our SuperClick class must extend the com.efg.framework.Game class. This will give it use of the GAME_OVER and NEW_LEVEL constants already set up in the Game class. It will also provide a structure of classes that can be overridden to ensure that Main.as can communicate with the SuperClick.as properly.

We have separated the variables into three different sections. The first section governs what we call game logic and flow. These variables are needed to make sure the game plays the way it is designed (the game logic).

```
//game logic and flow
private var score:int;
private var level:int;
private var percent:Number;
private var clicked:int;
private var gameOver:Boolean;
private var circles:Array;
private var tempCircle:Circle;
private var numCreated:int;
```

The score variable will hold the current score accumulated by the player. The level variable holds the current game level the player has reached. The percent variable holds the current percentage of blue circles the player has clicked while a game level is in progress. The clicked variable holds the number of blue circles the player has clicked during a game level. The gameOver variable is set to false unless one of the two previously discussed GAME_OVER over conditions occurs (see the section called "The checkForEndGame function definiton"). The circles array holds the list of Circle class references for the current game level. We will discuss the custom Circle class in the next section. The tempCircle variable is a class level variable that will hold the current Circle reference while iterating through the circles array. The numCreated variable holds the current number of Circle instances created during a game level. Not all circles are created at the same time, which you will see when we make use of the numCirclesOnScreen variable.

Next up, we have messaging variables. These are used to place an instance of the custom ScoreTextField class on to the game screen when the player clicks a blue circle. These will display the score the player received for clicking the circle based on its size and the maxScore variable. The scoreTexts variable will hold the current list of ScoreTextField instances that need to be displayed on the game screen. The tempScoreText is a class level variable that will hold a reference to the current ScoreTextField instance while iterating through the scoreTexts array. The textFormat holds the look of the text that will be applied to the ScoreTextField instances.

After that, we have the level difficulty variables. These variables were discussed in detail inside the game technical specification. One of these variables has been defined with a default value. This is the maxScore variable.

```
private var maxScore:int = 50;
```

The maxScore variable is set to 50 at the beginning of the game. This is the score the player will receive if a blue circle is clicked at its smallest size. As a Circle instance grows on the screen, its scale will be used to adjust the maxScore to a lower amount (we say that they have an inverse relationship).

Defining the constructor and init function for SuperClick.as

The constructor function for our game is an empty function that does not need to do any processing.

```
public function SuperClick() {

}
```

In later games, we might call other functions such as an initialization function (sometimes called init) that will set up variables and elements that the game needs before the framework calls the newGame function. Super Click is a very simple game that does not need to do this.

```
override public function newGame():void {
    trace("new game");
    level = 0;
    score = 0;
    gameOver = false;

    dispatchEvent(new CustomEventScoreBoardUpdate
     (CustomEventScoreBoardUpdate.UPDATE_TEXT,
     Main.SCORE_BOARD_SCORE,"0"));

    dispatchEvent(new CustomEventScoreBoardUpdate
     (CustomEventScoreBoardUpdate.UPDATE_TEXT,
     Main.SCORE_BOARD_CLICKED,"0/0"));

    dispatchEvent(new CustomEventScoreBoardUpdate
     (CustomEventScoreBoardUpdate.UPDATE_TEXT,
     Main.SCORE_BOARD_PERCENT_NEEDED,"0%"));

    dispatchEvent(new CustomEventScoreBoardUpdate
     (CustomEventScoreBoardUpdate.UPDATE_TEXT,
     Main.SCORE_BOARD_PERCENT_ACHIEVED,"0%"));
}
```

The first thing that might catch your eye in this code is the override directive in front of the function name. We must do this because the Game.as class that we extend to create SuperClick.as already has a newGame function stub created.

In this code, we reset the score and level variables to 0 and set the gameOver Boolean to false. These are the basic variables that almost all games will have to initialize in their newGame functions. Some games may not have a score, and some may not have levels, but almost all games will have some sort of game over state.

After the variable initialization, we dispatch the custom Event instances to the listeners in Main to update the scoreBoard and reset the values to the game start values. The key passed is a constant we have predefined in the Main.as class. For example, to update the score value on the scoreBoard, we pass in Main.SCORE_BOARD_SCORE as the key and 0 for the value.

If you recall from Chapter 2, the value is the same as the value in the ScoreBoard class when calling the ScoreBoard.update function. The SuperClick.as class does not call these directly, but dispatches an event that Main listens for (the scoreBoard is a child of the Main class, not Game or its subclasses like SuperClick). This allows the Main.as to also update and maintain the scoreBoard.

Decoupling SuperClick and scoreBoard, using Main as a controller and communication mechanism, is a major element in the basic framework, but you can use direct calls if you are more comfortable doing so. That can be accomplished with by passing a reference to the ScoreBoard instance from Main to the Game class. Or by providing public getter and setter functions inside of Main that allow the Game class and its subclasses to make indirect updated to the ScoreBoard instance.

Alternatively, if the ScoreBoard class was set up to listen for events from the Game class (instead of using Main.as as a message receiver), then ScoreBoard would need to have a reference to the Game class. None of these things are wrong *per se*, but once you have started to directly reference class instances and listen for or dispatch events to and from the Game and its own custom classes to the ScoreBoard you will start to create spaghetti of direct references that is difficult to maintain. For this reason, we use the Main class as a message gateway for a single flow of communication between the Game class and the associated classes in the framework. There certainly are other ways to handle this communication, such as using an individual mediator or controller classes that would handle communication between the Game.as subclasses (SuperClick.as in this example), ScoreBoard.as, and other framework classes. This might be useful in much larger games and applications to prevent the Main.as from becoming overburdened with message linking code between all of the classes. Our games will be simple enough that we can rely on Main.as as our message gateway.

Using root to access the main display content holder for the game is not recommended. If needed, the root and parent values are set and available for any object that has been added to a display list with add child. But we don't feel their use is necessary if this book's framework is followed.

Defining the newLevel function

The newLevel function is called by the Main class in the STATE_STSTEM_NEWLEVEL state. Its main job is to reset level-specific variables for the new level. It bases the game leveling on some very basic knobs.

The knob, or settings, idea will be explored the detail in the next chapter on the arcade style game, Flack Cannon. For now, all you need to know is that the knobs are basically variables that we set using the level progression calculations from the Super Click game design document. To recap, those are as follows:

Number of blue Circles per level (25 * level)

- Chance for a bad Circle: (level + 9 or 40% after level 25)
- Circle growth speed (.01 * level)
- Maximum Circle size (5 * level or 1 after level 5)
- Percent successful Clicks needed to move to next level (10 + (5 * level))
- Maximum number of Circles on screen: (10 * level)
- This function also sends custom Event instances for the following:
  - Sends custom events to Main reset ScoreBoard
  - Sends custom event to Main to update **Level Screen** text

117

Here is the complete code for the newLevel function:

```
override public function newLevel():void {
    trace("new level");
    percent = 0;
    clicked = 0;
    circles = [];
    scoreTexts = [];
    level++;
    numCircles = level * 25;
    circleGrowSpeed = .01*level;
    circleMaxSize = (level < 5) ? 5-level : 1;
    percentNeeded = 10 + (5 * level);
    if (percentNeeded > 90)  {
        percentNeeded = 90;
    }

    maxCirclesOnscreen = 10 * level;
    numCreated = 0;
    percentBadCircles = (level < 25) ? level + 9 : 40;

    dispatchEvent(new CustomEventScoreBoardUpdate↵
     (CustomEventScoreBoardUpdate.UPDATE_TEXT,↵
     Main.SCORE_BOARD_PERCENT_NEEDED, String(percentNeeded)));

    dispatchEvent(new CustomEventScoreBoardUpdate↵
     (CustomEventScoreBoardUpdate.UPDATE_TEXT,↵
     Main.SCORE_BOARD_CLICKED,String(clicked + "/" +numCircles)));

    dispatchEvent(new CustomEventLevelScreenUpdate↵
     (CustomEventLevelScreenUpdate.UPDATE_TEXT, String(level)));
}
```

The newLevel function begins by resetting the variables needed for the level to begin properly. The percent variable holds the current percentage of total blue circles clicked by the user. The clicked variable holds the actual number of blue circles clicked by the user on the level. The circles array holds all Circle instances (the blue and evil red ones). We increase the level variable by one (level++) and then jump into calculating the knobs values for the new level. The calculations behind these knobs were discussed in earlier in the game design specification portion of the chapter.

The circleMaxSize variable is used to control the game's difficulty. On the earlier levels, a Circle object can grow to be bigger than 100 percent of its size to make the game easier to play. When the player is on levels 1–4, we set the maximum size for the Circle objects to be 5 minus the level. So on level 1, the maximum size is 4 (or 400 percent). This keeps the Circle on the screen longer and makes it easier to click. When we get to the scoring though, you will see that the quicker the player clicks on a Circle (the smaller it is), the greater the score will be for clicking that Circle.

One interesting construct you may or may not have seen before is the ? operator (formally called the **ternary operator**). It is used in place of a simple if statement, for example:

```
circleMaxSize = (level < 5) ? 5-level : 1;
```

In the example, it works like this:

1. If level is greater than 5, circleMaxSize equals 5 minus the level value.

2. Otherwise, circleMaxSize equals 1.

The numCircles variable is calculated as 25 multiplied by the current level value. On higher levels, there will be many circles that need to be clicked. The game right now is pretty impossible to complete once you pass the third level, but conceivably, there could be hundreds of circles per level.

The circleGrowthSpeed is .01*level, so on level 1 (on each frame tick), the circles grow pretty slowly. You will see in the custom class Circle that the game circles start out at 50 percent of their size and grow from there. So, on level 1, it takes 5 frames for a circle to grow to its original size, and because the level 1 circleMaxSize is 4 (5 minus the level), it will have 45 frame ticks to complete its growth and leave the screen.

The percentNeeded starts at 10. Then the value (5 multiplied by the level) is added to it. This represents the percentage of the good (blue) circles that the player must click to move on to the next level. This calculation could go over 100, so we check see if it is greater than 90 (to be safe), and if it is, we set it back to 90.

The maxCirclesOnScreen variable is used to keep the game levels flowing and running a little longer than if all the circles just appeared on the screen one after another, or all at the same time.

The percentBadCircles variable uses another ? operator. We max out at 40 percent chance of a bad circle appearing instead of a good one on any frame where a circle needs to be created (if circles's length is less than maxCirclesOnScreen).

The final thing we do is to dispatch our custom events. First, we update the ScoreBoard by dispatching one event to update the newly calculated pecentNeeded value on the ScoreBoard and the other to reset the clicked value. The final dispatch is one you have not seen before. It makes use of the CuctomeEventLevelScreenUpdate.UPDATE_TEXT custom Event, which tells the levelInScreen instance of the BasicScreen class (a child of Main) to update its display of the level number to the current level value. The next time the levelInScreen is shown, the new level value will be displayed.

Calling the runGame function definition

The runGame function is repeatedly called by Main in the game loop during the STATE_SYSTEM_GAMEPLAY state.

```
override public function runGame():void {
    trace("run game");
    update();
    checkCollisions();
    render();
    checkforEndLevel();
    checkforEndGame();
}
```

On each game frame tick, each of these functions will be called in order. The update function will modify the values of the Circle and ScoreTextField instances on the game screen. The checkCollisions function will check to see which circles have been clicked by the player. The render function will update the display with a new scale value for all circles that have not been clicked by the user. The checkForEndLevel and checkForEndGame will evaluate the current game play and logic variables and fire off events to Main.as to change state if necessary. All of these functions will be discussed in detail next.

Defining the update function

The update function is called every frame tick during the by the Super Click runGame function (as discussed in the previous section). Its duties are to create new circles, update the size of the circles currently on the screen, and remove any circle that has reached its maximum size. It also handles updating the ScoreTextField instances and removes them if they have been on screen passed their frame tick life values.

```
private function update():void {

    if (circles.length < maxCirclesOnscreen && numCreated < ↵
     numCircles) {

        var newCircle:Circle;
        if (int(Math.random() * 100) <= percentBadCircles ) {
            newCircle=new Circle(Circle.CIRCLE_BAD)
        }else {
            newCircle=new Circle(Circle.CIRCLE_GOOD)
            numCreated ++;
        }
        addChild(newCircle);
        circles.push(newCircle);
    }

    // Checks circles every frame for size and adds
    //to their nextScale property
    // if nextScale is larger than the max, removes the circle
    var circleLength:int = circles.length-1;
    for (var counter:int = circleLength; counter >= 0; counter--) {
        tempCircle = circles[counter];
        tempCircle.update(circleGrowSpeed);
        if (tempCircle.nextScale > circleMaxSize || ↵

         tempCircle.alpha <0 ) {
         removeCircle(counter);
        }
    }

    var scoreTextLength:int = scoreTexts.length-1;
    for (counter= scoreTextLength; counter >= 0; counter--) {
        tempScoreText = scoreTexts[counter];
        if (tempScoreText.update()){ //returns true is life is over
            removeScoreText(counter);
        }
    }
}
```

Adding circles to the screen

If the number of on-screen Circle objects (both blue and red) is less than maxCirclesOnScreen variable and if the number of blue circles created (numCreated) so far on the level is less than the number of blue circles for the level (numCircles), a new Circle object is created.

If a Circle instance needs to be created, a random number from 0 to 99 is created and checked against the percentBadCircles variable. If the random number is less than or equal to the percentBadCircles variable, a red circle is created. If not, a blue circle is created.

The call to the new Circle constructor (a custom class we will look at as the final part of this chapter) takes a single integer parameter. Two static constants are defined in the Circle class: CIRCLE_BAD and CIRCLE_GOOD. Passing CIRCLE_BAD tells the Circle constructor to create a bad, red circle. Conversely, CIRCLE_GOOD tells the Circle constructor to create a good, blue circle. If a good circle is created, the numCreated variable is updated by 1. The newly created Circle instance is placed in a tempCircle variable, added to the circles array, and added to display list of Super Click with the addChil function call.

Updating the on-screen circles

After adding (or not adding) a new Circle class instance, the update function loops through all of the circles currently on the screen. It employs the use of the tempCircle class variable to hold the current Circle instance in the circles array. The tempCircle size is updated by calling its update function passing in the circleGrowthSpeed variable. The tempCircle instance will use this variable to increase the scale of tempCircle. After the update, it checks to see if the tempCircle has reached its maximum size and removes it from the screen if it has. We will examine the Circle class in detail in a later section.

If a Circle instance is to be removed, we call the removeCircle function and pass in the current counter.

Updating the ScoreTextField instances

The ScoreTextField instances will be placed on the screen when the player successfully clicks on blue circles. The ScoreTextField instances will display the click score for a short period of time (life) and then be removed from the screen. Much like the circles array, we will loop through the scoreTexts array placing a reference to the current ScoreTextField instance into the tempScoreText class variable. We will then call the update function of the tempScoreText reference. A true will be returned from this function of the life for the ScoreTextField is over. If so, it will be removed from the screen.

Optimizing the loops

For the loop through the Circle instances, we have employed a couple of loop optimizations that we have found useful over the years. The first optimization is the creation of the circleLength variable. Before we set up the for loop, we find the length of the circles array and subtract 1 from it. We then use this variable in the loop through the circles array. This does two things. First, we don't have to keep reevaluating the length of the array on each loop iteration (that takes up valuable processor time). Also, if we splice an array element from the circles array on one iteration, and try to reevaluate the circles.length value on the next iteration, we would have strange runtime errors that would be difficult to diagnose. This is because we might bypass the final element in the array now that the length is one less than it was when we started.

The other optimization is the loop backward through the `circles` array. By doing this, when we do splice a `Circle` instance from the array (because it has reached its maximum size), we won't skip the `Circle` instance in the array following the one we splice.

For example, let's say we are looping forward through our circles array and we find that the tenth element in the array needs to be removed. We will need to call the `splice` function on the array to remove it. When we do this, the eleventh `Circle` instance in the array now becomes the tenth, and subsequently, all of the elements that follow the eleventh have to shift a place also. Now, on the next loop iteration, we would bypass the new tenth (which was the eleventh) element and move on to the new eleventh (the one that was twelfth). We have skipped processing on the original eleventh element.

We also employ one more optimization. By using the `tempCircle` and setting it to reference the current `circles[ctr]` instance, we don't have to perform a lookup on the `circle` array on each `Circle` instance attribute access call. Array element access is a little slow slow but necessary, and we need to keep it to a minimum if possible.

> *Optimization! To optimize a loop, assign the length of your array to a variable and use it in the for loop instead of the `Array.length` attribute. Iterate backward through your `Array` instance if there is the possibility of removing an element from the array with splicing. Assign the value of your `Array[loop counter]` so the lookup does not have to occur more than one time. The lookup is very slow.*

Defining the removeCircle function

The `removeCircle` function takes in an integer parameter corresponding to the index of the `Circle` instance to be removed from the `circles` array. Its job is to cleanly dispose of `Circle` object instances.

```
private function removeCircle(counter:int):void {
    tempCircle = circles[counter];
    tempCircle.dispose();
    removeChild(tempCircle);
    circles.splice(counter, 1);
}
```

We remove `Circle` instances with three separate function calls. First, we simply call the `Circle` object's internal `dispose` function. You will see this function when we discuss the `Circle` class. The internal `dispose` function should set to `null` all internal objects and get rid of all event listeners.

Next, we simply remove the `Circle` from the `SuperClick` class display list with the `removeChild` function call. The last thing we do is to splice the `Circle` instance from the `circles` array.

Defining the removeScoreText function

The `removeScoreText` function takes in an integer parameter corresponding to the index of the `ScoreTextField` instance to be removed from the `scoreTexts` array. Its job is to cleanly disposes of `ScoreTextField` object instances.

```
private function removeScoreText(counter:int):void {
    tempScoreText = scoreTexts[counter];
    tempScoreText.dispose();
    removeChild(tempScoreText);
    scoreTexts.splice(counter, 1);
}
```

Like the removeCircle function, we remove ScoreTextField instances with three separate function calls. First, we simply call the ScoreTextField object's internal dispose function. We will see this function when we discuss the ScoreTextField class. The internal dispose function should set to null all internal objects and get rid of all event listeners.

Next, we simply remove the ScoreTextField from the SuperClick display list with the removeChild function call. The last thing we do is to splice the ScoreTextField instance from the scoreTexts array.

Defining the checkCollisions function

The checkCollisions function is called every frame tick from the SuperClick class runGame function inside the SYSTYEM_STATE_GAMEPLAY state of the Main class. It doesn't actually check real collisions between objects or the mouse pointer colliding with a Circle instance. It does loop through the Circle objects in circles and checks for instances that have their clicked variable set to true.

```
private function checkCollisions():void {
    var circleLength:int = circles.length-1;
    for (var counter:int = circleLength; counter >= 0; counter--){
        tempCircle = circles[counter];
        if (tempCircle.clicked && !tempCircle.fadingOut) {
            tempCircle.fadingOut = true;
            if (tempCircle.type==Circle.CIRCLE_GOOD && ⏎
             tempCircle.alpha==1) {

                var scoreAdjust:Number = 1 / tempCircle.scaleX;
                var scoreAdd:int=maxScore * scoreAdjust;
                addToScore(scoreAdd);

                tempScoreText = new ScoreTextField(String⏎
                 (scoreAdd), textFormat, tempCircle.x, ⏎
                 tempCircle.y, 20);

                scoreTexts.push(tempScoreText);
                addChild(tempScoreText);
            }else if (tempCircle.type==Circle.CIRCLE_BAD) {
                gameOver = true;
            }
        }
    }
}
```

The checkCollisions function continues our loop optimizations by using the circleLength local variable to hold the length of the circles.length-1 value. It also employs the tempCircle class reference variable and loops through the circles array backward. The loop's job is to check the current tempCircle instance in the iteration for a true value in its clicked variable. If the variable is set to true, the function removes it, calculates the new score (if blue), and disposes of it. If a red Circle was clicked, the function sets gameOver to true.

The call to the internal addToScore function will be discussed next, but the call takes a single parameter that represents the value to multiply the maxScore variable by when adding to the player's score. This value is calculated in a way that gives the player a higher score the smaller the circle that is clicked. The multiplier is 1/Circle.scaleX. So, if the scaleX of the circle is .7, the value passed in is 1 divided .7, or about 1.4 times the maximum score. At a scale of 1, the

123

multiplier would simply be 1, and after the circle starts to increase in size greater than 1, the score for the click will be less than the maximum. For example, if the scaleX of the circle is 2, then half of the value, or .5, will be passed in as the score multiplier.

> *Note that unlike in AS2, AS3 display objects do not use 0 to 100 scales for with the scaleX, scaleY, or alpha attributes. In AS3, the scale is 0 to 1 for these attributes: 1 represents that same value as 100 did in AS2. This may confusing at first, but once you get the hang of it, it is quite easy to remember.*

Fading out the circle

We don't remove the Circle instance from the screen right as it is clicked. We first want to fade out the Circle before it is removed from the screen. We do this by setting the tempCircle.fadingOut variable to true. When a Circle instance is first detected to be clicked, this fadingOut variable will be false. We will need to set it to true:

```
if (tempCircle.clicked && ! tempCircle.fadingOutCircle) {
    tempCircle.fadingOut=true.
```

When the alpha value of the Circle is still 1 (the maximum), we know that it has not started to fade out yet. We then set the fadingOut attribute of the Circle instance to true, add to our score, and create the ScoreTextField instance to display on the screen. We then want to check if the Circle is good (CIRCLE_GOOD) and if the alpha value is still set to 1. This means we have not yet processed it as a clicked circle:

```
if (tempCircle.type==Circle.CIRCLE_GOOD && tempCircle.alpha==1) {
    var scoreAdd:int=maxScore * scoreAdjust;
    addToScore(scoreAdd);

    tempScoreText = new ScoreTextField(String(scoreAdd), textFormat,↵
     tempCircle.x,tempCircle.y, 20);

    scoreTexts.push(tempScoreText);
    addChild(tempScoreText);
```

We create a new ScoreTextField instance by passing in the score value we calculated for the clicked Circle along with our precreated TextFormat object instance, the x and y values to place the ScoreTextField, and the life (20) in frames for the ScoreTextField to remain on the screen.

With the fadingOut attribute set to true, the update function in the Circle instance will start to decrement the alpha attribute of the Circle instance rather than increase its size. When the alpha value reaches 0, it will be removed from the screen.

Defining the addToScore function

The addToScore function is called by the checkCollisions function when a good (blue) circle has been clicked. It takes a single parameter, a multiplier for the maxScore variable. The value 1/scaleX of the clicked circle is passed. This allows the score received for the click to be based on the size of the Circle instance. The smaller the circle, the more points the player will earn for clicking it. ScoreBoard custom events are fired off to update display fields for score, clicked, and percentAchieved.

```
private function addToScore(scoreAdd:Number):void {
    score += scoreAdd;

    dispatchEvent(new CustomEventScoreBoardUpdate↵
    (CustomEventScoreBoardUpdate.UPDATE_TEXT,↵
    Main.SCORE_BOARD_SCORE,String(score)));

    clicked++;
    percent = 100 * (clicked / numCircles);

    dispatchEvent(new CustomEventScoreBoardUpdate↵
    (CustomEventScoreBoardUpdate.UPDATE_TEXT,↵
    Main.SCORE_BOARD_PERCENT_ACHIEVED, String(percent)));

    dispatchEvent(new CustomEventScoreBoardUpdate↵
    (CustomEventScoreBoardUpdate.UPDATE_TEXT,↵
    Main.SCORE_BOARD_CLICKED,String(clicked + "/" +numCircles)));
}
```

Once a blue circle has been clicked, this function is called into action. It actually does quite a lot. First, it must use the passed-in multiplier to add to the current score by casting the probably real number returned as an integer:

```
score += int(maxScore * val);
```

Once the new score value has been calculated, it dispatches a custom CustomEventScoreBoardUpdate.UPDATE_TEXT Event and passes the Main.SCORE_BOARD_SCORE as the key and the value of the score variable.

Next, it calculates the new values for the clicked and percent variables and dispatches custom CustomEventScoreBoardUpdate.UPDATE_TEXT events for each. For the clicked update, it passes in the key of Main.SCORE_BOARD_CLICKED and the value as a ratio in a String that represents the clicked variable divided by the number blue circles for the level. Finally, **percent achieved** on the scoreBoard is updated by passing the Main.SCORE_BOARD_PERCENT_ACHIEVED key and the current value of the percent variable as a String.

Defining the render function

The render function simply loops through Circle objects and sets scaleX and scaleY of each to its nextScale value.

```
private function render():void {
    var circleLength:int = circles.length-1;
    for (var counter:int = circleLength; counter >= 0; counter--){
        tempCircle = circles[counter];
        tempCircle.scaleX = tempCircle.nextScale;
        tempCircle.scaleY = tempCircle.nextScale;
    }
}
```

The render function employs our loop iteration optimizations, which are a recalculated circleLength variable and a tempCircle instance, and it iterates backward through the loop. Now, we didn't necessarily need to loop backward here, because the render loop does not splice any circle instances from the circles array, but we continued the application this for consistency. It could very well be coded with a for:each loop.

Defining the checkForEndOfGame function

The `checkforEndOfGame` function checks for gameOver==true and sends basic custom event to Main called `GAME_OVER`. This function is run in each frame tick from the `runGame` method of the Game class. The `runGame` function is called from the `SYSYEM_STATE_GAMEPLAY` state of `Main.as`.

```
private function checkforEndGame():void {
    if (gameOver) {
        dispatchEvent(new Event(GAME_OVER));
        cleanUp();
    }
}
```

The `checkForEndOfGame` function simply checks to see if the gameOver variable has been set to true. If it has been set, the `cleanup` function is called and dispatches a simple custom `Event` `GAME_OVER`. Main catches this event and then changes the state to `SYSYEM_STATE_GAMEOVER`. The gameOver variable will be set to false until the player clicks a red circle or until the `checkForEndOfLevel` function finds that a level has been completed but the percent variable is less that the `percentNeeded`. See the next section for details on the `checkForEndOfLevel` function.

Defining the checkforEndLevel function

The `checkforEndLevel` function handles the level end conditions:

1. It checks to see if there are no more circles on the screen (`circles.length == 0`) and if the number of circles created (`numCreated`) equals the number for the level.

2. If both are `true`, it checks to make sure the user clicked enough to move to next level.

3. Based on that evaluation, it either sets gameOver to `true` or dispatches the simple custom event `NEW_LEVEL`.

Here is the complete code for the `checkForEndOfLevel` function.

```
private function checkforEndLevel():void {
    if (circles.length == 0 && numCreated == numCircles && ↵
     scoreTexts.length == 0) {
        if (percent >= percentNeeded) {
            dispatchEvent(new Event(NEW_LEVEL));
        }else {
            gameOver = true;
        }
    }
}
```

If the level is over but the player didn't click enough blue circles to make it to the next level, the gameOver variable is set to `true`. If the player did click enough blue circles, a simple custom event (`NEW_LEVEL`) is dispatched. Main listens for this event and changes state to the `SYSYEM_STATE_NEWLEVEL` state.

Defining the cleanUp function

The `cleanUp` function loops through all of the `Circle` instances in the `circles` array. It removes and disposes of all of them. It is called from the `checkforEndGame` function if the gameOver criteria have been reached. It also removes and cleans up the `scoreTexts` array in the same manner.

```
        private function cleanUp():void {
            var circleLength:int = circles.length-1;
            for (var counter:int = circleLength; counter >= 0; counter--){
                removeCircle(counter);
            }
            var scoreTextLength:int = scoreTexts.length-1;
            for (counter= scoreTextLength; counter >= 0; counter--) {
                removeScoreText(counter);
            }
        }
    } // close class
} // close package
```

Using the same loop optimizations you have seen a few times in this chapter, the cleanUp function calls the removeCircle function for each Circle instance left in the circles array.

> *As with the final function on all of our classes, the final two closing brackets (}) close the class and the package respectively.*

That's It for the SuperClick game class. Now let's move on to the two final classes for this game. First up is the Circle.as class.

The Circle Class

The Circle class dynamically creates a circle shape. It extends the Sprite class, so it is clickable using the MouseEvent.CLICK event.

Defining the Circle class

These are the static constants needed for the Circle class: CIRCLE_GOOD and CIRCLE_BAD.

The following public attributes are needed:

- clicked: This Boolean is set to true when the circle is clicked.
- type: This integer holds one of the two static constants: CIRCLE_GOOD or CIRCLE_BAD. This could have simply be a Boolean using true for good and false for bad, but to make the attribute more extensible in the future, we have used constants to define the basic types. For example, later you might want to add a CIRCLE_POWER_UP constant that gives the player extra time.
- nextScale: This attribute holds the next scaleX and scaleY value for the Circle. It is updated in the internal update function that is called by the SuperClick.update function and is rendered in the render function of the SuperClick class.
- fadingOut: This Boolean value set to true once a CIRCLE_GOOD is clicked by the player.

For the constructor arguments, we need a passed-in type value that will be one of the two constants: CIRCLE_GOOD or CIRCLE_BAD.

Creating the Circle class in the package structure

As with all of Main.as and the SuperClick.as class files, the Circle.as class file will reside in the game specific package structure.

This is the Flash IDE folder structure:

/source/projects/superclick/flashIDE/com/efg/games/superclick/Circle.as

And this is the structure for the Flex SDK (using Flash Develop):

/source/projects/superclick/flexSDK/src/com/efg/games/superclick/Circle.as

Importing the classes and declaring variables for Circle.as

The properties needed for a new Circle are a type variable to hold the CIRCLE_GOOD or CIRCLE_BAD constant, a clicked variable that is set to false, a fadingOut variable set to false, and a nextScale property that will be updated in the Game.update function.

The Boolean clicked used in the collision detection portion of the game logic. If a Circle is clicked, this property is set to true and evaluated in a loop inside the game's checkCollisions function.

```
package   com.efg.games.superclick
{
    // Import necessary classes from the flash libraries
    import flash.display.Shape;
    import flash.display.Sprite
    import flash.events.MouseEvent;
    import flash.text.TextField;
    import flash.text.TextFormat;
    /**
    * ...
    * @author Jeff Fulton
    */

    public class Circle extends Sprite {
        //Constsants used to define circle type
        public static const CIRCLE_GOOD:int = 0;
        public static const CIRCLE_BAD:int = 1;

        public var type:int;
        public var clicked:Boolean=false;
        public var fadingOut:Boolean = false;

        public var nextScale:Number;
```

The nextScale variable is the first "update" variable you have seen. We could simply set the scale of the circles in the update function by applying the new scale value to the circle.scaleX and scaleY attributes directly. We have added a step to this process by actually updating a nextScale variable in the update portion of the game and then applying the nextScale to the circle.scaleX and circle.scaleY in the render portion of the game. Although there is no real need for this separation in Super Click, it is a good habit to get started with. As we progress through the games in this book, you will see this type of separation more often, and in some games, separate update and render functions will be applied to improve game performance. That's getting a little ahead of ourselves though. For now, it makes for good code organization and functions that don't attempt to do too many tasks.

Defining the constructor and init function for Circle.as

The constructor takes a single integer parameter representing either the CIRCLE_GOOD or CIRCLE_BAD static constant integers of the Circle class. Once, the init function is called to create the look of the circle.

```
public function Circle(typeval:int) {
    buttonMode = true;
    useHandCursor = true;
    init(typeval);
}

public function init(typeval:int):void {
    var shapeColor:Number;
    switch (typeval) {
        case CIRCLE_GOOD:
            //good circle
            shapeColor = 0x0000FF;
            type = typeval;
            break;

        case CIRCLE_BAD:
            //bad circle
            shapeColor = 0xFF0000;
            type - typeval;
            break;
    }

    graphics.clear();
    graphics.lineStyle(2, 0xffffff);
    graphics.beginFill(shapeColor);
    graphics.drawCircle(5, 5, 8);
    graphics.cndFill();

    x = int(Math.random() * 399);
    y = int(Math.random() * 399);

    scaleX = .5;
    scaleY = .5;
    nextScale = scaleX;

    addEventListener(MouseEvent.MOUSE_DOWN, clickedListener, ↵
      false, 0, true);
}
```

The real meat of the Circle class is in the init function. Before we get to that, notice that we set the buttonMode and userHandCursor to true for the Circle class. We have access to these properties because we extended the Sprite class.

The init function must first do a switch:case on the typeval passed in to set the properties of either a CIRCLE_BAD or a CIRCLE_GOOD circle. We use a switch:case statement here, because we might want to create more than just two circle types in the future if we ever consider expanding this game into a more elaborate creation.

We create a circle shape directly on the graphics attribute of the Sprite and fill it with the color set previously. We clear its contents with the clear function call and set up the style of our line (2 pixels wide and white).

Next, we fill the circle with either red or blue (set in the switch:case statement earlier in this function) with graphics.beginFill(shapeColor). After calling beginFill, every shape we create will be filled in with the shapeColor until we call endFill. So, we draw a circle at position 5,5 on the Sprite with a radius of 8, and end the fill.

```
graphics.drawCircle(5, 5, 8);
graphics.endFill();
```

Drawing dynamically is as simple as that. The rest of the init function goes like this:

1. Randomly pick a starting location for the x and y attributes of the Circle (not the shape we are drawing, but this Circle class instance as a whole).

2. Set the starting scaleX and scaleY each to .5, the starting scale for all game circles.

3. Set clicked to be false.

4. Create a listener for the click.

5. Set nextScale to equal the current scale at creation time.

Defining the update function for Circle.as

The update function is called from the SuperClick update function. As you have seen, the SuperClick update function will iterate through all of the Circle instances on the game screen and, in turn, call the Circle.update function on each. The Circle update function accepts a single parameter called growSpeed.

```
public function update(growSpeed:Number):void {
    if (fadingOut) {
        alpha -= .05;
    }else{
        nextScale += growSpeed;
    }
}
```

If the Circle instance fadingOut Boolean is set to true, the alpha value of the Circle instance is decremented by .05. If the Circle instance is in the normal mode (not fading out but growing), the nextScale attribute is incremented by the passed in growSpeed value.

Defining the dispose function for Circle.as

The dispose function gets rid of unwanted objects and readies them for Flash's built-in garbage collection. It is called from the Game class's removeCircle function.

```
public function dispose():void {
    removeEventListener(MouseEvent.MOUSE_DOWN, clickedListener);
}
```

Notice that we make sure remove all of our event listeners. By doing this, we free up all of the unused objects for possible garbage collection.

Updating the clickedListener function definition for Circle.as

When the circle is clicked, the MouseEvent.MOUSE_DOWN event is fired off. This function listens for that event and simply sets the clicked property of the circle to true. When the SuperClick class checkCollisions function is run, any Circle with clicked set to true will be removed from the screen.

```
    private function clickedListener(e:MouseEvent):void {
        clicked = true;
        removeEventListener(MouseEvent.MOUSE_DOWN, clickedListener);
    }
} //end class
} // end package
```

The ScoreTextField class

The ScoreTextField class dynamically creates a TextField that contains the score value the player receives for clicking a blue Circle instance. It stays in the display list for the number of frame ticks in its life attribute and then is removed from the screen.

Defining the ScoreTextField class

For the ScoreTextField class, the following private attributes are needed:

- textField: An instance of the TextField class that contains the actual text to be displayed for the score value
- life: The number of frame ticks for the ScoreTextField to exist before being removed
- lifeCount: Used to count from 0 frame ticks to the life value and updated once per frame

We also need the following constructor parameters:

- text: The text score value to display
- textFormat: The TextFormat for the textField that displays the score value
- x: The x location for the text
- y: The y location for the text
- life: The life value in frame ticks for the score text

Creating the ScoreTextField class in the package structure

As with all of Main.as and the SuperClick.as class files, the ScoreTextField.as class file will reside in the game-specific package structure.

This time, the Flash IDE folder structure is as follows:

/source/projects/superclick/flashIDE/com/efg/games/superclick/ScoreTextField.as

And this is the structure for the Flex SDK (using Flash Develop):

/source/projects/superclick/flexSDK/src/com/efg/games/superclick/ScoreTextField.as

Let's take a look at the entire ScoreTextField.as class file now.

```
package  com.efg.games.superclick
{
   import flash.text.TextField;
   import flash.text.TextFormat;
   import flash.display.Sprite;
   /**
   * ...
   * @author Jeff Fulton
   */
   public class ScoreTextField extends Sprite{
      private var textField:TextField = new TextField();
      private var life:int;
      private var lifeCount:int;

      public function ScoreTextField(text:String,↵
       textFormat:TextFormat,x:Number,y:Number,life:int) {

         this.x = x;
         this.y = y;
         this.life = life;
         this.lifeCount = 0;
         textField.defaultTextFormat = textFormat;
         textField.selectable = false;
         textField.text = text;
         addChild(textField);
      }

      public function update():Boolean {
         trace("scoreText update");
         lifeCount++;
         if (lifeCount > life) {
           return true;
         }else {
           return false;
         }
      }

      public function dispose():void {
         removeChild(textField);
         textField = null;
      }
   }
}
```

You have seen most of the code needed for this class in previous classes we have created. The private attributes (textField, life, and lifeCount) and constructor parameters (text, textFormat, x, y, and life) have been discussed previously. Aside from accepting parameters and assigning them to the private attributes, the constructor also creates the textField with the passed in text value and calls the addChild method to place it on the stage display list.

Defining the update function for ScoreTextField

The update function is called from the `SuperClick.update` function as it iterates through the `ScoreTextField` instances in its `scoreTexts` array. The `lifeCount` value of the `ScoreTextField` is incremented by 1 until it exceeds the `life` value. When it does, `true` is returned to the `SuperClick` update function.

Defining the dispose function for ScoreTextField

The `dispose` function is called by `SuperClick` when the `SuperClick.update` function removes `ScoreTextField` instance that have exceeded their `life` span.

Test it!

Make sure the all of the package classes are in the correct folders as described throughout this chapter (this structure will depend on the development environment you have chosen). Select to build the project, export the movie, or publish, or use the similar option in your development environment.

The most common problem will be class path errors. If you are having problems with the build process, start by rechecking the path to the framework package structure.

Summary

In this chapter, we finally created a full-blown game called Super Click using the framework package structure. We created two new classes: `Main.as` class that is a subclass of the `GameFrameWork.as` file and `SuperClick.as` that is a subclass of the `Game.as` class. We also created two new game-specific classes for the Super Click game: `Circle.as` and `ScoreTextField.as`.

In the next set of chapters, we will create an arcade blaster game called Flak Cannon and explore many more game development concepts such as using `BitmapData` and pixel perfect collision detection.

Part 2

Building Games

In Part 2, you will build a series of games that make use of and expand on the game framework we created in Part 1.

Chapter 4

Laying The Groundwork for Flak Cannon

In Part 1 of this book, you learned how to create a game framework and how to apply it to a very simple game. In this chapter, we will apply what you learned in Part 1 to a complete game in AS3, including graphics, sound, and collision detection. Now, it is time to put theory to work and make Flak Cannon (see Figure 4-1).

In this chapter, we will concentrate on the groundwork necessary to support the Flak Cannon game. This includes designing the game, creating assets, creating a sound manager, exploring the differences between the libraries in Flash and Flex, creating game difficulty, and creating moving and animated sprites. In the next chapter, we will put all of these concepts together into a functioning product.

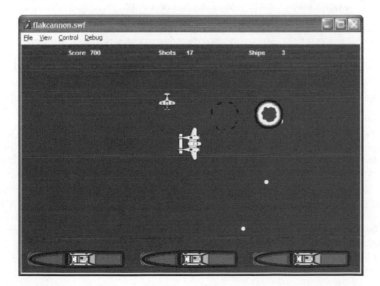

Figure 4-1. Flak Cannon

A short history of Missile Command

Atari was the first successful arcade video game company. They started in 1972 with the release of Pong, and continued perfecting the art of the arcade video games for the next 30 years (under several different names including Midway West). Atari had some very popular games through out the 1970s in the arcades including Gran Trak 10, Tank (under the Kee Games label), Breakout, Football, and in 1979, their best-selling game of all time, Asteroids. In 1980, they badly needed follow-ups to Asteroids to help them stay at the forefront of the video game industry.

To meet this demand, in 1980, Atari released two military themed games: Battlezone and Missile Command. While Battlezone was one of the very first 3D shooting games, Missile Command was something else entirely. The game echoed the same Cold War fear that played out on the nightly news and in the "drop and cover" drills of 1970s elementary school classrooms: Nuclear Holocaust. This was the same fear of the Generation X kids who were filling the arcades at the time, and this was one factor in making the game very popular. Another factor was that is a very enjoyable game to play.

Missile Command simulated a nuclear warhead attack on six cities that had to be defended by the player. The player was armed with three independent silos, each containing ten antiballistic missiles. Aiming with crosshairs controlled with a trackball, the player would launch missiles at incoming warheads, killer satellites, and nuclear bombers independently using three separate fire buttons. The antiballistic missiles were not fired directly at the incoming enemies, but instead at where they would be once the missile reached its destination. When the missile had finished its flight path, it would explode into an iridescent circle, destroying anything that touched it.

The unique game play led to players adopting all sorts of interesting strategies for getting a high score. Some players starting each level with a massive salvo of explosions meant to knock off as many incoming warheads as possible, while others would take a "cut your losses" strategy, defending only half of their cities in an attempt to conserve as many missile as possible for their chosen survivors. The three distinct missile bases also offered an interesting challenge: training three fingers to fire a missile from the base closest to the incoming warhead while still being accurate. Arguably, no arcade game before or since employed a shooting mechanism that offered so many nuanced ways for the player to plan defense.

Designed by Dave Theurer and Rich Adam, the game was released in mid 1980 to great success. While certainly not the size of Asteroids, it was still a huge hit with almost 20,000 units sold. The game certainly caught the imagination of the Cold War generation, and may have even acted as a kind of release for subconscious worries about nuclear annihilation. While the game has lost visibility over the subsequent 30 years, a recent episode of the NBC television show Chuck, centered around Missile Command and a fictional back story for the game involving spies and hidden codes, proves that game is very much embedded into the fabric of pop culture history.

For a shooter, Missile Command was also a very unique game. Oddly enough, while it was a very popular game for its time, there were not many sequels or copies of the game in the arcades during its heyday. However, there were a few commercial take-offs for home systems. Atlantis by Imagic for the Atari 2600 took the idea and had the player defend an underwater city. A few years later S.D.I. by Cinemaware created a cinematic story around a very similar contest for the Atari ST and Amiga computers. In the 1990s Atari tried (and failed) to re-create the success of the earlier game with Missile Command 3D for the Jaguar video game console. However, aside from these (and a few from a few slightly updated re-releases on various platforms) very few games have attempted to build on the basic playing style of Missile Command.

In the next two chapters, we will embark on an adventure to create a game based on the classic game play of Missile Command. Not a knock-off, our game will employ some of the unique elements of Missile command, while adding our own spin to the contest.

Designing the game

In our game, you play an off-screen defender of a fleet of Navy ships in World War II. Your job is to shoot down kamikaze airplanes before they reach your fleet. Here is the simple game design document for our project:

- **Game name**: Flak Cannon
- **Game genre**: Defense shooter
- **Game description**: The player defends a fleet of Naval ships from incoming Kamikaze attackers.
- **Player's goal**: Destroy the incoming planes before they hit and destroy the naval ships the player is defending.
- **Enemy description**: Enemy planes enter the screen from the top or sides and attempt to fly as fast as possible to the ships below. Enemy planes are dumb: they fly in straight lines and do not try to avoid flak. The enemy plan is to overwhelm the player's fleet.
- **Enemy's goal**: Destroy the naval fleet.
- **Level end**: A level ends automatically when all planes in that wave have made their attack runs. The player is awarded bonus points for shells remaining in the arsenal, and ships are replenished if a player has earned them as a bonus.
- **Game over conditions**: The game ends when all naval ships are destroyed.
- **Difficulty ramping**: The game difficulty is ramped through mathematical calculations. Enemy planes arrive on a timed basis, but their placement and flight path is random.
- **Bonus conditions**: There are three bonus conditions in the game.

    - Hitting multiple planes with one flak shot gains the player a bonus (in points) per plane destroyed.
    - Shooting a bonus plane that flies from right-left across the screen gains the player 10 extra flak shots.
    - The player is awarded an extra ship at 10,000 points.

Game development concepts in this chapter

While the chapters in Part 2 cover the development of different games using one game framework, certain game development topics are introduced in this chapter that will not be discussed elsewhere. We have done this both to maximize the amount of topics covered and to diversify the game engines developed as much as possible. Here is a brief rundown of the game development concepts we will cover in this chapter.

- Adding game assets to the library
- Handling library differences in Flash and Flex or Flash Develop

- Creating a basic sound manager
- Creating difficulty with "Settings"
- Creating sprites that move on a vector
- Creating animated sprites

We will start this project in a similar fashion to Super Click. You can build this game in the Flash IDE or with Flex or Flash Develop. We will note the differences in code for the two environments when required. This chapter will focus on building a game in the Flash IDE. However, the code we create will be easily transferrable to other development tools. Here are the properties of the new FLA:

- **Package**: com.efg.games.flackcannon
- **Game Class**: FlakCannon.as
- **Document Class**: Main.as
- **Size:** 600 × 400
- **FPS**: 30
- **Flex Asset Location**: src/com/efg/games/flakcannon/assets

This might be a good time to download the source from one of the web addresses from the back of the book. You can find the assets and code for this games in /source/projects/ch4_5_flakcannon. You will find both Flash IDE and Flex SDK versions in this directory.

Adding game assets to the library

In Super Click, we did not use any SWF library assets for the game. Everything was created on the fly, in code. While that is a nice way to work for demonstrations, it will most likely be necessary to create assets that you will use for your game. For Flak Cannon, we will use both graphics and sounds to create the game.

Creating graphics using Spritelib GPL

It would be nice if every person who plays a game could understand just how hard it is to program and overlook the graphics. Many programmers find it very hard to create visuals that are pleasing enough to keep players around long enough to experience all the cool stuff you have programmed for them.

Thankfully, the Internet provides some great resources for developers, many of them for free. One such resource is Spritelib GPL, maintained by Ari Feldman at www.flyingyogi.com/ fun/spritelib.html. This is a royalty-free graphics library, which means you can use the images in it for pretty much anything (save for distributing them as part of another sprite library). Several of the games in this book make use of this library. If you have a budget to spend, another good source of art is www.istockphoto.com.

Obviously, in a professional studio, you will have access to professionally designed art assets, so if you are working in that kind of an environment, you should not have to create anything yourself. In fact, in many studios, designers frown on programmer art. Know your surroundings and proceed with caution.

For our game, we will use the following graphics. Most are taken from Spritelib GPL:

- **Shot** (library class name: `ShotGif`): This is what the player will shoot at enemy planes. See Figure 4-2.

Figure 4-2. Player's cannon shot

- **Flak** (library class name `Exp1Gif. . .Exp7Gif`): The flak explosion is what the player will use to destroy the enemy. The shots themselves are harmless. Only their explosions can be used to defend the ships. Each of these images will form a single frame of a multiframe animation. See Figure 4-3.

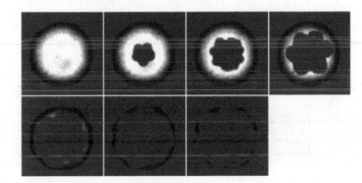

Figure 4-3. Flak explosion animation frames

- **Enemy plane** (library class name `PlaneGif`). This is the main enemy. It flies straight down at the player's fleet. See Figure 4-4.

Figure 4-4. Plane flying down

- **Enemy plane left** (library class name `PlaneLeftGif`): This plane flies in from the left. The lower it enters the screen, the harder it is to shoot down. See Figure 4-5.

Figure 4-5. Plane flying in from the left side

- **Enemy plane right** (library class name `PlaneRightGif`): This plane flies in from the right. The lower it enters the screen, the harder it is to shoot down. See Figure 4-6.

Figure 4-6. Plane flying in from the right side

- **Explosion** (library class name `Ex21Gif. . .Ex25Gif`): This is the animation we use when anything explodes in the game. See Figure 4-7.

Figure 4-7. Explosion animation frames

- **Ship** (library class name `ShipGif`): This is the ship the player must defend from the enemy planes. The player starts the game with three ships in the fleet. See Figure 4-8.

Figure 4-8. Ship

- **Bonus plane** (library class name `PlaneBonusGif`): The bonus plane always flies in from the left. If it is shot down, the player earns extra shots for the cannon. See Figure 4-9.

Figure 4-9. Bonus plane

- **Crosshairs** (library class name `CrosshairsGif`): The player controls this with the mouse. Shots fire directly to the center and explode into flak explosions when they reach that point. See Figure 4-10.

Figure 4-10. Crosshairs

Creating sounds using SFXR

Finding sounds to use in your games might be even harder than trying to find graphics. Most sound effects libraries and commercial programs have serious restrictions on how you can use the sounds included and can also be very expensive. In a professional environment or studio, you will probably have access to sounds created specifically for your game. You can also purchase sound libraries like the ones available at www.soundtrangers.com. However, just like for the graphics, there are some great free resources you can utilize to create royalty-free sounds for your games.

The first free sound resource we will explore is SFXR, which is shown in Figure 4-11. SFXR was developed by Tomas Pettersson and is available at www.cyd.liu.se/~tompe573/hp/ project_sfxr.html. There are versions for both the PC and Mac, so you have no excuses for not using it (except, I suppose, *you* Linux enthusiast).

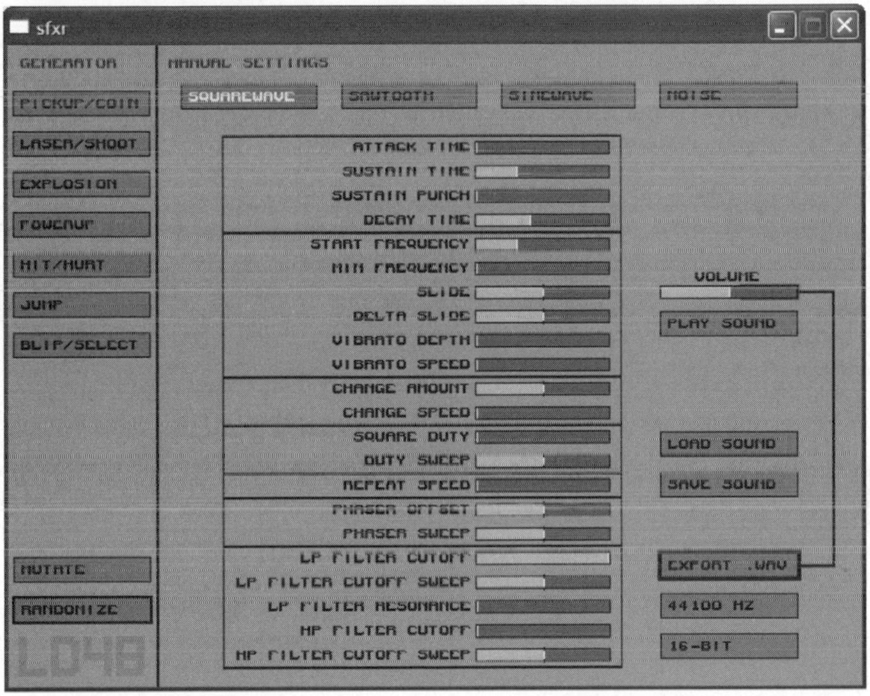

Figure 4-11. SFXR PC user interface

Described by the ludlumdare.com blog as "MS Paint for sound effects," SFXR helps you create random sound effects that you can export as WAV files and use in your games. After a sound is created, you have the ability to tweak some of the properties of the sound to customize it a little.

Using the program is fairly simple. You click one of the buttons on the left listed under **Generator** (e.g., **Pickup/Coin**, **Laser/Shoot**, and **Explosion**), and a sound is randomly generated for you. If you like the sound, you click the **Export** button to save it. If not, you can click one if the **Generator** buttons again, or you can manipulate the bars in the center of the screen to change the sound.

I used SFXR to create the sounds in Table 4-1 for Flak Cannon. It took me roughly 10 minutes to make all of these. Even if you are working in a professional studio environment, this can still be an invaluable tool for prototyping a game with placeholder sound effects.

Table 4-1. Flak Cannon Sounds and Their Flash Library Class Names

Library Class Name	Play Sound When
SoundBonus	The player shoots down a bonus plane and earns extra shots.
SoundBonusShip	The player earns an extra ship.
SoundExplodePlane	An enemy plane is shot down.
SoundExplodeFlak	A flak shell explodes.
SoundExplodeShip	A ship is destroyed.
SoundNoShots	The player has run out of shots.
SoundShoot	The player shoots the flak cannon.

Library differences in Flash and Flash Develop/Flex

Now that we have created graphics and sound files and put them into the library, you will need to reference them properly depending on what you are using to make our game: Flash or Flash Develop/Flex. Luckily, the library assets remain the same for both programming methods, but accessing them in the game classes is different. When you are working with sounds and graphics embedded in a game project, there are some minor differences between the Flash IDE and Flex framework methods of instantiating these assets.

For this game, we have started with the Flash IDE version with all of the necessary sounds and graphic elements embedded in the FLA library. To use those in the Flex version, we have to simply publish the SWF (with a new name, flackassets.swf) and place it an assets folder in the src directory of our Flash Develop/Flex project (src/com/efg/games/flakcannon/assets). This way, we can make use of the existing library of assets and not have to create a folder full of the originals. This concept is especially important for sounds other than MP3 files, as you cannot embed them directly. For instance, you cannot add WAV files into a Flex application unless they are part of a SWF file library.

You might now ask us, "Why is the /assets folder is inside the package class source location in Flex?" The reason is simple. If we had in the root /assets folder of the Flex projects, the references would look like this ../../../../assets/flackassets.swf because of how deep the code is inside the package directory. By storing the assets locally, the references will look much cleaner. If this bothers you, you can move the assets and adjust your code accordingly.

Using graphic assets

Let's start by looking at the graphical assets for Flak Cannon and how they will be embedded in both Flex and Flash. In the Game class, we need to embed the crosshairs.gif from the library. It looks like this:

```
//**Flex Framework Only
[Embed(source = "assets/flakassets.swf", symbol="CrosshairsGif")]
private var CrosshairsGif:Class;
```

The class designation under Embed is the same is the linkage name you would use in the Flash IDE. To create a linkage for a Flash asset in the library (see Figure 4-12), find the asset in the library, and click it to bring up the in-context selection menu. Then click the Linkage option. In the Class box, type the linkage name (see Figure 4-13). Since this is a class, you should style the name as you would the name of a class (i.e., beginning capital letter for each major word).

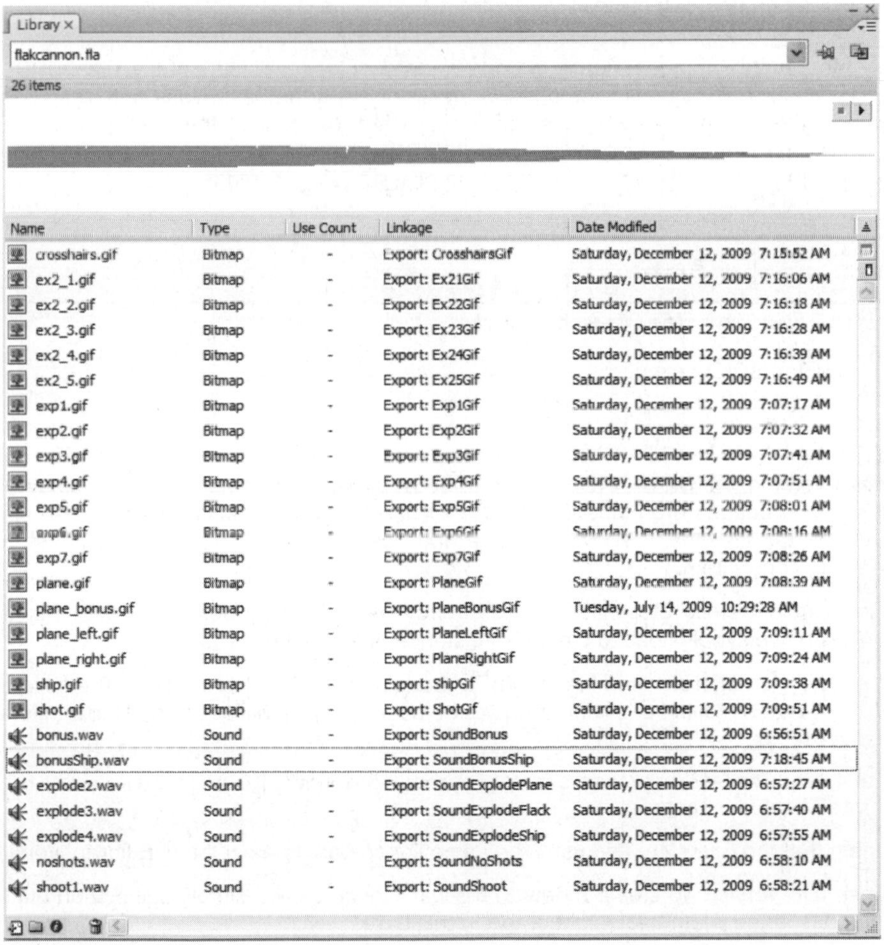

Figure 4-12. The FLA library with exported assets

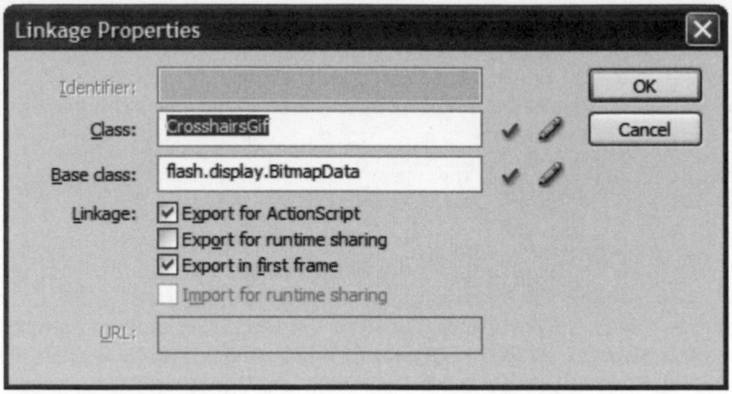

Figure 4-13. Exporting CrosshairsGif

The use of the image changes slightly in code when developing outside of the Flash IDE. This is because the Flash IDE embeds all images in the library with the base class of BitmapData, while Flex embeds them with the base class of BitmapAsset (a child of the BitmapClass). For this reason, if you first write your code to work in the IDE, you will need to translate the usage from BitmapData to Bitmap. Here is an example for the crosshairs.gif image:

- The Flash version:

```
private var crosshairs:Bitmap;
...
crosshairs = new Bitmap(new CrosshairsGif(0,0));
```

- The Flex SDK version:

```
private var crosshairs:Bitmap;
crosshairs = new CrosshairsGif();
```

In the Flash version, we want the crosshairs to be a Bitmap instance so we can display it on the screen. Because images are embedded in the IDE library with BitMapData as a base class, we need to create the crosshairs Bitmap instance and pass it a call to create a new version of the CrosshairsGif library item.

In the Flex version, since CrosshairsGif is already embedded by default as a BitmapAsset (a child of Bitmap), we simply need to create an instance of it and we are done.

Another example of differences in Flash/Flex embedding is in the Ship class. In the case of Ship, we want the imageBitmapData variable to hold an instance of BitmapData not Bitmap. Here is the embed code in Flex:

```
[Embed(source = "assets/flakassets.swf", symbol="ShipGif")]
private var ShipGif:Class;
```

Notice again that the Class created uses the same linkage name as in the IDE library version.

In the Flash IDE version, to create a new BitmapData instance, we simply call new on our linkage name and pass in the width and height of the BitmapData.

```
//**** Flash *****
imagebd = new ShipGif(0,0);
```

For Flex, BitmapData is an attribute of the BitmapAsset embedded in the library, so we just need to modify the call slightly. There is no need to pass in the width and height, we simply need to reference the bitmapData attribute of the ship_gif embedded asset when you create the imageBitmapData.

```
//***** Flex *****
imageBitmapData = new ShipGif().bitmapData;
```

Using sound

Sounds can be made to be compatible with both the IDE and Flex with a couple simple tips.

First, create new Sound instances with the Class types of Sound() rather than the linkage name in the library. This allows both IDE and Flex projects to use the same sound assets, even though the embedded types are slightly different.

For example, use the following

```
public var soundBonus:Sound=new SoundBonus();
```

instead of this

```
public var soundBonus:sound_bonus =new SoundBonus();
```

Second, for Flex, you must embed the sound of the SWF that contains the library.

```
[Embed(source = "assets/flackassets.swf", symbol="SoundBonus")]
private var SoundBonus:Class;
```

Don't worry if these tips do not make complete sense right now. We will cover all of this code in detail when we discuss the various classes that will make up the Flak Cannon game.

Creating a sound manager

SoundManager.as is a new support class that we will add to the game framework. This class is fairly self explanatory, as it will help us play sounds in our game. Why do we need this class? Because, while AS3 has a simple API to access sounds, there is no simple way to access sounds and work with them in a single place. Embedding sounds in Flash is different to doing so in Flex, so for Flex we will be using the Embed code style we described in the previous section.

The first thing we need to do is create a new class file named SoundManager.as with the in the default requisite package for the framework (com.efg.framework) with a constructor. There are several instance variables below that should be explained:

- sounds: This Array holds the sound objects that the SoundManager will play.
- soundChannels: This is an Array of SoundChannel objects. We keep sound channel objects, so we stop sounds and change soundtracks when we receive an event to do so.
- soundTrackChannel: This is a SoundChannel that we will use specifically for playing a soundtrack song. We will explain why we discuss soundtracks later in this chapter.
- soundMute: This Boolean a variable that will let us know if the sounds are currently muted or not.
- tempSoundTransform: This is a reusable SoundTransform object.

- **muteSoundTransform**: This is a SoundTransform object we will use for muting the sounds.
- **tempSound**: This is a reusable Sound object used to hold a sound we want to play.

We use the constructor only to initialize the sounds and soundChannels arrays:

```
package com.efg.framework
{
    import flash.media.*;
    public class SoundManager
    {
        private var sounds:Array;
        private var soundTrackChannel:SoundChannel=new SoundChannel();
        private var soundChannels:Array;
        private var soundMute:Boolean = false;
        private var tempSoundTransform:SoundTransform = new SoundTransform();
        private var muteSoundTransform:SoundTransform = new SoundTransform();
        private var tempSound:Sound;

    public function SoundManager()           {

        sounds = new Array();
        soundChannels = new Array();

        }
    }
}
```

We now need a function to add sounds to the sounds array. We will do this with an associative array. We will use the soundName as the index in the array, and then insert the sound object into that place in the array. soundName will be the value of a Main.SOUND_XXX static constant that we will define in the Main class for this game. We will discuss these in the next chapter.

There are several ways to tackle this type of function to add sounds. Since we have chosen to make the index of the array a String, that effectively makes this an associative array. Alternatively, you could use int as the index, as long as it matches the Main.SOUND_XXX value for the sound. We have chosen to use a String because we believe it makes the code easier to understand, but you need to be aware that is certainly not the only way to construct this functionality. Many modern Flash developers shy away from this type of construct, but we believe it still has its place.

```
public function addSound(soundName:String, sound:Sound):void {
    sounds[soundName] = sound;
}
```

First, we initialize the sounds array, and then we start adding sounds into it. Recall that SoundBonus() is the class we associated with the bonus sound in the Flash library. We then create six values in our array so that we can reference each Sound using the static const index values we have created for it.

Now, we have to create a way for someone to play one of the sounds in our sounds array on demand. We will do this with the playSound() function. In our game framework, this function will be called when a sound event is dispatched from our game to the Main class using the new CustomEventSound object (defined in the next section) where the type parameter set to CustomEventSound.PLAY_SOUND .

Now, let's look at the parameters we have created for playSound():

- soundName: This String contains the sound to play and should be one of the static constant we created in Main (ie, Main.SOUND_BONUS).
- isSoundTrack: This Boolean defines whether or not we play this sound as a soundtrack or not. Soundtracks are treated in a special way (see the end of this section).
- loops: This int defines the number of times to loop the sound (usually 1 for a single sound or 10000 for a soundtrack).
- offset: This Number defines the offset (in milliseconds) from which the sound will start playing (usually 0 unless you are using .mp3 files with Flex, then you might need to skip the leader).
- volume: This Number sets the volume at which to play the sound (between 0 and 1).

Here is the function definition for playSound():

```
public function playSound(soundName:String, isSoundTrack:Boolean=false, loops:int=1, ⏎
offset:Number=0, volume:Number=1):void {
```

This first two lines of code set up the temporary variables for this function: tempSoundTransform and tempSound. tempSound is simply set to the Sound object stored in the sounds array at the index specified by the soundName parameter. tempSoundTransform is a bit more complicated. The SoundTransform object is used to change the volume and pan properties of Sound object. You do not make changes to volume and pan directly in a Sound object, so you need this object to perform these functions.

```
tempSoundTransform.volume-volume;
tempSound = sounds[soundName];
```

Now, we need to make a decision based on the value of the isSoundTrack parameter passed to playSound(). If the sound is defined as a soundtrack, we are going to treat it differently than other sounds. We define a **soundtrack** as looping music or ambient that will play continuously for a specified amount of time. We have added this functionality because we find the process of playing soundtracks, especially when multiple songs will be treated as soundtracks and played at different times, a bit difficult to manage in AS3. The functionality we are looking for is this: We only want one soundtrack to play at a time. When a soundtrack is defined as playing, any other soundtracks playing will stop. This might sound simple, but since we are using a state machine for our games, the following situation could easily occur:

- You are playing soundtrack A at the title screen.
- You play soundtrack B while the game is playing.
- You play soundtrack C on the end screen.
- When the end screen closes, you go back to the title screen and soundtrack A plays again.

The problem with this scenario is that when the title screen plays the first time, no soundtrack is playing so we start playing soundtrack A. However, when the title screen displays the second time (after the end screen is displayed), soundtrack C is already playing, but we need to start playing soundtrack A again. It's very easy, in this situation, to start playing two soundtracks at once. You could have some logic to explicitly stop soundtrack C when the end screen is removed, or when title screen displays, but this can get out of hand as well. As the number of soundtracks and game states increases so does the number the complications with playing those soundtracks. Instead of managing all of this, functionality to simply play one soundtrack at a time starts looking very useful.

To facilitate this soundtrack functionality, we have created a single SoundChannel object named soundTrackChannel. If that soundTrackChannel is not null (which means a soundtrack is playing), we call the stop() function of soundTrackChannel. If it is null, we set soundTrackChannel equal to the value returned when we start playing the sound. However, this code begs the question, "What is a SoundChannel?"

SoundChannel objects in AS3 are used to differentiate sounds that are played, so you can set the volume and pan attributes separately for each sound. I know this might not sound like much, but this is a revelation after AS2. In AS2, you were forced to create separate sound objects attached to separate MovieClip objects to make this work correctly, and the code was still buggy in places. There were times when, no matter how hard we tried, every sound in a game would be set to the same volume or worse, no volume at all. With SoundChannel objects, all these limitations go away. However, the price you pay is slightly more complicated code than in previous versions of Flash.

The good news is this: a SoundChannel is provided for you every time you play a sound. All you need to do is set its properties once you have a reference to one. In our code, that reference is stored in the soundChannels array, keyed by the soundName parameter. We store these SoundChannel objects because, if we don't we will have no way to stop the sound from playing on request. We will cover this when we discuss the stopSound() function.

```
if (isSoundTrack) {
   if (soundTrackChannel != null) {
      soundTrackChannel.stop();
   }
   soundTrackChannel = tempSound.play(offset,loops);
   soundTrackChannel.soundTransform=tempSoundTransform;
}else {
   soundChannels[soundName] = tempSound.play(offset, loops);
   soundChannels[soundName].soundTransform=tempSoundTransform;
}
}
```

The stopSound() function is called by Main when it receives a CustomSoundEvent with the type parameter set to CustomEventSound.STOP_SOUND. The function looks to see if we should treat the stop as a soundtrack or not and then stops the sound accordingly. If it is a soundtrack, we ignore the soundName and just call the stop() function of soundTrackChannel. If not, we use soundName as the index into the soundChannels array to find the correct SoundChannel to stop.

```
public function stopSound(soundName:String, isSoundTrack:Boolean=false):void {
   if (isSoundTrack) {
      soundTrackChannel.stop();
   }else {
      soundChannels[soundName].stop;
   }
}
```

The muteSound() function is used to turn off all the sounds playing in a game. Just like with a sound channel, we need SoundTransform object to set the volume to mute all sounds. First, we check the soundMute Boolean. If it is true, we have already muted the sounds, and we will make them audible again. If it is false, it is time to mute everything. To mute, we set the muteSoundTransform.volume property to 0. To unmute, we set the muteSoundTransform.volume property to 1. Then, we set the flash.media.SoundMixer.soundTransform static property to the muteSoundTransform object we just configured. This goes the heart of Flash's ability to play sounds and turns the volume all the way up or down. We also set the soundMute to true or false, depending on which part if the if statement we dropped into, so that the next time this function is called we will know what to do.

```
public function muteSound():void {
    if (soundMute) {
        soundMute=false;
        muteSoundTransform.volume=1;
        flash.media.SoundMixer.soundTransform=muteSoundTransform;
    }else{

        muteSoundTransform.volume=0;
        flash.media.SoundMixer.soundTransform=muteSoundTransform;
        soundMute=true;
    }
}
```

And that is it for the SoundManager class. I know this was more complicated than it should be to simply play a sound, but we will reuse (and improve) this class later in this book, so we had to get it out of the way early.

However, we are not finished. We still need to create the custom event class that we will use to play sounds and stop sounds. The good news is that this event is very much like the custom events we created in Chapter 2. The differences are that we have two different types of events (PLAY_SOUND and STOP_SOUND) and we require a different set or parameters to be set when the event is dispatched:

- name: This String is the Main.SOUND_XXX static const that represents the sound we want to play. We will define our const variables in the next chapter.
- loops: This int defines the number of times to loop the sound. For a soundtrack, this should be something very high (i.e., 10000).
- offset: This Number defines the millisecond offset at which to start the sound playing.
- volume: This Number determines the volume to play the sound; it's value is between 0 and 1.
- isSoundTrack: If this Boolean is true, SoundManager will treat this as a soundtrack and will use the special SoundTrack channel to play it.

Here we will start the definition for the CustomEventSound class:

```
package com.efg.framework
{
    import flash.events.*;
    public class CustomEventSound extends Event
    {
        public static const PLAY_SOUND:String = "playsound";
        public static const STOP_SOUND:String = "stopsound";

        public var name:String;
        public var loops:int;
        public var offset:Number;
        public var volume:Number;
```

```
public var isSoundTrack:Boolean;

public function CustomEventSound(type:String,name:String, ⏎
    isSoundTrack:Boolean=false, loops:int=0,offset:Number=0, ⏎
        volume:Number=1, bubbles:Boolean=false,cancelable:Boolean=false)     {
        super(type, bubbles, cancelable);
    this.name = name;
    this.loops = loops;
    this.offset = offset;
    this.volume = volume;
    this.isSoundTrack = isSoundTrack;
}


public override function clone():Event {
    return new CustomEventSound(type, name,isSoundTrack,loops,offset, ⏎
    volume,bubbles,cancelable)
}

public override function toString():String {
    return formatToString(type, "type", "bubbles", "cancelable", ⏎
        "eventPhase",name,isSoundTrack,loops,offset,volume);
    }
}
```

Now, we have completed a fully functional SoundManager to add to the game framework and to use with our games. Flak Cannon might not use all of the functionality we have created, but we have finished this class so that it will be ready for more complicated uses of sound as this book progresses.

Creating difficulty with settings

Tuning the difficulty level of a game can be a very time-consuming process, and there are many ways to tackle the problem. In this game, we will use a method that was proposed to us by Rob Fulop in an impromptu game design class. Fulop was a programmer for the classic Atari VCS; he coincidentally programmed the Atari VCS version of Missile Command but is best known for the game Demon Attack, widely regarded as one of the best Atari VCS games ever made.

Fulop's suggestion was to make as many knobs as possible that you could use to turn up and down different parts of the game to suit your needs. Since we will not actually making physical knobs, we refer to them as settings. These settings can come in many forms, but for this game, they will be simple numerical variables, updated when a new level is created, that we will plug into our game code.

Difficulty settings

We will implement these settings as a group of variable tests that use to update set values for the current level of the game. Most of these difficulty settings use the following shortcut if:then format:

```
value = test:? true expression: false expression
```

This format makes it very easy to create settings where a limit is set that if reached, defaults to a set value. We do this so that the game maxes out at a certain difficulty level.

Now we are ready to starting turning the settings!

- numEnemies: This setting is used to set the number of enemies that will appear on any given level, with a maximum of 100. The first level would have 15, the next 30, then 45, and so on.

```
numEnemies =(numEnemies > 100) ? 100 :level * 10 + (level*5);
```

- enemyWaveDelay: This setting is used to set the time for the game to wait before another enemy shows up on the screen. The shorter the wait, the harder the game. The minimum is 20 frames. The first level is 60 frames, then 58, then 56, and so on.

```
enemyWaveDelay  =(enemyWaveDelay < 20)? 20:60 - (level-1)*2;
```

- enemyWaveMax: The maximum number of planes that will appear in each wave at the same time. The maximum set here is 8. We start with 2, then got to 3, 4, and so on. In the following code, we multiply by 1. Why? We don't have to do it, but that number is really just a placeholder. You could significantly increase the number of enemy planes per wave by tweaking this value.

```
enemyWaveMax  =(enemyWaveMax > 8) ? 8:1 * level+1;
```

- enemyWaveMultipleChance: This is the percentage chance that planes will arrive in multiple waves. There is a 10 percent increase in chance per level passed, starting at 10 percent.

```
enemyWaveMultipleChance =(enemyWaveMultipleChance > 100)? 100:10*level;
```

- enemySpeed: This defines the flight speed of enemy planes and is calculated in pixels per frame. We start at 2, then go to 2.5, 3, 3.5, and so.

```
enemySpeed  =(enemySpeed > 8)   ? 8:2 + (.5*(level-1));
```

- enemySideChance: This is the percentage chance that enemy planes will come from the side of the screen. There is a 10 percent increase in chance per level passed, starting at 0 (so the first level will have no planes coming in from the sides).

```
enemySideChance  =(enemySideChance > 70)? 70:10*(level-1);
```

- enemySideFloor: This is the closet position to the player's ships that enemy planes can enter the screen, from the side (lower levels are harder).

```
enemySideFloor =(enemySideFloor > 300)? 300:100 + 25*(level-1);
```

- bonusPlaneDelay: This one defines the time (in frames) to wait before sending a bonus plane onto the screen.

```
bonusPlaneDelay =(bonusPlaneDelay > 450)? 450:350 + 10*(level-1);
```

- bonusPlaneSpeed: This sets the speed of the bonus plane.

```
bonusPlaneSpeed  =(bonusPlaneSpeed > 12) ? 12   : 4 + (1*level);
```

- startShots: The number of shots added to the player's cannon when a new level starts.

```
startShots = 30;
```

- extraScore: The player earns an extra ship for the fleet at the score set here.

```
extraScore = 10000;
```

- baseEnemyScore: This score is awarded for destroying an enemy plane.

```
baseEnemyScore = 100;
```

- enemyHitBonus: This bonus score is awarded for hitting multiple planes with the same flak explosion.

```
enemyHitBonus  = 500;
```

- baseBonusPlaneScore: This score is awarded for destroying a bonus plane.

```
baseBonusPlaneScore = 500;
```

- maxBonusPlanes: This is the number of bonus planes on the screen at the same time.

```
maxBonusPlanes = 1;
```

- maxVisibleShips: This sets the number of ships that can be displayed on the screen at any one time.

```
maxVisibleShips = 3;
```

- bonusPlaneMaxY: The highest y value at which the bonus plane will enter the screen is defined here.

```
bonusPlaneMaxY = 350;
```

- shipYPadding: This determines the number of pixels of padding between the bottom of the ships and the bottom of the screen.

```
shipYPadding = 5;
```

We will define all of these settings variables in the newLevel() function that we will create in the next chapter. For now, you only need to understand that we will be using these variables to set the difficulty of the game. They are also a good place for you to start experimenting with the code and using it to craft your own game.

> *The more difficulty settings you create, the easier it will be to balance the levels in your game. At the same time, the more settings you create, the more chances you have to create complexity and bugs in your code. Your challenge as game developer is to find the right mix for your game.*

Creating sprites that move on a vector

We now need to create a set of game objects we will call static sprites. While these sprites might move, they have only one frame of animation. The Shot, Enemy, BonusPlane, and Ship objects in our game are all static sprites, and they are all defined in a similar way.

Defining a sprite that moves between two points

Here is a question for you. What is one very basic thing that you can do if you have two points? Well, I'm sure there are many, but the most important one we can do is: *draw a line*. This might not seem spectacular right now, but with a line we can determine the distance between two points. If we know the distance between two points, and if we know the velocity (speed) and direction (*vector*) that something will travel at along that line, we can figure out *how much to move* an object each frame in Flash.

The good news is that we can determine all of this on the fly and make sprites move from point to point. Let's start by looking at the very basic design of our Shot class.

Shot

The first sprite we will look at is Shot. This sprite represents the shell fired by the player when the mouse button is clicked. Shots always start at the bottom center of the screen, and they always travel to the center of the crosshairs. This means that we will always have two points to work with. This is very important, because these two points are going to make moving our sprites very easy.

First, we must import the classes necessary to work with Bitmap images and BitmapData, plus the Sprite base class.

```
package    com.efg.games.flakcannon
{
    import flash.display.Shape;
    import flash.display.Sprite
    import flash.events.MouseEvent;
    import flash.display.Bitmap:
    import flash.display.BitmapData;
    import flash.geom.Point;
    public class Shot extends Sprite
        {
```

Then, we must define all the variables we will need in the class. First, we need variables to hold the ShotGif() image, and the BitmapData associated with it. Alternatively, you could create Shot as a MovieClip in the Flash IDE and drag the bitmap image into it, but we are going to focus on doing this programmatically so the code will be portable to other tools. We will use image to hold the reference to the ShotGif instance, and imageBitmapData to hold a reference to its BitmapData.

```
    public var imageBitmapData:BitmapData;
    public var image:Bitmap;
```

Next, we need to define variables to hold the two points we will use to calculate the movement vector for the Shot. The easiest and cleanest way to do this is to create a Point object to hold each set. We will name these Point classes startLocation and endLocation.

```
    private var startLocation:Point;
    private var endLocation:Point;
```

155

Now we will need a couple variables to hold the amount to move Shot on the (x, y) plane on each frame. We will calculate and hold those variables in xunits and yunits.

```
private var xunits:Number;
private var yunits:Number;
```

Because we are going to calculate the next place to move our sprites before we actually move them, we need a place to store the next positions to move the Shot. We hold these in another Point class named nextLocation.

```
private var nextLocation:Point;
```

Now, we need to set a speed for the Shot (we default to 15 pixels per frame) and create a variable that holds the number of moves the Shot will make before it is finished. We also need a variable we can check from Game to see if the Shot has finished moving. We do that with the finished variable.

```
private var speed:int = 15;
private var moves:int = 0;
public var finished:Boolean;
```

Finally, if we are building this game in Flex, we will need to embed the ShotGif graphic. You will need to uncomment this code to make it work:

```
/*
//**Flex Framework Only
[Embed(source = "assets/flakassets.swf", symbol="ShotGif")]
private var ShotGif:Class;
*/
```

The constructor for this function is quite simple. It takes two points (startX, startY) and (endX, endY) and stores them in our instance variables: startLocation and endLocation. We also initialize the nextLocation instance of Point so we can use it later. Then we call init() where the most interesting stuff will happen.

```
public function Shot (startX:Number, startY:Number, endX:Number, endY:Number)
{
    startLocation = new Point(startX,startY);
    endLocation = new Point(endX,endY);
    nextLocation = new Point(0,0);
    init();
}
```

We just defined the very basics of the Shot class. Now, we will fill it out will all the necessary functions. The good news is that even though we have multiple moving objects in Flak Cannon, most of the objects use similar code, so some of this code will need to be described once.

The init() function is where we will calculate xunits and yunits for the Shot. The first thing we are going to do is to calculate the distance between the start point startLocation (when the Shot starts), and the end point endLocation, which is the middle of the crosshairs.

```
public function init():void
{
    x = startLocation.x;
    y = startLocation.y;
    var xd:Number  = endLocation.x - x;
    var yd:Number  = endLocation.y - y;
    var distance:Number  = Math.sqrt(xd*xd + yd*yd);
```

The `distance` variable is calculated with a standard geometric equation, as shown in Figure 4-14. We converted the equation to AS3, but it is the exact same calculation.

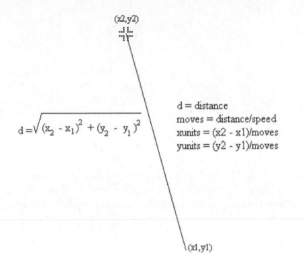

Figure 4-14. Using a distance equation to determine the **xunits** and **yunits** values

Now that we know the `distance` of the line, we can calculate how many frames it will take to get from the start point to the end point if we know the speed the `Shot` needs to travel. Luckily, we already know the speed.

```
moves = Math.floor(Math.abs(distance/speed));
```

Finally, we can get the exact number of pixels to move each frame by dividing (`endLocation.x - x`) by `moves` and (`endLocation.y - y`) by `moves`.

```
xunits = (endLocation.x - x)/moves;
yunits = (endLocation.y - y)/moves;
```

The nice thing about doing this calculation once is that, for the rest of the time this `Shot` exists in the game, it only has to do some simple arithmetic to move. All necessary values have already been calculated. There are other ways to calculate a vector and move a sprite, but this is one of the best methods we have found that will move an object on a line to reach an exact point. We will discuss a more general-purpose algorithm to move an object when we talk about the `Enemy` class.

Now we must finish up by actually getting the `ShotGif` graphic `BitmapData` from the library and attaching it to an instance of `Bitmap`. (Remember, in Flex, you need to uncomment the Flex code and comment out the Flash code).

```
//***** Flex *****
//imageBitmapData = new ShotGif().bitmapData;

//***** Flash *****
imageBitmapData = new ShotGif(0,0);

image = new Bitmap(imageBitmapData);
```

Finally, we add the image to the instance of Shot and set finished to false. This will get set to true once. The Shot has used up all its moves.

```
addChild(image);

finished = false;
}
```

Now it is time to write the update(), render() and dispose() functions for the Shot class. update() is called by the Game class (FlakCannon.as) to set the nextLocation Point. We do not actually move anything in update(). The reason is very simple. If we had to do any kind of look-ahead collision detection (e.g., testing for hitting walls), we would want to make sure that we have all the nextLocation values for our game objects beforehand. Even though we don't use look-ahead collision detection for this game, we will use the same conventions so you will get used to them.

The first thing we do in update() is test to see if there are still moves left. If not, we set finished to true. The next time Game checks to see if the Shot is finished, it will turn it into a Flak explosion. We'll discuss that process later. If the Shot is not finished, we update the nextLocation Point and decrement moves.

```
public function update():void {
   if (moves > 0) {
      nextLocation.x = x + xunits;
      nextLocation.y = y + yunits;
      moves--;
   } else {
      finished = true;
   }
}
```

We just told you that update() only sets the new movement values. render() actually does the work, which in this case is very simple. We set the x and y values of the Shot to value of nextLocation.x and nextLocation.y. Again, just like update(), render() is called by Game.

```
public function render():void {
   x = nextLocation.x;
   y = nextLocation.y;
}
```

Finally, we get to dispose(). When the Shot has finished moving, and it has been turned into a flak explosion, we need to remove it. While Game will remove the Shot from the screen and take it out of its aShot[] array, dispose() takes care of removing the Bitmap and BitmapData from memory. This clean up operation, while not required, helps initiate garbage collection in AS3. Without performing this action, eventually the game would start slowing down considerably as available memory becomes harder and harder to locate.

```
public function dispose():void {
   removeChild(image);
   imageBitmapData.dispose();
   image = null;
      }
   }
}
```

So that is all there is to the Shot class. However, we still need to talk about Enemy, Ship, and BonusPlane. Luckily, BonusPlane is nearly identical to Shot, so we will discuss that one next. Enemy and Ship also have some major similarities to Shot.

You may be thinking that if these classes are so close in structure, why didn't we create a class and inherit from it? Honestly, the answer is just for clarity. You could easily take the common elements of all these classes and create a base class for them that all of these objects would instantiate from. We will leave this to you so you can create a more complex object model that fits your particular style.

BonusPlane

We will use the code from Shot to create the code for the BonusPlane. The code changes to support BonusPlane are very few. The BonusPlane always flies across the screen from left to right. The only real difference then is the bonusValue instance variable (plus, obviously, the Flex embed). The bonusValue variable is the number of extra shots the player earns by shooting down the BonusPlane. We need to create an instance variable named bonusValue and pass in that value to the constructor.

```
package  com.efg.games.flakcannon
{
import flash.display.Shape;
import flash.display.Sprite
import flash.display.Bitmap;
import flash.display.BitmapData;
import flash.geom.Point;

public class BonusPlane extends Sprite
    {
    public var imageBitmapData:BitmapData;
    public var image:Bitmap;
    private var startLocation:Point;
    private var endLocation:Point;
    private var nextLocation:Point;
    private var xunits:Number;
    private var yunits:Number;
    private var speed:Number = 5;
    private var moves:int = 0;
    public var bonusValue:int = 0;
    public var finished:Boolean;
    /*
    [Embed(source = "assets/flakassets.swf", symbol="PlaneBonusGif")]
    private var PlaneBonusGif:Class;
     */

public function BonusPlane(startX:Number, startY:Number, endX:Number, endY:Number, ↵
speed:Number, bonusValue:int)    {
    startLocation = new Point(startX,startY);
    endLocation = new Point(endX,endY);
    nextLocation = new Point(0,0);
    this.speed=speed;
    this.bonusValue=bonusValue;
    init();
}
```

When init() is called, the only real difference is the Bitmapdata we use to create the image. This time it is PlaneBonusGif()

```
public function init():void
{
    x = startLocation.x;
    y = startLocation.y;
    var xd:Number  = endLocation.x - x;
    var yd:Number  = endLocation.y - y;
    var Distance:Number  = Math.sqrt(xd*xd + yd*yd)
    moves = Math.floor(Math.abs(Distance/speed));
    xunits = (endLocation.x - x)/moves;
    yunits = (endLocation.y - y)/moves;
    //***** Flex *****
    //imageBitmapData = new PlaneBonusGif().bitmapData;
    //***** Flash *****
    imageBitmapData = new PlaneBonusGif(0,0);
    image = new Bitmap(imageBitmapData);
    addChild(image);
    finished = false;
}
```

The rest of the functions from Shot remain essentially the same in BonusPlane.

```
public function update():void {
    if (moves > 0) {
        nextLocation.x = x + xunits;
        nextLocation.y = y + yunits;
        moves--;
    } else {
        finished = true;
    }
}

public function render():void {
    x = nextLocation.x;
    y = nextLocation.y;
}


public function dispose():void {
    removeChild(image);
    imageBitmapData.dispose();
    image = null;
    }
    }
}
```

Ship

Now we will discuss the Ship object. Ship is the easiest Sprite class because Ships do not move in Flak Cannon. They truly are static sprites! They simple stay in place, waiting to be destroyed (err, defended). That means that the only real differences are the Flex embed and the fact that we use ShipGif() to get our Bitmapdata.

```
package   com.efg.games.flakcannon
{

import flash.display.Shape;
import flash.display.Sprite
import flash.events.MouseEvent;
import flash.display.Bitmap;
import flash.display.BitmapData;

public class Ship extends Sprite
{
    public var imageBitmapData:BitmapData;
    public var image:Bitmap;

    /*
    //**Flex Framework Only
    [Embed(source = "assets/flakassets.swf", symbol="ShipGif")]
    private var ShipGif:Class;
    */

    public function Ship() {
        init();
    }


    public function init():void {
        //***** Flex *****
        //imageBitmapData = new ShipGif().bitmapData;
        //**** Flash *****
        imageBitmapData = new ShipGif(0, 0);

        image = new Bitmap(imageBitmapData);
        addChild(image);
    }

    public function dispose():void {
        removeChild(image);
        imageBitmapData.dispose();
        image = null;
    }
}

}
```

Creating objects that move on a continuous vector: Enemy

Unlike BonusPlane and Ship, Enemy has some major differences from the Shot class. Some of them come from the fact that we simulate three different types of Enemy planes with one class. We do this by supporting three directions for the Enemy planes: DIR_DOWN, DIR_RIGHT, or DIR_LEFT. The other major change is more substantial. We could have created the movement code in Enemy the same way we created the movement code in both Shot and BonusPlane. Instead though, we will introduce a new algorithm for movement that can support an object moving in almost any direction using an angle.

First, let's take a quick look at the class instance variables. Notice that we have added four new variables. `dir` is the direction the Enemy plane will fly, while `DIR_DOWN`, `DIR_RIGHT` and `DIR_LEFT` represent this direction. They are static variables so they can be referenced outside the Enemy class.

```
package  com.efg.games.flakcannon
{
    import flash.display.Shape;
    import flash.display.Sprite
    import flash.events.MouseEvent;
    import flash.display.Bitmap;
    import flash.display.BitmapData;
    import flash.geom.Point;

    public class Enemy extends Sprite
    {
        public var imageBitmapData:BitmapData;
        public var image:Bitmap;
        private var startLocation:Point;
        private var endLocation:Point;
        public var nextLocation:Point;
```

Notice that `nextLocation` is a public variable in the class. We do this so we can access it for collision detection. Since we will not be using look-ahead collision detection in this game, we will not make use of this feature, but it is something that should be noted. You need to remember to make variables that need to be accessed from the out public in some way, either by making them explicitly public, or by creating get/set methods for each

Another addition is the variable `angle`. We are now creating objects that move from one point in any particular direction until we tell them to stop, instead of moving from one point to another and stopping. To facilitate this, we will keep track of the current angle at which the object is travelling. This value will help us calculate the `nextLocation` point values in a brand new `render()` function.

```
        private var speed:int = 5;
        public var finished:Boolean;
        public var dir:Number;
        public var angle:Number;

        public static const DIR_DOWN:int = 1;
        public static const DIR_RIGHT:int =2;
        public static const DIR_LEFT:int  =3;
```

Another thing we need to do is embed the three different plane graphics if we are using Flex. Again, these three graphics are used for the three different directions from which an Enemy can fly onto the screen.

```
        /*
        //**Flex Framework Only
        [Embed(source = "assets/flakassets.swf", symbol="PlaneGif")]
        private var PlaneGif:Class;

        [Embed(source = "assets/flakassets.swf", symbol="PlaneLeftGif")]
        private var PlaneLeftGif:Class;

        [Embed(source = "assets/flakassets.swf", symbol="PlaneRightGif")]
        private var PlaneRightGif:Class;
        */
```

There are a couple small differences to the constructor as well. Instead of having a speed set in the class, we pass in a speed parameter from FlakCannon. This will allow Game to use its enemySpeed difficulty setting to set the speed of the Enemy planes as levels progress. We also pass in a value for dir (one of the static const values). This allows Game to use its enemySideChance difficulty setting as the levels progress.

```
public function Enemy(startX:Number, startY:Number, endY:Number, speed:Number, ↩
  dir:int) {
    startLocation = new Point(startX,startY);
    endLocation = new Point(0,endY);
    nextLocation = new Point(0,0);
    this.dir = dir;
    this.speed=speed;
    init();
}
```

Finally, we need to do something with the dir instance variable that defines the direction that the plane will fly on the screen. This happens in init() We use a switch() statement to decide which Bitmap to attach to the class depending on the value of dir. Notice again, that there is different code here for Flash and Flex. However, there is a much more important difference in this function than in the one we created for BonusPlane and Shot. Instead of using already calculated xunits and yunits, this function uses angle and speed values to resolve the vector that this object is moving on. This is a much more flexible way to handle vectors than point-to-point because you can calculate movement simply by changing the angle of an object.

To start, let's discuss how Flash views the angles. Flash uses a Cartesian coordinate system (basically a grid with x and y axes) to position objects on a 2D plane. We have already used this system many times by setting the x an y values of various sprites and MovieClips. However, when using angles, it is important to know how this system works in a bit more detail.

Angles in Flash are calculated with the origin of 0 degrees pointing directly to the right of the screen (as shown in Figure 4-15). This is because of the Cartesian coordinate system.

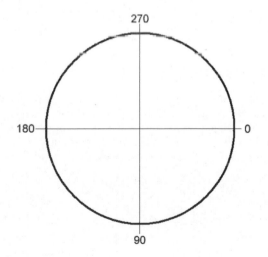

Figure 4-15. How Flash AS3 calculates angles

In Figure 4-16, you can see where the Flash 2D plane lies in that system. With x increasing in value to the right, and y increasing in value down, the screen falls into the lower right-hand portion of the grid. This means that a 45-degree angle, cut from the center, would travel through the grid as shown. This also means that 0 degrees is 45 degrees less than that line, which puts 0 to the direct right of the screen.

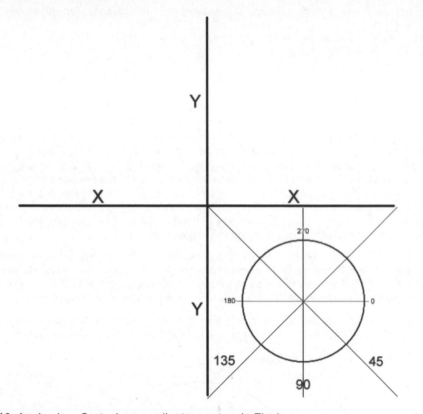

Figure 4-16. Angles in a Cartesian coordinates system in Flash

On the screen then, a rotation of 90 degrees will point directly down the screen. Since our Enemy planes will fly directly down, we need to note this value. We will also have Enemy planes that fly in from the right at a 45-degree angle, and from the left at 135-degree angle. These are the three angle values we will need for the Enemy class. As you can see in the following code, we use the dir value to set the angle we will need to move the Enemy:

```
public function init():void
{
    x = startLocation.x;
    y = startLocation.y;
    switch(dir) {
        case DIR_DOWN:
            //***** Flex *****
            //imageBitmapData = new PlaneGif().bitmapData;
            //**** Flash *****
```

```
            imageBitmapData = new PlaneGif(0,0);
            angle = 90;
            break;
        case DIR_RIGHT:
            //***** Flex *****
            //imageBitmapData = new PlaneRightGif().bitmapData;
            //**** Flash *****
            imageBitmapData = new PlaneRightGif(0,0);
            angle = 45;
            break;
        case DIR_LEFT:
            //***** Flex *****
            //imageBitmapData = new PlaneLeftGif().bitmapData;
            //**** Flash *****
            imageBitmapData = new PlaneLeftGif(0,0);
            angle=135;
            break;
    }
    image = new Bitmap(imageBitmapData);
    addChild(image);
    finished = false;
}
```

Now that we have values for angle and speed, we can calculate the next x and y values to move the Enemy. Recall that a vector needs both direction and velocity. Both angle and speed fulfill those requirements for Enemy.

The first thing we need to do is to change the value we have for angle into radians. Radians are a standard unit of measurement used in trigonometry to calculate the values for sine and cosine of an angle. It just happens that we can use sine and cosine to help us calculate nextLocation for the Enemy. A radian is equal to about 57.3 degrees, but for our game, you don't really need to know that. All you need to know is how to convert angle to radians which can be done like this:

```
radians = angle * Math.PI / 180;
```

To find the values for nextLocation, we will use sine and cosine with the radians value to find the change in x (Math.cos()) and the change in y (Math.sin()) given a velocity (speed). We then add those values back the current values for x and y, and we have the next location to move.

```
public function update():void {
    if (y < endLocation.y) {
        var radians:Number = angle * Math.PI / 180;
        nextLocation.x =  x  + Math.cos(radians) * speed;
        nextLocation.y =  y  + Math.sin(radians) * speed;
    } else {
        finished = true;
    }

}
```

While the description for this calculation might seem complicated, the good news is that this code is nearly plug and play among different platforms and programming languages. Once you know the basics how to find the nextLocation values using radians, sine, and cosine, the rest can be easily converted on nearly any platform. The advantage of this method over the point-to-point method is that we could easily change the angle of the Enemy and have it move in a different direction. The rest of the functions in enemy remain essentially unchanged from the Shot class.

```
public function render():void {
    x = nextLocation.x;
    y = nextLocation.y;
}

public function dispose():void {
    removeChild(image);
    imageBitmapData.dispose();
    image = null;
}
}
}
```

Creating animated sprites

In Flak Cannon, two game objects require multiple frames of animation: Flak and Explosion. Both are nearly identical, but they have some major differences from the moving (and in the case of Ship, not moving) static sprites.

Flash gives programmers some very easy ways to create animation using the built-in timeline and MovieClips. In Chapter 1, we created an explosion using this method. However, since this chapter begins our journey into the world of using bitmaps to make games, we are not going to cut corners. Creating MovieClips for animation is easy, but you pay a price in overheard for using them. Bitmaps can be fast and efficient, and we will make use of them throughout this book to create games.

For an animated sprite, we need multiple images that we can display over time to achieve the desired effect. Luckily, we already imported seven graphics that we can use for our Flak explosion. All we need now is a way to display them, one after another, controlling their order and how long they are displayed before the image is changed.

Flak

Recall that the flak explosion contains seven frames of animation that we added to the library (see Figure 4-3). These are the frames we need to run through to display the Flak explosion. To start off, the import statements for Flak are identical to the ones for Shot, as is the class definition.

```
package com.efg.games.flakcannon
{
// Import necessary classes from the flash libraries
import flash.display.Shape;
import flash.display.Sprite
import flash.events.MouseEvent;
import flash.display.Bitmap;
import flash.display.BitmapData;

public class Flak extends Sprite
    {
```

However, the similarities end when we start to define the instance variables. First of all, instead of a single image, we have an array named images. This will hold the frames of animation that Flak will run through. We do still need a single image variable to hold the current frame of animation, so image still exists. Also, we need `currentImageIndex`, which holds the index of the images array that we are current showing. We also need a `finished` Boolean, so `FlakCannon` can tell when the animation is complete and can start the process to remove it from the screen. `frameCounter` is used to define the number of frames that have passed since we have changed images. We use this in conjunction with `frameDelay` to define the length of the animation. Finally, we have another new variable named `hits`, it's a counter that we increment each time a plane is destroyed by this `Flak` explosion. Keeping track of `hits` allows us to give the player bonus points for destroying more than one plane with a `Flak` explosion. After these new variables, we have to embed the Flak explosion frames for Flex.

```
public var images:Array;
public var image:Bitmap;
public var currentImageIndex:int = -1;
public var finished:Boolean;
private var frameCounter:int = 0;
private var frameDelay:int = 2;
public var hits:int;

/*
//**Flex Framework Only
[Embed(source = "assets/flakassets.swf", symbol="Exp1Gif")]
private var Exp1Gif:Class;

[Embed(source = "assets/flakassets.swf", symbol="Exp2Gif")]
private var Exp2Gif:Class;

[Embed(source = "assets/flakassets.swf", symbol="Exp3Gif")]
private var Exp3Gif:Class;

[Embed(source = "assets/flakassets.swf", symbol="Exp4Gif")]
private var Exp4Gif:Class;

[Embed(source = "assets/flakassets.swf", symbol="Exp5Gif")]
private var Exp5Gif:Class;

[Embed(source = "assets/flakassets.swf", symbol="Exp6Gif")]
private var Exp6Gif:Class;

[Embed(source = "assets/flakassets.swf", symbol="Exp7Gif")]
private var Exp7Gif:Class;
*/
```

Since we do not need to move `Flak`, the constructor simply sets `hits` to 0 and calls `init()`. `hits` is a simple counter that we will use for scoring. Since a `Flak` explosion does not disappear when it hits an `Enemy`, it can effectively destroy many planes. Hits will be used to keep track of the number of `Enemy` planes that this `Flak` explosion has destroyed. We will give the player a bonus for hitting multiple `Enemy` objects with one `Flak` object.

```
public function Flak() {
  hits = 0;
  init();
}
```

A lot of the new interesting code for `Flack` lives in `init()`. We are going to create `image` as a holder for the current `Bitmap` and add it to the sprite. Then, we will fill the `images` array with all the bitmaps needed to run through the animation. Again, notice the different code for Flex and Flash. We then call setNextImage() to get the BitmapData for the current image, set frameCounter to 0 to start the animation timing, and set finished to false so that FlakCannon will not instantly remove it from the screen.

```
public function init():void
{
    image = new Bitmap();
    addChild(image);

    //***** Flex *****
    /*images = [new Exp1Gif().bitmapData,
    new Exp2Gif().bitmapData,
    new Exp3Gif().bitmapData,
    new Exp4Gif().bitmapData,
    new Exp5Gif().bitmapData,
    new Exp6Gif().bitmapData,
    new Exp7Gif().bitmapData
    ];
    */

    //***** Flash *****

    images = [new Exp1Gif(32,32),
    new Exp2Gif(0,0),
    new Exp3Gif(0,0),
    new Exp4Gif(0,0),
    new Exp5Gif(0,0),
    new Exp6Gif(0,0),
    new Exp7Gif(0,0)
    ];

setNextImage();
frameCounter=0;
finished=false;

}
```

setNextImage() increments the currentImageIndex counter and then checks to see if we have reached the end of the animation. If we have, we set finished to true. If not, we set image.bitMapData to the image at index = currebtImageIndex in the images array.

```
public function setNextImage():void {
    currentImageIndex++;
    if (currentImageIndex > images.length-1) {
        finished = true;
    } else {
        image.bitmapData = images[currentImageIndex];
    }

}
```

The update() function does not need to move anything. When it is called by FlakCannon, it simply updates the frameCounter. The interesting stuff will happen in render().

```
public function update():void {

    frameCounter++;
}
```

render() is interesting because it controls the flow of the animation. First, it checks to see if the frameCounter has reached the value of frameDelay. If so, setNextImage() is called, and the frameCounter is zeroed out so we can start counting frames for the next image in the images array.

```
public function render():void {
    if (frameCounter >= frameDelay && !finished) {
        setNextImage();
        frameCounter=0;
    }

}
```

Just like in Shot, dispose() gets rid of the objects we have used to help with garbage collection. The difference here is that we need to dispose of a whole array of images instead of just one. We use a for each loop here instead of a for loop. for each is new to AS3, but has been around in other languages for many years. The advantage of for each is that the code is a bit cleaner, and we get a typed variable (tempImage) to operate with. Also of note, the following call to tempImage.dispose() is a call to the built-in BitmapData class method. We named our function the same thing so that it would be clear as to the purpose of this code.

```
public function dispose():void {
    removeChild(image);

    for each ( var tempImage:BitmapData in images ) {
tempImage.dispose();
    }
    images = null;

    }

}

}
```

Explosion

Since Explosion is nearly identical to Flak, we will only talk about the differences between the two objects. However, there is very little to say. Besides using a different set of images and a different amount (five instead of seven), the only real difference is that there is no hits variable because we do not need to count the number of times the explosion hits anything. It is simply an animation that plays and nothing else. Recall that the Explosion has five frames of animation (see Figure 4-7). Here is the code for the Explosion class:

```
package  com.efg.games.flakcannon
{
    // Import necessary classes from the flash libraries
    import flash.display.Shape;
    import flash.display.Sprite
    import flash.events.MouseEvent;
```

```
import flash.display.Bitmap;
import flash.display.BitmapData;

public class Explosion extends Sprite
{
    public var images:Array;
    public var image:Bitmap;
    public var currentImageIndex:int = -1;
    public var finished:Boolean;
    private var frameCounter:int = 0;
    private var frameDelay:int = 1;

    /*
    //**Flex Framework Only
    [Embed(source = "assets/flakassets.swf", symbol="Ex21Gif")]
    private var Ex21Gif:Class;

    [Embed(source = "assets/flakassets.swf", symbol="Ex22Gif")]
    private var Ex22Gif:Class;

    [Embed(source = "assets/flakassets.swf", symbol="Ex23Gif")]
    private var Ex23Gif:Class;

    [Embed(source = "assets/flakassets.swf", symbol="Ex24Gif")]
    private var Ex24Gif:Class;

    [Embed(source = "assets/flakassets.swf", symbol="Ex25Gif")]
    private var Ex25Gif:Class;
    */

    public function Explosion()      {
        init();
    }

    public function init():void {
        image = new Bitmap();
        this.addChild(image);
        //***** Flex *****
        /*
        images = [
        new Ex21Gif().bitmapData,
        new Ex22Gif().bitmapData,
        new Ex23Gif().bitmapData,
        new Ex24Gif().bitmapData,
        new Ex25Gif().bitmapData
        ];
        */

        //***** Flash *****
        images = [
        new Ex21Gif(0,0),
```

```
            new Ex22Gif(0,0),
            new Ex23Gif(0,0),
            new Ex24Gif(0,0),
            new Ex25Gif(0,0)
            ];

            setNextImage();
            frameCounter=0;
            finished=false;

        }

    public function setNextImage():void{
        currentImageIndex++;
        if (currentImageIndex > images.length-1) {
            finished=true;
        } else {
            image.bitmapData = images[currentImageIndex];
        }
    }

    public function update():void {
        frameCounter++;
    }

    public function render():void {
        if (frameCounter >= frameDelay && !finished) {
            setNextImage();
            frameCounter=0;
        }
    }

    public function dispose():void {
        removeChild(image);
        for each ( var tempImage:BitmapData in images ) {
            tempImage.dispose();
        }
      images = null;
    }

    }
}
```

Summary

In this chapter, you learned some basic concepts for designing a game, managing game difficulty, creating and adding sounds and graphics, and supporting the differences between Flash and Flex libraries, plus how to move sprites using two different vector algorithms and how to animate sprites in code. In the next chapter, we will put all of this together to make our fourth game, Flak Cannon, the second project that utilizes our game framework.

Chapter 5

Building the Flak Cannon Game Loop

In Chapter 4, we built all the assets and classes we will need to make the Flak Cannon game. In this chapter, we will put everything together into something that we can play and build on. To recap a bit, Flak Cannon is a game much like the classic Atari Missile Command. Your job is to defend your fleet of ships against kamikaze planes that are trying to destroy them. To defend the ships, you use a flak gun. With the flak gun, the player does not shoot directly at the planes, but instead shoots where they will be. The flak explosion is the lethal part of the equation, not the shot itself.

We created a set of classes and objects in the previous chapter that we will use for this game. Let's quickly review what was created. SoundManager was a class to help play sounds easily in the game. We created that class and a new custom event named CustomEventSound that we will use in Flak Cannon. Shot was the class that represented the player's Flak shots from their off-screen cannon. We calculated a point-to-point vector for the path the Shot will fly up the screen. We made similar classes for Ship and BonusPlane. We created an Enemy class that uses angle and speed to calculate a vector on the fly. We also created animated sprite classes for Flak and Explosion. With all of those classes now complete, it is time to put them together into a functioning game.

Understanding the Flak Cannon game flow

Before we actually build the game, let's quickly go over the flow of the game loop and what we need to do to make Flak Cannon work.

The Main.as class is the beginning of the game framework. It contains our new game class FlakCannon.as, which contains the following methods:

- newGame(): Called by Main when a new game starts
- newLevel(): Called by Main when a new level starts

    - **Set difficulty settings**: Set up new a level
    - **Create crosshairs**: Put crosshairs on screen for the player

- `placeShips()`: Puts a player's fleet on the screen
- `runGame()`: Called by `Main` for the game loop
- `checkEnemies()`: Checks to see if an enemy plane should be created
- `checkBonusPlane()`: Checks to see if a bonus plane should be created
- `update()`: Calculates new positions for all objects
- `checkCollisions()`: Checks to see if objects have hit one another
- `addToScore()`: Adds a score for hitting planes
- `render()`: Physically places objects on the screen
- `checkforEndLevel()`: Checks to see if level has been completed
- `addToScore()`: Adds to the score for shots left over
- `cleanUpLevel()`: Cleans up objects for the next level
- `checkforEndGame()`: Checks to see if the player has lost the game.
- `shootListener()`: Listens for mouse button click to fire a shot
- `mouseMoveListener()`: Listens for mouse movement to update placement of crosshairs.

Updating GameFramework.as

Before we get into the core of the Flak Cannon–specific code, we need to discuss some updates to the game framework to support the `SoundManager` that we created in the last chapter. These changes are not specific to Flak Cannon, but they are specific to the game framework. We have placed this code in this chapter to enforce the point that the sound manager, while part of the game framework, can be used on its own. This section shows how we will integrate it into the rest of the code.

The first thing we need to do in `GameFrameWork.as` is to add a variable to hold the reference to `SoundManager`. This is named `soundManager` and will be placed in the properties definition section of the class.

```
public var soundManager:SoundManager;
```

Note This might be a good time to download the source fcode from one of the web addresses on the back cover of the book. You can find the final version of GameFramework.as in

`/source/class/com/efg/framework/`.

If you recall from Chapter 4, we created `CustomSoundEvent`, which was an event we could use with `SoundManager` to tell `Main.as` when a game needed to play a sound. We need to add a couple lines to a couple different functions from `GameManager.as` to use this event. The first function is `systemNewGame()`. We need to add `GameFrameWork` as an `EventListenter` to the game class (in this case, game is an instance of `FlakCannon`). We set `soundEventListener()` as the function to call when the event is dispatched.

```
public function systemNewGame():void {
    addChild(game);
    game.addEventListener(CustomEventScoreBoardUpdate.UPDATE_TEXT, ↵
        scoreBoardUpdateListener, false, 0, true);
    game.addEventListener(CustomEventLevelScreenUpdate.UPDATE_TEXT, ↵
        levelScreenUpdateListener, false, 0, true);
    game.addEventListener(CustomEventSound.PLAY_SOUND, soundEventListener, ↵
        false, 0, true);
    game.addEventListener(Game.GAME_OVER, gameOverListener, false, 0, true);
    game.addEventListener(Game.NEW_LEVEL, newLevelListener, false, 0, true);
    game.newGame();
    switchSystemState(FrameWorkStates.STATE_SYSTEM_NEW_LEVEL);
}
```

> *Note that many developers like to use naming convention onXxxxxEvent() to name callback functions for events. This is a fine way to name your events, and if you feel like renaming the events in this book to match that style you are more than welcome to do so.*

We also need to remove the EventListener when the game is over. To do that, we add another line of code to the gameOverListener() function:

```
public function gameOverListener(e:Event):void {
    switchSystemState(FrameWorkStates.STATE_SYSTEM_GAME_OVER);
    game.removeEventListener(CustomEventScoreBoardUpdate.UPDATE_TEXT, ↵
        scoreBoardUpdateListener);
    game.removeEventListener(CustomEventLevelScreenUpdate.UPDATE_TEXT, ↵
        levelScreenUpdateListener);
    game.removeEventListener(CustomEventSound.PLAY_SOUND, soundEventListener);
    game.removeEventListener(Game.GAME_OVER, gameOverListener);
    game.removeEventListener(Game.NEW_LEVEL, newLevelListener);
}
```

The soundEventListener() function is brand new in the GameFrameWork class. When the CustomEventSound event is dispatched, we will set all the properties of the CustomEventSound object necessary to play a sound. As a review, those properties follow:

- type: This String defines the type of event, either CustomSoundevent. PLAY_SOUND or CustomSoundevent.STOP_SOUND

- name: This String determines the sound to play. Values are static consts defined in Main.as: Main.SOUND_XXX

- isSoundTrack: This Boolean indicated whether to consider this sound a soundtrack when playing.

Note We will talk about playing sound tracks in Chapter 8.

- loops: This int sets the number of times to loop the sound when playing.

- offset: This Number defines the offset, in milliseconds, into the song to start. It can be useful for skipping an MP3 leader if you have loaded .mp3 sounds.
- volume: This Number sets the volume level to play the sound; it's value can be between 0 and 1.

When the soundEventListener() function is called, we look at the type parameter to see if we should play or stop the sound. Other than that, all the parameters are passed into soundManager.playSound() as is.

```
public function soundEventListener(e:CustomEventSound):void {
    if (e.type == CustomEventSound.PLAY_SOUND) {
        soundManager.playSound(e.name, e.isSoundTrack, e.loops, e.offset, e.volume );
    }else {
        soundManager.stopSound(e.name, e.isSoundTrack);
    }
}
```

Defining Main.as

Now, we start the specific code for Flak Cannon by defining the Main.as class. Recall that we have abstracted most of the game framework from Main. We did this so customizing the game would be easier, while leaving the framework itself untouched for a specific game (except for when we enhance the game framework itself with new features for all games).

The import statements are standard for Main.as classes for our games. Notice that we need to add the new SoundManager we created so we can use it for this game.

```
package com.efg.games.flakcannon
{
import com.efg.framework.FrameWorkStates;
import com.efg.framework.GameFrameWork;
import com.efg.framework.BasicScreen;
import com.efg.framework.ScoreBoard;
import com.efg.framework.Game;
import com.efg.framework.SideBySideScoreElement;
import com.efg.framework.SoundManager;

import flash.display.Bitmap;
import flash.display.BitmapData;
import flash.display.Sprite;
import flash.events.Event;
import flash.geom.Point;
import flash.utils.Timer;
import flash.events.TimerEvent;
import flash.text.TextFormat;
```

Recall that our Main.as class extends com.efg.framework.GameFrameWork. This means that we only need to override the functions that we will need to change; for Flak Cannon, that will only be the init() function.

```
public class Main extends GameFrameWork {

    //custom sccore board elements
```

The ScoreBoard elements that we will create for Flak Cannon, while different than previous games, operate the same. Here, we create some static const values that we will use the reference these elements inside our game.

```
public static const SCORE_BOARD_SCORE:String = "score";
public static const SCORE_BOARD_SHOTS:String = "shots";
public static const SCORE_BOARD_SHIPS:String = "ships";
```

One of the significant additions to Main.as for Flak Cannon is support for playing sounds. We need to create a static const that we will reference inside the FlakCannon class when we want to play a sound. We need to create one static const for each sound. Also, if you are using Flex, you will need to embed each sound individually.

```
//custom sounds
public static const SOUND_BONUS:String          =   "sound bonus";
public static const SOUND_BONUS_SHIP:String     =   "sound bonus ship";
public static const SOUND_SHOOT:String          =   "sound shoot";
public static const SOUND_NOSHOTS:String        =   "sound no shots";
public static const SOUND_EXPLODE_PLANE:String  =   "sound explode plane";
public static const SOUND_EXPLODE_FLAK:String   =   "sound explode flak";
public static const SOUND_EXPLODE_SHIP:String   =   "sound explode ship";


//**Flex Framework Only
/*
[Embed(source = "assets/flakassets.swf", symbol="SoundExplodePlane")]
private var SoundExplodePlane:Class;

[Embed(source = "assets/flakassets.swf", symbol="SoundExplodeFlak")]
private var SoundExplodeFlak:Class;

[Embed(source = "assets/flakassets.swf", symbol="SoundShoot")]
private var SoundShoot:Class;

[Embed(source = "assets/flakassets.swf", symbol="SoundNoShots")]
private var SoundNoShots:Class;

[Embed(source = "assets/flakassets.swf", symbol="SoundBonus")]
private var SoundBonus:Class;

[Embed(source = "assets/flakassets.swf", symbol="SoundBonusShip")]
private var SoundBonusShip:Class;

[Embed(source = "assets/flakassets.swf", symbol="SoundExplodeShip")]
private var SoundExplodeShip:Class;

*/


public function Main() {
    init();
}
```

Again, the only function we will override in `GameFrameWork` is init(), and even then, the override includes mostly specific customizations for Flak Cannon. The rest of the game framework remains untouched. The first change is that we pass the width and height (600 × 400) into the instance of `FlakCannon`. `FlakCannon` will use these values to set boundaries for objects in the game.

The rest of the changes highlighted below are size, positioning, and textual updates to support Flak Cannon specifically. The game is 600 × 400 pixels and requires the scoreboard to keep track of **Score**, **Shots**, and **Ships** fields. We use the text **Flak Cannon** on the title screen with buttons that say **Go!** and **Shoot The Enemy Planes!** On the instructions screen, there's a **Play!** button, and on the end screen, a **Game Over** label with a **Play Again** button.

```
override public function init():void {
    game = new FlakCannon(600,400);
    setApplicationBackGround(600,400,false, 0x0042AD);
    scoreBoard = new ScoreBoard();
    addChild(scoreBoard);
    scoreBoardTextFormat= new TextFormat("_sans", "11", "0xffffff", "true");
    scoreBoard.createTextElement(SCORE_BOARD_SCORE, new ⮐
    SideBySideScoreElement(80, 5, 15, "Score",scoreBoardTextFormat, 25, "0", ⮐
        scoreBoardTextFormat));
    scoreBoard.createTextElement(SCORE_BOARD_SHOTS, new ⮐
        SideBySideScoreElement(240, 5, 10, "Shots",scoreBoardTextFormat, 40, "0", ⮐
        scoreBoardTextFormat));
    scoreBoard.createTextElement(SCORE_BOARD_SHIPS, new ⮐
        SideBySideScoreElement(400, 5, 10, "Ships",scoreBoardTextFormat, 50, "0", ⮐
        scoreBoardTextFormat));

    screenTextFormat = new TextFormat("_sans", "14", "0xffffff", "true");
    screenButtonFormat = new TextFormat("_sans", "11", "0x000000", "true");

    titleScreen = new BasicScreen(FrameWorkStates.STATE_SYSTEM_TITLE, 600,400, ⮐
        false, 0x0042AD);
    titleScreen.createDisplayText("Flak Cannon",250,new Point(255,100), ⮐
        screenTextFormat);
    titleScreen.createOkButton("Go!",new Point(250,250),100,20, ⮐
        screenButtonFormat,0xFFFFFF,0xFF0000,2);
    instructionsScreen = new BasicScreen(FrameWorkStates.STATE_SYSTEM_INSTRUCTIONS, ⮐
        600,400, false, 0x0042AD);
    instructionsScreen.createDisplayText("Shoot The Enemy Planes!",300, ⮐
        new Point(210,100),screenTextFormat);
    instructionsScreen.createOkButton("Play",new Point(250,250),100,20, ⮐
        screenButtonFormat,0xFFFFFF,0xFF0000,2);
    gameOverScreen = new BasicScreen(FrameWorkStates.STATE_SYSTEM_GAME_OVER, ⮐
        600,400, false, 0x0042AD);
    gameOverScreen.createDisplayText("Game Over",300,new Point(250,100), ⮐
        screenTextFormat);
    gameOverScreen.createOkButton("Play Again", new Point(225,250),150,20, ⮐
        screenButtonFormat,0xFFFFFF,0xFF0000,2);
    levelInText = "Level ";
    levelInScreen = new BasicScreen(FrameWorkStates.STATE_SYSTEM_GAME_OVER, ⮐
        600,400, false, 0x0042AD);
```

```
levelInScreen.createDisplayText(levelInText,300,new Point(275,100), ↵
    screenTextFormat);
switchSystemState(FrameWorkStates.STATE_SYSTEM_TITLE);
waitTime= 40;
```

Here are the only actual code additions to init() that we need to discuss: We created a set of static const values that represent each sound we want to make available to play in Flak Cannon, but we still need to register those sounds with soundManager. We do this by calling soundManager.addSound() passing two parameters: the static const name for the sound, and a reference to the sound class as exported in the Flash library.

```
soundManager.addSound(SOUND_BONUS,new SoundBonus());
soundManager.addSound(SOUND_BONUS_SHIP, new SoundBonusShip());
soundManager.addSound(SOUND_SHOOT,new SoundShoot());
soundManager.addSound(SOUND_NOSHOTS,new SoundNoShots());
soundManager.addSound(SOUND_EXPLODE_PLANE,new SoundExplodePlane());
soundManager.addSound(SOUND_EXPLODE_FLAK,new SoundExplodeFlak());
soundManager.addSound(SOUND_EXPLODE_SHIP,new SoundExplodeShip());
```

```
frameRate = 30;
startTimer();
}
}
    }
```

FlakCannon.as

Every game we make will have a radically different class that extends from the Game class. For this game, we will create a class named FlakCannon for the purpose. Most of this chapter will cover how we build the FlakCannon.as class for the Flak Cannon game.

Importing classes

The first thing we need to do is to add the class import statements we use for the game. Some of these you have seen before when we made the Super Click game.

```
package com.cfg.games.flakcannon {
    import flash.display.Sprite;
    import flash.events.*;
    import flash.events.MouseEvent;
```

We are going to use the mouse to control the crosshairs that point to where the player will fire a shot. To do this, we must support the MouseEvent class. The rest of these imported classes are new. This rest of this section provides short run down of how we will make use of them.

First, we will be loading all of our game graphics in as bitmaps. We need the Bitmap class to support this procedure.

```
import flash.display.Bitmap;
```

Next, we will be using the bitmap-level collision detection available with the BitmapData object. To do this, we will need to define a Point (x,y) to check for collisions. The flash.geom package will allow us to do just that.

```
import flash.geom.Point;
```

We need to know the location of the mouse pointer on the screen so we will know to what point we need to fire a shot. `ui.Mouse` will give us that information.

```
import flash.ui.Mouse;
```

Finally, we import the classes we will need from the game framework and begin the FlakCannon class definition.

```
import com.efg.framework.Game;
import com.efg.framework.CustomEventLevelScreenUpdate;
import com.efg.framework.CustomEventScoreBoardUpdate;
import com.efg.framework.CustomEventSound;
public class FlakCannon extends com.efg.framework.Game {
```

Setting the FlakCannon.as properties and constructor

Now that we have gotten the imports out of the way, it is time to get into some of the actual game code. First, we must define the necessary variables in the properties section of the class. Most of these properties will be new for every game. The first two properties, game `Width` and `gameHeight`, will be used to store the width and height of the screen passed to `FlakCannon` by `Main`.

```
//constructor
private var gameWidth:int;
private var gameHeight:int;
```

Next, we will define some variables that we will use to track properties specific to Flak Cannon. The `score` will track the player's score. `level` is the game level that the player has currently reached. This will be used to create the difficulty settings. The `ships` variables tracks how many ships that player currently has (not necessarily how many are on the screen). `shots` tracks the number of shots the player has left to fire at the `Enemy` planes. We will report most of these back to `ScoreBoard` using a `CustomEventScoreBoardUpdate` event. `isGameOver` is simply a setting to tell `FlakCannon` that game has finished, while `extraCount` is a running total the number of extra ships the player has earned that we will use to calculate when and if they will earn an extra `Ship`.

```
//NewGame

private var score:int;
private var level:int;
private var ships:int;
private var shots:int;
private var isGameOver:Boolean = false;
```

The next variable is used to count how many extra ships the player has received by reaching the value in the scoreNeededForExtraShip variable. Since the player rarely achieves a score that is exactly the value of scoreNeededForExtraShip, we need to store how many extras the player has received so we don't award extra ships unnecessarily.

```
private var  extraShipCount:int = 0;
```

Now, we will create arrays and variables to hold the objects we will create in the game. Explosion objects are held in `explodeArray`, Shot objects in `shotArray`, Ship objects in `shipArray`, Flak explosions in `flakArray`, Enemy planes in `enemyArray`, and BonusPlane objects in `bonusPlaneArray`. The player will control the `Bitmap` held in the `crosshairs` variable.

```
//New Level
private var explodeArray:Array;
private var shotArray:Array;
private var shipArray:Array;
private var enemyArray:Array;
private var flakArray:Array;
private var bonusPlaneArray:Array;
private var crosshairs:Bitmap;
```

incomingCount holds a tally of the number of Enemy planes that have been created for the level. We check incomingCount to know when the level is over.

```
private var incomingCount:int;
```

All of the following settings that need to be made available to the entire FlakCannon class, so we need to define them as instance variables. These are the settings used to control the difficulty of the games. Refer to Chapter 4 for detailed descriptions.

```
//Difficulty Knobs/Settings
private var enemyWaveDelay:int = 30;
private var numEnemies:int;
private var enemyFrameCounter:int = 0;
private var enemySpeed:int = 0;
private var enemyWaveMax:Number    = 0
private var enemyWaveMultipleChance:Number = 0;
private var enemySideFloor:Number = 100;
private var enemySideChance:Number = 10;
private var bonusPlaneFrameCounter:Number = 0;
private var bonusPlaneDelay:Number = 1;
private var startShots:int = 30;
private var scoreNeededForExtraShip:int = 10000;
private var baseEnemyScore:int = 250;
private var enemyHitBonus:int  = 500;
private var baseBonusPlaneScore:int = 500;
private var maxBonusPlanes:int - 1;
private var maxVisibleShips:int = 3;
private var bonusPlaneMaxY:int =350;
private var bonusPlaneSpeed:int = 3;
private var shipYPadding:int = 0;
```

The next set of variables contains temporary holders that we will define once and reuse in many different functions. These will be use to hold an instance of our major objects (Shot, Flak, Enemy, Ship, Explosion, BonusPlane) when we iterate through the arrays designed to hold multiple instances of them.

```
private var tempShot:Shot;
private var tempFlak:Flak;
private var tempEnemy:Enemy;
private var tempShip:Ship;
private var tempExplode:Explosion;
private var tempBonusPlane:BonusPlane;
```

After that, we include flakassets.swf for Flex versions of the game.

```
/*
//**Flex Framework Only
[Embed(source = "assets/flakassets.swf", symbol="CrosshairsGif")]
```

```
private var CrosshairsGif:Class;
*/
```

Next, we define the constructor itself. Recall that this function sets gameWidth and gameHeight as passed in by Main but doesn't do anything else. A bit later, we will use gameWidth and gameHeight to calculate important values (i.e., where to place Enemy planes and Ship objects on the screen).

FlakCannon now waits for the Main class to call its functions. The first will be newGame().

```
public function FlakCannon(gameWidth:int,gameHeight:int) {
    this.gameWidth=gameWidth;
    this.gameHeight=gameHeight;
}
```

Starting a new game

The newGame() function is one of the places where the FlakCannon class interfaces with the Main class. If you recall from Part 1, an instance of a Game class (or a class extended from Game like FlakCannon) does nothing without receiving calls from the Main class. This allows Main to be in control (i.e., take care of the boring stuff like showing title screens), and it also allows FlakCannon to take care of the game logic (i.e., do the cool stuff like make Flak Cannon shells go boom!). Here is the full code for the function:

```
override public function newGame():void {
    level = 0 ;
    score = 0;
    ships = 3;
    shots = 0;
    extraShipCount=0;
    isGameOver = false;
    dispatchEvent(new CustomEventScoreBoardUpdate(↵
        CustomEventScoreBoardUpdate.UPDATE_TEXT,Main.SCORE_BOARD_SCORE,"0"));
    dispatchEvent(new CustomEventScoreBoardUpdate(↵
        CustomEventScoreBoardUpdate.UPDATE_TEXT,Main.SCORE_BOARD_SHOTS,String(shots)));
}
```

The code in newGame() is pretty simple, with only a couple minor changes from Super Click. First, we set the basic game variables to their initial values.

```
level = 0 ;
score = 0;
ships = 3;
shots = 0;
extraShipCount=0;
isGameOver = false;
```

Next, we set-up some events that we will use to tell Main some pertinent information about the player progress in the game.

```
dispatchEvent(new CustomEventScoreBoardUpdate(↵
    CustomEventScoreBoardUpdate.UPDATE_TEXT,Main.SCORE_BOARD_SCORE,"0"));
dispatchEvent(new CustomEventScoreBoardUpdate(↵
    CustomEventScoreBoardUpdate.UPDATE_TEXT,Main.SCORE_BOARD_SHOTS,String(shots)));
```

We created similar events to these in Super Click. The real difference here is that we will be sending the ScoreBoard class information about the number of ships the player has left in the fleet with the CustomEventScoreBoard event.

Starting a new level

newLevel() is where we will update all the game level settings. Before we make any changes to the settings. However, we must first initialize all the arrays that we will use to hold our game's objects. We also need to reset incomingCount (so we can count the Enemy planes on this level) and then update the level variable so that we can calculate the settings for this level correctly.

```
override public function newLevel():void {
    explodeArray = [];
    flakArray = [];
    shotArray = [];
    shipArray = [];
    enemyArray = [];
    bonusPlaneArray = [];
    incomingCount = 0;
    level++;
```

Here are the difficulty settings that described in Chapter 4; refer to that chapter for a full description of how these variables will be used. We also describe them in context when we talk about each function in the FlakCannon class. For now, just notice that we can alter the game play for Flak Cannon in many ways using these variable settings.

```
numEnemies = (numEnemies > 100) ? 100          : level * 10 + (level*5);
enemyWaveDelay = (enemyWaveDelay < 20)         ? 20    :60 - (level-1)*2;
enemyWaveMax = (enemyWaveMax > 8) ? 8          : 1 * level+1;
enemyWaveMultipleChance =(enemyWaveMultipleChance > 100)? 100          : 10*level;

enemySpeed = (enemySpeed > 8)          ? 8 :2 + (.5*(level-1));
enemySideChance = (enemySideChance > 70) ? 70 : 10*(level-1);
enemySideFloor = (enemySideFloor > 300) ? 300          : 100 + 25*(level-1);

bonusPlaneDelay = (bonusPlaneDelay > 450) ? 450          : 350 + 10*(level-1);
bonusPlaneSpeed = (bonusPlaneSpeed > 12) ? 12          : 4 + (1*level);

bonusPlaneFrameCounter = 0;
enemyFrameCounter = enemyWaveDelay;
startShots = 30;
shots+=startShots;
scoreNeededForExtraShip = 10000;
baseEnemyScore = 100;
enemyHitBonus  = 500;
baseBonusPlaneScore = 500;
maxBonusPlanes = 1;
maxVisibleShips = 3;
bonusPlaneMaxY =350;
shipYPadding = 5;
```

Handling mouse events and starting the crosshairs

The player in Flak Cannon will control `crosshairs` on the screen that they will use to target shots. The crosshairs will be controlled by the mouse; the mouse button will be used to fire a `Flak` shell at incoming `Enemy` planes.

The first thing we must do to support the `crosshairs` is to define a variable to hold the bitmap in the properties definition section of the `Game` class. Note, we already created this in the properties, this line of code is just for clarification.

```
private var crosshairs:Bitmap;
```

Now, in `newLevel()`, we will test to see if the crosshairs exists. If not, we will hide the mouse pointer using the `Mouse.hide()` function and then define a new instance of the crosshairs `Bitmap` that we can add to the screen. Notice that if you are using Flex, the call to create a new instance is slightly different than in Flash. This is because Flex already considers the `CrosshairsGif()` class to be a `Bitmap`, while in Flash, we need to create a new Bitmap instance by passing an instance of `CrosshairsGif()` . The difference is subtle, but both sets of code are necessary to support either technology.

```
if (crosshairs == null) {
    Mouse.hide();

    //***** Flex *****
    //crosshairs = new CrosshairsGif();

    //***** Flash *****
    crosshairs = new Bitmap(new CrosshairsGif(0,0));
```

Now, we need to position the crosshairs on the screen. This is the first place where we use `gameWidth` and `gameHeight` that we passed in from `Main`. We will then add crosshairs to the screen using `addChild()`. Finally, we will add a new event handler to the stage to listen for the `MouseEvent.MOUSE_MOVE` event, so we can move the crosshairs when the mouse is moved, making it appear to move with the mouse.

```
    crosshairs.x=gameWidth/2;
    crosshairs.y=gameHeight/2;
    addChild(crosshairs);
    stage.addEventListener(MouseEvent.MOUSE_MOVE, mouseMoveListener, false, 0, true);
}
```

Now that we have our crosshairs on the screen, we need to do one more thing to support user input. We need to listen for the mouse button click, so we know when to fire a flak shell for the player. We do this by listening for the `MouseEvent.MOUSE_DOWN` event. This event is better for a game like Flak Cannon than `MouseEvent.MOUSE_CLICK`, as that event will wait for the mouse button to be pressed and released, while `MouseEvent.MOUSE_DOWN` will fire when the mouse is pressed down. This will make the firing more responsive for the player.

```
stage.addEventListener(MouseEvent.MOUSE_DOWN, shootListener, false, 0, true);
```

Having now defined listeners for mouse event, we must also create functions for those listeners to call. The first function `mouseMoveListener()` is quite simple. It is called whenever the mouse moves to update the position of crosshairs.

```
public function mouseMoveListener(e:MouseEvent):void    {
   crosshairs.x = e.stageX-(crosshairs.width/2);
   crosshairs.y = e.stageY-(crosshairs.height/2);
}
```

There are a couple of interesting things to note about this function. The first is self-explanatory but should still be noted. We can find the position of the mouse relative to the stage using the stageX and stageY properties of the MouseEvent object. The second thing is more subtle. We need to subtract half of the width and height from stageX and stageY to position the crosshairs properly (see Figure 5-1).

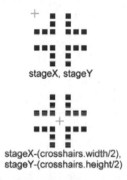

stageX, stageY

stageX-(crosshairs.width/2),
stageY-(crosshairs.height/2)

Figure 5-1. Adjusting the crosshairs into the center

We need to do this because of the way bitmaps are loaded dynamically in AS3. Without any adjustments, a bitmap image will load at its upper-left-hand registration point (see top of Figure 4-12). If we stopped there, shots fired would not explode in the center of the crosshairs, but in the upper-left. By performing the adjustment (see bottom of Figure 4-12), you can see that the center of the crosshairs is now where the mouse pointer would be and is also the point at which shots will explode.

Next, we need to write a function that will fire shots when the player presses the mouse button. That function is shootListener():

```
public function shootListener(e:MouseEvent):void {
```

The first thing we to do in this function is to check and see if the player has any shots left to fire from the cannon. This is quite easy to accomplish by simply creating an if:then statement to check the value of the shots variable:

```
   if (shots > 0) {
```

If shots are remaining, we drop into the if:then statement and create an instance of the Shot class, add it to the stage, push it into shotArray(), and then decrement the shot variable. Notice that we subtract (crosshairs.width/2) from mouseX and (crosshairs.height/2) from mouseY. We do this to center the shot in the middle of the crosshairs when it explodes into a Flak explosion.

```
   tempShot = new Shot(gameWidth/2,gameHeight,mouseX-↵
      (crosshairs.width/2),mouseY-(crosshairs.height/2));
   this.addChild(tempShot);
   shotArray.push(tempShot);
   shots--;
```

Finally, we send a message to the `ScoreBoard` telling it the new value of `shots`, so the value can be displayed correctly. We also dispatch a `CustomSoundEvent` to play the `Main.SOUND_SHOOT` to play the shooting sound for the cannon.

```
dispatchEvent(new CustomEventScoreBoardUpdate(CustomEventScoreBoardUpdate.UPDATE_TEXT,↵
    Main.SCORE_BOARD_SHOTS,String(shots)));
dispatchEvent( new CustomEventSound(CustomEventSound.PLAY_SOUND,Main.SOUND_SHOOT,↵
    false,1,0,.5));
```

Alternatively, if we do not drop into the then portion of the `if:then` statement (because there are no shots left), we drop into the `else` and play the annoying "no shots" sound, so the player knows the arsenal has been prematurely depleted.

```
} else {
    dispatchEvent( new CustomEventSound(CustomEventSound.PLAY_SOUND, ↵
    Main.SOUND_NOSHOTS,false,1,0,.75));
}

}
```

Placing the ships

One of the final things `newLevel()` must do is place the player's fleet of ships on the screen. We remove and replace the player's ships at the start of each level, so we can add ships to the fleet if they have been earned by reaching `scoreNeededForExtraShip` and reposition the ships, if necessary, according to how many the player has left.

No matter how many ships the player currently has in the fleet, only three are shown on the screen at any one time, as defined by the `maxVisibleShips` setting (note that you could make this value larger, but the ships would not all fit onto the screen). If there are less than three ships, the placement is adjusted so that they are centered on the screen.

To handle the ship placement, we must first call `placeShips()` in the `newLevel()` function.

```
placeShips();
```

Now, we need to define the `placeShips()` function itself. Recall that the idea behind this function is that we always want to place the remaining ships centered on the screen. To do this, we need to know how many ships are left and how big the screen is that we will be placing them onto. The good news is that we already know this information; we just need to use it properly.

The first thing we need to do is to define the function and then find out how many ships the player has left.

```
private function placeShips():void {
    var ctr:int;
    var xSpacing:int;
    var tShips:int = ships;
    if (tShips > maxVisibleShips) {
        tShips = maxVisibleShips;
    }
```

We don't care if the player has more than three ships at the start of a level; we are only going to use a maximum of three (as set in `maxVisibleShips`). The rest are in reserve and will be used on the next level. Now, we are going to start placing the ships.

```
xSpacing = (gameWidth/tShips);
```

xSpacing is a value calculated by splitting the screen size into as many parts as we have ships. We will use this in a second. First, we create a for:next loop to cycle through the ships. Then, we create a temporary ship (tempShip) that we can work with.

```
for (ctr = 0; ctr < tShips; ctr++) {
    tempShip = new Ship();
```

OK, now here is the big piece of code. To calculate the x value for a ship, we multiply the counter (ctr+1) by xSpacing to find out what part of the screen it belongs in. We then subtract xSpacing/2 to find the center of the area. After that, we again subtract half the width of a Ship so that that ship itself will be centered in the area (recall that bitmaps are loaded starting at the upper-left corner, so to find the center we need to subtract half the width).

```
tempShip.x =  ((xSpacing * (ctr+1)) - xSpacing/2) - (tempShip.width/2);
```

Now, we will clean up by setting the y value to specify the height of the ship (shipYPadding pixels) and put it into our shipArray array, and then add the ship the screen (see Figure 5-2). Recall that shipYPadding is the number of pixels between the bottom of the screen and the bottom of the ships. This is a constant setting, but there is no reason why the game could not be updated to increase this value at each level. This would increase the difficulty, as the higher the ships are up on the screen, the harder they will be to defend from the Enemy planes.

```
tempShip.y = gameHeight-tempShip.height- shipYPadding;
shipArray.push(tempShip);
this.addChild(tempShip);
}

}
```

Figure 5-2. Ship placement with 3, 2, and 1 ships left in the fleet

Handling newLevel events

Finally, we are almost done with newLevel(). The only thing left to do is to report the level, shots, and ships values back to ScoreBoard by dispatching events to update each one.

```
dispatchEvent(new CustomEventLevelScreenUpdate(↵
    CustomEventLevelScreenUpdate.UPDATE_TEXT,String(level)));
dispatchEvent(new CustomEventScoreBoardUpdate(↵
    CustomEventScoreBoardUpdate.UPDATE_TEXT, Main.SCORE_BOARD_SHOTS,String(shots)));
dispatchEvent(new CustomEventScoreBoardUpdate(↵
    CustomEventScoreBoardUpdate.UPDATE_TEXT, Main.SCORE_BOARD_SHIPS,String(ships)));
}
```

Testing out the game

Just to recap, we created four new functions: newLevel(), mouseMoveListener, shootListener, and placeShips(). If you compile and run the game right now, you will see something similar to Figure 5-3. If you click the mouse button, you will hear the sound of the shots firing, but no shots will fly because we have not coded that part of the game yet. You can also move the crosshairs with the mouse. When you are done, move onto the next section, so we can create a new level and finish the game.

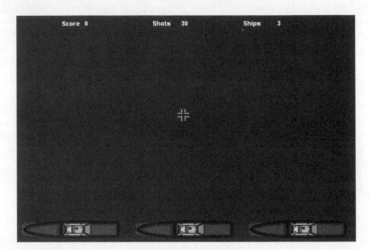

Figure 5-3. The crosshairs on the playfield while testing

Creating the game loop

Finally, it is time talk about the game itself. Like newGame() and newLevel(), runGame() is called by Main as part of the game framework's optimized game loop. The beauty of the game framework is that we do not have to worry about how or when runGame() gets called. We only need to know what do when it is called. We will discuss each of the function calls listed in the code for runGame() in detail. First, let's take a look at how the function is constructed.

```
override public function runGame():void {
    checkEnemies();
    checkBonusPlane();
    update();
    checkCollisions();
    render();
    checkforEndLevel();
    checkforEndGame();
}
```

Pretty simple, huh? Well, it's simple because all it does is call a bunch of functions we still need to define, but it was easy to write anyway. In the next sections, we will describe all of these functions and how they work together to create the Flak Cannon game.

Checking for enemies

The first thing we do in our runGame() function is call checkEnemies(). This function is designed to work with the enemyWaveDelay difficulty setting and the enemyFrameCounter variable. Its job is to test to see if a new enemy plane should be created to attack the player's fleet.

The first few lines of code set up the function and then test to see if we need to create an enemy. First, we increment enemyFrameCounter and test it against enemyWaveDelay. On the first level, enemyWaveDelay is set to 60. That means that 60 frames need to fire before an enemy is created. We also test incomingCount against numEnemies. incomingCount is incremented each time an enemy is created. numEnemies is another difficulty settings that represents the number of enemies per level. On the first level, this is set to 15.

```
private function checkEnemies():void {
    enemyFrameCounter++;
    if ((enemyFrameCounter >= enemyWaveDelay) && (incomingCount < numEnemies)) {
```

Now, we need to test to see if we are going to create a wave of multiple enemies, and if so, how many enemies we will create. For this, we will test the enemyWaveMultipleChance difficulty setting against a percentage chance random number (1–100). If the random number (chance) is less than or equal to enemyWaveMultipleChnace, the current wave we are creating will have multiple enemies at the same time. The more enemy planes that arrive at the same time, the harder it will be for the player to shoot them all down.

```
var chance:int = Math.floor(Math.random() * 100)+1;
var enemiesToCreate:int - 1;
```

Figure 5-4 shows what the screen will look like when Enemy planes start appearing in timed intervals.

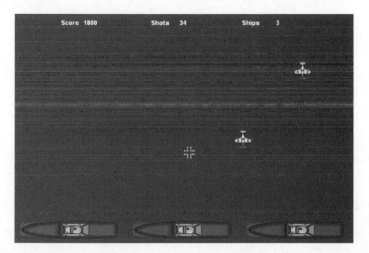

Figure 5-4. Single enemies flying down

If we do have multiple enemies, as shown in Figure 5-5, we will then find out how many by creating a random number with the maximum value using another difficulty setting, enemyWaveMax. We place that value into the local enemiesToCreate variable.

```
if (chance <= enemyWaveMultipleChance) {
        enemiesToCreate = Math.floor(Math.random() * enemyWaveMax)+1;
}
```

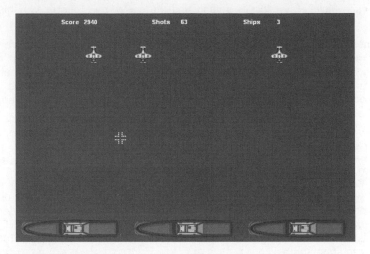

Figure 5-5. Multiple enemies flying down in a single wave

We then adjust the wave size to the number of enemies we have left on the current level (just in case the wave is bigger than how many are left). Recall, enemiesToCreate represents the number of Enemy objects that we need to create.

```
if (enemiesToCreate > (numEnemies-incomingCount)) {
    enemiesToCreate = (numEnemies-incomingCount);
}
```

Now, it is time to create the Enemy planes and put them on the screen. We will do this in a loop, with enemiesToCreate being the maximum number of iterations. If you recall, in Chapter 4, the Enemy class we created required a starting and ending point to define the vector on which the plane would move. This is where we will calculate those points. We start this by initializing startX and startY (the starting x and y values), endX and endY (the ending x and y values) plus dir, which represents the direction the plane will fly (Enemy.DIR_DOWN , Enemy.DIR_RIGHT, or Enemy.DIR_LEFT).

```
for (var ctr:int = 0; ctr < enemiesToCreate; ctr++) {
    var startX:int = 0;
    var startY:int = 0;
    var endX:int = 0;
    var endY:int = 0;
    var dir:int = 0;
    chance = Math.floor(Math.random() * 100)+1;
```

Now, we will use still another difficulty setting, enemySideChance, to test to see which direction this plane will be flying. We test against a percentage chance, just like we did with enemyWaveMultipleChance. If this plane does indeed come from the side, we will do another random test to see if the plane will come in from the left or right (leftOrRight).

```
if (chance <= enemySideChance) {
    var leftOrRight:int = Math.floor(Math.random() * 2);
```

startY is the starting y position of the Enemy plane. We have to incorporate another difficulty setting to calculate this value, enemySideFloor. enemySideFloor is the lowest point at which an Enemy plane will arrive on the screen from the side. The idea here is that the lower an Enemy enters the screen, the harder it will be to shoot down. The ending y value (endY) is always gameHeight, which means it will exit at the bottom of the screen. We don't need to find an endX value, because Enemy tests only the endY value to see if the Enemy has finished flying.

Now, depending on if the Enemy is flying to the left or right, we will create some slightly different values. If the plane is flying left, it will start at the extreme right of the screen. For that reason, startX equals gameWidth. If the plane is flying to the right, it will start at the extreme left (0) minus the width of the Enemy (−32). If you recall from Chapter 4, the Enemy class will select an angle for the Enemy to travel based on the direction (dir). Flying left to the left, the angle is 135 degrees (see Figure 5-6); from the right, it is 45 degrees.

```
startY = Math.floor(Math.random() * enemySideFloor)+1;
endY = gameHeight;
switch(leftOrRight) {
    case 0: //left
        startX = gameWidth;
        dir = Enemy.DIR_LEFT;
        break;
    case 1: //right
        startX = -32;
        dir = Enemy.DIR_RIGHT;
        break;
}
```

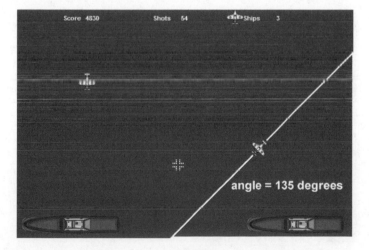

Figure 5-6. Enemy coming in from the left at a 135-degree angle

For Enemy planes that fly down (Enemy.DIR_DOWN), the values are quite easy to calculate. The starting x value (startX) is a random number generated that is the width of the screen (gameWidth) minus the width of the Enemy plane (32). This will keep the Enemy planes within the confines of the play field. The starting y value (startY) is simply –32, which means the entirety of the height of the Enemy will start off screen. The ending y value (endY) is the height of the screen.

```
    } else {
        startX = Math.floor(Math.random() * (gameWidth-32));
        startY = -32;
        endY = gameHeight;
        dir = Enemy.DIR_DOWN;
    }
```

Next, we create an instance of Enemy using the values we just calculated, add it to the display list with addChild(), and push it into our array of Enemy planes, enemyArray. We also update incomingCount so we can test it later to see if the level has been completed. Finally, we set the enemyFrameCounter to 0 so it can start counting again and be tested the next time checkEnemies() is called.

```
    tempEnemy = new Enemy(startX,startY,endY,enemySpeed,dir);
    this.addChild(tempEnemy);
    enemyArray.push(tempEnemy);
    incomingCount++;
    }
 enemyFrameCounter = 0;
    }
}
```

Checking for a bonus plane

A bonus plane, shown in Figure 5-7, arrives at a regular interval to give the player a chance to earn more shots for the flak cannon.

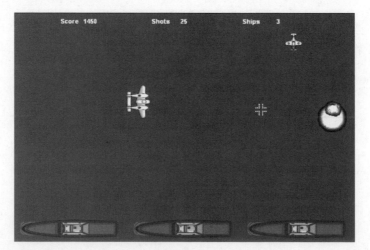

Figure 5-7. A bonus plane enters the screen

Here are the aspects of BonusPlane that make it different from Enemy:

- The BonusPlane always arrives flying from the left to the right.

192

- Shooting the `BonusPlane` awards the player 10 shots for the Flak cannon (note that the number of shots could be made into a difficulty setting).
- There can only ever be as many `BonusPlane` objects as set in the `maxBonusPlanes` setting.

Besides these rules, `checkBonusPlane()` acts a lot like `CheckEnemies()`. First of all, we will use a difficulty setting named `bonusPlaneDelay`. This setting tells us how long the game should wait before a `BonusPlane` arrives. We do not want it to come too early or too often, or the player will have an unfair advantage against the `Enemy` planes. The delay is calculated in frames. We use `bonusPlaneFrameCounter` to keep track of how frames have passed between `BonusPlane` arrivals.

```
private function checkBonusPlane():void {
    bonusPlaneFrameCounter++;
    if ( bonusPlaneFrameCounter >= bonusPlaneDelay) {
        if (bonusPlaneArray.length < maxBonusPlanes) {
```

Now, we get to create an instance of `BonusPlane`. The first thing we will do is set the starting y value for the plane. For this, we will simply get a random number between 0 and `bonusPlaneMaxY`. This difficulty setting represents the highest y value (lowest place on the screen) that a `BonusPlane` can fly. The starting x value is -32, which means it will always start off the right side of the screen, just far enough so the entire image is not visible. The ending x value is `gameWidth+32`, wihich means the plane will fly until it is entirely off the right side of the screen. Both the starting and ending y values are set to `randomY` because the y value will never change as the plane flies acrosss the screen.

```
    var randomY:int = Math.floor(Math.random()*bonusPlaneMaxY);
```

Wo aloo nood to oot the opeed of the BonusPlane. The speed of the plane will increase on every level. However, we do not want the plane to get too fast, or the player will not be able to shoot it down. Because of this, we use the `bonusPlaneSpeedMax` difficulty setting. If the `BonusPlane` speed is too fast, our code will set it to the maximum value.

The only thing left is to create an instance of `BonusPlane` and push it into `bonusPlaneArray`. Recall that we give the player ten extra shots when a `BonusPlane` is shot down. The last parameter in the call to `BonusPlane` is the literal 10, which represents this value. The `BonusPlane` could support different values for this bonus, but we are going to make it 10 every time. We then add It to the display list with `addChild()` and reset the `bonusPlaneFrameCounter` so we can test for another `BonusPlane` when the proper number of frames have passed.

```
    tempBonusPlane =new BonusPlane(-32,randomY,gameWidth+32,randomY,bonusPlaneSpeed,10);
    bonusPlaneArray.push(tempBonusPlane)
    this.addChild(tempBonusPlane);
    } else {
    bonusPlaneFrameCounter = 0;
    }
    }

}
```

Updating objects

The update() function is used to set all of the movement values for the game objects and to create Flak explosions from shots that have finished their movement cycle. The first part of the function tackles the Shot objects and their respective Flak explosions. The second part moves all the other objects.

```
private function update():void {
```

First, we start iterating through the shotArray using a for:each statement. This is useful here because for:each allows us to use a typed object that we would have to create manually using a for:next loop. Recall that tempShot was created as a class variable of type Shot, not local to this function. We did this to save the overhead of creating temporary variables every time we loop through our arrays of objects. We do the same for all the objects we will be updating in this function.

```
for each (tempShot in shotArray){
```

Recall that when any of our moving objects gets to the end of the vector (or finishes animating), they set their finished property to true. That makes it very easy for us to check to see if they should be removed from the screen. In the case of Shot, not only do we remove it from the screen but we also create an instance of Flak that needs to appear exactly where the Shot finished moving. Since Flak is 32 × 32 pixels, and it was created with its registration point at (0,0), we need to subtract half the width and height from x and y to make the center of the Flak explosion appear exactly where the Shot finished moving.

```
if (tempShot.finished) {
    tempFlak = new Flak();
    tempFlak.x = tempShot.x-(tempShot.width/2);
    tempFlak.y = tempShot.y-(tempShot.height/2);
```

Now, we will add the Flak explosion to the display list and push it into flakArray (see Figure 5-8). We then play the sound of flak exploding by dispatching CustomEventSound.PLAY_SOUND with Main.SOUND_EXPLODE_FLAK as the sound parameter. Notice that we have set the volume of the sound to .5. This is because the explosion sound, as recorded, is a bit louder than the other sounds. We could have fixed this with an audio program, but we adjusted the volume here to illustrate that you can make adjustments to some sound properties in code.

Next, we call a new function named removeItemFromArray() passing the item to remove and the array to remove it from. We will discuss this very useful function a bit later. For now, we can just say that the function will do everything necessary to make this instance of Shot disappear for good.

```
this.addChild(tempFlak);
flakArray.push(tempFlak);
dispatchEvent( new CustomEventSound(CustomEventSound.PLAY_SOUND, ↩
    Main.SOUND_EXPLODE_FLAK,false,1,0,.5));
removeItemFromArray(tempShot,shotArray);
```

If the Shot was not finished (finished==false), we simply call the update() function for the object. This will set up the movement values that will be applied when we call render() (the next function in the game loop). If you recall from the last chapter, update() will set the nextLocation point for the objects that move in our game. We will actually move the objects in the render() function discussed in the next section.

```
        } else {
            tempShot.update();
        }
    }
```

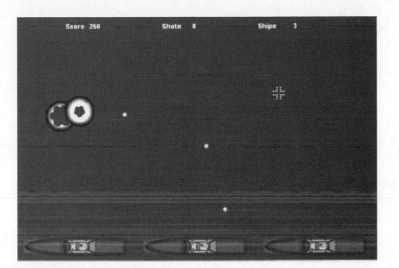

Figure 5-8. Shots exploding into Flak

Now, we need to iterate through our Flak explosions. Unlike Shot's, when Flak's explosions are set to finished, we simply remove them from the screen. We don't create anything else or play any sounds. You will notice that the rest of the objects we iterate through operate in a nearly identical manner.

```
    for each (tempFlak in flakArray){
        if (tempFlak.finished) {
            removeItemFromArray(tempFlak,flakArray);
        } else {
            tempFlak.update();
        }
    }
```

Updating Enemy, Explosion, and BonusPlane objects works just like updating Flack explosions.

```
    for each (tempEnemy in enemyArray){
        if (tempEnemy.finished) {
            removeItemFromArray(tempEnemy,enemyArray);
        } else {
            tempEnemy.update();
        }
    }

    for each (tempExplode in explodeArray){
        if (tempExplode.finished) {
            removeItemFromArray(tempExplode,explodeArray);
        } else {
            tempExplode.update();
```

```
        }
    }

    for each (tempBonusPlane in bonusPlaneArray){
        if (tempBonusPlane.finished) {
            removeItemFromArray(tempBonusPlane,bonusPlaneArray);
        } else {
            tempBonusPlane.update();
        }
    }
}
```

Removing objects

Now, we will create the removeItemFromArray() function to support removing the game objects from the screen. This is a general-purpose function that takes two values as parameters:

- item: This Object is the item to remove from the array
- group: This is the Array from which to remove the item.

The function takes the item and uses the Array.indexOf() function to find it. We call the dispose() method of the object, remove it from the screen with removeChild(), and then splice() it out of the array represented by group.

This function is by no means perfect. It would be better to use an explicit type instead of the generic Object type. However, this function saves a lot of time and code, so we have found it very useful in our projects.

```
private function removeItemFromArray(item:Object, group:Array) :void {
    var index:int = group.indexOf(item);
    group[index].dispose();
    removeChild(group[index]);
    group.splice(index, 1);
}
```

Detecting basic bitmap collisions

OK, so now we get to the most important function of this entire game, checkCollisions(). This is the function where nearly everything we have already created, literally, collides head on. This function is also quite intricate, so we will take it as slowly as possible.

To accomplish the necessary collision detection, we are going to use a built-in Flash function that is new to ActionScript programmers used to working with MovieClips only. In previous versions of ActionScript (and still in AS3), you could easily test for collisions using MovieClip.hitTest(). This used what is known as **bounding box collision detection**. With bounding box collision detection, you test only where the full box around a MovieClip hit another full box around another MovieClip. It does not matter how intricate the image is inside the box—all that matters were the boxes. If you draw a box around all the pixels in the image so that every pixel was included, and that box collided with a similar box around another object, a hit was registered. This actually works well for games where the objects are rectangular (e.g., Breakout), but for a game like Flak Cannon with intricately drawn sprites, collision detection with bounding boxes would prove to be far too inaccurate to be any fun to play at all. See the top of Figure 5-9.

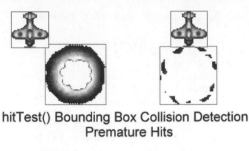

hitTest() Bounding Box Collision Detection
Premature Hits

bitmapData.hitTest() Collision Detection
Near Misses

Figure 5-9. Collision detection method comparison

When Bitmap support was included in ActionScript, it included a function for the BitmapData object named hitTest(). It is similar to MovieClip.hitTest() in name only. BitmapData.hitTest() tests for collisions based on the actual pixels in an image, not on bounding boxes. If you have an image with a transparent color, it will ignore that color when detecting collisions. See Figure 5-9, bottom section. Since we spent the time to create BitmapData for each of our objects, we can now use those objects to detect collisions.

There is one drawback to using BitmapData.hitTest(). While this function tests every pixel of a Bitmap image for a collision with every pixel of another Bitmap image, the Bitmap data to perform this operation is created once but not updated with any kind of transform (i.e., rotation). If you do try to transform an image with something like a rotation, the Bitmap data will remain in its original state, and false or incorrect hits will occur. The good news is that you can update the BitmapData manually when you transform an image (we will discuss this type of operation later in this book). Since we don't have to rotate any images or do any other kinds of transform on them, we do not need to worry about this for Flak Cannon. We can use the function as is.

Now, let's move on to the checkCollisions() function. Whenever you need to test against multiple types of objects, it is a good idea to try to group these objects so that, if possible, they can be tested at the same time. You can do this by nesting loops that iterate through the various lists of object. If these loops are nested properly, you can maximize the number of collisions checked per loop and minimize the number of loops that need to be completed. However, there is a point at which multiple nested loops become hard to maintain. We have taken a conservative approach in Flak Cannon. We have created three distinct loops, each illustrating a different set of collisions. There are ways we could have optimized this function further, but we would rather the code be clear to you, instead of just being tricky with some nested loops.

We are going to test three explicit bitmap collisions in this function grouped the following ways:

- Enemy hitting Flak or BonusPlane hitting Flak
- Enemy hitting Ship

We start the function by creating some variables to hold the lengths of the Array objects we will be testing.

```
private function checkCollisions():void {
    var enemyLength:int = enemyArray.length-1;
    var flakLength:int = flakArray.length-1;
    var shipLength:int = shipArray.length-1;
    var bonusPlaneLength:int = bonusPlaneArray.length-1;
```

Next, we begin iterating backward through the enemyArray array. Recall that tempEnemy is a class variable created one time so that we don't have to waste the processing cycles making a one every time we go through this loop. Notice the enemy: that precedes the for loop. This is a **label**. We will use this label to break out of a loop if the item we are testing has been removed from the array (this will be explained a bit when we talk about the break statement).

```
    enemy: for (var ctr2:int = enemyLength; ctr2 >= 0; ctr2--) {
```

The first collisions we are going to test are between the Flak explosions and the Enemy objects. First, we need to create an instance of the Point class. We need a Point class for each object that we are going to test for collisions. We will name this Point enemyPoint. This Point represents the upper-left-hand corner of the Enemy object. bitmapData.hitTest() requires this location as one of its parameters. Next, we start iterating through flakArray, setting tempFlak in every iteration.

```
tempEnemy = enemyArray[ctr2];
var enemyPoint:Point = new Point(tempEnemy.x, tempEnemy.y);
for (var ctr:int = flakLength; ctr >= 0; ctr--) {
    tempFlak = flakArray[ctr];
```

We also need a second Point that represents the upper left-hand corner of the Flak explosion. This is required by the bitmapData.hitTest() function, so it will know where to start its pixel-level collision detection.

```
    var flakPoint:Point = new Point(tempFlak.x, tempFlak.y);
```

Next comes the big boy for this function. This is the *gold*, where everything really happens. This is the actual bitmapData.hitTest() test (inside an if statement):

```
    if (tempFlak.image.bitmapData.hitTest(flakPoint,255,↵
        tempEnemy.image.bitmapData,enemyPoint)) {
```

Let's break down the actual test and parameters of the call to make it abundantly clear what is actually happening here:

- flackPoint: The upper-left hand corner of the Flak explosion we are testing.
- 255: This is the first alpha channel threshold. It needs to be the highest opaque value of the bitmap, which in our case is 255.
- tempEnemy.image.bitmapData: This is the bitmapData of the Enemy we are testing against.
- ePoint: This is the upper-left hand corner of the Enemy we are testing.

If a collision is detected, we then move into this section of code. The first thing we do is call the removeItemFromArray() function we created earlier passing tempEnemy and enemyArray array. Notice that we don't remove the Flak explosion. That is because a Flak explosion can keep destroying enemy planes as long as it stays on the screen. Then, we dispatch a `CustomEventSound` to play the `Main.SOUND_EXPLODE_PLANE` sound effect we created in Chapter 4.

```
removeItemFromArray(tempEnemy,enemyArray);
dispatchEvent( new CustomEventSound(CustomEventSound.PLAY_SOUND,↵
    Main.SOUND_EXPLODE_PLANE,false,1,0,.5));
```

The next two lines of code are for functions that we will create a bit later in this section. `makeExplosions()` will create an instance of `Explosion` at the specified (x,y) location passed as parameters to the function. Then, we call `addToScore()` passing the value that we want to add to the player's score. The player gets the value of the setting `baseEnemyScore` points per enemy destroyed (100 points by default), but we give a bonus of `enemyHitBonus` (500 points by default) for every enemy a single flak explosion destroys that is greater than 1. So for instance, hitting a single enemy with a flak explosion would net the player 100 points. However, hitting two enemy planes with the same flak explosion would score 700 points (100 × 2 + 500 × 1); hitting three enemy planes would score 1,300 points (100 × 3 + 500 × 2).

```
makeExplosion(tempEnemy.x,tempEnemy.y);
addToScore(baseEnemyScore+(tempFlak.hits*enemyHitBonus));
```

We then update the `hits` property of the current `Flak` explosion so we can give the player a bonus if more than one enemy is indeed hit. We need `hits` to be a property of `Flak`, not a local variable to the loop, because a `Flak` explosion stays around for multiple frames, which means multiple runs through this collision detection function. For that reason, `hits` needs to persist beyond the scope of this single call to `checkCollisions()`.

```
tempFlak.hits++;
```

Finally, we will make use of our label. The break statement will break us out of the current loop back to the enemy label. This essentially gets us out of testing the `Enemy` that was just destroyed against any more `Flak` explosions. We start with a new `Enemy`, and test all the `Flak` explosions again. Again, we need to do this so that the Flash runtime does not throw errors resulting from a null reference to an `Enemy` object that no longer exists (because it just blew up).

```
break enemy;
        }
    }
}
```

Now, we will test the `BonusPlane` objects against the `Flak` explosions. Because we had to test the `Flak` explosions in a nested loop inside `Enemy` when testing `Enemy` and `Flak` collisions, we now have to loop again through the `Flak` explosions. However, since there is not always a `BonusPlane` on the screen, there is a good chance that this check will not happen on any given frame.

The `bitmapData.hitTest()` test for the `BonusPlane` objects is nearly identical to the one we used for the `Enemy` objects, as is much of the code here. We play a different sound if the `BonusPlane` is hit (`Main.SOUND_BONUS`), and we add the value of `tempBonusPlane.bonusvalue` to the player's shots counts. We then dispatch an event to the scoreboard to tell it that `shots` has been updated. Another small difference is that we add `bonusPlaneScore` to the player's score instead of `baseEnemyScore`.

Also, notice that we want our `Explosion` to be directly over the `BonusPlane`. However, since the plane is 64 × 64 pixels and the explosion is only 32 × 32 pixels, we need to move it over by half its width and a quarter of its height to center it over the spot that the plane had been when it was destroyed.

```
bonusplane: for (ctr2 = bonusPlaneLength; ctr2 >= 0; ctr2--) {
    tempBonusPlane = bonusPlaneArray[ctr2];
    var bonusPlanePoint:Point = new Point(tempBonusPlane.x, tempBonusPlane.y);
    for (ctr = flakLength; ctr >= 0; ctr--) {
        tempFlak = flakArray[ctr];
        flakPoint = new Point(tempFlak.x, tempFlak.y);
            if (tempFlak.image.bitmapData.hitTest(flakPoint,255,↵
                tempBonusPlane.image.bitmapData,bonusPlanePoint)) {
                dispatchEvent( new CustomEventSound(CustomEventSound.PLAY_SOUND,↵
                    Main.SOUND_BONUS,false,1,0,1));
                shots += tempBonusPlane.bonusValue;
                dispatchEvent(new CustomEventScoreBoardUpdate(↵
                    CustomEventScoreBoardUpdate.UPDATE_TEXT,Main.SCORE_BOARD_SHOTS,↵
                    String(shots)));
                makeExplosion(tempBonusPlane.x + tempBonusPlane.width/2,↵
                    tempBonusPlane.y + tempBonusPlane.height/2);
                addToScore(baseBonusPlaneScore+(tempFlak.hits*enemyHitBonus));
                tempFlak.hits++;
                removeItemFromArray(tempBonusPlane,bonusPlaneArray);
                break bonusplane;
            }
    }
}
```

By the way, we could have made the bonus planes a special case Enemy object, instead of its own type. In that case, we would have only had to do the loop once. Finding ways to optimize the code beyond what is presented in this text is a good way to further hone your game development skills.

Now, we have to test the player's ships against the Enemy planes. Unfortunately, we have to loop through the enemyArray arrays again. Fortunately, we do this for a good reason. Since the Ship objects always sit at the same y coordinate on the screen, we can do a quick test to see if we have to do collision detection based on the current y location of an Enemy.

Notice the ship: that precedes the for loop. This is another label. Again, we will use this label to break out of a loop if the item we are testing has been removed from the array. Most of the rest of this should look familiar to you by now.

```
ship: for (ctr = shipLength; ctr >= 0; ctr--) {
    tempShip = shipArray[ctr];
    var sPoint:Point = new Point(tempShip.x, tempShip.y);
    enemyLength = enemyArray.length-1;
    for (ctr2 = enemyLength; ctr2 >= 0; ctr2--) {
        tempEnemy = enemyArray[ctr2];
```

Here is where this loop gets interesting. We will test to see if the current y position of the Enemy is close enough to the Ship objects for a collision to occur. Since the Ship objects are always in the same place, all we have to do is calculate the first point at which an Enemy could possible hit a Ship. Otherwise, we skip the test. To do this, we will take the gameHeight and subtract the height of a Ship plus subtract shipYPadding pixels (because Ships are shipYPadding pixels from the bottom of the screen). Then, we subtract the height of the Enemy plane because its registration point is in the upper-left hand corner. Figure 5-10 shows how we came to this calculation.

```
if (tempEnemy.y > gameHeight-tempShip.height-tempEnemy.height-shipYPadding) {
    enemyPoint = new Point(tempEnemy.x, tempEnemy.y);
    if (tempShip.image.bitmapData.hitTest(↵
        sPoint,255,tempEnemy.image.bitmapData,enemyPoint)) {
```

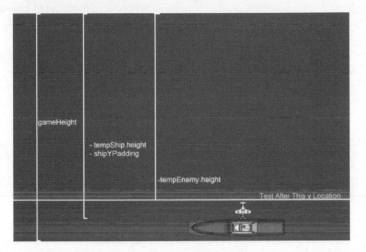

Figure 5-10. *Testing enemy planes only when they reach the y location of the ships*

If we detect a collision, we do a few things differently from previous collisions. First, we remove the Enemy plane. Unlike Flak, which stays around until its animation sequence is complete, the Enemy plane blows up along with the Ship. Second, we dispatch CustomEventSound.PLAY_SOUND to play Main.SOUND_EXPLODE_SHIP. Next, we make three Explosion objects. This is simply to drive home to the player that a Ship has been destroyed. One Explosion would have made it seem like the Enemy was destroyed, and that would not be enough of a visual cue for the player. We next remove the Ship by calling removeItemFromArray(), decrement the ships variable and dispatch an event to the ScoreBoard telling it to update the text. Finally, we call break ship. Again, this is done because we have removed the Ship from shipArray, and we do not need to test it again against any more Enemy planes.

```
                removeItemFromArray(tempEnemy,enemyArray);
                dispatchEvent( new CustomEventSound(CustomEventSound.PLAY_SOUND,↵
                    Main.SOUND_EXPLODE_SHIP,false,1,0,1));
                makeExplosion(tempEnemy.x,tempEnemy.y);
                makeExplosion(tempShip.x+25,tempShip.y+5);
                makeExplosion(tempShip.x+tempShip.width-40,tempShip.y+10);
                makeExplosion(tempShip.x+tempShip.width/2,tempShip.y+3);
                removeItemFromArray(tempShip,shipArray);
                ships--;
                dispatchEvent(new CustomEventScoreBoardUpdate(↵
                    CustomEventScoreBoardUpdate.UPDATE_TEXT,Main.SCORE_BOARD_SHIPS,↵
                        String(ships)));
                break ship;
                }
            }
        }
    }
}
```

We are finished with the checkCollisions() function, but we still need to create a few functions to support the code we just added. The first function is createExplosions(). This function accepts the (x,y) coordinates to place an instance of the Explosion object. Recall the Explosion class that we created in Chapter 4. It displays multiple frames of animation to simulate an explosion. Creating the explosion and putting it on the screen is a very straightforward operation. We have used similar code several times previously in Flak Cannon. Here is the full code for the function.

```
private function makeExplosion(explodeX:int,explodeY:int):void{
    tempExplode = new Explosion();
    tempExplode.x = explodeX;
    tempExplode.y = explodeY;
    this.addChild(tempExplode);
    explodeArray.push(tempExplode);
}
```

The addToScore() function is called whenever the player gains points by destroying Enemy planes. addToScore() accepts the value to add to the player's score as its only parameter. The score is updated, and an event is dispatched to tell the ScoreBoard to display a new score value. We also call checkBonusShips(). This function, described a bit further on in this chapter is used to check to see if the player has attained a score that will net an extra Ship for the fleet.

```
private function addToScore(val:Number):void {
    score += int(val);
    checkBonusShips();
    dispatchEvent(new CustomEventScoreBoardUpdate(↵
        CustomEventScoreBoardUpdate.UPDATE_TEXT,Main.SCORE_BOARD_SCORE,String(score)));

}
```

The checkBonusShips() function does a simple arithmetic test to see if the player has attained a score that will award an extra Ship. However, there is a trick to it that may not seem evident at first. We have created a difficulty setting named scoreNeededForExtraShip. For this game, scoreNeededForExtraShip is 10000, but it could be any score. It might seem logical that we would simply check to see if the player's score is equal to some multiple of scoreNeededForExtraShip (e.g., 10000, 20000, and 30000), and if so, award an extra Ship. However, we cannot be sure that the player's score will ever actually be equal to multiple of scoreNeededForExtraShip, so there is a good chance we will never award the player an extra Ship if we simply look at this value. Alternatively, if we look for a score that is greater-than-or-equal-to scoreNeededForExtraShip, we will continue to award the player an extra Ship every time we call this function, after the first multiple of scoreNeededForExtraShip is reached. Instead, we must use a combination of both checks to award the proper amount of bonus Ship objects to the player. Here is the calculation:

```
if ( (score-(extraShipCount*scoreNeededForExtraShip) >= scoreNeededForExtraShip) ) {
```

For this example, let's pretend the player has a score of 20,100 and has earned one bonus ship already in the game. Here it is translated into a more readable form:

```
If 20100-(1*10000) >= 10000
```

We could write this even more simply as follows:

```
If 10100 >= 10000
```

Since this statement is true, the player gets an extra Ship. However, the next time this calculation is called, called it would be like so:

```
If 20100-(2*10000) >= 10000
```

Even more simply, we could write it as follows:

`If 100 >= 10000`

This time, the statement is false, so no Ship would be awarded.

Besides this little detail, the rest of this function is self-explanatory.

```
private function checkBonusShips():void {
    if ( (score-(extraShipCount*scoreNeededForExtraShip) >= scoreNeededForExtraShip) )
    {
        ships++;
        extraShipCount++;
        dispatchEvent( new CustomEventSound(↵
            CustomEventSound.PLAY_SOUND,Main.SOUND_BONUS_SHIP,false,1,0,1));
        dispatchEvent(new CustomEventScoreBoardUpdate(↵
        CustomEventScoreBoardUpdate.UPDATE_TEXT,Main.SCORE_BOARD_SHIPS,String(ships)));
    }
}
```

Rendering objects

The `render()` function called by `runGame()` to actually move the objects on the screen. For each array of objects that either moves (Shot, Enemy, and BonusPlane) or animates (Flak and Explosion), we run through a separate `for:each` loop. We can use `for:each` here, because we are not removing anything from the arrays, we are only calling the render function of each object.

```
private function render():void {
    for each (tempShot in shotArray){
        tempShot.render();
    }
    for each (tempFlak in flakArray){
        tempFlak.render();
    }
    for each (tempEnemy in enemyArray){
        tempEnemy.render();
    }
    for each (tempExplode in explodeArray){
        tempExplode.render();
    }
    for each (tempBonusPlane in bonusPlaneArray){
        tempBonusPlane.render();
    }

}
```

Ending a level

The next to last function called by `runGame()` is `checkForEndOfLevel()`. This function looks to see if the all the conditions exist to advance to player to the next level of the game. There are two major variables that determine if the `level` has been completed: the length of the `enemyArray` array, and `incomingCount`. `incomingCount` is used to determine if the number of `Enemy` planes created for this level is equal to the difficulty setting `numEnemies`. If so, we know we will not create any more `Enemy` objects for this level. However, there could still be `Enemy` planes on the screen. Since they are tracked in `enemyArray`, we look at the `length` property of that array to determine if the there are any left on the screen.

However, that is not all. Even if all the Enemy planes are gone, ending the level abruptly can be jarring for the player. If there are Explosion objects or Flak still animating, Shot objects flying or a BonusPlane flying, we want to wait until those animations end before the level is over. This also gives the player a chance to shoot the BonusPlane one last time if it has arrived just when the level is over. We do this by simply checking the length properties of all the associated arrays for the objects. Also, as a quick bonus, we add 10 times the number of player's shots remaining to the score (this is another possible difficulty setting). Finally, we dispatch a Game.NEW_LEVEL event so that Main can take control and call newLevel().

```
private function checkforEndLevel():void {
    if (enemyArray.length <= 0 && incomingCount >= numEnemies ↵
        && explodeArray.length <=0 && flakArray.length <=0 && ↵
        shotArray.length <=0 && bonusPlaneArray.length <= 0) {

        addToScore(10*shots);
        cleanUpLevel();
        dispatchEvent(new Event(Game.NEW_LEVEL));
    }
}
```

You will notice in the preceding function that another function is called named cleanUpLevel(). This function removes all the objects from the screen and removes the EventListener we created to respond to the player shooting. We have separated this into a second function so it could be called from the checkForEndGame() function as well as from checkForEndOfLevel(). All of the code in this function should look very familiar to you. It is very similar to render(), in that we will loop through all of our arrays of objects. However, since we are removing the objects from the arrays, we can't use for:each. If we did use for:each (or a forward for:next loop) the loop will get out of sync as we remove items resulting in the array not being fully cleaned up. Instead, we must iterate backward through each array. For every item, we use our old friend removeItemFromArray(). Also, to be complete, at the end of the function, we remove the listener for the MouseEvent.MOUSE_DOWN.

```
private function cleanUpLevel():void {
    var ctr:int = 0;
    for (ctr = shotArray.length-1;ctr >=0;ctr--) {
        removeItemFromArray(shotArray[ctr],shotArray);
    }
    for (ctr = flakArray.length-1;ctr >=0;ctr--) {
        removeItemFromArray(flakArray[ctr],flakArray);
    }
    for (ctr = enemyArray.length-1;ctr >=0;ctr--) {
        removeItemFromArray(enemyArray[ctr],enemyArray);
    }
    for (ctr = explodeArray.length-1;ctr >=0;ctr--) {
        removeItemFromArray(explodeArray[ctr],explodeArray);
    }
    for (ctr = shipArray.length-1;ctr >=0;ctr--) {
        removeItemFromArray(shipArray[ctr],shipArray);
    }
    for (ctr = bonusPlaneArray.length-1;ctr >=0;ctr--) {
        removeItemFromArray(bonusPlaneArray[ctr],bonusPlaneArray);
    }

    stage.removeEventListener(MouseEvent.MOUSE_DOWN, shootListener);
}
```

Ending the game

The final function called by runGame() is checkForEndGame(). This function is very simple. It checks to see if the ships variable is less than or equal to 0 (<= 0). Why <= 0 and not just equal to 0 (==0)? Because, on the off chance that something goes wrong and the player's ships are decremented past 0, (that should never happen, but just in case), the game would never end. This simple code makes sure that bug never appears.

The rest of the code is pretty self-explanatory. First, we dispatch a Game.GAME_OVER event to the game framework (Main.as) so it can start the end game sequence. Recall that the Game.GAME_OVER (along with Game.NEW_LEVEL) const was defined in the base Game class that we extended for FlakCannon. We remove crosshairs from the screen with removeChild(crosshairs) and make the mouse pointer appear again with Mouse.show();. We remove the MOUSE_MOVE EventListener that moves the now nonexistent crosshairs. We then call the cleanUpLevel() function the same way we did in checkForEndLevel() to remove all the objects from the screen and finally set the crosshairs to null so that they will be re-created when the game restarts.

```
private function checkforEndGame():void {
    if (ships <=0) {
        dispatchEvent(new Event(Game.GAME_OVER));
        removeChild(crosshairs);
        Mouse.show();
        stage.removeEventListener(MouseEvent.MOUSE_MOVE, mouseMoveListener);
        cleanUpLevel();
        crosshairs = null;
    }
}
```

Finally, don't forget to finish-off your class with two concluding brackets after all the functions: one to end the class, and to end the package:

```
    }
}
```

Playing the game!

And there you have it. It's taken a very long time, but Flak Cannon has now been completed. After you type in all this code (or download the source code and compile it), start playing Flak Cannon. Enjoy a few rounds of the game; you deserve it!

As you play, note some things that you like and dislike about the game. While the game plays pretty well, there are definitely ways to improve on the design and game play. Flak Cannon is only a demonstration of how game like this might be created; it is not polished title ready for publication.

Summary

Over the last two chapters, we have spent a lot of time discussing how to take the game framework that we created in Chapters 2 and 3 and implement it by making a game based on Atari's venerable coin-operated game, Missile Command. Our game was not an exact copy of Missile Command by any means, but we used the ideas in that game as a jumping-off point to create Flak Cannon. In the process of making Flak Cannon, we covered many ways that you could update and alter the game to make it something entirely new.

If you start twiddling with the game to see how you can alter it, the best places to start are the difficulty settings. numEnemies and enemyWaveDelay are prime candidates, as they will set how many Enemy planes arrive and how quickly they show up. As soon as you change those values, you might want to alter startShots and scoreNeededForExtraShip to see how they affect the game. You can go crazy with these values. Set them impossibly high or impossibly low. A good way to see how hard a game can be is to set the value to what you think are maximum possible for the game and then scale them back until you find something playable.

Flak Cannon could be improved in a few ways that go beyond tweaking the variables. What could we do to fix up the game and make it better? Well, there is probably an infinite list of things that could be done, be here are a couple obvious ones:

- **More difficulty settings**: There are still a few places where magic numbers are used (e.g., the value of a BonusPlane and the bonus points awarded at the end of level for shots remaining) that could be turned into difficulty settings updated by the level value in newLevel(). We have left these for you to update and explore.

- **Reserve ships**: When all three ships get destroyed but the player has earned a reserve ship, the game continues until the level is over and then awards the extra ship for the next level. Functionally, this is exactly like the game Missile Command, but in practice, it seems bit weird. One idea would be to pause the game and allow the extra ship to enter the screen and then resume play. Another would be to send the game into a space mode, an alternate universe that can only escaped by fulfilling a particular goal, similar to the arcade game Defender.

- **Ships fire**: Instead of an off-screen cannon, you could instead have the ships fire at the planes themselves. You could do this in many ways. You could assign a key press for each ship or have the ship closest to the crosshairs fire a shot. Alternatively, you could have the shots fire automatically.

- **Different enemy planes**: Flak Cannon has only one Enemy. We randomized the way the enemy planes fly on the screen, but they always look the same and always take one hit to destroy. Adding different graphics for other enemies and increasing the number of hits they take before they are destroyed would not be very difficult and would add immensely to the game experience.

Chapter 6

Laying the Groundwork for No Tanks!

In the previous two chapters, we explored how to make a relatively simple arcade game using some advanced techniques. In this chapter and the next one, we will up the ante and dive further into the once-murky depths of optimized Flash game development. We are going to explore how to create a tile-based game world while constructing an arcade game called No Tanks!

In this journey, we will cover a lot of ground very quickly by introducing and explaining some new and advanced topics at a rapid pace. First, we are going to explore how to create and use a tile sheet and the code necessary for displaying it on the game screen. During this journey, we will cover the necessary steps for arranging game world graphics on a tile sheet and how to use free and open source tools to create levels for a game world. We will then cover how to use those tiles in an optimized Flash game using copyPixels and blitting methods.

In the next chapter, we will discuss the game logic necessary to allow the player and enemy to navigate the tile-based game world, including some basic tile-based artificial intelligence, and we'll finish off our game by letting the player and the enemy tanks chase and shoot at one another inside the maze. This will include adding some new classes to the reusable framework and creating a new Main.as class to integrate No Tanks! with that framework.

The No Tanks! game design

We are going to create a classic style game in the maze, or chase, genre. The most recognizable game in this category is Namco's Pac-Man. In our game, the main player will be a tank. Its goal is to collect a single piece of stolen treasure on each level while destroying enemy tanks and avoid being destroyed.

The maze will be made up of tiles, some of which can be moved on and some cannot. There will also be ammunition, and extra lives (tanks) for the player to pick up. We will construct the game engine so any number of levels can be created. As long as the level designer follows some simple rules, the levels will be playable in the game engine.

In many game engines of this type, the developer goes to great lengths to supply data along with the tiles for precoded movement possibilities. For example, four-way movement cross sections are precoded to tell the engine all of the possible directions the tank can move when it reaches that cross intersection. The advantage of coding maze-based movement in this manner is simplicity. The game maze is hard-coded and there is no need for the game developer to attempt to write code that will work in any conditions other than the ones precoded into the game. The disadvantage is that once the developer has created and hard-coded the logic for movement into the maze, building additional maze levels takes just as much time as building the first.

We will not do that here. We are going to create a game level engine and a set of maze movement algorithms that will be able to work dynamically—we mean that once we have created the logic rules for moving about the maze, all game levels will share that same logic. We will create an engine that works smoothly, no matter how the tiles are organized (to a point), so level creation will be as simple as drawing boxes on a screen.

Here's the basic information for this game:

- **Name**: No Tanks!
- **Genre**: Maze/chase/shooter
- **Description**: The player must traverse a 2D maze looking for the stolen artifact. Enemy tanks will be stationed in the maze to defend the artifact.
- **Player Goal**: Collect the artifact on each level to progress to the next. The player will have a limited amount of ammunition but can collect ammunition that has been left by the careless enemy. Surprisingly, both the player tanks and the enemy tanks use the same type of ammunition! The player starts with three tanks but can collect more that are scattered throughout the game levels.
- **Enemy description**: Enemy tanks will chase and fire on the player tank once it enters the zone that an enemy tank is guarding. The game screen will be split into four zones. Enemy tanks will employ a basic maze-chase artificial intelligence (AI) and will navigate around objects to find the player. If the player is in the line of site, the enemy tanks will fire at the player.
- **Enemy's goal**: Destroy the player's tanks.
- **Level end**: The level ends when the player has successfully collected the artifact.
- **Game over conditions**: The game ends when all of the player's tanks (lives) are destroyed.
- **Difficulty**: Game difficulty is ramped through level specific variable settings. The game level designer can add as many enemy tanks as desired to a level and can make ammunition scarce at higher levels. Also, the fire rate and intelligence of enemy tanks can be set in the level variable data.

Game development concepts in Chapters 6 and 7

Here is a brief rundown of the game development concepts we will cover in this chapter and the next:

- Chapter 6
  - Using tile sheets for game graphics
  - Creating a tile sheet in a graphics program

LAYING THE GROUNDWORK FOR NO TANKS!

- Creating a game level in the Mappy Level Editor
- Creating a library class for Flex projects
- Creating a `TileSheet` class
- Creating an `Level` base class
- Extending the `Level` base a class to hold the level specific data
- Blitting the game world tiles to a `BitmapData` output screen

■ Chapter 7

- Creating a `BlitSprite` class for game objects
- Extending the `BlitSprite` class with tile maze based game logic
- Animating a `Sprite` with bitmap tiles
- Moving a player and enemy around a user designed tile game level
- Creating basic chase AI using zones and logic
- Using line of site for enemy firing on the player
- Using look-ahead variables for collision detection and movement
- Finishing off the game with sound and screens
- Modifying the framework for No Tanks!

Adding game assets to the library

In Flak Cannon, we used assets from the Spritelib GPL library. We will use some of them again, but this time, we will place all of our assets on a sheet of 32 × 32 tiles rather than add them to the game as separate graphic objects. We will also be using the SFXR to tool to create the sounds for our game.

Using Spritelib GPL

As in the previous game, we will be using the Spritelib GPL, maintained by Ari Feldman and located here: http://www.flyingyogi.com/fun/spritelib.html. This is a royalty-free graphics library, which means you can use it for pretty much anything (save for distributing it as part of another sprite library). Several of the games in this book make use of this library.

Using a tile sheet

One of the most useful advances in ActionScript for game developers has been the use of raw bitmap data to render on-screen images. A **tile sheet** is a bitmap image file (GIF, JPG, PNG, etc.) that is organized into a series or rows and columns in a grid format. The most common tile sheet format is a set of rows and columns of square-sized images. For example, we will be using image tiles with a 32-pixel width and a 32-pixel height. We will call these tiles 32 × 32 tiles. We will create a sheet of these tiles that is organized into rows and columns (see Figure 6-1). The tiles will be used to create the background and sprite animations for our game.

Rather than importing each 32 × 32 bitmap tile into the Flash library individually we will import the entire tile sheet into our game as a single file. We will then cut out the tiles as we need them using code. This will be done using the `BitmapData` class in AS3.

The tile sheet will be referenced as a single dimensional array of tiles. So, the tile in the upper left-hand corner of Figure 6-1 will be tile 0, and the last tile in the grid will be file 31 (the lower right-hand corner).

Organizing game levels into tiles

Our game levels will be made up of a 20 × 15 grid of 32 × 32-sized tiles. The grid will be encoded into in a 2D array of tile ID numbers. The tile ID number will be the number 0–31 (see Figure 6-1) that represents a tile id on the tile sheet. A 2D array is what we call an array of arrays. ActionScript does not have built-in support for an array with more than a single dimension. We will create a 2D array by placing another array inside each element of our base array. The level screen size will be 640 (20 × 32) × 480 (15 × 32). This means that our level data will consist of 300 (20 × 15) tile ID numbers. We will have 15 rows and 20 columns. Here is an example of the 2D data format for the level we will create:

```
var backGroundMap:Array = [
[26,24,25,0,26,26,26,26,26,0,0,26,26,26,26,26,0,24,25,26],
[27,0,0,0,0,0,0,0,0,0,0,0,0,0,0,0,0,0,0,27],
[29,0,28,0,0,0,24,25,0,24,25,0,24,25,0,0,0,27,0,29],
[27,0,28,0,27,0,0,0,0,0,0,0,0,0,27,0,29,0,27],
[29,0,0,0,29,0,0,30,0,0,0,0,31,0,0,29,0,0,0,29],
[0,0,28,0,26,0,0,31,0,0,0,0,31,0,0,26,0,26,0,0],
[0,0,0,0,0,0,0,31,0,0,0,0,31,0,26,0,0,0,0,0],
[26,26,26,0,0,26,0,30,30,30,30,30,30,0,0,0,0,26,26,26],
[0,0,0,26,0,0,0,0,0,28,0,0,0,0,26,0,0,0],
[0,0,0,0,26,0,0,27,0,27,0,27,0,28,0,26,0,0,0,0],
[27,0,0,0,27,0,0,29,0,29,0,29,0,28,0,27,0,0,0,27],
[29,0,0,0,29,0,0,0,0,0,0,0,0,0,29,0,0,0,29],
[27,0,0,0,0,26,0,28,0,28,0,28,28,0,26,0,0,0,0,27],
[29,0,0,0,0,0,0,0,0,0,0,0,0,0,0,0,0,0,0,29],
[26,24,25,0,0,26,26,26,26,0,0,26,26,26,26,0,0,24,25,26]
]
```

Notice that there are exterior brackets ([]) surrounding the interior rows of tile IDs (each also inside their own set of brackets). The exterior set of brackets creates the array that will hold our 15 row arrays of column data. This creates a 2D array of rows and columns.

Our data will be organized into a set of rows and columns. We will use a 2D array for the level data, because accessing the grid of tiles programmatically is made much easier if we can simply reference the row and column the tile is located in. The row will be the first subscript of the 2D array, and the column will be the second subscript. For example, the method to access the tile in row 10 and column 5 would look something like this:

```
levelData[9][4] = 26
```

Since our arrays are **zero-relative**, meaning they start with 0 and not 1, 9 is the tenth row, and 4 is the fifth column. If you look closely at this, you might notice something odd. Rows are actually the y axis dimension of our grid, and columns are the x axis dimension, but we are accessing them by row and then column ([y][x]) rather than [x][y]. This has been debated for years by various game developers. In our experience, it is much easier and more straightforward to create tile-based worlds using the [row][column] context when using a 2D array in AS3. All you need to do in the level data to find the correct tile is count down (the first subscript of the 2D array) to find row 9 (starting at 0) and then count over (the second subscript in the 2D array) to find column 5 (starting at 0). The tile ID at row 9, column is 26.

Creating a level

Creating a game level is as simple as picking the tile ids we want and placing them into the 2D grid of rows and columns. This can be done pretty easily by hand, but it is much easier to do with a tile map editor. Some developers find that laying out tiles in a drawing tool or even the Flash IDE to be a suitable method for creating level data. Others actually create a level editor in Flash to create levels specific to the game they are creating. In our experience, we have come to really like using a tool called Mappy for level creation (full details for downloading and using Mappy will be given shortly). Unfortunately, there is no Mac OS version of Mappy. It can be used with Parallels or VMWare software, but there is no native Mac OS version of the software. It will also run using WINE in Linux and Mac OS X and is listed in the WINE software database as working in Mac OS. Even if you don't have a Windows machine, you should be able to make use of Mappy. There are some other good multiplatform level editors such as FLAN that you might want to check out also.

Creating a level with Mappy

We will first create a unique set of image tiles and export those tiles as a PNG file. Next, we will load those tiles into a map creation tool (Mappy) and use them to create a level screen for our game. We will then export the data from Mappy that represents the level we have created. This data will be used in AS3 to display build our game level.

For our game, we will use the following graphics. They have been cut from the Spritelib GPL files and placed onto our own tile sheet.

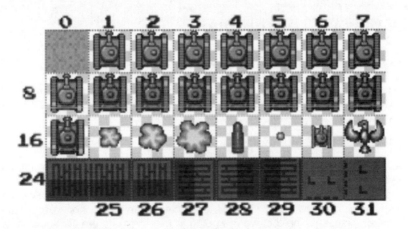

Figure 6-1. The entire set of tiles for No Tanks! (with tile ID numbers)

First of all, the name of this tile sheet is going to be tanks_sheet.png. It is stored in the /assets folder of our Flex SDK project. For the Flash IDE version, it will be embedded in our .fla library. It is a 256 × 128 PNG file with a transparent background.

Let's take the sheet row by row and describe each of the tiles:

- Row1 (tiles 0–7): Tile 0 is the road or floor tile. It is used as a background and as a walkable tile; this means a tile that the player and enemy tanks can move on. This row also contains the first seven frames for the player tank. On each of the frames, the tank tracks are slightly different. When played in succession this causes the tank to appear to be driving rather than sliding across the game screen.
- Row2 (tiles 8–15): This row contains the eighth frame for the player tank and then the first seven frames for the enemy tank. On each of the frames, the tank tracks are slightly different. Just like the player tank, this causes the tank to appear to be driving rather than sliding across the game screen.
- Row3 (tiles 16–23):

    - Tile 16 is the eighth and final frame for the enemy tank.
    - Tiles 17–19 are used for explosions.
    - Tile 20 is the ammunition pick up object.
    - Tile 21 is the missile that both the player and the enemy will fire at one another.
    - Tile 22 is the object representing extra tank pick-ups in the game.
    - Tile 23 is the artifact that the player seeks to find on each level.

- Row4 (tiles 24–31): This row contains eight tiles that can be used for walls. Neither the player nor the enemy can move onto these tiles.

Sprites vs. tiles vs. background

We will be using the term "sprite" to refer to any interactive object in our game. These sprites will not be part of the background of our level. They will be in the foreground. Sprites are made up of tiles in our tile sheet just the same as the background. The background for our game will be the walls and walkable tiles that the tanks can move on. The sprites will be the tanks, ammunition, missiles, explosions, and other objects in the game.

Creating the tile sheet

A tile sheet is basically the same as any other image, but it is set up in a unique manner. Our tile sheet will be 256 pixels in width and 128 in height. This will allow us to have four rows of 8 32 × 32 tiles to use. For the look of the tiles, we will copy images directly from the Spritelib GPL files and place them on to our new sheet. For this example, I wanted to choose tools that everyone would have at their disposal. The tool we are going to use to create the tile sheet is called GIMP. Photoshop and Fireworks are also tools used by many professionals for the same purpose. We will stop to give hints for those tools also along the way where we can.

GIMP is a free, community supported tool with many of the same features as Photoshop and Fireworks. You can download the latest version at http://www.gimp.org.

Detailed instructions on GIMP are beyond the scope of this book, but what follows are the steps necessary to create and save a tile sheet that we can use for our No Tanks! game.

You can use any tool that allows for you to create PNG files with transparency. Both Photoshop and Fireworks can do this. As well, other free tools such as Paint.net and Pixen will work for this purpose. We will give instruction on using GIMP, but please feel free to use you own favorite tool.

1. Start Up GIMP and create a new image. Make sure to select the advanced options as seen in Figure 6-2, so you can set the background fill to transparent.

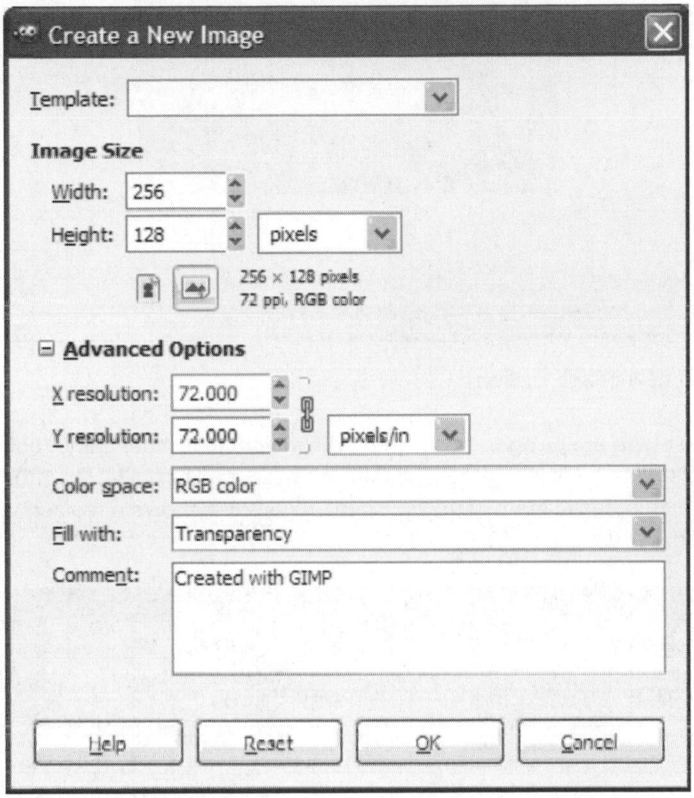

Figure 6-2. GIMP new image screen

2. Make sure you set the width of the new image to 256 and the height to 128. This will accommodate a tile sheet that's eight 32 × 32 tiles wide by four tiles tall.

3. After you have created the new image, set the grid properties to be 32 × 32 spacing in the **Image ➤ Configure Grid** menu option. Once that is complete, you should make sure that **Show grid** is check marked in the **View** menu. The image will look like Figure 6-3.

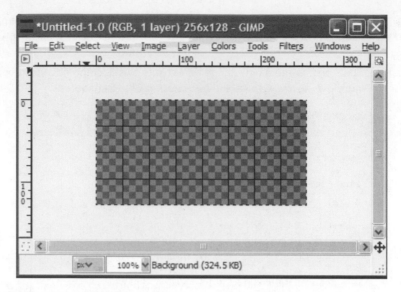

Figure 6-3. GIMP new image screen

The next steps are going to be very specific to your individual game, but in the case of No Tanks! I have copied some tiles from the maze/tankbrigade.bmp (from the Spritelib GPL) file and placed them in my tile sheet. Figure 6-4 shows a resized version of that sheet for reference:

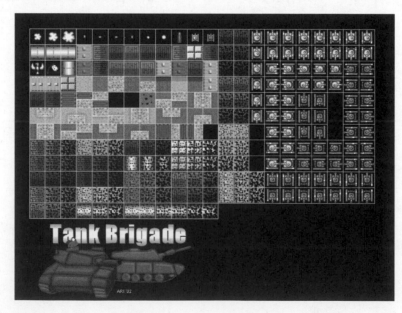

Figure 6-4. The Tank Brigade tile sheet

4. One problem with the Spritelib GPL tile sheets if that they are in the BMP format with no transparency. No matter, when we cut the tiles we need from the sheet, we will paste them into our sheet and then have to delete out the background color. Also notice that the tankbrigade.bmp file has actual border lines around each tile. Make sure to set your rectangle select tool to be 32 × 32 and zoom in to position your selected image so you just get the tile portion you need. See Figure 6-5.

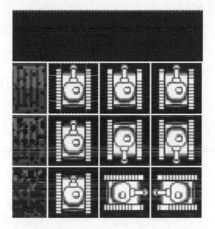

Figure 6-5. Slice a 32 × 32 image, but watch out for the grid lines.

5. Once you have selected the first image to copy, you can then paste it into the 256 × 128 sheet that we are creating. Continue to do this until you have created the sheet shown in Figure 6-6 sheet (note that we have deleted the background from these tiles).

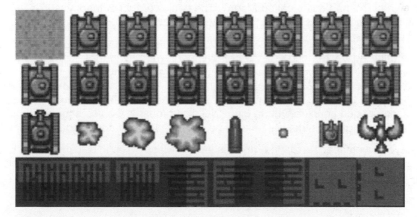

Figure 6-6. The tile sheet will look like this when completed.

215

It is very important that the first tile be a road or wall tile, not a sprite tile if you are using Mappy to create levels. We are going to be creating levels with two layers. The background layer will contain wall and road tiles while the foreground layer will only contain only our game sprites. The foreground will overlay on top of the background layer. All of the tiles on the foreground that do not contain a sprite will be blank and will be exported from Mappy with the tile id of 0. When our code parses the data for sprite placement, it will ignore any tile with an id of 0. If we have placed a sprite at tile 0 on our tile sheet then it will never be placed into game. So, we have placed the nonsprite road tile in the tile 0 spot. This concept will become clearer as we progress to the section on Mappy.

6. You will need to delete out the background color for the unused pixels behind the tiles to have transparency around your sprite objects. The best method to accomplish this is to use the erase tool in the 1 × 1 pixel configuration. Zoom in to 800% (or 8 to 1) and erase just the dark pixels around the images. You will start to see the transparent background show up where the deleted pixels once were. Other tools, such as the **Fuzzy Select** tool can also be used for this purpose and may speed the process up immensely. The **Magic Wand** tool in both Fireworks and Photoshop is also very much up to this task.

7. Save this file as a PNG named tank_sheet.png. Make sure to check **Merge Visible Layers** and not **Flatten Image** in the export dialog. **Flatten** will give the image a white background, and **Merge** will keep the transparent background. The option you want to use in Photoshop is **Save For Web**, while in Fireworks you can easily select **Save As** and select the **png** option.

Creating a game level with Mappy

One of the most useful weapons in the arsenal of any game developer is a good map editor. We like to rely on a great map editor called Mappy. The basic version of Mappy is free, but we highly suggest spending the $19.00 it costs to register the full version.

Details on Mappy can be found at the Mappy web site (http://www.tilemap.co.uk/). Complete instruction on all the features and nuances of Mappy is well beyond the scope of this book. We will go into enough detail so you will be able to use this as a starting point for you own projects though. We will cover the very basic steps that anyone can use to create a level map with Mappy. We are going to use the tank_sheet.png tile sheet we created in the previous section. The latest version of Mappy needs an extra DLL to use PNG files properly. So you should take careful note that there is a ZIP file of DLLs that will need to be downloaded and copied to the Mappy folder.

Once you have downloaded, unzipped, and placed the Mappy files in a folder (there is no official install program), you will need to unzip the libpng12.zip file (which can be obtained at http://www.tilemap.co.uk/pngfiles.html) to use PNG files with the program.

Now, let's create our level tile map:

1. Open Mappy.

2. In the **File** menu, select **New Map** and set the tile size to 32 × 32 and the map size to 20 × 15. The No Tanks! levels will fit in a 640 × 480 screen, or 32 × 20 width times 32 × 15 height.

3. Mappy will warn you that you will now need to import a tile sheet into the program. In the **File** menu, choose **Import** and then select the `tank_sheet.png` file we created in GIMP.

4. The tiles will show up in the right-hand window. Take a close look at the tile sheet, and you will notice that a blank tile has been inserted at the beginning of the tile sheet. This is useful for deleting tiles from your map but isn't an actual tile in your sheet. This detail will be important when we need to export our data for use in Flash.

Creating a two-layer map

We are going to use Mappy to create two layers for our level tile map. The first layer we will create (Layer 0) will be the background layer. The second layer (Layer 1) will be for all for the sprite objects.

Creating the background layer

This layer will consist of only the road tile (Mappy tile 1) and the wall tiles (Mappy tiles 25–32). You will notice that because Mappy has added the eraser tile at the beginning of the tile sheet that our Mappy tile numbers for our tiles are 1 greater than those in our tile sheet. Don't worry; when we export out tile map from Mappy, we will automatically subtract 1 from each our Mappy tile IDs so they will match our tile sheet IDs.

Using the road and wall tiles, create a tile map that looks something like Figure 6-7.

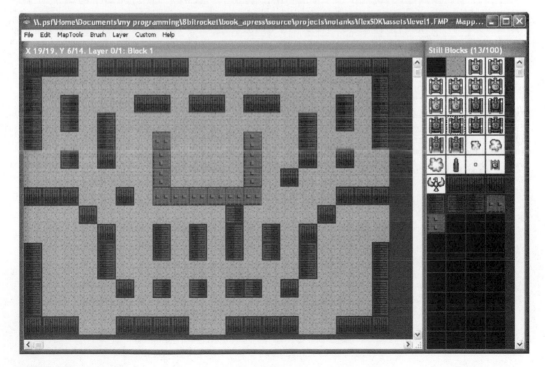

Figure 6-7. A sample level in Mappy for No Tanks!

217

Designing a level for No Tanks is pretty simple. Really, the only necessary sprites are a green tank and the gold bird-looking item that represents the artifact that must be recovered. The gray tiles are ones that all the tanks can move on, and the solid blue ones are wall tiles that no tanks can move on. All tiles that are not TILE_WALL or TILE_MOVE are considered sprites.

If you have a move tile (the only one is the gray road) on the outer edge on one side and on the other side in the same vertical (or horizontal) position, you will automatically create a warp tunnel in our engine. Some game engines make you specify a tile for the warp, but we will assume that any move tiles that match up on the top and bottom (or left and right) create a tunnel warp.

Creating the sprite layer

Once you have created the background layer, it is time to create the spite layer:

1. In Mappy, click the **Layer ➤ Add Layer** option in the **Layer** menu. This will add a **Layer 1** to your project. We will re-create the sprites on this layer.

2. Select the **Layer ➤ Onion Skin** option in **Layer ➤ Background Layers Darkened** option. This will become very useful when we start to edit the **Layer 1** sprite layer.

3. In the **Layer** menu, select the **Layer 1** option. You should now see **Layer 1** on top with the background layer underneath and darkened out. Since layer 1 is empty right now, there will be nothing in the foreground of the layer yet. See Figure 6-8 for an example of what this should look like.

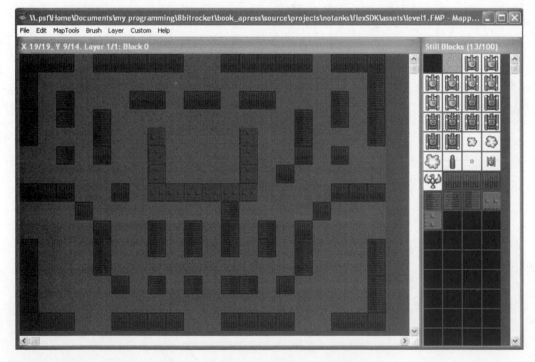

Figure 6-8. The Sprite layer (layer 1) is blank. Layer 0 is darkened.

4. Next, we need to start filling out the **Sprite** layer. This is the easy part. Follow the example in Figure 6-9.

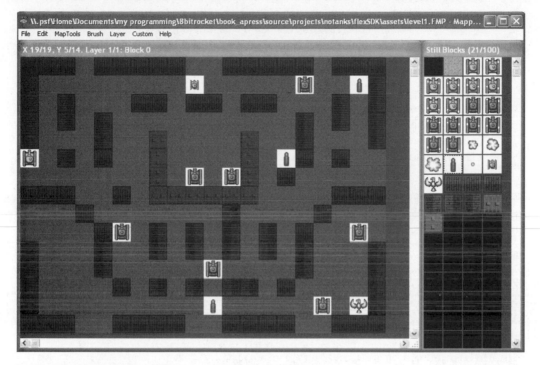

Figure 6-9. The Sprite layer (layer 1) filled out with sprites

5. The sprite layer is now complete. Now, we can export both layers to use in our game.

Saving the level .FMP file

The next step is to save the file as `level1.FMP`. This will save a file with both the created maze data and the tile sheet together, so you can go back in later to edit or update it.

Exporting the level from Mappy

We are going to export the background (layer 0) and sprite (layer 1) layers separately. There is an option in the Mappy **Custom** menu called **Export For ActionScript**. This will export the current selected layer as the 2D array we need for our level map data.

Exporting the background layer

Here are the steps for exporting the background layer.

1. The background layer (layer 0) should already be selected. If it is not, select it from the **Layer** menu.

2. Select the **Export For Actionscript** option in the **Custom** menu.

3. The first thing you will see is a warning that explains what you are going to be exporting is simply a flattened version of the map of the current layer; no animation will be exported. We did not create any animated tiles, but Mappy can do this and many other things we do not have space to cover.

4. Click **OK**, and type in a name for the .as file. For this example, use level1_back.as. Click **Save**.

5. Next, it will ask you how much to adjust the map values. This is an important question because Mappy added that extra blank tile to the beginning of our tile sheet. Because of this, the actual map values are 1 greater than they will be when we use the original tiles.png file as our source for tiles in Flash. For that reason, put –1 into this dialog box, and click on the **OK** button.

The ActionScript exported for this map will look something like this:

```
var map = [
[26,24,25,0,26,26,26,26,26,0,0,26,26,26,26,26,0,24,25,26],
[27,0,0,0,0,0,0,0,0,0,0,0,0,0,0,0,0,0,0,27],
[29,0,28,0,0,0,24,25,0,24,25,0,24,25,0,0,0,27,0,29],
[27,0,28,0,27,0,0,0,0,0,0,0,0,0,0,27,0,29,0,27],
[29,0,0,0,29,0,0,30,0,0,0,0,0,31,0,0,29,0,0,0,29],
[0,0,28,0,26,0,0,31,0,0,0,0,31,0,0,26,0,26,0,0],
[0,0,0,0,0,0,0,0,31,0,0,0,0,31,0,26,0,0,0,0,0],
[26,26,26,0,0,26,0,30,30,30,30,30,30,0,0,0,0,0,26,26,26],
[0,0,0,26,0,0,0,0,0,0,0,28,0,0,0,0,26,0,0,0],
[0,0,0,0,26,0,0,27,0,27,0,27,0,28,0,26,0,0,0,0,0],
[27,0,0,0,27,0,0,29,0,29,0,29,0,28,0,27,0,0,0,27],
[29,0,0,0,29,0,0,0,0,0,0,0,0,0,0,0,29,0,0,0,29],
[27,0,0,0,0,26,0,28,0,28,0,28,28,0,26,0,0,0,0,0,27],
[29,0,0,0,0,0,0,0,0,0,0,0,0,0,0,0,0,0,0,0,29],
[26,24,25,0,0,26,26,26,26,0,0,26,26,26,26,0,0,24,25,26]
]
```

Exporting the sprite layer

Here are the steps for exporting the sprite layer:

1. Select the sprite layer (layer 1) from the **Layer** menu.

2. Select the **Export For ActionScript** option in the **Custom** menu.

3. The first thing you will see is a warning that explains what you are going to be exporting is simply a flattened version of the map of the current layer; no animation will be exported. We did not create any animated tiles, but Mappy can do this and many other things we do not have space to cover.

4. Click **OK**, and type in a name for the .as file. For this example, use level1_sprites.as. Click **Save**.

5.   Next, it will ask you how much to adjust the map values. This is an important question because Mappy added that extra blank tile to the beginning of our tile sheet. Because of this, the actual map values are 1 greater than they will be when we use the original tiles.png file as our source for times in Flash. For that reason, put a –1 into this dialog box, and click the OK button.

The ActionScript exported for this sprite map will look something like the following code. Notice that 0 has been exported in each location where we had a blank space on the sprite layer. When we code the sprite placement routine in the next chapter, we will need to ignore any tiles in the map that have an id of 0.

```
var map = [
[0,0,0,0,0,0,0,0,0,0,0,0,0,0,0,0,0,0,0,0,0],
[0,0,0,0,0,0,0,0,0,22,0,0,0,0,0,9,0,0,20,0],
[0,0,0,0,0,0,0,0,0,0,0,0,0,0,0,0,0,0,0,0,0],
[0,0,0,0,0,0,0,0,0,0,0,0,0,0,0,0,0,0,0,0,0],
[0,0,0,0,0,0,0,0,0,0,0,0,0,0,0,0,0,0,0,0,0],
[1,0,0,0,0,0,0,0,0,0,0,0,0,0,0,20,0,0,0,0,0],
[0,0,0,0,0,0,0,0,0,9,0,9,0,0,0,0,0,0,0,0,0],
[0,0,0,0,0,0,0,0,0,0,0,0,0,0,0,0,0,0,0,0,0],
[0,0,0,0,0,0,0,0,0,0,0,0,0,0,0,0,0,0,0,0,0],
[0,0,0,0,0,9,0,0,0,0,0,0,0,0,0,0,0,0,9,0],
[0,0,0,0,0,0,0,0,0,0,0,0,0,0,0,0,0,0,0,0,0],
[0,0,0,0,0,0,0,0,0,0,9,0,0,0,0,0,0,0,0,0,0],
[0,0,0,0,0,0,0,0,0,0,0,0,0,0,0,0,0,0,0,0,0],
[0,0,0,0,0,0,0,0,0,0,20,0,0,0,0,0,9,0,23,0],
[0,0,0,0,0,0,0,0,0,0,0,0,0,0,0,0,0,0,0,0,0]
]]
```

Setting up our project

As with all of the games in this book, No Tanks! will use the framework package structure we created in Chapter 2. Let's begin by creating the package necessary for our game in both the Flash IDE and Flash Develop (for use with the Flex SDK).

Creating the No Tanks! game project in the Flash IDE

Here are the steps needed to create the game in the Flash IDE:

1.   Start up your version of Flash. I am using CS3, but this process should work exactly the same in CS4 and CS5.

2.   Create a .fla file in the /source/projects/notanks/flashIDE/ folder called notanks.

3.   In the /source/projects/notanks/flashIDE/ folder, create the package structure for your game: /com/efg/games/notanks/.

4.   Set the frame rate of the Flash movie to 30 FPS. Set the width to 640 and the height to 500.

5.   Set the document class to com.efg.games.notanks.Main.

6. We have not yet created the `Main.as` class, so you will see a warning. We are going to create this later in this chapter.

7. Next, add the framework reusable class package to the class path for the `.fla` file. First, in the publish settings, select **Flash ➤ ActionScript 3 in the Actionscript Version** dropdown, and click the **Settings** button.

8. Then, click the **Browse to Path** button, and find the `/source` folder we created in Chapter 2 for the package structure.

9. Finally, select the `classes` folder, and click the **Choose** button. Now the `com.efg.framework` package will be available for use when we begin to create our game.

Here is the folder structure for the Flash IDE version:

```
[source]
     [projects]
          [notanks]
               [flexIDE]
                         [com]
                              [efg]
                                   [games]
                                        [notanks]
```

Creating the No Tanks! game project in Flash Develop

Steps to create the No Tanks game in Flash Develop

1. Create a folder inside the `/source/projects/notanks/` folder called `flexSDK` (if you have not already done so).

2. Start Flash Develop, and create a new project. Begin by selecting **Flex 3 Project** and giving the project the name **notanks**. The location should be the `/source/projects/notanks/flexSDK` folder and the package should be `com.efg.games.notanks`.

   Do not have Flash Develop create a project folder automatically. Make sure the **Create Folder For Project** is *unchecked*.

   Click the **OK** button to create the project.

3. Add the class path to the framework to the project by selecting the **Project ➤ Properties ➤ Classpaths** menu item and clicking the **Add Classpath** button.

4. Next, find the `/source` we created earlier, and select the `classes` subfolder.

5. Click the **OK** button and then the **Apply** button.

6. Change the size of the output and frame rate by selecting the **Project ➤ Properties ➤ Classpaths** menu item. Set the Frame Rate to **30**, the width to **640**, and the height to **500**.

Here is the folder structure for the Flex SDK version (made with Flash Develop).

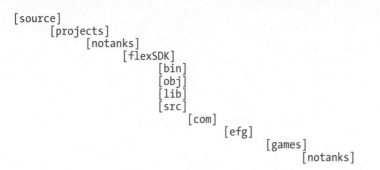

```
[source]
     [projects]
          [notanks]
               [flexSDK]
                    [bin]
                    [obj]
                    [lib]
                    [src]
                         [com]
                              [efg]
                                   [games]
                                        [notanks]
```

You now have the basic structure to start creating projects inside the framework. We are now going to discuss a few topics concerning the structure of the framework classes and then move into building the reusable framework code.

> *For Flex Builder, Flash Builder, or another IDE, please refer to the documentation provided for that product to create a new project and set the default compile class.*
>
> *Here's a note on the Flash Develop and Flash IDE workflow: A common method of Flash development is to use the Flash IDE for assets and organization and Flash Develop for code editing. If this is your workflow of choice, you will want to follow the Flash IDE folder and package structure rather than the Flex SDK folder structure.*

Describing our tile sheet in XML

Before we get to the ActionScript necessary to read our level1 tile map, we need a way to describe tile types that exist in our tile sheet to the game engine. One method that I have used in the past is to create a separate XML file to describe the type of tile that exists in each spot on the sheet. We will do this in an ActionScript class that our game can use.

Creating the TilesheetDataXML.as class

This class will simply be a set of XML data set as a static class variable. This type of construct is useful for encapsulating data into a class that you will not need to instantiate but contains data we will want to use in our game.

Here's the structure for the Flash IDE:

/source/projects/notanks/flashIDE/com/efg/games/notanks/TilesheetDataXML.as

And this is for the Flex SDK (using Flash Develop):

/source/projects/notanks/flexSDK/src/com/efg/games/notanks/TilesheetDataXML.as

Here is entire code listing for this class:

```
/**
* ...
* @author Jeff Fulton
* @version 0.1
* //file name TilesheetDataXML.as
*/
```

223

```
package com.efg.games.notanks {

    public class TilesheetDataXML {
        public static var XMLData:XML=

    <tilesheet>

    <tile id="0" name="road" type="walkable"></tile>
    <tile id="1" name="player" type="sprite"></tile>
    <tile id="2" name="player" type="sprite"></tile>
    <tile id="3" name="player" type="sprite"></tile>
    <tile id="4" name="player" type="sprite"></tile>
    <tile id="5" name="player" type="sprite"></tile>
    <tile id="6" name="player" type="sprite"></tile>
    <tile id="7" name="player" type="sprite"></tile>

    <tile id="8" name="player" type="sprite"></tile>
    <tile id="9" name="enemy" type="sprite"></tile>
    <tile id="10" name="enemy" type="sprite"></tile>
    <tile id="11" name="enemy" type="sprite"></tile>
    <tile id="12" name="enemy" type="sprite"></tile>
    <tile id="13" name="enemy" type="sprite"></tile>
    <tile id="14" name="enemy" type="sprite"></tile>
    <tile id="15" name="enemy" type="sprite"></tile>

    <tile id="16" name="enemy" type="sprite"></tile>
    <tile id="17" name="explode1" type="sprite"></tile>
    <tile id="18" name="explode2" type="sprite"></tile>
    <tile id="19" name="explode3" type="sprite"></tile>
    <tile id="20" name="ammo" type="sprite"></tile>
    <tile id="21" name="missile" type="sprite"></tile>
    <tile id="22" name="lives" type="sprite"></tile>
    <tile id="23" name="goal" type="sprite"></tile>

    <tile id="24" name="blueblock1" type="nonwalkable"></tile>
    <tile id="25" name="blueblock2" type="nonwalkable"></tile>
    <tile id="26" name="blueblock3" type="nonwalkable"></tile>
    <tile id="27" name="blueblock4" type="nonwalkable"></tile>
    <tile id="28" name="blueblock5" type="nonwalkable"></tile>
    <tile id="29" name="blueblock6" type="nonwalkable"></tile>
    <tile id="30" name="blueblock7" type="nonwalkable"></tile>
    <tile id="31" name="blueblock8" type="nonwalkable"></tile>

    <smallexplode tiles="17,18,17"></smallexplode>
    <largeexplode tiles="17,18,19,18,17"></largeexplode>
</tilesheet>;

        } // end class
}// end package
```

The purpose of this class is to describe (to the Game class) the type of tile in each position on the tile sheet This way, you can create your own, modified tile sheet for this game or any other game and not rely on the game hard-coding tile definitions.

Tile attributes

Inside the `<tile></tile>` data for each tile sheet element, we have defined three different attributes that describe the tile.

- id: The id is simply the tile number, starting at 0 and going up to 31. There are 32 tiles in the tile sheet: 4 rows of 8 tiles each. This number is not used by the game code but rather is a reference for the game developer and level designer to understand where that tile will be in the one-dimensional array of tile sheet tiles when we get to the game code.

- name: This represents the type of sprite that the tile is. Some tiles are not sprites, but they have names too. Those are used purely for reference for the game designer and programmer. The code we will create in the next chapter will use this name types and create custom class instances for each based on this name. This makes it easy for the level designer to place the player tank any place on the level. The same holds for the enemy, goal, ammunition, and lives sprites. The explosion and missile sprites should not be placed in the level. They are used for special FX in the game.

- type: There are three different tile types: sprite, walkable, and nonwalkable. All wall tiles must be set to nonwalkable; all road and passageway tiles must be set to walkable. Everything else should be set to sprite.

The final two attributes in the XML were not part of the data from Mappy:

```
<smallexplode tiles="17,18,17"></smallexplode>
<largeexplode tiles="17,18,19,18,17"></largeexplode>
```

We added these attributes. They describe to the game the tile sequences needed for two different explosion types using the tiles in the tile sheet. So, for example, the smallexplode animation sequence will play tile 17, then tile 18, then tile 17 again. We will go into detail on these two in the next section.

How this code works

TilesheetDataXML.as is a basic global type or static style class that we will never have to instantiate. The Game class will never need an instance of the class because our single variable, XMLData is defined as static. This allows the Game to simply use this XML data without needing to instantiate the class directly.

Why don't we just use an XML file and load it in? The focus of this book it to create final SWF files that need no external assets. This creates the easiest game content to spread 'round the World Wide Web. For this reason, we have gone to great lengths to make sure that the final SWF file has all of the needed assets embedded without the need to call external files.

Using the tile sheet data in code

We will now create some example code that will be fleshed out in the next chapter. The example code will parse the TileSheetDataXML.as XML data and place it into a one-dimensional array that can be used to describe the contents of the level XML files file to the Game.

Create the GameDemo.as class

Create a new ActionScript class file called GameDemo.as. For the rest of this chapter, you will want to set this class as the document class of the notanks.fla file if you are using the Flash IDE and the always-compile class if you are using the Flex SDK and Flash Develop. For any other development tools, follow the documentation provided for that environment, to set a base, main, or document class for your project.

Here's the folder structure for the Flash IDE:

/source/projects/notanks/flashIDE/com/efg/games/notanks/GameDemo.as

And this one is for the Flex SDK (using Flash Develop):

/source/projects/notanks/flexSDK/src/com/efg/games/notanks/GameDemo.as

Here is the first iteration of the entire GameDemo.as class. We will add to this class in following sections. Type the following code into the file and save it; we will discuss the code in the next section:

```
package com.efg.games.notanks
{
    import flash.display.Sprite;

    /**
     * ...
     * @author Jeff Fulton
     */
     public class GameDemo extends Sprite{

        public static const TILE_WALL:int = 0;
        public static const TILE_MOVE:int = 1;
        public static const SPRITE_PLAYER:int = 2;
        public static const SPRITE_GOAL:int = 3;
        public static const SPRITE_AMMO:int = 4;
        public static const SPRITE_ENEMY:int = 5;
        public static const SPRITE_EXPLODE:int = 6;
        public static const SPRITE_MISSILE:int = 7;
        public static const SPRITE_LIVES:int = 8;

        private var playerFrames:Array;
        private var enemyFrames:Array;
        private var explodeFrames:Array;
        private var tileSheetData:Array;

        private var missileTiles:Array=[];
        private var explodeSmallTiles:Array;
        private var explodeLargeTiles:Array;

        private var ammoFrame:int;
        private var livesFrame:int;
        private var goalFrame:int;

        public function GameDemo() {
            initTileSheetData();
```

```
            trace("tileSheetData.length=" + tileSheetData.length);
            trace("playerFrames.length=" + playerFrames.length);
            trace("enemyFrames.length=" + enemyFrames.length);
            trace("missileTiles.length=" +          missileTiles.length);
        }


        private function initTileSheetData():void {
            playerFrames = [];
            enemyFrames = [];
            tileSheetData = [];
            var numberToPush:int = 99;
            var tileXML:XML = TilesheetDataXML.XMLData;
            var numTiles:int = tileXML.tile.length();
            for (var tileNum:int = 0; tileNum < numTiles; tileNum++) {
                if (String(tileXML.tile[tileNum].@type) == "walkable") {
                    numberToPush = TILE_MOVE;
                }else if (String(tileXML.tile[tileNum].@type) == "nonwalkable") {
                    numberToPush = TILE_WALL;
                }else if (tileXML.tile[tileNum].@type == "sprite") {
                    switch(String(tileXML.tile[tileNum].@name)) {
                        case "player":
                            numberToPush = SPRITE_PLAYER;
                            playerFrames.push(tileNum);
                            break;
                        case "goal":
                            numberToPush = SPRITE_GOAL;
                            goalFrame = tileNum;
                            break;
                        case "ammo":
                            numberToPush = SPRITE_AMMO;
                            ammoFrame = tileNum;
                            break;
                        case "enemy":
                            numberToPush = SPRITE_ENEMY;
                            enemyFrames.push(tileNum);
                            break;
                        case "lives":
                            numberToPush = SPRITE_LIVES;
                            livesFrame = tileNum;
                            break;
                        case "missile":
                            numberToPush = SPRITE_MISSILE;
                            missileTiles.push(tileNum);
                            break;
                    }
                }
                tileSheetData.push(numberToPush);
            }
            explodeSmallTiles = tileXML.smallexplode.@tiles.split(",");
            explodeLargeTiles = tileXML.largeexplode.@tiles.split(",");
        }
    }
}
```

THE ESSENTIAL GUIDE TO FLASH GAMES

Reading the tile sheet data

This first set of code for GameDemo.as is used to read in and evaluate the tile sheet data. In the previous section, we examined the structure of the TileSheetDataXML.as file. In the preceding code, we create the first version of the GameDemo.as class that we will be using to demonstrate functionality for our future game, No Tanks!. None of this will go to waste, as we will be using the exact same code with some minor modifications in the next chapter as we build the game.

The constants

You will notice that we create some constants at the beginning of the code. These will be used in place of plain old integers to describe the contents of the tiles in the tile sheet. The only two basic background tile types are TILE_WALL and TILE_MOVE. These will be the lowest level components on the background of our game level. A tile can only be one or the other, but cannot be both. Any tile with type="walkable" in the XML will be designated with the TILE_MOVE value. Any tile with type="nonwalkable" in the XML will be designated with the TILE_WALL value. Any tile that either describes an interactive object or other game object that is not strictly used for creating the background of a level is give the type="sprite" value in the XML. Those tiles will be evaluated based on their name= XML attribute values.

The next seven constants (SPRITE_PLAYER through SPRITE_LIVES) are used to describe the sprites used in the game. Each sprite will use the tiles associated with it in a slightly different way. The name= attribute value in the tile XML will be used by the game engine to make use of the sprites for the game.

- **Player:** The player is the sprite that the user will control in the game. The array of tiles for the player creates the movement animation of the tank track that will simulate tank movement. The look of the player sprite is a series of tile sheet frame numbers that are all stored in the array, playerFrames. The game will assume that the tiles for the player are in the correct order on the tile sheet already. As the code reads in the tile sheet XML data, when it encounters a tile with type="sprite" and the name="player", it will add that tile to this array.

- **Enemy:** All of the enemy sprites will share the same look. The tiles for the enemy will be stored in the enemyFrames array and function exactly like the player tiles. The game engine assumes that the tiles are in the correct animation order on the tile sheet already. The code looks for type="sprite" and name="enemy" and adds all of those tiles to the array.

- **Missile**: Both the player and the enemy will share a single tile for the missile. The code will look for type="sprite" and name="missile". When it finds a missile tile, it will add it to the missileTiles array. Even though our game uses a single tile, we store it in an array so it can easily be swapped out to a multiframe animation with ease.

- **Explosion**: There are three tiles that are designated as type="sprite" and name="explode1","name="explode2", and name="explode3". These are handled differently than the other sprites in the game. We are going to allow game programmers to make use of these three tiles in any way that they desire. We have two arrays that we filled with actual tile numbers to create two different explosions.

```
private var explodeSmallTiles:Array;
private var explodeLargeTiles:Array;
```

They are both set by reading data from the XML:

```
explodeSmallTiles = tileXML.smallexplode.@tiles.split(",");
```

```
explodeLargeTiles = tileXML.largeexplode.@tiles.split(",");
```

The data looks like this:

```
<smallexplode tiles="17,18,17"></smallexplode>
<largeexplode tiles="17,18,19,18,17"></largeexplode>
```

The first explosion uses only the first two explosion tiles. We create a simple animation sequence by specifying that we play tile 17, then tile 18, and then tile 17 again. Let's look at our tile sheet again; see Figure 6-10.

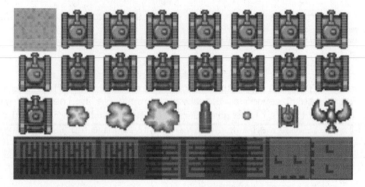

Figure 6-10. The tile sheet

If we play tile 17 (the smallest explosion tile), tile 18, and tile 17 again (and then display no tile), we will have a nice, relatively simple explode animation. This will be used for player and enemy missiles that hit a TILE_WALL and harmlessly explode.

The larger array of tiles is set up to play in this order: 17, 18,19,18, and 17. This will create a larger, longer animation that will be used when the player hits an enemy with a missile and when the player is destroyed.

We chose to set these in the TilesheetDataXML file to keep our game clean of any hard-coded data references. We could have easily just set all of these arrays up in code, but then the game would be less easily reused and reskinned.

The initTileSheetData function

The GameDemo constructor is set up to simply call the initTileSheetData function and then print out the lengths of the arrays that were created in that function. To assign data to these arrays, the initTilesheetData function simply loops through the XML represented by the tileXML variable. This variable is set to the static value of the TilesheetDataXML.XMLData variable. The purpose of this function is to create a one-dimensional array called tileSheetData that will hold the constant value assigned to each tile in the tile sheet in order.

XML data is pretty easy to traverse in AS3. We can simply loop through all of the nodes in the XML data that contain tile data as if they are part of an array. We first find the number of tiles in the data like this:

```
var numTiles:int = tileXML.tile.length();
```

Pretty simple, right? Next, we just loop though the XML as if it was an array and check out the attribute content of each <tile></tile> node in the XML data. Our first check is to see if the tile is walkable or nonwalkable. If either of those is the value of the type attribute, the corresponding constant is stored in our local numberToPush variable. The value will either be TILE_WALL or TILE_MOVE. If the tile type is sprite, we have to do a second check using the name of the tile. Depending on the name value, our switch:case statement will both assign values to our tile arrays (described in the previous section "The constants"), and assign the corresponding constant to the numberToPush variable. After a number constant has been assigned to the tile and any associated arrays have been updated, we finally add the constant value to the tileSheetData array.

You have seen the final two lines before. Those are for the explode arrays. We discussed those in detail in the previous section.

Testing it out

In either the Flash IDE or Flash Develop, you can test out this file with no changes. For Flash Develop, remember to set GameDemo.as the always-compile file. In The Flash IDE, make sure GameDemo is the document class of the game_demo.fla, and test the movie. You should see the output shown in Figure 6-11 in the trace window (unless you have modified the tile sheet for your own purpose).

```
tileSheetData.length=32
playerFrames.length=8
enemyFrames.length=8
missileTiles.length=1
explodeSmallTiles.length=3
explodeLargeTiles.length=5
```

Figure 6-11. The trace output for this demonstration publish or build

This output shows the lengths of the arrays we created after the initTileSheetData function was called. The first trace shows the length of the tileSheetData array (32). Next, we see the number of tiles for both the playerFrames array and enemyFrames array (8). The missileTiles array only contains a single tile id, while the explodeSmallTiles and the explodeLargeTiles arrays contain 3 and 5 respectively.

Displaying the level data on the screen

The next task we are going to tackle is reading the level data and displaying it on the game screen. This is going to make use some tile sheet blitting techniques that we will discuss shortly in the section called "Tile sheet blitting and sprites." We will again be using the GameDemo.as file and updating it to include the new code. We will require some slight differences between the Flex

SDK version of the game code and the Flash IDE game code, because the two technologies handle embedding assets in slightly different ways. For example, when you embed a PNG bitmap file in the Flash IDE library, the base class it is given is `BitmapData`. But when you embed the same asset in a Flex project, the base class is an instance of `BitmapAsset` (which is a child of `Bitmap`). So, we will need the code base for the two different applications to be slightly different. Let's start there.

Organizing your code

If you are using the Flex SDK, you will want to make sure that you are placing all the raw assets (only the `tank_sheet.png` file so far) are in the `/assets` folder. We have not created this folder yet. So let's do it now. Let's revisit those locations in the package structure:

```
[source]
      [projects]
            [notanks]
                  [flexSDK]
                        [assets]
                              tank_sheet.png
                        [bin]
                        [obj]
                        [lib]
                        [src]
                              [com]
                                    [efg]
                                          [games]
                                                [notanks]
                                                      GameDemo.as
```

Notice that we have created a new folder inside the `/source/projects/flexSDK` folder called `assets`. This folder is at the same level as the `/bin/`, `/obj/`, `/lib/`, and `/src/` folders for our Flex SDK project. We have also placed the `tank_sheet.png` file in the `assets` folder. The code for our game will need to find this folder to embed the image during compilation so the location is very important.

If you are using the Flash IDE we will simply embed the `tank_sheet.png` file in the FLA library. We will do this in the next section.

Adding the Library.as class for Flex projects only

The Flash IDE project will not need the `Library.as` class. The standard method for embedding assets in the Flash IDE (up until Flash CS4) was to embed them in the FLA library at design time. In Flex SDK projects, there is no library to embed assets at design time. For this reason, we will need to embed our assets at compile time for Flex SDK projects. This is also possible with Flash CS4 (and beyond) so if you are using a Flash IDE version more modern than CS3, you can also make use of the `Libray.as` class, we will create for our Flex SDK projects.

The theory behind the `Library.as` class is this: we want to mimic as closely as possible the Flash IDE style library with only Flex style embeds. Our library will be made up of static constant variable values that represent the embedded assets. You should create and save the `Library.as` class code in the same project folder as the `GameDemo.as` class.

Here's how the `Libray.as` file fits into the No Tanks! package structure:

`/source/projects/notanks/flexSDK/src/com/efg/games/notanks/Library.as`

Here is the entire set of Library class code:

```
package com.efg.games.notanks
{
    import flash.display.Bitmap;
    import flash.display.BitmapData;
    /**
    * ...
    * @author Jeff Fulton
    */
    public class Library {
        [Embed(source='../../../../../assets/tanks_sheet.png')]
        public static const TankSheetPng:Class;
    }
}
```

This class is really very simple. It embeds the tanks_sheet.png file and gives it an export class name of TankSheetPng. Notice the location of the PNG file is set relative to the package folder. This is very important to remember. We will use this static constant (TankSheetPng) in our game code in much the same way as the IDE library uses the class name when a library item is set for export.

Adding the library assets for the Flash IDE only

If you are using the Flash IDE, you will need to import the tanks_sheet.png file into the library and set the export name to be TankSheetPng. Notice that this is the exact same name we used for the Flex embed class name. Keeping these consistent will make porting from one technology to the other a trivial matter.

Using the library assets in Flex and the Flash IDE

Now that we have the asset in the library of Flash Develop/Flex or the Flash IDE, we are ready to use the asset. As a quick example, this is the code we will use in the Flex version to pass the TankSheetPng class instance to the TileSheet class that we will create in the next section.

```
//***** Flex *****
private var tileSheet:TileSheet= new TileSheet(new Library.TankSheetPng().bitmapData, ⏎
                    tileWidth, tileHeight);
//***** End Flex *****
```

Notice that the code creates a new instance of the TankSheetPng class and passes the bitmapData attribute of it directly into the TileSheet constructor. We do this because the TileSheet class constructor requires us to pass in a BitmapData instance, not a Bitmap instance. Since Flex only allows us to embed bitmap assets as a Bitmap class (actually BitmapAsset), to get to the bitmapData, we have to reference it with the dot (.) syntax.

Conversely, in the Flash IDE, bitmap assets in the library are given the base class of BitmapData. So, our call to the constructor or the TileSheet class is a little simpler.

```
//***** Flash IDE *****
//private var tileSheet:TileSheet = new TileSheet(new TankSheetPng(0,0), tileWidth, ⏎
                        tileHeight);
//***** End Flash IDE *****
```

The big difference is the constructor for the TankSheetPng requires that two parameters be passed or a compile-time error will occur. These values can be the actual size of the tank_sheet.png file, or they can be 0,0. Passing 0,0 works fine, so you don't have to hard-code the size of the tile sheet into your GameDemo.as class if you don't want to.

Tile sheet blitting and sprites

We are about to create the next reusable class for our framework, the TileSheet class. This class can be used to describe all of the attributes needed to copy cells from a tile sheet to other display objects. We will make heavy use of this class in this and some of the following chapters.

Before we venture into the code for the tile sheet class, let's define "tile sheet blitting" because you are going to see those words, and "blit," very often in the rest of this book.

Defining "blitting"

Blitting refers to techniques used in the late 1970s and throughout the 1980s and early 1990s for video and computer game development. Most arcade games, home systems, and computers used some type of tiles, sprite sheet, or character sheet for many of their games. Some games, such as early Atari games like Asteroids did *not* use a tile sheet. But, Atari home systems (Atari 2600, 5200, 7800, 800, etc.) used a form of blitting called Player Missile Graphics (PMGs). These PMGs were used to separate the background of the game from a limited number of free moving display objects in memory. Data to represent these objects was probably not held in any type of tile sheet in the early systems, but rather a machine language representation of the map of memory binary objects (on or off) was used to create single color display objects (Multicolor in Atari 7800 and Lynx games).

Throughout the 1980s, system after system used these techniques and called them various things: BOBs, sprites, blitter objects, OBJs, and so on. Some were derived from custom hardware chips, and some were simply created in software. For example, the first Atari ST machines were fast, but they had no hardware sprites. The games for the system were good but a little sluggish if created by an inexperienced developer, because software techniques, rather than dedicated hardware, were used to create game sprites. When the Commodore Amiga came along, it could blast fast hardware sprites in the form of BOBs to the screen, and this made creating high-speed arcade games for the machine relatively easy. The Nintendo Entertainment System (NES), probably the most popular system in the 1980s, was very powerful because it made extensive use of tiles, tile sheets, and blitting.

You probably won't find the word "blit" in any dictionary, but even if it means nothing to *Webster's*, it means a lot to game developers (and programmers alike). The verb **blit** means to take a map of bits (usually a 1D or 2D array or a single linked list) and move them around in memory really fast. The Amiga, Sega Genesis, and later Atari STE used this methodology in hardware to create some stunning 16-bit games. Most early second-generation game systems used tile sheets and blitting of some sort to create animated characters and backgrounds. The actual word "blit" comes from the 1974 Xerox Alto computer's ability to do this kind of data movement. It was termed as "bit block transfer," or "bit blit" for short. It has been shortened even further to just "blit." It used to be that blitting and sprites were two different methods of accomplishing the same thing. Sprites were actually hardware generated on top of the bitmapped display, while blits were written right to the display buffer with a hardware or software rendering techniques.

Defining "sprite" further

Sprites, in their original incarnation, were made popular on the Atari (called PMGs), Texas Instruments TI99/4A, Commodore 64, and NES (where they were called OBJs) computers and video game systems of the late 1970s and early 1980s. A company name Signetics was the first to create technology that acted like a sprite, though they did not use that name. In the early days, sprite was simply an extra set of display memory (usually based on display scan lines), independent from the bitmapped screen. It could be controlled independently from the screen background, and some early implementations even included collision detection, multicoloring, layering, and other features. Many early game systems made use of the sprite: the Atari 2600 had three: two players and one ball. Texas Instruments was the first company to use the term "sprite." A sprite was part of the hardware of the computer and was specifically used to display important game objects independently from the background. Usually, the hardware offered only a limited number of rather small sprites.

Understanding the differences between sprites and blitting

Many popular 1980s game systems and computers (like the Atari 520 ST and Apple IIGS) had no hardware sprites. This required game developers to use tile sheets and blitting techniques in software to achieve some of the same features of hardware sprites. The main difference between the two was that the hardware sprites were written to the display separately than the rest of the bitmapped screen. Some later computers (the Amiga and Atari STE) actually had hardware blitting capabilities that combined the best of both worlds—fast bit block transfer rendered to a bitmapped screen. Usually, systems with hardware blitting were replicating sprite capabilities with custom chips that were essentially moving bits around really fast in memory, but still displaying the screen as one big bitmap, with no separate sprite channels independent of the screen.

On systems with no hardware sprites or hardware blitting capabilities (or systems with too few of either), software techniques were used to replicate the same thing. These software techniques placed maps of bits on to the screen in a certain order, many times a second to achieve a blitted, animated screen. This is essentially what we do in Flash when we are doing a blit; we are replicating a classic software blit.

Tile sheets (or other image map representations) were used with both hardware and software driven sprites and or blitted memory maps of bits. In Flash, we will use tile sheets too (but there are certainly other methods of storing blit data). No matter what system is used (hardware sprites, hardware blitting, or software systems), blitting to the screen requires you to exercise control over the screen rendering to achieve the effects you wants to achieve.

Bringing Flash into the mix

In Flash, a `Sprite` is a built-in class. The Flash Player engine renders it, so you don't have to worry about manually refreshing the screen when a sprite is moved (or changed) on the screen. Unlike classic hardware sprites, the software only sprites actually are redrawn to the display background every frame and are not provided by hardware. Flash sprites share a name only with classic hardware sprites and are essentially a `MovieClip` without a timeline. Flash uses a technique called **screen invalidation** to mark areas of the screen that need to be refreshed rather than refreshing the entire screen with the vector render engine every frame.

If you right-click a Flash Movie that is playing in a browser (with the menu option turned on in the HTML embed), you will see an option called **Show Re-draw Regions**. *Click this option, and you can see screen invalidation in action. In a game that makes use of many display objects, you will see red outlined screen invalidation areas all over the screen. In games that make use of full screen blit techniques (you will see one in Chapter 11), you will see only a single red outline (or very few depending on the number of blit canvases used).*

Flash uses the vector render engine for all sprites unless they are specifically cached as a bitmap. If a `Sprite` is set to **Cache as Bitmap**, and its display changes (or animates in some way), it will need to be cached again each frame, causing the processor to do double duty. With a lot of objects moving and animating on the screen, the Flash vector render engine will have to invalidate almost every portion of the screen and redraw (and in cases of vectors cached as bitmaps, cache) repeatedly. Since the Flash vector render engine is not the most efficient method of displaying a bitmapped screen in this manner, we will explore different methods of using tiles sheets and blitting to optimize the process.

We won't ignore the Flash vector render engine entirely though. You will see a good advantage to using Flash sprites with a tile sheet in No Tanks!—rotation and scaling! Our game will not have hundreds of on-screen objects. It will only contain relatively few moving or animating sprites. For our game sprites (such as the tanks, missiles, and explosions), we will use a system we call **blitting to individual display objects**. This means we will be combining the advantages of a tile sheet with the advantages of the built-in Flash `Sprite` objects.

When we created our tile sheet for the tanks, we put in eight frames for each tank. Each frame displays the tank treads slightly offset to simulate animation. We did not create versions of these sprites on the tile sheet for the down, left, or right directions. We did this because when we blit from a tile sheet to a Flash `Sprite`, we have the advantage of using the vector renderer's rotation property to flip the `Sprite` to the desired direction.

In Chapter 11, we will create a game that blits to a single canvas (a full-screen blit). With a game like that, we will not be able to make use of the `Sprite` class and the built-in vector render engine for rotation. We will create our own system for rotation of blit objects to utilize rotation in that chapter.

Understanding the difference between tile and sprite sheets

You will hear both the terms "tile sheet" and "sprite sheet" used interchangeably. They are essentially the same thing: an image file logically and physically split into regions that can be used to display objects on the screen and animate them. Some tile-based games use a sheet full of background tiles for rendering. They might have a separate sheet for sprite frames. We have mixed background tiles on the same sheet as sprite frames for the No Tanks! game. It doesn't matter to me that they are mixed together. In fact, it actually saves memory to combine them into one.

There are various ways that we can use tile sheets for blitting in Flash games. We will use two of these techniques in this chapter:

A full screen blit

The full-screen blit is the most drastic version of blitting technique. It arguably provides the greatest render speed benefits but at a cost. It is the most complicated and limiting blitting procedure. It requires the developer to have *one* `BitmapData` object that we call a Canvas. All objects are placed on to this canvas with `copyPixels` operations. There are no `Sprites`, `MovieClips`, `Bitmaps`, or other objects added to the Flash display list other than a single `Bitmap` object to hold this canvas. This type of blitting operation requires the developer to pre-render all of the display assets and animations in tile sheets, or arrays of `BitmapData` before they can be displayed on the screen.

Individual object blits

Individual object blitting refers to using multiple display objects to render the game, each with its own canvas for displaying tile sheet or array based `BitmapData` objects. For example, if we `copyPixels` a 32 × 32 tile from our tile sheet to the `BitmapData` attribute of a `Bitmap` object in Flash, we are blitting from a tile sheet. If we add that `Bitmap` to a `Sprite` object and position it at an x location of `(width*.5)*-1` and y at `(height*.5)*-1`, then we have our 32 × 32 tile with the registration point in the center. Now, we can rotate, scale, and move that individual `Sprite` all we want. If we want to change its tile, we copy new pixels to the `BitmapData` attribute of the `Bitmap`. We do this individually for our game characters to reap the benefits of tile sheets and the benefits of the Flash `Sprite` at the same time.

Combining types of blits

I find that using a combination of the two blitting methods is the most flexible. I have created entire games with individual blit objects, and I have created entire games with a single canvas display object. Both work fine, but the game we are going to create in this chapter and the next one uses a combination of both techniques. We will be using a screen-sized single canvas for the level map. This will contain only the `TILE_WALL` and `TILE_MOVE` designated tiles. We will then create our own special class called `BlitSprite` to be used for the sprites in the game. This class will extend `Sprite` but use our `TileSheet` class to blit animations to the sprite. This structure will give us the flexibility to use the rotation property of the `Sprite` class and not have to prerender all of the rotations for each of the eight frames of out tanks.

Testing blitting render speed

Many people have asked us why we like to use blitting operations for animation and screen rendering. They point out that they are much more difficult than timeline-based animations and take more time to code and set up. Our answer is *power*. In 2008, We decided to answer those critics by doing a series of render tests on our web site, www.8bitrocket.com. We are not going to go into the full detail of the tests here, but we will show the results, which indicated a huge speed and frame rate performance gain by using some type of blitting (individual sprite or full screen) over using the go-to-and-stop method of timeline-style of animating `MovieClip` objects.

Each test was run by attempting to place increasingly more and more objects on the screen and timing the average frame rate while doing so. I did the test using 100, 500, 1,000, 5,000, 10,000, and finally 15,000 objects on the screen. All tests were completed inside the Flash IDE with the stage frame rate set to 120.

Testing the timeline-based method

This test used individual `MovieClip` objects. I put each tile of my animation on a separate frame of a `MovieClip`; see Table 6-1.

Table 6-1. The Average Frame Rates for Each Set of `MovieClips`

Number of Movie Clips	Average Frame Rates
100 `MovieClips`	107 FPS
500 `MovieClips`	22 FPS
1,000 `MovieClips`	9 FPS
5,000 `MovieClips`	Less than 1 FPS
10,000 `MovieClips`	Not tested
15,000 `MovieClips`	Not tested

Testing individual object blits

This test used individual `Sprite` objects. I placed a `Bitmap` object inside each `Sprite` and put each frame of the animation in a tile sheet. I used the `copyPixels` method of the `BitmapData` object attached to each `Bitmap` object to copy the frame of animation from the tile sheet to the `Bitmap` object.

The results are shown in Table 6-2.

Table 6-2. Results of the Individual Object Blit Test

Number of Sprites	Average Frame Rate
100	124 FPS
500	124 FPS
1,000	91 FPS
5,000	18 FPS
10,000	9 FPS
15,000	6 FPS

Testing the sprite full-screen blit

This test used a single `BitmapData` display canvas. The `copyPixels` method of the `BitmapData` object was used to copy the tiles for animation from a tile sheet. Results are in Table 6-3.

Table 6-3. Results of the full-screen blit test

Number of Sprites	Average Frame Rate
100	126 FPS
500	24 FPS
1,000	93 FPS
5,000	22 FPS
10,000	12 FPS
15,000	8 FPS

Making sense of these results

In our games, we should try to attempt to keep a constant frame rate of at least 30 frames a second. As you can see, with the timeline-based method, we can achieve a very nice frame rate with 100 objects, but as we progress toward 500 objects, the frame rate drops significantly. Both the individual sprite and full-screen blit methods offer a significant performance boost even with 1,000 objects on the screen. We have to add 5,000 objects to the screen in the full-screen blit method to lower our frame rate to the same rate the timeline-based method drops to at only 500 objects.

What does this mean? It means that we can squeeze high performance from the Flash Player if we need to. Not all games are going to need this performance boost, but throughout this book we will use the blitting and tile sheet methods to show how then can be used in almost any game. With the advent of new handheld and mobile devices that can make use of Flash Player games, we will see the need to squeeze performance from the Flash Player become more and more important.

> *If you are interested in trying the render speed tests with the latest Flash Player, the code and necessary files are included in the Chapter 6 book files on the download site. Flash 10 Player has added some significant improvement across the board for all three rendering techniques.*

The TileSheet class

The `TileSheet` class is the *core* of our blitting operations. It contains a reference to the `Library` item tile sheet and contains the necessary information for other display objects to use it for blitting operations. This class will be part of the overall game framework package. We will use this class in a few more games in this book.

Create the `TileSheet.as` file in the framework package structure we created in Chapter 2:

`/source/classes/com/efg/framework/TileSheet.as`

Let's take a look at the code for the class in its entirety first:

```
package com.efg.framework{
    import flash.display.BitmapData;import flash.geom.*;

    /**
     * ...
     * @author Jeff Fulton
     */

    public class TileSheet  {
        public var sourceBitmapData:BitmapData;
        public var width:int;
        public var height:int;
        public var tileWidth:int;
        public var tileHeight:int;
        public var tilesPerRow:int;

        public function TileSheet(sourceBitmapData:BitmapData,tileWidth:int, ↵
          tileHeight:int ) {
            this.sourceBitmapData = sourceBitmapData;
            width = sourceBitmapData.width;
            height =  sourceBitmapData.height;
            this.tileHeight = tileHeight;
            this.tileWidth = tileWidth;
            tilesPerRow = int(width / this.tileWidth);
        }
    }
}
```

Understanding the attributes of a TileSheet

To use a tile sheet as a source for game graphics, we need to define and have access to several variables. The constructor only receives three pieces of information:

```
(sourceBitmapData:DitmapData,tilewidth:int, tileheight:int)
```

```
private var sourceBitmapData:BitmapData;
```

In the constructor you will find this line of code:

```
this.sourceBitmapData=sourceBitmapdata;
```

The `sourceBitmapData` represents the actual PNG sheet of tiles that will be the source of out blitting operations. This variable holds a reference to the `BitmapData` instance that is passed into the constructor. For our game, we have a sheet that is 256 × 128. That is good for eight columns 32 × 32 tiles and four rows. The next two variables represent the actual width and height of the sheet.

```
private var width:int;
private var height:int;
```

In the constructor, these are set based on the width and height of the passed in `BitmapData`.

```
width = sourceBitmapData.width;
height =  sourceBitmapData.height;
```

The `tileWidth` and `tileHeight` are passed directly into the constructor.

```
private var tileWidth:int;
private var tileHeight:int;
```

In the constructor, they are assigned.

```
this.tileHeight = tileHeight;
this.tileWidth = tileWidth;
```

The `tilesPerRow` variable is very important for our blitting operations. It is used to calculate the row and column values for the needed tile based only on the location of the tile in a single dimensional array. For example, to locate the tile number 9 on the tile sheet, with a `tilesPerRow` value of 8, we find that we must look for the first tile on the second row of our tile sheet.

```
private var tilesPerRow:int;
```

That's all there is to the `TileSheet` class. Let's move on to reading the level data from our `Level1.as` class.

Reading the level data

All of the data for our level will reside in a class, just like the tile sheet data. We do this so our game can be distributed on a single SWF file and to make game portal integration very easy. We have a very basic base class for all of the No Tanks! levels called `Level`. Let's start by creating this class.

The Level class

The `Level` class will be the base class for all of the game levels we create. It will be created inside the No Tanks! package structure:

The Flash IDE:

/source/projects/notanks/flashIDE/com/efg/games/notanks/Level.as

The Flex SDK (using Flash Develop)

/source/projects/notanks/flexSDK/src/com/efg/games/notanks/Level.as

Here is the complete code for the `Level.as` class:

```
package com.efg.games.notanks
{
/**
 * ...
 * @author Jeff Fulton
 */

    public class Level {
        public var backGroundMap:Array;
        public var spriteMap:Array;
        public var backGroundTile:int;
        public var enemyIntelligence:int;
        public var enemyShotSpeed:Number;
        public var ammoPickUp:int;
```

```
    public function Level() {

    }
  }
}
```

This is a simple base class that only defines the variables that will be needed to store all of the data for each game level. Let's take a look at each variable.

```
public var backGroundMap:Array;
```

The `backGroundMap` array will store the 2D array of level data we created in Mappy for the background layer (layer 0) for the game level.

```
public var spriteMap:Array;
```

The `spriteMap` array will store the 2D array of level data we created in Mappy for the sprite layer (layer 1) for the game level.

```
public var backGroundTile:int;
```

The `backGroundTile` variable is used to tell the game engine which tile on the tile sheet should be ignored when drawing the sprite layer. Normally, this will be tile 0. If you recall, Mappy used tile 0 as tile ID for the blank tiles on the sprite layer. We will use 0 in our game, but if you use a different level editor, you might need to change this value.

```
public var enemyIntelligence:int;
```

The `enemyIntellgence` value is a number from 0–100. It is used to tell the game engine how often (in percentages) that the enemy will make a random movement rather than follow the rules of the tile-base chase AI we will cover in the next chapter. The higher the number the more intelligent the enemy will be.

```
public var enemyShotSpeed:Number;
```

The `enemyShotSpeed` is the number of pixels that the enemy missiles will travel per frame tick. The greater this number the faster the enemy shots will travel.

The `ammoPickUp` variable is the amount of ammunition that will be added to the player's reserves when an ammunition pickup sprite is collected.

Creating the Level1 class

The class that will hold our level 1 data is called `Level1.as`. This file will be part of the No Tanks! package structure. It will be a subclass of the `Level` class with the variables assigned to specific values for our game level.

This is the path for the Flash IDE:

```
[source][projects][notanks][flashIDE][com][efg][games][notanks]Level1.as
```

And here's the one for the Flex SDK (using Flash Develop):

```
[source][projects][notanks][flexSDK][src][com][efg][games] [notanks]Level1.as
```

Here is the complete code for the `Level1.as` class:

```
package com.efg.games.notanks
{
    /**
     * ...
     * @author Jeff Fulton
     */
    public class Level1 extends Level {

        public function Level1() {
            backGroundTile = 23;
            enemyIntelligence = 60;
            enemyShotSpeed = 2;
            ammoPickUp = 20;
            backGroundMap = [
[26,24,25,0,26,26,26,26,26,0,0,26,26,26,26,26,0,24,25,26],
[27,0,0,0,0,0,0,0,0,0,0,0,0,0,0,0,0,0,0,27],
[29,0,28,0,0,0,24,25,0,24,25,0,24,25,0,0,0,27,0,29],
[27,0,28,0,27,0,0,0,0,0,0,0,0,0,0,27,0,29,0,27],
[29,0,0,0,29,0,0,30,0,0,0,0,31,0,0,29,0,0,0,29],
[0,0,28,0,26,0,0,31,0,0,0,0,31,0,0,26,0,26,0,0],
[0,0,0,0,0,0,0,0,31,0,0,0,0,31,0,26,0,0,0,0,0],
[26,26,26,0,0,26,0,30,30,30,30,30,30,0,0,0,0,26,26,26],
[0,0,0,26,0,0,0,0,0,0,0,28,0,0,0,0,26,0,0,0],
[0,0,0,0,26,0,0,27,0,27,0,27,0,28,0,26,0,0,0,0],
[27,0,0,0,27,0,0,29,0,29,0,29,0,28,0,27,0,0,0,27],
[29,0,0,0,29,0,0,0,0,0,0,0,0,0,0,29,0,0,0,29],
[27,0,0,0,0,26,0,28,0,28,0,28,28,0,26,0,0,0,0,27],
[29,0,0,0,0,0,0,0,0,0,0,0,0,0,0,0,0,0,0,29],
[26,24,25,0,0,26,26,26,26,0,0,26,26,26,26,0,0,24,25,26]
];

        spriteMap = [
[0,0,0,0,0,0,0,0,0,0,0,0,0,0,0,0,0,0,0,0],
[0,0,0,0,0,0,0,0,0,0,22,0,0,0,0,0,9,0,0,20,0],
[0,0,0,0,0,0,0,0,0,0,0,0,0,0,0,0,0,0,0,0,0],
[0,0,0,0,0,0,0,0,0,0,0,0,0,0,0,0,0,0,0,0,0],
[0,0,0,0,0,0,0,0,0,0,0,0,0,0,0,0,0,0,0,0,0],
[1,0,0,0,0,0,0,0,0,0,0,0,0,0,0,20,0,0,0,0,0],
[0,0,0,0,0,0,0,0,0,9,0,9,0,0,0,0,0,0,0,0,0],
[0,0,0,0,0,0,0,0,0,0,0,0,0,0,0,0,0,0,0,0,0],
[0,0,0,0,0,0,0,0,0,0,0,0,0,0,0,0,0,0,0,0,0],
[0,0,0,0,0,9,0,0,0,0,0,0,0,0,0,0,0,0,9,0],
[0,0,0,0,0,0,0,0,0,0,0,0,0,0,0,0,0,0,0,0,0],
[0,0,0,0,0,0,0,0,0,9,0,0,0,0,0,0,0,0,0,0,0],
[0,0,0,0,0,0,0,0,0,0,0,0,0,0,0,0,0,0,0,0,0],
[0,0,0,0,0,0,0,0,0,0,0,20,0,0,0,0,0,9,0,23,0],
[0,0,0,0,0,0,0,0,0,0,0,0,0,0,0,0,0,0,0,0]
];
        }
    }
}
```

As you can see from this class, we have simply filled in values for all of the variables in the Level base class (notice that Level1 extends level). We have also copied the 2D array data from the level1_back.as file that we exported from Mappy and assigned it to the backGroundMap array. We did a similar operation with the level1_sprites.as file we exported from Mappy. For this data, we assigned it to the spriteMap array variable.

Updating the New GameDemo.as file

Now that we have an actual tile sheet created, a Library to put it in, a class to hold its instance, and level data to draw from, we can start to look at actually putting it on the screen. To do this, we are going to go back to the GameDemo.as file and add some code to paint the background with the tiles from the Level1.as file

Here are the three main steps we must accomplish in the following code to finally paint out background on the screen:

1. We must parse the level data and put it into a 2D array.

2. We must paint the 2D array of background tiles to our out output display canvas.

3. We must add the canvas to the stage.

The class imports

Replace the entire class import section in GameDemo.as with this set of code:

```
package com.efg.games.notanks
{
    import flash.display.Sprite;
    import flash.display.Bitmap;
    import flash.display.BitmapData
    import flash.geom.Rectangle;
    import flash.geom.Point;
    import com.efg.framework.TileSheet;
```

Notice that we have added a few new classes that will be needed for the blitting operations. The geom and display package classes will do the bulk of the work there. Also notice that we have imported the com.efg.framework.TileSheet class we created earlier and saved into the framework package structure.

The variable definitions

Replace the entire variable definition section from original GameDemo.as with the following:

```
public class GameDemo extends Sprite{

    public static const TILE_WALL:int = 0;
    public static const TILE_MOVE:int = 1;
    public static const SPRITE_PLAYER:int = 2;
    public static const SPRITE_GOAL:int = 3;
    public static const SPRITE_AMMO:int = 4;
    public static const SPRITE_ENEMY:int = 5;
    public static const SPRITE_EXPLODE:int = 6;
    public static const SPRITE_MISSILE:int = 7;
```

```
        public static const SPRITE_LIVES:int = 8;

        private var playerFrames:Array;
        private var enemyFrames:Array;
        private var explodeFrames:Array;
        private var tileSheetData:Array;

        private var missileTiles:Array=[];
        private var explodeSmallTiles:Array;
        private var explodeLargeTiles:Array;
        private var ammoFrame:int;
        private var livesFrame:int;
        private var goalFrame:int;

        //the map definition
        private var tileWidth:int = 32;
        private var tileHeight:int = 32;
        private var mapRowCount:int = 15;
        private var mapColumnCount:int = 20;

        //levels
        private var level:int = 1;
        private var levelTileMap:Array;
        private var levelData:Level;
        private var levels:Array = [undefined,new Level1()];

        //full screen blit
        private var canvasBitmapData:BitmapData=new BitmapData(tileWidth * É
                mapColumnCount, tileHeight * mapRowCount, true, 0x00000000);
        private var canvasBitmap:Bitmap = new Bitmap(canvasBitmapData);

        private var blitPoint:Point = new Point();
        private var tileBlitRectangle:Rectangle = new Rectangle(0, 0, É
          tileWidth, tileHeight);

        //***** Flex *****
        private var tileSheet:TileSheet= new TileSheet(new É
                Library.TankSheetPng().bitmapData,tileWidth, tileHeight);
        //***** End Flex *****

        //***** Flash IDE *****
        //private var tileSheet:TileSheet = new TileSheet(new É
                    TankSheetPng(0,0), tileWidth, tileHeight);
        //***** End Flash IDE *****
```

If you are using the Flash IDE, you will want to comment out the Flex line above and uncomment the Flash line for instantiating the TileSheet instance.

Let's take a look a quick look at these variables. We will go into detail on their use very soon, but it won't hurt to discuss them briefly here.

These are the *map definition variables*:

```
//the map definition
private var tileWidth:int = 32;
private var tileHeight:int = 32;
private var mapRowCount:int = 15;
private var mapColumnCount:int = 20;
```

These variables define the width and height in tiles of the game screen. The tileWidth * mapColumnCount equals the width of the BitmapData canvas for the background tile map (32 × 20 = 640). The tileHeight * mapRowCount equals the height of the BitmapData canvas for the background tile map (32 × 15 = 480).

These are the *level data variables*:

```
private var level:int = 1;
private var levelTileMap:Array;
private var levelData:Level;
private var levels:Array = [undefined,new Level1()];
```

These are used by the game engine to determine which game level to display and which array to place the data into. The levelTileMap will hold the background set of tiles from our game Level1.as file. The levelData variable holds a reference to the current Level subclass represented by the level variable. The levels array holds a reference to all of the individual Level subclasses. We have only one for this game, Level1.as. Notice that we have added an undefined value in what would be index 0 in the levels array. We do not have a level 0 on our game, so we put this in as a placeholder. The current level's data will be accessed through a construct like this:

```
levelData=levels[level];
```

These are the *full-screen blit variables*:

```
//full screen blit
private var canvasBitmapData:BitmapData=new BitmapData(tileWidth * ↵
          mapColumnCount, tileHeight * mapRowCount, true, 0x00000000);
private var canvasBitmap:Bitmap = new Bitmap(canvasBitmapData);

private var blitPoint:Point = new Point();
private var tileBlitRectangle:Rectangle = new Rectangle(0, 0, tileWidth, ↵
          tileHeight);

//***** Flex *****
private var tileSheet:TileSheet= new TileSheet(new ↵
          Library.TankSheetPng().bitmapData,tileWidth, tileHeight);
//***** End Flex *****

//***** Flash IDE *****
//private var tileSheet:TileSheet = new TileSheet(new ↵
          TankSheetPng(0,0), tileWidth, tileHeight);
//***** End Flash IDE *****
```

These variables are used to display the background tiles for the level with blitting operations. The canvasBitmapData defines a BitmapData object that will hold the 20 × 15 set of painted tiles for the game TILE_MOVE and TILE_WALL tiles. This is what we call the **full-screen blit canvas**. The canvasBitmap is the actual display object that will be added to the stage display list.

The `blitPoint` is used in `copyPixels` blitting operations to specify the top-left (x,y) position to start the painting of a tile sheet tile onto the `canvasBitmap`. The `tileBlitRectangle` will be used to specify the top-left (x,y) position on the tile sheet to start copying the 32 × 32–pixel `Rectangle`. This `Rectangle` will be placed on the `canvasBitmap` at the `blitPoint`. You have seen the `tileSheet` variable before; we instantiate the `tileSheet` by passing it an instance of the library item `TankSheetPng` along with `width` and `height` for our tile.

The constructor

The new constructor adds in code to call some new functions.

```
public function GameDemo() {
    initTileSheetData();
    readBackGroundData();
    readSpriteData();
    drawLevelBackGround();
    addChild(canvasBitmap);
}
```

First, we will read the background data in from the `Level` instance. Next, we will call a stub version of the `readSpriteData` function. We will not be implementing this function in this chapter, but we want to make sure we point out that the sprite data is not read in when we read in the background data. We will next draw our background to the `canvasBitmapData` with the `drawLevelBackGround` function and finally add the `canvasBitmap` to the stage.

The readBackGroundData function

The `readBackGroundData` function is completely new. We will use it to read through our level data and create the 2D `levelTileMap` array.

```
private function readBackGroundData():void {
    levelTileMap = [];
    levelData = levels[level];
    levelTileMap = levelData.backGroundMap;
}
```

The `readBackGroundData` function is very simple. In Chapter 7, we will add code to read more of the level-specific variables from the `Level` class instance, but for now, we will keep it very simple. We first initialize the `levelTileMap` array by assigning it the shortcut [] value. Next, we place a reference to the current `Level` object into the `levelData` `Level` class instance. Finally, we simply assign the `levelTileMap` array to reference the `levelData.backGroundMap` array. That is all we need to do to start using the level data.

The readSpriteData function

The `readSpriteData` function is only a stub placeholder that we will fill in when we get to Chapter 7.

```
private function readSpriteData():void {
    //place holder for reading sprite data and placing sprites on the screen
}
```

The drawLevelBackGround function

The drawLevelBackGround function is the heart of the screen-based blit operation that we have been discussing throughout this chapter. Here is the full code for the function, followed by a lengthy discussion of the anatomy of the logic behind it:

```
private function drawLevelBackGround():void {
    canvasBitmapData.lock();
    var blitTile:int;
    for (var rowCtr:int=0;rowCtr<mapRowCount;rowCtr++) {
        for (var colCtr:int = 0; colCtr < mapColumnCount; colCtr++) {
            blitTile = levelTileMap[rowCtr][colCtr];

            tileBlitRectangle.x = int(blitTile % tileSheet.tilesPerRow) * tileWidth;
            tileBlitRectangle.y = int(blitTile / tileSheet.tilesPerRow) * tileHeight;

            blitPoint.x=colCtr*tileHeight;
            blitPoint.y = rowCtr * tileWidth;

            canvasBitmapData.copyPixels(tileSheet.sourceBitmapData, ↵
                        tileBlitRectangle, blitPoint);
        }
    }
    canvasBitmapData.unlock();
}
```

Organizing our game rendering

The background level tiles that make up the walls and road for the tanks to move on will use a full-screen blit and be placed on a BitmapData canvas called canvasBitmapData. The canvasBitmapData instance will be an attribute of a Bitmap object called canvasBitmap. Only the canvasBitmap will be added to the display list for our game tiles. The individual tiles will all be placed on to the canvasBitmapData with copyPixels operations that paint each tile onto the canvasBitmapData layer, not to individual Sprites or MovieClips. This is contrary to some popular methods, such as the following

- Placing a 2D array of MovieClips on the screen and using gotoAndStop to find the necessary frame for display.
- Using individual Sprite (or Bitmap) objects in a 2D grid on the screen and bitmaps (or even a tile sheet) for the display of each tile.

This function is used to blit the background tiles (the walkable and nonwalkable tiles) individually to the canvasBitmapData. Here is the definition of this variable from the variable definition section:

```
private var canvasBitmapData:BitmapData = new BitmapData(tilewidth * mapcols, ↵
                    tileheight * maprows, true, 0x00000000);
```

It is a BitmapData object the size of the game screen (640 × 480). It has a transparent background and is filled with black (although you cannot see it is as it is completely transparent). We could have chosen any color, but we like to standardize on the number 0x00000000 for all of our transparent BitmapData canvas initializations. The stream of eight consecutive zeros helps drive home the fact that this is a blank canvas. If we wanted to actually have a black canvas, we would change the first two bits of this 32-bit number to FF. For example, the number 0xFF000000 would be a completely opaque black background. The background layer will not change during level play, so it will be copied a single time to the canvasBitmapData.

The code uses a nested loop structure to first loop through the rows of the levelTileMap array, and inside that loop, it iterates through the columns in the array. Remember, this is opposite of the [x-axis], [y-axis] special coordinate point systems. We do this because the rows of the 2D array are the first subscript, and the columns are the second. Over the years, I have found it much easier to work with 2D array data in rows and then columns, following the natural way an array is accessed in Flash. In other words, I like to use [row][column] rather than trying to force in a [column][row] style system.

Let's go through the code necessary to copy the data from our tile sheet to the canvasBitmapData in detail. The following lines are the most important piece of information in this chapter:

```
blitTile = levelTileMap[rowCtr][colCtr];
tileBlitRectangle.x = int(blitTile % tileSheet.tilesPerRow) * tileWidth;
tileBlitRectangle.y = int(blitTile / tileSheet.tilesPerRow) * tileHeight;
blitPoint.x=colCtr*tileHeight;
blitPoint.y = rowCtr * tileWidth;
canvasBitmapData.copyPixels(tileSheet.sourceBitmapData,↵
                           tileBlitRectangle, blitPoint);
```

This first line assigns the blitTile variable to hold the tile id from for the current [row][column] cell in the level data. The id value corresponds to the array index in the single dimensional array of tiles from the sheet (tileSheetData).

The tileBlitRectangle defines a square portion of the tile sheet to copy pixels from the tile sheet.

The next two lines use a little math trick to find the starting x and y locations for the tile on the tile sheet (the tileBlitRectangle's top-left corner). Since the sheet is actually 2D (eight columns by four rows), and our array (tileSheetData) is only a single dimension, we need to use this trick.

The x value for the start of the tile to copy is the integer value (technically rounded down) of the *remainder* of the blitTile divided number of tiles in a row on the sheet. We use modulo (%) operator rather than the division (/) operator to find this remainder value and cast it as an integer.

The y value for the start of the tile to copy is the integer value (technically rounded down) of the blitTile value using divided by the number of tiles in a row on the tile sheet.

See Figure 6-12 for a diagram of this concept.

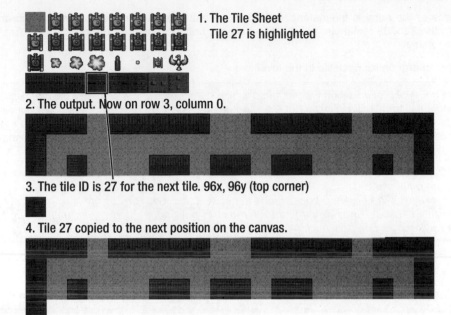

1. The Tile Sheet
   Tile 27 is highlighted

2. The output. Now on row 3, column 0.

3. The tile ID is 27 for the next tile. 96x, 96y (top corner)

4. Tile 27 copied to the next position on the canvas.

Figure 6-12. The anatomy of a tile sheet blit

So, what exactly is going on in Figure 6-12?

1. We see is our drawLevelBackground function in the middle of processing. It has copied two rows of data from the tile sheet to the canvasBitmapData based on the data in the levelTileMap 2D array.

2. The next tile to place is the first tile (tile 0) on the fourth row (row 3): levelTilemap[3][0] The row value is 3, and the column value is 0.

3. The blitTile variable is set to the contents of levelTilemap[3][0]. This is tile is 27 on our tile sheet.

4. Next, we need to find where to start copying from the tile sheet to get the 32 × 32–pixel square for that tile:

   - tileBlitRectangle.x=int(27 % 8)*32 or x= 3*32 = 96
   - tileBlitRectangle.y=int(27 / 8)*32 or y=3*32 = 96

   The location on our tile sheet to start copying is 96x, 96y. It's only a coincidence that they are the same value.

The blitPoint.x and blitPoint.y values set where the 32 × 32 set of pixels from the tile sheet will be placed on to the canvasBitmapData canvas; see Figure 6-13.

Finally, we copy the pixels from the tile sheet to background canvas:

```
backgroundBD.copyPixels(tilesheet.getsourcebitmap(),blitrectTile, blitpoint);
```

249

The source of the copy is the instance of the Tilesheet class we created to hold our library tile sheet. It's the 32 × 32 rectangle (tileBlitRectangle), and its location is the point (blitPoint) that we set previously.

We do this operation for each tile in the level.

> *Optimization! A big optimization we put into practice here was using a single Point class instance and a single Rectangle class instance. Creating objects is a very processor-intensive activity. By using a single instance of each of these two, we took up a little extra memory up front but saved a lot of processor in return. In the next chapter, we will be using these techniques to blit changes to the display objects on each frame and this optimization will come in very handy.*
>
> *The last thing you will notice is the canvasBitmapData.lock before the copyPixels operation and the canvasBitmapData.unlock after the copyPixels operation. This optimization will help in screen rendering. It allows the copyPixels operation to occur off screen. The lock tells all display objects that have this BitmapData as an attribute reference to not update themselves until the unlock is set. This will keep screen updates looking as smooth as possible.*

This is the final code for the chapter. If you type it all in, with no errors, and test move, build with Flash Develop/Flex, you will see the output shown in Figure 6-13.

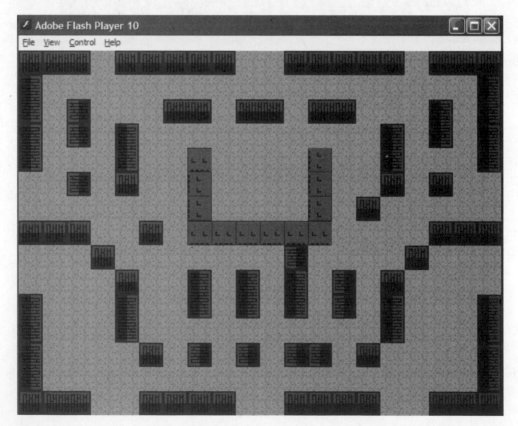

Figure 6-13. The output in Flash Develop

Summary

We covered quite a lot of ground in this chapter. You started by creating your own tile sheet and two-layer level using your drawing tool of choice and level editor. Next, we created a `TileSheet`, `Library`, and `Level` base classes and a `Level1` extension of the `Level` base class. All of those were used with our new `GameDemo.as` class to create the beginning of the No Tanks! game and to illustrate a full-screen blit. Along the way, we discussed various blitting screen display techniques and even took a look at some render profiling results.

By the end of the next chapter, we will have a fully working No Tanks! game. Keep reading, as there is more to learn about tile-based maze/chase games and blitting.

Chapter 7

Creating the Full No Tanks! Game

In the previous chapter, we covered a lot of ground in our No Tanks! game. We explored tile sheets, levels, XML, and blitting to a BitmapData canvas. In this chapter, we will finish up the game and cover some more advanced topics such as smooth tile-base grid movement and a "good enough" enemy chase AI. We are going to plow through a lot of code very quickly, and we'll need to be pretty efficient to fit all of the game logic and changes to the framework into the allotted space. So, hold on, read everything very carefully, and please check out the AS3 documentation provided by Adobe if you are stuck on any language concepts we skip over or only cover briefly.

We will have to cover a lot of ground fast to complete this game in the space allotted. To do so, we will cover some topics in detail, and only present the code and a brief description for others.

- Creating a BlitSprite class for game objects
- Extending the BlitSprite class for tile maze-based game logic
- Animating a Sprite with bitmap tiles
- Moving a the player and enemy around a user designed tile game level
- Creating basic chase AI using zones and logic
- Using line-of-site firing against the enemy player
- Using look-ahead variables for collision detection and movement
- Finishing off the game with sound and screens
- Modifying the framework for No Tanks!
- Extending the Library class

In the previous chapter, we started to create a file called GameDemo.as. We are going to continue modifying that file in the following sections until we have a complete game. The first thing you should do is open the GameDemo.as file in Flex, Flash Develop, or in the Flash IDE (along with the no_tanks.fla file for the IDE). We will eventually change the game file name from GameDemo.as to NoTanks.as and integrate it into the framework, but for now, you can leave it as is. Now that you've got the files open, let's get to work.

*In this chapter, we are going to take a unique approach to creating the final game code. We are going to start with the GameDemo.as file from Chapter 6 and add small pieces of code a little at a time that will build on one another. We call this building a game through **iteration**. There will be six iterations before we start the final section on completing the game. The result of each iteration will be a class file that we can compile and view to see the latest version of the game in progress. Before we get to the iterations, we will start with some theory on moving game characters on a 2D overhead tile-based grid.*

Tile-based movement theory

There are many ways to move game characters on the screen. As you saw in Chapter 6, we are creating a game that uses 32 × 32–pixel tiles to make up the game screen layout and the characters that will go on this screen.

Tile jumping

Tile jumping refers to a method employed by some early games' attempts to create tile-based maze/chase games. All of the characters in the game would jump from tile to tile on the grid instead of moving smoothly between the tiles. They didn't actually jump, of course, but their movement was limited to the center of each tile. So, each time the user pressed an arrow key, the on-screen character would simply move directly to the next tile (32 pixels at a time) in the direction specified. There was no fluid movement between the two screen positions, and it appeared to the player as if the game characters simply jumped to the next tile. There was no ability to move on the pixels in between the center positions on the tiles. Unless the animation is particularly well done (and even so), this type of movement is jarring to look at and is not particularly fun to control. The opposite of this type of tile-base maze movement would be in the classic Pac-Man game where the player seems to be able to fluidly move to any pixel on the screen. In any case, games that employed the tile-to-tile jumping scheme were actually solving two classic game programming problems:

- **System resource management**: The capabilities of the Flash Player (and early 8-bit systems) and the systems running it were limited enough to necessitate creating mostly simulated arcade games rather than real fast-action games.
- **Grid-based movement and logic**: Some grid-based movement is difficult to manage (especially turning corners) but can be made easier if the game characters make movement and logic decisions at the center of a tile.

For our No Tanks! game, we will employ a much smoother tile-to-tile movement style, much like the classic Pac-Man game. Even though the latest Flash Player and AS3 are pretty fast at rendering the screen and executing game logic, we will employ some of our own optimizations to make sure the game runs well. Also, the system we will use, smooth tile-to-tile movement, will look good to the user, play well, and allow us to use math and logic shortcuts associated with tile-to-tile grid-based movement.

Smooth tile-to-tile movement

Smooth tile-to-tile movement solves the ugly visual problems usually associated with tile jumping games but retains the programming convenience of using the center of a tile for grid-based movement logic. This allows for the game to appear to have free-flowing movement over a grid of tiles, as the game characters will move a specified number of pixels each frame tick until the center of the next time is reached. This system is a lot less limited than it seems, as it allows the player to reverse the character's direction at any time, even before the next tile center has been reached. We will not simply be playing an animation that shows the characters moving between the tiles, which would not allow for user interaction before the player stopped on the next tile and would make for an awkward game playing experience.

We will start by coding the movement of the main character on the level we created in Chapter 6. If you have not completed Chapter 6, it might be a good idea to look it over and download the final files from this book's web site.

The BlitSprite Class

The current GameDemo.as reads in the tile sheet and level data and then displays the level on the screen. There really isn't any game here yet, but it goes a long way toward getting us started. What we need now is a way to place sprites on the screen and control their look with a tile sheet. This class takes care of blitting from the tile sheet that represents the Sprite, allows tile sheet animation, and contains attributes necessary for controlling basic movement.

We will create the class as part of the reusable framework that was started in Chapter 2. The locations for the file in the framework will be as follows:

/source/classes/com/efg/framework/BlitSprite.as

Here is the complete code for the class:

```
package com.efg.framework
{
    import flash.display.Bitmap;
    import flash.display.BitmapData;
    import flash.display.Sprite;
    import flash.geom.Point;
    import flash.geom.Rectangle;

    /**
     * ...
     * @author Jeff Fulton
     */

    public class BlitSprite extends Sprite {
        private var bitmap:Bitmap;
        public var bitmapData:BitmapData;
        private var tileSheet:TileSheet;
        private var rect:Rectangle;
        private var point:Point;
        public var animationDelay:int=3;
        public var animationCount:int=0;
        public var animationLoop:Boolean=false;
        public var tileList:Array;
        public var currentTile:int;
        public var tileWidth:Number;
        public var tileHeight:Number;
        public var nextX:Number=0;
```

```
public var nextY:Number = 0;
public var dx:Number=0;
public var dy:Number = 0;
private var doCopyPixels:Boolean = false;
public var loopCounter:int = 0;
// counts the number of animation loops if useCounter is set to true;
public var useLoopCounter:Boolean = false;

public function BlitSprite(tileSheet:TileSheet, tileList:Array, firstFrame:int) {
    this.tileSheet = tileSheet;
    tileWidth = tileSheet.tileWidth;
    tileHeight = tileSheet.tileHeight;
    this.tileList = tileList;

    rect = new Rectangle(0, 0, tileWidth, tileHeight);
    point = new Point(0, 0);

    bitmapData = new BitmapData(tileWidth, tileHeight, true, 0x00000000);
    bitmap = new Bitmap(bitmapData);
    bitmap.x = -.5 * tileWidth;
    bitmap.y = -.5 * tileHeight;

    addChild(bitmap);
    currentTile = firstFrame;
    renderCurrentTile(true );
}

public function updateCurrentTile():void {

    if (animationLoop) {

        if (animationCount > animationDelay) {
            animationCount = 0;
            currentTile++;
            doCopyPixels = true;

            if (currentTile > tileList.length - 1) {
                currentTile = 0;
                if (useLoopCounter) loopCounter++;
            }

        }
        animationCount++;
    }
}

public function renderCurrentTile(forceCopyPixels:Boolean=false):void {

    if (forceCopyPixels) {
        doCopyPixels = true;
    }
```

```
    if (doCopyPixels) {
        bitmap.bitmapData.lock();

        rect.x=int(tileList[currentTile] % tileSheet.tilesPerRow)*tileWidth;
        rect.y=int(tileList[currentTile] / tileSheet.tilesPerRow)*tileHeight;

        bitmap.bitmapData.copyPixels(tileSheet.sourceBitmapData, rect, point);
        bitmap.bitmapData.unlock();
    }
    doCopyPixels = false;
}


public function dispose():void {
    bitmap.bitmapData.dispose();
    bitmap = null;
    rect = null;
    point = null;
    tileList = null;
    }
  }
}
```

The BlitSprite class is a basic building block of all of the game characters in the No Tanks! game. It is an extension of the built-in Sprite class, so we can utilize rotation and other features easily. It doesn't have a timeline, so we build our own way of animating characters by passing in an instance of our TileSheet class along with an array of tile ids and the id of the first tile to display in the list of tile ids. These tile ids will be used to reference tiles on the 8 × 4-tile sheet we created in Chapter 6. These tiles will be applied to the Bitmap object inside our BlitSprite instances by using the copyPixels method.

Animating with the BlitSprite class

We don't have the space to go into all the details (line by line) of the BlitSprite class so here are the essentials:

- The BlitSprite class requires a TileSheet instance passed to it. This will be stored in a private variable called tileSheet.
- It also requires an Array instance passed to it representing the list of tile sheet ids (a single-dimensional list in an array) that represent the sequence of frames for its animation. This is stored in the tileList array variable.
- It requires a frame value (firstFrame) passed to it that will be used to seed the currentTile public property.
- It contains a Bitmap (named bitmap) object that is centered on the origin of the Sprite (-.5* width, -.5*height). This enables the BlitSprite to rotate the Bitmap on its center axis when the BlitSprite itself is rotated.
- The Bitmap contains a BitmapData instance (named bitmapData) that will be used for blitting. Each time the look of the BlitSprite is to change to a new tile, the pixels are copied to the BitmapData from the TileSheet.

- The No Tanks! game class will call the `updateCurrentTile` function of the `BlitSprite` class on each frame tick.
- The `animationLoop` Boolean controls whether or not the `BlitSprite` should spend any cycles working to find a new tile for the `Sprite`. The `Player` and `Enemy` tanks don't want to animate their respective tank tracks when they are stationary, so in that instance, this variable will be set to `false`.
- The `animationCount` is used to count frames until the count is greater than the `animationDelay` variable. If it is greater, the `currentTile` value is updated to the next value in the `tileList` array. In this case, the `doCopyPixels` public attribute is set to `true`.
- The `renderCurrentTile` function is used to copy the new set of pixels to the `BitmapData` inside the `Bitmap` object. The No Tanks! game class will call this on each frame tick. If `true` is passed in, it will force the function to copy the current tile from the tile sheet.
- Next, the `doCopyPixels` Boolean value is evaluated. This is set in the `updateCurrentTile` function (or passed in as `true`). If it is `true`, then tile sheet pixels are copied from the `tilesheet` to the `bitmapData` inside the `bitmap` instance.
- We set the `bitmapData.lock` before the `copyPixels` and `bitmapData.unlock()` after. This is an optimization that will help with rendering speed. Essentially, when you do this, you are telling all objects that have the `BitmapData` instance as an attribute reference to *not* update themselves until the `unlock` is set. This smoothes out the animation and allows for the processor to not have to keep up with the `copyPixels` operation on all objects while the copy is being carried being carried out. After the `unlock` call, all of the pixel data is copied to the display objects.
- The `dispose` function is used to clean up the memory used by this object after it is deleted from the screen.

The TileByTileBlitSprite class

All of our game objects will use the `BlitSprite` class as a base class. Some of them though (the player and the enemy tanks) will use another class that is a subclass of the `BlitSprite` class. The `TileByTileBlitSprite` class is simply an extension of the `BlitSprite` class that contains some variables necessary for moving about the maze in a logical manner.

We will create the class as part of the reusable framework that was started in Chapter 2. The locations for the file in the framework will be as follows:

/source/classes/com/efg/framework/TileByTileBlitSprite.as

Here is the complete code for the class:

```
package com.efg.framework
{

    /**
     * ...
     * @author Jeff Fulton
     */
```

```
public class TileByTileBlitSprite extends BlitSprite {

    public var inTunnel:Boolean = false;
    public var currRow:int;
    public var currCol:int;
    public var nextRow:int;
    public var nextCol:int;

    public var moveDirectionsToTest:Array = [];

    public var missileDelay:Number = 100;
    public var missileTime:int;
    public var healthPoints:int;

    public var distinationX:Number;
    public var distinationY:Number;
    public var currDirection:int = 0;

    public var moveSpeed:Number = 2;
    public var currentRegion:int;

    public function TileByTileBlitSprite(tileSheet:TileSheet, tileList:Array, ↵
                    firstFrame:int) {
        super(tileSheet, tileList, firstFrame);
    }

    }

}
```

The TileByTileBlitSprite class very well could have just been part of the BlitSprite class, but by creating another class, we can make use of the BlitSprite class for non-tile-based games and without the slight overhead of the extra variables that would be unnecessary. Also, I added the healthPoints variable to this class because it is only needed for the player and enemy tanks. We will examine the use of all of these variables as we proceed through this chapter.

Moving the player character through the maze

We are going to create a system of movement for the player that will allow level designers the freedom to not worry about where they place tiles. By this, I mean we will have very few preset rules for creating a level. As long as a level contains TILE_WALL and TILE_MOVE tiles, a green Player tank, and a Goal, it should work without a problem. We won't set any other rules for level design. This will be similar to the methods employed by platform game engine designers.

Most classic versions of maze/chase games were created in such a way that preset math and logic were used to set the directions that a player or other character could move at intersections in the maze. This hard-coded information was used to simplify the math needed to turn the characters in the right directions and restrict allowable movement to the open corridors in the maze. You will see this type of logic coding if you Google Java and JavaScript versions of Pac-Man code. The classic Pac-Man game had only a single maze, so hard-coding movement logic made sense. We want our game engine to be extensible with as many different levels as possible, so we have chosen a different, more fluid method to code our movement logic.

The center tile trick

Since we are going to take a different approach than the old Pac-Man style, rather than create a maze level and then preset or hard-code allowable movement data into our maze, we are going to set up some ground rules for movement and let the game engine respond dynamically to the level design. We will do this by using a trick. The trick is to always evaluate movement logic when a character has reached the center of a tile. This concept works best with square tiles and tiles where the character sprites and the tiles are the same size. This might sound limiting, but this trick turns out to solve many problems with maze-based movement.

For example, if you have ever played Pac-Man, you will notice that that main hero cannot turn in any direction unless there is an open tile in that direction. This very important concept sets a ground rule for the movement and logic for the game. I don't know how Tōru Iwatani (the original Midway developer of Pac-Man) coded his movement, but we know how to mimic how he did it. The Pac-Man character cannot move into a space unless its entire body can move, but it doesn't need or use pixel-perfect collision detection. It uses tile-based collision detection. The game logic just needs to know what type of tile the next tile is and then it can evaluate if the character can move into that tile or not. The game doesn't need to check for the next tile when the character is not at the center of the current tile, because doing so would result in false positives and negatives as the character moves into the open space between the tiles or if the character is on two or more tiles at the same time.

Our game will go one step further and force our player character to stop at the center of each tile. You will see as we start to code and test the game elements that the player character will move in the direction indicated by pressing the arrows keys if the tile in the direction pressed is a TILE_WALK tile. The character will start to move and will continue to move on each subsequent frame tick until it has reached the center of the next tile and then stop. This will not be as limiting as it sounds, because if the user holds down a direction key (and there is an open space in the direction the player wants to move), the player will continue into that open space without stopping. This movement includes turning and going forward. Reversing direction is even smoother, as the player can reverse direction at any time, even before the center of the next tile is reached. This is slightly different than Pac-Man where the only time the player character stopped was when it hit a wall or corner and could not move any further.

The one caveat to doing this type of movement logic is that the number of pixels a character can move on each frame tick must be a number that divides evenly into the tile size. So, since we have 32 × 32 tiles, our game characters should move 1, 2, 4, 8, 16, or 32 pixels per frame. If they don't, they may never actually reach the center of a tile, and the logic will fail.

Adding the player (iteration 1)

We are now going to start by simply modifying the code to add the player to the screen in the GameDemo.as file, which is the first building block in our game. The player character will be a TileByTileBlitSprite instance. Let's start by adding some code to our variable definition section with all of the variables necessary to handle a player and movement for the player.

We are going to create this as a separate file called GameDemoIteration1.as.

Here's the path for the Flash IDE:

/source/projects/notanks/flashIDE/com/efg/games/notanks/GameDemoIteration1.as

And this one is for the Flex SDK (using Flash Develop):

```
/source/projects/notanks/flexSDK/src/com/efg/games/notanks/GameDemoIteration1.as
```

Changing the class name for iteration 1

We have a new file name for the game demonstration, so now we will need to change the class name to match. We will also need to change the name of the constructor function as follows. First, we will change the new class name.

```
public class GameDemoIteration1 extends Sprite
{
```

And then, we will change the constructor.

```
public function GameDemoIteration1() {
```

Adding the new framework classes to the import section

Here are the class imports needed to add the Framework functionality to this iteration:

```
// added iteration #1
import com.efg.framework.BlitSprite;
import com.efg.framework.TileByTileBlitSprite;
// end added iteration #1
```

Defining the iteration 1 variables

Add these variables to the variable definition section of the existing GameDemo.as file:

```
        //movement specific variables added in iteration #1
        public static const MOVE_UP:int = 0;
        public static const MOVE_DOWN:int = 1;
        public static const MOVE_LEFT:int = 2;
        public static const MOVE_RIGHT:int = 3;
        public static const MOVE_STOP:int = 4;
        //*** added iteration #1
        //player specific variables
        private var player:TileByTileBlitSprite;
        private var playerStartRow:int;
        private var playerStartCol:int;
        private var playerStarted:Boolean = false;
        private var playerInvincible:Boolean = true;
        private var playerInvincibleCountDown:Boolean = true;
        private var playerInvincibleWait:int = 100;
        private var playerInvincibleCount:int = 0;
        //*** end added iteration #1
```

Some of these variables, such as the ones controlling the invincibility of the player on restarts, will not be used yet, but they will come into play very soon.

Next, we will add some code in the constructor and create a few new functions that will be used later to handle interactions with the Main.as and framework classes. You will notice that we have moved everything from the constructor to a new init function and added a line to call init in the constructor. For this reason, the entire section is listed. You should delete the previous constructor function and replace it with all of the following code:

```
public function GameDemoIteration1() {
    init();
}

private function init():void {

    initTileSheetData();
    player = new TileByTileBlitSprite(tileSheet, playerFrames, 0);
    readBackGroundData();
    drawLevelBackGround()
    readSpriteData();
    addChild(canvasBitmap);
    newGame();
}

private function newGame():void {
    newLevel();
}

private function newLevel():void {
    restartPlayer();
    addChild(player);
}

private function restartPlayer(afterDeath:Boolean=false):void {
    trace("restart player");
    player.visible = true;
    player.currCol = playerStartCol;
    player.currRow = playerStartRow;
    player.x=(playerStartCol * tileWidth)+(.5*tileWidth);
    player.y = (playerStartRow * tileHeight) + (.5 * tileHeight);
    player.nextX = player.x;
    player.nextY = player.y;
    player.currentDirection = MOVE_UP;
    playerStarted = true;
    playerInvincible = true;
    playerInvincibleCountDown = true;
    playerInvincibleCount = 0;
}
```

You will notice that we are starting to simulate an actual game loop (new game, new level, restarts, and so on) with some stub functions that will later interact with the framework classes. Since there is no framework to deal with yet, we simply call the classes in order—init calls newGame, and newGame calls newLevel.

The init function for iteration 1

The new init function is basically a copy of the contents of the previous constructor function. We have added one line though:

```
player = new TileByTileBlitSprite(tileSheet, playerFrames, 0);
```

This line needs to exist in this exact spot. The player cannot be instantiated until the `playerFrames` is populated with the list of frames needed to animate the player. If you recall from Chapter 6, this is assigned in the `initTileSheet` function. Also, the `readSpriteData` function cannot execute unless the player has been created. A runtime error will occur if the player sprite is not created before the `readSpriteData` function executes, because the game engine needs to place the player on the screen and cannot do so unless it has been created.

The iteration 1 restartPlayer function

This function is used to restart the player for a new level or after death. We don't need the local `afterDeath` variable yet, but it will be necessary later because when the player actually dies, the new tank that replaces the old one will be given maximum `healthPoints` and some starting ammunition. When a player starts a new level without dying, these attributes are not affected. So, to use the same function for both occurrences, the `afterDeath` Boolean is passed in.

These six lines are the most important to discuss in setting up the player for a player for restart:

```
player.currCol = playerStartCol;
player.currRow = playerStartRow;
player.x=(playerStartCol * tileWidth)+(.5*tileWidth);
player.y = (playerStartRow * tileHeight) + (.5 * tileHeight);
player.nextX = player.x;
player.nextY = player.y;
```

The first thing we do here is to calculate the current row and column on the game grid that the player resides in. We can do this at the beginning of a level (or on restart after death) because we know the player is in the center of the current tile.

Next, we set the x and y coordinates for the player using the `player.currCol` and `player.currRow` variables we just set. Here, we find the x value of the top-left corner of the tile that the player needs to be in; `playerStartCol * tileWidth` is this location. We do a similar operation for the top-left corner of the y position. The player tank will not sit in this exact position though. Notice that the player's position is set an additional 0.5 multiplied by the `tileWidth` for x and 0.5 times the `tileHeight` for y. This offset is needed because the `Bitmap` inside the `BlitSprite` that represents the player has been moved to −0.5 multiplied by the width and −0.5 multiplied by the height center it on the registration point of the Sprite. If we don't reposition it further to the right and down, it would be 10 pixels off in left and down directions.

The `nextX` and `nextY` variables are set to be equal to the current x any y values for the player. These are important because they will be used in the update portion of the game loop. We will update the `nextX` and `nextY` values, then do collision detection based on them (as well as grid based logic movement evaluation), and finally set x and y to equal `nextX` and `nextY` for the render portion of the game loop. We will examine these in detail in a later iteration through the game code.

The readSpriteData function

The `readSpriteData` function was merely an empty stub in `GameDemo.as`. We are now going to fill it out with the necessary code to loop through the sprite data and place the player on the game screen:

```
private function readSpriteData():void {

    var tileNum:int;
    var spriteMap:Array = levelData.spriteMap;
```

```
for (var rowCtr:int = 0; rowCtr < mapRowCount; rowCtr++) {
    for (var colCtr:int = 0; colCtr < mapColumnCount; colCtr++) {
        tileNum = spriteMap[rowCtr][colCtr];

        switch(tileSheetData[tileNum]) {

            case SPRITE_PLAYER:
                player.animationLoop = false;
                playerStartRow= rowCtr;
                playerStartCol= colCtr;
                player.currRow = rowCtr;
                player.currCol = colCtr;
                player.currentDirection = MOVE_STOP;
                break;
        }
    }
}
```

This function is used to parse the 2D array of data in the `levelData.spriteMap` variable. As you might recall, this variable was assigned `readBackGroundData` function in the original `GameDemo.as` file. Here is a breakdown of what is happening in this function.

We will loop through this data using a nested loop structure. A nested loop structure contains an outer loop that will iterate though the rows in our sprite data, and inside each row, we will iterate through each column. This inside loop through the column data for each row is the **nested loop**.

1. We create a local variable called `tileNum`. This will hold the current tile id for the `[row][column]` on our sprite layer when we iterate through the level sprite data.

2. We assign the `spriteMap` class variable the value of the `levelData.spriteMap` contents.

3. We start our outer loop using the local `rowCtr` variable (starting at 0) while it is less than the `mapRowCount` amount (15).

4. The inner, or nested, loop through each column in the current row begins by using the `colCtr` variable to start at 0 and loop through all of the columns while it is less than `mapColumnCount` (20).

5. The current `tileNum` is the value in the array at `[rowCtr][colCtr]`.

6. That `tileNum` is plugged into the `tileSheetData` single dimensional array to find the type of sprite that is in that location. If you recall, the `initTileSheetData` function parsed the data in the `TileSheeDataXML.as` file as assigned a constant to the value of each sprite in the `tileSheetData` array.

7. We start a `switch:case` statement based on the constant.

8. The player variable is assigned with its starting values.

The player begins with its `animationLoop` variable set to false. The tank is stopped (`player.currDir=MOVE_STOP`) when the level begins. We don't want the tank treads to animate while the tank is stopped, so we set this to `false`.

We also set the player.startRow and player.startCol. These are used to place the player at the beginning of the level and when it is destroyed and a new player tank is added to the game screen.

The player.currCol and player.currRow represent the tile the player is currently on and will be used in many game calculations in the following iterations.

Testing iteration 1

Using your development environment of choice, test out the current iteration of the GameDemoIteration1.as file. This will need to be set as the document or always-compile file of your FLA or project. If you run this version, you should see something similar a game screen similar to Figure 7-1. Your level and or player tank placement might vary based on your own creation.

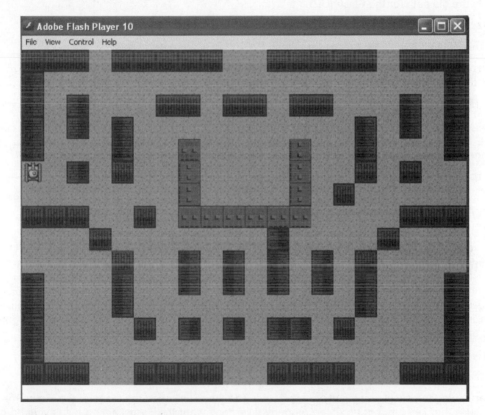

Figure 7-1. Iteration 1's game screen

THE ESSENTIAL GUIDE TO FLASH GAMES

Moving the player using key logic (iteration 2)

Now we are going to tackle moving the player about the maze and going through tunnels (they warp to the other side if the tile on the opposite side is an open one. Since we have not yet added this game to the framework, the first task we must tackle is setting up a simple ENTER_FRAME event for our game loop. This will be replaced later in the chapter when we integrate with the framework.

We will be changing the name of the file to GameDemoIteration2.as. You are not required to do this unless you want to have a keepsake of each iteration in the chapter. If you do create a new file, make sure the class name and constructor are changed to correspond to the new name. If you are using the IDE, you will need to make sure the document class attribute references the new class name.

This is the file path for the Flash IDE:

/source/projects/notanks/flashIDE/com/efg/games/notanks/GameDemoIteration2.as

And this one is for the Flex SDK (using Flash Develop):

/source/projects/notanks/flexSDK/src/com/efg/games/notanks/GameDemoIteration2.as

Changing the class name for iteration 2

We have a new file name for the game demonstration, so now, we will need to change the class name to match. We will also need to change the name of the constructor function. First, we will change the class name.

```
public class GameDemoIteration2 extends Sprite
{
```

Next, we will change the constructor.

```
    public function GameDemoIteration2() {
```

Adding a simple placeholder game timer

For the simple placeholder game timer, we will use a standard ENTER_FRAME event. Our game is being designed to eventually use the Main.as game timer, so all of this code will be replaced upon integration with the Main class. For now though, it can be used to demonstrate all game logic except starting new levels and new player tanks after they have been destroyed.

First, we must import the event package in import section of the code:

```
    import flash.events.*;
```

We are going to accept key input into our game. The game will need the focus of the Flash Player to ensure that key input is accepted properly. We don't want the focusRect to display when our game Sprite has focus, so we make sure it is turned off.

In the init function, you should add this line:

```
this.focusRect = false;
```

Next, we have to find a place to add in the temporary event listener. We have chosen to do it inside the restartPlayer function. Only a portion of the function is listed in this section. The bold code needs to be added. The ellipses represent all of the other code in the function, so we don't need to waste space repeating it; we will continue to use this formatting throughout this chapter.

```
private function restartPlayer(afterDeath:Boolean=false):void {

    player.visible = true;
    player.currCol = playerStartCol;
    playerInvincibleCountDown = true;
    playerInvincibleCount = 0;

    . . .

    /this is as good a place as any for now
    addEventListener(Event.ENTER_FRAME, runGame, false,0,true);

}
```

Next, we will add in the new very basic game loop function. Create the following new function:

```
public function runGame(e:Event):void {
    trace("run game");
}
```

If you test this code, you should see this output:

```
run game
run game
run game
run game
```

The output will continue repeatedly. So, we have the runGame function being called repeatedly, but we don't have it doing anything yet. Let's bite off moving the player about the maze in simple chunks.

Switching player move state with the arrow keys

Before we get to the actual movement of the player, we need to set up all of the necessary functions to control changing the state. The move state of the player is contained in the BlitSprite class instance attribute, currentDirection. The currentDirection variable can be set to be one of five states, which are the GameDemoInteration2.as constants: MOVE_UP, MOVE_DOWN, MOVE_LEFT, MOVE_RIGHT, and MOVE_STOP. The currentDirection variable doesn't actually represent the rotation of the tank (that is held in the Sprite.rotation property). For this reason, we can use STOP as a direction. A TileByTileBlitSprite can have a currentDirection of MOVE_STOP and a rotation of 0 (facing up). Also (for instance), a TileByTileBlitSprite can have a rotation of 90 (turned to the right) and a currentDirection of MOVE_RIGHT. But, a TileByTileBlitSprite cannot have a rotation of -90 (left) and a currentDirection of anything but MOVE_LEFT (for instance). These two properties, currentDirection and rotation, are used in conjunction to facilitate moving about the maze.

In a nutshell, unless the currentDirection is MOVE_STOP the currentDirection and rotation must match.

We are now going to add some functions and code to the game file in order to be able to check if the desired movement is valid and used to actually change the rotation of the player. Once you have put in the following code changes, it will appear that we are only rotating the player, but we will be setting the groundwork for moving the player about the maze.

Adding the keypress logic

The first code change is very simple. We need to add a variable to hold keypress values. Keypresses will be handled with simple key up and down events. When a key is pressed down, the Boolean true will be placed in an array called keyPressList (at the array index location represented by the ASCII key value) when a key up event is encountered, a false will be placed at the array index location. So, for instance, when the user presses down, the key code number 37 is sent to the event listener for key down events. That listener will then place true in the keyPressList[37] location. Let's check out the code changes necessary to get this working.

First, in the variable definition section, add in a line for the keyPressList variable:

```
//iteration#2 variables, moving the player around the maze
private var keyPressList:Array = [];
```

The only changes to the newGame function are the addition of KEY_DOWN and KEY_UP event listeners:

```
private function newGame():void {

    stage.addEventListener(KeyboardEvent.KEY_DOWN,keyDownListener);
    stage.addEventListener(KeyboardEvent.KEY_UP, keyUpListener);

    newLevel();
}
```

These two completely new listener functions must be added to the file:

```
private function keyDownListener(e:KeyboardEvent):void {

    trace(e.keyCode);

    keyPressList[e.keyCode]=true;
}

private function keyUpListener(e:KeyboardEvent):void {

    keyPressList[e.keyCode]=false;

}
```

Testing iteration 2

You will want to comment out the trace("run game"); statement in the runGame function to be able to see the key events in the output. If you run the code and press each of the arrow keys, you will see output like this:

```
38
40
39
37
```

The 38, 40, 39, and 37 represent pressing each of the arrow keys.

Updating the move states for player movement (iteration 3)

Now, we are going to start adding in quite a few new functions to handle the actual movement logic. First, let's take a look at the constant variables that we will use to control the current move state of the player. We are going to change to a new class name for this iteration.

As usual, we'll provide you with the file path for the Flash IDE:

/source/projects/notanks/flashIDE/com/efg/games/notanks/GameDemoIteration3.as

and for the Flex SDK (using Flash Develop):

/source/projects/notanks/flexSDK/src/com/efg/games/notanks/GameDemoIteration3.as

Changing the class name for iteration 3

We have a new file name for the game demonstration, so now, we will need to change the class name to match. We will also need to change the name of the constructor function. As before, we first change the class name.

```
public class GameDemoIteration3 extends Sprite
{
```

Next, we modify the constructor name.

```
    public function GameDemoIteration3() {
```

Adding the move state constants

The following states were already added to the variable definition section in iteration 1, but we have not discussed them much:

```
//movement specific variables
public static const MOVE_UP:int - 0;
public static const MOVE_DOWN:int = 1;
public static const MOVE_LEFT:int = 2;
public static const MOVE_RIGHT:int = 3;
public static const MOVE_STOP:int = 4;
```

We will use these states when evaluating the current and next directions for the game characters. We assign them as constants to make them easier to remember than strings or straight integers. Plus, if you are using an advanced editor (such as Flash Develop, Flex Builder, Flash Builder, or the CS5 IDE), constant variables show up in the code hinting to make them very easy to use.

Changing the runGame function for iteration 3

Now, we will add in some code to the runGame function to check the keyPressList array for the various movement directions on each frame tick:

```
    public function runGame(e:Event):void {
        if (playerStarted) {
            checkInput();
        }
    }
```

As you can see, we only want to run the `checkInput` function when `playerStarted` is set to true. This way, we don't evaluate keypresses for the player during level transitions and other time when we don't want the player to move on the screen.

Updating the checkInput function

The `checkInput` function is the heart of the code that sets, evaluates, and puts into motion changes to the `rotation` and `currentDirection` attributes of the player. Here is the code listing. We will point out the major concepts after you have examined (and hopefully typed in) all of this code. Note that some of the code is commented out; you should add these lines but leave them commented out for now. This code will be implemented later to play sounds and fire player missiles. Some `trace` statements are commented out also. They can be useful for debugging. We will be removing the comment designations as we progress through the iterations.

```
private function checkInput():void {
    //var playSound:Boolean = false;
    var lastDirection:int = player.currentDirection;

    if (keyPressList[38] && player.inTunnel==false) {
        if (checkTile(MOVE_UP, player )) {
            if (player.currentDirection == MOVE_UP || player.currentDirection ↵
            == MOVE_DOWN || player.currentDirection == MOVE_STOP  ) {

                switchMovement(MOVE_UP, player );
                //playSound = true;

            }else if (checkCenterTile( player)) {
                switchMovement(MOVE_UP, player );
                //playSound = true;
            }
        }else{
            //trace("can't move up");
        }
    }

    if (keyPressList[40] && player.inTunnel == false) {
        if (checkTile(MOVE_DOWN, player )) {
            if (player.currentDirection == MOVE_DOWN || player.currentDirection ↵
            == MOVE_UP || player.currentDirection == MOVE_STOP) {

                switchMovement(MOVE_DOWN, player );
                //playSound = true;

            }else if (checkCenterTile(player)) {

                switchMovement(MOVE_DOWN, player );
                //playSound = true;

            }
        }else {
            //trace("can't move down");
        }
    }
```

```
    if (keyPressList[39] && player.inTunnel==false) {
        if (checkTile(MOVE_RIGHT, player )) {
            if (player.currentDirection == MOVE_RIGHT || player.currentDirection
            == MOVE_LEFT || player.currentDirection == MOVE_STOP) {

                switchMovement(MOVE_RIGHT, player );
                //playSound = true;

            }else if (checkCenterTile( player)) {

                switchMovement(MOVE_RIGHT, player );
                //playSound = true;

            }
        }else {
            //trace("can't move right");
        }
    }

    if (keyPressList[37] && player.inTunnel==false) {
        if (checkTile(MOVE_LEFT,player )) {
            if (player.currentDirection == MOVE_LEFT || player.currentDirection
            == MOVE_RIGHT || player.currentDirection == MOVE_STOP) {

                switchMovement(MOVE_LEFT, player );
                //playSound = true;

            }else if (checkCenterTile(player)) {

                switchMovement(MOVE_LEFT, player );
                //playSound = true;
            }
        }else {
            //trace("can't move left");
        }
    }


    if (keyPressList[32]&& player.inTunnel==false) {
        //if (ammo >0) firePlayerMissile();
    }

    //if (lastDirection == MOVE_STOP && playSound) {
    //dispatchEvent(new CustomEventSound(CustomEventSound.PLAY_SOUND,
      Main.SOUND_PLAYER_MOVE, false, 1, 0));
    //}
}
```

There are many methods to do tile-based collision checking. We will implement a set of logic here that is very specific to this game type. It would not (for instance) be suitable for a free-moving overhead driving game. Luckily, we cover that topic in Chapter 10.

These are the major points you need to know about the `checkInput` function:

- The game does not accept player key input if the player tank is currently moving through a tunnel. This greatly simplifies the code that handles movement when the player is off the screen (in a tunnel). The `inTunnel` attribute of the `TileByTileBlitSprite` class is used in this evaluation. When the player leaves the screen and goes into a tunnel, this will be set to `true`.

- The `checkTile` function is used to check if the next tile the player is trying to move to is a valid `TILE_MOVE` tile (see Chapter 6 for the difference between `TILE_WALL` and `TILE_MOVE`).

- If the `checkTile` function returns `true` for the desired move direction, more evaluations are made. These evaluations mostly hinge on whether the player is trying to turn. Turning is the most complicated procedure in this type of movement structure, because the player should only be able to turn into an open space.

- If the direction to move is the same as the current direction the player is moving in, or the exact opposite direction, or if the player is stopped, the move is valid and the `switchMovement` function is called.

- If the direction to move is *not* the same as the current direction, is not the opposite of the current direction, or the player is not stopped, we must evaluate further. This means the player is trying to turn. The player will only be allowed to make the turn from the center of the current tile. This situation is handled with a call to the `checkCenterTile` function.

> *I coded the movement in this game to mimic a few of the attributes of Pac-Mac that I wanted to try out. In Pac-Man, the player cannot turn in a direction unless the next tile in that direction is a TILE_WALK tile. Some might think that this means the player tank cannot rotate to free itself when stuck in a corner. This assumption would be a false. Just like Pac-Man, the tank cannot get stuck in any corners because the player can always just press arrow for the opposite direction of movement with out having to rotate to that position.*

Adding the checkTile function

The `checkTile` function has a single purpose: to evaluate whether or not a `TileByTileBlitSprite` instance can legally move into a tile. It does this by first evaluating what the next tile will be and then checking the tile number in the `tileSheetData` array to see if it is a `TILE_MOVE` or `TILE_WALL` tile. The function accepts a direction represented by the integer value, `direction`, and an instance of the `TileByTileByTileSprite` class represented by the `object` variable.

```
private function checkTile(direction:int, object:TileByTileBlitSprite):Boolean {

    var row:int = object.currRow;
    var col:int = object.currCol;

    switch(direction) {
        case MOVE_UP:
            row--;
            if (row <0) {
                row = mapRowCount-1;
            }
```

```
            break;

    case MOVE_DOWN:
        row++;
        if (row == mapRowCount) {
            row = 0;
        }
        break;

    case MOVE_LEFT:
        col--;
        if (col <0) {
            col = mapColumnCount - 1;
        }
        break;

    case MOVE_RIGHT:
        col++;
        if (col == mapColumnCount) {
            col = 0;
        }
        break;
    }

    if (tileSheetData[levelTileMap[row][col]] == TILE_MOVE) {
        //trace("can move");
        return true;
    }else {
        //trace("can't move");
        return false;
    }
}
```

These are the major points you need to know about the checkTile function:

- The checkTile function runs a switch:case on the direction passed in.
- The first thing it does is set its local row and col variables to equal the currRow and currCol values from the object (the player in this case).
- Based on the direction the player is trying to go, the col or row value will either be incremented or decremented by one as follows:
    - **Left**: col--
    - **Right**: col++
    - **Up**: row --
    - **Down**: row++
- If the new value for the row or column happens to be off screen (a tunnel perhaps), the tile col or row value is set to the value on the opposite side of the game screen.
- After the switch:case statement, the tileSheetData array is evaluated. It plugs the row and col values into the 2D array of level tiles, levelTileMap, to get a single number representing the tile from the tile sheet (tileSheetData) on the level map. If that tile is a TILE_MOVE tile, true is returned by the function. If not, false is returned.

Adding the checkCenterTile function

The checkCenterTile function simply takes the passed in TileByTileBlitSprite instance and evaluates whether or not it is in the center of the current tile. If it is, it sends back true; if not, it sends back false.

```
private function checkCenterTile( object:TileByTileBlitSprite):Boolean {
    var xCenter:int = (object.currCol * tileWidth) + (.5 * tileWidth);
    var yCenter:int= (object.currRow * tileHeight) + (.5 * tileHeight);

    if (object.x == xCenter && object.y == yCenter) {
        //trace("in center tile");
        return true;

    }else {

        //trace("not in center tile");
        return false;
    }
}
```

The x and y values for a tile represent the top left-hand corner of the tile. To find the current x and y values, we multiply the currCol by the tileWidth and the currRow by the tileHeight. Then, we add half the tile width to the x value and half the tileheight to the y value. This calculates the xCenter and yCenter values, which are then checked against the x and y values for our object. The game objects are offset from the center of the tiles because they are centered around the midpoint of the Sprite holder. If they were not, we would have to add half the tileWidth and tileHeight to the x and y values of the object also.

Adding the switchMovement function

The switchMovement function takes in the direction variable as a parameter to represent the direction that object is going to move in. It also takes in a TileByTileBlitSprite reference as the object parameter variable. Based on the passed-in direction, the function simply sets properties of the object to match the new direction. Here is the code for the functions:

```
private function switchMovement(direction:int, object:TileByTileBlitSprite):void{
    switch(direction) {
        case MOVE_UP:
            //trace("move up");
            object.rotation = 0;
            object.dx = 0;
            object.dy = -1;
            object.currentDirection = MOVE_UP;
            object.animationLoop = true;
            break;

        case MOVE_DOWN:
            //trace("move down");
            object.rotation = 180;
            object.dx = 0;
            object.dy = 1;
            object.currentDirection = MOVE_DOWN;
            object.animationLoop = true;
            break;
```

```
                    case MOVE_LEFT:
                        //trace("move left");
                        object.currentDirection = MOVE_LEFT;
                        object.rotation = -90;
                        object.dx = -1;
                        object.dy = 0;
                        object.animationLoop = true;
                        break;

                    case MOVE_RIGHT:
                        //trace("move right");
                        object.currentDirection = MOVE_RIGHT;
                        object.rotation = 90;
                        object.dx = 1;
                        object.dy = 0;
                        object.animationLoop = true;
                        break;

                    case MOVE_STOP:
                        //trace("move stop");
                        object.currentDirection = MOVE_STOP;
                        object.dx = 0;
                        object.dy = 0;
                        object.animationLoop = false;
                        break;
                }

            object.nextRow = object.currRow + object.dy;
            object.nextCol = object.currCol + object.dx;
        }
```

These are the major points you need to know about the switchMovement function:

- Based on the passed in direction value, it sets the currentDirection of the passed in TileByTileBlitSprite object property to the matching constant move state variable.
- Based on the direction variable, it sets the rotation of the object to match.
- Based on the direction variable, the delta x (dx) and delta y (dy) attributes of the object are changed. These are used in the update function to move the object along the vertical or horizontal axis of the game play field. Because we only move up, down, right, or left, one will always be 1 (or −1), and the other will always be 0 unless the object is stopped. In this case, they will both be 0.
- If the object is moving in a direction (not stopped), its object.animationLoop property is set to true.
- If the object is stopped, the object.animationLoop property is set to false.
- Finally, the nextRow and nextCol attributes of the object are set.

Testing iteration 3

When you run this iteration, you will see that the tank can be rotated to any open position but not to one where a TILE_WALL tile is the next tile. In Figure 7-2, you will see the tank pointing down. It cannot point up, but it can point left and right. Don't worry if this looks limiting. When we add the tank movement in the next iteration, you will find the movement to be very well suited to this style of game.

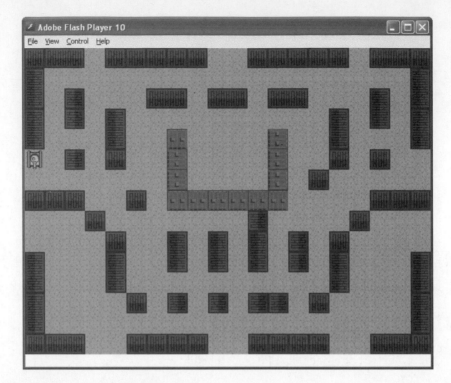

Figure 7-2. Iteration 3's game screen

Updating and rendering player movement (iteration 4)

Next, we are going to add the update and render functions to the game code. When we are done with these, the player Tank will smoothly navigate the maze, moving from tile center to tile center, negotiating tunnels like an expert tank commander.

In this section, we will be creating the updating and rendering portions of our game and including only the code needed for the player. We will also update the variable definition section and the runGame function to add in the new calls to the update and render functions.

Let's get started right away. Once again, we are going to change to a new class name for this iteration.

This is the path for our new class in the Flash IDE:

/source/projects/notanks/flashIDE/com/efg/games/notanks/GameDemoIteration4.as

And this is the path in the Flex SDK (using Flash Develop):

/source/projects/notanks/flexSDK/src/com/efg/games/notanks/GameDemoIteration4.as

Changing the class name for iteration 4

We have a new file name for the game demonstration, so now, we will need to change the class name to match. We will also need to change the name of the constructor function. First, we change the class name.

```
public class GameDemoIteration4 extends Sprite
{
```

And as before, we next change the constructor.

```
    public function GameDemoIteration4() {
```

Updating the variable definitions for iteration 4

We need to add some variables to indicate the extreme top, bottom, left, and right of our game screen. These are needed because all of the game characters are actually positioned at 16-pixel tileWidth and tileHeight offsets. These offsets were added to compensate the Bitmap inside the BlitSprite being positioned at -.5*tileWidth for x and -.5*tileWidth for y (to center it over the Sprite's registration point). We also set up some variables to hold the maximum and minimum positions (xMax, ymax, xMin, and yMin) for the game characters inside the tunnels.

For instance, the actual horizontal minimum is 16 (not 0) because the player and enemy tanks are offset −16 pixels on the BlitSprite to allow them to rotate around the center. If we used 0 as the minimum horizontal movement, half the tank would actually be off the screen at x=0 for the top left corner of the tank. The maximum horizontal movement location is 624 (624 + 16 = 640) for the same reason. The vertical maximum and minimum movement locations are similar.

The tunnel movement locations indicate how far off the screen to move the object before it should appear on the opposite side of the screen.

Add the following variables to the variable definition section of the GameDemoIteration4.as file:

```
//** added iteration #4
private var xMin:int = 16;
private var yMin:int = 16;
private var xMax:int = 624;
private var yMax:int = 464;
private var xTunnelMin:int = -16;
private var yTunnelMin:int = -16;
private var xTunnelMax:int = 656;
private var yTunnelMax:int = 496;
//** end iteration #4
```

You will soon see how these numbers will be used to confine the maximum and minimum movements for the game objects and allow the tunnel warping effects to look the same on all sides of the game level.

Updating the runGame function for iteration 4

We need to add two simple function calls to the runGame function to call the soon to be defined update and render functions. Here is what the entire new runGame function should look like:

```
public function runGame(e:Event):void {
    if (playerStarted) {
    checkInput();
    }
    //*** added iteration #4
    update();
    render();
    //** end added iteration #4
}
```

Adding the update function

The update function's primary task is to update the nextX and nextY attributes of the player (and other game moving objects). Once updated, these two variables will eventually be used in collision detection (not implemented until a later iteration).

Here is the full code for this iteration's update function. We'll cover the main points of the function after you have taken a look (and hopefully typed it in).

```
private function update():void {

    //*** added iteration #4
    player.nextX = player.x + player.dx*player.moveSpeed;
    player.nextY = player.y + player.dy * player.moveSpeed;

    if (player.y <yMin || player.y>yMax || player.x<xMin || player.x >xMax){
        player.inTunnel = true;
    }else {
        player.inTunnel = false;
    }

    if (player.inTunnel) {

        switch(player.currentDirection) {

            case MOVE_UP:
                if (player.nextY == yTunnelMin){
                    player.nextY=yTunnelMax
                }else if (player.nextY == yMax) {
                    player.inTunnel = false;
                }
                break;

            case MOVE_DOWN:
                if (player.nextY == yTunnelMax){
                    player.nextY = yTunnelMin;
                }else if (player.nextY == yMin) {
                    player.inTunnel = false;
                }
                break;

            case MOVE_LEFT:
                if (player.nextX == xTunnelMin){
                    player.nextX = xTunnelMax;
                }else if (player.nextX == xMax) {
```

```
                    player.inTunnel = false;
                }
                break;

            case MOVE_RIGHT:
                if (player.nextX == xTunnelMax) {
                    player.nextX = xTunnelMin;
                }else if (player.nextX == xMin) {
                    player.inTunnel = false;
                }
                break;

            case MOVE_STOP:
                trace("stopped");
                break;
        }
    }
    player.currRow = player.nextY / tileWidth;
    player.currCol = player.nextX / tileHeight;

    player.updateCurrentTile();
    //*** end added iteration #4
}
```

These are the major points you need to know about the update function:

- The nextX and nextY properties of the player object are updated by adding the dx and dy values multiplied by the moveSpeed of the object. The player.moveSpeed value is 2. It should be noted that the tile width and height must be evenly divisible by the moveSpeed of any object that when we are trying to detect the center of a tile. The moveSpeed value is set to 2 by default in the BlitSprite class, but it can be set to 1, 2, 4, 8, 16, and 32. 1, 2, 4, and 8 will have the best results and the most playable control for the character. *Do not* use an odd number other than 1, or the game objects may never detect the center of the tile.

- If you have played a poor implementation of a Pac-Man style game or even an emulated version with poor input controls, you will find that it is very easy to overshoot a tunnel when you actually want to turn. The control scheme we have implemented here goes to great lengths to ensure that this lack of control does not occur. We actually stop the player's forward movement when the character reaches the center of a tile unless a key is held down to move the character in a valid direction. If the player presses an arrow to move in a direction to turn, the turn will occur right away when the center is reached.

> *If we were making a Pac-Man style game, where the player does not stop at the center of each tile, we would just need to eliminate the swtitchMovement(MOVE_STOP) function call in the render function.*

- The bulk of the update code occurs if the player is in a tunnel, because once the player has moved off the screen, we need to take control of the character and force it to the other side. At the end of this iteration, you will notice that once you enter a tunnel, you cannot turn around until you have made it to the other side of the tunnel. It happens very fast, and the player will not notice this trick, but using it lets us detect when the player enters and leaves the tunnel and allows for the smooth animation into the tunnel and out on the other side.

- Whether or not the player is in a tunnel, we always set the `player.currRow` and `player.currCol` to the updated values based on the `nextX` and `nextY` attributes.

- The last thing we do is to call the `player.updateCurrentTile` function. Recall this function from the discussion of the `BlitSprite` class? If not, take a look at it again. If the `player.animationLoop` Boolean is set to `true`, the code looks to update the `currentTile` attribute if the `animationDelay` (three frames) has been reached. If it the tile is to be changed, the `doCopyPixels` Boolean variable is set to `true`. If not, it remains `false`.

Adding the render function

The `render` function takes care of three very important tasks, the most important of which is calling the `renderCurrentTile` function of the player object. Here is the full text of the `render` function for this iteration:

```
private function render():void {
    player.x = player.nextX;
    player.y = player.nextY;

    if (checkCenterTile(player)) {

        if (!player.inTunnel) {
            switchMovement(MOVE_STOP, player);
            //setCurrentRegion(player);
        }
    }

    player.renderCurrentTile();

}
```

These are the major points you need to know about the render function:

- The function will eventually be called after the `checkCollisions` function (not implemented yet). After collisions are checked against the `nextX` and `nextY` values, the actual x and y values of the `BlitSprite` object are updated and reflected directly on the game screen.

- The next task the `render` function undertakes is to check to see if the player is in the center of the current tile. This will only work for 32 × 32 tiles if the `moveSpeed` attribute of the tile is set to 1, 2, 4, 8, 16, or 32.

- If the tank character is in the center of the current tile but not in a tunnel, it is stopped. If the character is not in the center of the current tile, it does not stop. If the player holds down a key to move in a valid direction and the center of the tile is reached, the stop will not be noticeable, and the player tank will continue to move on the next frame.

- The last thing we do is to call the `player.renderCurrentTile` function. Recall this function from the discussion of the `BlitSprite` class too? If not, take a look at it again. If the `player.doCopyPixels` Boolean is set to `true`, the tank tracks will animate by copying the corresponding pixels from the `tileSheet` to the `bitmapData` attribute of the `bitmap` object inside the `BlitSprite` instance (in this case, the player).

- Notice that we have the `setCurrentRegion` function call commented out. We will be using this soon.

Testing iteration 4

When you run this iteration, you will find that the player tank can travel tile by tile smoothly around the screen and enter and exit tunnels on the other side (see Figure 7-3 for a screen shot of this iteration). Notice that the tank will not appear to stop if you hold down the movement keys while it moves between tiles. Also, if the tank is moving up and you want it to move into an open tunnel to the left (for example), you must take your finger off of the up key and press the left key. The tank will smoothly turn without stopping.

We have now completed the bulk of the code for moving game characters. The enemy tank code will be very similar. We will take a look at that briefly and go into the "good enough" enemy Tank AI in the next set of iterations.

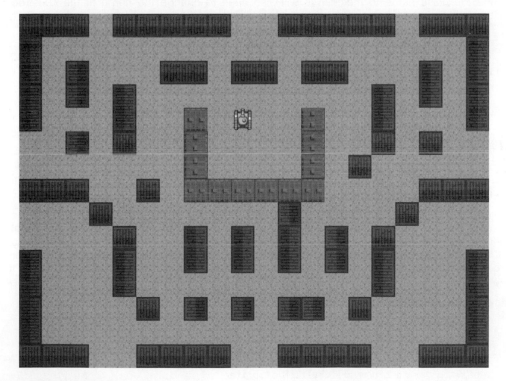

Figure 7-3. Iteration 4's game screen

Adding and moving enemy tanks (iteration 5)

The enemy tanks have one job—destroy the player tank. We will create our game logic for the tanks in a manner similar to the player tank. One difference will be that the enemy tanks will have some moderately smart AI code that will at least make them a moderate challenge against a human opponent.

In this iteration, we will be reorganizing the game a little to get closer to the final version. This means reordering and moving some of the current code and adding in code to place the enemy tanks on the screen.

Once again, we are going to change to a new class name for this iteration.

In the Flash IDE, this is the file path:

/source/projects/notanks/flashIDE/com/efg/games/notanks/GameDemoIteration5.as

And in the Flex SDK (using Flash Develop), it's this one:

/source/projects/notanks/flexSDK/src/com/efg/games/notanks/GameDemoIteration5.as

Changing the class name for iteration 5

We once again have a new file name for the game demonstration, so now, we will need to change the class name to match. We will also need to change the name of the constructor function. We first change the class name

```
public class GameDemoIteration5 extends Sprite
{
```

and then change the constructor name:

```
    public function GameDemoIteration5() {
```

Let's look at the changes to the variable definition section for this iteration.

Updating the variable definitions for iteration 5

There are a few variables we need to add to this iteration for the enemy tanks to be successfully added to the game screen. Also, we are going to add some variables that will contain region information for the game screen.

Regions will be discussed in detail when we get to the enemy AI portion of the code, but for now, just note that we have broken the game screen up into four regions. The regions are roughly made up the tiles that make up the TOP_LEFT, TOP RIGHT, BOTTOM LEFT, and BOTTOM RIGHT portions of the level map. These will be used to trigger enemy movement. If the player is in the same screen region as an enemy tank (or tanks), then the enemy tank (or tanks) will start to chase the player (more on this later in the section called "Chasing the player").

Add these variables to the variable definition section of the game code:

```
    //** added in iteration #5
     private var regions:Array;
     private var tempRegion:Object;
     private var enemyList:Array;
     private var tempEnemy:TileByTileBlitSprite;

     //end iteration #5
```

Updating the init, newGame, and newLevel functions

The changes to these functions for iteration 5 are all about structure and modifying the game code so it better resembles the code in the final version integrated with the Main class and the game framework. Please copy over these functions entirely:

```
private function newGame():void {

    //** changed in iteration #5
    setRegions();
    stage.addEventListener(KeyboardEvent.KEY_DOWN,keyDownListener);
    stage.addEventListener(KeyboardEvent.KEY_UP, keyUpListener);\
    addChild(canvasBitmap);
    newLevel();
    //** end changed in iteration #5

}

private function init():void {
    this.focusRect = true;
    initTileSheetData();
    newGame();
}

private function newLevel():void {
    //** changed in iteration #5
    enemyList = [];
    player = new TileByTileBlitSprite(tileSheet, playerFrames, 0);
    readBackGroundData();
    readSpriteData();
    drawLevelBackGround();
    restartPlayer();
    addChild(player);
    //** end changed in iteration #5
}
```

One change of note is the setRegions function call in the newGame function. We will examine that function next. It breaks up the game screen into four logical regions used for enemy AI chase logic. You have seen the rest of the code in these functions before. We have only reordered it to make it more compatible with the framework. We have also added a new line that resets the enemyList array back to the default empty [ ] setting. We will do this at the start of each level to ensure we have a clean, new array to store the enemy for the level.

Adding the setRegions function

We have broken up the tiles for the game level screen into the following four logical regions:

- The top-left region starts at column 0, row 0 and ends at column 9, row 7.
- The top-right region starts at column 10, row 0 and ends at column 19, row 7.
- The bottom-left region starts at column 0, row 8 and ends at column 9, row 14.
- The bottom-right region starts at column 10, row 8 and ends at column 19, row 14.

See Figure 7-4 for a closer view of the regions.

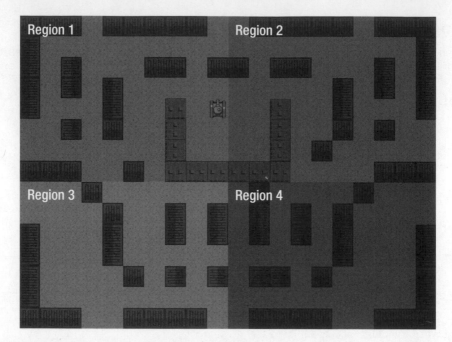

Figure 7-4. Iteration 5's regions depicted with different shaded areas

As Figure 7-4 shows, since we only have 15 vertical tiles (an odd number), we had to make the top region eight tiles high and the bottom seven tiles high. We could have done it a different way, but we chose this for ease of use. The horizontal length (ten tiles each) of the left and right regions is identical because we have 20 tiles, an even number.

Now, let's take a look at two functions that are needed for the regions. The first, setRegions, is used to create and populate the regions array. The second, setCurrentRegion, calculates the current region for an object. Type these into your GameDemoIteratio5.as file just as they are.

```
//** added in iteration #5
    private function setRegions():void {
        regions = [];

        //top left region
        var tempRegion:Object = { col1:0, row1:0, col2:9, row2:7 };
        regions.push(tempRegion);

        //top right region region
        tempRegion = { col1:10, row1:0, col2:19, row2:7 };
        regions.push(tempRegion);

        //bottom left region region
        tempRegion = { col1:0, row1:8, col2:9, row2:14 };
        regions.push(tempRegion);

        //bot right region region
        tempRegion = { col1:10, row1:8, col2:19, row2:14 };
```

```
      regions.push(tempRegion);
   }


   private function setCurrentRegion(object:TileByTileBlitSprite):void {

      var regionLength:int = regions.length - 1;

      for (var regionCtr:int = 0; regionCtr <= regionLength; regionCtr++) {
         tempRegion = regions[regionCtr];
         if (object.currCol >= tempRegion.col1 && ↵
            object.currCol <= tempRegion.col2 && ↵
            object.currRow >= tempRegion.row1 && ↵
            object.currRow <= tempRegion.row2) {

               object.currentRegion = regionCtr;

         }
      }
   }//** end added in iteration #5
```

The setCurrentRegion function takes a TileByTileBlitSprite in as a parameter called object. Using the currCol and currRow attributes of the object, it loops through the four regions in the regions array to find which region the object currently is in. The object's currentRegion attribute is changed to the detected region number.

Changing the readSpriteData function

We now need to modify the readSpriteData function to create new enemy tanks and add them to the enemyTanks array. In the existing switch:case statement inside the readSpriteData function, you will need to add a case for the enemy tanks. Add the following code below the case SPRITE_PLAYER code. We have included the SPRITE_PLAYER case for reference. It should match what you already have in the GameDemoIteration5.as file.

```
         case SPRITE_PLAYER:
            player.animationLoop = false;
            playerStartRow= rowCtr;
            playerStartCol= colCtr;
            player.currRow = rowCtr;
            player.currCol = colCtr;
            player.currentDirection = MOVE_STOP;
            break;

      //** added in iteration #5

      case SPRITE_ENEMY:

         tempEnemy = new TileByTileBlitSprite(tileSheet, enemyFrames, 0);

         tempEnemy.x=(colCtr * tileWidth)+(.5*tileWidth);
         tempEnemy.y = (rowCtr * tileHeight) + (.5 * tileHeight);

         tempEnemy.currRow = rowCtr;
         tempEnemy.currCol = colCtr;

         setCurrentRegion(tempEnemy);
```

```
            tempEnemy.currentDirection = MOVE_STOP;
            tempEnemy.animationLoop = false;

            addChild(tempEnemy);
            enemyList.push(tempEnemy);

            break;
            //** end added in iteration #5
```

Testing iteration 5

When you test this iteration, you should see all of the enemy tanks placed on the screen, as shown in Figure 7-5.

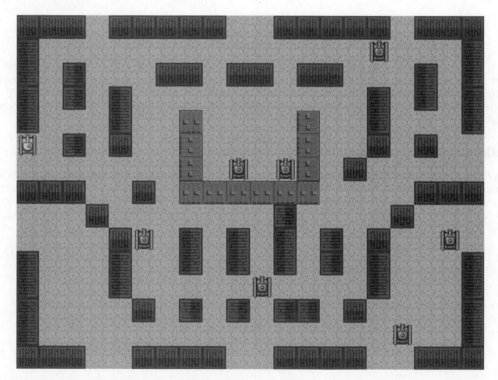

Figure 7-5. Iteration 5's game screen with tanks

Allowing enemy tank movement with the AI (iteration 6)

Now we are getting somewhere! The enemy tanks are on the screen, and we must get them to chase the player. One thing we have left out of the code so far is the player tank setting its own region. Once we have done that, we can add AI and movement code to the enemy tanks so they will start to chase the player tank if it is in the same region as an enemy tank (or tanks).

Once again, we are going to change to a new class name for this iteration.

This is the Flash IDE path:

/source/projects/notanks/flashIDE/com/efg/games/notanks/GameDemoIteration6.as

And this is for the Flex SDK (using Flash Develop):

/source/projects/notanks/flexSDK/src/com/efg/games/notanks/GameDemoIteration6.as

Changing the class name for iteration 6

We have a new file name for the game demonstration, so now, we will need to change the class name to match. We will also need to change the name of the constructor function. First, we again modify the class name.

```
public class GameDemoIteration6 extends Sprite
{
```

Then, we modify the constructor.

```
    public function GameDemoIteration6() {
```

Making additions to the restartPlayer function

First, we need to add a line to the restartPlayer function. You only need to add in the following bold code; the other code should already be in the function and is listed for reference:

```
        playerInvincibleCount = 0;

        //** added iteration 6
        setCurrentRegion(player);
        //** end added iteration 6

        //this is as good a place as any for now
        addEventListener(Event.ENTER_FRAME, runGame, false,0,true);
```

Next, we will look at the changes to the render function for setting the currentRegion attribute of the player. The line we need was already added to the render function. We have a comment mark in front of it though. Now it is time to remove the comment from the line.

```
        if (!player.inTunnel) {
            switchMovement(MOVESTOP, player);
            //*** uncommented in iteration #6
            setCurrentRegion(player);
            //*** end uncommented in iteration #6
            //once player gets to center, check the enemy chase AI
        }
```

Modifying the update and render functions for enemy tanks

Enemy tanks are updated in the same manner as the player. They can move about the maze in the same manner as the player and even utilize the warp tunnel off the sides, top, and bottom of the game screen. To render the enemy tanks, we first update the nextX and nextY values. Next, if the tank is in a tunnel, we check to see if it is out of the tunnel. Finally, we update the currRow and currCol attributes and call the updateTile function of the enemy tank. We do this to each enemy tank by looping through the enemyTanks array.

This is *not* a complete rewrite of the update function. You should add this code in the current update function under the existing section for the player rendering that we have already placed into the function. Here are the additions to the update function that will handle enemy tanks:

```
//** added iteration #6
var enemyLength:int = enemyList.length-1;
for (var ctr:int = enemyLength; ctr >= 0; ctr--) {
    tempEnemy = enemyList[ctr];

    tempEnemy.nextX = tempEnemy.x + tempEnemy.dx*tempEnemy.moveSpeed;
    tempEnemy.nextY = tempEnemy.y + tempEnemy.dy * tempEnemy.moveSpeed;

    //check to see is enemy off side of screen then set in tunnel
    if (tempEnemy.y <yMin || tempEnemy.y>yMax || ↵
     tempEnemy.x<xMin || tempEnemy.x >xMax){
        tempEnemy.inTunnel = true;
    }else {
        tempEnemy.inTunnel = false;
    }

    if (tempEnemy.inTunnel) {
        switch(tempEnemy.currentDirection) {

            case MOVE_UP:
                if (tempEnemy.nextY == yTunnelMin){
                    tempEnemy.nextY=yTunnelMax
                }else if (tempEnemy.nextY == yMax) {
                    tempEnemy.inTunnel = false;
                }
                break;

            case MOVE_DOWN:
                if (tempEnemy.nextY == yTunnelMax){
                    tempEnemy.nextY = yTunnelMin;
                }else if (tempEnemy.nextY == yMin) {
                    tempEnemy.inTunnel = false;
                }
                break;

            case MOVE_LEFT:
                if (tempEnemy.nextX == xTunnelMin){
                    tempEnemy.nextX = xTunnelMax;
                }else if (player.nextX == xMax) {
                    tempEnemy.inTunnel = false;
                }
                break;

            case MOVE_RIGHT:
                if (tempEnemy.nextX == xTunnelMax) {
                    tempEnemy.nextX = xTunnelMin;
                }else if (player.nextX == xMin) {
                    tempEnemy.inTunnel = false;
```

```
        }
        break;

    case MOVE_STOP:
        //trace("stopped");
        break;
    }
}

tempEnemy.currRow = tempEnemy.nextY / tileWidth;
tempEnemy.currCol = tempEnemy.nextX / tileHeight;
tempEnemy.updateCurrentTile();
}
//** end added iteration #6
```

Remember that this code needs to be added to the existing update function. We have not shown the final close bracket (}) to finish off the function because it is already in the existing code.

As you can see, the code to update the enemy and move them through tunnels is identical to the code for the player.

Here are the additions to the render function that will handle enemy tanks. The render function code for the enemy tanks is very similar to the render function code for the player. The biggest difference is the inclusion of two function calls that perform artificial intelligence operations for the enemy tanks. These two calls are chaseObject and the checkLineOfSight functions. Add this code to the pre-existing render function under the code for the player render logic:

```
//** added in iteration #6
var enemyLength:int = enemyList.length-1;
for (var ctr:int = enemyLength; ctr >= 0; ctr--) {

    tempEnemy = enemyList[ctr];
    tempEnemy.x = tempEnemy.nextX;
    tempEnemy.y = tempEnemy.nextY;
    setCurrentRegion(tempEnemy);

    if (checkCenterTile(tempEnemy)) {

        //trace("enemy @ center tile");
        if (!tempEnemy.inTunnel) {
            switchMovement(MOVE_STOP, tempEnemy);
            chaseObject(player, tempEnemy);
        }
    }

    //should enemy fire
    checkLineOfSight(player, tempEnemy);

    tempEnemy.renderCurrentTile();
}
    //** end added in iteration #6
```

Again, we have not shown the final } for the function, because it should already exist in the code.

Adding new functions for enemy tank AI

Two new functions will be added next that attempt to make the enemy tanks appear somewhat intelligent. We have not added every bit of conceivable AI to the enemy tanks, just enough to make them a small challenge. We call this "good-enough AI." Once you see how it works, it can be modified and extended to make the enemy tanks even smarter.

Chasing the player

We want the enemy tanks to chase the player tank if they are in the same region. We will accomplish this individually, for each enemy tank, by calculating the number of tiles an enemy tank is from the player tank. The difference in tiles left or right will be called the horizontalDiff. The difference in tiles up and down will be called the verticalDiff. See Figure 7-6 for a situational example.

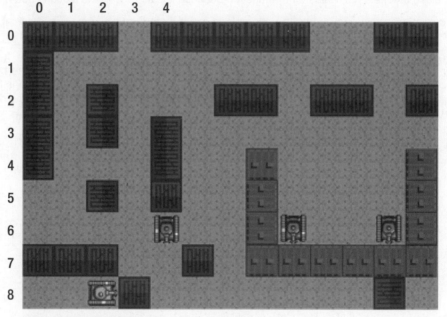

Prey at [row 8] [colum 2]
Predator at [row 6] [column 4]
Horizontal difference = 2 (4-2=3)
Vertical difference = -2 (6-8=-2)

Figure 7-6. Chase example

We will create a function called chaseObject that can be reused in other games that employ a tile-based structure. This function takes two parameters (TileByTileBlitSptite instances). The first object will be the prey object and the second will be the predator. The predator will chase the prey if they are in the same region. If they are in the same region, we attempt to create a list of possible moves for the predator. The list of possible moves will be prioritized using the direction the predator must move to find the prey and the distance between the two objects. We check the horizontal difference in tile locations and store it in the `horizontalDiff` variable and the vertical difference with the `vericalDiff` variable.

We will use the absolute value Math function to compare the `horizontalDiff` and the `verticalDiff`. We want the predator to move in the direction where the number of tiles between the player and the tank is the lowest One problem crops up when we try to compare directions, because we can't adequately compare negative values that result from the simple compare math against positive values. For instance, here are the steps the code needs to take for the example comparison in Figure 7-6:

1. The prey is in horizontal column 2 and vertical row 8.

2. The predator is at horizontal column 4 and vertical row 6.

3. `predator.currCol` minus `prey.currCol` equals 2.

4. If the prey's vertical row is 8 and the `preditor`'s is 6, then `pred.currRow` minus `prey.currRow` equals –2.

5. The difference really is simply 2 in both directions. The negative number results from the order in which we do the subtraction.

When we compare these to see which is smaller (the direction where the prey is closest to the predator), we must use the `Math.abs` (absolute value) function to ensure we are comparing the numbers properly. We do this because –2 will always be less than 2 unless we compare with the absolute value function, which ignores the sign of the integer. In looking at tile location differences, 2 and –2 are equivalent. Both indicate the same distance difference between predator and prey. Again, we only care about the number of tiles difference between the locations of the sprite; we don't care about the sign of the result of the difference calculation. The negative would cause this function to not work half the time.

When we have selected to move horizontally or vertically, we then need to choose which direction (left or right for horizontal and up or down for vertical) for the enemy tank to move.

First, we'll take a look at the code and then we'll discuss the major points from the function.

The chaseObject function

Here's the code for the `chaseObject` function:

```
private function chaseObject(prey:TileByTileBlitSprite, ↵
                predator:TileByTileBlitSprite):void {

    //trace("chase");

    if (prey.currentRegion == predator.currentRegion) {
        moveDirectionsToTest = [];
        var horizontalDiff:int = predator.currCol - prey.currCol;
        var verticalDiff:int = predator.currRow - prey.currRow;

        if (Math.abs(verticalDiff) < Math.abs(horizontalDiff)) {
            if (verticalDiff >0) {
                //trace("AI UP");
                moveDirectionsToTest.push(MOVE_UP);
                moveDirectionsToTest.push(MOVE_DOWN);
```

```
        }else if (verticalDiff < 0) {
        //trace("AI DOWN");
            moveDirectionsToTest.push(MOVE_DOWN);
            moveDirectionsToTest.push(MOVE_UP);

        }

        if (horizontalDiff > 0) {
            //trace("AI LEFT");
            moveDirectionsToTest.push(MOVE_LEFT);
            moveDirectionsToTest.push(MOVE_RIGHT);

        }else if (horizontalDiff < 0) {
            //trace("AI RIGHT");
            moveDirectionsToTest.push(MOVE_RIGHT);
            moveDirectionsToTest.push(MOVE_LEFT);
        }
    }

    if (Math.abs(horizontalDiff) < Math.abs(verticalDiff)) {
        if (horizontalDiff >0) {
            //trace("AI LEFT");
            moveDirectionsToTest.push(MOVE_LEFT);
            moveDirectionsToTest.push(MOVE_RIGHT);

        }else if (horizontalDiff < 0) {
            //trace("AI DOWN");
            moveDirectionsToTest.push(MOVE_RIGHT);
            moveDirectionsToTest.push(MOVE_LEFT);
        }

        if (verticalDiff > 0) {
            //trace("AI UP");
            moveDirectionsToTest.push(MOVE_UP);
            moveDirectionsToTest.push(MOVE_DOWN);

        }else if (verticalDiff < 0) {
            //trace("AI DOWN");
            moveDirectionsToTest.push(MOVE_DOWN);
            moveDirectionsToTest.push(MOVE_UP);
        }
    }


    //make an educated guess
    if (Math.abs(horizontalDiff) == Math.abs(verticalDiff)) {
        trace("AI Random");
        if (int(Math.random() * 2) == 0) {
            //vertical
            if (verticalDiff >0) {
                //trace("AI UP");

                moveDirectionsToTest.push(MOVE_UP);
                moveDirectionsToTest.push(MOVE_DOWN);
            }else if (verticalDiff < 0) {
```

```
                    //trace("AI DOWN");

                    moveDirectionsToTest.push(MOVE_DOWN);
                    moveDirectionsToTest.push(MOVE_UP);
                }
        }else {
            //horizontal
            if (horizontalDiff >0) {
                //trace("AI LEFT");

                moveDirectionsToTest.push(MOVE_LEFT);
                moveDirectionsToTest.push(MOVE_RIGHT);

            }else if (horizontalDiff < 0) {
                //trace("AI DOWN");

                moveDirectionsToTest.push(MOVE_RIGHT);
                moveDirectionsToTest.push(MOVE_LEFT);
            }
        }
    }

    if (horizontalDiff == 0 && verticalDiff == 0) {
        //trace("AI STOP");
        moveDirectionsToTest = [MOVE_STOP];
    }

    //as a final move for all, push in a MOVE_STOP
    moveDirectionsToTest.push(MOVE_STOP);

    //moveDirectionsToTest should now have a list of moves in it.
//loop though those, check them and set the dx and dy of the enemy.

    var moveFound:Boolean = false;
    var movePtr:int = 0;
    var move:int;

    while (!moveFound) {
        move = moveDirectionsToTest[movePtr];

        if (move==MOVE_UP && predator.inTunnel==false) {

            if (checkTile(MOVE_UP, predator)) {

                switchMovement(MOVE_UP, predator );
                moveFound = true;
            }
        }

        if (move==MOVE_DOWN && predator.inTunnel==false) {
//trace("player.currentDirection=" + player.currentDirection);
            if (checkTile(MOVE_DOWN, predator)) {

                switchMovement(MOVE_DOWN, predator );
```

```
                        moveFound = true;
                    }
                }

                if (move==MOVE_RIGHT && predator.inTunnel==false) {
                    if (checkTile(MOVE_RIGHT, predator )) {

                        switchMovement(MOVE_RIGHT, predator );
                        moveFound = true;
                    }
                }

                if (move==MOVE_LEFT && predator.inTunnel==false) {
                    if (checkTile(MOVE_LEFT,predator )) {

                        switchMovement(MOVE_LEFT, predator );
                        moveFound = true;
                    }
                }

                if (move==MOVE_STOP && predator.inTunnel==false) {
                    switchMovement(MOVE_STOP, predator );
                    moveFound = true;
                }

                movePtr++;
                if (movePtr == moveDirectionsToTest.length) {
                    switchMovement(MOVE_STOP, predator );
                    moveFound = true;
                }
            }
        }
    }
}
```

These are main points in the chaseObject function:

1. To begin, this function takes two parameters, both TileByTileBlitSprites. The first is the prey, and the second is the predator. The predator will chase the prey if they are in the same region.

2. The first section of the function searches for directions to fill up the moveDirectionsToTest array. This array of moves will be used in the second part of the function to find a direction to move in that is not blocked by a wall.

3. The horizontalDiff and verticalDiff local variables calculate the horizontal and vertical difference (in tiles) between the predator and the prey.

4. The two sets of if statements compare the absolute value (to compensate for negative values) of verticalDiff and horizontalDiff values, so we can determine in which direction the predator is closer to the prey. All we care about is which (verticalDiff or horizontalDiff) is a lower number.

5. The first set of if statements is for the vertical direction (to determine if the verticalDiff is less than the horizontalDiff). If verticalDiff is less than 0, the prey is above (up from) from the predator. If the verticalDiff is greater than 0, the prey is below (down from) the predator.

   If up is the shortest direction, we push MOVE_UP and then MOVE_DOWN for the up direction. If down is the shortest direction, we push MOVE_DOWN then MOVE_UP for the down direction.

   Why do we do this? This is where the "good enough AI" comes in. We want to give the predator a series of moves to test. The goal is to have the enemy tanks find at least one valid move (or stop) on each frame tick that they are in the center of a tile. We know that we really want the predator to move up, but if a wall blocks that direction, we want it to move down.

   So far, if the verticalDiff is smaller than the horizontalDiff, we will want to move in a vertical direction. If the verticalDiff is greater than 0, we want the predator to move up. If the predator cannot move up, we will have it try to move down as the next best choice.

6. The next task the code does is look to see what horizontal move to add to the moveDirectionsToTest array. The first two directions will already be MOVE_UP and MOVE_DOWN (not necessarily in that order), so to fill out the moveDirectionsToTest array, we look to see if horizontalDiff is greater or less than 0. MOVE_LEFT and MOVE_RIGHT are added based on this test.

7. The second set of if statements tests if horizontalDiff is less than verticalDiff. This occurs when the predator is closer to the prey in the horizontal direction rather than the vertical direction. These work exactly the same when the verticalDiff is less than the horizontalDiff, but prioritize horizontal movement over vertical movement.

8. If horizontalDiff and verticalDiff both equal 0 (), the predator is on top of the prey, and the predator doesn't move at all.

9. If the absolute value of horizontalDiff equals the absolute value if verticalDiff, we simply choose a direction based on a random value and take an educated guess. The random value chooses between vertical or horizontal. Within those random values, the code checks the value of the verticalDiff or horizontalDiff (depending on the random value) and chooses to move toward the player as the first move is possible.

10. MOVE_STOP is always added to the end of the moveDirectionsToTest array.

11. The final portion of the code uses a while loop to look for a valid move for the predator. If no move can be found, the predator will remain stopped.

The AI is somewhat limited but is enough for a small challenge to the player. It can be extended to not allow an enemy tank to move in the opposite direction from which it came (unless there are no other possible moves). This would prevent some of the back and forth pacing style movement of the tanks. We will not cover that in this chapter, but if now that you know how the movement list works, you can add that logic in if you need it. There are some very good path finding algorithms such as A* that can be used to find the shortest path between a predator and prey also.

The checkLineOfSight function

The checkLineOfSight function is used to allow the enemy to turn and fire at the player. What is the line of sight? The enemy tanks will turn and fire at the player only if there are no walls blocking their view of the player tank. We calculate this by finding the direction the player is in relation to the enemy tank, and then we loop though all of the tiles separating them in a straight line (only strictly vertical and horizontal). During this loop, if we hit a wall or go off the screen, then the enemy tank will *not* fire at the player. If we reach the same tile as the player, the enemy tank will fire at the player.

An attribute of the Level instance called enemyIntelligence will be used to determine the likelihood of the enemy using line of sight if it is not in the same region as the player. This number will be a value from 0–100. The greater the number, the better the chance is that the enemy will turn and fire at the player if it is in the line of sight of the enemy tank. We have not implemented any of the level-specific variables (such as enemyIntelligence) for the enemy yet, but those will be added when we clean up the final game later in this chapter. For now, we'll use a placeholder value of 50 for the enemyIntelligence, as this variable is named in the following code:

```
private function checkLineOfSight(prey:TileByTileBlitSprite, ↵
                predator:TileByTileBlitSprite):void {

    //rotation reference
    //up=0;
    //right=90;
    //down=180;
    //left=-90;

    var testDX:int;
    var testDY:int;
    var testRotation:int;
    var checkCol:int;
    var checkRow:int;
    var difference:int;
    var differenceCtr:int;
    var act:Boolean = false;

    //1. test if they are in the same col or row
    //2. if in same col (horizontalDiff), check if verticalDiff is pos or neg
    //3. if in same row (verticalDiff), check if horizontalDiff is pos or neg

    //**placeholder
    var enemyIntelligence:int = 50;

    if (prey.currentRegion == predator.currentRegion) {
        act = true;
    }else if (int(Math.random() * 100) < enemyIntelligence) {
        //trace("act based on intel");
        //if not in same region, then turn toward player
        //first be sure to turn toward the player

        var horizontalDiff:int = predator.currCol - prey.currCol;
        var verticalDiff:int = predator.currRow - prey.currRow;
        if (verticalDiff >0) {
```

```
        //trace("AI UP");
        predator.rotation = 0;

}else if (verticalDiff < 0) {
        //trace("AI DOWN");
        predator.rotation = 180;

    }else if (horizontalDiff > 0) {
        //trace("AI LEFT");
        predator.rotation = -90;

    }else if (horizontalDiff < 0) {
        //trace("AI RIGHT");
        predator.rotation = 90;
    }
    act = true;
}

if (act) {

    if (predator.currCol == prey.currCol) {
        //trace ("same col");
        difference = Math.abs(predator.currRow - prey.currRow);

        if (predator.currRow <prey.currRow) {
            testDX = 0;
            testDY = 1;
            testRotation = 180;
        }else if (predator.currRow > prey.currRow) {
            testDX = 0;
            testDY = -1;
            testRotation - 0;
        }else {
            testDX = 0;
            testDY = 0;
            testRotation = 99;
        }
    }else  if (predator.currRow == prey.currRow) {

        difference = Math.abs(predator.currCol- prey.currCol);
        // trace ("same row");

        if (predator.currCol<prey.currCol) {
            testDX = 1;
            testDY = 0;
            testRotation = 90;
        }else if (predator.currCol>prey.currCol) {
            testDX = -1;
            testDY = 0;
            testRotation = -90;
        }else {
            testDX = 0;
            testDY = 0;
            testRotation = 99;
        }
```

```
      }else {
         difference = 0;
      }

      checkCol = predator.currCol;
      checkRow = predator.currRow;

      for (differenceCtr = 0; differenceCtr <= difference; differenceCtr++) {
         checkCol += testDX;
         checkRow += testDY;

         if (checkCol < 0 || checkCol == mapColumnCount)  {
            break;
          //trace("col hit border");

         }else if (checkRow < 0 || checkRow == mapRowCount) {
            break;
            //trace("row hit border");

         }else if (tileSheetData[levelTileMap[checkRow][checkCol]] == TILE_WALL) {
            //trace("hit wall");
            break;

         }else if (checkCol == player.currCol && checkRow == player.currRow) {
         //if predator is facing the player then fire
            if (predator.rotation == testRotation) {
               fireMissileAtPlayer(predator);
            }
         break;

         }else {
          //trace("hit nothing");
          }
      }
   }
}
```

//** end added in iteration #6

These are the main points in the checkLineOfSight function:

1.   The predator and prey are passed in just as they are in the chaseObject function.

2.   If the predator and the prey are already in the same region, the local act variable is set to true to force the later code to test line of sight.

3.   If the predator and prey are not in the same region, the enemyIntel value is used to decide whether the predator object will test line of sight against the prey. The act variable is set to true if they share the same region or if the random generated value is less than enemyIntel). Also, the predator is rotated toward the prey, so it looks smart and the player can tell it is working.

4.   If act is true, we first check to see of the predator and prey are in the same column. If so, we set the local difference variable to be the absolute value of the difference

between their two tile locations. We then use a nested `if:else` structure to find which direction we need to test. The local `testDX` and `testDY` variables represent the number of tiles in each direction to move during each step of the test. The `testRotation` is the rotation the predator will need to assume to fire at the player if the test comes out true.

5. If the current column for `predator` and `prey` are not the same, next we check the rows in the same manner as in step 3.

6. Finally, if they are not in the same row or column, we set the `difference` to 0. This will prevent the `for` loop in the next section from firing, and we will end this `predator`'s line of sight test.

7. We loop from 0 to the `difference` (difference between the `predator` and `prey` tile locations was calculated in step 4). On each loop iteration, we add the `testDX` value to the `checkCol` and the `testDY` to the `checkRow`. If the enemy hits the player's current tile without stopping at a wall or going off the screen, it fires at the player (and turns in the direction of the player to do so).

The fireMissileAtPlayer stub function

We add the `fireMissileAtPlayer` function now as a placeholder until we add projectiles in the next section. It will contain a trace so we can see the enemy tank AI logic firing missiles at the player.

```
private function fireMissileAtPlayer(enemySprite:TileByTileBlitSprite):void {
    trace("fire at player");
}
```

Adding to the variable definitions

We still have not added the `moveDirections` array that was used in the `chaseObject` function to the variable definition section for this iteration. Add the following line to the variable definition section:

```
private var moveDirectionsToTest:Array;
```

Testing iteration 6

When you test this iteration, you should see all of the enemy tanks placed on the screen (see Figure 7-7). They should move toward the player if they are in the same region and also turn and fire (in a trace for now). You will notice that this will fire off *a lot* of trace statements. If this slows down your IDE or Flash Develop, be sure to remove some and test it again.

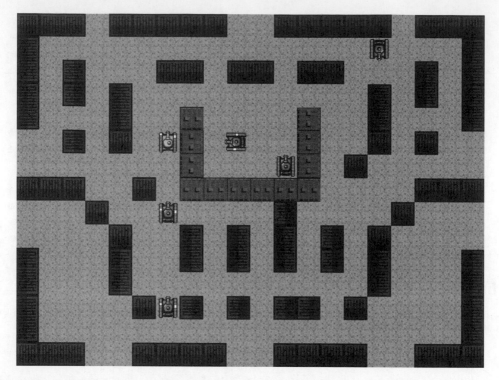

Figure 7-7. Iteration 6 game screen with enemy tanks moving toward the player

Integrating into the framework

Before we add the final touches to the game, such as projectiles firing from the player and enemy tanks, explosions, levels, ammunition, and other pick ups, it is time to add the game into the framework. To do so, we will be creating a `Main.as` file in the game-specific package structure. We will also be modifying the `Library` class the `TileSheetDataXML` class we created in Chapter 6.

Integrating onto the Main.as framework class

As usual, we'll start by telling you the file paths for the new class for the Flash IDE:

/source/projects/notanks/flashIDE/com/efg/games/notanks]Main.as

and for the Flex SDK (using Flash Develop):

/source/projects/notanks/flexSDK/src/com/efg/games/notanks/Main.as

We are not going to discuss this class in full, as we have done so in earlier chapters. We will highlight the major changes though, as we have added some new, unique code to handle playing sounds on the title screen.

```
package com.efg.games.notanks
{

    import flash.text.TextFormat;
    import flash.text.TextFormatAlign;
    import flash.geom.Point;

    import com.efg.framework.FrameWorkStates;
    import com.efg.framework.GameFrameWork;
    import com.efg.framework.BasicScreen;
    import com.efg.framework.ScoreBoard;
    import com.efg.framework.SideBySideScoreElement;
    import com.efg.framework.SoundManager;


    public class Main extends GameFrameWork {


        //custom sccore board elements
        public static const SCORE_BOARD_SCORE:String = "score";
        public static const SCORE_BOARD_AMMO:String = "ammo";
        public static const SCORE_BOARD_TANKS:String = "tanks";
        public static const SCORE_BOARD_HEALTH:String = "health";

        //custom sounds
        public static const SOUND_ENEMY_FIRE:String = "enemyfire";
        public static const SOUND_EXPLODE:String = "explode"
        public static const SOUND_PLAYER_EXPLODE:String = "playerexplode";
        public static const SOUND_PLAYER_FIRE:String = "playerfire";
        public static const SOUND_PLAYER_MOVE:String = "playermove";
        public static const SOUND_PICK_UP:String = "pickup";
        public static const SOUND_GOAL:String = "goal";
        public static const SOUND_HIT:String = "hit";
        public static const SOUND_MUSIC:String = "music";
        public static const SOUND_HIT_WALL:String = "hitwall";
        public static const SOUND_LIFE:String = "soundlife";


        public function Main() {
            init();
        }

        override public function init():void {
            game = new NoTanks();
            game.y = 20;
            setApplicationBackGround(640, 500, false, 0x000000);


            //add score board to the screen as the seconf layer
            scoreBoard = new ScoreBoard();
            addChild(scoreBoard);

                scoreBoardTextFormat= new TextFormat("_sans", "11", "0xffffff", "true");

                scoreBoard.createTextElement(SCORE_BOARD_SCORE, new ↵
```

301

```
    SideBySideScoreElement(80, 5, 20, "Score", scoreBoardTextFormat, 25, "0", ⏎
      scoreBoardTextFormat));

  scoreBoard.createTextElement(SCORE_BOARD_AMMO, new ⏎
    SideBySideScoreElement(180, 5, 20, "Ammo", scoreBoardTextFormat, 25, ⏎
  "0/0", scoreBoardTextFormat));

  scoreBoard.createTextElement(SCORE_BOARD_TANKS, new ⏎
  SideBySideScoreElement(280,5, 20, "Tanks", scoreBoardTextFormat, 25, ⏎
  "0%", scoreBoardTextFormat));

  scoreBoard.createTextElement(SCORE_BOARD_HEALTH, new ⏎
    SideBySideScoreElement(380, 5, 20, "Health", scoreBoardTextFormat, 25, ⏎
    "0%", scoreBoardTextFormat));

//screen text initializations
screenTextFormat = new TextFormat("_sans", "16", "0xffffff", "false");
screenTextFormat.align = flash.text.TextFormatAlign.CENTER;
screenButtonFormat = new TextFormat("_sans", "12", "0x000000", "false");

titleScreen = new BasicScreen(FrameWorkStates.STATE_SYSTEM_TITLE,640,500,⏎
  false,0x0000dd );

titleScreen.createOkButton("Play", new Point(250, 250), 100, 20, ⏎
  screenButtonFormat, 0x000000, 0xff0000,2);

titleScreen.createDisplayText("No Tanks!", 120,new Point(245,150), ⏎
  screenTextFormat);

instructionsScreen = new BasicScreen(FrameWorkStates. ⏎
  STATE_SYSTEM_INSTRUCTIONS,640,500,false,0x0000dd);

instructionsScreen.createOkButton("Start", new Point(250, 250), 100, 20, ⏎
  screenButtonFormat, 0x000000, 0xff0000,2);

instructionsScreen.createDisplayText("Find the treasure.\nDestroy the ⏎
  tanks!\nArrows and Space",250,new Point(180,150),screenTextFormat);

gameOverScreen = new BasicScreen(FrameWorkStates.STATE_SYSTEM_GAME_OVER,⏎
  640,500,false,0x0000dd);

gameOverScreen.createOkButton("Restart", new Point(250, 250), 100, ⏎
  20,screenButtonFormat, 0x000000, 0xff0000,2);

gameOverScreen.createDisplayText("Game Over",100,new Point(250,150),⏎
  screenTextFormat);

levelInScreen = new BasicScreen(FrameWorkStates.STATE_SYSTEM_LEVEL_IN, ⏎
  640, 500, true, 0xaaff0000);
                levelInText = "Level ";
levelInScreen.createDisplayText(levelInText,100,new Point(250,150), ⏎
  screenTextFormat);
```

```
        //set initial game state
        switchSystemState(FrameWorkStates.STATE_SYSTEM_TITLE);

        //wait
        waitTime = 30;

        //sounds
        //*** flex SDK
        soundManager.addSound(SOUND_ENEMY_FIRE,new Library.SoundEnemyFire);
        soundManager.addSound(SOUND_EXPLODE, new Library.SoundExplode);
        soundManager.addSound(SOUND_PLAYER_EXPLODE,new Library.SoundPlayerExplode);
        soundManager.addSound(SOUND_PLAYER_FIRE,new Library.SoundPlayerFire);
        soundManager.addSound(SOUND_PLAYER_MOVE,new Library.SoundPlayerMove);
        soundManager.addSound(SOUND_PICK_UP,new Library.SoundPickUp);
        soundManager.addSound(SOUND_GOAL,new Library.SoundGoal);
        soundManager.addSound(SOUND_HIT,new Library.SoundHit);
        soundManager.addSound(SOUND_MUSIC,new Library.SoundMusic);
        soundManager.addSound(SOUND_HIT_WALL,new Library.SoundHitWall);
        soundManager.addSound(SOUND_LIFE, new Library.SoundLife);
        //*** end flex sdk

    //***Flash IDE
    */
        soundManager.addSound(SOUND_ENEMY_FIRE,new SoundEnemyFire);
        soundManager.addSound(SOUND_EXPLODE, new SoundExplode);
        soundManager.addSound(SOUND_PLAYER_EXPLODE,new SoundPlayerExplode);
        soundManager.addSound(SOUND_PLAYER_FIRE,new SoundPlayerFire);
        soundManager.addSound(SOUND_PLAYER_MOVE,new SoundPlayerMove);
        soundManager.addSound(SOUND_PICK_UP,new SoundPickUp);
        soundManager.addSound(SOUND_GOAL,new SoundGoal);
        soundManager.addSound(SOUND_HIT,new SoundHit);
        soundManager.addSound(SOUND_MUSIC,new SoundMusic);
        soundManager.addSound(SOUND_HIT_WALL,new SoundHitWall);
        soundManager.addSound(SOUND_LIFE, new SoundLife);
    */



        //create timer and run it one time
        frameRate = 30;
        startTimer();
    }

    override public function systemTitle():void {
        soundManager.playSound(SOUND_MUSIC, false,999, 0, 1);
        super.systemTitle();
    }

    override public function systemNewGame():void {
        soundManager.stopSound(SOUND_MUSIC);
        super.systemNewGame();
    }
  }
}
```

The application background and game Sprite location

Now we will set the background color for the application and position the game `Sprite` on the screen.

1. In the variable definition section, we changed the application size to 640 × 500 pixels. We have added 20 pixels at the top of the screen for a scoreboard.

```
setApplicationBackGround(640, 500, false, 0x000000);
```

2. We have moved the game instance down to a y position of 20 to accommodate the 20-pixel scoreboard at the top of the game screen.

```
game.y = 20;
```

The ScoreBoard

We added four elements to our `ScoreBoard` to handle the `SCORE`, `AMMO`, `TANKS`, and `HEALTH` values that we want to display to the user. The constants were added to the variable definition section and the `createTextElement` calls were added to the `init` function.

Here are the four new elements we will be adding:

- **Score:** The player's score
- **Ammo:** The ammunition the player has left (starts with 50 on a new tank)
- **Health:** The health points left for the player tank (starts with 5)
- **Tanks:** The number of tanks the player has left

The Screens

We added text, locations, and buttons (if necessary) to the four screens (`titleScreen`, `instructionsScreen`, `gameOverScreen`, and `levelInScreen`).

The Sounds

We added constants for all of our sounds to the variable definition section and `addSound` function calls to the `init` function. Notice that we have added the `Library` class name to the front of all of the sounds in the Flex SDK code. This is an important difference between the Flash IDE and Flex SDK versions of the code, and we will explore this in detail in the next section on integrating sound.

The New Function Overrides for the Sounds

We have two very new functions that are overrides of functions in the `GameFrameWork.as` file. The `systemTitle` and `systemNewGame` functions are now set up to handle playing and stopping the `SOUND_MUSIC` sound. This is done by first making a `SoundManager` class function call to `playSound` or `stopSound` and then calling the `Super` version of each function in the `GameFrameWork.as`.

Finishing up the Library class

The sounds are special case, as they require assets, which you must either create yourself or download from the web site for this book. We will embedding .mp3 sounds directly inside Flex SDK AS3 applications (with a Flex embed) in Chapters 10 and 11. For now, we will use the same method we used in Chapters 4 and 5. You will need to embed your sounds in a .fla, give them the linkage names that match the Library.as class (which comes next), and export them as noTanks_assets.swf. You will need to place this file in the assets folder for the project. There is no need for this file if you are using the Flash IDE. In that case, simply import in the sounds and set the linkage identifiers to the names in the class (this code will come next).

Here is the location in the framework for this file:

/source/projects/notanks/flexSDK/assets/noTaks_assets.swf

We will add new assets to our Library.as to handle each of the sounds we need. As a refresher, the location for this file will be:

/source/projects/notanks/flexSDK/src/com/efg/games/notanks/Library.as

Here is the new Library.as file with the assets embedded using the noTanks_assets.swf as the source of the sounds:

```
package com.efg.games.notanks
{
    import flash.display.Bitmap;
    import flash.display.DitmapData;

    public class Library {

        [Embed(source='../../../../../assets/tanks_sheet.png')]
        public static const TankSheetPng:Class;

        [Embed(source = "../../../../../assets/noTanks_assets.swf", ↵
         symbol="soundEnemyFire")]
        public static const SoundEnemyFire:Class;

        [Embed(source = "../../../../../assets/noTanks_assets.swf", symbol="soundExplode")]
        public static const SoundExplode:Class;

        [Embed(source = "../../../../../assets/noTanks_assets.swf", ↵
         symbol="soundPlayerExplode")]
        public static const SoundPlayerExplode:Class;

        [Embed(source = "../../../../../assets/noTanks_assets.swf", ↵
         symbol="soundPlayerFire")]
        public static const SoundPlayerFire:Class;

        [Embed(source = "../../../../../assets/noTanks_assets.swf", ↵
         symbol="soundPlayerMove")]
        public static const SoundPlayerMove:Class;

        [Embed(source = "../../../../../assets/noTanks_assets.swf", symbol="soundPickUp")]
        public static const SoundPickUp:Class;
```

```
[Embed(source = "../../../../../assets/noTanks_assets.swf", symbol="soundGoal")]
public static const SoundGoal:Class;

[Embed(source = "../../../../../assets/noTanks_assets.swf", symbol="soundHit")]
public static const SoundHit:Class;

[Embed(source = "../../../../../assets/noTanks_assets.swf", symbol="soundMusic")]
public static const SoundMusic:Class;

[Embed(source = "../../../../../assets/noTanks_assets.swf", symbol="soundHitWall")]
public static const SoundHitWall:Class;

[Embed(source = "../../../../../assets/noTanks_assets.swf", symbol="soundLife")]
public static const SoundLife:Class;
    }
}
```

We created all of the sounds with the SFXR tool with the exception of the music. Chapters 4 and 5 had a nice discussion of this tool. The music was created with Sony Acid, using a Magix loop library. We saved the music as a .wav file, so it would loop properly when exported in the game SWF.

Finalizing the Level.as and Level1.as file

We created the Level.as file in the previous chapter. We need to add two new attributes to the level-specific data.

The first new attribute is called enemyShotDelay. It represents the delay in frames between times the enemy will fire at he player. The shorter the delay the harder the game level will be.

The second new attribute is called enemyHealthPoints. This represents the number of missile hits an enemy can take before being destroyed by the player

This file should already be located here:

/source/projects/notanks/flexSDK/src/com/efg/games/notanks/Level.as

Add the new line for enemyShotDelay to the existing file. Here is the entire Level.as file once again:

```
package com.efg.games.notanks
{
/**
* ...
* @author Jeff Fulton
*/
   public class Level{

       public var backGroundMap:Array;
       public var spriteMap:Array;
       public var backGroundTile:int;
       public var enemyIntelligence:int;
       public var enemyShotSpeed:Number;
       public var ammoPickUp:int;

       //***added in chapter 7
```

306

```
    public var enemyHealthPoints:Number;
    public var enemyShotDelay:int;

    public function Level() {
    }
  }
}
```

We now need to modify the `Level1.as` file to add in two new elements. Add the following code to the `Level1.as` file variable assignment section:

```
enemyShotDelay = 10;
enemyHealthPoints = 2;
```

Finishing up the NoTanks.as file

We are now going to quickly go through all of the code necessary to make the `GameDemoInteration6.as` file into a complete game. There are quite a few little things we need to do, but we have the most complicated code out of the way. When we are done, you will have a complete game that is ready for more levels and any enhancements you can think of.

Once again, we are going to change to a new class name for this iteration.

Here is the new class name and location for the Flash IDE:

`/source/projects/notanks/flashIDE/com/efg/games/notanks/NoTanks.as`

Here is the new class name and location for the Flex SDK:

`/source/projects/notanks/flexSDK/src/com/efg/games/notanks]NoTanks.as`

Changing the class name for NoTanks.as

We have a new file name for the game, so we will once again need to change the class name to match. We will also need to change the name of the constructor function.

It is very important that you change the NoTanks class to extend Game rather than Sprite. Here is the new class definition. First, we will change to the new class name

```
public class NoTanks extends Game
{
```

and then the constructor name:

```
    public function NoTanks() {
```

Adding to the class import section for NoTanks.as

The very top of your new `NoTanks.as` file should look exactly like the following; you don't need to type in the comments, but they are for reference if you need them:

```
package com.efg.games.notanks
{

    import flash.display.BitmapData;
```

```
import flash.geom.Point;
import flash.geom.Rectangle;
import flash.display.Bitmap;
import flash.display.Sprite;
import flash.events.*;
import com.efg.framework.CustomEventSound;
import com.efg.framework.Game;
import com.efg.framework.CustomEventLevelScreenUpdate;
import com.efg.framework.CustomEventScoreBoardUpdate;
import com.efg.framework.CustomEventSound;
import com.efg.framework.BlitSprite;
import com.efg.framework.TileByTileBlitSprite;
import com.efg.framework.TileSheet;


/**
 * ...
 * @author Jeff Fulton
 */
public class NoTanks extends Game {
```

Adding the new NoTanks.as variables

Add these variables to the variable definition section:

```
public static const EXPLODE_SMALL:int = 0;
public static const EXPLODE_LARGE:int = 1;
//game specific
private var score:int;
private var lives:int;
private var ammo:int;
private var playerStartLives:int = 2;
private var playerStartAmmo:int = 50;
private var playerStartHealthpoints:int = 5;
private var scoreEnemy:int = 25;
private var scoreGoal:int = 50;

//game loop
private var gameOver:Boolean = false;

//goal
private var goalReached:Boolean = false;
private var goalSprite:BlitSprite;

//level specific
private var enemyIntelligence:int;
private var enemyShotDelay:int;
private var enemyShotSpeed:int;
private var enemyHealthPoints:int;

//hit detection
private var playerHitPoint:Point = new Point(0, 0);
private var enemyHitPoint:Point = new Point(0, 0);
private var missileHitPoint:Point = new Point(0, 0);
```

```
private var pickupHitPoint:Point = new Point(0, 0);


//temps for loops
private var tempExplode:BlitSprite;
private var tempPickup:BlitSprite;

//explosions
private var explosionList:Array;

//pickups
private var ammoPickupList:Array;
private var lifePickupList:Array;
private var ammoPickupAmount:int;

//missiles
private var playerMissileList:Array;
private var tempMissile:BlitSprite;
private var enemyMissileList:Array;
//** end the final Game.as variables **
```

Adding the new NoTanks.as init function

The new init function is going to delete the newGame function call and set the focusRect to be false.

```
private function init():void {
    this.focusRect = false;
    initTileSheetData();
}
```

The newGame function is now called by Main.as and the focusRect will be set to false when the level starts.

Creating the newGame function

This function is almost a complete rewrite of the original newGame function. We have added code to reset the level, score, lives, and gameOver variables, as well as dispatch events to update the four scoreboard elements.

```
override public function newGame():void {
    setRegions();

    level = 0;
    score = 0;
    lives = playerStartLives;
    gameOver = false;

    stage.addEventListener(KeyboardEvent.KEY_DOWN,keyDownListener);
    stage.addEventListener(KeyboardEvent.KEY_UP, keyUpListener);

    addChild(canvasBitmap);
    dispatchEvent(new CustomEventScoreBoardUpdate(CustomEventScoreBoardUpdate.↵
     UPDATE_TEXT,Main.SCORE_BOARD_SCORE,"0"));
```

309

```
dispatchEvent(new CustomEventScoreBoardUpdate(CustomEventScoreBoardUpdate.
 UPDATE_TEXT,Main.SCORE_BOARD_AMMO,"0"));

dispatchEvent(new CustomEventScoreBoardUpdate(CustomEventScoreBoardUpdate.
 UPDATE_TEXT,Main.SCORE_BOARD_TANKS,"0"));

dispatchEvent(new CustomEventScoreBoardUpdate(CustomEventScoreBoardUpdate.
 UPDATE_TEXT,Main.SCORE_BOARD_HEALTH,"0"));
}
```

Creating the newLevel function

The newLevel function must make sure to reset all values for a new level. It also must make sure that if we are starting a new game (level==0) that we call restartPlayer with the right value (true) to ensure the player starts with the same ammo and healthPoints that a new tank would. We have added and changed quite a few lines, so it is best to rewrite the entire function just to be sure you have all of the new code.

```
override public function newLevel():void {

    stage.focus = this;
    var newGameStart:Boolean;

    //if new game then reset ammo and health
    if (level == 0) {
        newGameStart = true;
    }else {
        newGameStart = false;
    }

    if (level==levels.length-1) level = 0;
    level++;
    player = new TileByTileBlitSprite(tileSheet, playerFrames, 0);
    player.missileTime = 0;
    player.missileDelay = 2;

    enemyList = [];
    playerMissileList = [];
    explosionList = [];
    enemyMissileList = [];
    ammoPickupList = [];
    lifePickupList = [];
    goalReached = false;
    readBackGroundData();
    readSpriteData();
    drawLevelBackGround();
    goalReached = false;

    dispatchEvent(new CustomEventLevelScreenUpdate(CustomEventLevelScreenUpdate.
     UPDATE_TEXT, String(level)));

    restartPlayer(newGameStart);
    addChild(player);
}
```

This function also sends the level value as a string back to Main to be used in the levelInScreen by dispatching an instance of the CustomEventLevelScreenUpdate class. Also notice that we set the stage.focus=this to ensure that all key events will be captured from the game when it is in play.

Creating the restartPlayer function

The restartPlayer function just needs a few additions and changes. We are adding in the call to only reset the player.healthPoints value if the game is new or the player has just died. That way, on a new level, the player will not receive extra health and ammunition (you can change this in your version of the game if you wish). We also need to get rid of the ENTER_FRAME event listener creation. It will be replaced with the framework's timer. Be sure to copy over the entire function.

```
private function restartPlayer(afterDeath:Boolean=false):void {
    trace("restart player");
    player.visible = true;
    player.currCol = playerStartCol;
    player.currRow = playerStartRow;
    player.x=(playerStartCol * tileWidth)+(.5*tileWidth);
    player.y = (playerStartRow * tileHeight) + (.5 * tileHeight);
    player.nextX = player.x;
    player.nextY = player.y;
    player.currentDirection = MOVE_UP;
    playerStarted = true;
    playerInvincible = true;
    playerInvincibleCountDown = true;
    playerInvincibleCount = 0;

    //** added iteration 6
    setCurrentRegion(player);
    //** end added iteration 6

    //** added in Game.as final ***
    player.healthPoints - playerStartHealthpoints;
    if (afterDeath) {
        ammo = playerStartAmmo;
        player.healthPoints = playerStartHealthpoints;
    }
    //** end added in Game.as final **
}
```

Overwriting the runGame function

These three functions are brand new and should just be copied exactly as they are in this section and placed into the NoTanks.as file, overwriting the current runGame function.

The updateScoreBoard function simply refreshes the scoreBoard on each frame tick, while the checkInvincible function is used to count up the time the player tank cannot be harmed when a new level starts or a new tank starts. The effect we have in place (part of the update and render loop) is to blink the player tank when it is invincible.

The new runGame function has now has been fully fleshed out with calls to all of the necessary game loop functions. It also checks for the end of a level and the end of the game, and updates the scoreBoard. It does not accept keyboard input until the playerStarted Boolean is set to true.

```
        private function updateScoreBoard():void {

            dispatchEvent(new CustomEventScoreBoardUpdate(CustomEventScoreBoardUpdate.↩
            UPDATE_TEXT, Main.SCORE_BOARD_SCORE, String(score)));

            dispatchEvent(new CustomEventScoreBoardUpdate(CustomEventScoreBoardUpdate.↩
            UPDATE_TEXT,Main.SCORE_BOARD_AMMO,String(ammo)));

            dispatchEvent(new CustomEventScoreBoardUpdate(CustomEventScoreBoardUpdate.↩
            UPDATE_TEXT,Main.SCORE_BOARD_TANKS,String(lives)));

            dispatchEvent(new CustomEventScoreBoardUpdate(CustomEventScoreBoardUpdate.↩
            UPDATE_TEXT,Main.SCORE_BOARD_HEALTH,String(player.healthPoints) ↩
            + "/" + String(playerStartHealthpoints)));

        }

        override public function runGame():void {
            checkInvincible();
            if (playerStarted) {
                checkInput();
            }
            update();
            checkCollisions();
            render();

            checkforEndLevel();
            checkforEndGame();
            updateScoreBoard();

        }

        private function checkInvincible():void {
            if (playerInvincibleCountDown && playerInvincible) {
                playerInvincibleCount++
                if (playerInvincibleCount > playerInvincibleWait) {
                    playerInvincible = false;
                    playerInvincibleCountDown = false;
                    playerInvincibleCount = 0;
                    player.visible = true;
                }
            }
        }
```

Adding the CheckInput function

The checkInput function requires us to uncomment all of the lines for playing sounds and firing missiles. See the following bold code:

```
        private function checkInput():void {
            var playSound:Boolean = false;
            var lastDirection:int = player.currentDirection;

            if (keyPressList[38] && player.inTunnel==false) {
```

```
        if (checkTile(MOVE_UP, player )) {
            if (player.currentDirection == MOVE_UP || player.currentDirection ⏎
            == MOVE_DOWN || player.currentDirection == MOVE_STOP  ) {

                switchMovement(MOVE_UP, player );
                playSound = true;

            }else if (checkCenterTile( player)) {
                switchMovement(MOVE_UP, player );
                playSound = true;
            }
        }else{
            //trace("can't move up");
        }
    }

    if (keyPressList[40] && player.inTunnel == false) {
        if (checkTile(MOVE_DOWN, player )) {
            if (player.currentDirection == MOVE_DOWN || player.currentDirection ⏎
            == MOVE_UP || player.currentDirection == MOVE_STOP) {

                switchMovement(MOVE_DOWN, player );
                playSound = true;

            }else if (checkCenterTile(player)) {

                switchMovement(MOVE_DOWN, player );
                playSound = true;

            }
        }else {
            //trace("can't move down");
        }
    }

    if (keyPressList[39] && player.inTunnel==false) {
        if (checkTile(MOVE_RIGHT, player )) {
            if (player.currentDirection == MOVE RIGHT || player.currentDirection⏎
            == MOVE_LEFT || player.currentDirection == MOVE_STOP) {

                switchMovement(MOVE_RIGHT, player );
                playSound = true;

            }else if (checkCenterTile( player)) {

                switchMovement(MOVE_RIGHT, player );
                playSound = true;

            }
        }else {
            //trace("can't move right");
        }
    }
```

```
        if (keyPressList[37] && player.inTunnel==false) {
            if (checkTile(MOVE_LEFT,player )) {
                if (player.currentDirection == MOVE_LEFT || player.currentDirection ↵
                == MOVE_RIGHT || player.currentDirection == MOVE_STOP) {

                    switchMovement(MOVE_LEFT, player );
                    playSound = true;

                }else if (checkCenterTile(player)) {

                    switchMovement(MOVE_LEFT, player );
                    playSound = true;
                }
            }else {
                //trace("can't move left");
            }
        }


        if (keyPressList[32]&& player.inTunnel==false) {
            if (ammo >0) firePlayerMissile();
        }

    if (lastDirection == MOVE_STOP && playSound) {
        dispatchEvent(new CustomEventSound(CustomEventSound.PLAY_SOUND, ↵
        Main.SOUND_PLAYER_MOVE, false, 1, 0));
    }
}
```

Here is a list of changes we made:

- We uncommented this line for the variable that will signal whether or not to play the tank moving sound: var playSound:Boolean = false;
- There should be eight places inside the if:else clause to uncommented the line playSound = true;.
- At the bottom of the function, you should uncomment the line that calls the firePlayerMissile when the space bar is pressed: if (ammo >0) firePlayerMissile();.
- We uncomment the line for playing the SOUND_PLAYER_MOVE sound if playSound was set to true in step 2:

```
if (lastDir == MOVE_STOP && playSound) {
        dispatchEvent(new CustomEventSound(CustomEventSound.PLAY_SOUND, É
        Main.SOUND_PLAYER_MOVE, false, 1, 0));
}
```

Improving the update function

We need to add in code to update the invincibility for the player, the game missiles, and the explosions. Notice that when a missile hits a wall, it will create a small explosion and then is passed to the dispose function to be deleted. The same goes for explosions that have run their course through the frame animation. Add all of the following code to the current update function in the existing code:

```
//** added in the final Game.as **
if (playerInvincibleCountDown) {
   if (playerInvincibleCount % 2 == 0) {
      //blink player
      player.visible = !player.visible
   }
}
//player missiles
var playerMissileLength:int = playerMissileList.length - 1;

for (ctr = playerMissileLength; ctr >= 0; ctr--) {
   tempMissile = playerMissileList[ctr];
   tempMissile.nextX = tempMissile.x + tempMissile.dx ;
   tempMissile.nextY = tempMissile.y + tempMissile.dy ;

   if (tempMissile.nextY <= yMin-.5*tileHeight || ↵
      tempMissile.nextY >= yMax+.4*tileHeight || ↵
      tempMissile.nextX <= xMin-.5*tileWidth || ↵
      tempMissile.nextX >= xMax+.5*tileWidth) {

      playerMissileList.splice(ctr,1);
      dispose(tempMissile);
   }else if (checkHitWall(tempMissile)) {
      playerMissileList.splice(ctr, 1);

      createExplode(EXPLODE_SMALL, tempMissile.x, tempMissile.y);

      dispatchEvent(new CustomEventSound(CustomEventSound.PLAY_SOUND, ↵
       Main.SOUND_HIT_WALL, false, 1, 0));

      dispose(tempMissile);
   }
}

//enemy missiles
var enemyMissileLength:int = enemyMissileList.length - 1;

for (ctr = enemyMissileLength; ctr >= 0; ctr--) {
   tempMissile = enemyMissileList[ctr];
   tempMissile.nextX = tempMissile.x + tempMissile.dx;
   tempMissile.nextY = tempMissile.y + tempMissile.dy;

   if (tempMissile.nextY <= yMin-.5*tileHeight || ↵
       tempMissile.nextY >= yMax+.4*tileHeight || ↵
       tempMissile.nextX <= xMin-.5*tileWidth || ↵
      tempMissile.nextX >= xMax+.5*tileWidth) {

      enemyMissileList.splice(ctr,1);
      dispose(tempMissile);
   }else if (checkHitWall(tempMissile)) {
      enemyMissileList.splice(ctr, 1);
```

```
            createExplode(EXPLODE_SMALL, tempMissile.x, tempMissile.y);

            dispatchEvent(new CustomEventSound(CustomEventSound.PLAY_SOUND, ↵
            Main.SOUND_HIT_WALL, false, 1, 0));

            dispose(tempMissile);
        }
    }


        //explosions can be updated and rendered at the same time
        var explodeLength:int = explosionList.length - 1;

        for (ctr = explodeLength; ctr >= 0; ctr--) {
            tempExplode = explosionList[ctr];
            tempExplode.animationLoop = true;
            tempExplode.updateCurrentTile();

            if (tempExplode.loopCounter > 0) {
                explosionList.splice(ctr, 1);
                dispose(tempExplode);
            }else {
                tempExplode.renderCurrentTile();
            }
        }

        //** end added in the final Game.as
```

Adding the checkHitWall function

The checkHitWall function is used exclusively to test if missiles have hit a wall. It is much more simple than the checkTileFunction, which requires a TileByTileBlitSprite. Since the missiles use the BlitSprite class and do not need complicated AI movement logic, this function will be much faster (in terms of code execution) than trying to shoehorn missile hitting tile code into the checkTileFunction. It returns true if the current tile the missile is on is a TILE_WALL.

```
    private function checkHitWall(object:BlitSprite):Boolean {
        var row:int = int(object.nextY / tileWidth);
        var col:int = int(object.nextX / tileHeight);

        return tileSheetData[levelTileMap[row][col]] == TILE_WALL;
    }
```

The checkCollisions function

The checkCollisions function is new; you have not seen it before at all. You have seen similar functions in the last few chapters that do basically the same thing though—check for pixel-perfect collisions between BitmapData instances inside sprites. One thing we have added in this chapter is checking the nextX and nextY values rather than the current x and y values. While this check is not completely necessary in an action game like No Tanks!, it is a good exercise to keep in mind. If you do this, you will never have an instance where you move an object move too far in the update function and need to move it back because of a collision.

These are the collisions we look for in this function:

- **When any missile in the** playerMissiles **array hits an enemy tank**: Enemy tanks have healthPoints just like the player. When all healthPoints are gone, the enemy tank is destroyed.
- **Missiles in the** enemyMissiles **array hitting the** player: Each time the player is hit by an enemy missile, one of its healthPoints is removed. When all five are gone, the player tank explodes. If the player is out of lives, gameOver is set to true.
- **The** player **hitting the** goalSprite: As soon as the player hits the goalSprite, the level is over.
- **The** player **hitting any** BlitSprite **in the** ammoPickupList **array**: The ammo variable is increased by the ammoPickupAmount value when this is true.
- **The** player **hitting any** BlitSprite **in the** lifePickups **array**: The lives variable is increased by 1 when this is true.

Here's the new function's code:

```
private function checkCollisions():void {

    //loop through playerMissiles and check against enemy
    var playerMissileLength:int = playerMissileList.length - 1;
    playerHitPoint.x = player.nextX;
    playerHitPoint.y = player.nextY;

    var enemyLength:int = enemyList.length - 1;

missiles: for (var ctr:int = playerMissileLength; ctr >= 0; ctr--) {
        tempMissile = playerMissileList[ctr]

        for (var ctr2:int = enemyLength; ctr2 >= 0; ctr2--) {
            tempEnemy = enemyList[ctr2];
            missileHitPoint.x - tempMissile.nextX;
            missileHitPoint.y = tempMissile.nextY;
            enemyHitPoint.x = tempEnemy.nextX;
            enemyHitPoint.y = tempEnemy.nextY;

            if (tempMissile.bitmapData.hitTest(missileHitPoint, ↵
             255, tempEnemy.bitmapData, enemyHitPoint)) {

                //trace("hit enemy");
                tempEnemy.healthPoints--;
                if (tempEnemy.healthPoints < 1) {
                    createExplode(EXPLODE_LARGE, tempEnemy.x, tempEnemy.y);

                    dispatchEvent(new CustomEventSound(CustomEventSound.PLAY_SOUND, ↵
                     Main.SOUND_EXPLODE, false, 1, 0));

                    enemyList.splice(ctr2, 1);
                    dispose(tempEnemy);
                    score += scoreEnemy;
                }else {

                    createExplode(EXPLODE_SMALL, tempMissile.x, tempMissile.y);
```

```
                        dispatchEvent(new CustomEventSound(CustomEventSound.PLAY_SOUND, ↩
                          Main.SOUND_HIT, false, 1, 0));
                    }

                    playerMissileList.splice(ctr, 1);
                    dispose(tempMissile);

                    break missiles;
                }
            }
        }

        //loop through playerMissiles and check against enemy
        var enemyMissileLength:int = enemyMissileList.length - 1;

    emissiles:for (ctr = enemyMissileLength; ctr >= 0; ctr--) {
                tempMissile = enemyMissileList[ctr]
                missileHitPoint.x = tempMissile.nextX;
                missileHitPoint.y = tempMissile.nextY;

                if (tempMissile.bitmapData.hitTest(missileHitPoint, 255, ↩
                    player.bitmapData, playerHitPoint) && !playerInvincible) {

                    player.healthPoints--;
                    if (player.healthPoints < 1) {
                        createExplode(EXPLODE_LARGE, player.x, player.y);

                        dispatchEvent(new CustomEventSound(CustomEventSound.PLAY_SOUND, ↩
                          Main.SOUND_PLAYER_EXPLODE, false, 1, 0));

                        lives--;
                        if (lives > 0) {
                            restartPlayer();
                        }else {
                            gameOver = true;
                        }

                        player.visible = false;

                    }else {
                        createExplode(EXPLODE_SMALL, tempMissile.x, tempMissile.y)

                        dispatchEvent(new CustomEventSound(CustomEventSound.PLAY_SOUND, ↩
                          Main.SOUND_HIT, false, 1, 0));
                    }

                    enemyMissileList.splice(ctr, 1);
                    dispose(tempMissile);
                    break emissiles;
                }

            }
```

```
        if (player.hitTestObject(goalSprite)) {

            dispatchEvent(new CustomEventSound(CustomEventSound.PLAY_SOUND, ↵
            Main.SOUND_GOAL, false, 1, 0));

            dispose(goalSprite);
            score += scoreGoal;
            goalReached = true;
            playerInvincible = true;
        }

        var ammoPickupLength:int = ammoPickupList.length - 1;
        for (ctr = ammoPickupLength; ctr >= 0; ctr--) {
            tempPickup = ammoPickupList[ctr];
            pickupHitPoint.x = tempPickup.x;
            pickupHitPoint.y = tempPickup.y;

            if (tempPickup.bitmapData.hitTest(pickupHitPoint, 255, player.bitmapData, ↵
                playerHitPoint)){

                ammoPickupList.splice(ctr, 1);
                dispose(tempPickup);
                ammo += ammoPickupAmount;

                dispatchEvent(new CustomEventSound(CustomEventSound.PLAY_SOUND, ↵
                Main.SOUND_PICK_UP, false, 1, 0));

            }
        }

        var lifePickupLength:int = lifePickupList.length - 1;
        for (ctr = lifePickupLength; ctr >= 0; ctr--) {
            tempPickup = lifePickupList[ctr];
            pickupHitPoint.x - tempPickup.x;
            pickupHitPoint.y = tempPickup.y;

            if (tempPickup.bitmapData.hitTest(pickupHitPoint, 255, player.bitmapData, ↵
                playerHitPoint)){

                lifePickupList.splice(ctr, 1);
                dispose(tempPickup);
                lives += 1;

                dispatchEvent(new CustomEventSound(CustomEventSound.PLAY_SOUND, ↵
                Main.SOUND_LIFE, false, 1, 0));
            }
        }

    }
```

Updating the render function for NoTanks.as

The render function needs to be altered to add in a set of iterations through both the player and enemy missile arrays. Add the following code to the render function below the existing code but, of course, before the ending bracket for the render function:

```
//** added in final Game.as
var playerMissileLength:int = playerMissileList.length-1;

for (ctr = playerMissileLength; ctr >= 0; ctr--) {
   tempMissile = playerMissileList[ctr];
   tempMissile.x = tempMissile.nextX;
   tempMissile.y = tempMissile.nextY;
}

var enemyMissileLength:int = enemyMissileList.length - 1;
for (ctr = enemyMissileLength; ctr >= 0; ctr--) {
   tempMissile = enemyMissileList[ctr];
   tempMissile.x = tempMissile.nextX;
   tempMissile.y = tempMissile.nextY;

}

//** end added in final Game.as
```

Checking for the end of a level or game

We now need to add three brand new functions, as shown in the following code.

The checkForEndOfLevel function simply checks to see if the goalReached Boolean is set to true.

The checkForEndOfGame function checks for the gameOver Boolean to be true. It also checks to see if all of the explosions have finished. This is just added as an example of how to make transitions between games less abrupt. You will see that the levels end slightly abrupt manner, but the game-over sequence is a little smoother. You can add as many conditions you want to in the two functions to make the transition as smooth as you like.

The addToScore function takes in an integer value that is applied to the score.

```
private function checkforEndGame():void {

   if (gameOver  && explosionList.length==0) {
      dispatchEvent(new Event(GAME_OVER));
      disposeAll();
   }
}


private function checkforEndLevel():void {

   if (goalReached) {
      disposeAll();
      dispatchEvent(new Event(NEW_LEVEL));
   }
```

```
    }

    private function addToScore(val:Number):void {
        score += val;
    }
```

Creating functions to fire missiles

The firePlayerMissile and fireMissileAtPlayer functions are very similar. They actually could be combined into a single function with some modifications (for example, a switch:case statement when a player or enemy fires a missile), but since they have slightly different jobs, we have kept them separate. They both use the missileTime and missileDelay properties of the TileByTileBlitSprite class to determine if the object trying to fire can actually fire. It does this by comparing counting frame ticks with the TileByTileBlitSprite.missileTime. If the missileTime is greater than the missileDelay value, a missile will be fired. All missiles are instances of the BlitSprite class.

Once a missile is fired, its direction is set by the direction of the player or enemy firing the missile. All player missiles travel at 3 pixels per frame tick. This pixel per frame rate can be modified to come from a variable if you desire a power-up of some sort to make the player's missiles go faster. The enemy missile speed is governed by the enemyShotSpeed for the lLevel class instance

The firePlayerMissile function is brand new. Copy it completely. The fireMissileAtPlayer function already exists (as a stub with a trace).

```
    private function firePlayerMissile():void {
        if (player.missileTime++ > player.missileDelay) {
            ammo--;
            player.missileTime = 0;
            //trace("fire a missile");

            tempMissile = new BlitSprite(tileSheet, missileTiles, 0);

            switch(player.rotation) {

                case 0:
                    tempMissile.dx = 0;
                    tempMissile.dy = -3;
                    tempMissile.x = player.x;
                    tempMissile.y = player.y-10;
                    break

                case 90:
                    tempMissile.x = player.x+10;
                    tempMissile.y = player.y;
                    tempMissile.dx = 3;
                    tempMissile.dy = 0;
                    break;

                case 180:
                    tempMissile.x = player.x;
                    tempMissile.y = player.y+10;
                    tempMissile.dx = 0;
```

```
            tempMissile.dy = 3;
            break

        case -90:
            tempMissile.x = player.x-10;
            tempMissile.y = player.y;
            tempMissile.dx = -3;
            tempMissile.dy = 0;
            break;
    }

    tempMissile.nextX = tempMissile.x;
    tempMissile.nextY = tempMissile.y;
    playerMissileList.push(tempMissile);
    addChild(tempMissile);

    dispatchEvent(new CustomEventSound(CustomEventSound.PLAY_SOUND, ↵
      Main.SOUND_PLAYER_FIRE, false, 1, 0));
    }
}


    private function fireMissileAtPlayer(enemySprite:TileByTileBlitSprite):void {

        if (enemySprite.missileTime++ > enemySprite.missileDelay) {
            enemySprite.missileTime = 0;
            trace("fire a missile");
            tempMissile =new BlitSprite(tileSheet, missileTiles, 0);

            switch(enemySprite.rotation) {

                case 0:
                    tempMissile.dx = 0;
                    tempMissile.dy = -1*enemyShotSpeed;
                    tempMissile.x = enemySprite.x;
                    tempMissile.y = enemySprite.y-10;
                    break

                case 90:
                    tempMissile.x = enemySprite.x+10;
                    tempMissile.y = enemySprite.y;
                    tempMissile.dx = enemyShotSpeed;
                    tempMissile.dy = 0;
                    break;

                case 180:
                    tempMissile.x = enemySprite.x;
                    tempMissile.y = enemySprite.y+10;
                    tempMissile.dx = 0;
                    tempMissile.dy = enemyShotSpeed;
                    break

                case -90:
                    tempMissile.x = enemySprite.x-10;
                    tempMissile.y = enemySprite.y;
```

```
                tempMissile.dx = -1*enemyShotSpeed;
                tempMissile.dy = 0;
                break;
        }

        tempMissile.nextX = tempMissile.x;
        tempMissile.nextY = tempMissile.y;
        enemyMissileList.push(tempMissile);
        addChild(tempMissile);

        dispatchEvent(new CustomEventSound(CustomEventSound.PLAY_SOUND, ⏎
         Main.SOUND_ENEMY_FIRE, false, 1, 0));
    }
}
```

Changing the readBackGroundData function

Make sure the ReadBackGroundData function has a line for each of the five level-specific data variables from the Level class subclasses. Here is the entire function for reference, but the five variables to add are indicated in bold in the code:

```
private function readBackGroundData():void {
    levelTileMap = [];
    levelData = levels[level];
    levelTileMap = levelData.backGroundMap;

    //*** The five new variables
    enemyIntelligence = levelData.enemyIntelligence;
    enemyShotDelay=levelData.enemyShotDelay;
    enemyShotSpeed = levelData.enemyShotSpeed;
    enemyHealthPoints = levelData.enemyHealthPoints;
    ammoPickupAmount=levelData.ammoPickUp;
}
```

Changing the readSpriteData function

The readSpriteData function needs to be updated to handle the sprite types we have not added yet. Also, there are a couple lines for the enemy sprites that need to be uncommented.

First, uncomment these lines in the case SPRITE_ENEMY section:

```
empEnemy.missileDelay = enemyShotDelay;
tempEnemy.healthPoints = enemyHealthPoints;
```

Here is the entire new case for SPRITE_ENEMY for reference:

```
    case SPRITE_ENEMY:
        tempEnemy = new TileByTileBlitSprite(tileSheet, enemyFrames, 0);
        tempEnemy.x=(colCtr * tileWidth)+(.5*tileWidth);
        tempEnemy.y = (rowCtr * tileHeight) + (.5 * tileHeight);
        tempEnemy.currRow = rowCtr;
        tempEnemy.currCol = colCtr;
        setCurrentRegion(tempEnemy);
        tempEnemy.currentDirection = MOVE_STOP;
        tempEnemy.animationLoop = false;
```

```
        tempEnemy.missileDelay = enemyShotDelay;
        tempEnemy.healthPoints = enemyHealthPoints;
        addChild(tempEnemy);
        enemyList.push(tempEnemy);
        break;
```

Now, add in the AMMO, GOAL, and LIVES sprite case branches:

```
    case SPRITE_AMMO:
        tempPickup = new BlitSprite(tileSheet, [ammoFrame], 0);
        tempPickup.x=(colCtr * tileWidth)+(.5*tileWidth);
        tempPickup.y = (rowCtr * tileHeight) + (.5 * tileHeight);
        addChild(tempPickup);
        ammoPickupList.push(tempPickup);
        break;

    case SPRITE_GOAL:
        goalSprite = new BlitSprite(tileSheet, [goalFrame], 0);
        goalSprite.x=(colCtr * tileWidth)+(.5*tileWidth);
        goalSprite.y = (rowCtr * tileHeight) + (.5 * tileHeight);
        addChild(goalSprite);
        break;

    case SPRITE_LIVES:
        tempPickup = new BlitSprite(tileSheet, [livesFrame], 0);
        tempPickup.x=(colCtr * tileWidth)+(.5*tileWidth);
        tempPickup.y = (rowCtr * tileHeight) + (.5 * tileHeight);
        addChild(tempPickup);
        lifePickupList.push(tempPickup);
        break;
```

These three sprite types are all handled in a similar manner to the enemy and player sprites. The difference is that they are instances of the BlitSprite class rather than the TileByTileBlitSprite class. These don't have to move about the maze; they simply remain stationary.

Changing the checkLineOfSight function

We need to make one small change to the checkLineOfSight function. We previously used a placeholder local variable for the enemyIntelligence value. We can now remove that placeholder, because we read in a global enemyInteligence value in the readBackGroundData function. Please make sure to find the line below (under //**placeholder) and comment it out or remove it entirely:

```
//**placeholder
//var enemyIntelligence:int = 50;
```

Adding the createExplode function

The createExplode function is used to create both the smaller explosion that displayed when a wall or tank is hit and the larger explosion when one is destroyed. The function takes in three parameters. The first is an integer constant that represents the size: EXPLODE_SMALL or EXPLODE_LARGE. The second is the x location, and the final is the y location. Explosions are added to the explosionList array.

```
    private function createExplode(size:int, xloc:int, yloc:int):void {

        if (size==EXPLODE_SMALL) {
            tempExplode = new BlitSprite(tileSheet, explodeSmallTiles, 0);
        }else {
            tempExplode = new BlitSprite(tileSheet, explodeLargeTiles, 0);
        }

        tempExplode.x = xloc;
        tempExplode.y = yloc;
        tempExplode.animationLoop = true;
        tempExplode.useLoopCounter = true;
        explosionList.push(tempExplode);
        addChild(tempExplode);
    }
```

Coding the object cleanup functions

The **object cleanup functions** are dispose and disposeAll.

The dispose function takes in a single BlitSprite (or its child, TileByTileBlitSprite) and removes it from the screen and readies it for garbage collection. It calls the internal dispose function of the BlitSprite class and removes the object from the display list.

The disposeAll function calls dispose on all of the objects in the game. It is called at the end of each level and at the end of the game.

```
    private function dispose(object:BlitSprite):void {
        object.dispose();
        removeChild(object);
    }

    private function disposeAll():void {
        dispose(player);

        for each(tempEnemy in enemyList) {
            dispose(tempEnemy)
        }
        enemyList = null;

        for each(tempMissile in playerMissileList) {
            dispose(tempMissile)
        }
        playerMissileList = null;

        for each(tempMissile in enemyMissileList) {
            dispose(tempMissile)
        }
        enemyMissileList = null;

        for each(tempExplode in explosionList) {
            dispose(tempExplode)
        }
        explosionList = null;
```

```
for each (tempPickup in ammoPickupList) {
    dispose(tempPickup);
}
ammoPickupList = null;

for each (tempPickup in lifePickupList) {
    dispose(tempPickup);
}
lifePickupList = null;
}
```

Testing the final game

You now have a one-level game that should be playable. In your IDE of choice, select **Build**, **Publish**, or **Test Movie** to see what we have accomplished so far. You should first get the blue title screen with music playing in the background. Click through the screens to start the game.

Once the game starts, you should see a screen like the one shown in Figure 7-8. Use the arrow keys to move about the maze and the space bar to fire.

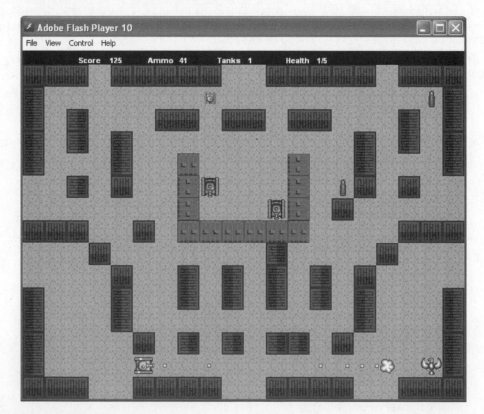

Figure 7-8. Final game screen

Extending the game

We have covered a lot in the last two chapters, and we did it at a very rapid pace. As you can see from the final game, it is lacking a little polish that you would expect from a finished arcade game. Some things, like a pause function and a mute button, will be covered in later chapters. We will also cover creating slightly better level transitions that are not as abrupt the ones in this game.

One thing that you can do for yourself right now is to create more levels. If you need a refresher, please refer to Chapter 6. If you do add more levels, you will need to do things to make sure they are implemented properly:

1. Create a new two-layer level in Mappy.

2. Save both layers out as ActionScript.

3. Create a new Level.as subclass, and call it Level2.as.

4. Make any level-specific changes to the new level; for example, you might want to update attributes such as enemyIntelligence.

5. Add the backGroundMap and spriteMap data from the exported Mappy files.

6. Add a new reference to Leve2 in the levels creation code:

```
private var levels:Array - [undefined,new Level1(), new Level2()]
```

7. Repeat these steps for all of the levels you create.

On to Color Drop

If you made it through these last two chapters completely unscathed, give your self a huge standing ovation. Remember all the way back when we covered the basics of a tile sheet? Between that topic and now we have completed an extendable game level creation system using GIMP and Mappy. We also created a set of code to handle levels and level data, explored how to move game characters around a tile-based maze, how to fire projectiles, how to code enemy chase AI specific to arcade maze games and much more.

In the next chapter, we will take a break from arcade-style games and create a casual game using the framework and many of the classes we have built so far.

Chapter 8

Creating the Color Drop Casual Puzzle Game

Although game developers need to make sure they do not use other people's graphics, sounds, or words without permission, the rules for borrowing game ideas are a lot less clear-cut, and in the next chapter, we will take a short looks at the legalities around using content that is not your own in the games you make. As a game designer, a good rule is that you should try to change up an idea enough to make it your own. However, this does not mean that you cannot be inspired by other games or use that inspiration as a building block for your work. Ideas for games exist not in a vacuum but on a continuum. There is no better example of this than the evolution of casual games.

In this chapter, we will start a two-game, two-chapter discussion of modern casual style puzzle games and build a simple casual puzzle game named Color Drop. In the next chapter, we'll finish up our casual gaming discussion by talking a bit about intellectual property before jump into a second casual style gamed named Dice Battle.

Understanding the Evolution of Casual Games

Most of the original video games from the 1970s, like Pong and Breakout, could be described in today's terms as **casual games**, but at the time they were just video games, with no real distinction of genre or style. With so few games at the time, there really was no reason to segment the offerings into well-known buckets. In fact, nearly every new game was a genre unto itself. At the same time, a good percentage of video games were designed to be played by two players. Their contest-like design belied the pool, darts, and pinball heritage of the bars and arcades where they could be played. However, somewhere around the time Space Invaders was released into the arcades in 1978, things started to change. Single-player games with high scores emerged, with the emphasis on beating the machine overtaking an emphasis on beating the other player. This trend continued with games like Tempest and Defender, which ramped up the difficulty and intensity to very high levels, creating the first wisps of what would one-day be known as hardcore games. This domination of single-player arcade contests transferred to home video games as well. By 1982, most home video games for major systems were arcade game translations or games based on other arcade games. The casual play of the first video games' era was overtaken by obsessively skill-based genres that took lightning-fast reflexes. In some ways, it can be argued that the over-emphasis in single-player skill-based arcade contests created a box for video game designers that led to public disinterest and helped to fuel the first video game crash (however, this is a simplistic view, as there were many other factors involved).

When Nintendo broke out big in the USA in 1986, it offered the public a new style of contest that would grow the simple arcade contest into what is now known as **core gaming** ("core gaming" is a term now used to describe dedicated gamers who thrive on games that usually involve high levels of difficulty and/or competition) Nintendo offered games such as Super Mario Brothers and Zelda that were loosely based on earlier games like Pitfall! and Adventure for the Atari VCS, and these games offered a much more compelling and engrossing game play experience that moved beyond the single-screen skill games of the video game golden age (roughly 1978–1983) and revitalized the video game industry. Ironically, these days, those core games are now considered casual, but such is the continuum of game design.

Casual gaming did not appear as a definable genre until Alexey Pajitnov's Tetris invaded the west from the Soviet Union in the late 1980s. While there are other examples of casual style puzzle games (for example, Flag Capture on the Atari VCS), they did not really break into the mainstream until Tetris. Tetris used a classic set of shapes made of four blocks each. As each block fell down the screen, the player had to manipulate them into an opportune spot. When a full line was made across the playfield, the blocks in that line would be removed. The player's satisfaction came from both matching the shapes with an open spot and with clearing the screen.

While called a puzzle game, Tetris was really more of an action game with puzzle elements that had to be matched. While Tetris itself was a brilliant game, it was also a sort of dead-end as far game design is concerned. Many other games have been created based on the ideas presented in Tetris, but none have matched its simple brilliance. The best versions of Tetris that exist today are only slight modifications on the original design. Tetris was one of the best selling games of the late 1980s and was released in some way on almost every platform available. When the Nintendo Game Boy was released in the United States in 1991 (1989 in Japan), the popularity of the Tetris pack-in game increased its popularity further and proved that it was the type of game that was great to play while traveling, waiting for the school bus, and other activities not normally associated with video game playing.

In this way, Tetris served as transition from the action-oriented video games of the early 1980s to the more cerebral style casual games to follow. One such game was Columns, created by Jay Geertsen in 1989 but popularized by Sega. Columns used lines of colored jewels that had to be matched, three-in-row, to be cleared from the screen. Columns took the basic idea of falling blocks from Tetris, but changed up the game enough to make it new.

While video game systems were evolving their own casual games, computer owners had been playing them for many years. Again, while there are many examples of casual style games prior to it, the most dominant casual game for the masses was the version of solitaire packed into Windows 3.0 released in 1990. This free game was probably biggest time waster of the early 1990s for computer professionals, secretaries, and home computer users. It was instantly accessible, easy to play, and could be completed in just a few minutes. When Windows 95 was released, it contained still another game that would further the casual genre: Minesweeper. Minesweeper was actually based on many similar games dating back many years on other computer systems. However, like solitaire, it was easily available and compelling. The game used a grid of blocks that needed to be clicked by the user. Clicking a block revealed information about bombs that were surrounding that block. The aim was to mark as many bombs as possible without clicking one, which ended the game. Minesweeper's idea of the using the mouse to select blocks on the grid, while not new, became mainstream, and thus acceptable as an interface to further the casual puzzle game genre.

At the turn of the twenty-first century, the people at PopCap devised the next great evolution combining some ideas from both Columns and Minesweeper to create Diamond Mine. In this game, the player was given a board consisting of colored gems that lined up row by row in square. The player's job was to swap two gems at a time, to make three in a row. When three gems were matched, they would disappear, and more gems would fall down into place from the top of the screen. While the concept of matching three remained from Columns, the action elements were removed to make a game based on thoughtful planning like Minesweeper. PopCap later revised this game as Bejeweled, and a ground-breaking game genre was born.

These **match-three games** have grown into their own genre complete with subcategories and designs, expansions into role-playing games, and many other manifestations beyond the concept of simply matching three items.

Although casual games come in many forms, games of this type generally have common features that make them instantly identifiable to game players:

- Objects appear in (or fall into) a grid-like form of some type.
- Objects fall down the screen in some way, either on their own or after user interaction.
- Matching items on the screen (not necessarily three) is part of core game play.
- In many instance, objects are controlled with the mouse.
- Time limits are generally not preferable, because they limit the thinking involved.
- The core process of clearing space is common denominator.

So while casual games have evolved and continue to evolve as a game genre, they have also built on the ideas of one another to create new and interesting games. There are more facets to casual games than just puzzles, but to follow up all the angles of their story could take an entire book itself. The fact is that many games currently considered casual can trace their lineage all the way through to the grid-style games we just described. We believe that there is no better way to design a game than to look at what has already been successful and attempt to design your own twist and functionality into the idea, so in this chapter, the game we will build—Color Drop—is a simple game based on this evolution of casual puzzle games.

Designing the game

For Color Drop, we will use ideas from match-three–style games to create our own style of game where the object is to create the biggest chain of connecting colored boxes as possible. Here is breakdown of the game design concepts behind Color Drop, and Figure 8-1 provides a screenshot:

- **Game name**: Color Drop
- **Game genre**: Click to remove matching colors games.
- **Game description**: A grid of colored blocks is presented to the player. When the player clicks a block, all blocks of that color that are touching that block in some way disappear.
- **Player's goal**: Make the number of blocks displayed in the **Score Needed** field disappear before all the plays are used up.
- **Enemy's description**: None
- **Enemy's goal**: None

- **Level end**: When the value displayed in the Score Needed field is reached
- **Game over conditions**: When the player has no more plays but has not reached the Score Needed vale
- **Difficulty ramping**: Level difficulty is specifically specified using Level classes.
- **Bonus conditions**: The player score extra points (which do count toward Score Needed) depending on the number of blocks removed from the screen in one play.

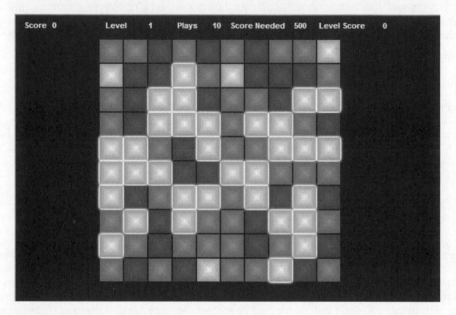

Figure 8-1. The Color Drop game screen

Game development concepts in this chapter

These are the game design concepts that this chapter will cover:

- Creating, maintaining, and managing a grid of objects the size of which can be easily redefined in code
- Effectively using 2D arrays for grid-style puzzle games
- Defining an efficient iterative loop that does not need recursion to test the connections
- Defining distinctive level ramping objects that can be controlled individually
- Creating a specific state machine for the ColorDrop class to assist in managing game flow

We will start this project in a similar fashion to other games in this book. You can build this game in the Flash IDE or with Flex/Flash Develop, and as usual, we will note the differences in code for the two environments when required. Create the new project (or FLA) with the following attributes:

- **Package**: com.efg.games.colordrop
- **Game Class**: ColorDrop.as

- **Size:** 600 × 400
- **FPS:** 40
- **Flex Asset Location:** src/com/efg/games/colordrop/assets

For Flash, be sure to use Main.as as the document class for the FLA.

Adding this game's assets to the library

This game does not require a lot of assets. We will embed the assets in the same way as previous games in this book. Flash assets are stored in the FLA library. Flex assets are stored in the assets.swf file included in the project.

Adding sounds

We only need a few sounds for this game. We are not going to make any significant change to the SoundManager either, so we will simply list the sounds that we are going to make use of for the game. All of these sounds were made with SFXR:

- SoundClick: Plays when the player clicks a block
- SoundBonus: Plays when a set of blocks disappears from the screen
- SoundLose: Plays when the player loses the game
- SoundWin: Plays when the player finishes a level

Adding graphics

We only have one sprite sheet for this game, and it is very simple. It includes seven 32 × 32–pixel colored blocks that we will cut apart in code to create the blocks the player will click in the game; the tile sheet is shown in Figure 8-2. We could have made this even simpler, with one block that we recolored in code, and the tradeoff would be more code to manage the colors. When programming gets down to this level of detail, it's really up to you as the programmer to decide which method is best for your development efforts.

Figure 8-2. Tile sheet for Color Drop game

Defining the classes for Color Drop

Before we get into the code, let's briefly discuss the set of classes we will create for Color Drop:

- ColorDrop: This is the main game class for ColorDrop. It will be called from Main and extend from com.efg.framework.Game.
- Block: This class will represent all of the on screen blocks for ColorDrop. The blocks will all use the same tile sheet for display.

■ CustomEventClickBlock: This is a custom event we will use to tell ColorDrop when a Block has been clicked.

■ GameStates: This class holds all the static const values that we will use for our in-game state machine for Color Drop.

Updating the Main class for Color Drop

Now, we will look at the Main class for ColorDrop. This class should look very familiar to you at this point. It extends GameFramework and has the same specific code for ColorDrop as the other games we have created thus far. The *major* changes in the code have to do with the ScoreBoard items and the sounds we will use in the game. The ScoreBoard will display the following items:

■ Main.SCORE_BOARD_SCORE: The player's total game score

■ Main.SCORE_BOARD_LEVEL: The current game level

■ Main.SCORE_BOARD_PLAYS: The number of clicks the player has left.

■ Main.SCORE_BOARD_THRESHOLD: The score the player must reach to finish the level

■ Main.SCORE_BOARD_LEVEL_SCORE: The current accumulated score for this level

We already talked a bit about the sounds we will use in the game, but again, they are SoundWin, SoundLose, SoundClick, and SoundBonus, and they will be referenced as Main.SOUND_WIN, Main.SOUND_LOSE, Main.SOUND_CLICK, Main.SOUND_BONUS respectively from ColorDrop.

Here is the full code for Main.as; other changes (such as screens and title text) for ColorDrop are highlighted in bold:

```
package com.efg.games.colordrop
{
    import com.efg.framework.FrameWorkStates;
    import com.efg.framework.GameFrameWork;
    import com.efg.framework.BasicScreen;
    import com.efg.framework.ScoreBoard;
    import com.efg.framework.Game;
    import com.efg.framework.SideBySideScoreElement;
    import com.efg.framework.SoundManager;

    import flash.display.Bitmap;
    import flash.display.BitmapData;
    import flash.display.Sprite;
    import flash.events.Event;
    import flash.geom.Point;
    import flash.utils.Timer;
    import flash.events.TimerEvent;
    import flash.text.TextFormat;

    public class Main extends GameFrameWork {

        public static const SCORE_BOARD_SCORE:String = "score";
        public static const SCORE_BOARD_LEVEL:String = "level";
        public static const SCORE_BOARD_PLAYS:String = "plays";
        public static const SCORE_BOARD_THRESHOLD:String = "threshold";
        public static const SCORE_BOARD_LEVEL_SCORE:String = "levelScore";
```

```
public static const SOUND_CLICK:String           =   "soundClick";
public static const SOUND_BONUS:String           =   "soundBonus";
public static const SOUND_WIN:String             =   "soundWin";
public static const SOUND_LOSE:String            =   "soundLose";

//**Flex Framework Only
/*
[Embed(source = "assets/colordropassets.swf", symbol="SoundClick")]
private var SoundClick:Class;

[Embed(source = "assets/colordropassets.swf", symbol="SoundBonus")]
private var SoundBonus:Class;

[Embed(source = "assets/colordropassets.swf", symbol="SoundWin")]
private var SoundWin:Class;

[Embed(source = "assets/colordropassets.swf", symbol="SoundLose")]
private var SoundLose:Class;
        */

public function Main() {
    init();
}

override public function init():void {
    game = new ColorDrop(600,400);
    setApplicationBackGround(600,400,false, 0x000000);
    scoreBoard = new ScoreBoard();
    addChild(scoreBoard);
    scoreBoardTextFormat= new TextFormat("_sans", "11", "0xffffff", "true");

    scoreBoard.createTextElement(SCORE_BOARD_SCORE, ⏎
      new SideBySideScoreElement(10, 5, 15, "Score", ⏎
      scoreBoardTextFormat, 50, "0", scoreBoardTextFormat));

    scoreBoard.createTextElement(SCORE_BOARD_LEVEL, ⏎
      new SideBySideScoreElement(125, 5, 15, "Level", ⏎
      scoreBoardTextFormat, 40, "0", scoreBoardTextFormat));

    scoreBoard.createTextElement(SCORE_BOARD_PLAYS, ⏎
      new SideBySideScoreElement(225, 5, 15, "Plays",⏎
      scoreBoardTextFormat, 40, "0", scoreBoardTextFormat));

    scoreBoard.createTextElement(SCORE_BOARD_THRESHOLD, ⏎
      new SideBySideScoreElement(300, 5, 15, "Threshold", ⏎
      scoreBoardTextFormat, 80, "0", scoreBoardTextFormat));

    scoreBoard.createTextElement(SCORE_BOARD_LEVEL_SCORE, ⏎
      new SideBySideScoreElement(425, 5, 15, "Level Score", ⏎
      scoreBoardTextFormat, 80, "0", scoreBoardTextFormat));

    screenTextFormat = new TextFormat("_sans", "14", "0xffffff", "true");
    screenButtonFormat = new TextFormat("_sans", "11", "0x000000", "true");
    titleScreen = new BasicScreen(⏎
     FrameWorkStates.STATE_SYSTEM_TITLE,
```

```
600,400, false, 0x000000);
titleScreen.createDisplayText("Color Drop",↵
250, new Point(255, 100), screenTextFormat);
titleScreen.createOkButton("Go!",new Point(250,250),100,20,  ↵
screenButtonFormat,0xFFFFFF,0x00FF0000,2);

instructionsScreen = new BasicScreen(↵
FrameWorkStates.STATE_SYSTEM_INSTRUCTIONS, 600,400, false, 0x000000);
instructionsScreen.createDisplayText("Click Colored Blocks",300, ↵
new Point(210,100),screenTextFormat);
instructionsScreen.createOkButton("Play",new Point(250,250),↵
100, 20, screenButtonFormat, 0xFFFFFF, 0xFF0000, 2);
gameOverScreen = new BasicScreen(↵
FrameWorkStates.STATE_SYSTEM_GAME_OVER,↵
600, 400, false, 0x000000);
gameOverScreen.createDisplayText("Game Over",300,↵
new Point(250, 100), screenTextFormat);
gameOverScreen.createOkButton("Play Again",↵
new Point(225, 250), 150, 20,↵
screenButtonFormat,0xFFFFFF,0xFF0000,2);
levelInText = "Level ";
levelInScreen = new BasicScreen(↵
FrameWorkStates.STATE_SYSTEM_GAME_OVER,↵
600,400, false, 0x000000);
levelInScreen.createDisplayText(levelInText,300,new Point(275,100),↵
screenTextFormat);

switchSystemState(FrameWorkStates.STATE_SYSTEM_TITLE);
waitTime= 40;

soundManager.addSound(SOUND_CLICK,new SoundClick());
soundManager.addSound(SOUND_BONUS, new SoundBonus());
soundManager.addSound(SOUND_WIN,new SoundWin());
soundManager.addSound(SOUND_LOSE,new SoundLose());

frameRate = 40;
startTimer();
}

}

}
```

Creating the Block class

We need to create only a couple extra classes for Color Drop. The first is the Block class. Because Block is a fairly complicated class, it's a good idea to get it out of the way first. Since most of Color Drop is played with colored blocks, this class is also the most important one that we will create for this game.

First, we create the class and import the proper classes. We are extending this class from BlitSprite that we created and put into the game framework in Chapter 7. Recall that BlitSpite is a class that itself extends from Sprite but is specifically used to both display and animate from a tile sheet. We are also going to use TileSheet class from the game framework.

```
package com.efg.games.colordrop
{

import flash.filters.GlowFilter;
import flash.events.MouseEvent;
import flash.display.Bitmap;
import flash.display.BitmapData;

import com.efg.framework.TileSheet;
import com.efg.framework.BlitSprite;

public class Block extends BlitSprite {
```

Now, we will create the instance variables for Block. blockColor is the color of the Block. Its value is one of the Block.BLOCK_COLOR_XXX static class variables defined in the next listing. Next, we have a set of two Boolean values that we will use to describe what the block is currently doing. These are the mini states of the Block, but they are so simple that we are not going to use a state machine. These two mini states are isFalling (the Block is moving down the screen) and isFading (the Block is fading out). For the actual fading of the Block, we have a variable named fadeValue that is set to the amount to fade the block on every frame. For falling, fallEndY is the y value on the screen that a Block must reach before isFalling is set to false. Finally, we have speed, which is how fast a block moves when falling; and nextYLocation, which is set in update and used in render like previous games in this book.

```
public var blockColor:Number;
public var isFalling:Boolean;
public var isFading:Boolean;
public var fadeValue:Number = .05;
public var fallEndY:Number;
public var speed:int = 10;
public var nextYLocation:int = 0;
```

Two other very useful instance variables are row and col. These two variables represent the current row and column in the grid kept in ColorDrop. They are critical for determining which blocks need to be tested to see if they are same color as the one clicked.

```
public var row:Number;
public var col:Number;
```

The class variables in Block are all static vars that represent the colors in the tile sheet (see Figure 8-2). These numbers will be used when calculating what part of the tile sheet to cut out to make the Block.

```
public static const BLOCK_COLOR_RED:int       = 0;
public static const BLOCK_COLOR_GREEN:int     = 1;
public static const BLOCK_COLOR_BLUE:int      = 2;
public static const BLOCK_COLOR_VIOLET:int    = 3;
public static const BLOCK_COLOR_ORANGE:int    = 4;
public static const BLOCK_COLOR_YELLOW:int    = 5;
public static const BLOCK_COLOR_PURPLE:int    = 6;
```

The constructor for Block requires information both for its superclass and for itself. blockColor, row, col, and speed are all pretty much self-explanatory from the previous descriptions. endY will be passed to startFalling, which will, in turn, set fallEndY to its value. However, tileSheet, an instance of the TileSheet object, needs some further discussion, as it is essential when we call super.

The TileSheet (ts) was created and passed to Block by ColorDrop. Block does not own its own TileSheet, which means we don't have to create multiple versions of the TileSheet for each Block and waste memory. Alternatively, we could have made tileSheet a static class variable. However, we think that passing in the value for the tileSheet helps keep the Block class a bit more universal and reusable. As well, it keeps us from having to write any code to determine if tileSheet exists yet and if it needs to be initialized as a class variable.

The next thing we need to do is determine the tile from the sheet that will represent this Block's color. Since the color is stored in blockColor, and the values of the Block.BLOCK_COLOR_XXX static constants represent the order of the colors on the tile sheet, we can easily calculate which tile will represent this Block like so: tile = blockColor;

Finally, we call the constructor of BlitSprite with the code super(tileSheet, [tile], 0). The first parameter is the TileSheet, which we have already described. The second parameter is an array of tile indexes for this instance to animate through. Since our Blocks do not animate, we simple put a single value in the array (the value of tile). The third parameter is the index of the starting tile in the tiles array. Since we only have one tile, the index is 0.

We also need to have this Block fire off a MouseEvent if the player clicks it, so we add a MOUSE_DOWN event that will call the function onMouseDownListener. We also set buttonMode and useHandCursor to true, so when the mouse pointer rolls over the Block, we will prompt to the user to click with a recognizable hand cursor. Finally, we call startFalling to have the Block start moving down the screen.

```
public function Block(color:Number,tileSheet:TileSheet,row:Number,col:Number,⤶
endY:Number,speed:Number) {

    blockColor = color;
    this.row = row;
    this.col = col;
    isFalling = false;
    isFading = false;
    var tile:Number = blockColor;
    super(tileSheet, [tile], 0);
    this.addEventListener(MouseEvent.MOUSE_DOWN, onMouseDownListener, false, 0, true);⤶
    this.buttonMode = true;
    this.useHandCursor = true;
    startFalling(endY,speed);
}
```

The startFalling function is the first link in developing this game into a drop-style game where blocks fall into place. The heart of the function is the speed and fallEndY instance variables. The distance between the starting y position of the Block (set by Game) and fallEndY should be evenly divisible by speed, but it does not have to be. If it is, the Blocks will fall into place smoother, but the gameplay won't be affected. We set the isFalling variable to true so that update and render functions will process the Block movement when they are called by Game.

```
public function startFalling(endY:Number,speed:Number):void {
    this.speed = speed;
    fallEndY = endY;
    isFalling = true;
}
```

The startFade function is called by ColorDrop to start the Block fading from the screen when the level ends. The fade is stopped by setting the isFading Boolean to true. The fadeValue passed as a parameter is the value used to decrement the alpha value of the Block when render is called by Game.

```
public function startFade(fadeValue:Number):void {
    this.fadeValue = fadeValue;
    isFading=true;
}
```

This update function is much like the update functions we have already written in this book. It looks to see if the Block's isFalling variable equals true, and if so, it updates nextYLocation to the current y position plus speed. The fading of the Block is not affected by render.

```
public function update():void {
    if (isFalling) {
        nextYLocation = y + speed;
    }
}
```

The render function is only slightly more complicated than update. If the Block is falling, update sets y to nextYLocation. If fallEndY is reached, the function makes sure the Block ends in the correct location by setting it exactly to the value in fallEndY. We do this because the last time the block moved, there is a good chance that that it overshot fallEndY, so we simply move it to where it should land. The isFalling property is set to false, so ColorDrop can test to see if all Block objects have stopped falling.

If the block is fading, we update the alpha value of the Block by subtracting the fadeValue. If the alpha value is reached (or goes negative), we set it to 0 and set isFading to false, so ColorDrop can test to see if all the fading Blocks are finished.

```
public function render():void {

    if (isFalling) {
        y = nextYLocation;
        if (y >= fallEndY) {
            y = fallEndY;
            isFalling = false;
        }
    }

    if (isFading) {
        alpha -= fadeValue;
        if (alpha <= 0) {
            alpha = 0;
            isFading = false;
        }
    }
}
```

The onMouseDownListener function is called when the player clicks on the Block with the mouse. This function dispatches a custom event that we will create in the next section of this chapter. The CustomEvent sends a reference to itself as the second parameter. ColorDrop will listen for this event, so it can start processing the Block objects to see which ones it should remove from the screen.

```
      public function onMouseDownListener(e:MouseEvent):void {↵
      dispatchEvent(new CustomEventClickBlock(CustomEventClickBlock.EVENT_CLICK_BLOCK,↵
      this));

          }
```

The makeBlockClicked function sets a GlowFilter around the block. This function is called from Game when that class is trying to determine which Blocks to light up when the player clicks a Block.

```
      public function makeBlockClicked():void {
      this.filters=[new GlowFilter(0xFFFFFF,70,4,4,3,3,false,false)]
  }
  }
}
```

Creating the CustomEventClickBlock class

To go along with the Block class, we need to create a new custom Event that will be dispatched when the player clicks a Block. The custom event will be similar to the custom events we created and put into the game framework in Chapter 2. However, we are going to put this event into the colordrop package instead of the game framework. Why? Well, it is specific enough to the ColorDrop game that it can live within the colordrop package.

This Event will include one property: a reference to the Block object that generated it. We will store this reference in the block property. We also need to create an identifier that will be used by the Block and ColorDrop classes to refer to this Event. This identifier will have the value of eventClickBlock and will be stored in a static const named EVENT_CLICK_BLOCK.

```
package com.efg.games.colordrop
{
    import flash.events.*;

    public class CustomEventClickBlock extends Event
    {
        public var block:Block;
        public static const EVENT_CLICK_BLOCK:String = "eventClickBlock";

        public function CustomEventClickBlock(type:String, block:Block,↵
        bubbles:Boolean=false,cancelable:Boolean=false)
        {
            super(type, bubbles,cancelable);
            this.block = block;
        }

        public override function clone():Event {
            return new CustomEventClickBlock(type, block, bubbles,cancelable)
        }

        public override function toString():String {↵
            return formatToString(type, "type", "bubbles", "cancelable", "eventPhase");
        }
    }
}
```

Controlling difficulty with a level class

We've shown you a couple different ways to create difficulty levels in a game already in this book, and with Color Drop, we will expand on these ideas even further. A simple DifficultyLevel class follows. We will create an array of these classes in ColorDrop to represent explicit difficulty levels that will ramp up when a level is completed.

Each DifficultyLevel contains three properties:

- allowedColors: This array holds all the possible colors of blocks that can occur on any given level.
- startPlays: This is the number of plays the player is awarded at the beginning of the level. When plays run out, the game is over
- scoreThreshold: The score must be reached on a level to advance to the next level. This score must be reached before the number of plays equals zero.

The DifficultyLevel class accepts all of these parameters in the constructor and sets the appropriate variables.

```
package com.efg.games.colordrop
{

    public class DifficultyLevel {

        public var allowedColors:Array;
        public var startPlays:Number;
        public var scoreThreshold:Number;

        public function DifficultyLevel(allowedColors:Array, startPlays:Number, ↩
        scoreThreshold:Number)
        {
            this.allowedColors = allowedColors;
            this.startPlays = startPlays;
            this.scoreThreshold = scoreThreshold;
        }
    }
}
```

Creating the GameStates class

GameStates is a class we will use to hold the static const values we will use in Color Drop to control the flow of the game. These values are the local states for the ColorDrop state machine. We will be creating a state machine local to this game that is used along with the state machine in Main, and these states (as well as the state machine) will be explained in full a bit later. For now, it is good to know that we will be making extensive use of these values very soon.

```
package com.efg.games.colordrop
{

public class GameStates {

    public static const STATE_INITIALIZING:int            = 10;
```

```
    public static const STATE_START_REPLACING:int        = 20;
    public static const STATE_WAITING_FOR_INPUT:int      = 30;
    public static const STATE_REMOVE_CLICKED_BLOCKS:int  = 40;
    public static const STATE_FADE_BLOCKS_WAIT:int       = 50;
    public static const STATE_FALL_BLOCKS_WAIT:int       = 60;
    public static const STATE_END_GAME:int               = 70;
    public static const STATE_END_LEVEL:int              = 80;
    public static const STATE_WAIT:int                   = 90;

    }
}
```

You might be wondering why these values are multiples of 10, while the static const values we created earlier in the Block class were multiples of 1. The reason is very simple. The const values we created in the Block class represented the colored blocks as they existed in a TileSheet. Those frames are multiples of 1, and need to be multiples of 1 for the code to work properly. However, the states in GameStates have arbitrary values, and they are numbered in roughly the order that they will be used. In this way, if you need to add a new state, you can fit it in between two other states and not have to renumber any of the other consts. While this spacing in value is not necessary, there is a historical significance to it. Back when BASIC was a popular language, all of the lines of code were numbered. It was a common practice at that time to number the lines of code in multiples of 10, for the same reason we numbered the states in multiple of 10—to allow the programmer to add lines of code in between other lines without having to renumber every line of code. In reality, you can number this states with any values, as long as all of them are unique.

Implementing the basic game structure

The structure of the ColorDrop class for Color Drop is very close to some of the other games we have created in this book so far. The game lives in the com.efg.games.colordrop package. The imports are mostly standard, but since we will be using the TileSheet class, we have imported that one specifically. TileSheet will be used with the Block class to display the colored blocks on the screen. gameWidth and gameHeight will be passed the colorDrop constructor from Main.

```
package com.efg.games.colordrop
{
    import flash.display.Sprite;
    import flash.events.*;

    import com.efg.framework.Game;
    import com.efg.framework.CustomEventLevelScreenUpdate;
    import com.efg.framework.CustomEventScoreBoardUpdate;
    import com.efg.framework.CustomEventSound;
    import com.efg.framework.TileSheet;

    public class ColorDrop extends com.efg.framework.Game
    {

        private var gameWidth:int;
        private var gameHeight:int;
```

Now we will define some very important const values that we will use for this game. These are also some of the more important values to understand if you want to reuse this game for another purpose, as they help define the position, size, and spacing of the grid of Blocks on the screen.

```
//Game Constants
```

The first two constants are X_PAD and Y_PAD. These two values define the starting (x, y) position of the grid of Blocks on the screen. These values will be added to the position of every Block when it is created so that it will be positioned correctly

```
private static const Y_PAD:int =              50;
private static const X_PAD:int =              135
```

ROW_SPACING and COL_SPACING define how many pixels of empty space we will leave in between each block on the screen.

```
private static const ROW_SPACING:int =              2;
private static const COL_SPACING:int =              2;
```

BLOCK_HEIGHT and BLOCK_WIDTH define the dimensions of each Block. These will also be used when we create our TileSheet object to define the dimensions of each tile.

```
private static const BLOCK_HEIGHT:int=              32;
private static const BLOCK_WIDTH:int =              32;
```

BLOCK_ROWS and BLOCK_COLS define how many rows and columns of blocks will appear on the screen. The way this game is written, you can easily change the amount of blocks on the screen by updating these values.

```
private static const BLOCK_ROWS:int    =        10;
private static const BLOCK_COLS:int     =        10;
```

The next set of variables is used for in-game housekeeping. We already described these values when we discussed the additions to the ScoreBoard in Main, but to review

- score is the player's total game score that we will report back to ScoreBoard.
- level is the current game level we will report back to ScoreBoard.
- plays are the number of clicks the player has left, which we will also report back to ScoreBoard.
- levelScore is the current accumulated score for this level that we report back to ScoreBoard. This score must be equal to or higher than DifficultyLevel.scoreThreshhold before plays have been exhausted for the player to advance to the next level.

```
private var score:int;
private var level:int;
private var plays:int;
private var levelScore:int;
```

Since we are going to manage the game's difficulty using DifficultyLevel objects stored in an array, we need to define some variable to hold these values. difficultyLevelArray will hold all of the DifficultyLevel objects we create. currentLevel will hold the DifficultyLevel class that represents the level the player is currently playing.

```
private var difficultyLevelArray:Array;
private var currentLevel:DifficultyLevel;
```

343

Now, we need to create some variables to represent the Blocks that the player will be clicking in the game. The clickedBlocksArray array will be used to hold the set of Blocks that we calculate are the same color as the Block the player has clicked and are somehow connected to it. board is a multidimensional array that will hold all the Blocks logically in their relative screen positions (row,col). This will make it much easier to calculate where one block is in reference to other blocks. tempBlock is an instance variable that we will use many times in the Game class. We create it to save the overhead of creating it every time we use it.

```
private var clickedBlocksArray:Array;
private var board:Array;
private var tempBlock:Block;
```

The next set of variables are used with the game states for the state machine. gameState is the current game state in Game. nextGameState is used with the GameStates.STATE_WAIT state to define the game state to revert to once GameStates.STATE_WAIT is finished. GameStates.STATE_WAIT is a special state that we will use to pause the game for a few frames to make the action smoother. Both framesToWait and framesWaited are used in conjunction with GameStates.STATE_WAIT.

```
private var gameState:int = 0;
private var nextGameState:int = 0;
private var framesToWait:int = 0;
private var framesWaited:int = 0;
```

Next, we will define a couple difficulty settings. We only have two of these in Color Drop, as we are using a DifficultyLevel class for most of the other settings. However, these settings are universal. The first, POINTS_PER_BLOCK is the number if points we will award the player per block that is clicked and matched. The second, BONUS_POINTS_PER_BLOCK is the amount of points we award the player for every successive block in the group they have clicked beyond the first. This essentially gives them a quarter-point bonus for every block beyond the first one.

```
private static var BONUS_PER_BLOCK:Number = .25;
private static var POINTS_PER_BLOCK:Number = 1;
```

Finally, we define the tileSheet variable we will be using for this game.

```
//***** Flex *****
//[Embed(source = 'assets/colordropassets.swf', symbol = 'ColorSheet')]
//private var ColorSheet:Class;
//***** End Flex *****

private var tileSheet:TileSheet;
```

The constructor for this game is very similar to the constructor of the previous games. We accept the game's gameWidth and gameHeight. We then set the gameState to GameStates. STATE_INITIALIZING and call init to set up the variables. We set the gameState to make sure that in the event that runGame is called by Main while initialize is being called. Remember, it's called in the game timer loop in Main so we don't have control over it from Game; Game will know what to do.

```
public function ColorDrop(gW:int,gH:int) {
        gameWidth=gW;
        gameHeight=gH
        init();
        gameState = GameStates.STATE_INITIALIZING;
        }
```

Initializing the game

The init function is called from the Game constructor to set up the initial variable values for Color Drop. We start by setting the value for tileSheet. As we discussed in the section about the Block class, we need to pass the tileSheet to Block instances when they are created. The parameters for TileSheet are the bitmap we are using for the tiles as set in the SWF library (in this case, ColorSheet) and the height and width of the tiles we are going to cut from the tile sheet. The Flex version of this code has been commented out but left in so you can see the differences.

```
public function init():void {
   //***** Flash IDE *****
   tileSheet = new TileSheet(new ColorSheet(0,0), BLOCK_WIDTH,BLOCK_HEIGHT);
   //***** End Flash IDE *****
   //***** Flex *****
   //tileSheet = new TileSheet(new ColorSheet().bitmapData, BLOCK_WIDTH,↵
   BLOCK_HEIGHT);      //***** End Flex *****
```

Now, we need to create the difficulty levels for the game. To do this, we first initialize our difficultyLevelArray array. Then, we simply create each level one at a time by pushing a new instance of DifficultyLevel into the array.

Since the object of the game Color Drop is to remove adjacent same-color blocks from the screen, the difficulty ramps by adding more colors that will appear per level. We do this by passing an array of Block.BLOCK_COLOR_XXX values as the first parameter for DifficultyLevel. The other parameters are startPlays, the number of plays added for the player when the level starts; and scoreThreshold, the score that must be reached on that level to advance to the next. We have left both of these values the same for every level. This would be the first place to tinker with this game, changing values to see if the difficulty for this game can be managed in a different way.

```
   difficultyLevelArray = new Array();
   difficultyLevelArray.push(new DifficultyLevel(↵
      [Block.BLOCK_COLOR_RED,Block.BLOCK_COLOR_GREEN,Block.BLOCK_COLOR_BLUE],10,500));
   difficultyLevelArray.push(new DifficultyLevel(↵
      [Block.BLOCK_COLOR_RED,Block.BLOCK_COLOR_GREEN,Block.BLOCK_COLOR_BLUE,↵
      Block.BLOCK_COLOR_VIOLET],10,500));
   difficultyLevelArray.push(new DifficultyLevel(↵
      [Block.BLOCK_COLOR_RED,Block.BLOCK_COLOR_GREEN,Block.BLOCK_COLOR_BLUE,↵
      Block.BLOCK_COLOR_VIOLET,Block.BLOCK_COLOR_ORANGE],10,500));
   difficultyLevelArray.push(new DifficultyLevel(↵
      [Block.BLOCK_COLOR_RED,Block.BLOCK_COLOR_GREEN,Block.BLOCK_COLOR_BLUE,↵
      Block.BLOCK_COLOR_VIOLET,Block.BLOCK_COLOR_ORANGE,Block.BLOCK_COLOR_YELLOW],↵
      10,500));
   difficultyLevelArray.push(new DifficultyLevel(↵
      [Block.BLOCK_COLOR_RED,Block.BLOCK_COLOR_GREEN,Block.BLOCK_COLOR_BLUE,↵
      Block.BLOCK_COLOR_VIOLET,Block.BLOCK_COLOR_ORANGE,Block.BLOCK_COLOR_YELLOW,↵
      Block.BLOCK_COLOR_PURPLE],10,500));

}
```

The newGame function is called from Main. For new game, we set level, score, and plays to 0. That is all we need to do for a new game.

```
override public function newGame():void {
    level = 0;
    score = 0;
    plays = 0;
}
```

Unlike `newGame`, `newLevel` has some very interesting code in the Color Drop game. We start `newLevel` by updating `level` and `plays` so that the game can start. For `level`, we increment the variable and then test it to see if it is larger than the final level we have stored in `difficultyLevelArray` (`difficultyLevelArray.length-1`). If so, we get the level values from the last available level in the `difficultyLevels` array. We use a variable named `tempLevel` to store the level locally, because while we want to retain the `level` value for the `ScoreBoard`, we need to read the level data from the last available level.

Next, we add the value of `startPlays` from `tempLevel` to the `plays` variable. Remember, the player gets to keep the `plays` left over from the last level for the current level. We then set `levelScore` to 0. `levelScore` is the calculation of the points the player has amassed for this level only. We use this variable to see if the player has equaled or passed the `scoreThreshold` for the current level and can advance to the next. Next, we dispatch events to report the new values for `plays`, `level`, and `threshold`.

```
override public function newLevel():void {
    level++;
    var tempLevel:int = level;
    if (tempLevel > (difficultyLevelArray.length-1)) {
        tempLevel = difficultyLevelArray.length-1
    }
    currentLevel = difficultyLevelArray[tempLevel-1];
    plays += currentLevel.startPlays;
    levelScore = 0;
    dispatchEvent(new CustomEventLevelScreenUpdate(↵
        CustomEventLevelScreenUpdate.UPDATE_TEXT, String(level)));
    dispatchEvent(new CustomEventScoreBoardUpdate(↵
        CustomEventScoreBoardUpdate.UPDATE_TEXT,Main.SCORE_BOARD_PLAYS,String(plays)));
    dispatchEvent(new CustomEventScoreBoardUpdate(↵
        CustomEventScoreBoardUpdate.UPDATE_TEXT,Main.SCORE_BOARD_LEVEL,String(level)));
    dispatchEvent(new CustomEventScoreBoardUpdate(↵
        CustomEventScoreBoardUpdate.UPDATE_TEXT,Main.SCORE_BOARD_THRESHOLD,↵
        String(currentLevel.scoreThreshold)));
```

Now, we need to initialize the blocks on the screen. We will store references to all the blocks on the screen in a 2D array named board. First, we initialize the array. Next, we create two nested for loops. The first for loop creates a new array for each row of blocks. The next for loop creates a null value in each spot in each row-column combination in each array (board[r][c] = null;). We will use these null values to determine if we need to create a Block to put in its place. We then initialize clickedBlocksArray. As we said before, we will use this array to hold the list of blocks that match the color of the Block the player has clicked on. Finally, we set the gameState to GameStates.STATE_START_REPLACING, which will actually put blocks on the screen.

```
    board = new Array();
    for (var r:int  = 0; r < BLOCK_ROWS; r++) {
        board[r] = new Array();
        for (var c:int = 0; c <BLOCK_COLS; c++) {
            board[r][c] = null;
        }
```

```
    }
    clickedBlocksArray = new Array();
    gameState = GameStates.STATE_START_REPLACING;
}
```

Adding the ColorDrop state machine

Before we talk about putting blocks on the screen, we should discuss the state machine we are going to create in the ColorDrop class. We have already created a state machine for our Main class. It controls Game and tells it when to start a new game, start a new level, and run its game loop by calling runGame. So far, this has been sufficient for most of our games. However, when it comes to casual puzzle-style games, it can be beneficial to further refine the runGame method into its own state machine. Before you close this book and run away screaming, let us explain.

If you recall from Chapter 1, we created a very simplified state machine using a switch statement. We explained why we think this is a good idea and showed you the code to implement it. To review, we believe the state machine helps keep the game flowing logically and takes the place of multiple Boolean variables and the messy tests involved to make sure they all have the right values. We further refined that state machine in Chapter 2 to make it run more efficiently by getting rid of the switch statement and using a systemFunction variable that is used to call the current state function.

We need something similar for Color Drop's Game class. The reason is simple: we need more control over the flow of the game. Since most of the time the game is waiting for user input, we want to restrict what can actually be happening at any given time. For example, when blocks are falling into place on the screen, we want to make sure the user cannot click on them. Without a state machine in Game, we would have the same problem that would plague Main: too many Boolean variables to test and keep updated. With a simple machine, all we need to do is to test the current gameState to see what input is valid and what the game should be doing.

For Color Drop, we are going to create a simple state machine much like the one from Chapter 1 with a switch statement. We decided to do this to show you, the now advanced Flash game-making *wunderkind*, that a switch statement style state machine can be very useful alongside the systemFunction style state machine.

Recall that we defined these states in the properties section of our GameStates class:

```
public static const  STATE_INITIALIZING:int             = 10;
public static const  STATE_START_REPLACING:int           = 20;
public static const  STATE_WAITING_FOR_INPUT:int         = 30;
public static const  STATE_REMOVE_CLICKED_BLOCKS:int     = 40;
public static const  STATE_FADE_BLOCKS_WAIT:int          = 50;
public static const  STATE_FALL_BLOCKS_WAIT:int          = 60;
public static const  STATE_END_GAME:int                  = 70;
public static const  STATE_END_LEVEL:int                 = 80;
public static const  STATE_WAIT:int                      = 90;
```

We will use these states to manipulate the flow of the game, in way that is similar to creating a small abstract programming language inside another programming language (AS3). One thing that you will notice is that we attempt (wherever possible) to control the changing of states within this switch statement. In that way, following the flow of the game is easier. While we can't always keep state changes in this function, that should be the goal.

GameStates.STATE_INITIALIZING is set by the ColorDrop class constructor and is a blanket state for everything that happens when the game is starting, and Main is calling newGame and newLevel.

```
override public function runGame():void {
    switch(gameState) {
        case GameStates.STATE_INITIALIZING:
        break;
```

The GameStates.STATE_START_REPLACING is set when blocks need to be put on the screen—at the beginning of every level and after the player has clicked to remove blocks from the grid. We have standardized this state so that it can work in both instances. The replaceBlocks function only gets the blocks on the screen, but they still need to fall into place. This is what the state GameStates.STATE_FALL_BLOCKS_WAIT is for. We set the nextGameState variable so that it is GameStates.STATE_WAITING_FOR_INPUT. GameStates.STATE_FALL_BLOCKS_WAIT will set gameState to nextGameState when it has calculated that all the blocks have stopped falling on the screen.

```
        case GameStates.STATE_START_REPLACING:
            replaceBlocks();
            nextGameState = GameStates.STATE_WAITING_FOR_INPUT;
            gameState = GameStates.STATE_FALL_BLOCKS_WAIT;
            break;
```

GameStates.STATE_WAITING_INPUT is the general state called when the player is thinking about what choice to make. If this was a timed game, you might update the clock here. We make a call to checkForEndLevel, because this is a convenient place to do it. This call could have gone right after the player clicked a Block, but we put it here because it's easier to understand the game flow when most of the calls are in game loop.

```
        case GameStates.STATE_WAITING_FOR_INPUT:
            checkforEndLevel();
            break;
```

GameStates.STATE_REMOVE_CLICKED_BLOCKS has a very descriptive name. This state is set when blocks are being removed from the screen. This state is used in conjunction with GameStates.STATE_WAIT (described in this section a bit later). We created this state so that we could have a slight pause between when the player clicked a block and when the blocks are removed from the screen. This lends each click a dramatic effect, as the player gets to see all the connecting blocks light up before they are removed from the screen. We call removeClickedBlock (described in "Adding blocks to the screen" section) to get rid of the current set of clicked blocks and then set the gameState to GameStates.STATE_START_REPLACING to put more blocks back on the screen.

```
        case GameStates.STATE_REMOVE_CLICKED_BLOCKS:
            removeClickedBlocks();
            gameState = GameStates.STATE_START_REPLACING;
            break;
```

GameStates.STATE_FADE_BLOCKS_WAIT is set when the entire group of blocks is clearing off the screen by fading them out using their alpha property. The state keeps calling checkForFadingBlocks, so it can set the state to nextGameState when all the blocks have faded off the screen.

```
        case GameStates.STATE_FADE_BLOCKS_WAIT:
            if (!checkForFadingBlocks()) {
            gameState = nextGameState;
            }
            break;
```

GameStates.STATE_FALL_BLOCKS_WAIT is a state set when blocks are falling on or off the screen, which happens when the level starts, after blocks are clicked, and when the game ends. The function continually calls checkForFallingblocks, so it can set the state to the value of nextGameState when all the blocks have stopped falling.

```
case GameStates.STATE_FALL_BLOCKS_WAIT:
    if (!checkForFallingBlocks()) {
    gameState = nextGameState;
    }
    break;
```

GameStates.STATE_END_LEVEL is set when ColorDrop has concluded that the player's levelScore is equal to or greater than currentLevel.scoreThreshhold. endLevel is called and then we put the gameState into GameStates.STATE_INTIALIZING so we can wait for Main to call nextLevel.

```
case GameStates.STATE_END_LEVEL:
    endLevel();
    gameState = GameStates.STATE_INITIALIZING;
    break;
```

GameStates.STATE_END_GAME is set when ColorDrop has concluded that plays are equal to 0 but levelScore is not equal to or greater than currentLevel.scoreThreshold. We call endGame, which takes care of the rest for us.

```
case GameStates.STATE_END_GAME:
    endGame();
    break;
```

GameStates.STATE_WAIT is a special state we have created that allows us to pause the game for a designated number of frames before continuing. This might sound useless at first, but for certain dramatic effects, it can be very useful. We will discuss what we use it for a bit later, but for now, we will just talk about how it works. The framesWaited variable is set to 0 before the gameState is set to GameStates.STATE_WAIT. Conversely, waitFrames is set to the maximum number of frames to pause the game. Also, nextGameState is set to the value of the STATE_XXX state that will go into effect after the GameStates.STATE_WAIT is finished. Every time that runGame gets called, framesWaited is incremented. When it is greater than or equal to waitFrames, we set gameState to nextGameState and then ColorDrop acts like this little waiting period never happened.

```
case GameStates.STATE_WAIT:
    framesWaited++;
    if (framesWaited >= framesToWait) {
    gameState = nextGameState;
    }
    break;
}
```

Finally, outside of our switch statement, we call both render and update. If we did not do this, we would have to make multiple calls to update and render inside of the states that needed those functions to be called. To be more efficient, we will make some changes to update and render to make sure they are only operating on objects that require their services.

```
    update();
    render();

}
```

checkForFallingBlocks is called when we need to find out if any Block objects on the screen are currently moving. The function loops through all the Blocks in the board 2D array, and if any one Block is still moving (isFalling = true), it returns false.

```
public function checkForFallingBlocks():Boolean {
    var isFalling:Boolean = false;
    for (var r:int  = 0; r < board.length; r++) {
        for (var c:int = 0; c < board[r].length; c++) {
            tempBlock =board[r][c];
            if (tempBlock.isFalling) {
                isFalling = true;
            }
        }
    }
    return isFalling;
}
```

checkForFadingBlocks is called when we need to find out if any Block objects on the screen are currently fading. The function loops through all the Blocks in the board 2D array, and if any one Block is still fading (isFading = true), it returns false.

```
public function checkForFadingBlocks():Boolean {
    var isFading:Boolean = false;
    for (var r:int  = 0; r < board.length; r++) {
        for (var c:int = 0; c < board[r].length; c++) {
            tempBlock =board[r][c];
            if (tempBlock.isFading) {
                isFading = true;
            }
        }
    }
    return isFading;
}
```

Adding blocks to the screen

When the gameState is equal to GameStates.STATE_START_REPLACING, runGame calls replaceBlocks to put our Block objects on the screen. We will write this function in a way that it will be universal for our game: no matter when blocks need to be replaced (at the beginning of a level or after the user clicks and removes blocks), it will operate the same way. We replace blocks very simply: we loop through our 2D array stored in board, and when we find a row, col combination that is equal to null (board[r][c] == null), we call addBlock(r,c) to fill it. That's it. addBlock then does most of the interesting work.

```
public function replaceBlocks():void {
    for (var r:int  = 0; r < board.length; r++) {
        for (var c:int = 0; c < board[r].length; c++) {
            if (board[r][c] == null) {
                board[r][c] = addBlock(r,c);
            }
        }
    }
}
```

addBlock might seem like a complex function at first, but it is really very simple. The code looks difficult because of all the constants we use to calculate the position of a Block. Let's get rid of the easy part first: finding the color of the block. We get a random color from the array CurrentLevel.allowedColors that we set in the DifficultyLevel class. First, we find an index into the allowedColors array like so:

```
var randomColor= Math.floor(Math.random()*currentLevel.allowedColors.length);
```

Then, we use that index to store that color for later use:

```
var blockColor = currentLevel.allowedColors[randomColor];
```

Now, we need to create an instance of Block and put it into tempBlock. Here is a rundown of the parameters we will pass to the Block constructor:

- blockColor: The color we just found from the currentLevel.allowedColors array
- tileSheet: A reference to the tile sheet we created that holds the graphics for the blocks
- row: The row index in the board array passed to us from replaceBlocks
- col: The col index in the board array passed to us from replaceBlocks
- (row*BLOCK_HEIGHT)+Y_PAD+(row*ROW_SPACING): The fallEndY property for Block

row*BLOCK_HEIGHT is the y value of the row position for this Block. Y_PAD is the distance from the top of the screen to the start of the Blocks in the grid. row*ROW_SPACING represents all the spaces between each row of Blocks. Add all of those values together to get the final position of the Block on the screen.

```
public function addBlock(row:Number, col:Number):Block {
    var randomColor:Number =
Math.floor(Math.random()*currentLevel.allowedColors.length);
    var blockColor:Number = currentLevel.allowedColors[randomColor];
    tempBlock = new Block(blockColor, tileSheet, row, col,↵
        (row*BLOCK_HEIGHT)+Y_PAD+(row*ROW_SPACING),(Math.random()*10)+10 );
```

Next, we will set the starting x value for the Block, which is very similar to the fallEndY value, except we use BLOCK_WIDTH, X_PAD, and COL_SPACING as our values to plug into the calculation. The starting y value is simply 0-BLOCK_HEIGHT so the Block will start just off the screen. Figure 8-3 shows how the constant values are used to calculate where blocks start and end in Color Drop.

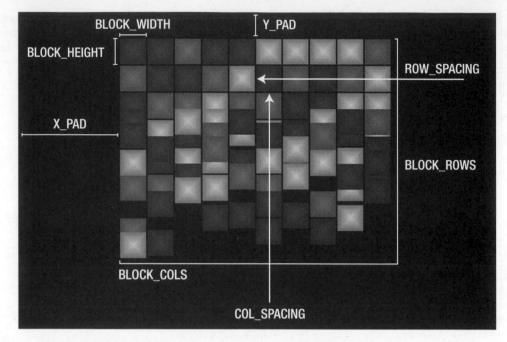

Figure 8-3. Blocks falling into place (annoted with const identifiers)

Next, we add an `EventListener` for the `CustomEventClickBlock.EVENT_CLICK_BLOCK` event we created earlier in the `CustomEventClickBlock` class. We will put into our `CustomEvent` class named `CUSTOMEVENT_CLICKBLOCK`. This is the same event that we had the `Block` class dispatch when it was clicked. The function `blockClickListener` will be used to handle that event. Finally, we put the `Block` on the screen with `addChild` and then return a reference to the `Block` to the caller. In our case, this is always `replaceBlocks`, which will store the reference in the `board` 2D array.

```
tempBlock.x=(col*BLOCK_WIDTH)+X_PAD+(col*COL_SPACING);
tempBlock.y= 0 - BLOCK_HEIGHT;
tempBlock.addEventListener(CustomEventClickBlock.EVENT_CLICK_BLOCK,⏎
    blockClickListener, false, 0, true);
this.addChild(tempBlock);
return tempBlock;
}
```

Expanding update and render for ColorDrop

The `update` and `render` functions for Color Drop are similar to ones created for other games in this book. However, we have expanded the logic a bit in both of them to assist with our local ColorDrop state machine. Recall, that these two functions are called regardless of the `gameState`. We do this because multiple states require these functions to be called, but it is messy to call them multiple times within the state `switch` statement. Instead, we put in some simple logic to test the `Block` objects to see if they need to have their `render` or `update` functions called.

For update, we loop through all of the Block objects in the board 2D array looking for any that are not null. This detail is important, because blocks can still be falling into (or out of) place moving before the entire grid has been replenished with new Block objects. If we do not test for null values in the array, the game will throw runtime exceptions because of the null object reference. If the Block is not null, then we test to see if tempblock.isFalling is true. If so, we call tempBlock.update. Otherwise, we do nothing.

```
public function update():void {
    for (var r:int  = 0; r < board.length; r++) {
        for (var c:int = 0; c < board[r].length; c++) {
            tempBlock = board[r][c];
            if (tempBlock != null) {
                if (tempBlock.isFalling) {
                    tempBlock.update();
                }
            }
        }
    }
}
```

The render function is very similar to update. First we check for null values, and then, we call tempBlock.render if tempBlock.isFalling or tempBlock.isFading is true. We did not test for tempBlock.isFading in update because tempBlock.update does not handle any of the alpha fading work for the block.

```
public function render():void {
    for (var r:int  = 0; r < board.length; r++) {
        for (var c:int = 0; c < board[r].length; c++) {
            tempBlock = board[r][c];
            if (tempBlock != null) {
                if (tempBlock.isFalling || tempBlock.isFading) {
                    tempBlock.render();
                }
            }
        }
    }
}
```

Waiting for user input

The game state GameStates.STATE_WAITING_FOR_INPUT is set when ColorDrop is in the game loop waiting for a mouse click. When one of the Block objects is clicked, CustomEventClickBlock.EVENT_CLICK_BLOCK is dispatched, and the function blockClickListener is called to handle it (see Figure 8-4).

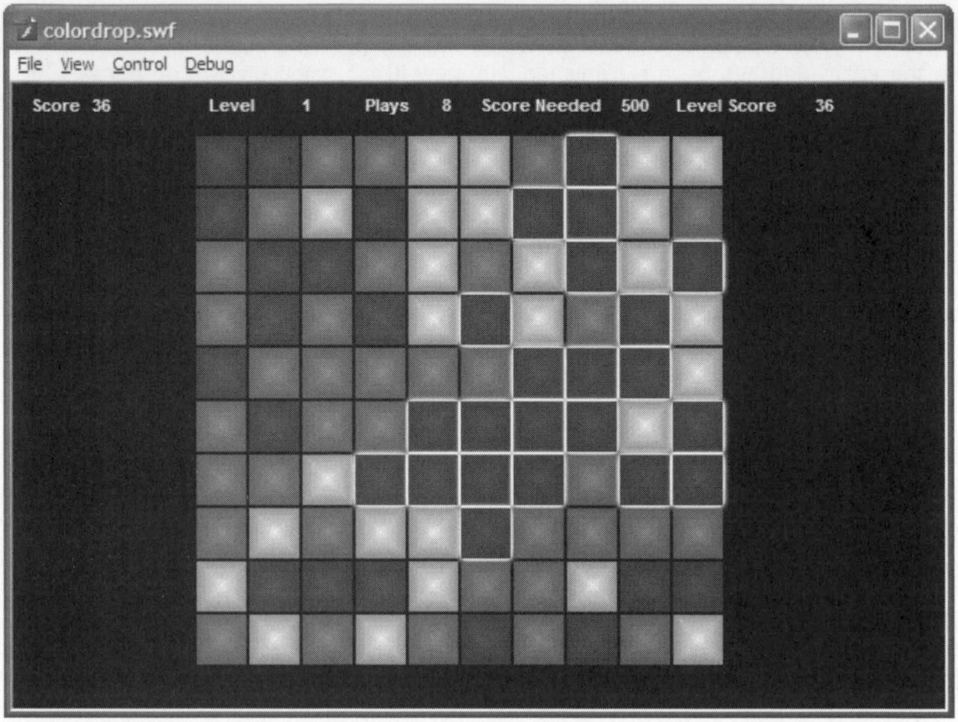

Figure 8-4. Clicking a colored block and selecting all similarly colored blocks touching it

The first thing we do in blockClickListener is test to see if we actually are in the GameStates.STATE_WAITING_FOR_INPUT game state. If so, we drop into the main part of the function and dispatch CustomEventSound.PLAY_SOUND event to play Main.SOUND_CLICK. This will to give the user audio feedback for each click of the mouse.

Next, we retrieve the reference to the Block that was clicked (e.block) and put it into tempBlock. We then fill clickedBlockArray by calling findLikeColoredBlocks and passing tempBlock as the lone parameter. We will discuss this function in moment, but first, we'll finish the last few lines of this function.

We then set all the necessary variables to create a GameStates.STATE_WAIT state (framesToWait = 15, framesWaited = 0, and nextGameState = GameStates. STATE_REMOVE_CLICKED_BLOCKS), decrement the plays variable (because the player just made a play by clicking on a block) and set the gameState to GameStates.STATE_WAIT. This wait time of 15 frames will give the game a dramatic pause between when the user clicks a Block, the blocks that match lighting up with a glow filter, and all the Block objects being removed from the screen in GameStates.STATE_REMOVE_CLICKED_BLOCKS.

```
public function blockClickListener(e:CustomEventClickBlock):void {
    if (gameState==GameStates.STATE_WAITING_FOR_INPUT) {
        dispatchEvent( new CustomEventSound(CustomEventSound.PLAY_SOUND,↵
        Main.SOUND_CLICK,false,1,0,1));
        tempBlock = e.block;
        clickedBlocksArray =      findLikeColoredBlocks(tempBlock);
```

```
        framesToWait = 15;
        framesWaited = 0;
        plays--;
        nextGameState = GameStates.STATE_REMOVE_CLICKED_BLOCKS;
        gameState = GameStates.STATE_WAIT;
    }
}
```

Using a nonrecursive function to test blocks

Normally, this section is where we would teach you about recursive functions and how they can be useful in a game like Color Drop. Recursive functions are functions that call themselves iteratively to perform a repeated action. You can imagine, in a game like Color Drop, that a recursive function might be useful. We need to test many blocks to see if they are connected. To do this, we need call some function, and it needs to be very intelligent on how it decides if a block is connected or not connected to the original block.

When you click a block in Color Drop, the ColorDrop class needs to look at all the Block objects around the clicked Block and all the Block objects those Block objects touch of the same color, to find every Block of that color that both touches and matches the original Block.

We could, for example, create a function named testBlock that would be passed a Block and its job would be to call testBlock for every Block that it was touching. If we did that, and looked at the execution stack, you might see something that looks like this:

```
testBlock()
    testBlockColor()
        testBlock()
            testBlockColor()
                testBlock()
                    testBlockColor()
                        testBlock()
```

This recursion would keep going until all blocks that had the color and were touching were tested. There is no problem with this, except that it uses a lot of resources. On most devices, calls to functions pass their parameters on the internal CPU stack. On devices with low amounts of memory (say, for example, an iPhone or other portable device), as the call stack gets larger, available memory can be used up very quickly. At the same time, informal tests (for other platforms) have shown that recursion is much slower than other options, like iteration (for an example, see http://shiman.wordpress.com/2008/05/28/recursion-vs-iteration/). However, even if recursion was faster than iteration, there is another very good reason to not use it for a game like Color Drop. Recursion in AS3 is limited to 256 levels. That means, at most, we could have 256 blocks on the screen to test (in the event that they were all the same color and all would be called recursively at once). Even though Color Drop only uses 100 blocks at a time, in theory a similar game could have many more blocks than 256. There is no reason to limit the objects in your game based on the levels of recursion that AS3 supports.

Instead, we are going to create a single function that can check every Block object iteratively. We are going to do this using three parallel arrays. These arrays will help us limit the number of Block objects we check and help us keep track of the Block objects that have matched or not matched the Block we are testing. Here are the arrays we are going to create:

- blocksToCheck: This is the list of Blocks that we determine are the same color as the clicked Block clicked and are also adjacent to that block or a block of that color that is adjacent to that block.
- blocksMatched: This array contains the list of Blocks that we have already determined match the clicked Block.
- blocksTested: This is list of Blocks we have already tested.

Why do we need all three arrays? They are used to make sure that our iterative function only makes the number of tests required and does not go into an infinite loop checking Block objects that have already been checked or matching Block objects that have already been matched.

```
public function findLikeColoredBlocks(blockToMatch:Block):Array {
    var blocksToCheck:Array = new Array();
    var blocksMatched:Array = new Array();
    var blocksTested:Array = new Array();
```

The next two arrays are also extremely important. They represent the row and column locations in the board 2D array that we are going to test for every Block. Since we allow any Block that is adjacent to the clicked Block (or a Block adjacent to that Block, etc.) to be considered connected, we need to test the nine spots around any Block to see if they contain Blocks with matching colors. Figure 8-5 illustrates the row and column locations that we need to test and how they relate to the values in rowList and colList.

```
    var rowList:Array = [-1, 0, 1,-1,1,-1,0,1];
    var colList:Array = [-1,-1,-1, 0,0, 1,1,1];
```

Figure 8-5. Row and column locations of surrounding blocks to check

In our first operation, we store the blockColor of the Block that was clicked in colorToMatch. We will use this very soon.

```
    var colorToMatch:Number = blockToMatch.blockColor;
```

Next, we push blockToMatch (the block passed as a parameter to this function) into the blocksToCheck array. We need to seed this array to get started with our iteration. The rest of the calculations will be taken care of completely by the while loop that follows.

```
    blocksToCheck.push(blockToMatch);
```

Now, we start the big loop. This is a pretty complicated loop, so why not stop for a bit? Take a breath, maybe even get a beverage then come back to this one. Done? Good. OK, let's get started.

Our big while loop lasts as long as there are Block objects in the blocksToCheck array. Since we seeded it with blockToMatch (the Block the user clicked), we drop into the loop and get started with it. The first thing we do in the loop is pop the last Block out of the blocksToCheck array and put it into tempBlock. We then check the color value of tempBlock (tempBlock.blockColor) to see if it matches the color of the Block the user clicked (colorToMatch).

Since we got the value for colorToMatch from the first Block, which also happens to be tempBlock, this comparison will be true. We then push tempBlock into the blocksMatched array (because it did indeed match) and call tempBlock.makeBlockClicked, which will light up the Block by adding the glow filter we created in the Block class. This test is only guaranteed to evaluate true the first time through the while loop. All subsequent iterations will be actual tests on Block objects other than the Block the user clicked.

```
while(blocksToCheck.length > 0) {
    tempBlock = blocksToCheck.pop();
    if (tempBlock.blockColor == colorToMatch) {
        blocksMatched.push(tempBlock);
        tempBlock.makeBlockClicked();
    }
```

Now we are going to test all the Block objects that surround tempBlock. Recall that we created two arrays, rowList and colList, and their values relate to the Blocks in Figure 8-5. First, we create a temporary Block object, tempBlock2, to use for this operation. Next, we create a for loop that iterates through the rowList array. Since rowList and colList have the same number of values, we don't need to specifically iterate through it, we will use the index (i) from the rowList iteration for colList.

The next if statement tests to see if the Block represented by rowList[i], colList[i] is within the bounds of the board. The values must be greater than 0 and less than BLOCK_ROWS and BLOCK_COLS (for columns and rows respectively). If we do not do this, an "array out of bounds exception" will be thrown at runtime.

```
var tempBlock2:Block;
    for (var i:int = 0;i < rowList.length;i++) {
    if ((tempBlock.row + rowList[i]) >= 0 && (tempBlock.row + rowList[i])↵
    < BLOCK_ROWS && (tempBlock.col + colList[i]) >= 0 &&↵
    (tempBlock.col + colList[i]) < BLOCK_COLS ) {
```

So now that we know we are looking at a legitimate place in the board 2D array, we set tr equal to the row calculation and tc equal to the column calculation. We now have two values that represent one of the Blocks in Figure 8-5. We set tempBlock2 equal to the Block object in the board array represented by the tr and tc indexes (board[tr][tc];).

```
var tr:int = tempBlock.row + rowList[i];
    var tc:int = tempBlock.col + colList[i];
    tempBlock2 = board[tr][tc];
```

Now, we are ready for our most important test. If the blockColor property of tempBlock2 is equal to colorToMatch (the color of the clicked Block), we are in business.

However, we are not ready to push this Block into the blocksToCheck array just yet. We also need to check to see if this Block is already in either blocksToCheck or blocksTested. If we did not check this, the same Block would be pushed into blocksToCheck multiple times, and this function would never complete.

A very easy way to check to see if a value already exists in an array is to use the `Array.indexOf` function. When we pass to this function the `Block` object we are checking (tempBlock2), it will return -1 if it is not found in the array. This is the value we want to see. By checking for -1 in `blocksToCheck .indexOf(tempBlock2)` and `blocksTested.indexOf(tempBlock2)`, we will know if we should push this `Block` into the `blocksToCheck` array.

```
        if (tempBlock2.blockColor == colorToMatch &&↵
            blocksToCheck.indexOf(tempBlock2) == -1 ↵
            && blocksTested.indexOf(tempBlock2) == -1) {
                blocksToCheck.push(tempBlock2);
            }
        }
    }
```

After we have tested this Block fully, we push it into the `blocksTested` array, and the loop continues to check the `blocksToCheck` array until it is exhausted of Block objects. When the loop is finished, we return the entire array of `blocksMatched` to the caller.

You might now be thinking, "Wait, why do I need both `blocksToCheck` *and* `blocksTested`? Why can't I just use `blocksTested`? Isn't it a list of the Block objects that we have already looked at?" Well, yes that is true, but remember, we are testing up to *eight* blocks every time we go through this loop. Any or all of those `Block` objects could be pushed into `blocksToCheck`, but only one, `tempBlock`, will be pushed onto `blocksTested`. Without checking `blocksToCheck`, we will get into an infinite loop nearly every time this function is executed, because multiple instances of Block objects already in `blocksToCheck`, but not in `blocksTested`, would be pushed into `blocksToCheck`. We would simply never get to the end of the `blocksToCheck` array.

```
        blocksTested.push(tempBlock);
        }
    return blocksMatched;
}
```

Removing blocks

The game state `GameStates.STATE_REMOVE_CLICKED_BLOCKS` is set when `ColorDrop` has finished its call to `findLikeColoredBlocks` and the `GameStates.STATE_WAIT` has finished its dramatic pause. We now have an array of `Block` objects named `clickedBlocks` that we can use to calculate the score for the player, remove `Block` objects from the screen, and then replenish the `Block` objects in the board 2D array. The call to `removeClickedBlocks` from the state machine `switch` statement in `runGame` starts this process.

`removeClickedBlocks` is a fairly simple function, as most of the real work is done by other functions. First, it calls `removeClickedBlocksFromScreen` to remove the `Block` objects in the, then calls `moveBlocksDown` to move the remaining `Block` objects in the `board` array to new positions based on the missing `Block` objects. We then reinitialize the `clickedBlocks` array, to be safe, but we have already removed the contents in the call to `removeClickedBlocksFromScreen` (as shown in the following code snippet). After that, we dispatch an event to `ScoreBoard` to update the `plays` display. When this function returns, the `switch` statement in `runGame` will change the `gameState` to `GameStates.STATE_START_REPLACING` so the board can be replenished with `Block` objects.

```
public function removeClickedBlocks():void {
    removeClickedBlocksFromScreen();
    moveBlocksDown();
    clickedBlocksArray = new Array();
```

```
dispatchEvent(new CustomEventScoreBoardUpdate(↵
    CustomEventScoreBoardUpdate.UPDATE_TEXT,Main.SCORE_BOARD_PLAYS,String(plays)));
}
```

The removeClickedBlocksFromScreen function is pretty straightforward. It contains a while loop that pops Block objects out of clickedBlocks and then calls removeBlock, passing a reference to those Block objects so they can be removed from the screen. It also plays the Main.SOUND_BONUS sound so the player gets some audio feedback from their move.

This function also contains the scoring code for Color Drop. We create a local variable named pointsPerBlock and set its initial value to the difficulty setting POINTS_PER_BLOCK. Inside the while loop, we increment pointsPerBlock by BONUS_PER_BLOCK for every connected block as a bonus for removing more blocks with one move. In our call to addToScore, we pass Math. floor(pointsPerBlock), which means the value rounds down until it reaches a whole number. By rounding, the player would receive one point per Block up until the fifth Block, receive two points per Block for five to nine blocks, and at for ten blocks or more, receive three points per block, and so on. This scoring prompts the player to try to configure the blocks to remove more on a single move if possible, because the score can ramp up pretty quickly on one turn.

```
public function removeClickedBlocksFromScreen():void {
    var blockLength:int = clickedBlocksArray.length 1;
    var pointsPerBlock:Number = POINTS_PER_BLOCK;
    dispatchEvent( new CustomEventSound(↵
        CustomEventSound.PLAY_SOUND,Main.SOUND_BONUS,false,1,0,1));
    while(clickedBlocksArray.length > 0) {
        addToScore(Math.floor(pointsPerBlock));
        tempBlock = clickedBlocksArray.pop();
        removeBlock(tempBlock);
        pointsPerBlock += BONUS_PER_BLOCK;
    }
}
```

The addToScore function simply increments score by the value passed, increments levelScore and then reports those values with dispatched events.

```
public function addToScore(val:Number):void {
    score += int(val);
    levelScore += int(val);
    dispatchEvent(new CustomEventScoreBoardUpdate(↵
        CustomEventScoreBoardUpdate.UPDATE_TEXT,Main.SCORE_BOARD_SCORE,String(score)));
    dispatchEvent(new CustomEventScoreBoardUpdate(↵
        CustomEventScoreBoardUpdate.UPDATE_TEXT,Main.SCORE_BOARD_LEVEL_SCORE,↵
        String(levelScore)));
}
```

The moveBlocksDown function is the second most intricate function in this game after findLikeColoredBlocks. The job of this function is to locate the missing blocks that were removed in removeClickedBlocksFromScreen and update how those missing Block objects relate to the rest of the Block objects on the screen. This exercise involves finding the missing Block objects in board, updating the existing Block objects to move into the empty positions left by the removed Block objects and mark the newly empty positions in the board 2D array as null so that replaceBlocks can replenish them.

First, we need to iterate through all the rows and columns in board and do it in the most efficient way we can manage. Because the blocks move down the screen, that means that the lowest blocks in the on-screen grid are the ones that will have a shorter distance to fall if a Block has been removed below them. For this reason, we are going to iterate backwards though the board 2D array. This means that we will be testing the right-most and bottom-most blocks first. By testing in that direction, we can be sure that we have counted the proper number of missing blocks below each block. We don't care how many blocks are missing above it, because the blocks above don't affect how far a block must fall to get into position. This little trick saves us tons of code and extra iterations though the board array.

We start by iterating through the columns in board, backward. For each column, we will then iterate through the rows in that column.

```
public function moveBlocksDown():void {
 var collength:int = BLOCK_COLS-1;
 for (var c:int = collength; c >= 0; c--) {
  var rowlength:int = BLOCK_ROWS-1;
  var missing:Number = 0;
  for (var r:int = rowlength; r >= 0; r--) {
   tempBlock=board[r][c];
```

When we find a row, col combination that is not null, we then we go ahead and test to see how many Block objects below it in the board 2D array are missing. We do this by creating another for loop that iterates through all the board[r][c] columns below the current Block (from r+1 to BLOCK_ROWS-1). If we find a missing Block, we increment the missing variable.

```
      if (tempBlock != null) {
         missing=0;
         if (r<BLOCK_ROWS) {
         for (var m:int = r+1; m < BLOCK_ROWS;m++) {
             if (board[m][c]==null) {
             missing++;
             }
         }
     }
   }
```

After we have calculated how many Block objects are missing in the column below the current Block represented by tempBlock, it is time to move it. First, we change the row and col properties of the Block to match the new position it will be in when it is finished falling.

```
      if (missing > 0) {
         tempBlock.row = r+missing;
         tempBlock.col = c;
```

Then, we update the new position of the Block in board where the tempBlock logically now exists and set the current position to null so the proper Block will be replaced.

```
         board[r+missing][c] = tempBlock;
         board[r][c] = null;
```

Finally, we call the startFalling function of tempBlock with the new position on the screen of the Block, which will, in turn, have it start falling into position.

```
         tempBlock.startFalling(tempBlock.y+↵
            (missing*BLOCK_HEIGHT)+(missing*ROW_SPACING),10);
            }
         }
      }
   }
  }
}
```

The `removeBlock` function is similar to other remove style function we have written in this book already. We pass in a reference to the `Block` we want to remove from the `board` array (`blockToRemove`). We then have to iterate through both arrays until we locate the `Block` that matches the `Block` (`blockToRemove`) we want to remove. Our next job is to clean up as much as possible behind this `Block`. We remove its `EventListener`, remove it from the display list with `removeChild(tempBlock)`, call its `dispose` function (which will clean up the `bitmapData`), and then set its `board` position in the multidimensional array to `null`.

```
public function removeBlock(blockToRemove:Block):void {
  for (var r:int = 0; r < board.length; r++) {
  for (var c:int = 0; c < board[r].length; c++) {
      tempBlock = board[r][c];
      if (tempBlock == blockToRemove) {
        tempBlock.removeEventListener(↵
       CustomEventClickBlock.EVENT_CLICK_BLOCK, blockClickListener);
        tempBlock.dispose();
        removeChild(tempBlock);
        board[r][c]= null;
      }
    }
  }
}
```

In Figure 8-6, you can see what it might look like when blocks are added back into the board after they have been removed from the screen.

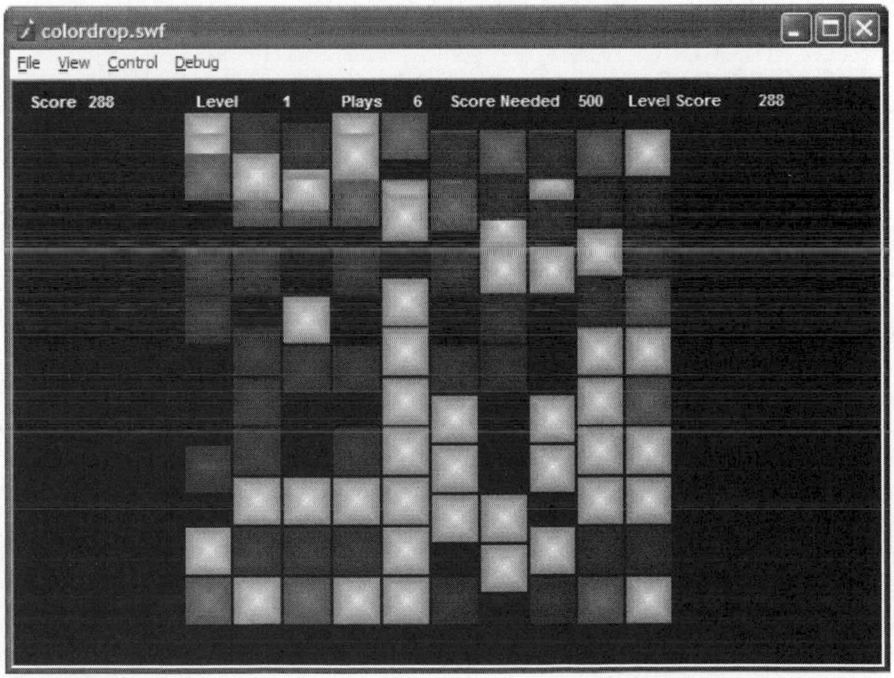

Figure 8-6. Blocks added back onto the screen

Ending a level or the game

So now we have put blocks on the screen, removed them, and added blocks back to take their place. The only thing left to do is to test to see if the level or the game has ended. We do this in the GameStates.STATE_WAITING_FOR_INPUT game state by calling checkForEndLevel.

This function does two things. First, it checks to see if the levelScore is equal to or greater than currentLevel.scoreThreshold. If so, the level has been completed. We play a sound, set the nextGameState to GameStates.STATE_END_LEVEL, call fadeBlocks, and set the gameState to GameStates.STATE_FADE_BLOCKS_WAIT. Recall that GameStates.STATE_FADE_BLOCKS_WAIT continually checks to see if all the Blocks have faded from the screen before continuing to the gameState set in nextGameState.

If the level has not been finished, we check to see if plays has been exhausted. If so, the game is over. We perform similar operations to the ones to end a level but, this time, to end the game. We play a different sound; we set the nextGameState to GameStates.STATE_END_GAME, call makeBlocksFall, and set the gameState to GameStates.STATE_FALL_BLOCKS_WAIT.

```
public function checkforEndLevel():void {
  if (levelScore >= currentLevel.scoreThreshold) {
   dispatchEvent( new CustomEventSound(CustomEventSound.PLAY_SOUND,↵
   Main.SOUND_WIN,false,1,0,1));
   nextGameState = GameStates.STATE_END_LEVEL;
   fadeBlocks();
   gameState = GameStates.STATE_FADE_BLOCKS_WAIT;
  } else if (plays <= 0) {
   nextGameState = GameStates.STATE_END_GAME;
   dispatchEvent( new
  CustomEventSound(CustomEventSound.PLAY_SOUND,Main.SOUND_LOSE,false,1,0,1));
   makeBlocksFall()
   gameState = GameStates.STATE_FALL_BLOCKS_WAIT;
  }
}
```

The fadeBlocks function iterates through all the blocks in the board 2D array and sets every Block to fade by calling the startFade function of each Block; see Figure 8-7. The Block.startFade function accepts a fadeValue (between 0 and 1) that will decrement the alpha value for the Block over a series of frames. We send this as a random value so that the fadeout does not appear completely uniform.

```
public function fadeBlocks():void {
  for (var r:int = 0; r < board.length; r++) {
  for (var c:int = 0; c < board[r].length; c++) {
      tempBlock = board[r][c];
      tempBlock.startFade((Math.random()*.9)+.1);
  }
 }
}
```

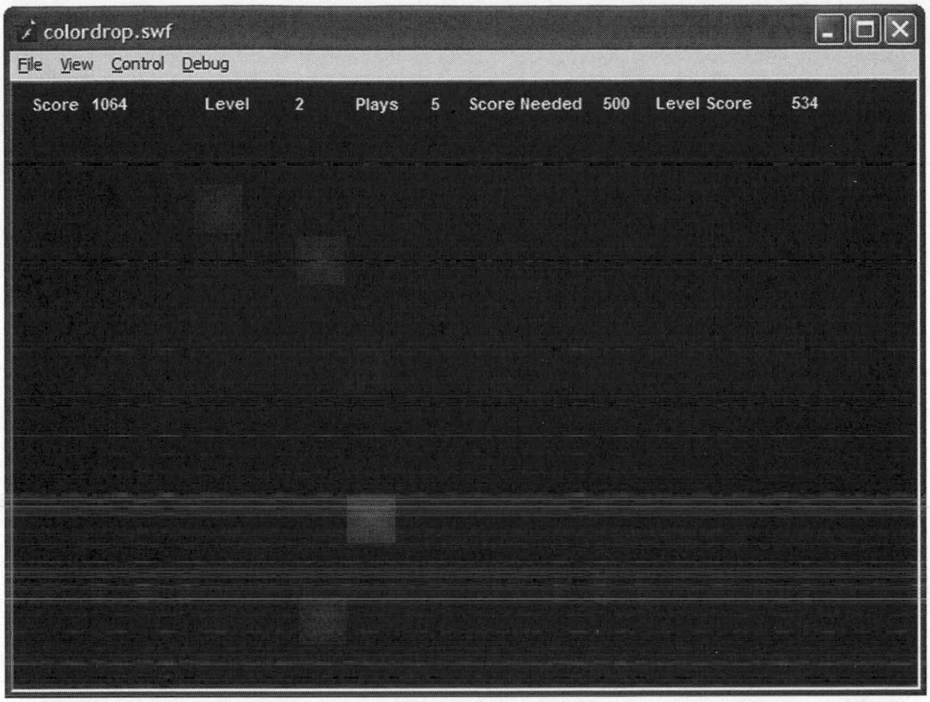

Figure 8-7. Blocks fading out to end a level

The makeBlocksFall function is very similar to fadeBlocks. It iterates through all of the Block objects in the board 2D array. Instead of calling startFade, it calls startFalling, passing the bottom of the screen plus the height of a Block (gameHeight + BLOCK_HEIGHT) as the first parameter (fallEndY). We pass this value so that the entire object will leave the screen before it is removed from the screen. The second parameter is a random value that will be used for the speed of the Block (to make the falling not look completely uniform).

```
public function makeBlocksFall():void {
 for (var r:int = 0; r < board.length; r++) {
  for (var c:int = 0; c < board[r].length; c++) {
      tempBlock = board[r][c];
      tempBlock.startFalling(gameHeight + BLOCK_HEIGHT, (Math.random()*15)+10);


  }
 }
}
```

Finally, we have come to endGame and endLevel function. Both functions call cleanUpevel before they dispatch the proper event to Main. The cleanUpLevel function iterates through all the Block objects in the board 2D array by calling removeBlock.

```
public function endGame():void {
 cleanUpLevel();
 dispatchEvent(new Event(GAME_OVER));
```

```
}
public function endLevel():void {
 cleanUpLevel();
 dispatchEvent(new Event(NEW_LEVEL));
}
public function cleanUpLevel():void {
 for (var r:int = 0; r < board.length; r++) {
  for (var c:int = 0; c < board[r].length; c++) {
        tempBlock = board[r][c];
        removeBlock(tempBlock);
  }
 }
}
```

You should also finish off the class definition with the following brackets c at the end of ColorDrop.as:

```
    }
}
```

Test it!

OK, now you have all the code for a casual puzzle style game written in ActionScript 3.0 using a reusable game framework. Once you've typed in all the code (or downloaded it), try the game. Notice that the game starts out very easy and gets difficult very quickly. By experimenting with the values in the DifficultyLevel classes, you can alter the game play and difficulty significantly.

Summary

In this chapter, we have built a unique game based on casual games that we discussed at the beginning of the chapter. We have built an internal game state machine and an iterative solution for matching like objects in a grid. And we have done this while keeping our code within the game framework that we have already built.

Notice, that while the Color Drop game is very simple, the code and ideas behind it are not. They lay the groundwork for nearly any game of this type that you might want to make. Sure, the iterative and recursive functions to test the blocks after the player had made a move might be different for another game, but the seeds are here for you to explore these types of games.

Here are some questions for you to ponder:

- What could be done make this game more fun to play for a longer amount of time?
- How would you make it easier to play?
- How could you change the game to disallow diagonal Block matches?
- What could be added to make this a truly addictive game?

We are finished with Color Drop but not with this style of game. In the next chapter, we will explore some of these ideas further by taking this basic engine and evolving it into another game style that has furthered the casual genre in the past couple years.

Chapter 9

Creating the Dice Battle Puzzle Game

There seems to be a lot of confusion among indie game developers about copyright, trademark, and patent issues regarding games. While we are not lawyers, there are some common sense ideas around these topics that every game developer should know, and a golden rule to remember that trumps all of them.

Let's say you want to make a game that involves five dice that are rolled three times to make poker hands. We'll call it Poker Dice. Sound familiar? You might know that games like this exist, but do you know if you have the legal right to make one? By doing a little research, you would find there is a classic game named Yacht that is played with five dice. Players roll the dice a successive (but limited number) times to make poker-like hands and score points. This game has been played for hundreds of years under all sorts of names but was popularized by the commercial versions Kizmet and Yahtzee. In light of this, let's explore the prospect of making a game like Poker Dice, from the perspective of copyrights, trademarks, and patents.

Getting started with intellectual property law

To find out if we can make Poker Dice, we'd first look to see what is covered under U.S. copyright law.

Considering copyright

Copyright is a way for authors to protect the stuff they have created. This "stuff" is usually referred to as **intellectual works**. Here is how the United States Copyright Office defines copyright at http://www.copyright.gov/circs/circ1.pdf:

"Copyright is a form of protection provided by the laws of the United States (title 17, U. S. Code) to the authors of 'original works of authorship,' including literary, dramatic, musical, artistic, and certain other intellectual works. This protection is available to both published and unpublished works. . . . It is illegal for anyone to violate any of the rights provided by the copyright law to the owner of copyright."

Copyright laws in other countries will vary. However, because of pressure from international business interests, many are moving towards a model similar to the United States'.

Hmm. Interesting. So "intellectual works" fall under copyright law. It appears that would cover a game like Poker Dice, because someone has obviously made one, and you can go play it and buy it right now. From this simplified view, you *would not* be able to make this game. However, games are special. They are not songs or paintings or even books, where the interaction between the consumer and the work is one-way (seeing, hearing, reading); a game could be all of these and more. Furthermore, a game is defined by rules that govern its play and the universe it exists within. In that case, there must be some specific information regarding games, right? Yes in fact, there is. The United States Copyright Office has this to say on the matter of copyrighting games at http://www.copyright.gov/fls/fl108.html:

> *"Copyright does not protect the idea for a game, its name or title, or the method or methods for playing it. Nor does copyright protect any idea, system, method, device, or trademark material involved in developing, merchandising, or playing a game. Once a game has been made public, nothing in the copyright law prevents others from developing another game based on similar principles. Copyright protects only the particular manner of an author's expression in literary, artistic, or musical form."*

Wow. Read that again. Digest it. What that means is, pretty much, as far as copyright law is concerned, anyone can make any game. You cannot copy the art, music, or words in the game (which fall under copyright law in their own way anyway), but the *idea* of game itself cannot be copyrighted. Wow, free rein then right? This appears to say that you could make a game named Yahtzee because the name and rules cannot be copyrighted. However, there is another method of protection for intellectual property, and that is a trademark.

Considering trademarks

Trademarks are used in commerce to define a unique idea that cannot be used by another party. According to the United States Patent and Trademark Office, trademarks are used to "protect words, names, symbols, sounds, or colors that distinguish goods and services from those manufactured or sold by others and to indicate the source of the goods. Trademarks, unlike patents, can be renewed forever as long as they are being used in commerce" (http://www.uspto.gov/main/glossary/#t).

From this definition, it would seem that, while the name "Yahtzee" does not fall under copyright law, it does fall under trademark law. That is, if the name has indeed been trademarked. To find this out, you must search for a trademark. How do you do this? Copyright and trademark searches are usually the duty of the law department of major corporations. Again, we are not lawyers, but there are still some useful resources available to you that can be used to find out if a term has been trademarked.

The United States Trademark and Copyright office has an online system named Trademark Electronic Search System (TESS) that can be used for simple trademark searches. You can find it here: http://tess2.uspto.gov/bin/gate.exe?f=tess&state=4004:eka3g9.1.1.

By searching TESS for the word "Yahtzee," you will find the following information (and more):

- **Word mark**: YAHTZEE
- **Goods and services**: IC 028. US 022. G & S: POKER DICE GAMES. FIRST USE: 19560403.
- **First use in commerce**: 19560403
- **Registration date**: March 19, 1957
- **(LAST LISTED OWNER)** HASBRO, INC. CORPORATION BY MERGER WITH RHODE ISLAND 1027 NEWPORT AVENUE PAWTUCKET RHODE ISLAND 02862
- **Renewal**: 3RD RENEWAL 20070323
- **Live/Dead Indicator**: LIVE

From this information, you can see that not only is Yahtzee trademarked, but the category it is trademarked under is "poker dice games," and the record indicates that it is *live*—bingo. This means that as a game developer, you cannot make a game named "Yahtzee" because that name is trademarked and still in use. This is a very simple example, but it illustrates our point. If you think you can get away with naming your game something that already exists, you may be in for trouble. It should be noted that even if you *don't* find a trademark in the TESS database, one might still exist. If you want to be sure that a trademark does not exist, or if you want to trademark something of your own, you should consult an intellectual property attorney.

Besides the trademark though, we can still make a game with the "idea" of Yahtzee because, as you saw in the "Getting started with copyright" section, a game idea cannot be copyrighted, only the specific implementation of a game can. This means that, while you can't make a game named Yahtzee that looks and plays exactly like the commercial game, you can make game named Poker Dice that is essentially the same thing, as long as all the graphics, words, and so on are your own. However, there still might be an instance when this would not be legal, and that is when a patent is involved.

Adding patents to the mix

Patents are used to protect inventions for the inventor. Specific algorithms and unique game mechanics might fall under a patent. According to the United States Patent And Trademark Office, a patent is "a property right granted by the Government of the United States of America to an inventor 'to exclude others from making, using, offering for sale, or selling the invention throughout the United States or importing the invention into the United States' for a limited time in exchange for public disclosure of the invention when the patent is granted" (http://www.uspto.gov/main/glossary/#p).

So, the question arises, have any game ideas, mechanics, and algorithms been patented in the past? In short, the answer is "yes." Many patents involve games. A quick search of the United States Patent database (http://patft.uspto.gov/) will bring up hundreds of records with the word "game" in them. It could be exhausting to look through all those patents to see if any of them resemble your game. By limiting your search to something like "poker dice," you get smaller list that includes many interesting patent descriptions including these:

- **Patent 5,456,467**: Method of playing a poker dice game
- **Patent 6,605,001**: Dice game in which categories are filled and scores awarded
- **Patent 7,331,860**: Game of skill and chance and system and method for playing such game

All of these appear to be patents for a "poker dice" game. However, upon further inspection, you will notice that these patents describe ways to "play" or "package" a poker dice game, not the game idea itself. While we *did not* examine *every record* in the patent database, there is most likely a very good reason that the poker dice game idea isn't patented—**prior art**.

Simply put, a patent cannot be issued if any "prior art" has existed about the idea before someone applies for the patent. A simple example would be a wheel. No one could patent a wheel because its mere existence is one of the cornerstones of modern society. Someone might be able to patent a device that uses a wheel as part of the design, but not the wheel itself. In this way, the game Yacht, which we noted has been around for hundreds of years, is most likely the "prior art" that would make patenting a "poker dice" game impossible. The existence of Yacht does not mean people couldn't try to patent poker dice; it just means they probably won't get their patent, and even if they did, it would be nearly impossible to defend. So in light of this information, it would probably be OK for us to make our own poker dice game.

So, what should you do with all of this legal mumbo jumbo? Will it stop you in your tracks from making a game? Well, if you follow the Golden Rule, you should be OK most of the time.

Following the Golden Rule

Many developers are ignorant or laws that govern intellectual property. They think that if other people have "borrowed" ideas, it is OK for them to do so. They think that if they find something on the Internet, it is in the public domain and can be used freely. They may also assume that their game is small so no one will find out or that using just "a little" will be OK. None of this is true. In fact, the laws of intellectual property vary from country to country. The Internet is worldwide, and it can be very difficult to abide by the minefield intellectual property laws in every country. However, by following the golden rules, you should be safe:

The golden rule of intellectual property is *use your own stuff*.

We've shown that game ideas cannot be cannot be copyrighted. However, that does not mean that someone won't try to sue you anyway. For instance, if you make a game with the exact rules of Pac-Man that operates exactly the same way as Pac-Man and looks very similar, Namco still might try to sue you to get rid of it. They might not win, but the legal battle with probably bankrupt you anyway. In fact, recently Namco has started to send "Cease and Desist" letters to Flash game portals owners who display games that illegally use their intellectual property. As the game industry moves away from physical to digital distribution and downloadable and online games become more commonplace, we expect this to happen on an even wider scale.

The best way to make sure that does not happen is, again, to remember this: the golden rule of intellectual property is *use your own stuff*.

Even if it is *legal* for you to use the exact same rules as another game, you might still be in trouble if you violate a trademark or patent. However, even beyond the legal matters, it is simply *not very creative* to use other people's ideas alone. Discerning game players will see that you have simply remade someone else's idea in another form. Fellow game developers will start to recognize you as someone who leeches ideas from others. It is very common to read developers complain about peers who create copies of their games without permission. Believe us, word gets around. Portals and publishers do not want to get entangled in legal fights about games, so they will start to recognize you as possible source of trouble. None of this will be good for your career as a game developer. We will say it one more time: the golden rule of intellectual property is *use your own stuff*.

Even if you base your game on another idea, you should change it up enough so that it is all your own. Change the rules; add layers, levels, difficulties, and challenges of your own design. We suppose you could have a career making games in which you simply copy the game ideas, verbatim, from other developers, but it sure wouldn't be a very interesting one.

Still, you should be aware of the possible legal details involved with your games. If you are concerned about your idea, the tools and databases we have mentioned in this section should get you started on your research about the legal standing of your game idea, name, and so on.

What will this cost? Well, if you live in the United States, and you want to copyright a single work with the United States Copyright Office, the basic price in 2010 is roughly $50. Through the United States Patent and Trademark Office, the starting price of processing a trademark is about $400, and the basic fee to file a patent is about $350. However patents are very tricky to file, and with the necessary legal help, it will probably cost in the neighborhood of $2500–$15,000 when all is said and done. And one more time, to be safe in these legal matters, you might want to consult a lawyer.

Designing the Dice Battle game

For Dice Battle, which is shown in Figure 9-1, we will use ideas from poker dice, drop-style games like Bejeweled and our own game Color Drop, but we will make a game that is fully our own design. In the previous chapter, we discussed the history of casual games, but we left it at match-three style games like Bejeweled. That game became so popular that further genres have been iterated beyond it, using its basic play style. One of those genres is the battle puzzle. Games like Book Worm Adventures and Puzzle Quest have taken the idea of the drop-style puzzle game, but put it into the context of a larger quest. The game we will create, Dice Battle, is an iteration on Color Drop that adds features that take it a few steps closer to being one of these battle puzzle games.

Actually, to be honest, we have not checked every one of the thousands of games on the Internet to see if there is not one just like this. However, the intention here is to make our game built on some foundational ideas, but add our own flair. Here's the basic game design, which is shown in Figure 9-1:

- **Game name**: Dice Battle
- **Game genre**: Drop-style battle puzzle game
- **Game description**: Battle through a succession of enemies by taking turns playing a game on a grid of dice.
- **Player's goal**: To click a die that connects to the most like-numbered, like-colored dice as possible. Points are scored for a play, and those points equal the number of hit points removed from the enemy.
- **Enemies' description**: The enemies are a succession of creatures that can play the dice game better and better.
- **Enemies' goal**: The enemies seek to make the best move that will remove hit points the player. The ultimate goal of the enemies is to remove all the player's hit points.
- **Level end**: When the enemies have lost all their hit points
- **Game over conditions**: When the player has lost all hit points

- **Difficulty ramping**: Difficulty is ramped through specific level objects. Enemy AI is created by finding the perfect move and then scaling back that move depending on the skill level of the enemy.
- **Bonus conditions**: The number of dice connected on a single play results in a bonus per die.

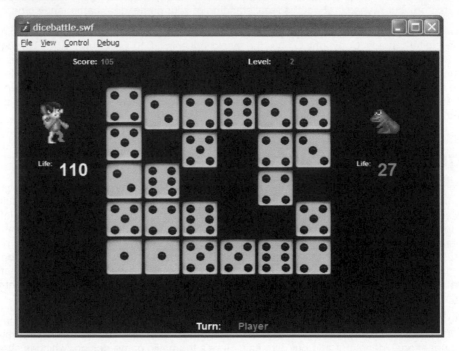

Figure 9-1. The Dice Battle game screen

Game development concepts in this chapter

Dice Battle is an iteration of Color Drop from the last chapter. While we include all of the code to create Dice Battle in this chapter, we will refer to Color Drop and Chapter 8 on many occasions. While it is possible to understand Dice Battle as a stand-alone game, we strongly suggest that you work through the topics covered in Chapter 8 and build Color Drop, before trying to tackle Chapter 9 and Dice Battle.

While creating Dice Battle, we will cover the following game design and development topics:

- Iterating an existing game to create another
- Playing soundtracks
- Creating a computer opponent
- Taking turns
- Algorithm-based AI

For Dice Battle, we will create the following classes:

- `DiceBattle`: The main game class for the Dice Battle game. This will extend `com.efg.framework.Game`.
- `DifficultyLevel`: This class will define the difficulty levels for the game. Dice Battle has ten different levels of difficulty.
- `Character`: This class extends from `com.efg.framework.BlitSprite`. It will be used to display the player and computer characters on the screen.
- `Die`: We will use this class to represent each die on the screen. This class is much like `Block` from the last chapter except that a `Die` class also has both a value and a color.
- `CustomEventClickDie`: This is a custom event we dispatch when a `Die` is clicked on the screen.
- `GameStates`: This class will hold all of the static const values that represent the internal game states for the Dice Battle game state machine.

Adding game assets to the library

Unlike Color Drop, in which very few assets were required, Dice Battle requires a lot of graphics and a few extra sounds. A description of both follows.

Adding Graphics for Dice Battle

For Dice Battle, we need two different tile sheets. The first tile sheet contains the different colored dice we will use in the game. As the levels progress, we will add different colored dice to the screen. Only dice of the same color can match, so with more colors, it becomes harder to find big matches of many dice. We could have colored the dice in code to save us the trouble of loading in three sets, but it is not always easy to get the same effects in code that you can get by just creating the graphics yourself. Each die is 50 × 50 pixels, and the tile sheet is shown in Figure 9-2. The library name for this sheet is `diceSheet`.

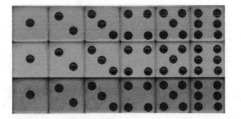

Figure 9-2. Dice tile sheet

The second tile sheet is the set of characters we will use in the game. The first character is the player. All subsequent characters are the enemies that player will fight in the game. We have created ten enemies, so there are effectively ten levels in this game. Like other graphics in this book, these characters were taken from Ari Feldman's SpriteLib GPL. Each character is 64 × 64 pixels, and the tile sheet is shown in Figure 9-3. The library name for this sheet is `Characters`.

Figure 9-3. Dice Battle Player character plus Enemy characters tile sheet

Adding sound for Dice Battle

Most of the sounds for Dice Battle are the same as Color Drop. However, we have added three new ones. SoundHit is the sound that is plays when the computer takes a turn. It's a clunk sound that makes it feel like the player is being bashed on the head. The other two sounds are SoundTrack1 and SoundTrack2. These are two looping songs that we will use for the soundtrack in the game. We consider the soundtrack to be a special sound, and in a later section, we will show you a strategy that will help you work with multiple soundtracks that need to be played at different times in your game. The complete list of sounds can be found in Table 9-1.

Table 9-1. Battle Dice Sounds

Library Class Name	Description
SoundBonus	Plays when the player connects dice
SoundClick	Plays when the player clicks dice
SoundWin	Plays when the player wins a battle
SoundLose	Plays when the player loses a battle
SoundHit	Plays when the computer connects dice
SoundTrack1	Soundtrack for title screen
SoundTrack2	Soundtrack for main game

Playing Soundtracks in Main.as

The first major piece of code we will discuss is Main.as. Much of the Main.as class for Dice Battle is similar to that of Color Drop. However, there are two major differences that we are going to discuss: the ScoreBoard and playing soundtracks.

Revamping ScoreBoard

For Dice Battle, are going to create a scoreboard that is more elaborate than anything we have created thus far. While this code is not intricate or tricky, we are going to discuss this because it demonstrates how the ScoreBoard object can be used for more intricate designs than we have previously created.

Notice the game screen for Dice Battle in Figure 9-4 where we have highlighted the five scoreboard elements.

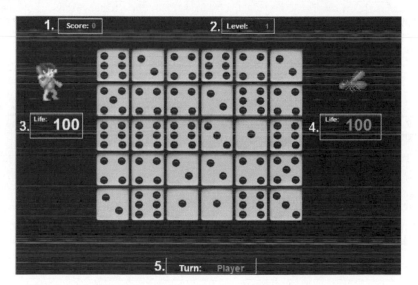

Figure 9-4. Dice Battle screen with scoreboard text highlighted

These are the Dice Battle scoreboard elements:

- The player's score
- The current game level
- Player's hit points
- Computer hit points
- Turn indicator

All of these elements are necessary to let the player know what is happening in the game. To support these elements we need to create some additional TextFormat objects.

```
var scoreBoardTextFormat1:TextFormat = new TextFormat("_sans", "11", "0xffffff", "true");
var scoreBoardTextFormat2:TextFormat = new TextFormat("_sans", "11", "0xff0000", "true");
var scoreBoardTextFormat3:TextFormat = new TextFormat("_sans", "14", "0xffffff", "true");
var scoreBoardTextFormat4:TextFormat = new TextFormat("_sans", "14", "0xff0000", "true");
var scoreBoardTextFormat5:TextFormat = new TextFormat("_sans", "10", "0xffffff", "true");
var scoreBoardTextFormat6:TextFormat = new TextFormat("_sans", "25", "0x00ff00", "true");
var scoreBoardTextFormat7:TextFormat = new TextFormat("_sans", "25", "0xff0000", "true");

scoreBoard.createTextElement(SCORE_BOARD_SCORE, new SideBySideScoreElement(↵
    75, 5, 15, "Score:",scoreBoardTextFormat1, 25, "0", scoreBoardTextFormat2));
scoreBoard.createTextElement(SCORE_BOARD_LEVEL,new SideBySideScoreElement(↵
    325, 5, 10, "Level:", scoreBoardTextFormat1, 50, "0", scoreBoardTextFormat2));
scoreBoard.createTextElement(SCORE_BOARD_TURN, new SideBySideScoreElement(↵
    250, 380, 10, "Turn:", scoreBoardTextFormat3, 50, "0", scoreBoardTextFormat4));
scoreBoard.createTextElement(SCORE_BOARD_PLAYER_LIFE, new SideBySideScoreElement(↵
    25, 150, 10, "Life:",scoreBoardTextFormat5, 20, "0",scoreBoardTextFormat6));
scoreBoard.createTextElement(SCORE_BOARD_COMPUTER_LIFE, new SideBySideScoreElement(↵
    480, 150, 10, "Life:",scoreBoardTextFormat5, 20, "0", scoreBoardTextFormat7));
```

Playing SoundTracks

Recall that, back in Chapter 4, we created the SoundManager class with the ability to play a soundtrack (background music). Many games in the battle puzzle genre like Dice Battle contain elaborate soundtracks that change to set the mood of the current state of the game. However, managing the play back of these different soundtracks can be quite a trick when you are using a state machine to run your game.

We have two different soundtracks represented by the static constants of SOUND_SOUND_TRACK_1 and SOUND_SOUND_TRACK_2 in Main:

```
public static const SOUND_SOUND_TRACK_1:String =   "soundTrack1";
public static const SOUND_SOUND_TRACK_2:String =   "soundTrack2";
...
soundManager.addSound(SOUND_SOUND_TRACK_1,new SoundTrack1());
soundManager.addSound(SOUND_SOUND_TRACK_2,new SoundTrack2());
```

We are going to play these soundtracks in different states of the game; see Table 9-2.

Table 9-2. Soundtracks for Main.as

State Description	State Function	Soundtrack to Play
Title screen shows	systemTitle	SoundTrack1
New game starts	systemNewGame	SoundTrack2
Game over	systemGameOver	SoundTrack2
Title screen shows	systemTitle	SoundTrack1

Notice that systemTitle will be called after systemGameOver, yet they both play the same soundtrack. Now, this is why we needed to create special functionality for playing soundtracks in SoundManager. Because the game states in GameFrameWork (the class Main extends) are independent, systemTitle has no idea that systemGameover was the last state, nor should it know that information. In fact, there could be other states in the middle (e.g., show a high score screen and nag for microtransactions). However, both states need SoundTrack1 to play, which is why we created the isSoundTrack Boolean parameter for the SoundTrack.playSoundTrack function. The function is designed to play only one soundtrack at a time. Recall, from Chapter 4, that it does this by creating a single SoundChannel that is used to play soundtracks exclusively. Not only does it work for playing the soundtracks, but it helps keep the separate functions in our state machine from having to know too much specific information about how the game states flow.

To support playing these soundtracks in Main, we need to override systemTitle, systemNewGame, and systemGameOver. Each of these new function calls soundManager.playSound directly and then calls super.[function name] to play its respective namesake function, so that Main can operate just like it has in previous games in this book.

```
override  public function systemTitle():void {
    soundManager.playSound(Main.SOUND_SOUND_TRACK_1,truc,1000,0,1);
        super.systemTitle();
}

override  public function systemNewGame():void {
    soundManager.playSound(Main.SOUND_SOUND_TRACK_2,true,1000,0,1);
    super.systemNewGame();
}

override public function systemGameOver():void {
    soundManager.playSound(Main.SOUND_SOUND_TRACK_1,true,1000,0,1);
    super.systemGameOver();
}
```

Updating the Main.as class

Here is the full code listing for Main. We have styled in bold the major changes between this version and the one in Chapter 8 for Color Drop:

```
package com.efg.games.dicebattle
{
    import com.efg.framework.FrameWorkStates;
    import com.efg.framework.GameFrameWork;
    import com.efg.framework.BasicScreen;
    import com.efg.framework.ScoreBoard;
    import com.efg.framework.Game;
    import com.efg.framework.SideBySideScoreElement;
    import com.efg.framework.SoundManager;
    import com.efg.framework.CustomEventSound;

    import flash.display.Bitmap;
    import flash.display.BitmapData;
    import flash.display.Sprite;
    import flash.events.Event;
    import flash.geom.Point;
    import flash.utils.Timer;
```

```
import flash.events.TimerEvent;
import flash.text.TextFormat;

public class Main extends GameFrameWork
{
    //custom sccore board elements
    public static const SCORE_BOARD_SCORE:String = "score";
    public static const SCORE_BOARD_LEVEL:String = "level";
    public static const SCORE_BOARD_TURN:String = "turn";
    public static const SCORE_BOARD_COMPUTER_LIFE:String = "computerLife";
    public static const SCORE_BOARD_PLAYER_LIFE:String = "playerLife";

    //custom sounds

    public static const SOUND_CLICK:String              =   "soundClick";
    public static const SOUND_BONUS:String              =   "soundBonus";
    public static const SOUND_WIN:String                =   "soundWin";
    public static const SOUND_LOSE:String               =   "soundLose";
    public static const SOUND_HIT:String                =   "soundHit";
    public static const SOUND_SOUND_TRACK_1:String      =   "soundTrack1";
    public static const SOUND_SOUND_TRACK_2:String      =   "soundTrack2";
//**Flex Framework Only
/*
[Embed(source = "assets/dicebattleassets.swf", symbol="SoundClick")]
private var SoundClick:Class;

[Embed(source = "assets/dicebattleassets.swf", symbol="SoundBonus")]
private var SoundBonus:Class;

[Embed(source = "assets/dicebattleassets.swf", symbol="SoundWin")]
private var SoundWin:Class;

[Embed(source = "assets/dicebattleassets.swf", symbol="SoundLose")]
private var SoundLose:Class; //chnaged

[Embed(source = "assets/dicebattleassets.swf", symbol="SoundHit")]
private var SoundHit:Class;

[Embed(source = "assets/dicebattleassets.swf", symbol="SoundTrack1")]
private var SoundTrack1:Class;

[Embed(source = "assets/dicebattleassets.swf", symbol="SoundTrack2")]
private var SoundTrack2:Class;
*/


// Our construction only calls init(). This way, we can re-init the ↩
    entire systemif necessary

public function Main() {
    init();
}
```

```
// init() is used to set up all of the things that we should only↵
        need to do one time

    override public function init():void {
            game = new DiceBattle(600,400);

            setApplicationBackGround(600,400,false, 0x000000);
            //add application background to the screen as the bottom layer

            //add score board to the screen as the seconf layer

            scoreBoard = new ScoreBoard();
            addChild(scoreBoard);

    var scoreBoardTextFormat1:TextFormat = new TextFormat("_sans", "11", "0xffffff", "true");
    var scoreBoardTextFormat2:TextFormat = new TextFormat("_sans", "11", "0xff0000", "true");
    var scoreBoardTextFormat3:TextFormat = new TextFormat("_sans", "14", "0xffffff", "true");
    var scoreBoardTextFormat4:TextFormat = new TextFormat("_sans", "14", "0xff0000", "true");
    var scoreBoardTextFormat5:TextFormat = new TextFormat("_sans", "10", "0xffffff", "true");
    var scoreBoardTextFormat6:TextFormat = new TextFormat("_sans", "25", "0x00ff00", "true");
    var scoreBoardTextFormat7:TextFormat = new TextFormat("_sans", "25", "0xff0000", "true");

            scoreBoard.createTextElement(SCORE_BOARD_SCORE, ↵
                new SideBySideScoreElement(75, 5, 15, "Score:",↵
                scoreBoardTextFormat1, 25, "0", scoreBoardTextFormat2));

            scoreBoard.createTextElement(SCORE_BOARD_LEVEL,↵
                new SideBySideScoreElement(325, 5, 10, "Level:", ↵
                scoreBoardTextFormat1, 50, "0",scoreBoardTextFormat2));
            scoreBoard.createTextElement(SCORE_BOARD_TURN, ↵
                new SideBySideScoreElement(250, 380, 10, "Turn:", ↵
                scoreBoardTextFormat3, 50, "0", scoreBoardTextFormat4));
            scoreBoard.createTextElement(SCORE_BOARD_PLAYER_LIFE, ↵
                new SideBySideScoreElement(25, 150, 10, "Life:", ↵
                scoreBoardTextFormat5, 20, "0",scoreBoardTextFormat6));
            scoreBoard.createTextElement(SCORE_BOARD_COMPUTER_LIFE,  ↵
                new SideBySideScoreElement(480, 150, 10, "Life:", ↵
                scoreBoardTextFormat5, 20, "0", scoreBoardTextFormat7));

            //screen text initializations
            screenTextFormat = new TextFormat("_sans", "14", "0xffffff", "true");
            screenButtonFormat = new TextFormat("_sans", "11", "0x000000", "true");
            titleScreen = new BasicScreen(FrameWorkStates.STATE_SYSTEM_TITLE,↵
                600,400, false, 0x000000);
            titleScreen.createDisplayText("Dice Battle! ", 120,new Point(255,↵
                150),screenTextFormat);
            titleScreen.createOkButton("Go!",new Point(250,250),100,20,↵
                screenButtonFormat,0xFFFFFF,0x00FF0000,2);

            instructionsScreen = new BasicScreen(↵
                FrameWorkStates.STATE_SYSTEM_INSTRUCTIONS, 600,400, false, 0x000000);
            instructionsScreen.createDisplayText("Beat The Computer!",↵
                250,new Point(230, 150),screenTextFormat);
```

```
            instructionsScreen.createOkButton("Play",new Point(250,250),100,20,↵
                screenButtonFormat,0xFFFFFF,0xFF0000,2);

            gameOverScreen = new BasicScreen(FrameWorkStates.STATE_SYSTEM_GAME_OVER,↵
                600,400, false, 0x000000);
            gameOverScreen.createDisplayText("Game Over",300,new Point(250,100),↵
                screenTextFormat);
            gameOverScreen.createOkButton("Play Again",new Point(225,250),150,20, ↵
                screenButtonFormat,0xFFFFFF,0xFF0000,2);

            levelInText = "Level ";
            levelInScreen = new BasicScreen(FrameWorkStates.STATE_SYSTEM_GAME_OVER,↵
                600,400, false, 0x000000);
            levelInScreen.createDisplayText(levelInText,300,new Point(275,100),↵
                screenTextFormat);

            //set initial game state
            switchSystemState(FrameWorkStates.STATE_SYSTEM_TITLE);
            waitTime= 40;

            soundManager.addSound(SOUND_CLICK,new SoundClick());
            soundManager.addSound(SOUND_BONUS, new SoundBonus());
            soundManager.addSound(SOUND_WIN,new SoundWin());
            soundManager.addSound(SOUND_LOSE,new SoundLose());
            soundManager.addSound(SOUND_HIT,new SoundHit());
            soundManager.addSound(SOUND_SOUND_TRACK_1,new SoundTrack1());
            soundManager.addSound(SOUND_SOUND_TRACK_2,new SoundTrack2());

            frameRate = 40;
            startTimer();

        }


    override public function systemTitle():void {
     soundManager.playSound(Main.SOUND_SOUND_TRACK_1,true,1000,0,1);
     super.systemTitle();
    }

    override public function systemNewGame():void {
     soundManager.playSound(Main.SOUND_SOUND_TRACK_2,true,1000,0,1);
     super.systemNewGame();
    }

    override public function systemGameOver():void {
     soundManager.playSound(Main.SOUND_SOUND_TRACK_1,true,1000,0,1);
     super.systemGameOver();
    }


    }

}
```

Creating AI difficulty with a class

If you recall from the last chapter, we created a `DifficultyLevel` class. We are going to create a new version of that class for Dice Battle. However, as well as describing the colors that will be on each level, we also need to describe the AI of the computer player for each level.

Since this class has no functions, we will simply describe the properties and how they relate to the Dice Battle game:

- `allowedColors`: This is an array of `Die.DIE_COLOR_xxx` color values that will be valid for this level. There are only three different color values for this game.
- `enemyLife`: This is the value for the hit points for this enemy. When all the enemy hit points are knocked off, the player wins the level.
- `aiBonus`: This is a percentage bonus that this enemy receives when we decide which move the computer should make. This bonus is what helps make the AI ramp up on each successive level.
- `minValue`: This is the minimum value of a move the computer player will make, if possible. This helps ramp up the difficulty on each successive level.
- `enemyTile`: This is the in the tile sheet that will be displayed on the screen for this level.

Here is the full code for the `DifficultyLevel` class:

```
package com.efg.games.dicebattle
{

    public class DifficultyLevel
    {

    public var allowedColors:Array;
    public var enemyLife:Number;
    public var aiBonus:Number;
    public var minValue:Number;
    public var enemyTile:Number

    public function DifficultyLevel(allowedColors:Array, enemyLife: Number,↵
        enemyTile:Number, aiBonus:Number, minValue:Number) {
        this.allowedColors = allowedColors;
        this.enemyLife = enemyLife;
        this.aiBonus = aiBonus;
        this.enemyTile = enemyTile;
        this.minValue = minValue;
    }
  }
}
```

Creating the Die class

The `Die` class is nearly identical to the `Block` class from Color Drop. In the spirit of the *second game theory* and the importance of iteration we have tried to emphasize in this book so far, we are going to use `Block` as the basis for the `Die` class. We will now highlight differences to `Block` that we have made to support the fact that we are playing with dice and not simple colored blocks.

Obviously, the main difference between colored dice and colored blocks is that dice have *value*. That value is represented by the face of the die. Avid role-playing gamers should know that dice can have faces that range from 4 to 20 sides and more. However, for this game, we are using standard 6-sided dice with values ranging from one to six. To represent value in the Die class, we will create a property named dieValue.

```
public var dieValue:Number;
```

We also need to create the color values for the dice. Recall that there will be three different colored dice in Dice Battle: white, blue and green. To support this, we will create DIE_COLOR_XXX static variables that can be referenced outside the Die class:

```
public static var DIE_COLOR_WHITE:int = 0;
public static var DIE_COLOR_GREEN:int = 1;
public static var DIE_COLOR_BLUE:int  = 2;
```

In the constructor for the Die class, we need to set the value and find the proper tile to display for that Die. The first part is really easy. We just set this.dieValue to the parameter dieValue:

```
this.dieValue = dieValue;
```

However, finding the proper face tile in the tile sheet is a bit trickier. Here is the code that does it:

```
var tile:int = (dieValue-1) + (dieColor)*6;
```

This code needs a bit of illustration. Let's say that the Die constructor is passed the following value for dieColor and dieValue:

- dieValue: 5
- dieColor: DIE_COLOR_GREEN (which equals 1)

Notice in Figure 9-5 that the dice in the TileSheet are in numerical order with each color in a separate row. What we need to do to find the correct tile is to calculate the proper column location in proper row. Recall that the tiles in a TileSheet are in a zero-based array. That means that we have to subtract 1 from the value to find the right place in a row for a die. Thus, the first part of the calculation is dieValue-1.

Next, we need to find the proper row for the color of the Die. Since the colors static const values start at 0 (DIE_COLOR_WHITE = 0;), if we add dieColor*6, we will find the proper row.

In our example, dieValue equals 5 and dieColor equals 1. Plugging those values into the equation we get (5 − 1) + (1 * 6) = 10.

Again, since the tiles are in a zero-based array, the chosen tile would be the eleventh one in the tile sheet, as illustrated in Figure 9-5.

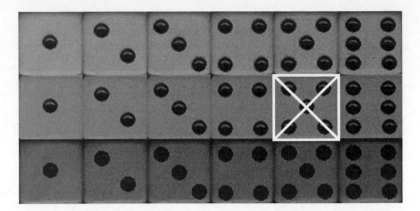

Figure 9-5. The dice tile sheet with the chosen tile highlighted (for illustration only)

There is one more significant addition to the Block class that we made to create the Die class. It is the following function:

```
public function makeDieClickedComputer() : void {
    this.filters=[new flash.filters.GlowFilter(0xFF0000,70,4,4,3,3,false,false)];
}
```

Notice, that this function is nearly identical to the following function:

```
public function makeDieClicked() : void {
    this.filters=[new flash.filters.GlowFilter(0xFFFF00,70,4,4,3,3,false,false)];
}
```

makeDieClickedComputer simply makes the dice red instead of yellow when they are clicked. Why two function instead of one? It's lazy coding folks, end of story. We apologize. We could have passed in the color value to change instead of making two functions, but we thought this example would help illustrate the computer AI a bit more than strictly optimized code.

The full code of the Die class follows:

```
package com.efg.games.dicebattle

{

import flash.filters.GlowFilter;
import flash.events.MouseEvent;
import flash.display.Bitmap;
import flash.display.BitmapData;

import com.efg.framework.BlitSprite;
import com.efg.framework.TileSheet;


public class Die extends BlitSprite {

    public var dieColor:Number;
    public var dieValue:Number;
```

```
//Action vars

public var isFalling:Boolean;
public var isFading:Boolean;
public var fadeValue:Number = .05;
public var fallEndY:Number;
public var speed:int = 10;
public var nextYLocation:int = 0;

//Board Info

public var row:Number;
public var col:Number;


public static var DIE_COLOR_WHITE:int        = 0;
public static var DIE_COLOR_GREEN:int        = 1;
public static var DIE_COLOR_BLUE:int         = 2;


public function Die(dieValue:Number, dieColor:Number,tileSheet:TileSheet,⏎
    row:Number,col:Number,endY:Number,speed:Number) {
this.dieColor = dieColor;
this.dieValue = dieValue;
this.row = row;
this.col = col;
isFalling = false;
isFading = false;
var tile:int = (dieValue-1) + (dieColor)*6;
super(tileSheet, [tile], 0);
this.addEventListener(MouseEvent.MOUSE_DOWN, onMouseDownListener, false, 0, true);
this.buttonMode = true;
this.useHandCursor = true;
startFalling(endY,speed);

}

public function startFalling(endY:Number,speed:Number) : void{
    this.speed = speed;
    fallEndY = endY;
    isFalling=true;
}

public function startFade(fadeValue:Number) : void {
    this.fadeValue = fadeValue;
    isFading=true;
}

public function update() : void {
    if (isFalling) {
        nextYLocation = y + speed;
```

```
        }
    }

    public function render() : void {

        if (isFalling) {
            y=nextYLocation;
                if (y >= fallEndY) {
                    y = fallEndY;
                    isFalling=false;
                }
        }

        if (isFading) {
            alpha -= fadeValue;
            if (alpha <=0) {
                alpha = 0;
                isFading = false;
            }
        }

    }

    public function onMouseDownListener(e:MouseEvent) : void {
        dispatchEvent(new CustomEventClickDie(CustomEventClickDie.EVENT_CLICK_DIE, this));
    }

    public function makeDieClicked() : void {
        this.filters=[new flash.filters.GlowFilter(0xFFFF00,70,4,4,3,3,false,false)];
    }

    public function makeDieClickedComputer() :void {
        this.filters=[new flash.filters.GlowFilter(0xFF0000,70,4,4,3,3,false,false)];
    }
    }
}
```

By the way, with a few changes, we could have used the Block class as the basis for Die and extended it in an object-oriented fashion. However, we will leave that effort for you to explore yourself.

Creating the CustomEventClickDie class

The CustomeEventClickDie class is a minor rewrite of the CustomEventClickBlock class from Color Drop in Chapter 8. In theory, we could have simply reused CustomEventClickBlock, or even created a reusable class and put it into the com.efg.framework package. However, we chose to simply rewrite the class here, because we wanted to reinforce the idea that you can create these kinds of custom events for your games. While the game framework is a very helpful tool, it will not write games for you. There will always be times to create classes that are local to your game class.

The only real difference in this class is the use of a `Die` class instead of `Block` class as the single variable property in the class.

```
package com.efg.games.dicebattle
{
    import flash.events.*;

    public class CustomEventClickDie extends Event
    {

        public var die:Die;
        public static const EVENT_CLICK_DIE:String = "eventClickDie";

        public function CustomEventClickDie(type:String, die:Die, ⏎
            bubbles:Boolean=false,cancelable:Boolean=false)
        {
            super(type, bubbles,cancelable);
                this.die = die;
            }

        public override function clone():Event {
            return new CustomEventClickDie(type, die, bubbles,cancelable)
        }

        public override function toString():String {
            return formatToString(type, "type", "bubbles", "cancelable", "eventPhase");
        }
    }
}
```

Creating the Character class

The `Character` class is very simple class that we will use to represent the tile from the characters tile sheet in the library. In a way, it is simply a subclass of `BlitSprite`. We created this class so that it could be potentially expanded upon in a further iteration of this game. You should keep this thought in mind as you progress through this chapter, "What are some ways I could improve this game with my own ideas and code?"

```
package com.efg.games.dicebattle
{

    import flash.display.Shape;
    import flash.display.Sprite;
    import flash.display.Bitmap;
    import flash.display.BitmapData;

    import com.efg.framework.BlitSprite;
    import com.efg.framework.TileSheet;


    public class Character extends BlitSprite {

        public function Character(ts:TileSheet, tile:Number) {
```

```
        super(ts, [tile], 0);
    }

    }
}
```

Adding the GameStates class

To support a computer AI player, we need to create some new game states for Dice Battle. In Chapter 9, for Color Drop, we introduced the idea of a game state machine: a substate machine used inside the game class independent of the one in Main. We created the states as a separate class so that they would be easier to manage and identify within the code of ColorDrop. We are going to utilize these concepts again for Dice Battle. However, for Dice Battle, we need to expand that state machine we created for Color Drop with two additional states specific to Dice Battle's functionality for playing against the computer.

The two states we need are STATE_CHANGE_TURN, where we decided whose turn to accept input for (player or computer), and STATE_START_AI, where we start the process of creating a computer move. The rest of the new states are really just name changes from Color Drop. Instead of BLOCK, we use the word DICE, but these are essentially the same states that we discussed in detail in Chapter 8 for Color Drop.

```
package com.efg.games.dicebattle
{

public class GameStates {

    public static const STATE_INITIALIZING:int        = 10;
    public static const STATE_CHANGE_TURN:int          = 20;
    public static const STATE_START_REPLACING:int      = 30;
    public static const STATE_START_AI:int             = 40;
    public static const STATE_WAITING_FOR_INPUT:int    = 60;
    public static const STATE_REMOVE_CLICKED_DICE:int  = 70;
    public static const STATE_CHECK_FOR_END:int        = 80;
    public static const STATE_FADE_DICE_WAIT:int       = 90;
    public static const STATE_FALL_DICE_WAIT:int       = 100;
    public static const STATE_END_GAME:int             = 110;
    public static const STATE_END_LEVEL:int            = 120;
    public static const STATE_WAIT:int                 = 130;
    }
}
```

Setting up the game in Game.as

Now we will start looking at the Game class to see what kinds of changes we will have to make to iterate it from Color Drop to Dice Battle. The first place that we need to make changes is in the class properties and the constructor. We will now step through the first part of Game.as, highlighting the major changes along the way.

The class starts exactly like the ColorDrop.as In fact, it's not until we get to the specific code that defines how the board is going to look that we get to any real changes. We will have far fewer Die objects than we did `Block` objects in Color Drop with a total of 30 (5 rows and 6 columns). Other than that, the specific changes to the variables are for display only.

```
package com.efg.games.dicebattle
{
    import flash.display.Sprite;
    import flash.events.*;

    import com.efg.framework.Game;
    import com.efg.framework.CustomEventLevelScreenUpdate;
    import com.efg.framework.CustomEventScoreBoardUpdate;
    import com.efg.framework.CustomEventSound;
    import com.efg.framework.TileSheet;


    public class DiceBattle extends Game
    {

    private var gameWidth:int;
    private var gameHeight:int;


    private static const Y_PAD:int        =    75;
    private static const X_PAD:int        =    150;
    private static const ROW_SPACING:int =    4;
    private static const COL_SPACING:int =    4;
    private static const DIE_HEIGHT:int =    50;
    private static const DIE_WIDTH:int =    50;
    private static const DIE_ROWS:int    =    5;
    private static const DIE_COLS:int    =    6;
```

The first significant differences in the class are CHAR_WIDTH and CHAR_HEIGHT. These two variables define the size of the character tiles that we will cut from the Characters tile sheet. We will use these in the init function. The next new variables will hold the hit points for both the player (playerLife) and the computer (computerLife). We will report these values back to the scoreboard with our custom event so they can be displayed properly. turn is a text variable that will hold the text for the current turn (**Player Turn** or **Computer Turn**). These values are held in the two static constants, TURN_PLAYER and TURN_COMPUTER. We will use this for both display and a logic test in our state switch statement.

```
    private static const CHAR_WIDTH:int = 64;
    private static const CHAR_HEIGHT:int = 64;

    private var score:int;
    private var level:int;
    private var playerLife:int;
    private var computerLife:int;
    private var turn:String;

    private static const TURN_PLAYER:String = "Player's";
    private static const TURN_COMPUTER:String = "Computer's";

    private var difficultyLevelArray:Array;
    private var currentLevel:DifficultyLevel;
```

The next set of new variables contains settings for the difficulty of the game. These could have also been created as difficulty settings, but since we have used the DifficultyLevel class for this game, doing so was really not necessary. playerLifeStart is the number of hit points the player will start with at the beginning of each level (added to the number of hit points left at the end of the previous level). DICE_BONUS is the number of bonus points awarded for each connected die (over one) that the player or computer plays on a single turn. The other new variables here are simply renamed from Color Drop: clickedDiceArray was clickedBlockArray, and tempDie was tempBlock. We do this a lot in the code for this game, so get ready for it.

```
private var playerLifeStart:int = 100;
private const DICE_BONUS:int = 2;

private var clickedDiceArray:Array;
private var board:Array;

private var tempDie:Die;

private var gameState:int = 0;
private var nextGameState:int = 0;
private var framesToWait:int = 0;
private var framesWaited:int = 0;
```

By the way, do you think you could take the code for this game and Color Drop and turn it into a base class that could be used to derive many different games of this type? How would you go about doing that? Think about it as you read this chapter.

Recall that we have two tile sheets to utilize in the game, DiceSheet and Characters. The following code creates variables to hold those sheets. It also creates two variables to hold instances of the Character class we defined earlier, one for the player's one screen character (playerTile), and one for the computer's onscreen character (enemyTile).

```
private var tileSheet:TileSheet;
private var charSheet:TileSheet;

private var enemyTile:Character;
private var playerTile:Character;

//***** Flex *****
//[Embed(source = 'assets/dicebattleassets.swf', symbol = 'Characters')]
//private var Characters:Class;
//[Embed(source = 'assets/dicebattleassets.swf', symbol = 'DiceSheet')]
//private var DiceSheet:Class;
//***** End Flex *****
```

The constructor for Dice Battle is nearly identical to that of Color Drop. The code for it follows:

```
public function DiceBattle(gameWidth:int,gameHeight:int) {
    this.gameWidth=gameWidth;
    this.gameHeight=gameHeight;
    init();
    gameState = GameStates.STATE_INITIALIZING;
}
```

The init function for Dice Battle acts pretty much like the other init function we have created for previous games: it sets up tile sheets and creates the difficulty levels. Besides having two tiles sheets (DiceSheet and Characters), there is little new to discuss on that front. However, the

DifficultyLevel classes are bit more interesting. Here is a sample of a DifficultyLevel we are going to create:

```
difficultyLevelArray.push(new DifficultyLevel([Die.DIE_COLOR_WHITE],150,3,20,7));
```

Now let's review the parameters that are passed to DifficultyLevel, as we will make use of these fairly quickly:

- [Die.DIE_COLOR_WHITE]: An array of the colors of dice that will be on this level
- 150: The hit points (life) for this enemy
- 3: The tile from characters to display on this level for the enemy
- 20: The AI bonus to append to the random value generated from 0–99 to help choose the computer's move
- 7: The lowest value this enemy will accept when making a move (if there are values equal to or above it)

We created ten levels for this game, and all of them follow a similar pattern. To make the game harder, we could add more dice colors to make matching harder, add enemies with more hit points, and increase the AI bonus and the low score threshold. All of these things can (and should) be tweaked to balance the game. Because this game involves AI, we have only really scratched the surface of how this game could be tweaked using these values. You should experiment to see how small changes to in this section affect the overall difficulty in the game.

```
public function init():void
{
    //***** Flash IDE *****
    tileSheet = new TileSheet(new DiceSheet(0,0), DIE_WIDTH,DIE_HEIGHT);
    charSheet = new TileSheet(new Characters(0,0), CHAR_WIDTH,CHAR_HEIGHT);
    //***** End Flash IDE *****

    //***** Flex *****
    //tileSheet = new TileSheet(new DiceSheet().bitmapData, DIE_WIDTH, DIE_HEIGHT);
    //charSheet = new TileSheet(new Characters().bitmapData, CHAR_WIDTH, CHAR_HEIGHT);
    //***** End Flex *****    difficultyLevelArray = new Array();

    difficultyLevelArray = new Array();
    difficultyLevelArray.push(new DifficultyLevel([Die.DIE_COLOR_WHITE],100,1,0,0));
    difficultyLevelArray.push(new DifficultyLevel([Die.DIE_COLOR_WHITE],125,2,10,6));
    difficultyLevelArray.push(new DifficultyLevel([Die.DIE_COLOR_WHITE],150,3,20,7));
    difficultyLevelArray.push(new DifficultyLevel([Die.DIE_COLOR_WHITE,↩
        Die.DIE_COLOR_BLUE],175,4,30,7));
    difficultyLevelArray.push(new DifficultyLevel([Die.DIE_COLOR_WHITE,↩
        Die.DIE_COLOR_BLUE],200,5,40,7));
    difficultyLevelArray.push(new DifficultyLevel([Die.DIE_COLOR_WHITE,↩
        Die.DIE_COLOR_BLUE],225,6,50,7));
    difficultyLevelArray.push(new DifficultyLevel([Die.DIE_COLOR_WHITE,↩
        Die.DIE_COLOR_BLUE],250,7,60,7));
    difficultyLevelArray.push(new DifficultyLevel([Die.DIE_COLOR_WHITE,↩
        Die.DIE_COLOR_BLUE,Die.DIE_COLOR_GREEN],275,8,70,7));
    difficultyLevelArray.push(new DifficultyLevel([Die.DIE_COLOR_WHITE,↩
        Die.DIE_COLOR_BLUE,Die.DIE_COLOR_GREEN],300,9,80,7));
    difficultyLevelArray.push(new DifficultyLevel([Die.DIE_COLOR_WHITE,↩
        Die.DIE_COLOR_BLUE,Die.DIE_COLOR_GREEN],325,10,90,7));

}
```

The newGame function does very little new in Dice Battle except initialize both playerLife and computerLife. These values will be set in newLevel.

```
override  public function newGame():void {
    level = 0;
    score = 0;
    playerLife=0;
    computerLife=0;
}
```

Creating a computer player

The majority of the big changes to DiceBattle class from ColorDrop class have to do with the creation of the computer AI player for the human player to battle. These changes begin to take serious shape in the newLevel function.

```
override public function newLevel():void {

    level++
    var tempLevel:int = level;
    if (tempLevel > (difficultyLevelArray.length-1)) {
        tempLevel = difficultyLevelArray.length-1
    }
    currentLevel = difficultyLevelArray[tempLevel-1];
```

The first new thing we need to do is calculate bonusLife. bonusLife is the number of extra hit points we give the player when a new level starts. For this game, the player gets 10 percent of the hit points left over from the previous level added to the value of playerStartLife. We also set computerLife, to the value of enemyLife set in the instance of DifficultyLevel held in currentLevel.

```
var bonuslife:int = (Math.ceil(playerLife/10));
playerLife = playerLifeStart + bonuslife;
computerLife = currentLevel.enemyLife;
turn ="";

board = new Array();
for (var r:int  = 0; r < DIE_ROWS; r++) {
    board[r] = new Array();
    for (var c:int = 0; c <DIE_COLS; c++) {
        board[r][c] = null;
    }
}
```

Now, we need to get the enemyTile and the playerTile so we can display those graphics on the screen. To do this, we create new Character classes for each and pass in a reference to the tile we want to set for them. Recall that the playerTile is always the first tile in the Characters tile sheet, while the enemyTile is set to the enemyTile property set when we created the instance of DifficultyLevel referenced in currentLevel.

```
clickedDiceArray = new Array();
enemyTile = new Character(charSheet,currentLevel.enemyTile);
playerTile = new Character(charSheet,0);
```

```
playerTile.x = 50;
playerTile.y = 100;
enemyTile.x  = 525;
enemyTile.y  = 100;

this.addChild(playerTile);
this.addChild(enemyTile);
```

Finally, we send off events to update the scoreboard. `playerLife` and `computerLife` are two new values that we track in Dice Battle that we set here in `newLevel`. We also need to determine whose turn it is to play, but we will do that in the new game state to `GameStates.STATE_CHANGE_TURN`. It which will decide which player (the human or computer) gets to play the board next.

```
dispatchEvent(new CustomEventLevelScreenUpdate(↵
   CustomEventLevelScreenUpdate.UPDATE_TEXT, String(level)));
dispatchEvent(new CustomEventScoreBoardUpdate(↵
   CustomEventScoreBoardUpdate.UPDATE_TEXT,Main.SCORE_BOARD_SCORE,String(score)));
dispatchEvent(new CustomEventScoreBoardUpdate(↵
   CustomEventScoreBoardUpdate.UPDATE_TEXT,Main.SCORE_BOARD_LEVEL,String(level)));
dispatchEvent(new CustomEventScoreBoardUpdate(↵
   CustomEventScoreBoardUpdate.UPDATE_TEXT,Main.SCORE_BOARD_COMPUTER_LIFE,↵
   String(computerLife)));
dispatchEvent(new CustomEventScoreBoardUpdate(↵
    CustomEventScoreBoardUpdate.UPDATE_TEXT,Main.SCORE_BOARD_PLAYER_LIFE,↵
    String(playerLife)));

gameState = GameStates.STATE_CHANGE_TURN;
}
```

Taking turns using new game states

The `runGame` function of Dice Battle has been updated to account for the fact that two players take turns in this game, the human player and the computer player. While this is not a two-player hot-seat game, with just a few minor changes it could easily be one. We will run through a short description of the major changes after you take a look at the following code:

```
override public function runGame():void {
   switch(gameState) {
      case GameStates.STATE_INITIALIZING:
         break;
```

The new gameState, `GameStates.STATE_CHANGE_TURN` was set in the `newLevel` function. Since turn is set to an empty string ("") when the level starts, the first turn is always "Player". From then on, we simply switch between the value of `TURN_PLAYER` and the value of `TURN_COMPUTER` until the level or game is over. We also dispatch an event to the scoreboard to update the **Turn** text at the bottom of the screen.

```
case GameStates.STATE_CHANGE_TURN:
   if (turn == TURN_COMPUTER || turn == "") {
      turn = TURN_PLAYER;
   } else {
      turn = TURN_COMPUTER
   }
```

```
dispatchEvent(new CustomEventScoreBoardUpdate(↵
    CustomEventScoreBoardUpdate.UPDATE_TEXT, Main.SCORE_BOARD_TURN, String(turn)));
gameState = GameStates.STATE_START_REPLACING;
        break;
```

After new dice are replaced, we look at whose turn it is at that moment. If it is TURN_PLAYER, we simply listen for mouse input by setting the gameState to GameStates.STATE_WAITING_FOR_INPUT. If it is the TURN_COMPUTER, we need to create an AI move, an AI move is created by setting the gameState to GameStates.STATE_START_AI. We then set the gameState to GameStates.STATE_FALL_DICE_WAIT to wait for the replaced dice to fall into place. We did the same thing in Color Drop.

```
case GameStates.STATE_START_REPLACING:
    replaceDice();
    if (turn == TURN_PLAYER) {
        nextGameState = GameStates.STATE_WAITING_FOR_INPUT;
    } else {
        nextGameState = GameStates.STATE_START_AI;
    }
    gameState = GameStates.STATE_FALL_DICE_WAIT;
    break;
case GameStates.STATE_WAITING_FOR_INPUT:
    break;
```

The next new gameState is GameStates.STATE_START_AI. This state essentially creates the move for the computer player. To create the computer move, we call createAIMove.

```
case GameStates.STATE_START_AI:
    createAIMove();
    framesToWait = 15;
    framesWaited = 0;
    nextGameState = GameStates.STATE_REMOVE_CLICKED_DICE;
    gameState = GameStates.STATE_WAIT;
    break;
case GameStates.STATE_REMOVE_CLICKED_DICE:
    removeClickedDice();
    gameState= GameStates.STATE_CHECK_FOR_END;
    break;
```

Checking for the end (of a level or the game) is a bit more complicated now, as shown in the following code. Since now we do not know if the game or level is over until the player or computer has completed a turn, we need to do both checks right here in the GameStates.STATE_CHECK_FOR_END state. The rest of the states remain essentially unchanged from Color Drop.

```
case GameStates.STATE_CHECK_FOR_END:
    if (checkforEndLevel()) {
        nextGameState = GameStates.STATE_END_LEVEL;
        fadeDice();
        gameState = GameStates.STATE_FADE_DICE_WAIT;
    } else if (checkForEndGame() ) {
        nextGameState = GameStates.STATE_END_GAME;
        makeDiceFall()
        gameState = GameStates.STATE_FALL_DICE_WAIT;
    } else {
        gameState= GameStates.STATE_CHANGE_TURN;
    }
```

```
      break;
   case GameStates.STATE_FADE_DICE_WAIT:
      if (!checkForFadingDice()) {
         gameState = nextGameState;
      }
      break;
   case GameStates.STATE_FALL_DICE_WAIT:
      if (!checkForFallingDice()) {
         gameState = nextGameState;
      }
      break;
   case GameStates.STATE_END_LEVEL:
      endLevel();
      gameState = GameStates.STATE_INITIALIZING;
      break;
   case GameStates.STATE_END_GAME:
      endGame();
      break;
   case GameStates.STATE_WAIT:
      framesWaited++;
      if (framesWaited >= framesToWait) {
         gameState = nextGameState;
      }
      break;
   }
   update();
   render();
}
```

Capturing and scoring a player move

Besides the fact that nearly every line of code in dieClickListener has been changed to include the word "die" or "dice" instead of "block," the function of the code is almost identical to blockClickListener in Color Drop. One minor but important difference is that this function accepts an instance of CustomEventClickDie instead of CustomEventClickBlock. However, the big difference is that we now calculate the score in this function instead of in removeClickedDice (removeClickedBlocks in Color Drop), because we will use removeClickedDice for both the player and computer move. By moving the score calculation here, removeClickedDice can remain a universal function instead of having to know the context in which it was called.

The important code that we have added follows. First, we get the value of the dice by calling getDiceValue passing clickedDiceArray as the parameter to get dicevalue. Then, we call addToScore passing dicevalue.

```
var dicevalue:Number = getDiceValue(clickedDiceArray);
dispatchEvent(new CustomEventScoreBoardUpdate(↵
   CustomEventScoreBoardUpdate.UPDATE_TEXT,Main.SCORE_BOARD_COMPUTER_LIFE,↵
   String(computerLife)));

addToScore(dicevalue);
```

Here is the full code listing for dieClickListener:

```
public function dieClickListener(e:CustomEventClickDie):void {
    if (gameState == GameStates.STATE_WAITING_FOR_INPUT) {
        dispatchEvent( new CustomEventSound(CustomEventSound.PLAY_SOUND,↵
        Main.SOUND_CLICK,false,1,0,1));
        tempDie = e.die;
        clickedDiceArray = findLikeColoredDice(tempDie);
        for (var i:int =0; i< clickedDiceArray.length; i++) { //changed dice battle
            clickedDiceArray[i].makeDieClicked(); //changed dice battle
        }
        var dicevalue:Number = getDiceValue(clickedDiceArray);
        dispatchEvent(new CustomEventScoreBoardUpdate(↵
        CustomEventScoreBoardUpdate.UPDATE_TEXT,Main.SCORE_BOARD_COMPUTER_LIFE,↵
        String(computerLife)));

        addToScore(dicevalue);
        framesToWait=15;
        framesWaited=0;
        dispatchEvent( new CustomEventSound(CustomEventSound.PLAY_SOUND,↵
        Main.SOUND_BONUS,false,1,0,1));
        nextGameState = GameStates.STATE_REMOVE_CLICKED_DICE;
        gameState = GameStates.STATE_WAIT;
    }
}
```

The findLikeColoredDice function is very much like the findLikeColoredBlocks function from Color Drop. The main difference is that we need to consider the diceValue of each Die class when testing matches as well as the diceColor. To do this, we will perform a check similar to this in two places:

```
if (tempDie.dieColor == tColor && tempDie.dieValue == tValue)
```

Basically, we are testing both dieColor and dieValue to find a match for Die objects in board. If there is match, we will push the Die object into the appropriate array for our test.

To fully understand how this code works, please refer to the discussion of findLikeColoredBlocks in Chapter 8.

```
private function findLikeColoredDice(tDie:Die):Array {
    var diceToCheck:Array = new Array();
    var diceMatched:Array = new Array();
    var diceTested:Array = new Array();
    var rowList:Array = [-1, 0, 1, -1, 1, -1, 0, 1];
    var colList:Array = [-1, -1, -1, 0, 0, 1, 1, 1];

    var tColor:Number = tDie.dieColor;
    var tValue:Number = tDie.dieValue;
    diceToCheck.push(tDie);
    while(diceToCheck.length > 0) {
        tempDie = diceToCheck.pop();
        if(tempDie.dieColor == tColor && tempDie.dieValue == tValue){ //changed for dice drop
            diceMatched.push(tempDie);
        }

        var tB2:Die;
```

```
        for (var i:int = 0; i < rowList.length; i++) {
            if ((tempDie.row + rowList[i]) >= 0 && (tempDie.row + rowList[i]) < DIE_ROWS && ⏎
                (tempDie.col + colList[i]) >= 0 && (tempDie.col + colList[i]) < DIE_COLS) {
                var tr:int = tempDie.row + rowList[i];
                var tc:int = tempDie.col + colList[i];
                tB2 = board[tr][tc];
                if(tB2.dieColor == tColor && tB2.dieValue == tValue && diceToCheck.indexOf(tB2)⏎
                    == -1 && diceTested.indexOf(tB2) == -1){
                    diceToCheck.push(tB2);
                }
            }
        }
        diceTested.push(tempDie);
    }
    return diceMatched;
}
```

The getDiceValue function is brand new for Dice Battle. This function was not necessary in Color Drop, because the colored blocks in that game did not have values. This function takes an array of Die objects as it a parameter. It looks through the array and calculates the value of all the dice based on the dieValue plus bonusPoints, which are incremented by DICE_BONUS for every Die in the array after the first one. Incrementing bonusPoints in this way means that a move made that includes multiple dice will have a bonus over a similar move with dice of the same dieValue with fewer dice in the set.

```
public function getDiceValue(tdice:Array):Number {
    var value:int = 0;
    var bonusPoints:int = 0;
    for (var d:int = 0;d< tdice.length;d++) {
        tempDie = tdice[d];
        value += (tempDie.dieValue+bonusPoints);
        bonusPoints += DICE_BONUS;
    }
    return value;

}
```

The addToScore function is very close to the same function in Color Drop. The main difference is that computerLife is decremented by the amount of the score (to take hit points away from the computer), and it is reported back to the ScoreBoard.

```
private function addToScore(val:Number):void {
    score += int(val);
    computerLife -= int(val);
    dispatchEvent(new CustomEventScoreBoardUpdate(⏎
        CustomEventScoreBoardUpdate.UPDATE_TEXT,Main.SCORE_BOARD_SCORE,String(score)));
    dispatchEvent(new CustomEventScoreBoardUpdate(⏎
        CustomEventScoreBoardUpdate.UPDATE_TEXT,Main.SCORE_BOARD_COMPUTER_LIFE,⏎
        String(computerLife)));
}
```

Creating the computer's minimax-style AI

The `createAIMove` function is called when the `GameStates.STATE_START_AI` game state is set as the `gameState`. The job of `createAIMove` is to simulate a move exactly like the player and score it just like we would a player move. The difference being that the AI move will subtract the value of the move from `playerLife` instead of from `computerLife`, thus reducing the player's hit points.

When trying to decided how to create the AI for this game, one thought kept coming to us: The computer making a move is no different than the player making a move; just the way we handle the outcome is different. Furthermore, if we could simulate the act of the player choosing the proper die to click that will score the most points, we could in effect, create AI that could play against a human. This kind of AI in commonly referred to as **minimax**, which really stands for "min or max."

This type of AI is great for games where the AI player has the full information of the board and can calculate the most optimal move to make (max) and the least optimal move (min) and then make a decision on how to move based on this information. This type of AI usually involves a decision tree that includes all the possible moves for an entire game, thus allowing the AI player to calculate the best move at any given moment and still know what the outcome will be in the end.

However, using this type of AI for our game presents a problem. The AI player only has full information for the dice displayed on the board currently. It has no information about the dice that will be generated once a move is made and dice are replenished. This limitation exists because we made the new dice have random color and values. Therefore, we can only generate a list of AI moves based on how the board currently looks at any given time. This means our minimax AI only has one pile (a set of moves that we can sort by value) at any given time. Also, we are going to augment this AI by scaling it back so that the computer does not always make the best move, thus allowing us to have difficulty levels for the game. This is why we call it a minimax-style AI: while it is related to minimax, it is not an exact implementation of a minimax algorithm.

Analyzing the Dice Battle AI

To figure how to create the AI for the computer player in Dice Battle, we first sat down to discuss the things we needed the computer to know about the game:

- When it is the computer's turn to make a move
- All the possible moves it could make on its turn
- The value of all the moves (i.e., how many hit points each would remove from the player)
- Its own ability to choose the best (max) move
- Its own ability to not make a terrible (min) move

We then set out to solve each of these problems one at a time.

The first problem, letting the computer know to make a move, was very easy to solve. As we stated before, we created the turn variable and the `GameStates.STATE_CHANGE_TURN` game state to solve this problem. Basically, the computer is told by a call to `createAIMove` that it is time for it to make a decision.

The next problem, knowing all the possible moves the computer could make on its turn, was a bit more difficult. We already have the function `findLikeColoredDice` that accepts an instance of `Die` as its parameter. That function returns an array of `Die` classes that are touching with the same value and the same color. By creating a collection of all of these sets of dice (moves), we would know every move the computer could make on any one turn.

The next problem, knowing the value of all the moves the computer can make, is related to the previous one. By having a collection of all the possible moves, we would also know the values of those moves. We could then sort those moves to find out which move was worth the most (max), second worst, third worst, and so on.

The last two problems, know the computer's ability to choose the best (max) move to avoid a terrible (min) move, were both addressed with the DifficultyLevel properties aiBonus and minValue.

With all of the questions tentatively answered, we moved onto create some code that could make all this a reality.

Discussing the Dice Battle AI

To illustrate how the computer AI chooses a move, let's take a look at the sample screen in Figure 9-6. From the information provided on the screen, you can tell that it is the computer's turn, and the player has reached level 3.

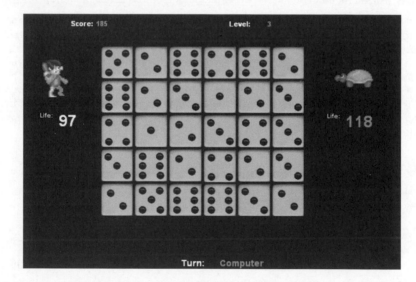

Figure 9-6. When it's the computer's turn, it calculates the AI move.

At this point, createAIMove is called, and the code will perform the following functions.

First, we find all the possible moves that the computer can make. We do this first by looping through all the Die objects on the board with two nested for loops. We take each Die on the board and call findLikeColoredDice(tempDie) to find the set of Die objects that match the Die tested. We consider these sets moves, because if we pretend like the computer clicked the tempDie, the set of Die objects returned would constitute a move the computer would make.

These moves only include each Die once. We make sure of this by using this test before we drop into the code that calls findLikecoloredDice:

```
if (diceTested.indexOf(tempDie) == -1) {
```

The `Array.indexOf` function will find the `Die` in the `diceTested` array if it exists. If it does, we will not make the test. For example, if a three is touching another three, only the first three will be added to the set of moves, because the clicking the second three would create the exact same move. By doing this, we significantly cut down the number of moves we need to calculate and handle.

```
public function createAIMove():void {

    var dieSets:Array = new Array();
    var diceTested:Array = new Array();
    var testSet:Array = new Array();
    var testValue:Number = 0;
    for (var r:int  = 0; r < board.length; r++) {
        for (var c:int = 0; c < board[r].length; c++) {
            tempDie = board[r][c];
                if (diceTested.indexOf(tempDie) == -1) {
                    testSet = findLikeColoredDice(tempDie);
                    testValue = getDiceValue(testSet);
                    dieSets.push([Number(testValue),tempDie]);
                    while(testSet.length > 0) {
                        diceTested.push(testSet.pop())
                    }
                }
        }
    }
}
```

The dieSets array is created as multidimensional array. The first dimension is the value of the move (the value of the dice). The second dimension is the Die object that will give us this set if we decide it will be our move.

If we printed out the values and `Row,Col` of the first die in each set, we would get the following list (with labels added to each value for illustration):

```
Moves:18
Value:5 Row:0 Col:0
Value:20 Row:3 Col:2
Value:6 Row:0 Col:2
Value:4 Row:0 Col:3
Value:6 Row:0 Col:4
Value:6 Row:1 Col:4
Value:6 Row:1 Col:0
Value:8 Row:2 Col:3
Value:1 Row:1 Col:3
Value:24 Row:4 Col:4
Value:4 Row:2 Col:0
Value:1 Row:2 Col:1
Value:10 Row:3 Col:3
Value:3 Row:3 Col:0
Value:24 Row:4 Col:3
Value:6 Row:4 Col:5
Value:2 Row:4 Col:0
Value:5 Row:4 Col:1
```

Now, we sort all the moves from lowest to highest value. The higher the value, the better the move. Sorting the values in the array will make it much easier for us to decide which move the computer should make. The `sortOn` function will work on multidimensional arrays if the numeric sort value is the first dimension. In our case, the first dimension is the value of the move, so we can use sortOn to put the moves in ascending order.

```
dieSets.sortOn("0",Array.NUMERIC);
```

Here is the traced output of dieSets array after it has been sorted (with labels added to each value for illustration):

```
Sorted Moves: 18
Value:1 Row:1 Col:3
Value:1 Row:2 Col:1
Value:2 Row:4 Col:0
Value:3 Row:3 Col:0
Value:4 Row:2 Col:0
Value:4 Row:0 Col:3
Value:5 Row:0 Col:0
Value:5 Row:4 Col:1
Value:6 Row:1 Col:0
Value:6 Row:0 Col:2
Value:6 Row:4 Col:5
Value:6 Row:1 Col:4
Value:6 Row:0 Col:4
Value:8 Row:2 Col:3
Value:10 Row:3 Col:3
Value:20 Row:3 Col:2
Value:24 Row:4 Col:3
Value:24 Row:4 Col:4
```

Next, we strip out all the like values from the list of moves to makes our calculation even easier. There is no reason why we need to choose from several moves that have the same value. Performing this action is quite easy. We created a lastValue variable that we will set in a for loop that loops through all the moves in order by value (remember we just sorted the array). If the current value of the move is the same as lastValue, we splice it out of the array because we don't need it.

```
var lastValue:Number = 0;
for (var ii:int = dieSets.length-1; ii >= 0; ii--) {
    if (dieSets[ii][0] == lastValue) {
        dieSets.splice(ii,1);
    } else {
        lastValue = dieSets[ii][0];
    }
}
```

Here is the traced output of dieSets array after we have removed all the like values (with labels added to each value for illustration):

```
No Like Values Moves:10
Value:1 Row:2 Col:1
Value:2 Row:4 Col:0
Value:3 Row:3 Col:0
Value:4 Row:0 Col:3
Value:5 Row:4 Col:1
Value:6 Row:0 Col:4
Value:8 Row:2 Col:3
Value:10 Row:3 Col:3
```

```
Value:20 Row:3 Col:2
Value:24 Row:4 Col:4
```

Finally, we remove any moves that are below the minValue set for the level (but only if it leaves one move to make at the end). For this level (level 3), the currentLevel.minValue is 7. This means that the computer will always choose a move that scores 7 or more (if one exists. With the values under currentLevel.minValue removed, we are left with four moves for the computer to choose from:

```
if (dieSets[dieSets.length-1][0] > currentLevel.minValue) {
    for (ii = dieSets.length-1; ii >= 0; ii--) {
        if (dieSets[ii][0] < currentLevel.minValue) {
            dieSets.splice(ii,1);
        }
    }
}
```

Here is the traced output of dieSets array after we have removed all the values below minValue (with labels added to each value for illustration):

```
minValue removed Moves:4
Value:8 Row:2 Col:3
Value:10 Row:3 Col:3
Value:20 Row:3 Col:2
Value:24 Row:4 Col:4
```

Now we get a random value from 0–99. In this case, it is 28. We test to see if (dieSets > 1), because we don't need to figure out which move to make if there is only one.

```
var aiVal:Number = 0;
if (dieSets.length > 1) {
    var pChance:Number = Math.floor(Math.random() * 100);
```

Here is the traced output of pChance (with a label added for illustration):

```
pChance without aiBonus:28
```

We now add the aiBonus for this level to that value. The higher the number, the better move the computer will make. The aiBonus for level 3 is 20 so we add that to pChance to make 48.

```
pChance += currentLevel.aiBonus;
```

Here is the traced output pChance with aiBonus added (with a label added for illustration):

```
pChance with AIbonus:48
```

Now, we simply divide 99 by the number of moves we have: Math.floor(99/dieSets.length), or 99 / 4, which makes 24. We put that in to pVal to get the multiplier for each move. We then divide pChance by pVal to get the move the computer will make and put that value into AIval. In this case, it would be 2. However, since our array is zero-based, the move we have chosen for the computer would be at index 1.

```
        var pVal:Number = Math.floor(99/dieSets.length);
        aiVal = Math.floor(pChance/pVal);
        if (aiVal > dieSets.length-1) {
            aiVal = dieSets.length-1;
        }
    } else {
        aiVal = 0;
    }
```

Here is the traced output aiVal when the algorithm is complete (with a label added for illustration):

Chosen dieSet:1

This output means this is the move the computer will make is at dieSets[1], which has a value of 10. This means we are going to knock 10 points from the player's hit points:

```
tempDie = dieSets[aiVal][1];
```

The rest of createAIMove does the simulation of the computer actually making a move. You will notice that some of this code looks familiar. This is because it is essentially the same as when the player makes a move. The main difference is that we subtract from, and report to ScoreBoard, playerLife instead of computerLife. We also play a different sound and call that lazy function in the Die class makeDieClickedComputer.

```
    clickedDiceArray = findLikeColoredDice(tempDie);
    for (var cd:int =0; cd< clickedDiceArray.length; cd++) {
    clickedDiceArray[cd].makeDieClickedComputer();
    }
playerLife -= dieSets[aiVal][0];
dispatchEvent( new CustomEventSound(CustomEventSound.PLAY_SOUND,Main.SOUND_HIT, ↩
    false,1,0,1));
dispatchEvent(new CustomEventScoreBoardUpdate( ↩
    CustomEventScoreBoardUpdate.UPDATE_TEXT,Main.SCORE_BOARD_PLAYER_LIFE, ↩
    String(playerLife)));
}
```

Figure 9-7 shows how the screen appears when the computers makes a move. Notice the red boxes that highlight the dice the computer has chosen. That comes from the call clickedDiceArray[cd].makeDiceClickedComputer.

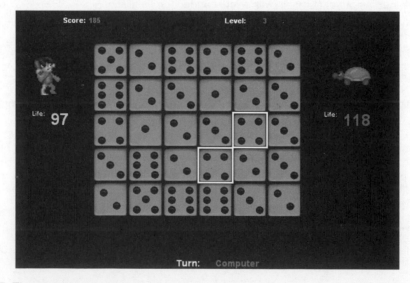

Figure 9-7. The computer chosen move

Ending the level or game

The functions checkForEndLevel and checkForEndGame are called from the gameState GameStates.STATE_CHECK_FOR_END. The level is over if the hit points for the computer (computerLife) are less than or equal to 0. Alternatively, the game is over if the players hit points (playerLife) is less than or equal to 0.

```
private function checkforEndLevel():Boolean { //changed
    var retval:Boolean = false;
    if (computerLife <= 0) {
        dispatchEvent( new CustomEventSound(CustomEventSound.PLAY_SOUND,Main.SOUND_WIN,↵
            false,1,0,1));
        retval = true;
    }
    return retval;
}

private function checkForEndGame():Boolean { //new
    var retval:Boolean = false;
    if (playerLife <= 0) {
        dispatchEvent( new CustomEventSound(CustomEventSound.PLAY_SOUND,Main.SOUND_LOSE,↵
            false,1,0,1));
        retval = true;
    }
    return retval;
}
```

Viewing the rest of the code for Dice Battle

We covered only the major changes from the Color Drop code to create Dice Battle in this chapter. However, there are a lot of code changes necessary to create the game where we simply renamed "block" to "die" so that it would be consistent for the game. Another good strategy here would be to take the context out of these functions and make some generic names like "objects" and create a drop-style game class that could be extended and reused for more games of this type.

At any rate, here is the code that remains essentially the same from Color Drop, except for name changes to existing variables and functions to match the content:

```
private function checkForFallingDice():Boolean {
    var falling:Boolean = false;
    for (var r:int  = 0; r < board.length; r++) {
        for (var c:int = 0; c < board[r].length; c++) {
            tempDie =board[r][c];
            if (tempDie != null) { //Changed Die Battle
                if (tempDie.isFalling) {
                    falling = true;
                }
            }
        }
    }
    return falling;
}
```

```
private function checkForFadingDice():Boolean {
    var fading:Boolean = false;
    for (var r:int  = 0; r < board.length; r++) {
        for (var c:int = 0; c < board[r].length; c++) {
            tempDie =board[r][c];
            if (tempDie != null) {
                if (tempDie.isFading) {
                    fading = true;
                }
            }
        }
    }
    return fading;
}


private function replaceDice():void {
    for (var r:int  = 0; r < board.length; r++) {
        for (var c:int = 0; c < board[r].length; c++) {
            if (board[r][c] == null) {
                board[r][c] = addDie(r,c);
            }
        }
    }
}

private function addDie(row:Number, col:Number):Die {
    var randomColor:Number = Math.floor(Math.random()*currentLevel.allowedColors.length);
    var dieColor:Number = currentLevel.allowedColors[randomColor];
    var dieValue:Number = Math.floor(Math.random() * 6)+1;
    tempDie = new Die(dieValue, dieColor, tileSheet, row, col,↵
        (row*DIE_HEIGHT)+Y_PAD+(row*ROW_SPACING),(Math.random()*10)+10 );
    tempDie.x=(col*DIE_WIDTH)+X_PAD+(col*COL_SPACING);
    tempDie.y= 0 - DIE_HEIGHT;
    tempDie.addEventListener(CustomEventClickDie.EVENT_CLICK_DIE, dieClickListener,↵
        false, 0, true);
    this.addChild(tempDie);
    return tempDie;
}

private function update():void {
    for (var r:int  = 0; r < board.length; r++) {
        for (var c:int = 0; c < board[r].length; c++) {
            tempDie = board[r][c];
            if (tempDie != null) {
                if (tempDie.isFalling) {
                    tempDie.update();
                }
            }
        }
    }
}

private function render():void {
    for (var r:int  = 0; r < board.length; r++) {
```

```
            for (var c:int = 0; c < board[r].length; c++) {
               tempDie = board[r][c];
               if (tempDie != null) {
                  if (tempDie.isFalling || tempDie.isFading) {
                     tempDie.render();
                  }
               }
            }
         }
      }
   }


   private function fadeDice():void {
      var boardLength:int = board.length;
      for (var r:int  = 0; r < boardLength; r++) {
         for (var c:int = 0; c < board[r].length; c++) {
            tempDie = board[r][c];
            if (tempDie != null) { //Changed Die Battle
               tempDie.startFade((Math.random()*.9)+.1);
            }
         }
      }
   }

   private function makeDiceFall():void {
      var boardLength:int = board.length;
      for (var r:int  = 0; r < boardLength; r++) {
         for (var c:int = 0; c < board[r].length; c++) {
            tempDie = board[r][c];
            if (tempDie != null) { //Changed Die Battle
               tempDie.startFalling(gameHeight + DIE_HEIGHT, (Math.random()*15)+10);
            }
         }
      }
   }

   private function removeDie(rd:Die):void {
      var boardLength:int = board.length;
      for (var r:int  = 0; r < boardLength; r++) {
         for (var c:int = 0; c < board[r].length; c++) {
            tempDie = board[r][c];
            if (tempDie == rd) {
               tempDie.removeEventListener(CustomEventClickDie.EVENT_CLICK_DIE,↵
                  dieClickListener);
               tempDie.dispose();
               removeChild(tempDie);
               board[r][c]= null;
            }
         }
      }
   }

   private function cleanUpLevel():void {
      var boardLength:int = board.length;
      for (var r:int  = 0; r < boardLength; r++) {
```

```
                for (var c:int = 0; c < board[r].length; c++) {
                    tempDie = board[r][c];
                    if (tempDie != null) {
                        removeDie(tempDie);
                    }
                }
            }
        }

    public function moveDiceDown():void {
        var collength:int = DIE_COLS-1;
            for (var c:int = collength; c >= 0; c--) {
                var rowlength:int = DIE_ROWS-1;
                var missing:Number=0;
                for (var r:int = rowlength; r >= 0; r--) {
                    tempDie=board[r][c]
                    if (tempDie != null) {
                        //find number of null spots in this column
                        missing=0;
                        if (r<DIE_ROWS) {
                            for (var m:int = r + 1;m < DIE_ROWS;m++) {
                                if (board[m][c]==null) {
                                    missing++;
                                }
                            }
                        }
                        if (missing > 0) {
                            tempDie.row = r+missing;
                            tempDie.col = c;
                            board[r+missing][c] = tempDie;
                            board[r][c] = null;
                            tempDie.startFalling(tempDie.y+(missing*DIE_HEIGHT)+↵
                              (missing*ROW_SPACING),10);
                        }
                    }
                }
            }
        }

public function removeClickedDice():void {
    removeClickedDiceFromScreen();
    moveDiceDown();
    clickedDiceArray = new Array();
    }

public function removeClickedDiceFromScreen():void {
    var dieLength:int = clickedDiceArray.length-1;
    while(clickedDiceArray.length > 0) {
        tempDie = clickedDiceArray.pop();
        removeDie(tempDie);
        }
    }

    private function endGame():void {
        cleanUpLevel();
```

```
      dispatchEvent(new Event(GAME_OVER));
   }

   private function endLevel():void {
      cleanUpLevel();
      dispatchEvent(new Event(NEW_LEVEL));
   }
```

You should also finish off the class definition with the following brackets c at the end of DiceBattle.as:

```
   }
}
```

Test it!

If you test Dice Battle, you'll notice that game starts really easy, but gets very hard very fast until it is very difficult. How do you think you could change this? How could you create levels that would ramp up in a smoother way?

There are many ways to further iterate games of this type into many other games. Color Drop and Dice Battle use very simply gameplay mechanics that could be expanded on in many ways. What about creating a game where you need to select multiple blocks or dice to make a hand, as you would in a card game? What if, instead of falling, the dice and blocks entered the screen from different directions? Alternatively, what would you do to take this game and iterate it into a Poker Dice puzzle role-playing game?

Summary

There you have it. First we talked about the legal aspects of games and intellectual property, an important but often misunderstood topic for any would-be game developer. We then iterated Color Drop into a completely different game where you battle computer AI using dice name Dice Battle. The minimax-style AI for the computers moves we used is just the tip of the iceberg when it comes to computer AI. Entire volumes have been written on the subject. If you are interested in taking game AI further, here are some links to web sites that might be of value to you:

- **AI Depot**: http://ai-depot.com/
- **AI Magazine**: http://www.aaai.org/ojs/index.php/aimagazine/index

We hope with the last two chapters we have sparked your interest in making games of this type. Now, we will move onto some really exciting games that push the game framework to its limit. Get ready to scroll, drive, fly into space, and then make some money with a viral Flash game!

Chapter 10

Blit Scrolling In a Tile-Based World

In this chapter, we will start with the tile-based single screen game theory we covered in Chapters 6 and 7 and extend it to a scrolling tile-based world. The game we are going to create is called Drive She Said. Drive She Said includes a top-down perspective and will feature a physics-based car that will navigate through the scrolling world. The car will be an extension of the BlitSprite class we created in Chapter 7, and the world will be a fully blit BitmapData canvas much like the one discussed in Chapter 6. Only this time, it will be much bigger than a single screen and will require us to scroll the viewable window as user navigates the car through the world.

Designing and getting started with Drive She Said

Let's get started by taking a look at a screenshot (see Figure 10-1), sample outline game design, and technical specification document for our game.

These are the basic game design specifications for this game:

- **Game name**: Drive She Said
- **Game type**: Driving through a tile-based world
- **Game inspiration**: The first scrolling world driving game we played was Auto Racing on the Mattel Intellivision. This was a great game, hampered by the deficiencies of the Intellivision control disc. We (Jeff in particular) were always interested in how the world was created and was especially excited when I found Rally Speedway on the Atari 800 and Super Cars on the Atari ST—both similar games that intrigued us with their simple premise: Race around a top-down scrolling world. Drive She Said is actually a driving adventure style game rather than a racing game, but the technical concept is the same.
- **Game objective**: You have made your girlfriend or boyfriend mad (once again). Before time runs out, collect all of the hearts on the level. If you collect enough before time runs out and make it to the finish, your date might accept your apology.

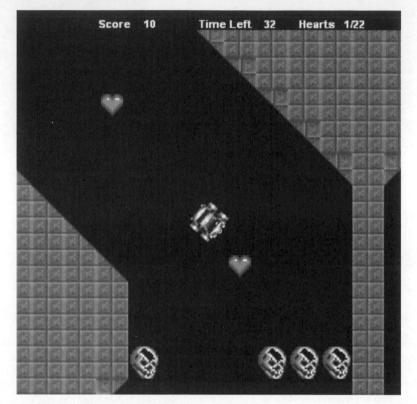

Figure 10-1. The Drive She Said game screen

- **Game play**: The player navigates the scrolling world in a car that implements basic physics properties to move about the world. Hearts will be scattered about the streets. Pick them up for points and to finish the level. Skulls will stop your car, and clocks will add precious seconds to your timer.

  The drivable world will be much larger than a single screen. The player will not have to do laps on the roadway but will simply need to get from the start to the finish under the time limit, having collected enough hearts to make it to the next level.

- **Level Progression**: Variables for the levels will be stored in XML and will be preconfigured by the level designer:

    - Percent of hearts needed to complete level
    - The start number of seconds on the countdown timer for the level
    - The score for collecting a heart
    - The amount of time added for collecting a clock
    - The negative speed adjustment and bounce back for hitting a skull
    - The negative speed adjustment and bounce back for hitting a wall

The basic technical design information follows:

- **Tile size**: 32 by 32 pixels
- **World size:** 50 tiles wide by 50 tiles high
- **Camera size:** 12 tiles by 12 tiles
- **Scrolling tile**: Tile-based to a `BitmapData` canvas
- **User control**: Keyboard arrow keys
- **Level data format**: XML
- **Tile sheet data format**: XML

Game development concepts in this chapter

While creating Drive She Said, we'll cover the following game development concepts in this chapter:

- Extending the `BlitSprite` class for car-based movement
- Moving the sounds into a the `Library` class (Flex only)
- Moving the player smoothly around a scrolling world (not tile to tile movement)
- Tile-based blit scrolling with a logical camera
- The basic physics of car movement
- Collision detection tricks for free form tile movement
- Transitions between levels with a simple state machine
- Creating a `BasicTimer` class (for counting down seconds)
- Creating a `LookAheadPoint` class
- Integrating Drive She Said into to the game framework

Defining new classes

We'll need to add these new gameplay, helper, and utility classes:

- `LookAheadPoint`: Used for collision detection between car and tiles
- `Camera2D`: Used to orient the display buffer to the correct tiles for screen display
- `CarBlitSprite`: An extension of the Chapter 7 `BlitSprite` class for car movement
- `BasicFrameTimer`: A very simple countdown counter for the game clock
- `CustomEventHeartsNeeded`: A new custom `Event` class that will pass the number of hearts the player needs to collect on a level back to the `Main.as` to display on the `levelInScreen`

Integrating with the game framework

For Drive She Said, we need the following basic screens:

- **Title screen**: Contains a `Play` button and display the text **Drive She Said**

- **Instructions screen**: Contains a Start button and the text Drive over all hearts before timer runs out.
- **Game over screen**: Contains Time Up text plus a Restart button

We need to add the following score board text elements:

- A Score display
- A Hearts display, shown as hearts collects / hearts needed
- A Time display, shown in seconds

Modifying the Library class

We will add sounds for Flex into the Library class and eliminate the need for the asset SWF from Flash.

Adding the custom LevelInScreen Class

We will add code to Main to modify the LevelInScreen dynamically. This will allow us to add a new text field to tell the user the number of hearts that must be collected on the level.

Transitioning between levels

Main.as will need to be modified to allow the Game.as class to move onto to screen and for the LevelInScreen to fade out.

Understanding free-form tile-based movement

There are many ways to move game characters on the screen. In Chapter 7, we created the No Tanks! game with smooth tile-to-tile movement. In that type of movement, we limited the tank movement to the center of each tile but smoothly animated the tank between tile centers. In this chapter, we will use a different tile-based movement called free-form tile-based movement.

Defining how free-form tile-based movement works

In **free-form tile-based movement**, the game world characters can move and make decisions on any pixel on the screen, which requires a completely different set of code and algorithms from Chapters 6 and 7. We will forego all code that checks for the tile location based on the center of the tile and instead use a system of look-ahead points to check against the next tile (or tiles) the player might run into.

Our car can rotate and move 360 degrees in an overhead view. We sometimes call this type of movement n-**way movement**, because the game character can be coded to move in any number of directions—not just the four directions from Chapters 6 and 7.

Tile scrolling is a method by which the game output screen is made up of a small portion of the actual game world. The world is made up of a 2D array of tile values.

Using art-based MoveClip stage scrolling

In one type of traditional scrolling (in Flash at least), the game world would be laid out on a `MovieClip` representing the entire world. This `MovieClip` would sit on the main timeline and would be moved up down right and left to simulate scrolling. Because the main time line display window was much smaller than the game world, scrolling was simulated. When done efficiently, this was (and is) an easy but limited way to scroll a screen. With a large world made up of many vectors the render engine would slow to just a few frames a second.

> *Note that newer versions of the Flash Player have cleaned up the art-based scrolling technique somewhat. It is now possible to have a stage that scrolls many hundreds of MovieClips with those outside the viewable space being ignored. Still though, this method only allows for a limited size game word as opposed to the blitted world we will create that essentially has limitless boundaries.*

GAS (GotoAndStop) tiles

One solution was to move to a tile-based method of timeline scrolling. The best way to represent a 2D array of tiles was by placing each different tile skin (road, building, etc.) on a frame of a tile clip and then use the "Go to and stop" method of jumping to a tile frame to change its display. When tiles were placed in a 2D array on the screen and scrolled, a tile-based world was created. "Go to and stop" (GAS) refers to the Flash time line control command, `MovieClip.gotoAndStop`.

We can think of the GAS method as a very early (for Flash) tile sheet. Each tile was put on its own frame inside a `MovieClip` with a `stop` command in the **Actions** panel for the frame the tile was on. Essentially, this created one, long timeline-based tile sheet. When the developer laid a grid of tiles on the screen and then looped through them to change the look by using the `gotoAndStop` command to change the viewable tile on each.

There were and are multiple different implementations of this method. Some placed *all* of the world tiles on the timeline and moved them every frame (less efficient), and others placed just the necessary ones on the screen (a view or camera) and changed just the needed ones. When Flash started to be used for fast-action, high-speed games, both of these methods started to show their deficiencies. The Flash engine was just not fast enough to sustain a high frame rate with that many `MovieClips` on the screen or create a very large world.

Using tile-based blit scrolling

There are a few different ways to use a blit canvas to scroll the screen. In this chapter, we will discuss tile-based blit scrolling. In the next chapter, we will explore something called screen-based blit scrolling. Tile-based blit scrolling is very similar in concept to a well-implemented GAS scrolling design but allows for a much higher frame rate. We will use a 2D array of tiles (or tile ids) that represent our world. We will not display the entire world anywhere on the screen but rather copy the needed tiles for the current camera position to a buffer canvas, scroll the buffer to the exact pixel location inside a 32 × 32 edge tile, and finally copy the buffer to our output canvas.

The World

The world is a 2D array (50 × 50) of tile values in our game. Each tile value (very similar to No Tanks! in Chapters 6 and 7) is associated with a constant value such as WALL, ROAD, HEART, and SKULL.

The Camera

The camera is just a set of variables that represent a subset of the world tiles using x and y values to indicate the start point for the current display.

The Buffer

The buffer is a `BitmapData` canvas that is 13 tiles wide and 13 tiles high (one extra in each direction). Because the player's car moves smoothly about the world, we cannot simply copy from an array of 12 × 12 exact tiles to the output canvas without this buffer. We know the start tile, but we don't know how far to the right or down the start tile needs to offset before copying pixels. For this reason, we need a thirteenth tile row and column. This 13 × 13 grid of 32 × 32 pixels is copied to the buffer.

The Output Canvas

The output canvas is 12 × 12 tiles (32 × 32 tiles = 384 × 384 dimensions). Using an offset from the top, left-hand corner, the output canvas copies from the buffer in one operation. This is where the thirteenth row and column in the buffer come into play. Since we moved right and down in the first tile to start our copy, the only way to display 384 × 384 pixels is to copy from the thirteenth tile in each direction. Take a look at Figure 10-2 for an example.

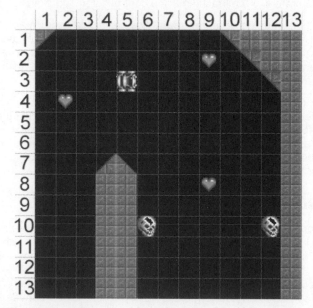

Figure 10-2. The buffer bitmap data

Figure 10-2 shows the contents for the buffer canvas for this example game output screen. As the player car moves from left to right, we must scroll the top left start point of our buffer. As you can see, the buffer contains 13 rows and 13 columns of bitmap data Let's say, for example, that the actual camera is not on these exact tile boundaries, but starts at 10x and 12y of the first tile.

412

Figure 10-3 shows what would be copied to the output canvas to shows the parts for tile first and thirteenth tiles for both the rows and the columns.

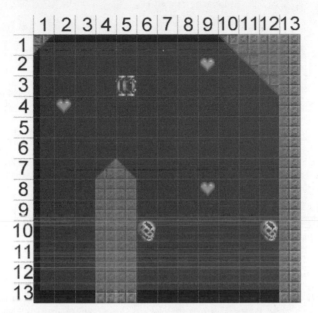

Figure 10-3. The buffer Rectangle that is copied to the canvas BitmapData

The shaded portion of Figure 10-3 is the actual area copied from the buffer to the output canvas. It represents the actual x and y coordinates of the camera and the offsets from the left top of the first tile. This is why the buffer needs to be 13 rows and 13 columns. We use this technique to product smooth tile-based blit scrolling for our game.

Creating the game world

The game world for Drive She Said will once again consist of tiles from Ari Feldman's Spritelib GPL. We have taken a few different sprites from his various sheets to create the tile sheet. We have modified some of them to fit our own needs, so you won't find all of these exact tiles in his library. You will also notice that we have created some tiles with angled walls. Tiles that don't fill up the entire tile space usually prove to be a challenge when using tile-based collision detection. We are going to use some relatively simple tricks to mitigate this challenge, but in doing so, we will also create some simple constraints on level design. We'll discuss these details soon. First, let's look at the tile sheet.

Creating the Tile Sheet

Figure 10-4 shows the 32 × 32 tile sheet that we will be using for our game.

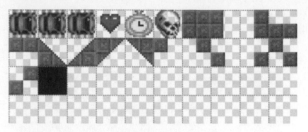

Figure 10-4. The 320 × 128 tile sheet for Drive She Said

The first three tiles represent the player's car with the tires animating slightly in the forward direction. We will code our car movement so this animation runs faster the more velocity the car has and slower when the car slows and stops. Also, our car can go in reverse, so we will run them backward when the car's velocity is a negative number. We will discuss this further in the section on the basic physics for our game car.

The heart, clock, and skull sprites are next, followed by 15 various tiles for making walls. The all black tile will be used for our drivable road, and the final two tiles represent the finish line tile in two different directions.

Detecting collisions on the WALL tiles

The wall tiles (the 15 tiles with gray boxes and a transparent background in Figure 10-4) will be used to mark the undrivable areas of our game world. The background tile for our game (the all black tile) will show through this transparency. The black color is very important, not just because it matches the road color. The color is used to depict which pixels are drivable and which are not in the WALL tiles. If we simply used tile-based collision detection on the wall tiles any time one of our look-ahead points hit any part of a WALL tile, our car would stop. This might be fine for the one tile that is completely filled with gray wall, but none of the other tiles would work very well with this type of collision detection.

So, we will use the black color around the WALL tiles as a collision buffer. If the car collides with the WALL tile, but the color of the pixel it is colliding with is black (0x00000000), the collision is not registered. The color of this buffer is selectable and can be set per level. Also, there is no reason why the code cannot be modified to provide for many buffer colors. Since the color number is a 32-bit number, you can use transparency to create very seamless worlds. Even with our simple black color, we have created a nice, seamless environment to drive in. You are not limited to simply using the background color for this detection. For instance, you could paint nontransparent pixels on the wall tiles as a buffer in any color you want and use those. You would just need to change the color specified in the level XML or change the Game.as class slightly to look at more than one color for the noncollision colors. One thing is certain though, the edge of the walls that need to be checked for collisions cannot contain the collision pass through color or the WALL tiles will not work properly.

Note that the background for our game will be on a separate layer than the foreground. By doing this, we eliminate the need to repaint the background on each frame tick. This also negates the collision detection between the background tile and the car look-ahead points. The actual foreground tile color will act as our collision pass-through color in this instance. If you find you are having trouble with collision points based on color values, set the background color of the canvasBD to the same color as the pass-through color if your wall tiles have transparent regions. An alternative is to fill the transparent regions of the wall tiles with the pass-through color.

Defining the game levels

Like the game levels in No Tanks (Chapters 6 and 7), we will use Mappy to create our levels. See Chapter 6 for a full set of information on using Mappy. You don't have to use Mappy or any other tool we suggest to create your levels; they can be designed by hand or with any tools you desire.

Unlike in Chapter 6 and 7, we will not be creating two layers for our world. There is only one sprite in our game, the player's car. Everything else, even the pick-up objects, is part of the game background. This allows us to easily scroll the screen with blitting and not have to keep track of a series of offsets for all of the game objects.

In our rules for level design, each level must contain the following

- 50 rows and 50 columns of 32 × 32 tiles
- A wall around the entire outside of each level (no warping as in NoTanks!)
- One and only one of the first three car sprites
- At least one heart sprite
- At least one of the yellow-line goal sprites

Make sure that the all black road tiles are tile 22 (the black square), not tile 0 from the Mappy tile library. It is very important that no tiles are left the Mappy default blank tile.

Obtaining the level data

Like the level data in No Tanks!, our levels will be stored in a 2D array by using the **Export For ActionScript** option in the **Custom** menu. The data for each tile row must be structured like the following code snippet. The 6 is the tile number. Tile row happens to be the top of the world, so the entire row id tile 6.

```
map = [
[6,6,6,6,6,6,6,6,6,6,6,6,6,6,6,6,6,6,6,6,6,6,6,6,6,6,6,6,6,6,6,6,6,6,6,6,6,6,6,6,6,6,6,↩
6,6,6,6,6,6,6,6]
[6,13,21,21,21,21,21,21,21,21,21,21,21,21,21,21,21,21,21,21,21,21,21,21,21,21,21,21,14,↩
6,6,6,6,6,6,6,6,6,6,13,21,21,21,21,21,21,21,21,14,6,6,6],
[6,0,21,21,21,21,21,21,21,21,21,21,21,21,21,21,3,21,21,21,21,21,21,21,21,21,21,21,14,↩
6,6,6,6,6,6,6,6,13,21,21,21,21,21,21,21,21,3,21,14,6,6],
[6,21,21,21,21,21,21,21,21,21,21,21,21,21,21,21,21,21,21,21,21,21,21,21,3,21,21,21,↩
21,14,6,6,6,6,6,13,21,21,21,21,21,21,21,21,21,21,21,21,14,6],
[6,11,21,21,21,21,21,21,21,21,21,21,21,21,21,21,21,21,21,21,21,21,21,21,21,21,21,↩
21,21,21,14,6,6,6,13,21,21,21,3,21,21,21,21,21,21,21,21,21,6],
[6,6,6,6,6,6,6,6,6,6,6,6,6,6,6,6,6,6,6,6,11,21,21,21,21,21,21,21,21,21,14,6,13,↩
21,21,21,21,21,21,21,21,21,21,21,21,21,6],,
...];
```

The level we will create is much too large to show on a single screen, so Figure 10-5 shows a miniature consolidation image of the entire level 1.

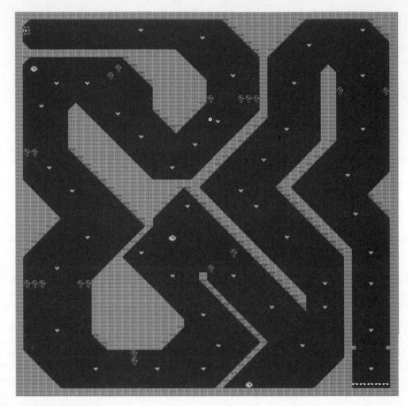

Figure 10-5. The entire level 1

Figure 10-5 was compiled from more than one image to show how we fit the tiles together to make level 1. You can attempt to mimic this level exactly or create one of your own.

Note that the Drive She Said engine can be used to make loopable tracks that require the player to do multiple laps before the yellow finish line tiles register the level as complete.

Applying basic car physics to our game

We want to make the car in our game behaves at least close to how the general game player feels a car should move. We don't have to attempt to mimic all of the real-world physics involved in car movement, just enough to give our game a sense of realism. We explored these concepts somewhat in Chapter 6 and 7 when we moved the tank forward though the maze. We didn't discuss them in detail then, so we will cover that topic a little more closely in here.

Moving forward and backward

Our car will begin stopped, and its velocity will be 0. When the up arrow key is pressed, we will add acceleration to the velocity value. The velocity will have a maximum (such as 8 pixels per frame). When the maximum velocity is reached, the car will not be able to accelerate any further. When the up arrow key is not pressed, a deceleration value will be subtracted from the velocity until it reaches 0. By pressing the down arrow key, the player will slowly begin to stop and then start to move in the reverse direction. There is a separate reverse maximum velocity that is roughly half the forward maximum velocity. Our car cannot turn or rotate unless it has some forward or reverse velocity.

Moving in a direction

Our velocity value is really just a scalar value that represents the current speed of the car. In reality, velocity is actually a vector value that includes values for moving along the x and y axis of a graph.

The direction the player car is facing and the amount to move in that direction will be considered the vector value for our movement. A **vector** is a number that includes a magnitude (amount) and a direction. We will have a variable in our game called velocity, but it really is just half of the value we need to move our car. Our vectors for movement will be stored as a number and a sign for both the x and y directions. The number will represent the magnitude, and the sign will represent the direction. So, for the horizontal direction we might have a value that is −1. This would represent 1 pixel in the left direction. We might have a vertical value of 3 (no sign means positive). This would represent a value of 3 pixels up the screen.

When the car is turned or rotated to a new position by pressing the arrow keys, we will need to calculate the vectors for moving in that new direction. To find the vector value to move in this new direction, we need to know the angle our car is currently moving.

We will store the vector for moving our car in a rotated direction in two variables. One will be used for the x direction and one will be used for the y direction. These two values are sometimes referred to as deltaX (dx) and deltaY (dy). These represent the change (or delta) in direction and location on each frame for our car. This value is derived using some basic trigonometry to determine the angle our car should move based on its current rotation. The speed of our car (the velocity attribute of our car) will be multiplied by the dx and dy values to achieve the actual movement in both the x and y directions.

Let's do an example where our car has been rotated to a 30-degree angle, and now we need to calculate the dx and dy values to move it in that direction on the next frame.

Let's take a look at some example code and the output to illustrate this point:

```
var velocity:Number = 2;
var rotation:Number = 30;
var carRadians:Number = (rotation / 360) * (2.0 * Math.PI);

trace("rotation=" + rotation);
trace("carRadians=" +carRadians);
trace("Math.cos(carRadians)=" + Math.cos(carRadians));
trace("Math.sin(carRadians)=" + Math.sin(carRadians));

var dx:Number=Math.cos(carRadians)*velocity;
var dy:Number= Math.sin(carRadians) * velocity;

trace("dx=" + dx);
trace("dy=" + dy);
```

And here's the traced output:

```
rotation=30
carRadians=0.5235987755982988
Math.cos(carRadians)=0.8660254037844387
Math.sin(carRadians)=0.49999999999999994
dx=1.7320508075688774
dy=0.9999999999999999
```

There are some key things to note about this output.

First, Flash uses degrees to indicate angles on display objects, but we must first translate that value to radians in order for it to be used in our calculations:

```
Radians = (rotation in degrees / 360) * (2 * pi)
```

So, for our example

```
Radians = 30/360 * (2 *pi)
Radians =   .083 * (6.28)
Radians = .0.523
```

Next we find the vector for the x axis. If you remember from basic trigonometry (if you have had the pleasure), the x axis and the cosine of the angle are closely related. The cosine of our angle will be the magnitude in pixels on the x axis for our car to move. The dx value is going to be the cosine of our radians multiplied by our velocity. When our car is moving with a velocity of 2 (in this example), we get this calculation:

```
dx=cos(.523) * 2
dx=,866*2
dx=1.73;
```

Now, let's look at the dy vector. The axis and the sine of the angle are closely related. The sine of our angle will be the magnitude in pixels our car will move in the y direction.

```
dy=sin(.523)*2
dy=.499 * 2
dy=0.999
```

To move our car at a 30-degree angle at a speed of 2 pixels, we would need to move 1.73 pixels along the x axis and .999 pixels on the y axis.

Preparing to create our Drive She Said game

Our game will make use of the framework classes (with some modifications) and will use some new custom classed that were mentioned earlier in the chapter.

No matter if you are using Flex, Flash Develop, Flash Builder, or the Flash IDE, you should create a new project folder to hold all of the code for this game.

As with all of the games in this book, Drive She Said will use the framework package structure we created in Chapter 2. Let's begin by creating the package necessary for our game in both the Flash IDE and Flash Develop (for use with the Flex SDK).

Creating the game project in the Flash IDE

By now, these steps to create the project in the Flash IDE should look very familiar to you:

1. Start up your version of Flash. We are using CS3, but this should work exactly the same in CS4 and CS5.

2. Create a .fla file in the /source/projects/driveshesaid/flashIDE/ folder called driveshesaid.

3. In the /source/projects/driveshesaid/flashIDE folder, create the package structure for your game: com/efg/games/driveshesaid/.

4. Set the frame rate of the Flash movie to **30** FPS. Set the width to **384** and the height to **404**.

5. Set the document class to com.efg.games.driveshesaid.Main.

6. We have not yet created the Main.as class, so you will see a warning. We are going to create this later in this chapter.

7. Now, we need to add the framework reusable class package to the class path for the FLA file. In the **Publish** settings select **Flash ➤ ActionScript 3 Setting.**

8. Click the **Browse to Path** button and find the /source folder we created in Chapter 2 for the package structure.

9. Select the classes folder and click the **Choose** button. Now the com.efg.framework package will be available for use when we begin to create our game.

Creating the game project in the Flash Develop

Here are the steps for creating the project in Flash Develop:

1. Create a folder inside the /source/projects/driveshesaid/ folder called [flexSDK] (if you have not already done so).

2. Start Flash Develop and create a new project; select **Flex 3 Project**, and give it the name **driveshesaid**. The location should be the /source/projects/driveshesaid/flexSDK folder, and the package should be com.efg.games.driveshesaid.

   Do not have Flash Develop create a project folder automatically. Make sure the **Create Folder For Project** is *unchecked*. Click the **OK** button to create the project.

3. Now, we need to add the class path to the framework to the project. Go to the **Project ➤ Properties ➤ Classpaths** menu item.

4. Click the **Add Class Path** button. Find the /source we created earlier, and select the classes subfolder.

5. Click the **OK** button and then the **Apply** button.

6. Next, change the size of the output and frame rate. Go to the **Project ➤ Properties ➤ Classpaths** menu item again, and set the frame rate to 30, the width to 384, and the height to 404.

You now have the basic structure to start creating projects inside the framework. We are now going to discuss a few topics concerning the structure of the framework classes and then move into building the reusable framework code.

> *For Flex Builder, Flash Builder, or another IDE, please refer to the documentation provided for that product to create a new project and set the default compile class.*
>
> *In a Flash Develop / Flash IDE workflow, a common method of Flash development is to use the Flash IDE for assets and organization and Flash Develop for code editing. If this is your workflow of choice, you will want to follow the Flash IDE folder and package structure rather than the Flex SDK folder structure.*

This is the folder structure for the Flash IDE:

`/source/projects/driveshesaid/flashIDE/com/efg/games/driveshesaid/`

and for the Flex SDK (using Flash Develop):

```
/source/projects/driveshesaid/flexSDK/
                                assets/
                                bin/
                                obj/
                                lib/
                                src/com/efg/games/driveshesaid/
```

Updating the Main.as class for Drive She Said

We will be making the most significant changes to the `Main.as` so far in the book. It is still going to be a subclass of `GameFrameWork.as`, but we will be adding in some new functionality for fading and moving the game screen as well as adding new text to the `LevelInScreen`.

Here is the file name and location for the Flash IDE.

`/source/projects/driveshesaid/flashIDE/com/efg/games/driveshesaid/Main.as`

Here is the file name and location for the Flex SDK.

`/source/projects/driveshesaid/flexSDK/src/com/efg/games/driveshesaid/Main.as`

And here's the entire `Main.as` class for Drive She Said:

```
package com.efg.games.driveshesaid
{

    import flash.text.TextFormat;
    import flash.text.TextField; //new
    import flash.text.TextFormatAlign;
    import flash.geom.Point;
    import flash.events.Event;

    import com.efg.framework.FrameWorkStates;
```

```
import com.efg.framework.GameFrameWork;
import com.efg.framework.BasicScreen;
import com.efg.framework.ScoreBoard;
import com.efg.framework.SideBySideScoreElement;
import com.efg.framework.SoundManager;


public class Main extends GameFrameWork {

    //custom score board elements
    public static const SCORE_BOARD_SCORE:String = "score";
    public static const SCORE_BOARD_TIME_LEFT:String = "timeleft";
    public static const SCORE_BOARD_HEARTS:String = "hearts";

    //custom sounds

    public static var SOUND_TITLE_MUSIC:String = "titlemusic";
    public static var SOUND_CAR:String = "car";
    public static var SOUND_CLOCK_PICKUP:String = "clockpickup";
    public static var SOUND_HEART_PICKUP:String = "heartpickup";
    public static var SOUND_GAME_LOST:String = "gamelost";
    public static var SOUND_LEVEL_COMPLETE:String = "levelcomplete";
    public static var SOUND_SKULL_HIT:String = "skullhit";
    public static var SOUND_PLAYER_START:String = "playerstart";
    public static var SOUND_HIT_WALL:String = "hitwall";

    //level in screen additions
    private var heartsToCollect:TextField = new TextField();

    public function Main() {
        init();
    }

    override public function init():void {
        game = new DriveSheSaid();
        game.y = 20;
        game.x = 404; //added
        setApplicationBackGround(384, 404, false, 0x000000);

        game.addEventListener(CustomEventHeartsNeeded.HEARTS_NEEDED, heartsNeededListener,↵
         false, 0, true);

        //add score board to the screen as the seconf layer
        scoreBoard = new ScoreBoard();
        addChild(scoreBoard);
        scoreBoardTextFormat = new TextFormat("_sans", "11", "0xffffff", "true");

        scoreBoard.createTextElement(SCORE_BOARD_SCORE, new SideBySideScoreElement↵
         (80, 5, 20,"Score", scoreBoardTextFormat, 25, "0", scoreBoardTextFormat));

        scoreBoard.createTextElement(SCORE_BOARD_TIME_LEFT, new SideBySideScoreElement↵
         (180, 5, 20, "Time Left", scoreBoardTextFormat, 45, "0", scoreBoardTextFormat));
```

421

```
scoreBoard.createTextElement(SCORE_BOARD_HEARTS, new SideBySideScoreElement↵
(280,5, 20, "Hearts", scoreBoardTextFormat, 25, "0", scoreBoardTextFormat));


//screen text initializations
screenTextFormat = new TextFormat("_sans", "16", "0xffffff", "false");
screenTextFormat.align = flash.text.TextFormatAlign.CENTER;
screenButtonFormat = new TextFormat("_sans", "12", "0x000000", "false");

titleScreen = new BasicScreen(FrameWorkStates.STATE_SYSTEM_TITLE,↵
 384,404,false,0x000000 );

titleScreen.createOkButton("Play", new Point(150, 250), 100, 20, ↵
 screenButtonFormat, 0x000000, 0xff0000,2);

titleScreen.createDisplayText("Drive She Said", 200, new Point(100, 150), ↵
 screenTextFormat);

instructionsScreen = new BasicScreen(FrameWorkStates.↵
 STATE_SYSTEM_INSTRUCTIONS,384,404,false,0x000000);

instructionsScreen.createOkButton("Start", new Point(150, 250), ↵
 100, 20,screenButtonFormat, 0x000000, 0xff0000,2);

instructionsScreen.createDisplayText("Drive over all harts\nbefore ↵
 timer\nruns out.",200,new Point(100,150),screenTextFormat);

gameOverScreen = new BasicScreen(FrameWorkStates.STATE_SYSTEM_GAME_OVER,↵
 640,500,false,0x0000dd);

gameOverScreen.createOkButton("Restart", new Point(150, 250), 100, 20,↵
 screenButtonFormat, 0x000000, 0xff0000,2);

gameOverScreen.createDisplayText("Time up\nGame Over",100,new Point(150,150),↵
 screenTextFormat);

levelInScreen = new BasicScreen(FrameWorkStates.STATE_SYSTEM_LEVEL_IN, ↵
 384, 404, true, 0xbbff00ff);

levelInText = "Level ";
levelInScreen.createDisplayText(levelInText,100,new Point(150,150),↵
 screenTextFormat);

heartsToCollect.defaultTextFormat = screenTextFormat;
heartsToCollect.width = 300;
heartsToCollect.x = 50;
heartsToCollect.y = 200;

levelInScreen.addChild(heartsToCollect);

//set initial game state
switchSystemState(FrameWorkStates.STATE_SYSTEM_TITLE);
```

```
    //sounds
    //*** Flex SDK

      soundManager.addSound(SOUND_TITLE_MUSIC,new Library.SoundTitleMusic);
      soundManager.addSound(SOUND_CAR, new Library.SoundCar);
      soundManager.addSound(SOUND_CLOCK_PICKUP,new Library.SoundClockPickup);
      soundManager.addSound(SOUND_HEART_PICKUP,new Library.SoundHeartPickup);
      soundManager.addSound(SOUND_GAME_LOST,new Library.SoundGameLost);
      soundManager.addSound(SOUND_LEVEL_COMPLETE,new Library.SoundLevelComplete);
      soundManager.addSound(SOUND_SKULL_HIT,new Library.SoundSkullHit);
      soundManager.addSound(SOUND_PLAYER_START,new Library.SoundPlayerStart);
      soundManager.addSound(SOUND_HIT_WALL,new Library.SoundHitWall);

    //*** Flash IDE SDK

      //soundManager.addSound(SOUND_TITLE_MUSIC,new SoundTitleMusic);
      //soundManager.addSound(SOUND_CAR, new SoundCar);
      //soundManager.addSound(SOUND_CLOCK_PICKUP,new SoundClockPickup);
      //soundManager.addSound(SOUND_HEART_PICKUP,new SoundHeartPickup);
      //soundManager.addSound(SOUND_GAME_LOST,new SoundGameLost);
      //soundManager.addSound(SOUND_LEVEL_COMPLETE,new SoundLevelComplete);
      //soundManager.addSound(SOUND_SKULL_HIT,new SoundSkullHit);
      //soundManager.addSound(SOUND_PLAYER_START,new SoundPlayerStart);
      //soundManager.addSound(SOUND_HIT_WALL,new SoundHitWall);


    //create timer and run it one time
    frameRate = 40;
    startTimer();
}

override public function systemTitle():void {
    soundManager.playSound(SOUND_TITLE_MUSIC, false,999, 20, 1);
    super.systemTitle();
}

override public function systemNewGame():void {
    soundManager.stopSound(SOUND_TITLE_MUSIC);
    super.systemNewGame();
}

override public function systemLevelIn():void {
    levelInScreen.alpha = 1
    super.systemLevelIn();
}

override public function systemWait():void {

    if (lastSystemState == FrameWorkStates.STATE_SYSTEM_LEVEL_IN) {
        game.x -= 2;
        if (game.x < 100) {
            levelInScreen.alpha -= .01;
            if (levelInScreen.alpha < 0 ) {
                levelInScreen.alpha = 0;
            }
```

```
        }
        if (game.x <= 0) {
          game.x = 0;
          soundManager.playSound(SOUND_PLAYER_START, false,1,20, 1);
          dispatchEvent(new Event(EVENT_WAIT_COMPLETE));
        }
      }

    private function heartsNeededListener(e:CustomEventHeartsNeeded):void {
      heartsToCollect.text = "Collect " + e.heartsNeeded + " Hearts";
      heartsToCollect.width = 300;
      heartsToCollect.x = 50;
      heartsToCollect.y = 200;
    }
  }
}
```

We have made some new alterations to the Main class that will change the way the game interacts with the framework, and we have made the same sort of game-specific changes that we have seen throughout the book.

Adding ScoreBoard elements

As with all of the games so far, we have added scoreboard elements for the text fields we want to display at the top of the screen; there are three in this game: SCORE_BOARD_SCORE will display the number of points the player has earned by colleting hearts. SCORE_BOARD_TIME_LEFT will display the number of seconds left for the player to reach the finish line having collected enough hearts to move on to the next level. SCORE_BOARD_HEARTS will display the number of hearts the player has collected so far.

```
public static const SCORE_BOARD_SCORE:String = "score";
public static const SCORE_BOARD_TIME_LEFT:String = "timeleft";
public static const SCORE_BOARD_HEARTS:String = "hearts";
```

Modifying the screens

The screens have been modified to display the new messaging we want for this game. These are all pretty straightforward and very similar to the screens in previous games.

Modifying the sounds

We have added nine new sound constants and have added these sounds to the SoundManager. Unlike in the previous chapter, where the Flex SDK version used an embedded SWF with all of the sounds included, we will use straight MP3 files this time around. These assets will be embedded into the library (at design time) of the Flash IDE version but will be embedded at compile-time in the Flex SDK version.

```
//*** Flex SDK

soundManager.addSound(SOUND_TITLE_MUSIC,new Library.SoundTitleMusic);
soundManager.addSound(SOUND_CAR, new Library.SoundCar);
soundManager.addSound(SOUND_CLOCK_PICKUP,new Library.SoundClockPickup);
soundManager.addSound(SOUND_HEART_PICKUP,new Library.SoundHeartPickup);
```

```
soundManager.addSound(SOUND_GAME_LOST,new Library.SoundGameLost);
soundManager.addSound(SOUND_LEVEL_COMPLETE,new Library.SoundLevelComplete);
soundManager.addSound(SOUND_SKULL_HIT,new Library.SoundSkullHit);
soundManager.addSound(SOUND_PLAYER_START,new Library.SoundPlayerStart);
soundManager.addSound(SOUND_HIT_WALL,new Library.SoundHitWall);

//*** Flash IDE SDK

//soundManager.addSound(SOUND_TITLE_MUSIC,new SoundTitleMusic);
//soundManager.addSound(SOUND_CAR, new SoundCar);
//soundManager.addSound(SOUND_CLOCK_PICKUP,new SoundClockPickup);
//soundManager.addSound(SOUND_HEART_PICKUP,new SoundHeartPickup);
//soundManager.addSound(SOUND_GAME_LOST,new SoundGameLost);
//soundManager.addSound(SOUND_LEVEL_COMPLETE,new SoundLevelComplete);
//soundManager.addSound(SOUND_SKULL_HIT,new SoundSkullHit);
//soundManager.addSound(SOUND_PLAYER_START,new SoundPlayerStart);
//soundManager.addSound(SOUND_HIT_WALL,new SoundHitWall);
```

If you are using the Flash IDE, you will want to comment out the Flex SDK addSound function calls and uncomment the Flash IDE versions.

Again, like in the previous chapters, we created override functions for the systemTitle and systemNewGame functions to handle the title screen music.

Transitioning to the LevelInScreen

One of the biggest changes in this version of Main is the coding on the leveInScreen transition in the. Our game class instance will be positioned at 404x to begin the game.

game.x = 404;

We have also created an override function for the systemWait function.

During the STATE_SYSTEM_LEVEL_IN state, this new function will move the game screen from the right-hand side of the stage to the 0 x position where the game play will start. Also, the game levelInScreen will fade out by decrementing its alpha value.

```
if (lastSystemState -- FrameWorkStates.STATE_SYSTEM_LEVEL_IN) {
    game.x -= ?;
    if (game.x < 100) {
        levelInScreen.alpha -= .01;
        if (levelInScreen.alpha < 0 ) {
            levelInScreen.alpha = 0;
        }
    }
    if (game.x <= 0) {
    game.x = 0;

    soundManager.playSound(SOUND_PLAYER_START, false,1,20, 1);
    dispatchEvent(new Event(EVENT_WAIT_COMPLETE));
    }
}
```

Notice also that once the levelInScreen is in its final position we have a sound that plays (SOUND_PLAYER_START) to indicate the level has begun.

We needed to also create an override function for the `systemLevelIn` function that would set the alpha of the `levelInScreen` back to 1 at the beginning of each `STATE_SYSTEM_LEVEL_IN` state.

```
override public function systemLevelIn():void {
   levelInScreen.alpha = 1
   super.systemLevelIn();

}
```

Updating the LevelInScreen text

We have added a new message to the `levelInScreen`. This message displays the number of hearts that need to be collected during the level. To do this we first made sure to import in the `TextField` class:

```
import flash.text.TextField;
```

Next, we added the heartsToCollect variable to the variable definition section.

```
private var heartsToCollect:TextField = new TextField();
```

In the init function, we have set the `defaultTextFormat` of the `heartsToCollect` field to be the same as the screen text.

```
heartsToCollect.defaultTextFormat = screenTextFormat;
heartsToCollect.width = 300;
heartsToCollect.x = 50;
heartsToCollect.y = 200;
```

The `heartsToCollect` `TextField` also needs to be added to the `levelInScreen`'s display list:

```
levelInScreen.addChild(heartsToCollect);
```

We also added an event listener into the init function that will listen for a new custom event class called `CustomEventHeartsNeeded`. When this event is dispatched, the number of hearts the player needs to collect for the level will be sent along with it.

```
game.addEventListener(CustomEventHeartsNeeded.HEARTS_NEEDED, heartsNeededListener, ↵
 false, 0, true);
```

The `heartsNeededListener` function was also added to `Main.as`:

```
private function heartsNeededListener(e:CustomEventHeartsNeeded):void {
   heartsToCollect.text = "Collect " + e.heartsNeeded + " Hearts";
}
```

This function will change the `heartsToCollect.text` to the passed in value (from the custom Event)

Increasing the game Frame Rate

As we transition into games that require more and more system resources, we are going to experiment with using the `Timer` class to create a frame rate different than the Stage frame rate (30).We are going to set the frame rate to 40 for this game. Remember that the `updateAfterEvent` function call inside the `GameFrameWork`'s game loop will help smooth out the look of the screen updates when we choose a frame rate higher than the `Stage` frame rate. In the next chapter, will we create a new type of timer that will really push the limits of the `Stage` frame rate.

```
frameRate = 40;
```

Creating the CustomEventHeartsNeeded.as class

This class will be very similar to the custom `Event` classes we created in Chapter 2. This one will be part of the Drive She Said package rather than the framework package.

Here is the file name and location for the Flash IDE:

`/source/projects/driveshesaid/flashIDE/com/efg/games/driveshesaid/CustomEventHeartsNeeded.as`

Here is the file name and location for the Flex SDK (using Flash Develop):

`/source/projects/driveshesaid/flexSDK/src/com/efg/games/driveshesaid/CustomEventHeartsNeeeded.as`

This class is a very simple subclass of the `Event` class. Here is the full source:

```
package com.efg.games.driveshesaid
{
    import flash.events.Event;

    /**
     * ...
     * @author Jeff Fulton
     */

    public class CustomEventHeartsNeeded extends Event{
        public static const HEARTS_NEEDED:String = "hearts needed";

        public var heartsNeeded:String;

        public function CustomEventHeartsNeeded(type:String,heartsNeeded:String,↵
         bubbles:Boolean=false,cancelable:Boolean=false) {

            super(type, bubbles,cancelable);
            this.heartsNeeded = heartsNeeded;
        }


        public override function clone():Event {
            return new CustomEventHeartsNeeded(type,heartsNeeded, bubbles,cancelable)
        }
    }
}
```

When an instance of this class is created, the `heartsNeeded` value is passed in and the listening function will be able to retrieve it. You'll see this in action when we get to the `newLevel` function in the `DriveSheSaid` class.

Creating the Library.as class

The `Library.as` class is only necessary for those using the Flex framework. It is not used for Flash IDE projects. The changes to the library have to do with adding the sounds as `static const` assets rather than having them inside an exported SWF from the IDE. By doing this, we free the game from needing the IDE at all. The one drawback to using assets embedded at run-time is the inability of the Flex framework to import `.wav` files. By using `.mp3` files, we mitigate this limitation, but with the added headache of trying to avoid the space of silence at the beginning of the .mp3 file. We will use a a an offset to skip this space when we play our sounds.

> *Here's a note about MP3 silence space: MP3-formatted files have a section of data at the beginning where the ID3 tag and other file specific information are stored. When you play the file, there is a short silence at the beginning of the file before the sound starts. This silence is almost unnoticeable when you play a song that does not loop. When a looping sound or piece of music is played, this silence will be pronounced and cause an audible delay between the end of the sound play and the start of the next play of the sound. Luckily, the AS3 sound handler functions allow us to skip into the play of a sound by an offset, which helps us to skip the silence when we loop a sound.*
>
> *Some MP3 file encoders also leave some silence at the end of the file. Unfortunately, there is no built-in ending offset in the AS3 sound handlers.*

If you are using the Flash IDE, you should import the sounds into the library and use the class names in the Library class as your linkage names. You do not need the Library class for the Flash IDE version.

This is the folder structure for this file in the Flex SDK (using Flash Develop):

/source/projects/driveshesaid/flexSDK/src/com/efg/games/driveshesaid/Library.as

Use the following code to create the file at that location:

```
package com.efg.games.driveshesaid
{
    public class Library {
    [Embed(source = "../../../../../assets/tile_sheet.png")]
    public static const TileSheetPng:Class;

    [Embed(source="../../../../../assets/sound_titlemusic.mp3")]
    public static const SoundTitleMusic:Class;

    [Embed(source="../../../../../assets/sound_car.mp3")]
    public static const SoundCar:Class;

    [Embed(source="../../../../../assets/sound_clockpickup.mp3")]
    public static const SoundClockPickup:Class;

    [Embed(source="../../../../../assets/sound_heartpickup.mp3")]
    public static const SoundHeartPickup:Class;

    [Embed(source="../../../../../assets/sound_gamelost.mp3")]
    public static const SoundGameLost:Class;

    [Embed(source="../../../../../assets/sound_levelcomplete.mp3")]
    public static const SoundLevelComplete:Class;

    [Embed(source="../../../../../assets/sound_skullhit.mp3")]
    public static const SoundSkullHit :Class;

    [Embed(source="../../../../../assets/sound_playerstart.mp3")]
    public static const SoundPlayerStart:Class;
```

```
[Embed(source="../../../../../assets/sound_hitwall.mp3")]
public static const SoundHitWall:Class;
}
}
```

You must ensure that you have moved the tile sheet and all of the sound assets to the /assets folder for the project, and placed the folder into the following structure for the Flex SDK (using Flash Develop):

```
[source]
    [projects]
        [driveshesaid]
            [flexSDK]
                [assets]
                    [bin]
                    [obj]
                    [lib]
                    [src]
                        [com]
                            [efg]
                                [games]
                                    [driveshesaid]
```

Remember, the assets folder is at the same level in the directory structure as the src, bin, obj, and lib folders. It will not be created automatically; you will need to create it yourself.

Creating the new framework classes

We will be creating some new classes that can be reused in future projects. These classes are the BasicFrameTimer class, the LookAheadPoint class, the CarBlitSprite class and the Canvas2D class.

Creating the BasicFrameTimer class

The BasicFrameTimer class is going to be used to create a countdown clock for our game. The class is very simple but is designed to work with counting up as well as the counting down we need for this game. It doesn't have any viewable interface, only logical data. For this reason, it extends the EventDispatcher class.

It does not make use of the getTimer class, because this mixing of time-based logic with frame-based code would be unfair for players on slower machines. With a real time-based countdown, the clock would be accurate, but if the game slowed down, the player might not be able to reach the goal in time. Also, mixing frame-based and time-based code allows cheaters to figure out methods to slow the game clock but keep the game frame rate running at the correct speed, which would allow almost unlimited time to complete a level.

What we will do is use a frame-based countdown. The constructor for our game will accept in a parameter that represents the frame rate our game is set to run at. A single second of time will be based on this number rather than 1,000 real milliseconds. If the frame rate speeds up or slows down, our frame-based second will do the same. This will allow players on all machines a fair attempt at the game.

This is the file location:

/source/classes/com/efg/framework/BasicFrameTimer.as

And here is the complete class code:

```
package   com.efg.framework
{
   import flash.events.*;


   public class BasicFrameTimer extends EventDispatcher {

      public static const  TIME_IS_UP:String = "timesup";

      public var countUp:Boolean = false;
      public var min:int = 0;
      public var max:int = 0;
      public var seconds:int;
      private var frameCount:int;
      public var started:Boolean = false;
      private var framesPerSecond:int;

      public function BasicFrameTimer(framesPerSecond:int) {
         this.framesPerSecond = framesPerSecond;
      }

      public function start():void {
         frameCount = 0;
         started = true;
      }

      public function stop():void {
         started = false;
      }

      public function reset():void {
         if (countUp) {
            seconds = max;
         }else {
            seconds = min;
         }
      }

      public function update():void {
         frameCount++;
         if (started) {
            if (frameCount > framesPerSecond) {
               frameCount=0;
               if (countUp) {
                  seconds++;
                  if (seconds == max) {
                     stop();
                     dispatchEvent(new Event( TIME_IS_UP));
                  }
               }else {
```

```
                    seconds--;
                    if (seconds == min) {
                        stop();
                        dispatchEvent(new Event( TIME_IS_UP));
                    }
                }
            }
        }
    }
}
```

The class is takes in a single parameter representing the `framesPerSecond`. The user simply needs to set a maximum and a minimum value for seconds and start and stop the timer as necessary. It contains an attribute called `countUp` that starts set to `false`. The game loop must call the update function of the timer for it to work. In the update cycle, the class uses the `frameCount` variable to count up until it is equal to the passed in `framesPerSecond`. When it is, we consider a second of game time to have passed. If so, the current value for `seconds` is either increased or decreased.

If the `seconds` variable reaches maximum (counting up) or minimum (counting down) the `TIME_IS_SUP` event constant is dispatched. The `Game` will listen for this event and (in our case) set the `gameOver` variable in the `DriveSheSaid` class to `true`.

Creating the LookAheadPoint class

The `LookAheadPoint` class is used for collision detection between the player's car and all of the tiles in the game. We will use three of these, placed at the front middle, left, and right of the car if it is moving with a positive velocity. If it is moving with a negative velocity, we will place these at the rear of the car. This class will extend `Sprite` because we want to be able to see these points while coding and testing. This way, we can turn on a circle that will wrap around the point for visual reference. This will allow us to visually see the points where the car will come into contact with the game level tiles and will help to test out the collision detection.

This is the file location:

`/source/classes/com/efg/framework/LookAheadPoint.as/`

Here's the complete code for the class:

```
package  com.efg.framework
{
    import flash.display.*;
    /**
     * ...
     * @author Jeff Fulton
     *
     */
    public class LookAheadPoint extends Sprite {

        public var parentContainer:Sprite;
        private var circle:Shape;
        private var circleColor:Number;

        public function LookAheadPoint(x:Number, y:Number, parentContainer:Sprite, ↵
          circleColor:Number=0xffff00) {
```

```
            this.x = x;
            this.y = y;
            this.parentContainer = parentContainer;
            this.circleColor = circleColor;
            circle = new Shape();
            circle.graphics.clear();
            circle.graphics.lineStyle(1, circleColor);
            circle.graphics.drawCircle(-1, -1, 2);
            addChild(circle);
        }

        public function show():void {
            parentContainer.addChild(this);
        }

        public function hide():void {
            parentContainer.removeChild(this);
        }
    }
}
```

This class takes in a four parameters:

- The x value for its screen location
- The y value for its screen location
- The parent display object that it will add and remove its self from
- A color value for the viewable circle around the point

The LookAheadPoint instances need not show themselves to the player. They are turned off and on with calls to the public show and hide functions.

Creating the CarBlitSprite class

The CarBlitSprite class is a child of the BlitSprite class introduced in Chapter 7. We have added in some attributes that will be used by the game for controlling the car. These will be identified in the DriveSheSaid.as code later in the chapter when they come into use. We have also created an override of the updateTile function from the BlitSprite class to handle the reverse direction for our car.

This added functionality will allow us to move the animation of the car tiles backward as well as forward through the tileList array. The backward direction will allow us to display the car with wheels moving in the opposite direction than the forward motion. To the player, the car will appear to be moving in reverse.

This is the file location:

/source/classes/com/efg/framework/CarBlitSprite.as

And here is the source code for this class:

```
package com.efg.framework
{
    import com.efg.framework.BlitSprite;
    import com.efg.framework.TileSheet;
```

```
public class CarBlitSprite extends BlitSprite{

    public var reverse:Boolean = false;
    public var velocity:Number = 0;
    public var deceleration:Number = 0;
    public var acceleration:Number=0;
    public var maxVelocity:Number=0;
    public var nextRotation:Number=0;
    public var turnSpeed:Number = 0;
    public var maxTurnSpeed:Number;
    public var minTurnSpeed:Number;
    public var move:Boolean = false;
    public var reverseVelocityModifier:Number = 0;
    public var radius:int = 0;
    public var worldX:Number;
    public var worldY:Number;
    public var worldNextX:Number;
    public var worldNextY:Number

    public function CarBlitSprite(tileSheet:TileSheet, tileList:Array,
firstFrame:int) {
        super(tileSheet,tileList,firstFrame);
    }

    override public function updateCurrentTile():void {

        if (animationLoop) {
            if (animationCount > animationDelay) {
                animationCount = 0;
                if (reverse) {
                    currentTile--
                }else {
                    currentTile++;
                }
                doCopyPixels = true;
                if (currentTile > tileList.length - 1) {
                    currentTile = 0;
                    if (useLoopCounter) loopCounter++;
                }
                if (currentTile < 0) {
                    currentTile = tileList.length - 1;
                    if (useLoopCounter) loopCounter++;
                }
            }
            animationCount++;
        }
    }
}
```

Let's discuss the new updateTile function in detail because it illustrates some major points about how we are going to animate and move the car in our game.

1. First, if the animationLoop variable is set to true, the code will continue through the rest of the condition.

433

2. Next, if `animationCount` is greater than `animationDelay`, we will move to the next tile in the `tilelist` array by updating the `currentFrame` property. If the car is going forward, we will add 1 to the `currentFrame` property. If the car is going backward, we'll subtract 1.

3. The `animationDelay` property will be set dynamically in the `Game.as` based on the velocity of the car. The higher the value, the slower the wheels will appear to move. We will see this code in the render function of the `Game` class.

4. The `loopCounter` variable can be used to only animate through a set of frames for a set amount of times. It is not used in this game.

Creating the Camera2D class

The `Camera2D` class doesn't look like much at first glance. It is little more than a structured set of variables encapsulated into a class for convenience. It is how we use those variables in the game that provides the power of the class. Currently, we are using it as a way to keep all of the necessary variables for the camera in a single place for organization. You might find this to be an odd way to organize code. That's OK; you can rip all of these variables out and put them directly in your game class with very few changes. We have them separated because we assume in the future that this will be a very nice base class for more elaborate child classes.

> For old guys like us, this camera class would have been a perfect use of a struct in the C language. In the 1990s, we created quite a few DOS games (mostly unreleased experiments while in school and just starting out in programming). Most of our code ideas come from those days (as you can tell). C is not an object-oriented language (though its cousin C++ is), The struct was a way to create a sort of class by packaging up a series of variables together that could be used as a unit. The Camera2D class is almost an exact duplicate of a struct Jeff used for the same purpose in a scrolling Asteroids-like C game that he never finished. When looking for things to write in this book, we searched through some of our old code and came across it. It was the inspiration for the game we will create in the next chapter.

The Camera2D class is located here:

`/source/classes/com/efg/framework/Camera2D.as`

And this is the code for the class:

```
package  com.efg.framework
{
    import flash.display.*;
    import flash.geom.*;
    /**
     * ...
     * @author Jeff Fulton
     */

    public class Camera2D {
        public var width:int;
        public var height:int;
        public var cols:int;
        public var rows:int;
        public var x:Number;
        public var y:Number;
```

```
        public var startX:Number;
        public var startY:Number;
        public var nextX:Number;
        public var nextY:Number;

        //the buffer is 1 tile longer and higher than the camera
        //well first copy all of the tiles to the buffer
        //then copy just the portion we need to the camera
        //buffer
        public var bufferBD:BitmapData;
        public var bufferWidth:int;
        public var bufferHeight:int;
        public var bufferRect:Rectangle;
        public var bufferPoint:Point;

        public function Camera2D() {
        }
    }
}
```

As we described earlier, the Camera2D class is simply a BitmapData canvas that will be used to hold the current set of tile data before it is copied to the output window. The x and y coordinates indicate where on the 50 × 50 grid of 32 × 32 pixels (1,600 pixels in each direction) tiles to start the copy of tiles to the buffer. The buffer actually contains enough space to hold 13 tiles. So, for the x dimension, the buffer will contain 416 pixels (13 × 32 = 416), and the same in the y direction. When the buffer is copied to the final output canvas, we move over to the actual start pixels in the x and y dimensions on the buffer and only copy 384 × 384 pixels.

Double (and triple) buffering

The Camera2D class also acts like a double buffer for the game display. You will notice in the game code that we copy all of the tiles to the screen each frame. By using the buffer, we also eliminate any chance of screen flicker because the draw operation of each tile occurs off screen. The loop through the tiles and the individual copyPixel operations for all 144 tiles 40 times a second takes some processor power. We do this off screen to reduce the processor needed and to eliminate the player from seeing any of the draw in sometimes associated with scrolling. If you have seen the crawling up or down the screen on the edge tiles on some scrolling games, you know what we am talking about here.

When we get to the game code, you will see that we will also use another type of buffer for our display. You have seen this in previous chapters in the book. Before we copy the buffer to the canvas, we will call the canvas lock method. This prevents the output Bitmap instance that holds the canvas from being updated until the entire copy operation is complete. So, to create our triple buffer we first copy all of the tiles to the off screen buffer in the Camer2D class, and then we lock the canvas and copy the needed pixels from the camera buffer to the output canvas off screen. Finally, we place the pixels on the screen with the canvasBD.unlock.

Creating the classes specific to Drive She Said

The rest of the classes for the game are specific to Drive She Said and will be created inside the project folder along with the Main.as and Library.as classes.

The TileSheeDataXML class

In Chapter 6, we created a version of this class for the No Tanks! game. The version for this game will be very similar. It simply describes the attributes of each tile in the tile sheet we created earlier in the chapter.

Here's the path for the Flash IDE:

/source/projects/driveshesaid/flashIDE/com/efg/games/driveshesaid/TileSheetDataXML.as

And this one is for the Flex SDK (using Flash Develop):

/source/projects/driveshesaid/flexSDK/src/com/efg/games/driveshesaid/TileSheetDataXML.as

And here's our TileSheetDataXML class code:

```
package com.efg.games.driveshesaid{

    public class TilesheetDataXML {
    public static var XMLData:XML=
    <tilesheet>

    <tile id="0" name="player" type="sprite"/>
    <tile id="1" name="player" type="sprite"/>
    <tile id="2" name="player" type="sprite"/>
    <tile id="3" name="heart" type="sprite"/>
    <tile id="4" name="clock" type="sprite"/>
    <tile id="5" name="skull" type="sprite"/>
    <tile id="6" name="wall" type="nonwalkable"/>
    <tile id="7" name="wall" type="nonwalkable"/>
    <tile id="8" name="wall" type="nonwalkable"/>
    <tile id="9" name="wall" type="nonwalkable"/>

    <tile id="10" name="wall" type="nonwalkable"/>
    <tile id="11" name="wall" type="nonwalkable"/>
    <tile id="12" name="wall" type="nonwalkable"/>
    <tile id="13" name="wall" type="nonwalkable"/>
    <tile id="14" name="wall" type="nonwalkable"/>
    <tile id="15" name="wall" type="nonwalkable"/>
    <tile id="16" name="wall" type="nonwalkable"/>
    <tile id="17" name="wall" type="nonwalkable"/>
    <tile id="18" name="wall" type="nonwalkable"/>
    <tile id="19" name="wall" type="nonwalkable"/>

    <tile id="20" name="wall" type="nonwalkable"/>
    <tile id="21" name="road" type="walkable"/>
    <tile id="22" name="goal" type="sprite"/>
    <tile id="23" name="goal" type="sprite"/>
    <tile id="24" name="none" type="nonwalkable"/>
    <tile id="25" name="none" type="nonwalkable"/>
    <tile id="26" name="none" type="nonwalkable"/>
    <tile id="27" name="none" type="nonwalkable"/>
    <tile id="28" name="none" type="nonwalkable"/>
    <tile id="29" name="none" type="nonwalkable"/>
    </tilesheet>;
    } // end class
}// end package
```

The Level.as class

For the level data (just like chapter 6), we will store our level specific data in a class. We do this to keep our final delivery as a single SWF file. This will be the base class that all of the game levels will extend:

This is the file location for the Flash IDE:

/source/projects/driveshesaid/flashIDE/com/efg/games/driveshesaid/Level.as

And here's the one for the Flex SDK (using Flash Develop)

/source/projects/driveshesaid/flexSDK/src/com/efg/games/driveshesaid/Level.as

The code for the Level.as class follows:

```
package com.efg.games.driveshesaid
{
    /**
     * ...
     * @author Jeff Fulton
     */
    public class Level{
        public var map:Array;
        public var backGroundTile:int;
        public var percentNeeded:Number;
        public var playerStartFacing:int;
        public var timerStartSeconds:int;
        public var heartScore:int;
        public var clockAdd:int;
        public var wallAdjust:Number;
        public var skullAdjust:Number;
        public var wallDriveColor:uint;

        public function Level() {
        }
    }
}
```

Let's quickly move on to the Level1.as class and use it to help define and describe the level-specific variables in the Level class.

The Level1.as Class

The Level1 class is a subclass of the Level base class. We will store our entire 2D array of level data in the map variable, along with definitions for the level-specific variables.

The file's location for the Flash IDE is this:

/source/projects/driveshesaid/flashIDE/com/efg/games/driveshesaid/Level1.as

And this one is for the Flex SDK (using Flash Develop):

/source/projects/driveshesaid/flexSDK/src/com/efg/games/driveshesaid/Level1.as

We have not written out each of the 50 rows for this level. You can download the actual level from this book website, or you can get creative and make your own. Only 5 rows are displayed in partial Level1.as class example, which follows:

```
package com.efg.games.driveshesaid
{
    /**
     * ...
     * @author Jeff Fulton
     */
    public class Level1 extends Level {

    public function Level1() {

        backGroundTile = 21;
        percentNeeded = .50;
        playerStartFacing = 0;
        timerStartSeconds = 60;
        heartScore = 10;
        clockAdd = 10;
        wallAdjust = .3;
        skullAdjust = .20;
        wallDriveColor = 0x00000000;

        map = [
[6,6,6,6,6,6,6,6,6,6,6,6,6,6,6,6,6,6,6,6,6,6,6,6,6,6,6,6,6,6,6,6,6,6,6,6,6,6,6,6,6,6,6↵
,6,6,6,6,6,6,6,6],
[6,13,21,21,21,21,21,21,21,21,21,21,21,21,21,21,21,21,21,21,21,21,21,21,21,21,21,↵
 14,6,6,6,6,6,6,6,6,6,13,21,21,21,21,21,21,21,21,14,6,6,6],
[6,0,21,21,21,21,21,21,21,21,21,21,21,21,21,21,3,21,21,21,21,21,21,21,21,21,21,21,↵
 14,6,6,6,6,6,6,6,13,21,21,21,21,21,21,21,21,3,21,14,6,6],
[6,21,21,21,21,21,21,21,21,21,21,21,21,21,21,21,21,21,21,21,21,21,21,21,3,21,21,21,↵
 21,14,6,6,6,6,6,13,21,21,21,21,21,21,21,21,21,21,21,14,6],
[6,11,21,21,21,21,21,21,21,21,21,21,21,21,21,21,21,21,21,21,21,21,21,21,21,21,21,↵
 21,21,21,14,6,6,6,13,21,21,21,3,21,21,21,21,21,21,21,21,6],
]
...;
        }
    }
}
```

The important thing to note is that if when you create your own levels, they must you must match the structure of this class, especially the level-specific variables at the top of the class. Here is a rundown of how we will make use of each:

- backGroundTile: This is the tile on the tile sheet that will be used to create the background behind all of our transparent tiles.
- percentNeeded: This is the percentage of total hearts that needed to be collected on the level.
- playerStartFacing: This is the angle (0 is facing to the right) for the starting position of the player car.
- timerStartSeconds: This is the number of seconds on the timer when the level starts.
- heartScore: This variable holds the score the player receives for collecting a heart.
- clockAdd: This one holds the number of seconds added to the level timer for collecting a clock.

- `wallAdjust`: For the collision reaction code when the player hits a wall tile, this is the percent that will be subtracted from the player velocity and dx and dy values.
- `skullAdjust`: This variable functions like the `walladjust` value, but for reactions with the skulls.
- `wallDriveColor`: This 32-bit number (so it includes an alpha channel) represents the color in the wall tiles that player's car can drive on. If the tiles are completely transparent in the wall buffer areas, this should match the color of the canvas background.

Iterating the Game class

We are about to create a brand new Game sub class called `DriveSheSaid.as` file. We will quickly piece together the final game by building it in iterations. Some of the code you will encounter is very similar to code we have already been through a number of times in previous chapters. Some will be new. We will present all of the coded need for each of the iterations, but we will only stop to discuss the new code in detail.

Here is the location and path for the file in the Flash IDE:

/source/projects/driveshesaid/flashIDE/com/efg/games/driveshesaid/DriveSheSaid.as

Here is the location and path for the file in Flex SDK (using Flash Develop)

/source/projects/driveshesaid/flexSDK/src/com/efg/games/driveshesaid/DriveSheSaid.as

Creating the Game class shell, variables, and constructor (iteration 1)

We will discuss the new and most important variables after you have taken a look at the following iteration 1 code:

```
package com.efg.games.driveshesaid
{
    import flash.display.*;
    import flash.geom.Point;
    import flash.geom.Rectangle;
    import flash.events.Event;
    import flash.utils.getTimer;
    import flash.events.KeyboardEvent;
    import com.efg.framework.CustomEventSound;
    import com.efg.framework.Game;
    import com.efg.framework.CustomEventLevelScreenUpdate;
    import com.efg.framework.CustomEventScoreBoardUpdate;
    import com.efg.framework.CustomEventSound;
    import com.efg.framework.BlitSprite;
    import com.efg.framework.TileSheet;
    import com.efg.framework.Camera2D;
    import com.efg.framework.BasicFrameTimer;
    import com.efg.framework.LookAheadPoint;
    import com.efg.framework.CarBlitSprite;
    /**
    *
```

```
 * ...
 * @author Jeff Fulton
 */
public class DriveSheSaid extends Game {

    public static const KEY_UP:int = 38;
    public static const KEY_DOWN:int = 40;
    public static const KEY_LEFT:int = 37;
    public static const KEY_RIGHT:int = 39;

    public static const TILE_WALL:int = 0;
    public static const TILE_MOVE:int = 1;
    public static const SPRITE_PLAYER:int = 2;
    public static const SPRITE_GOAL:int = 3;
    public static const SPRITE_CLOCK:int = 4;
    public static const SPRITE_SKULL:int = 5;
    public static const SPRITE_HEART:int = 6;

    public static const STATE_SYSTEM_GAMEPLAY:int = 0;
    public static const STATE_SYSTEM_LEVELOUT:int = 1;

    private var systemFunction:Function;
    private var currentSystemState:int;
    private var nextSystemState:int;
    private var lastSystemState:int;

    private var level:int = 0;
    private var levelData:Level;
    private var levels:Array = [undefined,new Level1()];

    //tiles
    private var mapTileWidth:int=32;
    private var mapTileHeight:int=32;

    //display
    private var canvasBitmapData:BitmapData;
    private var backgroundBitmapData:BitmapData;
    private var canvasBitmap:Bitmap;
    private var backgroundBitmap:Bitmap;

    //world
    private var world:Array=new Array();
    private var worldCols:int=50;
    private var worldRows:int=50;
    private var worldWidth:int=worldCols*mapTileWidth;;
    private var worldHeight:int=worldRows*mapTileHeight;

    //camera
    private var camera:Camera2D = new Camera2D();

    //for drawing cameraAreaTiles
    private var tileRect:Rectangle;
    private var tilePoint:Point;
    private var tileSheetData:Array;
```

440

```
//game specific
private var heartsTotal:int = 0;
private var heartsNeeded:int = 0;
private var heartsCollected:int = 0;
private var timeLeft:int = 0;
private var score:int;
private var goalReached:Boolean = false;

//*** level specific ***
private var levelHeartScore:int;
private var levelPlayerStartFacing:int;
private var levelTimerStartSeconds:int;
private var levelSkullAdjust:Number;
private var levelWallAdjust:Number;
private var levelClockAdd:int;
private var levelBackGroundTile:int;
private var levelPrecentNeeded:Number;
private var levelWallDriveColor:Number;

//** player car stuff
private var player:CarBlitSprite;
private var playerFrameList:Array;
private var playerStarted:Boolean = false;

//*sounds
private var carSoundDelayList:Array = [90,80,70,60,50,40,30,20,15,10,0];
private var carSoundTime:int = getTimer();

//** keyboard input
private var keyPressList:Array = [];
private var keyListenersInit:Boolean = false;

//** game loop
private var gameOver:Boolean = false;

//** look ahead points
// The Vector class requires Flash Player 10 publishing
// It can be swapped with an Array is only Flash Player 9 publishing is available.
/// private var lookAheadPoints:Array=[];

private var lookAheadPoints:Vector.<LookAheadPoint>=new Vector.<LookAheadPoint>↵
(3,false);

//**count down timer
private var countDownTimer:BasicFrameTimer = new BasicFrameTimer(40);

//***** Flex *****
private var tileSheet:TileSheet = new TileSheet(new Library.TileSheetPng().↵
 bitmapData, mapTileWidth, mapTileHeight);
//***** End Flex *****

//***** Flash IDE *****
//private var tileSheet:TileSheet = new TileSheet(new TileSheetPng(0,0), ↵
  tilewidth, tileheight);
//***** End Flash IDE *****
```

```
public function DriveSheSaid() {
    init();
    this.focusRect = false;
}
```

Keypress constants

We have created a set of constant values that represent the keyCode returned when the four directional keys are pressed.

```
public static const KEY_UP:int = 38;
public static const KEY_DOWN:int = 40;
public static const KEY_LEFT:int = 37;
public static const KEY_RIGHT:int = 39;
```

The internal state machine

The first two variables we want to discuss are used for creating an internal Game.as state machine that works identically like the Main.as state machine:

```
public static const STATE_SYSTEM_GAMEPLAY:int = 0;
public static const STATE_SYSTEM_LEVELOUT:int = 1;

private var systemFunction:Function;
private var currentSystemState:int;
private var nextSystemState:int;
private var lastSystemState:int;
```

The only two states we need are for the actual game play (STATE_SYSYTEM_GAMEPLAY) and for the animation of the game screen move itself off of the screen during the level out sequence (STATE_SYSTEM_LEVELOUT). The other four variables are used to set and manipulate the state when needed.

The tiles, display, and world

The variables for the tiles, display, and world are similar to those in the No Tanks! game but have been modified for Drive She Said.

The mapTileHeight and mapTileWidth simply specify the height and width of a tile on tile sheet and the world. These were called tileWidth and tileHeight in No Tanks! The display variables are identical to the ones in No Tanks! with one exception. We have added an actual Bitmap instance (backgroundBitmap) to hold the backgroundBitmapData in a separate layer in Drive She Said. We do this so the backgroundBitmapData will not have to be redrawn each frame as we move the camera window and repaint the screen. The world array is just a new name for the No Tanks! array called levelTileMap. We also need new variables to specify the columns, rows, height and width for the world because they are not the same as the canvasBitmapData (like they were in No Tanks!).

```
//tiles
private var mapTileWidth:int=32;
private var mapTileHeight:int=32;

//display
private var canvasBitmapData:BitmapData;
```

```
private var backgroundBitmapData:BitmapData;
private var canvasBitmap:Bitmap;
private var backgroundBitmap:Bitmap;

//world
private var world:Array=new Array();
private var worldCols:int=50;
private var worldRows:int=50;
private var worldWidth:int=worldCols*mapTileWidth;
private var worldHeight:int=worldRows*mapTileHeight;
```

The camera

The camera is simply an instance of the Camera2D class that we discussed earlier:

```
//camera
private var camera:Camera2D = new Camera2D();
```

Car sounds

The car sounds are going to be handled in a unique manner. Based on the velocity of the player car, we will loop the car sound with a different wait between plays: The faster the car's velocity, the shorter the wait (in milliseconds).

```
//*sounds
private var carSoundDelayList:Array = [90,80,70,60,50,40,30,20,15,10,0];
private var carSoundTime:int = getTimer();
```

The carSoundDelay array holds the number of milliseconds between plays of the car's sound. For example, at velocity 0 (car idle), there is a 90-millisecond delay between plays of the car sound.

Creating a working class (hero?) in iteration 2

In this iteration, we will add enough code to the DriveSheSaid.as to allow us to compile the application and see it fire the runGame function repeatedly. We are going to create stub functions for all of the in-game processes. We are also going to setup and begin use of the internal state machine. Simply add all of this under the constructor:

```
private function init():void {}

override public function newGame():void {
    switchSystemState( STATE_SYSTEM_GAMEPLAY );
}

override public function newLevel():void {
    stage.focus = this;
}

private function restartPlayer():void {}

private function updateScoreBoard():void {}

override public function runGame():void {
    systemFunction();
}
```

```
public function switchSystemState(stateval:int):void {
    lastSystemState = currentSystemState;
    currentSystemState = stateval;
    switch(stateval) {
        case STATE_SYSTEM_GAMEPLAY:
            systemFunction = systemGamePlay;
            break;

        case STATE_SYSTEM_LEVELOUT :
            systemFunction = systemLevelOut;
            break;
    }
}

private function systemGamePlay():void {}

private function systemLevelOut():void {}

private function levelOutComplete():void {}

private function checkInput():void {}

private function checkforEndGame():void {}

private function checkforEndLevel():void {}


private function update():void {}

private function checkCollisions():void {}

private function render():void {}

private function drawCamera():void {}

private function drawPlayer():void {}

private function addToScore(val:Number):void {}

private function initTileSheetData():void {}

private function setupWorld():void {}

private function dispose(object:BlitSprite):void {}

private function disposeAll():void {}

private function timesUpListener(e:Event):void {}

private function keyDownListener(e:KeyboardEvent):void {
    keyPressList[e.keyCode]=true;
}
```

```
        private function keyUpListener(e:KeyboardEvent):void {
            keyPressList[e.keyCode]=false;
        }
    }
}
```

The only real code worth noting in this set of stub functions relates to the internal game state machine. Just like the Main class, the systemFunction function reference is called each game timer tick. The switchSystemFunction function is used to change to a new state.

If you run this code, you should see a pretty much black game screen after the purple level in screen fades away. You will need to click trough the title and instructions screens first. Figure 10-6 is an example of this less-than-exciting game screen.

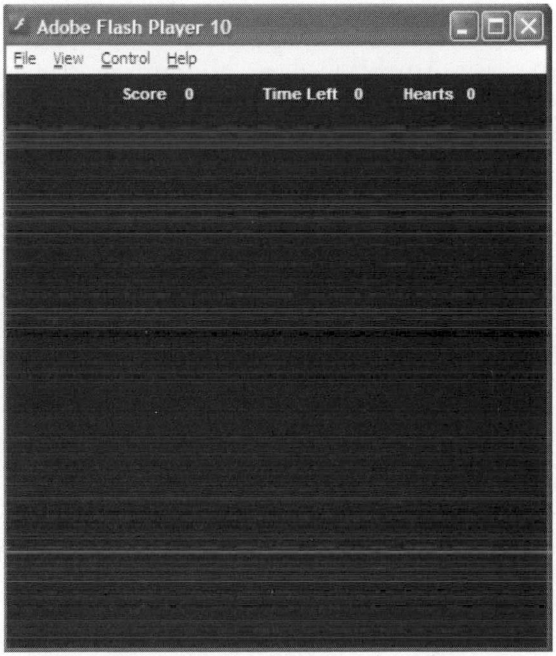

Figure 10-6. The stub game in action

Setting up the game (iteration 3)

The final output of this iteration will be to place the player's car on the screen. Don't let looks be deceiving though; this iteration accomplishes much more than that. We will initialize a new game, read in the tile sheet data, read the first levels, and prepare to play the level.

The init function

The full code for the init function follows:

```
        private function init():void {
            camera.width=384;
```

```
    camera.height=384;
    camera.cols=12;
    camera.rows=12;
    camera.x=0;
    camera.y=0;
    camera.bufferBD=new BitmapData(camera.width+mapTileWidth,↩
     camera.height+mapTileHeight,true,0x00000000);

    camera.bufferRect=new Rectangle(0,0,camera.width,camera.height);
    camera.bufferPoint=new Point(0,0);

    tileRect=new Rectangle(0,0,mapTileWidth,mapTileHeight);
    tilePoint=new Point(0,0);

    //canvasBitmap

    canvasBitmapData=new BitmapData(camera.width,camera.height,true,0x00000000);
    canvasBitmap=new Bitmap(canvasBitmapData);

    backgroundBitmapData = new BitmapData(camera.width, camera.height, ↩
     false, 0x000000);

    backgroundBitmap = new Bitmap(backgroundBitmapData);

    addChild(backgroundBitmap);
    addChild(canvasBitmap);

    //look ahead points
    lookAheadPoints[0] = new LookAheadPoint(0, 0, this);
    lookAheadPoints[1] = new LookAheadPoint(0, 0, this);
    lookAheadPoints[2] = new LookAheadPoint(0, 0, this);

    //to show look ahead points in development
    lookAheadPoints[0].show();
    lookAheadPoints[1].show();
    lookAheadPoints[2].show();
}
```

Here is a detailed description of the main points of this function:

- The camera is initialized by setting its width and height to be the viewable screen width and height (384 × 384). The number of rows and columns are set to be the number of rows and columns in the viewable area (12 × 12).
- The camera.bufferBitmapData is initialized with a size that is one tile width and one tile height greater than the canvas will be. This is how our smooth scrolling will work. If we did not do this, we would only be able to scroll 32 pixels at a time, rather than the smooth single pixel at a time needed for our game.
- The camera.bufferRect and buffer.point instances are initialized. The bufferPoint will always stay at 0,0 because it will start painting into the canvas at the same spot each frame tick. The bufferRect's width and height will always be 384 each, but the x and y values will be between 0 and 31 to provide for our smooth scrolling in each direction.

- The `tileRect` and `tilePoint` instances will be used to blit each tile to the screen in the right place inside of our render loop. The `tileRect` will always be a 32 × 32 square, but the `tilePoint` x and y values will change based on the location of the tile (column and row) in the screen buffer.
- The `canvasBitmap` will be added to the Game's display list and will contain the 384 × 384 `canvasBitmapdata` of our main output canvas. The `camera.bufferBitmapData` will be painted into this on each frame tick.
- The `backgroundBitmap` will be added to the display list behind the `canvasBitmap`. It will contain the `backgroundBitmapData` that in turn will be filled with the 12 × 12 background tiles specified in the level data XML.
- The `backgroundBitmap` and the `canvasBitmap` are added to the display list.
- Our `lookAheadPoints` list is set to contain three `LookAheadPoint` instances. All three are added to the display list, but you will want to comment out these three lines when your testing is complete. This is created using the ActionScript 3.0 (Flash Player 10 and above only) `Vector` class. The `Vector` class allows the developer to create an optimized array with a predefined size and only a single data type. Flash can manage memory better and is much faster at accessing data that is organized in this manner. We have used it here as an example. If you are using Flash Player 9, it can be swapped out with an `Array` class instance.

The newGame function

This is the full code for the `newGame` function:

```
override public function newGame():void {
    switchSystemState( STATE_SYSTEM_GAMEPLAY );
    initTileSheetData();

    player = new CarBlitSprite(tileSheet, playerFrameList, 0);

    addChild(player);
    level = 0;
    score = 0;
    gameOver = false;

    dispatchEvent(new CustomEventScoreBoardUpdate(CustomEventScoreBoardUpdate.
    UPDATE_TEXT, Main.SCORE_BOARD_SCORE, String(score)));
    dispatchEvent(new CustomEventScoreBoardUpdate(CustomEventScoreBoardUpdate.
    UPDATE_TEXT,Main.SCORE_BOARD_TIME_LEFT,"00"));

    dispatchEvent(new CustomEventScoreBoardUpdate(CustomEventScoreBoardUpdate.
    UPDATE_TEXT,Main.SCORE_BOARD_HEARTS,String(0)));

    //key listeners
    if (!keyListenersInit) {
        stage.addEventListener(KeyboardEvent.KEY_DOWN,keyDownListener);
        stage.addEventListener(KeyboardEvent.KEY_UP, keyUpListener);
```

```
            keyListenersInit = true;
        }

        countDownTimer.addEventListener(BasicFrameTimer.TIME_IS_UP, timesUpListener, ↵
            false, 0, true);
    }
```

Here is a detailed description of the main points of this function:

1. First, we set the internal state machine to SYSTEM_STATE_GAMEPLAY with a call to the switchSystemState function.

2. Next, we call the initTileSheetData function, which we will cover in the next section.

3. We initialize our player CarBlitSprite instance by passing in a reference to the tileSheet; the playerFrameList that will be set in the initTileSheetData function and the start frame from the car animation loop.

4. After that, we add the player to the display list and reset the score, level, and gameOver variables to their default new games values.

5. We dispatch three custom event instances to reset our ScoreBoard fields to their default new games values.

6. We add the key listeners to the game only before the first game. Because our Game instance's constructor is called in Main before the stage is ready, we cannot initialize these in the init function. We do it here because we are certain that the stage is initialized, but we only need to do it for the first game.

7. We add a listener to the DriveSheSaid class to listen for the TIME_IS_UP event in the CountDownTimer class instance.

The initTileSheetData function

This is the complete code listing for the initTileSheetData function:

```
private function initTileSheetData():void {
    playerFrameList = [];
    tileSheetData = [];
    var numberToPush:int = 99;
    var tileXML:XML = TilesheetDataXML.XMLData;
    var numTiles:int = tileXML.tile.length();

    for (var tileNum:int = 0; tileNum < numTiles; tileNum++) {
        if (String(tileXML.tile[tileNum].@type) == "walkable") {
            numberToPush = TILE_MOVE;
        }else if (String(tileXML.tile[tileNum].@type) == "nonwalkable") {
            numberToPush = TILE_WALL;
        }else if (tileXML.tile[tileNum].@type == "sprite") {
            switch(String(tileXML.tile[tileNum].@name)) {

                case "player":
                    numberToPush = SPRITE_PLAYER;
                    playerFrameList.push(tileNum);
```

```
            break;

        case "goal":
            numberToPush = SPRITE_GOAL;
            break;

        case "heart":
            numberToPush = SPRITE_HEART;
            break;

        case "skull":
            numberToPush = SPRITE_SKULL;
            break;

        case "clock":
            numberToPush = SPRITE_CLOCK;
            break;
        }
    }
    tileSheetData.push(numberToPush);
    }
}
```

Here is a detailed description of the main points of this function:

This function is very similar to the same named function in the No Tanks! game. Its job is to read in the `TileSheetDataXML` class and place a constant representing the tile type into each cell of a single-dimensional array (`tileSheetData`) representing our tile sheet tiles.

1. First, it initializes the `playerFrameList` and the `tileSheetData` arrays. The `playerFrameList` array will eventually contain the ids 0,1, and 2. Those are the first three frames in our tile sheet for animating the car and its wheels.

2. Next, it loops through all of the tile nodes in the XML as if they are in an array. This is a powerful feature of the ActionScript 3.0 XML class.

3. During this loop, we first check to see if the tile is one of the two basic types: `TILE_MOVE` or `TILE_WALL`. If it isn't one of those two, but is a sprite type, we drop into the switch/case and set the tile type based on the `name` attribute.

4. Finally, the local `numberToPush` (representing the constant value for this tile) is pushed into the `tileSheetData` array.

The newLevel function

Now, let's look at the complete code for the `newLevel` function:

```
override public function newLevel():void {

    stage.focus = this;
    if (level ==levels.length-1) level = 0;

    level++;
    heartsTotal = 0;
```

```
heartsNeeded = 0;
heartsCollected = 0;
setupWorld();

countDownTimer.seconds = levelTimerStartSeconds;
countDownTimer.min = 0;

goalReached = false;

dispatchEvent(new CustomEventLevelScreenUpdate(CustomEventLevelScreenUpdate.↵
  UPDATE_TEXT, String(level)));

dispatchEvent(new CustomEventHeartsNeeded(CustomEventHeartsNeeded.↵
  HEARTS_NEEDED, String(heartsNeeded)));

restartPlayer();
}
```

A detailed description of the main points of this function follows. The `stage.focus = this;` code ensures that the game will have keyboard focus and accept events without the user having to click the stage.

1. First, we check for the level rollover. If the previous level was the final level for the game, we reset to the first level.

2. We set our variables for collecting the hearts—heartsTotal, heartsCollected, and heartsNeeded—back to 0. heartsTotal represents a count of all the hearts in the level. heartsNeeded is heartsTotal multiplied by the `levelPrecentNeeded` variable. heartsCollected will count up the hearts the player collects on the level.

3. Next, we call the setupWorld function that will read in and format the tile data. We will cover this one next.

4. We reset the countDownTimer by setting the start seconds to levelTimerStartSeconds; the minimum for the counter is 0.

5. We set goalReached to be false. This will be set to true when heartsCollected is greater than or equal to heartsNeeded and the goal sprite has been reached.

6. We dispatch a custom event to reset the hearts needed on the scoreboard.

7. We call the restart player function.

The setUpWorld function

The setupWorld function that follows is a combination of the readBackGroundData and the readSpriteData functions from the No Tanks! game in Chapters 6 and 7. It reads in the level and parses it to create the current level.

```
private function setupWorld():void {
    world = [];
    var tileNum:int;
    var numberToPush:int;
    levelData = levels[level];
```

```
        levelBackGroundTile = levelData.backGroundTile;
        levelTimerStartSeconds = levelData.timerStartSeconds;
        levelHeartScore = levelData.heartScore;
        levelPlayerStartFacing = levelData.playerStartFacing;
        levelSkullAdjust = levelData.skullAdjust;
        levelWallAdjust =levelData.wallAdjust;
        levelClockAdd = levelData.clockAdd;
        levelPercentNeeded = levelData.percentNeeded;
        levelWallDriveColor = levelData.wallDriveColor;

        for (var rowCtr:int=0;rowCtr<worldRows;rowCtr++) {
            var tempArray:Array=new Array();
            for (var colCtr:int = 0; colCtr < worldCols; colCtr++) {
                tileNum = levelData.map[rowCtr][colCtr];
                if (int(tileSheetData[tileNum]) == TILE_WALL || ↵
                 int(tileSheetData[tileNum]) == TILE_MOVE ) {

                    numberToPush = tileNum;
                }else {
                    switch(tileSheetData[tileNum]) {
                        case SPRITE_PLAYER:
                            numberToPush = levelBackGroundTile;
                            player.worldX = (colCtr * mapTileWidth) + (.5*mapTileWidth);
                            player.worldY = (rowCtr * mapTileHeight) + (.5 * mapTileHeight);
                            break;

                        case SPRITE_HEART:
                            numberToPush = tileNum;
                            heartsTotal++;
                            break;

                        case SPRITE_SKULL:
                            numberToPush = tileNum;
                            break;

                        case SPRITE_GOAL:
                            numberToPush = tileNum;
                            break;

                        case SPRITE_CLOCK:
                            numberToPush = tileNum;
                            break;
                    }
                }
                tempArray.push(numberToPush);
            }
            world.push(tempArray);
        }
        heartsNeeded = int(heartsTotal * levelPrecentNeeded);
    }
```

Here is a detailed description of the main points of this function:

1. First, we reset of the world array and initialize local variables for the loop through the
    tiles. The tileNum will hold the current tile number from the tile sheet that corresponds

to the world tile. The `numberToPush` variable holds the number to put into the `world` array for the current row and column. Most of the time, this number will be the same as `tileNum`, with the exception of the player car tile. The player car tile will be replaced with the `levelBackGroundTile`.

2. We use the `levelData = levels[level]` setting to create a reference to the current Level data.

3. We assign values from the current level to our level-specific variables (discussed earlier in the section on the Level class).

4. Next, we loop through all of the rows nodes in the `levelData.map` 2D array for the level and create another nested for loop to iterate through each column inside the row. We create a temp array (`tempArray`) to hold all of the column data. It will be pushed into the `world` array on completion of each row loop iteration.

5. If the tile is a `TILE_WALL` or `TILE_MOVE` tile, we simply push the `tileNum` into the `tempArray`. If it is not, we drop down into the `switch:case` for sprites.

6. Unlike No Tanks! where all of the game objects were individual AS3 Sprites, only the player will be a separate display object. All of the other sprites will simply be tiles in the world. We will use the `LookAheadPoint` instances to do tile-based collision detection between these sprite tiles and the car rather that the `BitmapData` collision detection we used in the No Tanks! games.

7. The `switch:case` statement is used to determine the tile type and set up variables associated with each type.

8. At the end of the inner loop, the `numberToPush` variable is inserted into the `tempArray`.

9. At the end of the outer loop, the `tempArray` is pushed into the `world` array creating a 2D array of 50 × 50 tiles for our world.

10. Finally, we multiply the `heartsTotal` value by the `levelPrecentNeeded` to get the `heartsNeeded` for the level.

The restartPlayer function

The `restartPlayer` function contains quite a bit of logic associated with positioning the player car on the screen in the correct location. Player positioning is a very important topic that we will explore in some detail after you look at the code. The player object needs to be positioned to the viewable screen (384 × 384) but also in relation to full world. When the player object moves on the screen, the player does not move; the camera does instead. This forces the player to stay in the middle of the screen, which cannot happen properly if the player drives near the edge of the world. We compensate for this limitation by allowing the player move freely when near the edge of the world; in turn, the camera does not move.

You will see this logic when we explore the `update` function. For the `restartPlayer` function, we simply need to realize that the same rules apply. Since, most of the time, the player will probably start a level near the edge of the screen, at least one direction (vertical or horizontal or both) will need to offset from an edge of the screen, pushing or pulling the player away from the center. If we didn't do this, the player would not show up in the correct starting tile.

Moving the car and game world together

When our car moves about the scrolling world, we will want to simulate movement in a manner very different from how we have done it in games so far in the book.

The game output screen (called `canvasBitmapData` in our game) is one 384 × 384 `BitmapData` instance. The world is 50 tiles by 50 tiles or 1,600 × 1,600 pixels. Again, the trick we need to perform is to keep the player car in the center of the screen for most of the game. And as we said, this is simply done by moving the camera position to scroll the world rather than moving the car about the game screen, but this solution poses a problem when the car is near the edge of the screen. At that point, we cannot scroll the screen to keep the player in the middle anymore. In this instance, we will give up control back to the car for only the axis direction that is affected.

How does this work in practice?

Let's say the car is supposed to be at the position 700 × 900 in the game world. In this instance, the car sprite would be centered on the output screen at 192 × 192. The camera would need to offset 700 × 900 to find the upper x and y coordinates for it to start. Let's step through the process:

1. First, `player.worldX` equals 700, and `player.worldY` equals 900.

2. Then `camera.x` equals `player.worldX` minus .5 times `camera.width`, that is, 508. And `camera.y` equals `player.worldY` minus .5 times `camera.height`, that is, 708.

3. So the camera would start a 508,708 and need thus show from 508 to 892 on the x axis and 708 to 1102 the y axis. This example is illustrated in Figure 10-7.

camera 0, 0 on canvas
camera 508, 708 on world

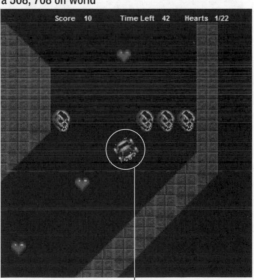

player at 192, 192 on canvas
player at 700, 900 on world

Figure 10-7. Player centered on canvas in the world

453

When we start the player for the first time on a level, we will use very similar logic. The only problem we face is when the player is positioned near an edge when it is started. Let's look at that example now:

1. The player's starting position in world is in row 2, column 3, or 64x and 96y.

2. The game logic will first try to position the camera so the player is in the center of the screen. The problem in this example is that this would offset the camera outside to viewable screen area.

```
camera.x = player.worldX - (.5 * camera.width)  = 64 - 192 = -128
camera.y = player.worldY - (.5 * camera.height) or 96 - 192 =  -86
```

3. The camera cannot be position here, so we need to re-orient it for it sits at 0,0:

```
camera.x = 0;
```

The player now must be offset from this new starting position for the camera:

```
player.x = player.worldX + camera.x = 64 + 0 = 64
```

The same goes for the y axis:

```
camera.y = 0
player.y = playerWorldY + camera.y = 96 + 0 = 96
```

Figure 10-8 illustrates this example.

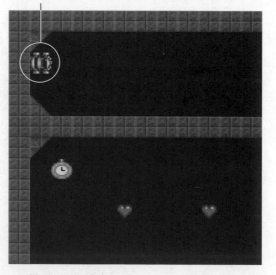

Figure 10-8. Player start position example

Here is the full code for the restartPlayer function:

```
private function restartPlayer():void {
    //find the region of the map the player is i

    camera.x = player.worldX - (.5 * camera.width);
    camera.y = player.worldY - (.5 * camera.height);

    if (camera.x < 0) {
        camera.x = 0;
        player.x = player.worldX + camera.x;
    }else if ((camera.x+camera.width) > worldWidth) {
        camera.x = worldWidth - camera.width;
        player.x = player.worldX - camera.x;
    }else {
        player.x = .5 * camera.width;
    }

    if (camera.y < 0) {
        camera.y = 0;
        player.y = player.worldY + camera.y;
    }else if ((camera.y+camera.height) > worldHeight) {
        camera.y = worldHeight - camera.height;
        player.y = player.worldY - camera.y;
    }else {
     player.y = .5 * camera.height;
    }

    camera.nextX = camera.x;
    camera.nextY = camera.y;

    player.nextX = player.x;
    player.nextY = player.y;
    player.worldNextX = player.worldX;
    player.worldNextY = player.worldY;

    player.dx = 0;
    player.dy = 0;
    player.nextRotation=levelPlayerStartFacing;
    player.turnSpeed = .3;
    player.maxTurnSpeed = .6;
    player.minTurnSpeed = .3;
    player.maxVelocity=10;
    player.acceleration =.05;
    player.deceleration=.03;
    player.radius = .5 * player.width;
    player.reverseVelocityModifier = .3;
    player.animationDelay = 3;
    player.velocity = 0;

    //reset Look Aheads
    lookAheadPoints[0].x = lookAheadPoints[0].y = 0;
    lookAheadPoints[1].x = lookAheadPoints[1].y = 0;
    lookAheadPoints[2].x = lookAheadPoints[2].y = 0;
```

```
        player.visible = false;

        drawCamera(); // draw the level so it will roll in from the side
    }
```

Here is a detailed description of the main points of this function:

1. First, we attempt to execute code as described previously: we orient the camera so the player is in the center of the screen.

2. If the player cannot be centered in either the x or y direction (or both), the camera is set to start at 0 on that axis, and the player position is set accordingly. If the player is not near an edge on an axis, it is centered on that axis.

3. You will start to notice the use of the nextX and nextX variables for the player.x, player.y, player.worldX, and player.worldY. We will always update these first and then do collision detection and set the player.x and player.y values to the nextX and nextY only if the car is allowed to move in that direction.

4. Next, we set all of the default values for car attributes. Here is a brief description of each:

   - player.dx = 0: The dx is the vector value for movement along the x axis.
   - player.dy = 0: The dy is the vector value for movement along the y axis.
   - player.nextRotation=levelPlayerStartFacing: This will be set when the player attempts to turn the car.
   - player.turnSpeed=.3: The turn speed will adjust based on the velocity of the car. This is the number of degrees the rotation of the car is changed then a left or right arrow is pressed.
   - player.maxTurnSpeed=.6: This is the maximum value for turn speed. This value is linear and related to velocity directly.
   - player.minTurnSpeed=.3: This is the minimum speed the car will turn while moving (the car cannot turn when velocity equals 0).
   - player.maxVelocity=8: This is the maximum number to multiply the sine and cosine of the radians of the current player rotation to obtain the dx and dy values.
   - player.acceleration=.05: The acceleration of the car is added every frame as long as the up key is pressed and held.
   - player.deceleration=.03: The deceleration is subtracted from the velocity then the up key is not pressed.
   - player.reverseVelocityModifier = .3: This is the percentage of the maximum velocity that applies to the reverse velocity; the car cannot go as fast in reverse as it can going forward unless you set this to 1.
   - player.radius = .5 * player.width: We use the radius to find the positions of the side LookAheadPoint instances.

- `player.animationDelay = 3`: The animation delay will adjust based on the velocity of the car. It will be greater when the car is moving slower and smaller when the car is moving faster.
- `player.velocity = 0`: With this, we're simply setting the velocity of the car to start at 0.

5. Next, we initialize the `LookAheadPoint` instances.

6. We set the player to be invisible for the next step, which is the animation of the `Game.as` screen onto the viewable area.

7. We make sure to draw the current background to the screen so it will display when the level animates onto the screen.

The systemGamePlay function

The full game loop for DriveSheSaid follows; it is associated with the `STATE_SYSTEM_GAMEPLAY` state of the internal DriveSheSaid state machine.

```
private function systemGamePlay():void {
    if (!countDownTimer.started) {
        countDownTimer.start();
        playerStarted= true;
        player.visible = true;
    }

    if (playerStarted) {
        checkInput();
    }

    update();
    checkCollisions();
    render();
    checkforEndLevel();
    checkforEndGame();
    countDownTimer.update();
    updateScoreBoard();
}
```

Here is a detailed description of the main points of this function:

1. If the countDownTimer has not started yet, this run must be the first one through the function for the game level. We set the player visible start the timer in this instance.

2. Only if the player is started do we want to accept input.

3. We run through the rest of the game loop functions.

Testing game iteration 3

When you build or test the movie, you should see the level screen fade out and the player car sitting in its starting spot, as shown in Figure 10-9. You will not see the level yet, because the drawCamera function is currently a blank stub. We are going to add in the update / render loop in iteration number 4 and then finish out the game in iteration 4.

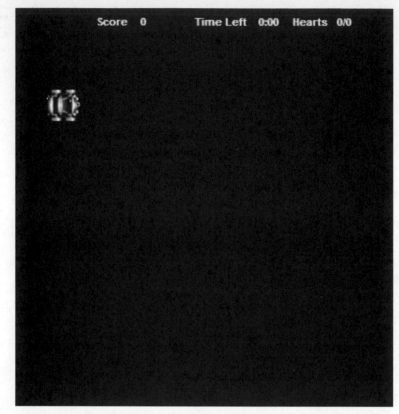

Figure 10-9. Iteration 3 in action—well, not much action yet

Adding player input and the update / render loop (iteration 4)

In this iteration, you will finally start to see things come alive in our game. By the time we are finished, you will be able to drive around the world and scroll it in all directions but without any collision detection.

The update function

The update function contains a lot of very important logic for simulating movement for the car and the world:

```
private function update():void {
    player.move = true;

    //*** update turnSpeed based on velocity
    if (player.velocity == 0) {
        player.turnSpeed = 0;
    }else {
        player.turnSpeed = player.minTurnSpeed + (Math.abs(player.velocity/10));
```

```
        if (player.turnSpeed > player.maxTurnSpeed) {
          player.turnSpeed = player.maxTurnSpeed;
        }
}

player.rotation=player.nextRotation;

var carRadians:Number = (player.nextRotation / 360) * (2.0 * Math.PI);
var lookRadians:Number;

player.dx=Math.cos(carRadians)*player.velocity;
player.dy=Math.sin(carRadians)*player.velocity;

player.worldNextX += player.dx;
player.worldNextY += player.dy;

camera.nextX = player.worldNextX - (camera.width * .5);
camera.nextY = player.worldNextY - (camera.height * .5);

if (camera.nextX <0) {
    camera.nextX = 0;
    player.nextX += player.dx;
}else if (camera.nextX > (worldWidth - camera.width - 1)) {
    camera.nextX = (worldWidth - camera.width - 1);
    player.nextX += player.dx;
}

if (camera.nextY <0) {
    camera.nextY = 0;
    player.nextY += player.dy;
}else if (camera.nextY > (worldHeight - (camera.height - 1))) {
    camera.nextY = (worldHeight - (camera.height - 1));
    player.nextY += player.dy;
}

if (player.velocity < 0) {
    player.reverse = true;
    lookRadians = ((player.nextRotation-45) / 360) * (2.0 * Math.PI);
    lookAheadPoints[0].x=(player.nextX-Math.cos(lookRadians)*player.radius);
    lookAheadPoints[0].y = (player.nextY - Math.sin(lookRadians) * player.radius);

    //lookradians the same as carRadians for middle
    lookAheadPoints[1].x=player.nextX-Math.cos(carRadians)*player.radius;
    lookAheadPoints[1].y = player.nextY - Math.sin(carRadians) * player.radius;

    lookRadians = ((player.nextRotation+45) / 360) * (2.0 * Math.PI);
    lookAheadPoints[2].x = (player.nextX - Math.cos(lookRadians) * player.radius);
    lookAheadPoints[2].y = (player.nextY - Math.sin(lookRadians) * player.radius);

}else {
    player.reverse = false;
    lookRadians = ((player.nextRotation-45) / 360) * (2.0 * Math.PI);
    lookAheadPoints[0].x=(player.nextX+Math.cos(lookRadians)*player.radius);
    lookAheadPoints[0].y = (player.nextY + Math.sin(lookRadians) * player.radius);
```

```
        //lookradians the same as carRadians for middle
        lookAheadPoints[1].x=player.nextX+Math.cos(carRadians)*player.radius;
        lookAheadPoints[1].y = player.nextY + Math.sin(carRadians) * player.radius;

        lookRadians = ((player.nextRotation+45) / 360) * (2.0 * Math.PI);
        lookAheadPoints[2].x = (player.nextX + Math.cos(lookRadians) * player.radius);
        lookAheadPoints[2].y = (player.nextY + Math.sin(lookRadians) * player.radius);
    }
}
```

This is the detailed description of the main points of the update function:

1. The player.move Boolean is set to true. When we do collision detection, we will set this to false if any one of the three LookAheadPoint references returns true for a WALL hit.

2. Next, we set the turn speed for the player. This relates directly to the actual velocity of the car. The maximum turn speed is .6 and minimum is .3, and we can set these speeds in a simple linear relation to the velocity. We simply divide the current velocity by 10 and add it to the player.minTurnSpeed. Then we check to make sure it isn't over our player.maxTurnSpeed.

3. Exactly as in the previous section in this chapter on moving the car about the world (see "Adding basic car physics to our game"),we calculate the new dx and dy values using the player.nextRotation value and the current velocity of the player. We update the player.worldNextX and player.worldNextY with the dx and dy values. The camera.nextX and camera.nexty values are based on this new world position for the player.

4. Next, we set the nextX of the camera in a similar fashion to how we described orienting it in the discussion in iteration 2. If the camera.nextX or camera.nextY is off the top, bottom, right, or left of the screen, we orient the associated axis back to 0 and move the player instead.

5. The final thing we do is set the three look ahead points to the front, middle, left, and right of the car if it is going forward (velocity greater than 0) and to the rear of the car if the velocity is less than 0.

We find these mathematically by calculating the radians for a 45-degree angle from the center of the car in each of the positive and negative directions and multiply this number by the radius we calculated earlier (16). The middle LookAheadPoint simply uses the radians for the current rotation.

See Figure 10-10 for an example.

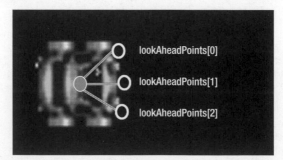

Figure 10-10. Calculated LookAheadPoint instances

Our drawn 45-degree angles in Figure 10-10 are not exact, but they demonstrate basically where the look-ahead points would be on a 0-degree angle for our player object.

The checkInput function

The checkInput function is called on each frame tick by the STATE_SYSTEM_GAMEPLAY state. It evaluates key presses stored in the keyPressList array.

```
private function checkInput():void {

    if (keyPressList[KEY_UP]){

    player.velocity+=player.acceleration;
    if (player.velocity >player.maxVelocity) player.velocity=player.maxVelocity;}
    if (!keyPressList[KEY_UP] && player.velocity >0) {
        player.velocity-=player.deceleration;
        if (player.velocity <0) player.velocity=0;

    }

    if (keyPressList[KEY_DOWN]){
        player.velocity-=player.acceleration;
      if (player.velocity < -player.maxVelocity*player.reverseVelocityModifier)↩
      player.velocity - -player.maxVelocity*player.reverseVelocityModifier;
    }

    if (!keyPressList[KEY_DOWN] && player.velocity <0) {
        player.velocity+=player.deceleration;
        if (player.velocity > 0) player.velocity = 0;
    }

    if (keyPressList[KEY_LEFT]){
        player.nextRotation-=(player.velocity)*player.turnSpeed;
    }

    if (keyPressList[KEY_RIGHT]){
        player.nextRotation+=(player.velocity)*player.turnSpeed;
    }
}
```

Here is a detailed description of the main points of this function:

- If the up key is pressed, we add acceleration (player.acceleration) to the velocity until the velocity is at the maximum value. The velocity variable we use simple holds the current speed of the car. It is not a true vector.
- If the up key in not pressed and the velocity greater than zero, we subtract the deceleration value from the velocity.
- If the down key is pressed, we subtract the acceleration from the velocity until the velocity is at the minimum value (velocity * reverseVelocityModifier).
- If the velocity is less than 0 and the down key is not pressed, we add the deceleration to the velocity until it reaches 0.

461

■ If the left or right keys are pressed, we calculate the next rotation by multiplying the player's velocity times the turnSpeed for the player. We add that to the rotation for rotating right and subtract it for rotating left.

The render functions

The render process is broken up into two parts: rendering the screen (drawCamera) and rendering the player car (drawPlayer).The render function simply calls these on order.

```
private function render():void {

    drawCamera();
    drawPlayer();

}

private function drawCamera():void {

    //calculate starting tile position
    if (player.move) {
        camera.x = camera.nextX;
        camera.y = camera.nextY;
    }

    //find starting tiles
    var tileCol:int=int(camera.x/mapTileWidth);
    var tileRow:int = int(camera.y / mapTileHeight);

    var rowCtr:int=0;
    var colCtr:int=0;
    var tileNum:int;

    //camera buffer is 1 tile larger (51 rows).
    //For last tile row, make sure to only copy 50
    //here we simply catch the exception

    for (rowCtr = 0; rowCtr <= camera.rows; rowCtr++) {
        if (rowCtr+tileRow == worldRows) break;

        for (colCtr = 0; colCtr <= camera.cols; colCtr++) {
            if (colCtr + tileCol ==worldCols ) break;

            tileNum = world[rowCtr + tileRow][colCtr + tileCol];
            tilePoint.x=colCtr*mapTileWidth;
            tilePoint.y=rowCtr*mapTileHeight;
            tileRect.x = int((tileNum % tileSheet.tilesPerRow))*mapTileWidth;
            tileRect.y = int((tileNum / tileSheet.tilesPerRow)) * mapTileHeight;
            camera.bufferBD.copyPixels(tileSheet.sourceBitmapData, ↵
            tileRect, tilePoint);
        }
    }
```

```
        //put buffer rect in corrct position what pixel
        //to start the copy on in the left-hand top tile
        camera.bufferRect.x=camera.x % mapTileWidth;
        camera.bufferRect.y = camera.y % mapTileHeight;

        //trace(bufferRect.x + "," + bufferRect.y);

        canvasBitmapData.lock();
        canvasBitmapData.copyPixels(camera.bufferBD,camera.bufferRect,↵
            camera.bufferPoint);
        canvasBitmapData.unlock();
    }

    private function drawPlayer():void {

        if (player.velocity == 0) {
            player.move = false;
        }

        if (player.move) {

            player.animationDelay = player.maxVelocity - player.velocity;
            player.animationLoop = true;

            player.updateCurrentTile();
            player.renderCurrentTile();

            player.x = player.nextX;
            player.y = player.nextY;

            player.worldX = player.worldNextX;
            player.worldY = player.worldNextY;
        }else {

            player.animationLoop = false;
        }

        if (getTimer() > carSoundTime + ↵
            carSoundDelayList[Math.abs(int(player.velocity))]) {

            dispatchEvent(new CustomEventSound(CustomEventSound.PLAY_SOUND, ↵
            Main.SOUND_CAR, false, 1, 0));

            carSoundTime = getTimer();
        }
    }
```

The drawCamera function

The drawCamera function is the core of the screen rendering code. The process we need run through on each frame looks like this:

1. Update the camera starting position.

2. Find the starting tile row and tile column for the camera.

3. Loop through the rows and columns and copy them to the buffer.

4. Paint the buffer to the canvas.

If the `player.move` variable (which is set to `false` in `checkCollisions` if the player hits a wall) is true, we update the `camera.x` and `camera.y` to the `nextX` and `nextY` values for the camera.

Next, we find the `tileCol` and `tileRow` variables. These represent the row and column to start copying from the `world array` to the `camera.bufferBitmapData`.

Now, we loop through 13 rows and 13 columns of tiles and paint them to the buffer. The 13 rows start at `tileRow` and run through `tileCol` plus 12. The 13 columns start at `tileCol` and run through `tileCol` plus 12. Notice the check for a `rowCtr` or `colCtr` that is greater than 50 (`worldRows` or `worldCols`). We do this because when we near the edge of the screen and only have 12 rows or columns left in the world, we can't build a buffer with 13 columns or rows in the direction that is near the edge. In this instance, we break from the associated loop.

Next, we find the point that represents the location on the screen to paint the tile and the rectangle that represents the location on the tile sheet to copy from. Finally, we paint the tile with a `copyPixels` call to the `camera.bufferBitmapData`.

Once the `bufferBitmapData` is complete, we set the `camer.bufferRect` rectangle to start on the correct pixel in the first tile. The x value to start at is the remainder of `camera.x / mapTileWidth` and y is the remainder of `camera.y / mapTileHeight`. The width and height of the buffer have already been set at 384 × 384 and need not change. Finally, we lock our `canvasBitmapData` and copy the entire 384 × 384 `bufferBitmapData` to the `canvasBitmapData` starting at 0,0.

The drawPlayer function

The `drawPlayer` function is the core of the player render functionality. It takes care of selecting and painting the correct frame of animation from the tile sheet to display for the player and also plays the car sound based on its speed.

1. If the player is not stopped, we should animate the player (move the wheels by changing the frame of animation for the car from the time sheet).

2. If it is OK to animate the player, update the player animation delay based on the inverse of its `velocity` (the greater the `velocity` the lower the delay between frames).

3. Update the player's current tile from the `tileSheet`.

4. Render the player's current tile to the `player.bitmapData`.

5. Set the player's new x and y coordinates. We also update the `player.worldX` and `player.worldY` values.

6. Play the car sound faster or slower based on the player's new `velocity` (speed.

In the `checkCollisions` function, we will set the `player.move` to be true or false based on the result (or lack thereof) a collision with a wall tile. If the player is able to move, we update the player attributes.

The `animationDelay` is the number of frames between changes to the player's tile from the tile sheet. The three car tiles when played forward (or backward) simulate the car's relative speed. Since the `velocity` and the *number of frames* are both linear, we can use the inverse of the velocity to calculate the delay.

Only if the player is allowed to move do we update the nextX and nextY values for the player. Note that if the player is not near the edge of the screen, the nextX and nextY values will always be the same as the x and y values for the player. This is because we want the player to remain in the center of the screen unless it is in a column or row that forces the scrolling to stop.

The sound for the player car is played based on the delay value from an array. We populated this array earlier:

```
private var carSoundDelayList:Array = [90,80,70,60,50,40,20,10,0];
```

The delay is pulled from this array based on the player velocity. This is similar to how we do the animationDelay for the wheels, but since we needed larger numbers and wanted to test each, we used an array look up table.

Testing iteration 4

When you build or test this movie, you should see the level screen fade out and the player car sitting in its starting spot. You will need to click the screen with the mouse before you can control the car with the keys. You can scroll all over the world without any collision detection. Figure 10-11 shows iteration 4.

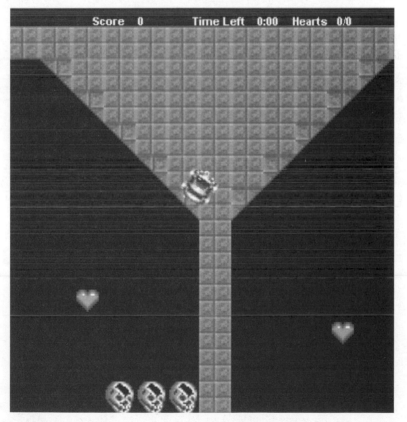

Figure 10-11. Iteration 4 in action—there is no collision detection yet, so drive on the walls!

Detecting collisions and the end of a level or the game (iteration 5)

In this iteration, we will build out most of the rest of our game logic. At the end of iteration 4, we had completed the update and render functions for our game. The car can now drive around the scrolling game world but will not be affected by the walls, hearts, or other sprites.

The collision detection routine for Drive She Said will use the three LookAheadPoint objects we created earlier. They are positioned at points that represent the next location for our player car. We have three of them to insure proper coverage across the surface of the car that will most likely hit an object. We will check the tile type that each of the three will be located in based on the player.nextX and player.nextY values that are updated in the update function. We also set the player.move variable to true in the update function. During the collision detection, if any of the three points hits a wall, this will be set to false.

If we had handled collisions another way, such as setting player.move to false first and then checking collisions and setting it to true if any of the LookAheadPoints was not on a wall, we would get strange behavior if one point was on the wall and one was not.

Let's take a look at the code for this now.

The checkCollisions function

This is the code for the checkCollisions function:

```
private function checkCollisions():void {

    var lookAheadLength:int = lookAheadPoints.length;
    var row:int;
    var col:int;
    var tileType:int;

    //loop through all three look ahead points

    for (var ctr:int = 0; ctr < lookAheadLength; ctr++) {

        row = (lookAheadPoints[ctr].y+camera.y) / mapTileHeight;
        col = (lookAheadPoints[ctr].x + camera.x) / mapTileWidth;

        tileType = tileSheetData[world[row][col]];

        switch(tileType) {

            case TILE_MOVE:
                //do not need to do anything
                break;

            case TILE_WALL:

                if (canvasBitmapData.getPixel(lookAheadPoints[ctr].x, ↵
                lookAheadPoints[ctr].y) != levelWallDriveColor) {

                    if (Math.abs(player.velocity) > 1) {
                        //don't keep on playing sound if close to a wall
```

```
        dispatchEvent(new CustomEventSound(CustomEventSound.PLAY_SOUND,↵
          Main.SOUND_HIT_WALL, false, 1, 0));
      }

      //check for stuck cars=

      if (player.reverse && player.velocity >.1) {
          player.velocity = -1;
      }else if (!player.reverse && player.velocity < .1){
          player.velocity = 1;
      }

      trace("player.velocity=" + player.velocity);
      player.velocity *= -levelWallAdjust;

      player.dx *= -levelWallAdjust;
      player.dy *= -levelWallAdjust;
      player.move = false;
    }
    break;

case SPRITE_SKULL:
    player.velocity *= -levelSkullAdjust;
    player.dx *= -levelSkullAdjust;
    player.dy *= -levelSkullAdjust;

    dispatchEvent(new CustomEventSound(CustomEventSound.PLAY_SOUND, ↵
      Main.SOUND_SKULL_HIT, false, 1, 0));

    break;

case SPRITE_CLOCK:
    countDownTimer.seconds += levelClockAdd;

    dispatchEvent(new CustomEventSound(CustomEventSound.PLAY_SOUND, ↵
      Main.SOUND_CLOCK_PICKUP, false, 1, 0));

    world[row][col] - levelBackGroundTile ,
    break;

case SPRITE_HEART:
    heartsCollected++;
    score += levelHeartScore;

    dispatchEvent(new CustomEventSound(CustomEventSound.PLAY_SOUND, ↵
      Main.SOUND_HEART_PICKUP, false, 1, 0));

    world[row][col] =  levelBackGroundTile ;
    break;

case SPRITE_GOAL:
    if (heartsCollected >= heartsNeeded  ) {
      goalReached = true;
```

```
                         dispatchEvent(new CustomEventSound(CustomEventSound.PLAY_SOUND, ↵
                         Main.SOUND_LEVEL_COMPLETE, false, 1, 0));

                         break;
                     }
                 }
             }
         }
```

For the collision detection we are going to loop through each of the three LookAheadPoint references and check the tile type that each is colliding with.

1.   If the tile is the TILE_MOVE type, we do nothing. This part of the switch:case statement added just for reference.

2.   If the tile is the TILE_WALL type, we do a second check to see if the pixel located at the same place as the point is a color other than the levelWallDriveColor. If it is, we assume that it is part of the wall and proceed with the collision reaction code:

     If the velocity of the player is greater than 1, we will play the sound for hitting the wall. We only want to do this one time per hit, so the code that follows will also make sure the velocity is less than 1 on the next frame tick. We use Math.abs so this will work in both for forward and reverse directions.

     In the event that the car overshoots the wall and is stuck and moving too slow to be bounced back, we make sure that the player's car is at least moving with velocity of 1 in its current direction. This will force the next lines of code to bump the player away from the wall.

     To ensure that the velocity for the player will be less than 1 on the next frame tick, we add the inverse of the levelWallAdjust to player.velocity, player.dx, and player.dy to effectively move the player car back in the opposite direction it was moving then it hit the wall.

     We make sure the player.move variable is set to false for this frame tick. On the next tick, the player will move back.

3.   If the player hits a SKULL sprite we add the inverse of the levelSkullAdjust variable to the player.dx, player.dy, and player.velocity in a similar manner as the wall hit. We also switch the tile out with the background tile so it will not be on the screen anymore and play the associated sound for the skull hit.

4.   If the player hits a CLOCK sprite, we add seconds to the countDownTimer: countdownTimer.seconds += levelClockAdd. We also switch the tile out with the background tile so it will not be on the screen anymore and play the associated sound for the clock hit.

5.   If the player hits a HEART sprite, we add seconds to add to the heartsCollected variable and to the score. We also switch the tile out with the background tile so it will not be on the screen anymore and play the associated sound for the heart hit.

6. If the player hits a GOAL sprite and has collected enough hearts, the goalReached variable will be set to true. We also play the associated sound for reaching the goal.

The rest of the game functions

The final functions add virtually no new game logic that you have not already seen. The only real new concept is the systemLevelOut function that is used in the STATE_SYSTEM_LEVELOUT state that begins once the goalReached variable has been set to true.

Add the rest of these functions to your DriveSheSaid.as file, and then follow the instructions for finalizing the build to package and run the final game

First, add the code for the complete addToScore function:

```
private function addToScore(val:Number):void {
    score += val;
}
```

Next, add the dispose function:

```
private function dispose(object:BlitSprite):void {

    object.dispose();
    removeChild(object);

}
```

Now comes the disposeAll function:

```
private function disposeAll():void {

    if (gameOver) {
        countDownTimer.removeEventListener(BasicFrameTimer.TIME_IS_UP,↵
         timesUpListener);
        dispose(player);
    }
}
```

The timesUpListener will fire off when the CountDownTimer instance reaches 0 and will signal the game to be over; add it now:

```
private function timesUpListener(e:Event):void {

    countDownTimer.stop();
    gameOver = true;

}
```

The full checkforEndGame function comes next:

```
private function checkforEndGame():void {

    if (gameOver ) {

        dispatchEvent(new CustomEventSound(CustomEventSound.PLAY_SOUND, ↵
         Main.SOUND_GAME_LOST, false, 1, 0));
```

```
            dispatchEvent(new Event(GAME_OVER));
            countDownTimer.stop();
            disposeAll();
        }
    }
```

Now, you can add the checkForEndLevel function:

```
    private function checkforEndLevel():void {

        if (goalReached) {
            disposeAll();
            switchSystemState( STATE_SYSTEM_LEVELOUT );
            countDownTimer.stop();
        }
    }
```

The systemLevelOut function moves the DriveSheSaid.as Sprite off the screen's until it is at completely off the viewable stage (an x value of 404). When it is, it calls the levelOutComplete function. Here's the code for this faction:

```
    private function systemLevelOut():void {
        this.x += 4;
        if (this.x >= 404) {
            this.x = 404;
            levelOutComplete();
        }
    }
```

The levelOutComplete function also needs to be added:

```
    private function levelOutComplete():void {
        dispatchEvent(new Event(NEW_LEVEL));
        switchSystemState( STATE_SYSTEM_GAMEPLAY );
    }
```

Finally, add the updateScoreBoard function:

```
    private function updateScoreBoard():void {

        dispatchEvent(new CustomEventScoreBoardUpdate(CustomEventScoreBoardUpdate.↵
        UPDATE_TEXT, Main.SCORE_BOARD_SCORE, String(score)));

        dispatchEvent(new CustomEventScoreBoardUpdate(CustomEventScoreBoardUpdate.↵
        UPDATE_TEXT,Main.SCORE_BOARD_TIME_LEFT,String(timeLeft) ));

        dispatchEvent(new CustomEventScoreBoardUpdate(CustomEventScoreBoardUpdate.↵
        UPDATE_TEXT,Main.SCORE_BOARD_HEARTS,String(heartsCollected) + "/" + ↵
        String(heartsNeeded)));

        timeLeft = countDownTimer.seconds;
    }
```

Testing the final game

You now have a one-level game that should be playable, as shown in Figure 10-12. When you test it, you should be able to drive around the environment, collecting hearts and clocks. Avoid the skulls and walls. You need to make it to the finish line before time runs out having collected enough hearts for the level.

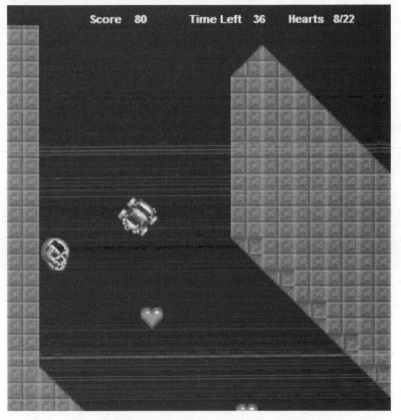

Figure 10-12. Iteration 5 (the final game) in action. Jeff just ran into a skull!

Extending the game

We will cover adding pause and mute functions to the framework in the next chapter, so those might be a good addition to this game. Also, more things to collect, new wall tiles on different levels, more hazards and possible more power ups for speed and steering might make the game more fun and extend it playability.

One thing you can do right now is create more levels for the game.

1. Create an XML file for the level in Mappy.

2. Make a copy of the Level1.as file and rename it Level2.as.

3. Replace the Level1 map variable data with the new 2D array of tile data, exported from Mappy with the **Export to ActionScript** option in the **Custom** menu for Level2.

4. Make any level-specific changes you want to the nontile variables in the file.

5. Make sure to add an instantiation for Level2 to the variable definition section of the DriveSheSaid.as:

```
private var levels:Array = [undefined, new Level1(), new Level2()];
```

6. Repeat this process for each of the levels you create.

Summary

We have covered a lot in this chapter, and we did it at a very rapid pace. To create this game, we extended the BlitSprite class and used the blitting techniques that we have been evolving throughout this book for car-based movement and created code to move it around a scrolling tile-based world. We created collision routines based on the tiles but also extended the collision detection to the actual color of the pixels on each tile. The game evolved some advanced screen render code and collision detection routines to allow free 360-degree fluid movement across the world. We used three look-ahead points across the front and rear of the car to determine exactly what tiles and pixel colors on those tiles the car would collide with if moved in the forward or reverse direction. We also moved our sounds into a custom class called Library (for the Flex SDK only) and embedded MP3 files rather than WAV files.

In the next chapter, we will up the ante and create the most optimized game in this book. Blaster Mines is a geometry wars–style blasting contest that will make use of a new optimized game loop timer as well as object pooling techniques and particles for explosions.

Chapter 11

Creating an Optimized Post-Retro Game

In this chapter, we will be creating a post-retro game. This genre of modern game takes a classic retro idea and improves it for the modern age. Two good examples of this are Bit Trip Beat and Geometry Wars. In Bit Trip Beat, the classic game Pong is re-created and combined with modern rhythm-based music gameplay to create an instant modern classic. In Geometry Wars, the classic game Asteroids is given a new coat of paint, a new set controls, a larger scrolling play field, and heart-pumping music to create a game that modern audiences enjoy as much as the classic game.

In this chapter, we will create our own post-retro game, or retro-evolved game to use the phrase coined by Geometry Wars. Our game will also be based on Asteroids. We will focus our technical efforts on creating an optimized screen-based blit scrolling game. The screen-based scrolling engine we will create doesn't use tiles (as in Drive She Said) but uses a screen-sized window area to display the viewable portion of the larger game world.

We will also focus on some optimizations for rendering speed and memory consumption. The techniques in this chapter can be applied to games on any platform that supports the Flash Player. Some techniques are better suited for memory consumption limits and some for render and execution speed. We are going to discuss how to use both for the game in this chapter. You will want to carefully consider which techniques to employ based on the platform your game will be targeted at.

Understanding post-retro games

Many people have the sense these days that the concept of retro games is disappearing. This does not mean that there are no retro-inspired games being made, but it means that "retro" has been enveloped into the mainstream and does not really exist any longer as its own genre. Retro is mainstream. At E3 2009, games that would have been shoved off into far corners and dismissed as retro in years past were right up front (i.e., Super Mario Wii, Nostalgia, and Final Fantasy VII). This proved that the term "retro" is so all-encompassing that it means almost nothing if applied to these games. These are just games (good games, mind you) and are tagged "retro" only for the most superficial reasons. In a sense, these are classic games with classic gameplay, that don't necessarily need to have a retro aesthetic.

At the same time, there still is a very healthy community for actual retro gaming: playing games on old systems and emulators or writing games specifically for old hardware. This truly is a retro activity and should be treated as such.

However, a new game design movement is emerging that is very difficult to describe with the current set of accepted game genres (e.g., casual, core, retro, viral, and mobile). The new movement consists of new concepts, presented in retro fashion but is not made up of classic retro games. These are not remixes, arrangements, remakes of old games with new graphics, or retro collections. Nor are they home-brew games made to run on retro consoles. These games are something entirely different and compose a genre we like to call "post-retro."

Defining post-retro

Post-retro games are games that utilize a retro aesthetic mixed with both retro and modern gameplay elements to create a wholly new experience. The term "post-retro" relates to "postmodern" in that these games have "moved beyond" the pure nostalgia element of the retro game era and instead use retro as a platform for new ideas.

Exploring the features of post-retro games

Post-retro games can, and have been, implemented in a variety of ways, making the boundaries of this genre a bit undefined at this point. However, there are some general features that many of these games contain. Not all games in this genre contain all of what is listed here, but they contain enough of them so that they are identifiable as part of the genre:

- **Plays retro and modern**: These are games with play that feels retro but also feels not retro at the same time (a paradox!). There is a sense that the game could have been made in a prior era but was not ever made, possibly because game design concepts have evolved over time .

- **Retro aesthetic**: Typically, these games utilize a retro graphical look (usually 8-bit, 16-bit, or vector) and sound effects that match.

- **Modern music**: Music is one interesting factor that sets these games apart from retro remakes and straight retro games. Most games from the original golden age consoles had little or no music (some computer games did, but that is a different story). While many of these games retain the 8- or 16-bit look of older games, they replace the relative background silence with music that is usually trippy and/or hypnotic. Sound effects are still in place, but the sound mix puts them in the back behind the music, instead of in front. Sound effects usually match the retro look of the game.

- **Hypnotic state**: Another feature that many of these games have is sped-up, almost flowing gameplay. In most games, lives and scores are still important, but you get many more lives than you would have received in a traditional retro game. In a sense, these games are more about experiencing a state of post-retro gameplay than about strictly being retro-inspired games.

- **Background images**: Hypnotic, moving background images fill void space that once existed in retro games.
- **Particle effects**: Massive particle effects are often present. They do not add much to gameplay but add a kinetic and chaotic feel that did not necessarily exists in games from the classic era.
- **No nostalgia for nostalgia's sake**: While these games might elicit a nostalgic feeling in certain gamers, they are designed as new experiences using (in part) a retro or nostalgic aesthetic.
- **No remakes**: This genre does not include straight retro remakes. If a post-retro game is a version if an older game, the gameplay has been changed significantly so that it is recognizable as part of this genre.

Emerging post-retro game features

Here are some emerging, but currently less widespread, features of post-retro games:

- **Automatic shooting or movement**: These features are fairly new, and they remove some of the classic gameplay burden from players so they can concentrate on the modern features.
- **Retro as the starting point**: This is another fairly new concept and refers to using the concept of retro games as the platform to create an entirely new game. We don't want to sound elitist here, but in some cases, there is a literary or artistic feel to the games. This feeling can occur as a deconstruction where the whole idea of certain games are torn apart and turned around or given multiple meanings. The game might serve as a metaphor, where it takes on completely different meaning than what is presented, or even be transcendent, where games are taken to a place beyond what they were initially created to do. (Note that obviously this area is up for debate.)

Tracing the history of post-retro games

While the history of post-retro has not been fully examined yet, most of the features of post-retro games can be found in Jeff Minter's Tempest 2000 for the Atari Jaguar from 1993.

Seeing this game in action is like viewing a time capsule into the future from 1993. Minter's game includes nearly all aspects of the post-retro genre. While the gameplay is very much like the classic Tempest, new elements are added as well. While still a bit basic, this game was a template for what post-retro would became 15 years later.

Still, while this game might be the spiritual forerunner of the post-retro aesthetic, it's difficult to trace all of this genre directly back to that game because not much else happened in between its release in 1993 and the appearance of these types of games *en masse* in about 2007.

Instead of going the route of Tempest 2000, retro games took some different turns in the ensuing years. When Hasbro bought the Atari assets in 1998, it started to create modern versions of Atari classics like Missile Command, Pong, Breakout, and Centipede. At the same time, Activision took up the idea to do the same thing with Battlezone and Asteroids. While some of these were fine games, they were not really post-retro, because they were more like remakes with modern paint jobs.

The same can be said of retro collections: multiple retro games in a single package that gained much popularity on the PS2 (e.g., Activision Anthology, Capcom Classics, Namco Museum). While some of the collections offered remixed or arrangement versions of games with slight upgrades, for the most part, they prided themselves on duplicating an exact classic gaming experience on a console.

While other examples of post-retro games are bound to exist (send them to us if you have them), it was not until the current generation of consoles that we started seeing games in this movement taking shape. The real ground zero for these games was the emergence of the console downloadable era on the Xbox Live Arcade, PlayStation Store, and WiiWare, as well as the viral, Web Flash gaming explosion.

Here are some post-retro game examples you might be familiar with:

- **Geometry Wars**: One of the best, first examples of post-retro would be Geometry Wars. First released on Xbox Live Arcade in 2007, this game was a smash hit that proved marketable games could be created by a very small team and could be successful on the Xbox Live Arcade. This game has a definite retro look and feel, but it adds a modern control mechanism, hypnotic music, and other effects. It's one of the first and best examples of the new post-retro movement. It was also the both a creative and financial inspiration for many of the games on this list.

- **Space Giraffe**: Since we credit Jeff Minter as one of the founder's of this genre, it would only be fair to add one of his own games to this list. Space Giraffe is an evolution of Tempest 2000, and that might also be its downfall. While this game contains most of the post-retro aesthetic (including actual 8-bit sounds from one of Minter's original computer games), and while it is does contain some major changes to the Tempest template, its gameplay is very close to a classic retro game. There is so much going on however, that it becomes a very tough game to play rather quickly. That might explain its limited appeal and slow sales as compared to some of the other games on this list.

- **Pac-Mac Championship Edition (CE)**: Pac-Man CE is an odd but addictive beast, and it is a very good example of one strain of post-retro—the classic game reborn. This game takes the main ideas of Pac-Man (eat all the dots; eat power-ups to kill ghosts), and keeps them mostly unchanged. However, it changes the gameplay just enough by adding morphing mazes and progressive gameplay to make it an entirely different game than the original. You never finish a level in Pac-Man CE, you just finish a portion of a level, and then the play field alters itself, and you keep going. This not insignificant change to the core gameplay makes a wholly different and addictive game. You get the sense while playing this game that this should have been the sequel to Pac-Man, but the state of game design at the time just could not have spawned this game. This is an important distinction for some of the best examples of post-retro: the sneaking feeling that some of these games could have saved the golden age of video games.

- **Bit Trip Beat and Bit Trip Core**: Bit Trip Beat takes the game of Pong and turns it into a journey through an 8-bit landscape filled with all sorts of challenges related to a ball and paddle. However, calling this "Pong" is like calling Geometry Wars "Asteroids." You can see the inspiration, but there really is no comparison. While it has nearly every feature on the post-retro list, the most striking aspect of this game is that it feels like an Atari 2600 game that was never made but could have been made (without the obvious modern effects) if only the idea had occurred to game developers back in the early 1980s. However, at the same time, the game could not have been made, because its reliance on music and musical timing would have been nearly impossible to achieve on golden-age game consoles. Because of this, Bit Trip Beat might be the quintessential post-retro game on this list.

  The sequel, Bit Trip Core, is a similar take on shooters but with the same feel as its older brother.

- **Space Invaders Extreme and Galaga Legions**: Both of these games take classic shooters and give them a post-retro makeover. Both have hypnotic soundtracks layered over classic sounds and graphics. Galaga Legions tends toward classic gameplay, while Space Invaders Extreme takes the whole concept of the original and deconstructs it. What is interesting is that both games have been made and remade over and over again for the past 25 years, but these post-retro versions stand out far above any previous efforts.

- **Mark Essen's FlyWrench from IndieCade**: FlyWrench takes a seemingly simple concept and turns it into a fascinating post-retro game. Your job is to fly your avatar through vector-graphic–looking levels, morphing the shape to match the current obstacle that you need to overcome. The game is very difficult and very addictive. It layers modern music over classic graphics and sound effects. A few seconds after seeing this game at E3, we knew it was part of this emerging trend. The game is striking example of how to take retro concepts to make a very new and interesting game.

- **Retro Game Challenge**: Retro Game Challenge is very good example of another emerging trend in post-retro games—transcendence. There are many meanings for "transcendence," but in this case, it means to go beyond. Basically, games of this type take the act of playing a retro game and make it into something much more. In Retro Game Challenge, you play a young boy in the 1980s who is visited by a man from the future that challenges you to play through eight different retro games, trying to achieve certain objectives. These challenges are set up in such a way that playing the games themselves takes a backseat to the act of playing a retro video game within a game. You get hints from virtual magazines; you input cheat codes, find hidden items, and so on. However, most of these things happen inside the retro games that are inside Retro Game Challenge not in the actual game of Retro Game Challenge itself. The difference here is that an entirely new game was created based on retro games, but the game itself is not a retro game; it's a modern one. The retro genre is transcended to a completely new place, post-retro.

- **Bit Boy**: Bit Boy is a lot like Retro Game Challenge in that it takes the players through several levels, each inspired by a different era of video game graphics and gameplay. While it does not contain multiple games, it does take the player on a journey through retro games (and beyond), transcending the genre to make something totally new.
- **Post-retro viral Flash games**: Besides these commercial games, many viral Flash games also fall into this category of post-retro. A great example is the recent hit Retroshoot. We, ourselves, also have a game that sort of fits into this category named Retro Blaster, created more than two years ago. A secondary offshoot of this genre would be the turn-the-tables retro games like Asteroids Revenge and Anti-Pac-Man. These games are good examples of a minor form of deconstruction in post-retro viral Flash games, where the multiple meanings for the game world exist simply by having the player take the nontraditional role of the bad guy from those classic games.

What the post-retro genre means to developers

To us, there is no doubt the genre of post-retro games exists and is only growing. What, then, can game developers learn from it?

Well, first of all, the fact that many (but not all) of these games have been very successful cannot be overlooked. It seems that people who buy downloadable games and play viral Flash games like this genre very much. It could also mean that the audience for retro games is getting much more sophisticated. You might not be able to settle on a pure retro-inspired game and hope for it to build any kind of audience. Most likely, you need to add something more to mix to get your game noticed.

If you are interested in making a game in this genre, here is our advice: Take a look at a couple of old games, and try to visualize what they would look like as post-retro games. What would you add to the classic concept that could not have been achieved when the game was first released? Would it transcend or deconstruct the original game, layer modern game design elements on top, both, or neither? We're truly fascinated by this emerging trend, and we look forward to playing any new games in this genre.

In this chapter, we will be making game in the vein of these post-retro, or retro-evolved, games called Blaster Mines.

Designing Blaster Mines

Let's get started by taking a look at a screen shot for our Blaster Mines game in Figure 11-1.

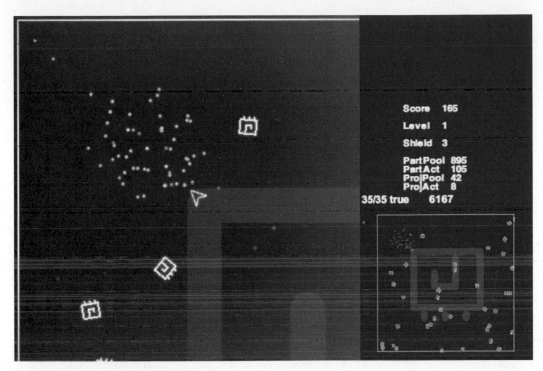

Figure 11-1. Blaster Mines game screen

Blaster Mines is going to be a game in the style of Asteroids or Geometry Wars. The basic technical specification outlines the game's name, type, inspiration, objectives, and play in these short paragraphs:

- **Game name:** Blaster Mines
- **Game type:** Arcade blaster in a 360-degree scrolling world
- **Game inspiration**: Atari's Asteroids was and will always be one of our all-time favorite arcade games. We have probably built ten different Asteroids variants in just the last four years. This style of game is great for a simple five to ten minute game session, but more importantly, it is a great way to test game optimizations. We will probably always come back to this style of game when we are starting out with a new development language or environment, just to see how much we can squeeze out of the game development platform. Games in this genre are all about blasting never-ending waves of on-screen attackers for as long as possible. The arrival of Geometry Wars contributed to this game genre lore by adding in new control schemes, scrolling, power ups, and more. This style of game is deceptively difficult to program correctly. A decent programmer, in under a day, can build a simple Asteroids game. The difficult part comes when the developer wants to add hundreds of missiles, particles, and enemies to the game screen. This can cause the Flash engine to slow way down.

- **Game objective:** You are a lone space Marine left trying to find your way home through a never-ending series of 360-degree scrolling mine fields.
- **Gameplay:** The player must fly a ship through the 360-degree scrolling world and blast all of the mines on each level to progress to the next.
- **Level progression:** Levels progress with simple calculations that increase the number and speed of the mines. There will be ten levels. The background color and color of the mines will change on each level.

And these are the basic technical design specifications:

- **World size:** 800 × 800 (no tiles)
- **Camera size:** 400 × 400
- **Scrolling type:** Screen-based to BitmapData canvas
- **User control:** Player will follow the mouse with automatic firing
- **Asset format:** Vectors cached to arrays of BitmapData (or single BitmapData instances)

Game development concepts in this chapter

In this chapter, we will cover the following:

- Managing garbage collection
- Optimizing render speed optimization
- Optimizing memory consumption
- Creating a time-base step timer with render profiling
- Adding a frame rate timer to the framework
- Drawing vector assets in code
- Caching vector assets into arrays of BitmapData for rendering
- Optimized Screen-based scrolling on BitmapData canvas with ScrollRect
- Using the power of BitmapData to create a simple radar screen
- Using look-up tables
- Creating a simple particle engine
- Pooling objects

Modifying the game framework

We are going to add the following functionality to our ever-evolving game framework:

- **Mute functionality:** This will be controlled by Main and will trigger a new function inside the SoundManager class.
- **Pause functionality:** This will be implemented in GameFrameWork.as and will be available only to games that use the time-based step timer created in this chapter. We have done this so the GameFrameWork file will remain compatible with all of the games previously created with the standard timer.

- **Time-based step timer**: This will replace the Timer-based game timer with an ENTER_FRAME-based step timer. The goal of this type of timer is to keep the game rendering and object movement constant when played at various frame rates.
- **Frame rate profiler**: This will test the player's machine capabilities before the game is played. The result will be passed into the Game class and can be used to increase or decrease game effects based on the profiled frame rate.
- **Frame counter**: The frame counter is used to calculate the current frame tick rate. It is used by the frame rate profiler and can also be displayed during gameplay.

> Note: The Entire GameFrameWork.as class code is re-printed at the end of this chapter. We recommend that you use that version after reading through the changes.

Checking stage access

The first modification we will make to the GameFrameWork.as file is to add code that Main can call when the stage is available. We do this because the GameFrameWork.as will need to add stage listeners for the **Pause** and **Mute** keys. The stage must be available for this to happen properly.

Creating the New addedToStage function

Place this new function inside the GameFrameWork.as file:

```
public function addedToStage(e:Event = null):void {
    stage.addEventListener(KeyboardEvent.KEY_DOWN,keyDownListener);
    this.focusRect=false;
    stage.focus = stage;
    trace("gamFrameWork added to stage");
}
```

The main purpose of this function is to add references to the stage object only after it is available to the SWF file. We have done this to ensure that Main's init() function is not called before the stage is available.

When we get to the "Adding pause and mute functionality to the framework" section of this chapter, we will examine how this function is called. The Main class will override this to call its own version of this function and then call this version with the super.addToStage() call.

Adding pause and mute functionality to the framework

Mute functionality will be added by placing a new set of key listeners in to the GameFrameWork.as class. These listeners will detect when the M key is pressed and then call a function in the SoundManager. These same listeners will be used for the pause functionality using the P key, which will trigger the pause functionality.

The actual pausing of the gameplay will be handled by the Game class. In the Main.as class for a game that implements pause functionality, we will override the systemGamePlay function and pass the paused class variable to the Game class when we call the runGame function. This will actually be a function called runGameTimeBased for the new step timer.

To ensure the games in the book that were created before this chapter will still compile within the framework we will only add pause functionality to the new `runGameTimeBased` function that we will create for the time-based step timer rather than the `runGame` function we have used for all of the previous games.

These are the public variables for the pause and mute functionality:

```
public static const KEY_MUTE:int = 77;  // added chapter 11
public static const KEY_PAUSE:int = 80; //added chapter 11
public var paused:Boolean = false;
public var pausedScreen:BasicScreen;
```

Let's now look closely at the five new functions needed to handle pause and mute:

- `private function keyDownListener(e:KeyboardEvent):void`: This function will use a `switch:case` statement to determine if any action needs to be taken for the key that was pressed. It will act on the M key for mute and the P key for pause by calling the handler functions described next.

- `private function pausedKeyPressedHandler():void`: When the P key is pressed, this handler function is called. It sets the new class Boolean variable, `paused`, to `true`. It also puts the `pausedScreen` on display. The `pausedScreen` is a simple instance of the `BasicScreen` class, so we can listen for the click of the OK button on the screen. This is the signal that the game player wants to close the `pausedScreen`. This function adds this listener for the click on the OK button on the `pausedScreen`:

```
pausedScreen.addEventListener(CustomEventButtonId.BUTTON_ID , pausedScreenClickListener,↵
false, 0, true);
```

This function also adds the pausedScreen to the display list:

- `public function pausedScreenClickListener(e:Event):void`: This function will remove the `pausedScreen` from the display list, remove the event listener for the OK button on the `pausedScreen` and set the paused class variable to `false`.

- `private function muteKeyPressedHandler():void`: When the M key is pressed, this handler will call the `soundManager.muteSound` function Look for a description of this function in the section on changes to the `SoundManager` class.

- We also need to add this line to the com.efg.framework.FrameWorkStates.as file with the rest of the constants:

```
public static const STATE_SYSTEM_PAUSE:int = 99;
```

For the full source to the `Main` class, see the section titled "The Main class." For the full source to the `GameFrameWork` class, see the section titled "The full `GameFrameWork` class code."

Adding the time-based step timer

In Chapter 2, we introduced the basic timer we use for our game loop. This timer is implemented with an instance of the `Timer` class that is set to run at an interval based on the `frameRate` variable. If we set the `frameRate` variable to 40, the timer will run at a 1,000/40-millisecond interval. The result was a decent timer that runs the current set of games in a nice manner. But, if the games are played on a variety of machines and Flash Player versions, there will be noticeable differences in frame rate. This will cause the game sprites to move faster or slower than we intended.

When using this timer, we split the game tick into even slices of time for each game loop iteration and hoped that the game would be able to process all code and render everything to the screen inside each even time slice. So, when we moved the car in Drive She Said (for example) at its speed of 4 pixels per tick, we simply moved the car 4 pixels every frame tick and hoped that in a single second the car would travel 30 × 4 (our frame rate times the pixels-per-second speed value). Since Drive She Said really was not a processor-intensive game, we were able to achieve the 120 pixels per second movement rate that we desired. This is not always the case though. As you will see with Blaster Mines, we are going to create a game with many moving objects that some systems and platforms might not be able to handle properly. Because of this, we will add some functionality to the time slice frame tick to ensure that all objects move the desired distance in a single second. As a result, objects will not always move the exact same distance on each frame tick, but in a single second, we will ensure that the objects move the distance we'd like. So, even if the Flash Player is running at a slower frame rate than desired, we can ensure that our game objects will move distance we want.

In this chapter, we are going to create a new type of timer that we call the **time-based step timer**. This timer will implement the standard `ENTER_FRAME` event rather than the `Timer` class. Instead of relying on interval time from the `Timer` call, we will use the stage frame rate to run our game. We will not simply rely on this stage frame rate to keep our game running smoothly though. We will be profiling the time it takes to run each frame tick and modifying the number of pixels our game character move based on this information.

First, we will need to change the `startTimer` function to add in the ability to use the new timer:

```
public function startTimer(timeBasedAnimation:Boolean=false):void {
    stage.frameRate = frameRate;
    if (timeBasedAnimation) {
        lastTime = getTimer();
        addEventListener(Event.ENTER_FRAME, runGameEnterFrame);
    }else{
        timerPeriod = 1000 / frameRate;
        gameTimer=new Timer(timerPeriod); //*** changed removed in new chapter 2
        gameTimer.addEventListener(TimerEvent.TIMER, runGame);
        gameTimer.start();
    }
}
```

The `startTimer` function now accepts a Boolean parameter that allows us to switch between the original timer and the new time-based step timer. By passing true, we switch to the ENTER_FRAME version. Our game loop will now called the runGameEnterFrame function rather than the original runGame function on each frame tick.

Adding the runEnterFrame function

The `runEnterFrame` function uses a `getTimer` call to time the number of milliseconds that have passed after each frame tick has run. This is stored in the `timeDifference` class level variable.

```
public function runGameEnterFrame(e:Event):void {

    timeDifference = getTimer() - lastTime
```

```
lastTime = getTimer();
systemFunction();
frameCounter.countFrames();
}
```

The `Main.as` class for each game will override the `systemGamePlay` state function from `GameFrameWork` and pass this `timeDifference` as well as the `paused` variable (used to pause the game if set to `true`) into the `BlasterMines` `runGameTimeBased` function. This is the new function that we will add to the `Game` base class. Here is an example of that function from the `Main.as` that will we will create for `BlasterMines`:

```
override public function systemGamePlay():void {
    game.runGameTimeBased(paused,timeDifference);

}
```

We will be creating this `runGameTime`-based function in the `Game` base class, and we will override it in each game that needs to implement this timer. The `runGameTimeBased` function in `BlasterMines.as` will look like the following:

```
override public function
runGameTimeBased(paused:Boolean=false,timeDifference:Number=1):void {
    if (!paused) {
        systemFunction(timeDifference);
    }
}
```

This function is part of the BlasterMines.as internal state machine. The systemFunction will reference the current state function. These functions must accept in the paused and timeDifference values. Here is an example of the BlasterMines.as systemGamePlay function. Notice that the pause functionality is applied in the previous runGameTimeBased function, so systemGamePlay will not be called if the paused value is true.

```
private function systemGamePlay(timeDifference:Number=0):void {
    update(timeDifference);
    checkCollisions();
    render();
    updateScoreBoard();
    checkforEndLevel();
    checkforEndGame();
}
```

The update function for Blaster Mines must accept in the `timeDifference` value. Here is a snippet of this function for demonstration:

```
private function update(timeDifference:Number = 0):void {

    //time based movement modifier calculation
    var step:Number = (timeDifference / 1000)*timeBasedUpdateModifier;
    trace("timeDifference= " + timeDifference);
    trace("timeDifference/1000=" + String (timeDifference / 1000));
    trace("timeBasedUpdateModifier=" + timeBasedUpdateModifier);
    trace("step=" + step);

    …
```

Here is where the real processing takes place. The timeDifference is passed into the update function, and then we calculate how this value will affect the step of each game character's movement. This step value is calculated using a variable called timeBasedUpdateModifier, which we will create in the Game.as base class. This variable is the number of slices we want the game to update per second. This is the same as the game's frame rate. This value will be assigned by the Main class based on the stage frame rate.

We calculate the local step variable by dividing the timeDifference by 1,000 (the number of milliseconds in a second) and multiplying this by the timeBasedUpdateModifier. This will be the step modifier for the movement of each game character.

For example, if the timeDifference is 20, meaning that it took 20 milliseconds to run the last frame, and we have an example frameRate of 40 (timeBasedUpdateModifier = 40), let's see what the step would be:

```
timeDifference= 20
timeDifference/1000=0.02
timeBasedUpdateModifier=40
step=0.8
```

The step is the percentage of the distance we want each of our game characters to move this frame tick. The calculated movement distance for each game character will be multiplied by this value. Here is an example of this calculation for the Mine enemy characters from Blaster Mines; it is in a class called Mine that we will create for the game:

```
public function update(step:Number=1):void {
    //trace("updateModifier=" + updateModifier);
    nextX+=dx*speed*step;
    nextY+=dy*speed*step;
```

As you can see in the code, the nextX and nextY values are calculated and then multiplied by the step value. This calculation allows us to modify the percentage of the distance moved based on the current frame rate. The complete code for all of these functions will be presented as we create the final Blaster Mines game.

Optimizing using render profiling

The FrameRateProfiler class we will create is used to profile the user's system to check if it can play the game at the desired frame rate.

Let's create this class as the first new file for the Blaster Mines game. It will be part of the game framework package structure.

Here is the class file name and location:

/source/classes/com/efg/framework/FrameRateProfiler.as

Here is the complete code for the FrameRateProfiler class. We will discuss it in detail after you have taken a look at all of the code:

```
package com.efg.framework
{
    import flash.display.*;
    import flash.events.*;
    import flash.utils.Timer;
```

```
import flash.geom.*;
import flash.events.*;
import flash.utils.getTimer;
import flash.text.*;
import flash.events.EventDispatcher;
/**
 * ...
 * @author Jeff Fulton
 */

public class FrameRateProfiler extends Sprite {

    public static const EVENT_COMPLETE:String = "profile complete";

    private var profileTimer:Timer;

    //public preperties
    public var profilerRenderObjects:int = 500;
    public var profilerRenderLoops:int = 10;
    public var profilerDisplayOnScreen:Boolean = false;
    public var profilerXLocation:int = 0;
    public var profilerYLocation:int = 0;

    public var profilerFrameRateAverage:int = 0;

    private var profilerFrameRate:int = 40;
    private var profilerRenderFrames:int = 0;

    private var profilerBackground:BitmapData = new BitmapData(400, 400, false, 0x000000);
    private var profilerCanvas:BitmapData = new BitmapData(400, 400, false, 0x000000);
    private var profilerBitmap:Bitmap = new Bitmap(profilerCanvas);

    private var profilerObject:BitmapData = new BitmapData(20, 20,false, 0xff0000);
    private var profilerFrameRateTotal:int=0;
    private var profilerFrameRateEventCounter:int = 0;
    private var profilerFrameCount:int = 0;
    private var profilerTempObject:Object;
    private var profilerObjectArray:Array = [];
    private var profilerRenderPoint:Point = new Point(0, 0);
    private var profilerFrameRateArray:Array= [];

    private var format:TextFormat=new TextFormat();
    private var messageTextField:TextField = new TextField();

    private var frameCounter:FrameCounter = new FrameCounter(); //added chapter 11

    public function FrameRateProfiler() {
        addChild(frameCounter);
        frameCounter.x = 0;
        frameCounter.y = 0;
    }

    public function startProfile(frameRate:int):void {
        trace("start profile");
        profilerFrameRate = frameRate;
```

```
    if (profilerDisplayOnScreen) {
        profilerBitmap.y = 20;
        profilerBitmap.x = 0;
    }else {
        profilerBitmap.x = stage.width + 10;
    }

    addChild(profilerBitmap);
    format.align = "center";
    format.size=24;
    format.font="Arial";
    format.color = 0xffffff
    format.bold = true;
    messageTextField.defaultTextFormat = format;
    messageTextField.text = "Profiling\nOptimal\nFrame Rate";

    messageTextField.width=200;
    messageTextField.height = 200;
    messageTextField.x = 100;
    messageTextField.y = 100;
    addChild(messageTextField);


    for (var ctr:int = 0; ctr < profilerRenderObjects; ctr ++) {
        profileAddObject()
    }
    profilerRenderFrames = profilerRenderLoops * profilerFrameRate;
    addEventListener(Event.ENTER_FRAME, runProfile);
}

private function runProfile(e:Event):void {
    profileUpdate();
    profileRender();

    if (frameCounter.countFrames()) {
        profilerFrameRateTotal += frameCounter.lastframecount;
        profilerFrameRateEventCounter++;

        messageTextField.text = "Profiling\nOptimal\nFrame Rate\n" + ↵
         String(int(profilerFrameCount / profilerRenderFrames * 100)) + "%";

        profilerFrameRateArray.push(frameCounter.lastframecount);
    }

    profilerFrameCount++;

  if (profilerFrameCount > profilerRenderFrames) {
      profileCalculate();
    }
}

private function profileCalculate():void {

    profilerFrameRateAverage = profilerFrameRateTotal / profilerFrameRateEventCounter;
    dispose();
```

```
        dispatchEvent(new Event(EVENT_COMPLETE));
    }


    private function profileAddObject():void {
        var profilerTempObject:Object = new Object();
        profilerTempObject.x=(Math.random() * 399);
        profilerTempObject.y=(Math.random() * 399);
        profilerTempObject.speed = (Math.random() * 5) + 1;

        profilerTempObject.dx=Math.cos(2.0*Math.PI*((Math.random()*360)-90)/360.0);
        profilerTempObject.dy = Math.sin(2.0 * Math.PI * ((Math.random()*360) - 90) ↵
            / 360.0);

        profilerObjectArray.push(profilerTempObject);
    }


    private function profileUpdate():void {

        for each (profilerTempObject in profilerObjectArray) {
            profilerTempObject.x += profilerTempObject.dx * profilerTempObject.speed;
            profilerTempObject.y += profilerTempObject.dy * profilerTempObject.speed;

            if (profilerTempObject.x > profilerCanvas.width) {
                profilerTempObject.x = 0;
            }else if (profilerTempObject.x < 0) {
                profilerTempObject.x = profilerCanvas.width;
            }

            if (profilerTempObject.y > profilerCanvas.height) {
                profilerTempObject.y = 0;
            }else if (profilerTempObject.y < 0) {
                profilerTempObject.y = profilerCanvas.height;
            }
        }
    }

    private function profileRender():void {
        profilerCanvas.lock();
        profilerRenderPoint.x = 0;
        profilerRenderPoint.y = 0;

        profilerCanvas.copyPixels(profilerBackground, profilerBackground.rect, ↵
            profilerRenderPoint);

        for each (profilerTempObject in profilerObjectArray) {
            profilerRenderPoint.x = profilerTempObject.x;
            profilerRenderPoint.y = profilerTempObject.y;
            profilerCanvas.copyPixels(profilerObject, profilerObject.rect, ↵
                profilerRenderPoint);
        }
```

```
            profilerCanvas.unlock();

        }


        public function dispose():void {

            removeEventListener(Event.ENTER_FRAME, runProfile);

            for (var ctr:int = 0; ctr < profilerObjectArray.length; ctr++) {
                profilerObjectArray[ctr] = null;
                profilerObjectArray.splice(1, 0);
            }

            removeChild(profilerBitmap);
            removeChild(messageTextField);
            profilerObjectArray = null;
            profilerBackground.dispose();
            profilerBackground = null;
            profilerCanvas.dispose();
            profilerBitmap = null;
            profileTimer = null;
            format = null;
            messageTextField = null;
            frameCounter = null;
        }
    }
}
```

Designing the FrameRateProfiler technical design

Let's first take a look at the variables and functions we need to define for our profiler.

These are the public variables:

- `public var profilerRenderObjects:int = 500;`: The number of objects to use in the profile
- `public var profilerRenderLoops:int = 10;`: The number of iterations to run the profile
- `public var profilerDisplayOnScreen:Boolean = false;`: Toggles the display of the render profiling on the screen
- `public var profilerXLocation:int = 0;`: Sets the upper left-hand corner x position for the profiler
- `public var profilerYLocation:int = 0;`: Sets the upper left-hand corner y position for the profiler
  This and the four previous variables can be set to custom values in the `Main.as` of the game before the profile is started. These values will be custom for each game you create.
- `public var profilerFrameRateAverage:int = 0;`: Holds the result of the profile when it is complete, that is, the average frame rate of the user's machine over the duration of the profile

These are the private variables:

- `private var profilerFrameRate:int = 40;`: The desired frame rate for the game
- `private var profilerRenderFrames:int = 0;`: The number of frames to run the profiler, calculated based on the passed in `profilerRenderLoops` value
- `private var profilerBackground:BitmapData = new BitmapData(400, 400, false, 0x000000);`: Background for the profiling screen
- `private var profilerCanvas:BitmapData = new BitmapData(400, 400, false, 0x000000);`: The `BitmapData` canvas to display objects for profiling
- `private var profilerBitmap:Bitmap = new Bitmap(profilerCanvas);`: Display object to show profiling
- `private var profilerObject:BitmapData = new BitmapData(20, 20,false, 0xff0000);`: The look (a square) for the profiled objects
- `private var profilerFrameRateTotal:int=0;`: The total of all frame rates collected in the profile session
- `private var profilerFrameRateEventCounter:int = 0;`: The number of profile events (An event is triggered each second.)
- `private var profilerFrameCount:int = 0;`: The total frames the profiler has run
- `private var profilerTempObject:Object;`: A temporary render object for the profiler render phase
- `private var profilerObjectArray:Array = [];`: An array of render profile objects
- `private var profilerRenderPoint:Point = new Point(0, 0);`: The shared point used to blit render objects to the screen
- `private var profilerFrameRateArray:Array = [];`: An array of frame rates calculated 1 per second
- `private var format:TextFormat = new TextFormat();`: The format for displayed text
- `private var messageTextField:TextField = new TextField();`: The text field for the render percentage text display
- `private var frameCounter:FrameCounter = new FrameCounter();`: A `FrameCounter` instance (a new custom class)

These are the public functions:

- `public function FrameRateProfiler()`: The constructor takes in no parameters. It adds an instance of the `FrameCounter` class that we will create in the next section. It also positions it on the screen.

```
addChild(frameCounter);
frameCounter.x = 0;
frameCounter.y = 0;
```

- public function startProfile(frameRate:int):void: This function requires that the needed frameRate be passed in. The profiler will use this value to evaluate ability of the user's machine to run at that frame rate. This function sets up the text and location for the profile and then starts the profile. There are five very important lines at the end of the function:

```
for (var ctr:int = 0; ctr < profilerRenderObjects; ctr ++) {
   profileAddObject()
}
```

Here we are creating the actual objects to render to the screen based on the preset profilerRenderObjects value.

- profilerRenderFrames = profilerRenderLoops * profilerFrameRate;: Here, we are calculating the number of frames we want the profile to run. This is based on the number of profile iterations we want to run and the frame rate we want to run them at.
- addEventListener(Event.ENTER_FRAME, runProfile);: The profile is started with the ENTER_FRAME event and will call the runProfile function on each iteration. It will run for profileRenderLoops number of iterations.

These are the private functions:

- private function runProfile(e:Event): This function is the game loop for the profiler. Its job it to calculate the frame rate for each set of render loops and store that data for analysis after the profile has completed.

```
if (frameCounter.countFrames()) {
   profilerFrameRateTotal += frameCounter.lastframecount;
   profilerFrameRateEventCounter++;
   messageTextField.text = "Profiling\nOptimal\nFrame Rate\n" + 
   String(int(profilerFrameCount / profilerRenderFrames * 100)) + "%";

   profilerFrameRateArray.push(frameCounter.lastframecount);
}
```

When the frameCounter returns a true in the if conditional, 1,000 milliseconds have passed since the last frame rate event. A frame rate event is simply a call to calculate the current frame rate once 1,000 milliseconds have passed. It is not an actual Event instance but rather our made up term to signify when a single second of processing has been completed. Since we don't know exactly how the system will perform under the profile, we cannot assume that the number of loops desired for the test will actually be the number run. We don't know how the system will actually perform under the stress of the test. For this reason, we keep our own count of events using the profilerFrameRateEventCounter. We add the frameCounter's last calculated frame rate to the total, profilerFrameRateTotal, and we update the on-screen text for the profile. Each frame rate is also placed in the profilerFrameRateArray array to be used in the adjusted average. See Figure 11-2.

- `private function profileCalculate():void`: Once the profiling is complete, we must calculate the average frame rate, making sure to use the actual number of frame rate events. We then call `dispose` and dispatch an event that `Main` will listen for so it can jump to the next framework state.

```
profilerFrameRateAverage = profilerFrameRateTotal / profilerFrameRateEventCounter;
dispose();
dispatchEvent(new Event(EVENT_COMPLETE));
```

- `private function profileAddObject():void`: This function adds objects for profiling. It is only used internally by the profile system.
- `private function profileUpdate():void`: This internal function is used in profiling the system. This updates the positions of the profile objects.
- `private function profileRender():void`: This blits the profile objects to the canvas when profiling is running.
- `public function dispose():void`: This is used to dispose of objects used in profiling to free up memory.

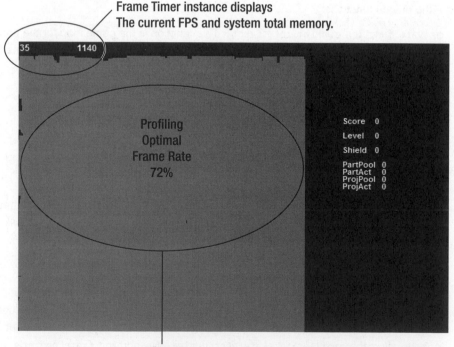

Frame Timer instance displays
The current FPS and system total memory.

If SBP display is set to true, the profiling will be shown to the user. The mass of red is actually 4000 blitted objects.

Figure 11-2. The render profiler in action

Monitoring frame rate and memory usage

There are two relatively simple tools we can use to examine the health of a game running in Flash. The first is to view the current frame rate the system is running under, and the second is to view changes in the total memory used by the system. Optimizations you have seen throughout the book and in this chapter will affect both of these numbers. We will now create a simple class that you can display on the screen (if you like) to show the current state of these two important metrics.

The FrameCounter class is used by the FrameRateProfiler to do execute frame rate events for profiling. A frame rate event is triggered every 1,000 milliseconds (1 second). We also have the ability to also add a FrameCounter on the screen while the game is running. It displays the profiled frame rate, the current frame rate, and the current memory used by the system. Figure 11-3 shows it in action.

Let's create this class as the next new file for the Blaster Mines game. It will be part of the game framework package structure.

Here is the class file name and location:

/source/classes/com/efg/framework/FrameCounter.as

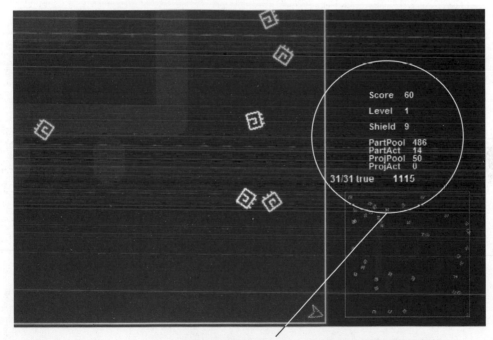

Under the ScoreBoard we have placed the FrameTimer instance. The current frame rate is 31 the desired frame rate is 31. The true means that updateAfterEvent is on. 1115 pages of 4096 memory is being consumed.

Figure 11-3. The FrameCounter class in action

493

The FrameCounter class also displays the current system memory used by the game and the Flash Player.

Here is the complete code for the FrameCounter class. We will discuss it in detail after you have taken a look at all of the code:

```
/**
 * ...
 * @author Jeff Fulton
 * @version 0.1
 */

package com.efg.framework {
    import flash.display.*;
    import flash.events.*;
    import flash.system.System;
    import flash.utils.getTimer;
    import flash.text.TextField;
    import flash.text.TextFormat;

    public class FrameCounter extends Sprite{
        private var format:TextFormat=new TextFormat();
        private var framectrText:String;
        private var textColor:uint = 0xffffff;
        private var memoryUsedText:String;
        private var framectrTextField:TextField = new TextField();
        private var memoryUsed:TextField = new TextField();
        public var lastframecount:int = 0;
        private var frameLast:int = getTimer();
        private var frameCtr:int = 0;
        public var showProfiledRate:Boolean = false;
        public var profiledRate:int;

        public function FrameCounter():void {

            format.size=12;
            format.font="Arial";
            format.color = String(textColor);
            format.bold = true;

            framectrText="0";
            framectrTextField.text=framectrText;
            framectrTextField.defaultTextFormat = format;
            framectrTextField.width=80;
            framectrTextField.height = 20;
            addChild(framectrTextField);

            memoryUsedText = "0";
            memoryUsed.text=memoryUsedText;
            memoryUsed.defaultTextFormat = format;
            memoryUsed.width=100;
            memoryUsed.height = 20;
            memoryUsed.x = 80;
```

```
        addChild(memoryUsed);

    }

    public function setTextColor(color:uint):void {
        format.color = String(color);
    }

    public function countFrames():Boolean {

        frameCtr++;
        if (getTimer() >= frameLast + 1000) {
            lastframecount = frameCtr;
            if (showProfiledRate) {
                framectrText = frameCtr.toString() + "/" + profiledRate;
            }else{
                framectrText = frameCtr.toString();
            }

            framectrTextField.text =framectrText;
            frameCtr = 0;
            frameLast = getTimer();

            memoryUsedText = String(System.totalMemory / 1024);
            trace(memoryUsedText);
            memoryUsed.text=memoryUsedText+"kb";
            return(true);
        }else {
            return(false);
        }
    }
    } // end class

} // end package
```

Let's take a look at the technical specification for the FrameCounter class, starting with the public variables:

- public var lastframecount:int: This variable holds the frame count for the most recent completed 1,000-millisecond event.
- public var showProfiledRate:Boolean: This Boolean is set outside, in Main, to determine whether or not to show the frame rate as **current/profiled** if true. If false, it will just show the current rate.
- public var profiledRate:int: This one holds the rate-profiled frame rate if it needs to be displayed.

The private variables come next:

- private var format:TextFormat: The format for text display
- private var framectrText:String: The String representing the current frame count value

- `private var memoryUsedText:String`: The `String` representing the current memory used value
- `private var framectrTextField:TextField`: The field to display the `framectrText` `String`
- `private var memorypagesField:TextField`: The field to display the `memorypagesText` `String`
- `private var frameLast:int`: Contains the `getTimer` milliseconds of the last count event
- `private var frameCtr:int`: Counts the number of frames that occur between 1,000-millisecond events

These are the public functions:

- `public function FrameTimer():void`: The constructor takes in no parameters. Its function is to set up the text fields for displaying the frame rate counter and memory usage indicator.
- `public function countFrames():Boolean`: The `countFrames` function doesn't take in any parameters, but it returns `true` if 1,000 milliseconds have passed since the last frame count event. For the `FrameCounter` to work properly, `countFrames` needs to be called at the end of each game timer, in `Main` or in the `FrameRateProfiler` (or in any class you created that needs the FPS monitored).

   The entire contents of the function are surrounded by a conditional that checks to see if 1,000 milliseconds (1 second) have passed since that last frame count event.

```
if (getTimer() >= frameLast + 1000) {
   ... do all of the frame count event code
   return(true);
}else {
   frameCtr++;
   return(false);
}
```

If 1,000 milliseconds have not passed since the last frame count event, we simply add 1 to the frameCtr variable.

What happens when there is a frame count event? This not an actual `Event` in the ActionScript context but just our name for each time a single second has passed. This event occurs when 1,000 milliseconds, or 1 second, has passed since the last frame count event.

Inside this event we want to display the number of frames that have been counted in the last second (frameCtr) and provide that information to the world outside the class in the lastframecount variable.

We also want to display the current amount of memory used and reset the counters for the next frame count event.

```
if (showProfiledRate) {
   framectrText = frameCtr.toString() + "/" + profiledRate;
}else{

   framectrText = frameCtr.toString();
}
```

```
framectrTextField.text =framectrText;
frameCtr = 0;
frameLast = getTimer();

memoryUsedText = String(System.totalMemory / 1024);
trace(memoryUsedText);
memoryUsed.text=memoryUsedText+"kb";

return(true);
```

That's the full extent of the functionality for this class. Now, let's move on to the changes necessary in the com.efg.framework.Game.as class file.

Changing the game class

Several changes are needed to the Game.as base class to support the functionality we are adding in this chapter. Let's take a quick look at all of them now.

Here is the entire com.efg.framework.Game.as class:

```
package  com.efg.framework
{

    // Import necessary classes from the flash libraries
    import flash.display.MovieClip;
    import com.efg.framework.CustomEventScoreBoardUpdate;
    import com.efg.framework.CustomEventLevelScreenUpdate;

    /**
    * ...
    * @author Jeff Fulton and Jeff Fulton
    */

    public class Game extends MovieClip {

        //Create constants for simple custom events
        public static const GAME_OVER:String = "game over";
        public static const NEW_LEVEL:String = "new level";

        public var timeBasedUpdateModifier:Number = 40;
        public var frameRateMultiplier:Number = 1;

        //Constructor calls init() only
        public function Game() {}

        public function setRendering(profiledRate:int, framerate:int):void {}

        public function newGame():void {}

        public function newLevel():void {}

        public function runGame():void {}
```

497

```
        public function runGameTimeBased(paused:Boolean=false,timeDifference:Number=1):void {}

    }
}
```

We added these two public variables:

```
    public var timeBasedUpdateModifier:Number = 40;
    public var frameRateMultiplier:Number = 1;
```

The `timeBasedUpdateModifier` was discussed in the section called "Adding the time-based step timer." It is the number of timer ticks we want the game to run at per second. It is the desired frame rate of the game, but we don't call it frame rate, so it will not be confused with the actual frame rate from the `FrameCounter` class.

The `frameRateMultiplier` variable has been added to allow the game designer to make use of the profiled frame rate. For example, in Blaster Mines, if the profiled frame rate is 85 percent of the desired frame rate then this multiplier is set to 2. This doubles the particles used in explosions.

These are the new public functions:

```
    public function setRendering(profiledRate:int, framerate:int):void {}
```

```
    public function runGameTimeBased(paused:Boolean=false,timeDifference:Number=1):void {}
```

The `setRendering` function is used to set the `frameRateMultiplier` variable. It takes in the `profiledRate` and the `frameRate` desired for the game. By overriding this function the developer will use this information in a custom manner to set the game quality. Blaster Mines contains a good example of this that we will see when we take a look at the game code in detail.

The `runGameTimeBased` function was discussed in the "Adding the time-based step timer" section. It accepts in the paused value from `Main` along with the `timeDifference` from the `GameFrameWork`'s `runGameEnterFrame` function.

Getting Started with the Blaster Mines Project

As with all of the games in this book, Blaster Mines will use the framework package structure we created in Chapter 2. Let's begin by creating the package necessary for our game in both the Flash IDE and Flash Develop (for use with the Flex SDK).

Creating the Blaster Mines game project in the Flash IDE

Here are the steps needed to create the game in the Flash IDE

1. Start up your version of Flash. We are using CS3, but this process should work exactly the same in CS4 and CS5.

2. Create a `.fla` file in the `/source/projects/blastermines/flashIDE/` folder called `blastermines`.

3. In the `/source/projects/blastermines/flashIDE/` folder, create the package structure for your game: `/com/efg/games/blastermines/`.

4. Set the frame rate of the Flash movie to 40 FPS. Set the width to **600** and the height to **400**.

5. Set the document class to `com.efg.games.blastermines.Main`.

6. We have not yet created the `Main.as` class, so you will see a warning. We are going to create this later in this chapter.

7. Next, add the framework's reusable class package to the class path for the `.fla` file. First, in the **Publish** settings, select **Flash ➤ ActionScript 3** in the **ActionScript Version** drop-down, and then click the **Settings** button

8. After that, click the **Browse to Path** button, and find the `/source` folder we created in Chapter 2 for the package structure.

9. Finally, select the `classes` folder, and click the **Choose** button. Now, the `com.efg.` framework package will be available for use when we begin to create our game.

Here is the folder structure for the Flash IDE version:

```
[source]
    [projects]
        [blastermines]
            [flexIDE]
                [com]
                    [efg]
                        [games]
                            [blastermines]
```

Creating the Blaster Mines game project in Flash Develop

Follow these steps to create the Blaster Mines game in Flash Develop:

1. Create a folder inside the `/source/projects/blastermines/` folder called `flexSDK` (if you have not already done so).

2. Start Flash Develop, and create a new project. Begin by selecting **Flex 3 Project** and giving the project the name **blastermines**. The location should be the `/source/projects/blastermines/flexSDK` folder, and the package should be `com.efg.games.blastermines`.

    Do not have Flash Develop create a project folder automatically. Make sure the **Create Folder For Project** is *unchecked*.

    Click the **OK** button to create the project.

3. Add the class path to the framework to the project by selecting the **Project ➤ Properties ➤ Classpaths** menu item and clicking the **Add Class Path** button.

4. Next, find the `/source` we created earlier, and select the `classes` subfolder.

5. Click the **OK** button and then the **Apply** button.

6. Change the size of the output and frame rate by selecting the **Project** ➤ **Properties** ➤ **Classpaths** menu item. Set the Frame Rate to **40**, the width to **600**, and the height to **400**.

Here is the folder structure for the Flex SDK version (made with Flash Develop).

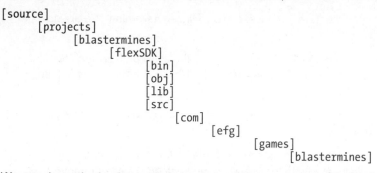

```
[source]
    [projects]
        [blastermines]
            [flexSDK]
                [bin]
                [obj]
                [lib]
                [src]
                    [com]
                        [efg]
                            [games]
                                [blastermines]
```

We now have the basic structure to start creating projects inside the framework, so we are going to discuss a few topics concerning the structure of the framework classes and then move into building the reusable framework code.

> *For Flex Builder, Flash Builder, or another IDE, please refer to the documentation provided for that product to create a new project and set the default compile class.*
>
> *As mentioned previously, a common method of Flash development is to use the Flash IDE for assets and organization and Flash Develop for code editing. If this is your workflow of choice, you will want to follow the Flash IDE folder and package structure rather than the Flex SDK folder structure.*

Creating the Main.as class for Blaster Mines

As with each game covered so far we must create a unique `Main.as` class for Blaster Mines. It will be based on the `Main.as` from Chapter 10, but there are many changes specific to Blaster Mines and many changes specific to the game framework.

Let's create this class as the next new file for the Blaster Mines game package. Here is the class file name and location for the Flash IDE:

/source/projects/blastermines/flashIDE/com/efg/games/blastermines/Main.as

And this is for the Flex SDK (using Flash Develop):

/source/projects/blastermines/flexSDK/src/com/efg/games/blastermines/Main.as

Here is the entire `Main.as` class. Well look at the changes after you have taken a look at all of the code for the class:

```
package com.efg.games.blastermines
{

    import com.efg.framework.FrameCounter;
    import com.efg.framework.FrameRateProfiler;
    import com.efg.framework.GameFrameWorkAdvancedTimer;
    import flash.text.TextFormat;
```

```
import flash.text.TextField;
import flash.text.TextFormatAlign;
import flash.geom.Point;
import flash.events.Event;

import com.efg.framework.FrameWorkStates;
import com.efg.framework.GameFrameWork;
import com.efg.framework.BasicScreen;
import com.efg.framework.ScoreBoard;
import com.efg.framework.SideBySideScoreElement;
import com.efg.framework.SoundManager;

public class Main extends GameFrameWork {

    //custom sccore board elements
    public static const SCORE_BOARD_SCORE:String = "score";
    public static const SCORE_BOARD_LEVEL:String = "level";
    public static const SCORE_BOARD_SHIELD:String = "shield";
    public static const SCORE_BOARD_PARTICLE_POOL:String = "particlepool";
    public static const SCORE_BOARD_PARTICLE_ACTIVE:String = "particleactive";
    public static const SCORE_BOARD_PROJECTILE_POOL:String = "projectilepool";
    public static const SCORE_BOARD_PROJECTILE_ACTIVE:String = "projectileactive";

    //custom sounds
    public static const SOUND_MINE_EXPLODE:String="SoundMineExplode";
    public static const SOUND_MUSIC_IN_GAME:String="SoundMusicInGame";
    public static const SOUND_MUSIC_TITLE:String="SoundMusicTitle";
    public static const SOUND_PLAYER_ENTER:String = "SoundPlayerEnter";
    public static const SOUND_PLAYER_EXPLODE:String="SoundPlayerExplode";
    public static const SOUND_PLAYER_HIT:String="SoundPlayerHit";
    public static const SOUND_PLAYER_SHOOT:String = "SoundPlayerShoot";
    // Our construction only calls

    public function Main() {

        //added in chapter 11
        if (stage) addedToStage();
        else addEventListener(Event.ADDED_TO_STAGE, addedToStage,false,0,true);
    }

    //function added in chapter 11
        override public function addedToStage(e:Event = null):void {
        if (e != null) {
            removeEventListener(Event.ADDED_TO_STAGE, addedToStage);
        }
        super.addedToStage();
        trace("in blastermines added to stage");
        init();
    }

    // init() is used to set up all of the things that we should only need to do one time

    override public function init():void {
        trace("init");
        game= new BlasterMines();
```

```
setApplicationBackGround(600, 400, false, 0x000000);

//add score board to the screen as the second layer
scoreBoard = new ScoreBoard();
addChild(scoreBoard);
scoreBoardTextFormat = new TextFormat("_sans", "11", "0xffffff", "true");

scoreBoard.createTextElement(SCORE_BOARD_SCORE, new SideBySideScoreElement(450,↵
    100, 20, "Score", scoreBoardTextFormat, 25, "0", scoreBoardTextFormat));

scoreBoard.createTextElement(SCORE_BOARD_LEVEL, new SideBySideScoreElement(450,↵
    120, 20, "Level", scoreBoardTextFormat, 25, "0", scoreBoardTextFormat));

scoreBoard.createTextElement(SCORE_BOARD_SHIELD, new SideBySideScoreElement(450,↵
    140, 20, "Shield", scoreBoardTextFormat, 25, "0", scoreBoardTextFormat));

scoreBoard.createTextElement(SCORE_BOARD_PARTICLE_POOL, new ↵
    SideBySideScoreElement(450, 160, 20, "PartPool", scoreBoardTextFormat, ↵
    50, "0", scoreBoardTextFormat));

scoreBoard.createTextElement(SCORE_BOARD_PARTICLE_ACTIVE, new ↵
    SideBySideScoreElement(450, 170, 20, "PartActive", scoreBoardTextFormat, ↵
    50, "0", scoreBoardTextFormat));

scoreBoard.createTextElement(SCORE_BOARD_PROJECTILE_POOL, new `CCC
    SideBySideScoreElement(450, 180, 20, "ProjPool", scoreBoardTextFormat, ↵
    50, "0", scoreBoardTextFormat));

scoreBoard.createTextElement(SCORE_BOARD_PROJECTILE_ACTIVE, new ↵
    SideBySideScoreElement(450, 190, 20, "ProjActive", scoreBoardTextFormat, ↵
    50, "0", scoreBoardTextFormat));


//screen text initializations
screenTextFormat = new TextFormat("_sans", "16", "0xffffff", "false");
screenTextFormat.align = flash.text.TextFormatAlign.CENTER;
screenButtonFormat = new TextFormat("_sans", "12", "0x000000", "false");

titleScreen = new BasicScreen(FrameWorkStates.STATE_SYSTEM_TITLE,400,400,↵
    false,0x000000 );

titleScreen.createOkButton("Play", new Point(150, 250), 100, 20, ↵
    screenButtonFormat, 0x000000, 0xff0000,2);

titleScreen.createDisplayText("Blaster Mines", 200, new Point(100, 150), ↵
    screenTextFormat);

instructionsScreen = new BasicScreen(FrameWorkStates.STATE_SYSTEM_INSTRUCTIONS,↵
    400,400,false,0x000000);

instructionsScreen.createOkButton("Start", new Point(150, 250), 100, 20,↵
    screenButtonFormat, 0x000000, 0xff0000,2);
```

```
instructionsScreen.createDisplayText("Shoot everything\nDon't get hit.",↵
    200,new Point(100,150),screenTextFormat);

gameOverScreen = new BasicScreen(FrameWorkStates.STATE_SYSTEM_GAME_OVER,↵
    400,400,false,0x0000dd);

gameOverScreen.createOkButton("Restart", new Point(150, 250), 100, 20,↵
    screenButtonFormat, 0x000000, 0xff0000,2);

gameOverScreen.createDisplayText("Game Over",100,new Point(150,150),↵
    screenTextFormat);

levelInScreen = new BasicScreen(FrameWorkStates.STATE_SYSTEM_LEVEL_IN, ↵
    400, 400, true, 0xbbff00ff);

levelInText = "Level ";

levelInScreen.createDisplayText(levelInText,100,new Point(150,150),↵
    screenTextFormat);

pausedScreen = new BasicScreen(FrameWorkStates.STATE_SYSTEM_PAUSE,400,400,↵
    false,0xff000000 );

pausedScreen.createOkButton("UNPAUSE", new Point(150, 250), 100, 20, ↵
    screenButtonFormat, 0x000000, 0xff0000,2);

pausedScreen.createDisplayText("Paused", 200, new Point(100, 150), ↵
    screenTextFormat);

//set initial game state
switchSystemState(FrameWorkStates.STATE_SYSTEM_TITLE);


//sounds
//*** Flex SDK

soundManager.addSound(SOUND_MINE_EXPLODE,new Library.SoundMineExplode);
soundManager.addSound(SOUND_MUSIC_IN_GAME, new Library.SoundMusicInGame);
soundManager.addSound(SOUND_MUSIC_TITLE,new Library.SoundMusicTitle);
soundManager.addSound(SOUND_PLAYER_ENTER,new Library.SoundPlayerEnter);
soundManager.addSound(SOUND_PLAYER_EXPLODE,new Library.SoundPlayerExplode);
soundManager.addSound(SOUND_PLAYER_HIT,new Library.SoundPlayerHit);
soundManager.addSound(SOUND_PLAYER_SHOOT,new Library.SoundPlayerShoot);

//flash IDE
//soundManager.addSound(SOUND_MINE_EXPLODE,new SoundMineExplode);
//soundManager.addSound(SOUND_MUSIC_IN_GAME, new SoundMusicInGame);
//soundManager.addSound(SOUND_MUSIC_TITLE,new SoundMusicTitle);
//soundManager.addSound(SOUND_PLAYER_ENTER,new SoundPlayerEnter);
//soundManager.addSound(SOUND_PLAYER_EXPLODE,new SoundPlayerExplode);
//soundManager.addSound(SOUND_PLAYER_HIT,new SoundPlayerHit);
//soundManager.addSound(SOUND_PLAYER_SHOOT,new SoundSkullHit);

//framerate profiler
frameRate = 40;
```

```
            frameRateProfiler = new FrameRateProfiler();
            frameRateProfiler.profilerRenderObjects = 4000;
            frameRateProfiler.profilerRenderLoops = 7;
            frameRateProfiler.profilerDisplayOnScreen= true;
            frameRateProfiler.profilerXLocation = 0;
            frameRateProfiler.profilerYLocation = 0;
            addChild(frameRateProfiler);
            frameRateProfiler.startProfile(frameRate);

            frameRateProfiler.addEventListener(FrameRateProfiler.EVENT_COMPLETE, ↩
                frameRateProfileComplete, false, 0, true);
        }

    override public function frameRateProfileComplete(e:Event):void {
        trace("profiledFrameRate=" + frameRateProfiler.profilerFrameRateAverage);
        game.setRendering(frameRateProfiler.profilerFrameRateAverage, frameRate);
        game.timeBasedUpdateModifier = frameRate;

        removeEventListener(FrameRateProfiler.EVENT_COMPLETE, frameRateProfileComplete) ;
        removeChild(frameRateProfiler);

        //frame counter
        frameCounter.x = 400;
        frameCounter.y = 200;
        frameCounter.profiledRate = frameRateProfiler.profilerFrameRateAverage;
        frameCounter.showProfiledRate = true;
        addChild(frameCounter);

        startTimer(true);
    }


    override public function systemGamePlay():void {
        game.runGameTimeBased(paused,timeDifference);
    }

    override public function systemTitle():void {
        soundManager.playSound(SOUND_MUSIC_TITLE, true,999, 20, 1);
        super.systemTitle();
    }

    override public function systemNewGame():void {
        trace("new game");
        soundManager.stopSound(SOUND_MUSIC_TITLE,true);
        super.systemNewGame();
    }

    override public function systemLevelIn():void {
        levelInScreen.alpha = 1;
        super.systemLevelIn();
    }

    override public function systemWait():void {
        //trace("system Level In");
        if (lastSystemState == FrameWorkStates.STATE_SYSTEM_LEVEL_IN) {
```

```
            levelInScreen.alpha -= .01;
            if (levelInScreen.alpha < 0 ) {
                dispatchEvent(new Event(EVENT_WAIT_COMPLETE));
                levelInScreen.alpha = 0;
            }
        }
    }
  }
}
```

We have made many changes to the Main.as class for Blaster Mines. The screen and sounds are pretty straightforward and very much like the changes we have made for all of the previous games. We will spend little time on those and focus on the changes needed to add in the pause, mute, time-based step timer, FrameRateProfiler, and FrameCounter functionality.

We'll need the following basic screens:

- **Title screen**: Contains a Play button and the text **Blaster Mines**
- **Instructions screen**: Contains a Start button and the text **Shoot everything. Don't get hit. . .**
- **Game-over screen**: Contains the text **Game Over** and a **Restart** button

And we also need these instances of the BasicScreen class:

- **Level-in screen**: Contains only the text **Level** plus the level variable
- **Paused screen**: Contains text such as **Paused** and a button to click to unpause the system

These are the modifications we need to make to the ScoreBoard class:

- Score indicator
- Level indicator
- Shield indicator
- Particle pool indicators
- Projectile pool indicators

We also need several new constants in the variable definition section for the new scoreBoard elements and sounds. These are added to the variable definition section:

```
//custom sccore board elements
public static const SCORE_BOARD_SCORE:String = "score";
public static const SCORE_BOARD_LEVEL:String = "level";
public static const SCORE_BOARD_SHIELD:String = "shield";
public static const SCORE_BOARD_PARTICLE_POOL:String = "particlepool";
public static const SCORE_BOARD_PARTICLE_ACTIVE:String = "particleactive";
public static const SCORE_BOARD_PROJECTILE_POOL:String = "projectilepool";
public static const SCORE_BOARD_PROJECTILE_ACTIVE:String = "projectileactive";


//custom sounds
public static const SOUND_MINE_EXPLODE:String="SoundMineExplode";
public static const SOUND_MUSIC_IN_GAME:String="SoundMusicInGame";
public static const SOUND_MUSIC_TITLE:String="SoundMusicTitle";
public static const SOUND_PLAYER_ENTER:String = "SoundPlayerEnter";
public static const SOUND_PLAYER_EXPLODE:String="SoundPlayerExplode";
public static const SOUND_PLAYER_HIT:String="SoundPlayerHit";
public static const SOUND_PLAYER_SHOOT:String = "SoundPlayerShoot";
```

Implementing the pause and mute functionality

We have discussed the pause and mute functions previously, but in the Main.as class, we now must change the init function and add in an override of the addedToStage functionality. These are necessary so we can add key listeners for the pause and mute functionality after we know the Flash stage is available. One note, you will need to add the line

```
public static const STATE_SYSTEM_PAUSE:int = 99;
```

to the com.efg.framework.FrameWorkStates.as file if you have not already done so.

Adding the new constructor function

We will replace the current constructor function in the Main.as with this one.

```
public function Main() {
    //added in chapter 11
    if (stage) addedToStage();
    else addEventListener(Event.ADDED_TO_STAGE, addedToStage,false,0,true);
}
```

The new constructor sets up a listener to wait until the stage is available. When it is available (or if it is already available when the constructor is first run), the addedToStage function is called.

Adding the addedToStage function

This function will override the GameFrameWork.as version of the addedToStage function and then call it with super:

```
override public function addedToStage(e:Event = null):void {
    if (e != null) {
        removeEventListener(Event.ADDED_TO_STAGE, addedToStage);
    }
    super.addedToStage();
    trace("in blastermines added to stage");
    init();
}
```

The main purpose of this function is to add references to the stage object only after it is available to the SWF file. We call the GameFrameWork class's addedToStage function with the super.addedToStatge call and call the init function for our game.

Notice that we have moved the call to the init function to the end of the addedToStage function. This ensures that we don't try to initialize the game until the GameFrameWork's addedStage function has been called.

Next, we need to add in the pausedScreen. This instance of the BasicScreen framework class is created in the GameFrameWork.as file, but it is instantiated in Main to allow color and size customizations. You can also use addChild to add any custom elements that you feel you need to this screen; it does not have to be just a plain screen with a background color, a button, and a little text. This advice actually goes for all of the BasicScreen instances.

```
pausedScreen = new
BasicScreen(FrameWorkStates.STATE_SYSTEM_PAUSE,400,400,false,0xff000000 );
pausedScreen.createOkButton("UNPAUSE", new Point(150, 250), 100, 20, screenButtonFormat, ↵
    0x000000, 0xff0000,2);
pausedScreen.createDisplayText("Paused", 200, new Point(100, 150), screenTextFormat);
```

The pause functionality requires that the paused variable of the GameFrameWork class be passed into the Game class instance. Let's take a look at what is necessary to add in functionality for the time-based step timer and see how this functions.

Implementing the time-based step timer for Blaster Mines

We need to override the systemGamePlay function to pass both the paused and the timeDifference variables into the Game class:

```
override public function systemGamePlay():void {
    game.runGameTimeBased(paused,timeDifference);
}
```

As we have discussed previously, the Game base class will be modified to add a function called runGameTimeBased. This function will act on these two variables.

Also, the startTimer function call has been moved to a new function called frameRateProfileComplete. Let's start our discussion of implementing the FrameRateProfiler next.

Customizing FrameRateProfiler for Blaster Mines

We need to add some new code in the init function to customize the FrameRateProfiler for the current game. These alterations are somewhat subjective and will change based on the game you are creating and the system you are creating them on. First, we'll look at the lines of code, and then we will examine the theory behind their use:

```
frameRate = 40;

frameRateProfiler = new FrameRateProfiler();
frameRateProfiler.profilerRenderObjects = 4000;
frameRateProfiler.profilerRenderLoops = 7;
frameRateProfiler.profilerDisplayOnScreen= true;
frameRateProfiler.profilerXLocation = 0;
frameRateProfiler.profilerYLocation = 0;
```

First, we set the desired frameRate value for our game. This should match or be below the frame rate setting you have place in the publish options for your SWF. The profileRenderObjects value is the most important setting we have for the FrameRateProfiler. We will need to experiment with this number just a small amount to see how it affects the render profile. The reason for this experimentation is that each machine and plug-in version combination will end up with a different FrameRateProfiler result. For this reason, you will need to base the number of objects to profile on your own machine or machines available to you. You will need to calibrate the profiler for your own development environment.

How do we calibrate the profileRenderObjects value? For example, if we want the game to play to at 40 FPS, we will need to set the number of objects in the profile to an arbitrary number (let's say 4,000) and then run the profile and the game. If the profiled frame rate comes out to be 35, but when we play the game our machine keeps the frame rate at 40, we will need to use less objects in my profile. This indicated that the number of objects in the profile was too high. We overtaxed the profiler in a way that was not representative of our gameplay. You might want to play the game multiple times and note to frame rate during play. The goal is to have the profiled rate and the rate the game runs on your machine match. This calibration is necessary to ensure that the number of objects in the profile is a good indication of how the various users' machines will play your game.

The time-based step timer will keep the game objects running at the same speed across all machines. We will also use the profiled rate and pass it into the setRendering function of the Game class. This will allow us to add or subtract game effects based on the profile of the user's machine.

The final three lines for the FrameRateProfiler add it to the stage display list, start it up, and add a listener for when it is complete.

```
addChild(frameRateProfiler);
frameRateProfiler.startProfile(frameRate);

frameRateProfiler.addEventListener(FrameRateProfiler.EVENT_COMPLETE, ↵
    frameRateProfileComplete, false, 0, true);
```

When the profile is complete the frameRateProfileComplete function is called. Let's take a look at this function now.

Creating the frameRateProfileComplete function

When the FrameRateProfiler has completed its work, the frameRateProfileComplete function is called. Let's take a line-by-line look at how it does its work and what it accomplishes.

When the profile is complete, the first thing we do is call the new function called setRendering that we added to the Game class. We pass in the profilerAverageFrameRate and the actual frameRate we desire for the game. We can use these two values and set customized options for game effects quality if needed. We will do this in the Blaster Mines game.

```
game.setRendering(frameRateProfiler.profilerFrameRateAverage, frameRate);
game.timeBasedUpdateModifier = frameRate;
```

In these two lines, we are simple removing the FrameRateProfiler from the screen and removing the event listener:

```
removeEventListener(FrameRateProfiler.EVENT_COMPLETE, frameRateProfileComplete) ;
removeChild(frameRateProfiler);
```

These five lines add the optional FrameCounter instance to the stage:

```
//frame counter
frameCounter.x = 400;
frameCounter.y = 200;
frameCounter.profiledRate = frameRateProfiler.profilerFrameRateAverage;
frameCounter.showProfiledRate = true;
addChild(frameCounter);
```

Finally, we start the game timer. By passing in true, we will use the new time-based step timer rather than the original game timer we created in Chapter 2:

```
startTimer(true);
```

Creating the Library.as class

The Library.as class file is only necessary for those using the Flex SDK framework. It is not used for Flash IDE projects. The changes to the library concern adding the sounds as static const assets rather than having them inside an exported SWF from the IDE. By doing this, we free the game from needing the IDE at all. The one drawback to decoupling the game and IDE is the inability of the Flex framework to import .wav files. By using .mp3 files, we mitigate this limitation but with the added headache of trying to avoid the space of silence at the beginning of the .mp3 file. We will use the offset setting when we play sounds to bypass this silent space. We went over this limitation in more detail in Chapter 10 when we also added the Drive She Said sounds to the library as MP3 files.

> Note that if you are using the Flash IDE, you will need to import all of the .mp3 sounds and create linkage names that match the class names listed in the Library class.

Let's create this class as the next new file for the Blaster Mines game package. Here is the class file name and location.

And this is for the Flex SDK (using Flash Develop):

/source/projects/blastermines/flexSDK/src/com/efg/games/blastermines/Library.as

Here is the entire Library.as class; we'll look at the changes after you have taken a look at all of the code for this class:

```
package com.efg.games.blastermines
{
    public class Library {

        [Embed(source='../../../../../assets/mineExplode.mp3')]
        public static const SoundMineExplode:Class;

        [Embed(source = '../../../../../assets/musicIngame.mp3')]
        public static const SoundMusicInGame:Class;

        [Embed(source='../../../../../assets/musicTitle.mp3')]
        public static const SoundMusicTitle:Class;

        [Embed(source='../../../../../assets/playerEnter.mp3')]
        public static const SoundPlayerEnter:Class;

        [Embed(source='../../../../../assets/playerExplode.mp3')]
        public static const SoundPlayerExplode:Class;

        [Embed(source='../../../../../assets/playerHit.mp3')]
        public static const SoundPlayerHit:Class;

        [Embed(source='../../../../../assets/playerShoot.mp3')]
        public static const SoundPlayerShoot:Class;
    }
}
```

Notice that, just like all of the library class constructions so far, we need to ensure that the class names for the sounds match those in the Main.as and that we have used the correct path to the assets folder.

Modifying the SoundManager class

The SoundManger class in the game framework needs to be modified to allow the mute functionality to work properly. Remember, this class is in the com.efg.framework package. We need to add two new private variables: Private var soundMute:Boolean and private var muteSoundTransform:SoundTransform = new SoundTransform();.

The `Private var soundMute:Boolean` variable will be turned from `true` to `false` and vice versa when the `muteSound` function is called.

The `private var muteSoundTransform:SoundTransform = new SoundTransform();` variable is an instance of the `SoundTransform` class. It will be used to set the volume between 0 (soundMute=true) and 100 (soundMute=false).

Now, let's take a look at the `muteSound` public function:

```
public function muteSound():void {
    //trace("sound manager got mute event");
    if (soundMute) {
        soundMute=false;
        muteSoundTransform.volume=1;
        SoundMixer.soundTransform=muteSoundTransform;

    }else{

        muteSoundTransform.volume=0;
        SoundMixer.soundTransform=muteSoundTransform;
        soundMute=true;
    }
}
```

Notice that we are setting the global `SoundMixer`'s volume by setting its `soundTransform` attribute to the value of our own `muteSoundTransform` variable. We must import the `SoundMixer` class to do this. Add this line to the class import section of the class:

```
import flash.media.SoundMixer;
```

Before we start to look at the details of the new gameplay-related classes that we are going to add to the game framework and the Blaster Mines package, let's take a look at some more optimization theory that we will implement for our game.

Optimizing with object pooling

Object pooling is an optimization technique that helps conserve both system memory and processor execution time. The method we will use to pool objects will be to create an `Array` of our objects types in a so called "pool." When we need to use an object, we will take it from the pool. If no objects are left in the pool, we will not be able to display an object. This is perfect for effects like particles that don't affect gameplay.

Conserving processor execution time

Creating new objects is a very processor-intensive activity. By reducing the need for objects to be reinstantiated each time they are needed, we reduce the overall execution time for the game.

Conserving memory

It is not obvious up front why object pooling would save memory, because we are going to create a pool of global objects that will be around, using up system memory and won't be garbage collected until we dispose of them. More memory is used up when the game begins, because the object pools will be filled and ready for use. The way we conserve memory with this technique is twofold and subtle.

First, if we set the pool size to a limited amount, we stop the system from creating too many objects and using up all of the available memory. This can be handled other ways such as setting maximum values variables that are checked when objects need to be created, but it works for the pool also.

Second, the pool of objects helps smooth out the garbage collection process for the system. If we are constantly creating and the disposing of hundreds of particles (for instance), it will take some time before the disposed objects are actually collected. We could actually be using twice the memory without the pool if we dispose of 100 objects and then reinstantiate 100 for the next particle explosion, because the garbage collection process has not necessarily freed up memory for the disposed objects in time for the next batch to be instantiated.

If we pool the objects, the garbage collector has much less to do, and we will be far less likely to experience large hiccups in rendering as the garbage collection process starts up and removes all of the discarded unpooled objects.

Implementing object pooling in our game

We will be using object pools for the player's projectile missiles and the particles for explosions. The game will set a base amount of objects for each pool. The particle pool will be doubled if the `FrameRateProfiler`'s `frameRateProfilerAverage` can run at 85 percent or more of the desired frame rate. This is just a very small example of how we can use the render profiling in conjunction with other optimizations to affect the overall performance of the game on the target player's system.

> *Note that you can also use the profiled rate as an indication of how to set the stage.quality attribute to low, medium, high, or best. This affects the quality of the vectors and bitmaps drawn on the stage. We will use this in the Blaster Mines game.*

Creating the technical specifications for object pooling in Blaster Mines

We will be creating separate manager classes for the pooled objects in our game. These manager classes will encapsulate the variables needed for object pooling and also the draw creation functions for the pooled objects.

There will also be a manager class for the `Mine` enemy craft that the player must shoot, but we will not be implementing a pool for those objects.

As an example, let's take a look at the pooling code from the `ParticleManager` class. This class code will be displayed in its entirely in the section called "Designing the Particle Manager class."

Adding the private variables

The following private variables will be created in the variable definition section of the `com.efg.games.blastermines.ParticleManager` class:

- `private var particleBitmapData:BitmapData`: Holds the look of the particle drawn into a `BitmapData` canvas

- private var particleAnimationFrames:Array: Holds the faded animation frames for the particles
- private var particles:Array: The *active* particle array
- private var particlePool:Array: The *inactive* particle array
- private var particleCount:int: Used for loops the active arrays
- private var particlePoolCount:int: Used for loops through the inactive arrays
- private var tempParticle:BasicBiltArrayParticle: A temporary object used in loops
- private var particlePoolMax:int = 500: The total for the pool
- private var particlesPerExplode:int = particlePoolMax / 20: The number of particles needed for an explosion

Instantiating a particle in the pool

The createParticlePool function is called at the start of each level to ensure that the particles created match the color of the enemy for that level. This function will be in the com.efg.games.blastermines.ParticleManager class:

```
public function createParticlePool(maxParticles:int):void {
   particlePool = [];
   particles = [];

   for (var particleCtr:int=0;particleCtr<maxParticles;particleCtr++) {
      var tempParticle:BasicBiltArrayParticle = new BasicBiltArrayParticle(0,799,0,799);
      particlePool.push(tempParticle);
   }
}
```

The function loops through a count of the passed in (maxParticles) and pushes them into the particlePool array.

Making a particle active

When a Mine is destroyed in the game, an explosion is created. The createExplode function does this job. This function will be part if the com.efg.games.blastermines.BlasterMines class:

```
private function createExplode(xval:Number,yval:Number,parts:int):void {
   for (var explodeCtr:int=0;explodeCtr<parts;explodeCtr++) {

      particleManager.particlePoolCount = particleManager.particlePool.length-1;
      if (particleManager.particlePoolCount > 0) {
         tempParticle=particleManager.particlePool.pop();
         tempParticle.lifeDelayCount=0;
         tempParticle.x=xval;
         tempParticle.y = yval;
         tempParticle.nextX=xval;
         tempParticle.nextY=yval;
         tempParticle.speed = (Math.random() * 3) + 1;
         tempParticle.frame = 0;

         tempParticle.animationList = particleManager.particleAnimationFrames;
         tempParticle.bitmapData = tempParticle.animationList[tempParticle.frame];
```

```
        var randInt:int = int(Math.random() * 359);

        tempParticle.dx = rotationVectorList[randInt].x;
        tempParticle.dy = rotationVectorList[randInt].y;

        particleManager.particles.push(tempParticle);
      }
   }
}
```

The function loops though the passed-in parts number to create an explosion that starts at the xval and yval passed in coordinates as the center. Particles will randomly choose a direction to move and then shoot out from this point.

First, the createExplode function checks to make sure that the pool contains a Particle instance for use. If there is no Particle left in the pool, no Particle is created. If possible, it takes a Particle from the pool, changes its properties and adds it to the particles array. It does so by assigning the tempParticle variable a reference to the last particle in the particlePool array by popping the next particle from the particlePool array and setting the tempParticle to reference it. After the attributes of tempParticle are set, it is placed in the particles array.

Making a particle inactive

When a particle has used up its life, it will be moved from the particles array back to the particlePool array. This occurs in the update function of the BlasterMines.as class:

```
particleManager.particleCount = particleManager.particles.length-1
   for (var ctr:int = particleManager.particleCount; ctr >= 0; ctr--) {

   tempParticle = particleManager.particles[ctr];

   if (tempParticle.update(step)) { //return true if particle is to be removed
      tempParticle.frame = 0;
      particleManager.particlePool.push(tempParticle);
      particleManager.particles.splice(ctr,1);
   }
}
```

Optimizing with single-unit processing and memory conservation

Sometimes, we call the concept of optimizing with single-unit processing "a pool of one." Throughout this book, we have created numerous class-level variables that are reused for processing. By "class-level," we mean a variable with global scope that every function in the class can use. We tend to do this for objects such as Point and Rectangle instances, because they are created and used a lot (30 to 40 times a second for each blitted object, for instance). By creating a single one of each to use, we are essentially creating a pool of one. This technique is a somewhat controversial, because (as with the object pools) by saving the processor time in creating these objects, we are also using up more memory, or creating a larger memory footprint, when our game initializes. The same theory from the pool section holds here though. Overall, we are reducing memory consumption by creating these "pools of one," because the total amount of objects at any one time will always be constant rather than fluctuating wildly at the whims of the garbage collection process, which would be the case if we created local objects on each frame tick.

Throughout this book, we have created quite a few custom Event calls for each ScoreBoard class element update. In Blaster Mines, we will create a single reusable event for each of these update events. Let's take a closer look at what we mean now.

Reusing global event objects

The BlasterMines.as class sends off a lot of events to update ScoreBoard on each frame tick. We are going to reduce the overall memory footprint, as well as processor and execution time, by reusing the events that fire off to update each of the ScoreBoard elements.

We will take the score element as an example, but this will apply to all ScoreBoard display elements in our Game class:

1. First, we need to create a reusable object event for the score update:

```
private var customcoreBoardEventScore:CustomEventScoreBoardUpdate = new ↵
   CustomEventScoreBoardUpdate(CustomEventScoreBoardUpdate.↵
   UPDATE_TEXT,Main.SCORE_BOARD_SCORE, "");
```

2. When we make a call to update the Main.SCORE_BOARD_SCORE text element on the score, we need to set the value property of the event to the current score value:

```
customScoreBoardEventScore.value = score.toString()
```

3. Finally, we need to dispatch the event:

```
dispatchEvent(customScoreBoardEventScore);
```

As you can see, we are simply going to reuse the same class level event variable every time we update the score and create a new event each time.

Optimizing with look-up tables

Look-up tables can be a very easy source of optimization when calculating complex mathematical values. It is somewhat debatable whether or not AS3 is faster at math than at array look-ups, but by using the FrameCounter, we were able to see a small difference of 1 FPS when using the single look-up table that we will use for rotational radian vector values. If applied to a much larger application, you might see a much greater improvement. We will use the Vector class for our look-up table, which in our experience allows even faster array look-ups. If you do not have access to a Flash Player 10–compatible publishing system, you can swap the Vector for an Array instance.

We are already going to use the BlitArrayAsset class to create rotational arrays of 360 images for our player's ship. Because of this, we will be able to use the same frame attribute of the BasicArrayBlitObject class to pick out the vector values needed to more our player in the direction is it facing.

Creating the movement vector look-up table

Follow these steps to create the movement lookup table:

1. We will add a global Array or Vector variable to our BlasterMines.as class that will hold Point object instances with the dx and dy values needed to move our game objects in direction of their rotation. The x of the Point will be our dx value and the y of the point will be our dy value. This uses slightly less memory than a generic Object instance, because it is Finalized and not dynamic, which saves the Flash Player from having to allocate memory just in case the generic Object instance needs to add properties on the fly. All of the following code will be in the com.efg.games.blastermines.BlasterMines.as file. First we have the lines from the variable definition section:

```
//math look up tables
//private var rotationVectorList:Array = [];
private var rotationVectorList:Vector.<Point>=new Vector.<Point>(360,false);
```

2. The init portion of the BlasterMines.as class will call a function that will create the look-up table:

```
createLookupTables();
```

3. The createLookUpTables function will loop through 0 to 359 and calculate the dx and dy vector values needed to move an object to that rotation:

```
private function createLookupTables():void {
    for (var ctr:int = 0; ctr < 359; ctr++) {
        var point:Point = new Point();
        point.x = Math.cos((Math.PI * ctr) / 180);
        point.y = Math.sin((Math.PI * ctr) / 180);
        rotationVectorList[ctr] = point;
    }
}
```

When one of the game objects needs to move into a particular direction based on a rotated angle, it will use the rotationVectorList instead of calculating the dx and dy values on the fly. Let's take a look at an example of this in the next section.

Accessing the vectorRotationList look-up table

All of the display objects will be moved at angles in the game. Let's look at how the Projectile object instances will be created and access this table.

The player's projectile missiles are automatically fired each frame tick with a three-frame delay between each shot. The projectiles will be pooled much like the particles. In the update function of BlasterMines.as, the projectiles will be created. Here is the code that does just that; this code will be in the com.efg.games.blastermines.BlasterMines.as file:

```
//*** auto fire
projectileManager.projectilePoolCount = projectileManager.projectilePool.length - 1;

if (projectileManager.lastProjectileShot > 3 && projectileManager.projectilePoolCount ⏎
    > 0 && playerStarted && mineManager.mineCount > 0) {
```

```
    dispatchEvent(new CustomEventSound(CustomEventSound.PLAY_SOUND, ⏎
    Main.SOUND_PLAYER_SHOOT, false, 0, 8, 1));

    tempProjectile = projectileManager.projectilePool.pop();
    var projectileRadians:Number = (player.frame / 360) * 6.28;

    //+ 16 to get it to the center of a 32x32 sprite
    tempProjectile.x=(player.point.x+16)+Math.cos(projectileRadians);

    tempProjectile.y =(player.point.y+16) + Math.sin(projectileRadians);

    tempProjectile.x = player.x+16;
    tempProjectile.y = player.y + 16;
    tempProjectile.nextX = tempProjectile.x;
    tempProjectile.nextY = tempProjectile.y;

    tempProjectile.dx = rotationVectorList[player.frame].x;
    tempProjectile.dy = rotationVectorList[player.frame].y;

    tempProjectile.speed = 5;
    tempProjectile.frame = 0;
    tempProjectile.bitmapData = tempProjectile.animationList[0];
    projectileManager.projectiles.push(tempProjectile);
    projectileManager.lastProjectileShot=0;
  }else {
    projectileManager.lastProjectileShot+=step;
  }
```

The preceding function is the actual entire projectile firing code. We only need be concerned with these two lines:

```
    tempProjectile.dx = rotationVectorList[player.frame].x;
    tempProjectile.dy = rotationVectorList[player.frame].y;
```

The player object's current frame index is the rotated BitmapData in the player.animationList array that represents the player's current rotated direction. The projectiles pull their dx and dy values from the rotationVectorList array using the same index using the x value for dx and the y value for dy.

Optimizing screen-based blit scrolling with ScrollRect

There are many ways to scroll a screen when programming in AS3. In the previous chapter, we looked at tile-based blit rendering over a 360-degree scrolling playfield. In this chapter, we will look at an optimized method to scroll a screen that is not necessarily made up of tiles (although it could be). We are going to draw all of our assets for the game as vector shapes, add some simple glow filters, and cache those as BitmapData. We will draw all of these game objects to a world-sized Bitmapdata canvas, but only display the current viewable window to the user. We will scroll our screen using a different method than the Camera2D class from Chapter 10.

In our experience, the fastest way to scroll a bitmap screen in AS3 is to use the scrollRect Rectangle property of the Bitmap instance that holds our world canvas. We simply change the x and y coordinates of the top-left corner of the Rectangle that represents the scrollRect for the Bitmap. In Chapter 10, we used a copyPixels offset to scroll the viewable window about the world canvas. We noticed a 2 to 3 frames per second increase in speed using the scrollRect method over the copyPixels method when testing it with Blaster Mines.

This method also greatly simplifies and reduces the number of operations we have to go through to scroll our screen. In Blaster Mines, the viewable screen is 400 × 400 while the entire world is 800 × 800. We are not using tiles as in Drive She Said, so we don't need a buffer with extra tiles to ensure smooth scrolling. All we really need to do is this:

1. Update the player's nextX and nextY values based on the position of the mouse.

2. The player is rendered to the 800 × 800 canvasBitmapData world at its current position. Its x and y coordinates are updated to be the same as its nextX and nextY coordinates

3. The top-left corner of the canvasBitmap (the display object holder of our canvasBitmapData blit canvas) is set to be player.x-200, player.y-200. The size is always set to 400 × 400. This sets our player in the middle of the screen.

4. When the player moves, we simply change the x and y coordinates of the upper corner of this scrollRect Rectangle. This will simulate scrolling over the entire world:

```
if (playerStarted) {
    canvasRect.x = player.x - 200;
    canvasRect.y = player.y - 200;
    if (canvasRect.x < 0) canvasRect.x = 0;
    if (canvasRect.y < 0) canvasRect.y = 0;
    if (canvasRect.x > 399) canvasRect.x = 399;
    if (canvasRect.y > 399) canvasRect.y = 399;
    canvasBitmap.scrollRect = canvasRect;
}
```

To ensure that the canvasBitmap.scrollRect does not go outside the boundaries of our world canvasBitmapDdata, we make sure to keep the upper left-hand corner between 0 and 399 for both the x and y directions.

Notice that we update a Rectangle instance called canvasRect rather than the canvasBitmap.scrollRect directly. The properties of the scrollRect cannot be changed directly. You must change the properties of a second Rectangle instance and then assign the canvasBitmap.scrollrect to equal that canavsRect (the last line of the code).

This simple scrolling technique is very powerful and, as we said, could save 2 to 3 frames per second over using the camera buffer method from Chapter 10.

Optimizing BitmapData reuse for the radar screen

The Blaster Mines game contains an entire miniature version of the game world to the right of the gameplay screen. This was actually very simple to create using a full-screen blitting technique.

First, let's discuss a traditional Flash method of scrolling the screen and creating an associated radar style screen. If we had chosen to use a Sprite canvas rather than a blit canvas, we would have a Sprite holder for our game screen with hundreds of other individual Sprites (or Bitmap objects) attached to its display list.

We very well could scroll the screen using the scrollRect property of the Sprite holder instance. However, we would lose the reusability of the canvasBitmapData world BitmapData canvas. With the scrollable Sprite canvas and individual Sprite objects attached to its display list we would have had to draw the Sprite holder's contents into a radarBD BitmapData on every frame we wanted to update the radar. Alternatively, we could have created a miniature version of the Sprite holder with a second Sprite object to represent each Sprite canvas object. Both of these ideas would be OK implementations, but they would be much slower than just reusing the canvasBitmapData as the BitmapData reference for out radarBitmap.

> *Obviously, the method of using a second Bitmap object to display the entire game world as a radar only works if you want the radar screen to be a miniature version of the actual game screen. If you want the radar to be an abstract representation of the game screen, you will have to employ a different method.*

When we create our radarBitmap, we set the reference to the canvasBitmapData:

```
private var radarBitmap:Bitmap = new Bitmap(canvasBitmapData);
```

As long as the canvasBitmapData has already been created, this line of code will work fine.

In the init function, we simply resize and place the radarBitmap on the screen. We then never have to worry about it again. It will always be updated when the canvasBitmapData is updated.

```
radarBitmap.x = 420;
radarBitmap.y = 230;
radarBitmap.scaleX = .2;
radarBitmap.scaleY = .2;
addChild(radarBitmap);
```

Creating the new game classes

The following classes, although created for this specific game's needs, are engineered to be generic pieces that can be reused by any game that needs them. Some will be added to the framework, and some will be in the Blaster Mines package.

Designing the BlitArrayAsset class

The BlitArrayAsset class is located in com.efg.famework and is the equivalent of a TileSheet for assets created in code. This helper class is used only to create arrays of assets. Instances of this class will always be temporary and only local to the functions that we create them in. The class doesn't even need a constructor; it is used like a library. BlitArrayAsset will be added to the framework package and will have two public functions. The first is

```
public function createRotationBlitArrayFromBD(sourceBitmapData:BitmapData, inc:int, ↵
    offset:int = 0):Array {
```

This function requires a BitmapData (sourceBitmapData) instance to be passed in along with an increment value and an angle offset for creating the rotation. The BitmapData represents a static graphic that will be turned into an array of rotated BitmapData values. The inc (or increment value) represents the degrees to skip on each object rotation. For example, an inc value of 1 would create an array of 360 rotations (offset by 1 degree each), while an inc value of 10 would only create an array of 36 rotations (offset by 10 degrees each).

The offset value is used to ensure that our object rotation values match the actual appearance of the object. You will notice (a little later in this chapter) that the player's ship is drawn facing up. We want this to be the 0 rotation value. Flash actually uses the facing-right value as the 0 rotation. By passing 90 in as the offset, we can mitigate this behavior and create the correct rotation values for our object. This way, our values will match the look-up table of precalculated vector values created for optimization of object movement. If the graphic that needs to be rotated was drawn facing right rather than up, this offset would not be needed. We will draw our graphics for the game facing up, because we find it much easier to draw via code in this manner. This offset also allows you the option of using images that are pointed at any angle as the source for the rotation array.

This function will use a Matrix to first translate the BitmapData (move to a position at -1/2 width for x and -1/2 height for y), rotate the original by the new increment, and then translate it back to its original position. It uses the original sourceBitmapData for each rotation to keep skewing and bitmap degradation to a minimum. The code for the Matrix looks like this:

```
var angleInRadians:Number = Math.PI * 2 * (rotation / 360);
var rotationMatrix:Matrix = new Matrix();
rotationMatrix.translate(-sourceBitmapData.width*.5,-sourceBitmapData.height*.5);
rotationMatrix.rotate(angleInRadians);
rotationMatrix.translate(sourceBitmapData.width*.5,sourceBitmapData.height*.5);
```

Our second public function is

```
public function createFadeOutBlitArrayFromBD(sourceBitmapData:BitmapData,
    steps:int ):Array{
```

Like the createRotationBlitArrayFromBD function, this one creates an array of faded out (alpha channel) BitmapData assets from the passed in sourceBitmapData. The steps value represents the number of frames of animation for the fade out. For example, if the value 10 is passed in, the function will degrade the alpha of the passed in BitmapData (sourceBitmapData) by .1 on each iteration.

This function uses a ColorMatrixFilter instance to apply the alpha fade to the sourceBitmapData. A full description of Matrix operations is beyond the scope of this book, but the following Matrix will fade out the sourceBitmapData when applied to it by the alpha value.

```
var alpha:Number=1 - (ctr*stepAmount)
var alphaMatrix:ColorMatrixFilter = new ColorMatrixFilter(
[1, 0, 0, 0, 0,
 0, 1, 0, 0, 0,
 0, 0, 1, 0, 0,
 0, 0, 0, alpha, 0]);
```

Here is the complete source code for this class:

```
package com.efg.framework
{
    import flash.display.*;
    import flash.geom.*;
    import flash.filters.ColorMatrixFilter;

    public class BlitArrayAsset {

        public var tileList:Array;
        private var point0:Point = new Point(0, 0);
```

```
public function createRotationBlitArrayFromBD(sourceBitmapData:BitmapData, ↵
    inc:int, offset:int = 0):Array {

    tileList = [];
    var rotation:int = offset;

    while (rotation<(360+offset)){
        var angleInRadians:Number = Math.PI * 2 * (rotation / 360);

        var rotationMatrix:Matrix = new Matrix();
        rotationMatrix.translate(-sourceBitmapData.width*.5,-sourceBitmapData.height*.5);
        rotationMatrix.rotate(angleInRadians);
        rotationMatrix.translate(sourceBitmapData.width*.5,sourceBitmapData.height*.5);

        var matrixImage:BitmapData = new BitmapData(sourceBitmapData.width, ↵
            sourceBitmapData.height, true, 0x00000000);

        matrixImage.draw(sourceBitmapData, rotationMatrix);
        tileList.push(matrixImage.clone());
        rotation += inc;
        matrixImage.dispose();
        matrixImage = null;
        rotationMatrix = null;
    }
    return(tileList);
}

public function createFadeOutBlitArrayFromBD(sourceBitmapData:BitmapData, ↵
    steps:int ):Array{

    var stepAmount:Number = 1 / steps;
    tileList = [];

    for (var ctr:int = 0; ctr <= steps; ctr++) {

        var alpha:Number=1 - (ctr*stepAmount)

        var alphaMatrix:ColorMatrixFilter = new ColorMatrixFilter(
            [1, 0, 0, 0, 0,
             0, 1, 0, 0, 0,
             0, 0, 1, 0, 0,
             0, 0, 0, alpha, 0]);

        var matrixImage:BitmapData = new BitmapData(sourceBitmapData.width, ↵
            sourceBitmapData.height, true, 0x00000000);

        matrixImage.applyFilter(sourceBitmapData, matrixImage.rect, point0, ↵
            alphaMatrix);

        tileList.push(matrixImage.clone());
        matrixImage.dispose();
        matrixImage = null;
        alphaMatrix = null;
    }
```

```
        return(tileList);
    }
  }
}
```

The `createRotationBlitArray` and `createFadeOutBlitArray` methods you have just seen will be used to create the objects in our games that will store their look and feel in arrays of `BitmapData` objects.

Next, we will take a look at the base class for all of our game objects. The base class will be called `BasicBlitArrayObject`. The `BlitArrayAsset` class will used create the look of these `BasicBlitArrayObjects` inside the "Manager" classes that we will discuss later in this section.

Designing the BasicBlitArrayObject class

Instead of a tile sheet for the game in this chapter, we will be drawing our graphics in code and using an `Array` of `BitmapData` instances to simulate animation. `BasicBlitArrayObject` is a base class for objects that are animated as an array of `BitmapData` objects. It contains four public functions and an assortment of public properties that are necessary to move the object on the screen and animate its appearance with an array of `BitmapData` objects. This class will be added to the framework package.

The package location is `com.efg.famework`.

These are the public attributes:

- `public var x:Number`: The x location (top-left corner) of the object for blitting to the `canvasBitmapData`
- `public var y:Number`: The y location (top-left corner) of the object for blitting to the `canvasBitmapData`
- `public var nextX:Number`: Updated in the update cycle of the game and applied to x in the render
- `public var nextY:Number`: Updated in the update cycle of the game and applied to y in the render
- `public var dx:Number`: The change in x to apply to `nextX` in the update cycle
- `public var dy:Number`: The change in y to apply to `nextY` in the update cycle
- `public var frame:int`: The current index of the `animationList` array
- `public var bitmapData`: A local reference to the `BitmapData` represented by `animationList[frame]`
- `public var animationList:Array`: The local Array of `BitmapData` references to loop through for animation
- `public var point:Point`: The global `Point` reference for the `copyPixels` operation
- `public var speed:Number`: The value to add to dx and dy on each update
- `public var xMax:int`: The maximum x blit location for the object
- `public var yMax:int`: The maximum y blit location for the object
- `public var xMin:int`: The minimum x blit location for the object
- `public var yMin:int`: The minimum y blit location for the object

These are the public functions:

- `public function BasicBlitArrayObject(xMin:int,xMax:int, yMin:int, yMax:int  ):`
  The constructor takes in values to set the maximum and minimum blit location (both x
  and y) for the object. It is up to the children of this base class to decide what to do with
  the attributes during the update cycle.
- `public function updateFrame(inc:int):void :` The `updateFrame` function takes in the
  `inc` (increment) and sets the frame property of the object. The `bitmapData` is then
  assigned a reference to the `animationList[frame]` item.
- `public function render(canvasBitmapData:BitmapData):void:` The render function
  takes a single `BitmapData` instance, `canvasBitmapData`. The object's `bitmapData` is
  copied to the `canvasBitmapData` with a `copyPixels` operation

Here is the full source code to the `BlitArrayObject` class:

```
package  com.efg.framework
{
    import flash.display.BitmapData;
    import flash.geom.Point;
    import flash.events.EventDispatcher;
    import flash.geom.Rectangle;

    public class BasicBlitArrayObject extends EventDispatcher{

        public var x:Number = 0;
        public var y:Number = 0;
        public var nextX:Number = 0;
        public var nextY:Number = 0;
        public var dx:Number = 0;
        public var dy:Number = 0;
        public var frame:int = 0;
        public var bitmapData:BitmapData;
        public var animationList:Array=[];
        public var point:Point = new Point(0, 0);
        public var speed:Number=0;
        public var xMax:int=0;
        public var yMax:int=0;
        public var xMin:int=0;
        public var yMin:int=0;


        public function BasicBlitArrayObject(xMin:int,xMax:int, yMin:int, yMax:int  ) {
            this.xMin = xMin;
            this.xMax = xMax;
            this.yMin = yMin;
            this.yMax = yMax;
        }

        public function updateFrame(inc:int):void {
            frame += inc;
            if (frame > animationList.length-1) {
                frame = 0;
```

```
        }
        bitmapData = animationList[frame];
    }


    public function render(canvasBitmapData:BitmapData):void {
        x = nextX;
        y = nextY;
        point.x = x;
        point.y = y;
        canvasBitmapData.copyPixels(bitmapData, bitmapData.rect, point);
    }

    public function dispose():void {
        bitmapData.dispose();
        bitmapData = null;
        animationList = null;
        point = null;
    }
  }
}
```

The next two classes, BasicBlitArrayParticle and Basic BlitArrayProjectile, will be subclasses of the BasicBlitArrayObject class. They are generic enough to be part of the framework rather than the Blaster Mines page package.

Designing the BasicBlitArrayParticle class

The BasicBlitArrayParticle class is a subclass of the BlitArrayObject that will be used in our game for basic explosion particles. This class will be added to the framework package and will be located here: com.efg.famework.

Here are its public attributes:

- public var lifeDelayCount:int: The count of frames between changes in animation
- public var lifeDelay:int: The number of fames to count in lifeDelayCount

Here is the private attribute:

- private var remove:Boolean: remove will be set to true if the particle needs to be removed from the screen.

And these are the public functions:

- public function BasicBiltArrayParticle(xMin:int,xMax:int, yMin:int, yMax:int): The constructor for all of the children of BasicBlitArrayObject accepts in the same parameters as their parent and pass them off with a call to super(): super(xMin, xMax, yMin, yMax);.

523

- public function update(timeBasedModifier:Number=1):Boolean: The update function's job is to apply the dx and dy (along with the speed) values to the object's nextX and nextY attributes. The nextX and nextY values will be multiplied by the timeBasedModifier. This value is used to keep the distance that objects move in a single second constant no matter what frame rate the game SWF is playing at. This concept will be discussed in the section called "Creating the time-based step timer."

```
nextX+=dx*speed*timeBasedModifier;
nextY+=dy*speed*timeBasedModifier;
```

It will update the lifeDelayCount variable and change the bitmapData of the object. The animationList array length is used as the life span of the particle. If the current frame of the object is greater than the animationList length, the remove is set to true. Also, if the particle's nextX or nextY values are outside the boundaries set with the xMax, yMax and xMin, yMin sets of variables, remove is also set to true. The function returns the remove value back to the caller.

Here is the full source for this class:

```
package com.efg.framework
{
    import com.efg.framework.BasicBlitArrayObject;

    public class BasicBiltArrayParticle extends BasicBlitArrayObject{

        public var lifeDelayCount:int = 0;
        public var lifeDelay:int=0;

        private var remove:Boolean = false;

        public function BasicBiltArrayParticle(xMin:int,xMax:int, yMin:int, yMax:int  ) {
            super(xMin, xMax, yMin, yMax);
        }

        public function update(step:Number=1 ):Boolean {
            remove = false;
            nextX+=dx*speed*step;
            nextY+=dy*speed*step;

            if (lifeDelayCount > lifeDelay) {
                lifeDelayCount = 0;
                frame++;
                if (frame == animationList.length) {
                    remove = true;
                }else {
                    bitmapData = animationList[frame];
                }
            }else {
             lifeDelayCount++;
            }

            if (nextX > xMax || nextX < xMin || nextY > yMax || nextY < yMin) {
                remove = true;
            }
```

```
        return(remove);
    }
  }
}
```

Designing the BasicBlitArrayProjectile class

The `BasicBlitArrayProjectile` class is also a subclass of `BasicBlitArrayObject`. It is used for the projectile missiles that the player ship will fire during our game. This class will be added to game framework package and is located in `com.efg.famework`.

There are no additional public attributes for this class, but here are the public functions:

- The constructor is identical to the `BasicBlitArrayParticle` version.
- `public function update(xAdjust:Number, yAdjust:Number,timeBasedModifier: Number=1 ):Boolean {`

The update function accepts in xAdjust and yAdjust values. These are used to modify the speed of the projectile (if needed) and add the player's speed to the projectiles. This way, you never have projectiles that are slower than the object firing them. The nextX and nextY values will be multiplied by the `timeBasedModifier`. This value is used to keep the distance that objects move in a single second constant no matter what frame rate the game SWF is playing at. This was discussed in the section called "Creating the time-based step timer."

The algorithm looks like this.

```
nextx+=(dx*(speed+Math.abs(xAdjust))) *timeBasedModifier;
nexty+=(dy*(speed+Math.abs(yAdjust))) *timeBasedModifier;
```

To determine whether or not to remove the projectile from the screen, the new nextX and nextY attributes are matched against maximum and minimum x and y values for the object; true is passed back to the caller if the object is outside these boundaries.

```
if (nextX > xMax || nextX < xMin || nextY > yMax || nextY < yMin) {
    remove = true;
}

return(remove);
```

Here is the full source for this class:

```
package com.efg.framework
{
    import com.efg.framework.BasicBlitArrayObject;
    import com.efg.framework.BasicBiltArrayProjectile;

    public class BasicBiltArrayProjectile extends BasicBlitArrayObject{

        public function BasicBiltArrayProjectile(xMin:int,xMax:int, yMin:int, yMax:int  ) {
            super(xMin, xMax, yMin, yMax);
        }

        public function update(xAdjust:Number, yAdjust:Number,step:Number=1 ):Boolean {
            //x adjust and y adjust change speed of projectile.
            //in this case they are used to ensure that sprojetciles are as fast
```

```
                    //or faster than the player ship
                    //add xMove to dx and dy so the missiles fire faster if ship is moving faster
                    nextX+=(dx*(speed+Math.abs(xAdjust)))*step;
                    nextY+=(dy*(speed+Math.abs(yAdjust)))*step;

                    if (nextX > xMax || nextX < xMin || nextY > yMax || nextY < yMin) {
                        return(true)
                    }else {
                        return(false);
                    }
                }
            }
        }
```

Designing the BlitArrayPlayerFollowMouse class

The `BlitArrayPlayerFollowMouse` class is the most complicated subclass of the `BasicBlitArrayObject` class. It contains some very specific code for the Blaster Mines game, so it will be part of the Blaster Mines game package rather than the framework package.

`BlitArrayPlayerFollowMouse` relies on a calculated offset passed in to the `update` function to move the player in the correct direction and speed to follow the mouse. The current mouse position will be passed into the `update` function along with a `delay` value that is used to slow the speed of the player ship so it doesn't just attach itself directly to the mouse pointer. This provides a little more realistic movement for the ship.

Using the mouse for control and allowing automatic firing of missiles is a relatively new and mostly Flash-based control mechanism. It is also a good one to employ when targeting any handheld touch-screen devices that might have a Flash Player capable of running game applications.

The package location is `com.efg.games.blastermines`.

These are the public attributes:

- `public var xMove:int`: The calculated new change in x based on the mouse position
- `public var yMove:int`: The calculated new change in y based on the mouse position
- `public var shipBitmapData:BitmapData`: Holds the `BitmapData` version of the drawingCanvas for the player ship
- `public var shieldBitmapData:BitmapData`: Holds the `BitmapData` version of the ship's shield
- `public var shieldRender:Boolean`: Tells the `render` function to display the shield around the player ship if the player's ship is hit by a `Mine` instance
- `public var shieldCount:int`: Counts from 0 to the `shieldLife` frame ticks before setting `shieldRender` to `false` so the shield will stay engaged for the `shieldLife` value
- `public var shieldLife:int`: The number of frame ticks for the shield to be active when the player is hit by a `Mine`

And these are the private attributes:

- `private var xChange:int`: The difference between the mouseY value and the object's y value
- `private var yChange:int`: The difference between the mouseX value and the object's x value
- `private var radians:Number`: Holds the degree in radians for the current rotation of the player
- `private var degrees:int`: Holds the degrees for the current rotation of the player
- `private var drawingCanvas:Shape`: Constructs the vector ship look and shield before they are drawn in the `shipBitmapData` variable

And there are three public functions.

First, the constructor is identical to the `BasicBlitArrayParticle` version.

This is the second function:

```
public function update(mousePositionX:Number, mousePositionY:Number, delay:int,
    timeBasedModifier:Number=1):void
```

This function takes in the current mouse x and y positions as well as a delay value. As mentioned before, the delay is used to control the speed of the player ship. The `timeBasedModifier` will be used to keep objects moving at a constant rate per second no matter at what frame rate the game is running.

The new rotation and movement change values are calculated for the ship based on these three passed in values. Here is the algorithm:

1. We calculate the radian value for the new rotation of the ship using the difference between the mouse x and y positions and the player's x and y positions. This uses the `Math.atan2` function.

2. Next we calculate the degrees (0 – 360) value of the newly calculated radian value:

```
radians = Math.atan2((mousePositionY)-y,(mousePositionX)-x);
degrees= (radians * (180 / Math.PI));
```

3. Then, we calculate the difference in the x and y values between the mouse and player:

```
yMove=(yChange/delay)*timeBasedModifier;
xMove=(xChange/delay)*timeBasedModifier;
```

4. The xMove and yMove values are multiplied by the `timeBasedModifier`. This calculation keeps the distance that objects move in a single second constant no matter what frame rate the game SWF is playing at. This concept was be discussed further in the "Creating the time-based step timer" section.

5. Next, we apply the difference divided by a delay so the ship doesn't just attach itself to the mouse:

```
yMove=yChange/delay;
xMove=xChange/delay;
```

6. The nextX and nextY values are changed to add xMove and yMove respectively and are checked against the minimum and maximum x and y values. There is no warping to the opposite side of the screen in this game (unlike Atari Asteroids), so the player ship object is stopped if it tries to go outside these boundaries.

```
nextX+=yMove;
nextY+=xMove;
if (nextY > xMax) {
    nextX = xMax;
}else if (nextX < +xMin) {
    nextX = xMin;
}
if (nextY > yMax) {
    nextY = yMax;
}else if (nextY < yMin) {
    nextY = yMin;
}
```

7. Finally, the new frame of animation (a rotated BitmapData instance) from the animationList array is selected based on the new degrees for the object. If the degree number is less than 0, we need to offset it by 359, so it will represent the appropriate array index for the animated frame.

```
frame = degrees;
if (degrees < 0) {
    frame = 359+degrees;
}
bitmapData=animationList[frame];
```

And this is the third function in BlitArrayPlayerFollowMouse:

```
public function createPlayerShip(spriteGlowFilter:GlowFilter):void
```

This function will draw the ship as a vector shape and then use the BlitArrayAsset class to create a 360-degree rotation of the ship as 32 × 32 BitmapData objects.

Here is the code that creates this array:

```
shipBitmapData.draw(drawingCanvas);

shipBitmapData.applyFilter(shipBitmapData, shipBitmapData.rect, new Point(0,0), ↩
spriteGlowFilter);

animationList=tempBlitArrayAsset.createRotationBlitArrayFromBD(shipBitmapData, 1,90);
```

Once the ship has been drawn into the drawingCanvas, we use the BitmapData.draw method to copy it to the shipBitmapData. We will examine this in the section called "Adding the Blaster Mines game init functions."

Here is the full source code for this class:

```
package  com.efg.games.blastermines
{
    import com.efg.framework.BasicBlitArrayObject;
    import com.efg.framework.BlitArrayAsset;
    import flash.display.BitmapData;
```

```
import flash.display.Shape;
import flash.geom.Point;
import flash.filters.GlowFilter;

public class BlitArrayPlayerFollowMouse extends BasicBlitArrayObject{

    public var xMove:int;
    public var yMove:int;
    private var xChange:int;
    private var yChange:int;
    private var radians:Number;
    private var degrees:int;

    private var drawingCanvas:Shape = new Shape();

    public var shipBitmapData:BitmapData = new BitmapData(32, 32, true, 0x00000000);

    public var shieldBitmapData:BitmapData = new BitmapData(32, 32, true, 0x00000000);
    public var shieldRender:Boolean - false;
    public var shieldCount:int = 0,
    public var shieldLife:int = 5;

    public function BlitArrayPlayerFollowMouse(xMin:int,xMax:int, yMin:int, yMax:int ) {
        super(xMin, xMax, yMin, yMax);
    }

    public function update(mousePositionX:Number, mousePositionY:Number, ↵
      delay:int,step:Number=1):void {

        radians = Math.atan2((mousePositionY)-y,(mousePositionX)-x);
        degrees= (radians * (180 / Math.PI));

        yChange= (mousePositionY-y);
        xChange= (mousePositionX-x);

        yMove=(yChange/delay)*step;
        xMove=(xChange/delay)*step;

        nextY+=yMove;
        nextX+=xMove;

        if (nextX > xMax) {
            nextX = xMax;
        }else if (nextX < +xMin) {
            nextX = xMin;
        }

        if (nextY > yMax) {
            nextY = yMax;
        }else if (nextY < yMin) {
            nextY = yMin;
        }

        frame = degrees;
```

```
        if (degrees < 0) {
           frame = 359+degrees;
        }

        bitmapData=animationList[frame]
    }

    public function createPlayerShip(spriteGlowFilter:GlowFilter):void {

        var tempBlitArrayAsset:BlitArrayAsset = new BlitArrayAsset();
        drawingCanvas.graphics.clear();
        drawingCanvas.graphics.lineStyle(1, 0xffffff);
        drawingCanvas.graphics.moveTo(15, 7);
        drawingCanvas.graphics.lineTo(7, 24);
        drawingCanvas.graphics.lineTo(15, 19);
        drawingCanvas.graphics.moveTo(16, 19);
        drawingCanvas.graphics.lineTo(24, 24);
        drawingCanvas.graphics.lineTo(16, 7);

        trace("drawingCanvas.height=" + drawingCanvas.height);
        trace("drawingCanvas.width=" + drawingCanvas.width);

        shipBitmapData.draw(drawingCanvas);
        shipBitmapData.applyFilter(shipBitmapData, shipBitmapData.rect, new Point(0,0),↵
           spriteGlowFilter);

        animationList=tempBlitArrayAsset.createRotationBlitArrayFromBD↵
           (shipBitmapData, 1,90);

        //*** end player ship

        //*** shield
        drawingCanvas.graphics.clear();
        drawingCanvas.graphics.lineStyle(3, 0xffffff);
        drawingCanvas.graphics.drawCircle(15, 15, 14);
        shieldBitmapData.draw(drawingCanvas);
        //*** end shield
    }
  }
}
```

As we progress through this game code, we will discuss this class in even more detail. Next up, we will create three manager classes for our game that will encapsulate functionality for groups of objects. The first is the MineManager class. This class will manage the Mine enemy ships that the player must destroy.

As these classes are core to the Blaster Mines game, they will be discussed in detail when we go though the game code. For now, let's briefly look at the code for each and a short description of the public and private attributes and function that each contains.

Designing the MineManager class

The `MineManager` class will hold the list of active `Mine` instances that the player must destroy. The `Mines` will each be an instance of the `Mine` class, which we will discuss in the following section. This class will be in the Blaster Mines game package: `com.efg.games.blastermines`.

These are the public attributes:

- `public var mineBitmapData:BitmapData`: This will be a `BitmapData` representation of the mine look after it has been constructed on the `drawingCanvas`.
- `public var mineAnimationFrames:Array`: This will hold the 360 frames of rotated `BitmapData` objects representing the `Mine`'s rotations.
- `public var mines:Array`: This will hold all of the active `Mine` class instances.
- `public var tempMine:Mine`: This is a class-shared variable used in all operations where a tempMine will be needed.
- `public var mineCount:int`: This one holds the current `length` of the mines array so is doesn't have to be recalculated inside each loop iteration.

These are the private attributes:

- `private var drawingCanvas:Shape`: The canvas where the vector mine look will be constructed before it is drawn into the `mineBitmapData`.
- `private var point0:Point`: This shared point instance at `0x,0y` can be used by all drawing and filter operations on the `mineBitmapData`.

And these are the public functions:

- `public function MineManager`: The constructor doesn't do any processing.
- `public function createLevelMines(spriteGlowFilter:GlowFilter,level:int, levelColor:uint):void`: This function creates all of the `Mine` instances for the current game level and constitutes the look of the mine by drawing it to the `drawingCanvas`. It uses the `BlitArrayAsset` class to create an array of 360 rotations stored as individual `BitmpaData` instances.

We will dive into the detail of this class when we explore the `BlasterMines.as` game. It will make much more sense and have a greater impact to see how it works with the `BlasterMines` class.

Here is the full source code for this class:

```
package com.efg.games.blastermines
{
    import flash.display.BitmapData;
    import flash.filters.GlowFilter;
    import flash.display.Shape;
    import flash.geom.Point;

    import com.efg.framework.BlitArrayAsset;

    public class MineManager {

        public var mineBitmapData:BitmapData;
```

```
public var mineAnimationFrames:Array = [];
public var mines:Array;
public var tempMine:Mine;
public var mineCount:int;

private var drawingCanvas:Shape = new Shape();
private var point0:Point = new Point(0, 0);

public function MineManager() {}

public function createLevelMines(spriteGlowFilter:GlowFilter,level:int, ⏎
    levelColor:uint):void {

    //*** Mines look
    mineBitmapData= new BitmapData(32, 32, true, 0x00000000);
    var tempBlitArrayAsset:BlitArrayAsset = new BlitArrayAsset();
    drawingCanvas.graphics.clear();

    drawingCanvas.graphics.lineStyle(2, 0xffffff);
    drawingCanvas.graphics.moveTo(6, 6);
    drawingCanvas.graphics.lineTo(25, 6);
    drawingCanvas.graphics.lineTo(25, 22);
    drawingCanvas.graphics.lineTo(6, 22);
    drawingCanvas.graphics.lineTo(6, 6);
    drawingCanvas.graphics.moveTo(18, 8);
    drawingCanvas.graphics.lineTo(18, 16);
    drawingCanvas.graphics.lineTo(12, 16);
    drawingCanvas.graphics.lineTo(12, 12);
    drawingCanvas.graphics.moveTo(9, 23);
    drawingCanvas.graphics.lineTo(9, 25);
    drawingCanvas.graphics.moveTo(15, 23);
    drawingCanvas.graphics.lineTo(15, 25);
    drawingCanvas.graphics.moveTo(21, 23);
    drawingCanvas.graphics.lineTo(21, 25);

    spriteGlowFilter.color = levelColor;
    mineBitmapData.draw(drawingCanvas);

    mineBitmapData.applyFilter(mineBitmapData, mineBitmapData.rect, point0, ⏎
        spriteGlowFilter);

    tempBlitArrayAsset = new BlitArrayAsset();

    mineAnimationFrames=tempBlitArrayAsset.createRotationBlitArrayFromBD⏎
        (mineBitmapData, 1,90);

    //*** end of mines look

    //*** create mines for level
    mines = [];

    for (var ctr:int=0;ctr<30+20*level;ctr++) {
        var tempMine:Mine=new Mine(5,765,5,765);

        tempMine.dx=Math.cos(6.28*((Math.random()*360)-90)/360.0);
```

```
            tempMine.dy = Math.sin(6.28 * ((Math.random() * 360) - 90) / 360.0);
            if (level % 2 == 0) {
               tempMine.y = 700
            }else {
               tempMine.y = 100
            }

            tempMine.x = 100;
            tempMine.nextX = tempMine.x;
            tempMine.nextY = tempMine.y;
            tempMine.frame = int((Math.random() * 359)) ;
            tempMine.animationList = mineAnimationFrames;

            tempMine.bitmapData = tempMine.animationList[tempMine.frame];
            tempMine.speed = (Math.random()*1)+2+level;
            mines.push(tempMine);
         }
      }
   }
}
```

Designing the ParticleManager class

The ParticleManager class will contain the design of the particles for Mine instance explosions. It will institute an object pool for memory optimization. We will present the basic outline of the class here, and the detailed discussion will be presented as we proceed through the BlasterMines.as class. Particles will be instances of the BasicBlitArrayParticle class. Their look will be unique per level to match the color of the Mine instances that the player must destroy.

The package location is com.efg.games.blastermines.

The public attributes for this class are as follows:

■ public var particleBitmapData:BitmapData: This is the BitmapData look for the Particles. These will be a unique color on each level to match the color of the Mines.

■ public var particleAnimationFrames: Particles will fade out as their life expires. The fade animation frames will be stored in this array. It will be created with the BlitArrayAsset class.

■ public var particles:Array: This array contains the current active Particles.

■ public var particlePool: This attribute contains an array of the Particles in the pool.

■ public var particleCount: This class-level variable will hold the length of the particles array.

■ public var particlePoolCount: This class-level variable will hold the length of the particlePool array.

■ public var tempParticle:BasicBiltArrayParticle: This reusable class-level Particle instance for loops through array the Particle arrays.

■ public var particlePoolMax: This attribute stores the total number of Particle instances that can be on the screen at a single time.

- `public var particlesPerExplode`: This is the number of `Particle` instances that will be created for each explosion.

And these are the private attributes:

- `private var drawingCanvas:Shape`: The canvas where the particle look will be constructed
- `private var point0:Point`: A reusable `Point` instance for drawing operations

This class's public functions follow:

- `public function ParticleManager()`: The constructor is an empty function.
- `public function createParticlePool(maxParticles:int):void`: The `BlasterMines.as` class will call this function before each new level to create the particle pool. We will see this in action and discuss it more when we go through the `BlasterMines.as` code.
- `public function createLevelParticles(spriteGlowFilter:GlowFilter, levelColor:uint):void`: This function is called by `BlasterMines.as` before each new level. It creates the look of the `particles` to match the color on the `Mine` instances.

Here is the full source code for this class:

```
package com.efg.games.blastermines
{
    import flash.display.BitmapData;
    import com.efg.framework.BlitArrayAsset;
    import com.efg.framework.BasicBiltArrayParticle;
    import flash.display.BitmapData;
    import flash.display.Shape;
    import flash.geom.Point;
    import flash.filters.GlowFilter;

    public class ParticleManager {

        public var particleBitmapData:BitmapData;
        public var particleAnimationFrames:Array = [];
        public var particles:Array = [];
        public var particlePool:Array = [];
        public var particleCount:int=0;
        public var particlePoolCount:int=0;
        public var tempParticle:BasicBiltArrayParticle
        public var particlePoolMax:int = 500;
        public var particlesPerExplode:int = particlePoolMax / 20;

        private var drawingCanvas:Shape = new Shape();
        private var point0:Point = new Point(0, 0);

        public function ParticleManager() {}

        public function createParticlePool(maxParticles:int):void {

            particlePool = [];
```

```
        particles = [];

        for (var particleCtr:int=0;particleCtr<maxParticles;particleCtr++) {

            var tempParticle:BasicBiltArrayParticle = new BasicBiltArrayParticle↵
                (0,799,0,799);

            particlePool.push(tempParticle);
        }
    }
    public function createLevelParticles(spriteGlowFilter:GlowFilter, ↵
        levelColor:uint):void {

        var tempBlitArrayAsset:BlitArrayAsset = new BlitArrayAsset();
        particleBitmapData = new BitmapData(8, 8, true, 0x00000000);

        drawingCanvas.graphics.clear();
        drawingCanvas.graphics.lineStyle(1, 0xffffff);
        drawingCanvas.graphics.drawRect(3, 3, 2, 2);
        particleBitmapData.draw(drawingCanvas);
        spriteGlowFilter.color = levelColor;

        particleBitmapData.applyFilter(particleBitmapData, particleBitmapData.rect, ↵
            point0, spriteGlowFilter);

        tempBlitArrayAsset= new BlitArrayAsset();
        tempBlitArrayAsset.createFadeOutBlitArrayFromBD(particleBitmapData, 30);

        particleAnimationFrames = tempBlitArrayAsset.tileList;
    }
  }
}
```

Designing the ProjectileManager class

The structure of the `ProjectileManager` class is almost identical to that of the `ParticalManager` class. The major difference is that the `projectilePool` is only created a single time per game session unlike the particle pool, which is recreated every level. The `projectiles` will be instances of the `BasicBlitArrayProjectile` class.

The location for this package is `com.efg.games.blastermines`.

The public attributes for this class are

- `public var projectileBitmapData:BitmapData`: This is the `BitmapData` look for the Projectiles.
- `public var projectileAnimationFrames`: Projectiles rotate as they fly through the air. The rotation animation frames will be stored in this array. It will be created with the `BlitArrayAsset` class.
- `public var projectiles:Array`: This attribute contains an array of the current active Projectiles.

535

- `public var projectilePool`: This one contains an array of the `projectiles` in the pool.
- `public var projectile Count`: This class-level variable will hold the length of the projectiles array.
- `public var projectile PoolCount`: This class-level variable will hold the length of the `projectilePool` array.
- `public var tempProjectile:BasicBiltArrayProjectile`: This reusable class-level `Projectile` instance for loops through array the `Projectile` arrays.
- `public var projectilePoolMax`: This attribute holds the total number of `projectiles` that can be on the screen at a single time.

The private attributes are

- `private var drawingCanvas:Shape`: The canvas where the `projectile` look will be constructed
- `private var point0:Point`: A reusable `point` instance for drawing operations

And these are the public functions:

- `public function Projectile Manager()` : The constructor is an empty function.
- `public function createProjectilePool(maxParticles:int):void`: The `BlasterMines.as` class will call this function before in its `init` function to create the projectile pool. We will see this in action and discuss it more when we go through the `BlasterMines.as` code.
- `public function createProjectilePool(maxProjectiles:int):void`: This function is called by `BlasterMines.as` before `init`. It creates the look of the projectiles.

Here is the full source code for this class:

```
package com.efg.games.blastermines
{
    import flash.display.BitmapData;
    import com.efg.framework.BlitArrayAsset;
    import com.efg.framework.BasicBiltArrayProjectile;
    import flash.display.BitmapData;
    import flash.display.Shape;
    import flash.geom.Point;
    import flash.filters.GlowFilter;

    public class ProjectileManager {
        public var projectileBitmapData:BitmapData = new BitmapData(8, 8, true, 0x00000000);
        public var projectileAnimationFrames:Array = [];
        public var projectiles:Array=[];
        public var lastProjectileShot:Number = 0;
        public var projectileCount:int;
        public var tempProjectile:BasicBiltArrayProjectile;
        public var projectilePool:Array = [];
        public var projectilePoolCount:int;

        private var drawingCanvas:Shape = new Shape();
        private var point0:Point = new Point(0, 0);
```

```
public function ProjectileManager() {}

public function createProjectiles(spriteGlowFilter:GlowFilter):void {

    //projectile look
    var tempBlitArrayAsset:BlitArrayAsset = new BlitArrayAsset();

    drawingCanvas.graphics.clear();
    drawingCanvas.graphics.lineStyle(1, 0xffffff);
    drawingCanvas.graphics.drawRect(3, 3, 2, 2);

    projectileBitmapData.draw(drawingCanvas);

    projectileBitmapData.applyFilter(projectileBitmapData, ↵
        projectileBitmapData.rect, point0, spriteGlowFilter);

    tempBlitArrayAsset= new BlitArrayAsset();

    projectileAnimationFrames=tempBlitArrayAsset.createRotationBlitArrayFromBD↵
        (projectileBitmapData, 10,0);
}

public function createProjectilePool(maxProjectiles:int):void {

    for (var projectileCtr:int = 0; projectileCtr < maxProjectiles; projectileCtr++) {

        var tempProjectile:BasicBlitArrayProjectile=new BasicBlitArrayProjectile↵
            (0,799,0,799);

        tempProjectile.animationList=projectileAnimationFrames;

        tempProjectile.bitmapData = tempProjectile.animationList[0];
        projectilePool.push(tempProjectile);
    }
  }
 }
}
```

The ProjectileManager class completes the manager classes. Now, we will take a look at the final custom class for our game—the Mine class.

Designing the Mine class

The Mine class is an extension of the BasicBlitArrayObject class with an update function customized to implement the step modifier from the time-based step timer. The class is so simple we will just show the code here and describe the update function when we get to the BlasterMines update function.

This is the package location: com.efg.games.blastermines.

Here is the complete code for the class:

```
package com.efg.games.blastermines
{
    import com.efg.framework.BasicBlitArrayObject;
```

537

```
public class Mine extends BasicBlitArrayObject{

    public function Mine(xMin:int,xMax:int, yMin:int, yMax:int) {
        super(xMin, xMax, yMin, yMax);
    }

    public function update(step:Number=1):void {

        nextX+=dx*speed*step;
        nextY+=dy*speed*step;
        //bounce
        if (nextX > xMax) {
            nextX = xMax;
            dx *= -1;
        }else if (nextX < xMin) {
            nextX = xMin;
            dx *= -1;
        }

        if (nextY > yMax) {
            nextY = yMax;
            dy *= -1;
        }else if (nextY < yMin) {
            nextY = yMin;
            dy *= -1;
        }
    }
  }
}
```

The most important thing to note about this class is the code that bounces the Mine around the screen when it hits the edge of the world. When a Mine hits the edge of the world, it is sent off at the inverse angle from where it came. We only do this for the axis of the side of the world the Mine collided with. This way, it will not simply bounce back but reflect around the world.

That's the Mine class. Now, we will take a look at the BlasterMines Game.as subclass and all of the logic we will implement to create the game. For the BlasterMines.as class technical design, we are going to iterate through code in sections and describe any new parts for functions that have not been discussed so far. You will find that we have covered much of BlasterMines.as already.

Building the Blaster Mines class

We are going to build the BlasterMines.as class in small, bite-sized chunks. This workflow will not be exactly the same as in previous chapters, where we iterated though a working game file. In this chapter, we want to move quickly though a lot of code that you have seen previously, stopping to point out implementations of the theory discussed earlier in the chapter and any new code or theory that has not already been discussed. Because we cover a lot of advanced topics in this chapter, if you have not read the earlier chapters, you might want to verse yourself on some of them before attempting to go straight to this optimized game code.

Let's create this class as the next new file for the Blaster Mines game package. Here is the class file name and location for the Flex SDK (using Flash Develop):

/source/projects/blastermines/flexIDE/com/efg/games/blastermines/BlasterMines.as

And this is for the Flex SDK (using Flash Develop):

/source/projects/blastermines/flexSDK/src/com/efg/games/blastermines/BlasterMines.as

Creating the Blaster Mines class shell

The shell contains the class import section, variable definition section, and constructor functions for the BlasterMines.as class file:

```
package com.efg.games.blastermines
{
    import com.efg.framework.Game;
    import com.efg.framework.GameFrameWork;
    import com.efg.framework.BasicBiltArrayParticle;
    import com.efg.framework.BasicBiltArrayProjectile;


    import flash.display.*
    import flash.events.*;
    import flash.geom.*;
    import flash.filters.*;


    import com.efg.framework.BasicBlitArrayObject;
    import com.efg.framework.BlitArrayAsset;
    import com.efg.framework.CustomEventLevelScreenUpdate;
    import com.efg.framework.CustomEventScoreBoardUpdate;
    import com.efg.framework.CustomEventSound;
    /**
    * ...
    * @author Jeff Fulton
    */
    public class BlasterMines extends Game{

        public static const GAME_OVER:String = "game over";
        public static const NEW_LEVEL:String - "new level";

        public static const STATE_SYSTEM_GAME_PLAY:int = 0;
        public static const STATE_SYSTEM_PLAYER_EXPLODE:int = 1;

        private var systemFunction:Function;
        private var currentSystemState:int;
        private var nextSystemState:int;
        private var lastSystemState:int;

        //** game loop
        private var gameOver:Boolean = false;

        //leveldata

        private var levelColors:Array = [NaN, 0xff0000, 0x00ff00, 0x0000ff, 0xffff00, ⏎
          0x00ffff, 0xffaa00, 0xaaff00, 0x00ffaa, 0x00aaff];
```

```
        private var levelColor:uint;

        private var level:int = 0;
        private var score:int = 0;
        private var shield:int = 10;
        private var maxLevel:int = levelColors.length;
        private var playerStarted:Boolean = false;
        private var playerExplosionParticles:Array = [];


        //Canvas and background

        private var backgroundBitmapData:BitmapData = new BitmapData(800, 800, false, ↵
           0x000000);

        private var canvasBitmapData:BitmapData = new BitmapData(800, 800, false, 0x000000);
        private var canvasBitmap:Bitmap = new Bitmap(canvasBitmapData);
        private var canvasRect:Rectangle = new Rectangle(0,0,400,400);

        //drawing
        private var drawingCanvas:Shape = new Shape();

        //player

        private var player:BlitArrayPlayerFollowMouse = new BlitArrayPlayerFollowMouse↵
         (1, 767, 1, 767);

        //mineManager
        private var mineManager:MineManager = new MineManager();
        public var tempMine:Mine;

        //projectileManagere
        private var projectileManager:ProjectileManager = new ProjectileManager();
        private var tempProjectile:BasicBiltArrayProjectile;

        //particleManager.particles
        private var particleManager:ParticleManager = new ParticleManager();
        private var tempParticle:com.efg.framework.BasicBiltArrayParticle;

        //reused rectangles/points
        private var rect32:Rectangle = new Rectangle(0, 0, 32, 32);
        private var point0:Point = new Point(0, 0);

        private var spriteGlowFilter:GlowFilter = new GlowFilter(0x0066ff, 1, 3 , 3, 3, ↵
           3, false, false);

        private var canvasBitmapGlowFilter:GlowFilter=new GlowFilter(0x0066ff, .5, 400, ↵
           400, 1, 1, true, false);

        //scoreBoard objects - for optimization

        private var customScoreBoardEventScore:CustomEventScoreBoardUpdate = new ↵
           CustomEventScoreBoardUpdate(CustomEventScoreBoardUpdate.UPDATE_TEXT,↵
           Main.SCORE_BOARD_SCORE, "");
```

```
    private var customScoreBoardEventShield:CustomEventScoreBoardUpdate = new ↵
        CustomEventScoreBoardUpdate(CustomEventScoreBoardUpdate.UPDATE_TEXT, ↵
        Main.SCORE_BOARD_SHIELD, "");

    private var customScoreBoardEventLevel:CustomEventScoreBoardUpdate= new ↵
        CustomEventScoreBoardUpdate(CustomEventScoreBoardUpdate.UPDATE_TEXT,↵
        Main.SCORE_BOARD_LEVEL, "");

    private var customScoreBoardEventParticlePool:CustomEventScoreBoardUpdate = new ↵
        CustomEventScoreBoardUpdate(CustomEventScoreBoardUpdate.UPDATE_TEXT,↵
        Main.SCORE_BOARD_PARTICLE_POOL,"");

    private var customScoreBoardEventParticleActive:CustomEventScoreBoardUpdate = new ↵
        CustomEventScoreBoardUpdate(CustomEventScoreBoardUpdate.UPDATE_TEXT,↵
        Main.SCORE_BOARD_PARTICLE_ACTIVE,"");

    private var customScoreBoardEventProjectilePool:CustomEventScoreBoardUpdate = ↵
        new CustomEventScoreBoardUpdate(CustomEventScoreBoardUpdate.UPDATE_TEXT,↵
        Main.SCORE_BOARD_PROJECTILE_POOL, "");

    private var customScoreBoardEventProjectileActive:CustomEventScoreBoardUpdate = ↵
        new CustomEventScoreBoardUpdate(CustomEventScoreBoardUpdate.UPDATE_TEXT,↵
        Main.SCORE_BOARD_PROJECTILE_ACTIVE, "");


    //math look up tables
    //private var rotationVectorList:Array = [];
    private var rotationVectorList:Vector.<Point>=new Vector.<Point>(360,false);

    //radar
    private var radarBitmap:Bitmap = new Bitmap(canvasBitmapData);

    public function BlasterMines() {
        trace("constructor");
        init();
    }
  }
}
```

The variable declaration section is very similar to the others you have seen so far in this book. We have broken it up into sections for easier digestion. We have also discussed many of them previously in the preceding sections of this chapter. As we progress through the rest of the code for the BlasterMines.as class, we will discuss new concepts in detail and briefly go over any that we have not previously covered in this or preceding chapters.

Adding the Blaster Mines game init functions

The BlasterMines.as init functions set up the class for all games that will be played during this session. It includes the render profile setup code, as well as functions to create the ship assets, projectile assets, and the pool of projectile objects.

First, we will look at the setRendering function. We have discussed this briefly a few times earlier in this chapter:

```
override public function setRendering(profiledRate:int, framerate:int):void {
    var percent:Number=profiledRate / framerate
    trace("framepercent=" + percent);
    trace("stage=" + stage);
    if (percent>=.85) {
        frameRateMultiplier = 2;
    }
    trace("frameRateMultiplier=" + frameRateMultiplier);
}
```

The setRendering function is public and called from the Main.as class. It passed in the profiledRate from the FrameRateProfiler class as well as the desired frameRate for the game. If the profiledRate rate is equal to or greater than 85 percent of the desired frameRate, the frameRateMultipler variable is set to 2. This setup allows us to double the number of particles for explosions. We will also double the size of the particle pool. This function serves as just a small example of how you can use the profiled information to create a unique experience for different powered computers.

We can't access the stage variable yet, because when the init function is called, the BlasterMines.as game has not been added to the Main.as stage display list. The stage will be available when the newGame function is called. In that function, we will set the stage.quality based on this new frameRateMultiplier value.

Next up is the init function where we create objects and set up the manager classes:

```
private function init():void {

    this.focusRect = false;

    //init radar
    radarBitmap.x = 420;
    radarBitmap.y = 230;
    radarBitmap.scaleX = .2;
    radarBitmap.scaleY = .2;

    createLookupTables();
    player.createPlayerShip(spriteGlowFilter);
    projectileManager.createProjectiles(spriteGlowFilter);
    projectileManager.createProjectilePool(50);

    canvasBitmap.scrollRect = new Rectangle(200,200,400,400);

    addChild(canvasBitmap);
    addChild(radarBitmap);

}
```

The init function sets up all of the initial information for the game. We previously discussed radarBitmap and canvasBitmap.scrollRect in the optimization sections. The createLookupTables function was also discussed previously, and you will see the createPlayerShip, createProjectiles, and createProjectilePool functions in detail when we look at the associated manager classes very shortly. One thing to note about all of these is that they only need to be called and created one time for the entire gaming session. There will never be a need to call them again.

The final task for this function is to add the two Bitmap holders to the screen. If you recall, they both are holders for the canvasBitmapData. The canvasBitmapData is the 800 × 800 blit canvas for the entire game world. The canvasBitmap will scroll over this 800 × 800 world using a 400 × 400 scrollRect, while the radarBitmap will show a resized version of the entire world to the right of the game screen.

Now, we will take a look at the createLookUpTables function:

```
private function createLookupTables():void {
   for (var ctr:int = 0; ctr < 359; ctr++) {
      var point:Point = new Point();
      point.x = Math.cos((Math.PI * ctr) / 180);
      point.y = Math.sin((Math.PI * ctr) / 180);
      rotationVectorList[ctr] = point;
   }
}
```

We have examined this function in detail previously. Its job is to create the vectorRotationList Vector Array of Point object instances that represent 360 directions of rotational movement vectors.

Also in the BlasterMines.as init function, we call the player.createPlayerShip method of this class to draw the player ship onto a vector drawing canvas. The player object is an instance of the BlitArrayPlayerFollowMouse. This canvas will be placed into a BitmapData holder and then an array of BitmapData instance will be created that represent 360 degrees of rotation for the ship. We have already taken a quick look at this function inside the BlitArrayPlayerFollowMouse class. Let's review it and dig a little deeper into its functionality:

```
public function createPlayerShip(spriteGlowFilter:GlowFilter):void {
   var tempBlitArrayAsset:BlitArrayAsset = new BlitArrayAsset();
   drawingCanvas.graphics.clear();
   drawingCanvas.graphics.lineStyle(1, 0xffffff);
   drawingCanvas.graphics.moveTo(15, 7);
   drawingCanvas.graphics.lineTo(7, 24);
   drawingCanvas.graphics.lineTo(15, 19);
   drawingCanvas.graphics.moveTo(16, 19);
   drawingCanvas.graphics.lineTo(24, 24);
   drawingCanvas.graphics.lineTo(16, 7);

   shipBitmapData.draw(drawingCanvas);

   shipBitmapData.applyFilter(shipBitmapData, shipBitmapData.rect, new Point(0,0), ↵
      spriteGlowFilter);

   animationList=tempBlitArrayAsset.createRotationBlitArrayFromBD(shipBitmapData, 1,90);
   //*** end player ship

   //*** shield
   drawingCanvas.graphics.clear();
   drawingCanvas.graphics.lineStyle(3, 0xffffff);
   drawingCanvas.graphics.drawCircle(15, 15, 14);
   shieldBitmapData.draw(drawingCanvas);
   //*** end shield

}
```

543

This is an interesting function. Its job is to draw the player's ship as a vector shape and use the BlitArrayAsset class to create an Array of 360 rotations for the ship. Each of those will be a separate BitmapData object that will be used for blitting to the canvasBitmapData at render time. Which one of the 360 is blitted is based on the rotation angle of the player ship.

We drew the player's ship in Adobe Fireworks (our favorite Bitmap tool) first; see Figure 11-4. Then we used the bitmap graphic we created to plot out the lines on the drawCanvas shape instance in the createPlayerShip.

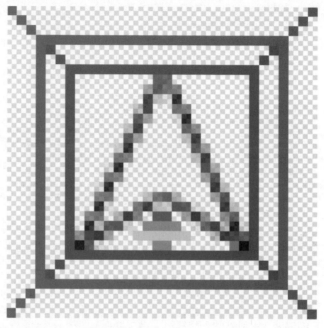

Figure 11-4. The 32 × 32 player ship blown up in Fireworks design mode

The player ship's design is actually on a 32 × 32 pixel canvas in Fireworks, blown up sixteen times its normal size in the design view. The blue line represents the place where the glow filter will end, and the red line is a buffer area for rotation so drawing the object won't cause clipping.

All of our game objects will be drawn in the color white, and the global class-level BlasterMines.as GlowFilter instance spriteGlowFilter will be changed as needed to the correct color for the object's glow effect. The ship's glow is a blue color. When the game begins, spriteGlowFilter is set to a blue color, so there is no need to change it here. We will reset it for other objects, so we need to set the color before we draw those. Next, we draw vector lines in the drawCanvas, and when finished, we use the BitmapData.draw method to draw the object into a BitmapData holder. We then create the animationList array for the player with a temporary BlitArrayAsset instance.

The shield for the player is created in a similar manner (with a drawCanvas.graphics.drawCircle function call). It is drawn into a BitmapData instance (shieldBitmapData) and will be blitted to the canvasBitmapData directly when the player's shield is turned on.

Now, we will examine the projectileManager.createProjectiles function:

```
public function createProjectiles(spriteGlowFilter:GlowFilter):void {
    //projectileManager.projectiles
    var tempBlitArrayAsset:BlitArrayAsset = new BlitArrayAsset();

    drawingCanvas.graphics.clear();
    drawingCanvas.graphics.lineStyle(1, 0xffffff);

    drawingCanvas.graphics.drawRect(3, 3, 2, 2);

    projectileBitmapData.draw(drawingCanvas);

    projectileBitmapData.applyFilter(projectileBitmapData, projectileBitmapData.rect, ⏎
        point0, spriteGlowFilter);

    tempBlitArrayAsset= new BlitArr`ayAsset();

    projectileAnimationFrames=tempBlitArrayAsset.createRotationBlitArrayFromBD⏎
        (projectileBitmapData, 10,0);
}
```

Projectiles are drawn in a very similar manner to the player's ship. These are a simple rectangle with a blue GlowFilter (spriteGlowFilter) to match the ship's glow.

Here is the projectileManager.createProjectilePool function:

```
public function createProjectilePool(maxProjectiles:int):void {

    for (var projetcileCtr:int = 0; projetcileCtr < maxProjectiles; projetcileCtr++) {

        var tempProjectile:BasicBiltArrayProjectile=new BasicBiltArrayProjectile(0,799,0,799);
        tempProjectile.animationList=projectileAnimationFrames;
        tempProjectile.bitmapData = tempProjectile.animationList[0];
        projectilePool.push(tempProjectile);
    }
}
```

The projectilePool is very similar to the particle pool described earlier. There are two Arrays that hold the projectiles. The projectilePool holds the inactive projectiles, and the projectiles Array holds the active projectiles that are in use.

Adding the newGame and newLevel functions

The BlasterMines.as newGame function sets up the defaults for a new game. The new level functions set up a new level based on a simple algorithm to change the color, speed, and number of enemy the player must face.

```
override public function newGame():void {

    //cannot do this until the game has been added to the stage.
    if (frameRateMultiplier==2) {
        stage.quality = StageQuality.BEST;
    }else {
        stage.quality = StageQuality.MEDIUM;
    }

    trace("new game");
```

```
   switchSystemState(STATE_SYSTEM_GAME_PLAY);
   score = 0;
   level = 0;
   shield = 10;
   gameOver = false;
   playerExplosionParticles = [];
   playerStarted = false;

   customScoreBoardEventShield.value = shield.toString()
   customScoreBoardEventScore.value = score.toString()
   customScoreBoardEventLevel.value = level.toString()

   dispatchEvent(customScoreBoardEventScore);
   dispatchEvent(customScoreBoardEventShield);
   dispatchEvent(customScoreBoardEventLevel);
}
```

This function is pretty simple, but we'd like to point out a few things. First, we use the frameRateModifier value to set the stage.quality. This is a simple example of using the profiled information to change the quality of the game for each user's machine. There are four settings for the stage.Quality: LOW, MEDIUM, HIGH, and BEST. We have chosen to use MEDIUM unless the setRendering function found that the frameRateModifier could be set to 2 for the user's machine.

Also notice that we have the first uses of the class level reusable score board update events in this function.

Here is the newLevel function:

```
override public function newLevel():void {
   stage.focus = this;
   trace("new level");
   mineManager.mines = [];
   projectileManager.projectiles = [];
   stage.focus = this;
   level++;
   if (level > maxLevel) {
      level = 1;
   }

   levelColor = levelColors[level];

   spriteGlowFilter = new GlowFilter(levelColor, .75, 2 , 2, 1.5, 2, false, false);
   createLevelbackground();
   mineManager.createLevelMines(spriteGlowFilter, level, levelColor);
   particleManager.createLevelParticles(spriteGlowFilter,levelColor);

   particleManager.createParticlePool(particleManager.particlePoolMax*↵
      frameRateMultiplier);

   canvasBitmapGlowFilter.color = levelColor;
   canvasBitmap.filters = [canvasBitmapGlowFilter];

   player.x = 400;
   player.y = 400;
   player.nextX = player.x;
   player.nextY = player.y;
   playerStarted = true;
```

```
player.bitmapData = player.animationList[0];
render();

dispatchEvent(new CustomEventLevelScreenUpdate(CustomEventLevelScreenUpdate.↵
    UPDATE_TEXT, String(level)));

dispatchEvent(new CustomEventSound(CustomEventSound.PLAY_SOUND, ↵
    Main.SOUND_MUSIC_IN_GAME, true, 999, 8, 1));

customScoreBoardEventLevel.value = level.toString();
dispatchEvent(customScoreBoardEventLevel);
}
```

The newLevel function does a lot of game logic. Let's step through the major actions of this function:

1. First, it adds 1 to the current level value. If the current level is greater than maxLevel, it will be set back to 1.

2. Using the current level integer value, we pull a color from the levelColors array and set the levelColor class variable. This will be used for the Mine glow, the Particle glow, and for a glow around the entire level. Here is the levelColors Array from the variable definition section.

```
private var levelColors:Array = [NaN, 0xff0000, 0x00ff00, 0x0000ff, 0xffff00, 0x00ffff, ↵
    0xffaa00, 0xaaff00, 0x00ffaa, 0x00aaff];
```

3. The spriteGlowFilter is set with the new levelColor value, and then the mine, particle, and background assets are drawn for the level with their respective creation functions. The particle pool is also created.

4. The special glow filter for the entire canvasBitmap is set to the levelColor, and then it is applied by adding to the filters array for the cavasBitmap.

5. The player object is initialized to the center of the screen and it set to the 0 frame (facing up).

6. The render function is called to ensure that the screen is drawn for the level transition fade in.

7. Events are fired off to set the levelScreen text, play the in-game music, and change the level value text on the scoreBoard. Notice that we are using the class-level shared event for the scoreBoard update.

> Note that we have only created class level shared events for the scoreBoard updates, but we could actually make them for the soundManager events and even the levelScreen update if we wanted to continue to utilize these optimizations.

Let's take a look at the createLevelBackground function now:

```
private function createLevelbackground():void {
    //*** background
    drawingCanvas.filters = [spriteGlowFilter];

    //draw symbol on background
```

```
drawingCanvas.graphics.clear();
drawingCanvas.graphics.lineStyle(2, 0xaaaaaa);
drawingCanvas.graphics.moveTo(6, 6);
drawingCanvas.graphics.lineTo(25, 6);
drawingCanvas.graphics.lineTo(25, 22);
drawingCanvas.graphics.lineTo(6, 22);
drawingCanvas.graphics.lineTo(6, 6);
drawingCanvas.graphics.moveTo(18, 8);
drawingCanvas.graphics.lineTo(18, 16);
drawingCanvas.graphics.lineTo(12, 16);
drawingCanvas.graphics.lineTo(12, 12);
drawingCanvas.graphics.moveTo(9, 24);
drawingCanvas.graphics.lineTo(9, 25);
drawingCanvas.graphics.moveTo(15, 24);
drawingCanvas.graphics.lineTo(15, 25);
drawingCanvas.graphics.moveTo(21, 24);
drawingCanvas.graphics.lineTo(21, 25);

//enlarge scale drawn symbol and place in center of the background
var scaleTranslateMatrix:Matrix = new Matrix();
scaleTranslateMatrix.scale(20, 20);
scaleTranslateMatrix.translate(100, 100);

var faceColorTransform:ColorTransform = new ColorTransform(1, 1, 1, .2 );

backgroundBitmapData.draw(drawingCanvas, scaleTranslateMatrix, faceColorTransform, ↵
    BlendMode.LAYER)

scaleTranslateMatrix = null;
faceColorTransform = null;

//draw box around background
drawingCanvas.graphics.clear();
drawingCanvas.graphics.lineStyle(2,0xffffff);
drawingCanvas.graphics.drawRect(5, 5, 790, 790);
backgroundBitmapData.draw(drawingCanvas);

//draw 800 random stars on the background
for (var ctr:int = 0; ctr < 800; ctr ++) {

backgroundBitmapData.setPixel32(int(Math.random() * 799), ↵
 int(Math.random() * 799), 0x0066ff);
 }
}
```

The backgroundBitmapData instance is used as the giant eraser for our blitting operations instead of a plain black background, so on every frame tick, the entire 800 × 800 background will be copied to canvasBitmapData and each of the objects will be copied to it.

Here is a rundown of how we will construct this background. The rendering portion will occur in the render function:

1. First, we paint the mine symbol (described in the next section) on the drawingCanvas.

2. Next, we enlarge and move the symbol to the center of the backgroundBitmapData with a scale and translate matrix.

3. We draw a rectangle box around the entire backgroundBitmapData to give it a thin border.

4. We draw 800 random blue stars (single pixels) to the backgroundBitmapData.

Now, we will take a look at the MineManager class function, createLevelMines. This function creates a certain number of Mine class instances based on the level value:

```
public function createLevelMines(spriteGlowFilter:GlowFilter,level:int, ↵
    levelColor:uint):void{

    //*** Mines look
    mineBitmapData= new BitmapData(32, 32, true, 0x00000000);
    var tempBlitArrayAsset:BlitArrayAsset = new BlitArrayAsset();
    drawingCanvas.graphics.clear();

    drawingCanvas.graphics.lineStyle(2, 0xffffff);
    drawingCanvas.graphics.moveTo(6, 6);
    drawingCanvas.graphics.lineTo(25, 6);
    drawingCanvas.graphics.lineTo(25, 22);
    drawingCanvas.graphics.lineTo(6, 22);
    drawingCanvas.graphics.lineTo(6, 6);
    drawingCanvas.graphics.moveTo(18, 8);
    drawingCanvas.graphics.lineTo(18, 16);
    drawingCanvas.graphics.lineTo(12, 16);
    drawingCanvas.graphics.lineTo(12, 12);
    drawingCanvas.graphics.moveTo(9, 23);
    drawingCanvas.graphics.lineTo(9, 25);
    drawingCanvas.graphics.moveTo(15, 23);
    drawingCanvas.graphics.lineTo(15, 25);
    drawingCanvas.graphics.moveTo(21, 23);
    drawingCanvas.graphics.lineTo(21, 25);

    spriteGlowFilter.color = levelColor;
    mineBitmapData.draw(drawingCanvas);

    mineBitmapData.applyFilter(mineBitmapData, mineBitmapData.rect, point0, ↵
        spriteGlowFilter);
    tempBlitArrayAsset = new BlitArrayAsset();

    mineAnimationFrames=tempBlitArrayAsset.createRotationBlitArrayFromBD↵
        (mineBitmapData, 1,90);

    //*** end look

    //create mines for the level
    mines = [];

    for (var ctr:int-0;ctr<30+20*level;ctr++) {

        var tempMine:Mine=new Mine(13,787,13,787);
```

```
//find a random roation value for the mine.
tempMine.dx=Math.cos(6.28*((Math.random()*360)-90)/360.0);
tempMine.dy = Math.sin(6.28 * ((Math.random() * 360) - 90) / 360.0);

if (level % 2 == 0) {
    tempMine.y = 700
}else {
    tempMine.y = 100
}

tempMine.x = 100;
tempMine.nextX = tempMine.x;
tempMine.nextY = tempMine.y;
tempMine.frame = int((Math.random() * 359)) ;
tempMine.animationList = mineAnimationFrames;

tempMine.bitmapData = tempMine.animationList[tempMine.frame];
tempMine.speed = (Math.random()*1)+2+level;
mines.push(tempMine);
    }
}
```

Based on the level value, a set of Mine instances is created for the level. Mine instances for the level are created starting at 30 and increasing by 20*level. This makes for a very difficult game at higher levels.

The mines will be created inside a loop before each level is created. The number of mines is based on a starting amount of 30, plus 20 multiplied by the level number:

```
for (var ctr:int=0;ctr<30+20*level;ctr++) {
… // interior loop code to create all mines for the level
}
```

The mine speed will be calculated as follows to allow it to be increased per level:

```
tempMine.speed = (Math.random()*1)+2+level;
```

This function also creates the look of our enemy mines (see Figure 11-5) based on a 32 × 32–pixel symbol. This symbol was created in a similar manner to the player object in Fireworks. It is also drawn to a drawCanvas Shape instance, placed into a BitmapData instance (mineBitmapData), and rotated with an instance of the BlitArrayAsset class. The 360 rotated BitmapData instances from the BlitArrayAsset.createRotationArray call are placed into the global mineAnimation Array.

Each new Mine instance is also given random dx and dy values. If the level value is an odd number, we start all of the mines in the upper left-hand corner (y=100). If the level is an even number, we start the mines in the lower left-hand corner (y=700).

Also, each mine is given a random frame to start in the animationList array (0–359). The speed of each mine is also random with a maximum based on the level value. All of these calculations make for a set of mines that will not be completely predictable to the game player.

Next, we will examine the particleManager.createParticlePool function. Here is the complete code for the function; you have seen much of this code previously in the section called "Optimizing with object pooling":

```
public function createParticlePool(maxParticles:int):void {
    particlePool = [];
    particles = [];

    for (var particleCtr:int=0;particleCtr<maxParticles;particleCtr++) {
        var tempParticle:BasicBiltArrayParticle = new BasicBiltArrayParticle(0,799,0,799);
        particlePool.push(tempParticle);
    }
}
```

A new pool of Particle instances is created for each level. The number of objects in this pool is based on the maxParticles value passed in.

Now, look at the particleManager.createLevelParticles function:

```
public function createLevelParticles(spriteGlowFilter:GlowFilter, levelColor:uint):void {
    var tempBlitArrayAsset:BlitArrayAsset = new BlitArrayAsset();
    particleBitmapData = new BitmapData(8, 8, true, 0x00000000);
    drawingCanvas.graphics.clear();
    drawingCanvas.graphics.lineStyle(1, 0xffffff);
    drawingCanvas.graphics.drawRect(3, 3, 2, 2);
    particleBitmapData.draw(drawingCanvas);
    spriteGlowFilter.color = levelColor;

    particleBitmapData.applyFilter(particleBitmapData, particleBitmapData.rect, ↵
        point0, spriteGlowFilter);

    tempBlitArrayAsset= new BlitArrayAsset();
    tempBlitArrayAsset.createFadeOutBlitArrayFromBD(particleBitmapData, 30);
    particleAnimationFrames = tempBlitArrayAsset.tileList;

}
```

The appearance of the particles is based on the levelColor for the Mines. That color is passed into the function along with the BlasterMines spriteGlowFilter instance. The particles use the BlitArrayAsset class's createFadeOutArrayFrameBD to create an array of faded frames. When played in succession over a number of frame ticks, the particles will appear to fade and burn out as they move away from the center of the explosion.

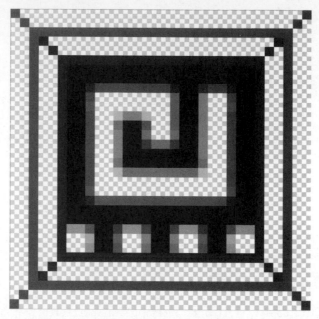

Figure 11-5. The 32 × 32 Mine graphic blown up in design mode

Updating the game loop and internal state machine

While the game loop and internal state machine for Blaster Mines are similar to ones in previous chapters, we have updated this one to make use of the time-based step timer. You must override the runGameTimeBased function in the Game.as class with one specific to your game. Add this function to the BlasterMines.as file:

The runGameTimeBased function was added to the Game.as base class to be used in place of the runGame function for games that make use of the time-based step timer.

```
override public function runGameTimeBased(paused:Boolean=false,timeDifference:Number=1):void {
    if (!paused) {
    systemFunction(timeDifference);
    }
}
```

The heart of both the pause functionality and the time-based step timer is in this function. The paused Boolean and the timeDifference value are both passed into the function from Main. The current systemFunction is run and will make use of the timeDifference if necessary.

The switchSystemState function is used to switch between the two basic game states: GAMEPLAY and PLAYEREXPLODE.

```
private function switchSystemState(stateval:int):void {
    lastSystemState = currentSystemState;
    currentSystemState = stateval;

    switch(stateval) {
```

```
   case STATE_SYSTEM_GAME_PLAY:
       systemFunction = systemGamePlay;
       break;

   case STATE_SYSTEM_PLAYER_EXPLODE :
       systemFunction = systemPlayerExplode;
       break;
   }
}
```

The systemGamePlay function makes use of the timeDifference variable by passing it into the update function.

```
private function systemGamePlay(timeDifference:Number=0):void {
   trace("in game play");
   update(timeDifference);
   checkCollisions();
   render();
   updateScoreBoard();
   checkforEndLevel();
   checkforEndGame();
}
```

The checkForEndGame function is unique to this game. When the player runs out of shields, the game is over. The checkCollisions function will set the gameOver Boolean to true when the shield variable is less than 0. We have a special explode function for the player that displays 300 particles. It reuses the projectile BitmapData for the look of the particles. The internal game state machine is set to run in the STATE_SYSYTEM_PLAYEREXPLODE state rather than the normal STATE_SYSTEM_GAMEPLAY state when the player is in the process of exploding.

```
private function checkforEndGame():void {
   if (gameOver ) {

   dispatchEvent(new CustomEventSound(CustomEventSound.STOP_SOUND, ↵
      Main.SOUND_MUSIC_IN_GAME, true));

   dispatchEvent(new CustomEventSound(CustomEventSound.PLAY_SOUND, ↵
      Main.SOUND_PLAYER_EXPLODE, false, 1, 8, 1));

   canvasBitmapData.copyPixels(backgroundBitmapData, new Rectangle(0,0,32,32), ↵
      player.point);

   createPlayerExplode(player.x + 16, player.y + 16, 300);
   playerStarted = falset
   switchSystemState(STATE_SYSTEM_PLAYER_EXPLODE);
   }
}
```

The checkForEndLevel function decides if the player is ready to proceed to the next game level. The level ends when all of the mines have been destroyed. We don't want the level to end too abruptly, so we wait until there are only 24 particles left on the screen and then start the new level. The player is erased from the screen by copying the background under the player back on top of its current location.

```
private function checkforEndLevel():void {

    if (mineManager.mines.length == 0 && particleManager.particles.length < 25 ) {

        dispatchEvent(new CustomEventSound(CustomEventSound.STOP_SOUND, ↵
            Main.SOUND_MUSIC_IN_GAME, true));
        disposeAll();
        playerStarted = false;

        //erase player from screen

        canvasBitmapData.copyPixels(backgroundBitmapData, new Rectangle(0,0,32,32), ↵
            player.point);

        dispatchEvent(new Event(NEW_LEVEL));
    }
}
```

When the gameOver variable is set to true, the checkForEndGame function will switch the currentSystemState to STATE_SYSTEM_PLAYEREXPLODE. While in the STATE_SYSTEM_PLAYEREXPLODE state, the systemFunction is set to the systemPlayerExplode function. This function will continue to call the update and render functions on each frame tick until all of the particles that make up the player's explosion have left the screen.

```
private function systemPlayerExplode(timeDifference:Number=0):void {
    update(timeDifference);
    render();
    if (playerExplosionParticles.length == 0) {
        playerExplodeComplete();
    }
}
```

The playerExplodeComplete function is called by the systemPlayerExplode state function when there are no more player explosion particles left. Main will change the framework system state when it receives this event. Also, the disposeAll function is called. It will clean up all of the object instances and get ready for a new game.

```
private function playerExplodeComplete():void {
    dispatchEvent(new Event(GAME_OVER));
    disposeAll();
}
```

Adding the update, autoShoot, render, and collision functions

The update, autoShoot, render, and collision functions are very similar to ones you have seen in previous games. We have also described most of the functionality previously in this chapter. We will go over the highlights and any new and previously not mentioned subjects.

```
private function update(timeDifference:Number = 0):void {
    //time based movement modifier calculation
    var step:Number = (timeDifference / 1000)*timeBasedUpdateModifier;

    //*** auto fire
```

```
    autoShoot(step);

    if (playerStarted) {

    player.update(this.mouseX + canvasBitmap.scrollRect.x, this.mouseY + ~cc
        canvasBitmap.scrollRect.y, 20,step);
    }

    for each (tempMine in mineManager.mines) {
        tempMine.update(step);
        tempMine.updateFrame(5);
    }

    particleManager.particleCount = particleManager.particles.length-1

    for (var ctr:int = particleManager.particleCount; ctr >= 0; ctr--) {
        tempParticle = particleManager.particles[ctr];

        if (tempParticle.update(step)) { //return true if particle is to be removed
            tempParticle.frame = 0;
            particleManager.particlePool.push(tempParticle);
            particleManager.particles.splice(ctr,1);
        }
    }

    var projectileLength:int = projectileManager.projectiles.length - 1;
        for (ctr=projectileLength;ctr>=0;ctr--) {
        tempProjectile = projectileManager.projectiles[ctr];

        if (tempProjectile.update(player.xMove, player.yMove,step)) {
            // returns true if needs to be removed
            tempProjectile.frame = 0;
            projectileManager.projectilePool.push(tempProjectile);
            projectileManager.projectiles.splice(ctr,1);
        }else {
            tempProjectile.updateFrame(1);
        }
    }

    for (ctr = playerExplosionParticles.length-1; ctr >= 0; ctr--) {
        tempParticle = playerExplosionParticles[ctr];

        if (tempParticle.update()) { //return true if particle is to be removed
            tempParticle=null
            playerExplosionParticles.splice(ctr,1);
        }
    }
}
```

The update function cycles through all of our game objects and updates them as follows:

1. The first thing update does is calculate the step value modifier for this frame tick. We
    have discussed this in detail earlier in this chapter, but for clarification, the step is the

percentage of the actual calculated distance we want each game object to move on this frame tick, which is based on the results of the time-based step timer.

2. The player's ship shoots projectiles automatically. Projectiles are taken from the `projectileManager.projectilePool` and fire from the ship's location every three frames. The `autoShoot` function is called to fire the projectiles.

3. The player object is updated by passing in the current `mouseX` and `mouseY` values and a `delay` value for the speed of the player relative to the mouse. The larger the `delay` value, the slower the ship will follow the mouse.

4. Each mine's position is updated. Then, each mine's frame is updated by passing the value 5 into the `updateFrame` function of the mine, which causes the mine to spin faster by skipping 5 frames of animation on each frame. This 5 value is arbitrary. It simply tells the `Mine` to rotate 5 degrees at a time. The value can be set to anything you like to create different `Mine` spin rates.

5. The projectiles are updated.

6. If the player has exploded, the player's exploding particles are updated.

Notice that each of the `update` functions is passed the `step` value to use in calculating the distance to move the object this frame tick.

Next up is the `autoShoot` function that is called on each frame tick. It will fire projectiles after a three-frame delay automatically if there are any left in the `projectileManager.projectilePool`.

```
private function autoShoot(step:Number):void {

    projectileManager.projectilePoolCount = projectileManager.projectilePool.length - 1;
    mineManager.mineCount = mineManager.mines.length;

    if (projectileManager.lastProjectileShot > 3 && projectileManager.projectilePoolCount⤸
       > 0 && playerStarted && mineManager.mineCount > 0) {

        dispatchEvent(new CustomEventSound(CustomEventSound.PLAY_SOUND, ⤸
            Main.SOUND_PLAYER_SHOOT, false, 0, 8, 1));

        tempProjectile = projectileManager.projectilePool.pop();
        var projectileRadians:Number = (player.frame / 360) * 6.28;

        //+ 16 to get it to the center
        tempProjectile.x=(player.point.x+16)+Math.cos(projectileRadians);
        tempProjectile.y =(player.point.y+16) + Math.sin(projectileRadians);
        tempProjectile.x = player.x+16;
        tempProjectile.y = player.y + 16;
        tempProjectile.nextX = tempProjectile.x;
        tempProjectile.nextY = tempProjectile.y;
        tempProjectile.dx = rotationVectorList[player.frame].x;
        tempProjectile.dy = rotationVectorList[player.frame].y;

        tempProjectile.speed = 5;
        tempProjectile.frame = 0;

        tempProjectile.bitmapData = tempProjectile.animationList[0];
```

```
            projectileManager.projectiles.push(tempProjectile);
            projectileManager.lastProjectileShot=0;
        }else {
            projectileManager.lastProjectileShot+=step;
        }
    }
}
```

Also notice that we add the step value to projectileManager.lastProjectileShoot counter instead of the standard 1 per frame tick. This way, we keep the fire rate of the player timed to the step timer rather than the frame rate. If we tied it directly to the frame tick rate, users on faster machines would get to fire more often in the same time frame than users on slower machines. In our game, each player will fire the same number of projectiles each second no matter what frameRate the game is played at.

Now, we are going to take a look at the checkCollisions functions:

```
private function checkCollisions():void {

    mineManager.mineCount = mineManager.mines.length - 1;
    projectileManager.projectileCount = projectileManager.projectiles.length - 1;

    mines: for (var mineCtr:int = mineManager.mineCount; mineCtr >= 0; mineCtr--) {
            tempMine mineManager.mines[mineCtr];
            tempMine.point.x=tempMine.x;
            tempMine.point.y=tempMine.y;

    projectiles: for (var projectileCtr:int=projectileManager.projectileCount;↵
                projectileCtr>=0;projectileCtr--) {

                tempProjectile=projectileManager.projectiles[projectileCtr];
                tempProjectile.point.x=tempProjectile.x;
                tempProjectile.point.y=tempProjectile.y;

                //use pixel hit because circle circle for
                //these was causing false negatives on ship shield hit

                if (tempProjectile.bitmapData.hitTest(tempProjectile.point,255,↵
                 tempMine.bitmapData,tempMine.point,255)) {

                    dispatchEvent(new CustomEventSound(CustomEventSound.PLAY_SOUND, ↵
                     Main.SOUND_MINE_EXPLODE, false, 0, 8, 1));

                    createExplode(tempMine.x+16, tempMine.y+16, particleManager.↵
                     particlesPerExplode*frameRateMultiplier);

                    tempMine=null;
                    mineManager.mines.splice(mineCtr, 1);
                    tempProjectile.frame = 0;
                    projectileManager.projectilePool.push(tempProjectile);
                    projectileManager.projectiles.splice(projectileCtr,1);

                    score += 5 * level;
```

```
                                 break mines;
                                 break projectiles;
                             }
                         }

              if (circleCheck(player.point.x, tempMine.point.x, player.point.y, ↵
                 tempMine.point.y, 12, 12)) {

              dispatchEvent(new CustomEventSound(CustomEventSound.PLAY_SOUND, ↵
                 Main.SOUND_MINE_EXPLODE, false, 0, 8, 1));

              createExplode(tempMine.x+16, tempMine.y+16, particleManager.↵
                 particlesPerExplode*frameRateMultiplier);

              tempMine=null;
              mineManager.mines.splice(mineCtr, 1);
              score += 5 * level;

              //trace("hit");
              if (!player.shieldRender) {
                 //trace("start shield");
                 shield--;

                 if (shield < 0) {
                     shield = 0;
                     gameOver = true;
                 }else {
                     dispatchEvent(new CustomEventSound(CustomEventSound.PLAY_SOUND, ↵
                        Main.SOUND_PLAYER_HIT, false, 0, 8, 1));

                     player.shieldRender = true;
                     player.shieldCount = 0;
                 }

              }else {
                 //trace("shield already started");
              }
          }
      }
   }
}
```

Let's now step through what's happening in the preceding code:

1. First, we loop though all of the mines and check them against all of the projectiles with a circle-to-circle mathematical check. We do this, because they are roughly circle shaped. They are removed if a hit occurs, and the player's score is updated. The particles and projectiles are placed back in their respective pools for reuse.

2. The player ship and the mines are checked for collisions using BitmapData pixel-perfect collisions. We use this type of collision detection because the player's ship is a triangle and the circle-to-circle check is far too inaccurate.

3. If the player's ship is hit by a Mine instance, its shield is displayed for a few frame ticks. If the player.shieldCount variable is less than 1, the gameOver Boolean is set to true.

```
private function render():void {

    canvasBitmapData.lock();
    canvasBitmapData.copyPixels(backgroundBitmapData, backgroundBitmapData.rect, point0);

    if (playerStarted) {
        player.render(canvasBitmapData);
    }

    for each (tempMine in mineManager.mines) {
        tempMine.render(canvasBitmapData);
    }

    for each (tempParticle in particleManager.particles) {
        tempParticle.render(canvasBitmapData);
    }

    for each (tempProjectile in projectileManager.projectiles) {
        tempProjectile.render(canvasBitmapData);
    }

    for each (tempParticle in playerExplosionParticles) {
        tempParticle.render(canvasBitmapData);
    }

    if (player.shieldRender) {
        //trace("render shield");
        canvasBitmapData.copyPixels(player.shieldBitmapData, player.
          shieldBitmapData.rect, player.point);

        player.shieldCount++;

        if (player.shieldCount > player.shieldLife) {
            player.shieldCount = 0;
            player.shieldRender = false;
        }
    }

    canvasBitmapData.unlock();

    if (playerStarted) {
        canvasRect.x = player.x - 200;
        canvasRect.y = player.y - 200;

        if (canvasRect.x < 0) canvasRect.x = 0;

        if (canvasRect.y < 0) canvasRect.y = 0;

        if (canvasRect.x > 399) canvasRect.x = 399;

        if (canvasRect.y > 399) canvasRect.y = 399;

        canvasBitmap.scrollRect = canvasRect;
    }
}
```

The `render` function simply locks our canvas, loops through all of the game objects, and blits them to the `canvasBitmapData`. The final task it completes is to make sure the `scrollRect` of the `canvasBitmap` is positioned in the right location to simulate scrolling.

Adding auxiliary functions

Many of the remaining auxiliary functions are very similar to ones you have seen in other games. As usual, we will describe the major differences and new functions.

```
private function updateScoreBoard():void {

    customScoreBoardEventScore.value = score.toString();
    customScoreBoardEventShield.value =shield.toString()
    customScoreBoardEventParticlePool.value = String(particleManager.particlePool.length);
    customScoreBoardEventParticleActive.value = String(particleManager.particles.length);
    customScoreBoardEventProjectilePool.value = String(projectileManager.↵
        projectilePool.length);

    customScoreBoardEventProjectileActive.value = String(projectileManager.↵
        projectiles.length);

    dispatchEvent(customScoreBoardEventScore);
    dispatchEvent(customScoreBoardEventShield);
    dispatchEvent(customScoreBoardEventParticlePool);
    dispatchEvent(customScoreBoardEventParticleActive);
    dispatchEvent(customScoreBoardEventProjectilePool);
    dispatchEvent(customScoreBoardEventProjectileActive);
}
```

The `ScoreBoard` is updated using our new set of global custom `Events`.

```
private function addToScore(val:Number):void {
    score += val;
}
```

The `addToScore` function simply accepts in a value to add to the current score.

```
private function circleCheck(x1:Number, x2:Number, y1:Number, y2:Number, ↵
    radius1:Number, radius2:Number):Boolean {

    var dx:Number = x2 - x1;
    var dy:Number = y2 - y1;
    var dist:Number = Math.sqrt(dx * dx + dy * dy);
    return dist < radius1 + radius2
}
```

The `circleCheck` function takes in the location of two objects and the radius of each. It returns true if they intersect, signaling a collision.

```
private function createExplode(xval:Number,yval:Number,parts:int):void {
    for (var explodeCtr:int=0;explodeCtr<parts;explodeCtr++) {

        particleManager.particlePoolCount = particleManager.particlePool.length-1;
        if (particleManager.particlePoolCount > 0) {

            tempParticle=particleManager.particlePool.pop();
```

```
                tempParticle.lifeDelayCount=0;
                tempParticle.x=xval;
                tempParticle.y = yval;
                tempParticle.nextX=xval;
                tempParticle.nextY=yval;
                tempParticle.speed = (Math.random() * 3) + 1;
                tempParticle.frame = 0;

                tempParticle.animationList = particleManager.particleAnimationFrames;
                tempParticle.bitmapData = tempParticle.animationList[tempParticle.frame];

                var randInt:int = int(Math.random() * 359);

                tempParticle.dx = rotationVectorList[randInt].x;
                tempParticle.dy = rotationVectorList[randInt].y;

                tempParticle.lifeDelay = int(Math.random() * 10);
                particleManager.particles.push(tempParticle);
        }
    }
}
```

The `createPlayerExplode` function creates an explosion using `Particles` from the `particlePool` (if enough are left in the pool).

```
private function createPlayerExplode(xval:Number,yval:Number,parts:int):void {
    for (var explodeCtr:int=0;explodeCtr<parts;explodeCtr++) {

        var tempParticle:BasicBiltArrayParticle = new BasicBiltArrayParticle(0,799,0,799);
        tempParticle.lifeDelayCount=0;
        tempParticle.x=xval;
        tempParticle.y = yval;
        tempParticle.nextX=xval;
        tempParticle.nextY=yval;
        tempParticle.speed = (Math.random() * 10) + 1;
        tempParticle.frame = 0;

        tempParticle.animationList = projectileManager.projectileAnimationFrames;
        tempParticle.bitmapData = tempParticle.animationList[tempParticle.frame];

        var randInt:int = int(Math.random() * 359);
        tempParticle.dx = rotationVectorList[randInt].x;
        tempParticle.dy = rotationVectorList[randInt].y;
        tempParticle.lifeDelay = int(Math.random() * 5);
        playerExplosionParticles.push(tempParticle);
    }
}
```

The `createPlayerExplode` function creates an explosion where the player ship used to be. We use the first frame of the `projectileAnimation` array of `BitmapData` instances. Instead of creating a new particle, we use a `Projectile` `BitmapData` because it is already the same color as the player.

```
private function disposeAll():void {

    particleManager.particleCount = particleManager.particles.length-1

    // remove particle pool
    for (var ctr:int = particleManager.particleCount; ctr >= 0; ctr--) {
        tempParticle = particleManager.particles.pop();
        tempParticle.frame = 0;
        particleManager.particlePool.push(tempParticle);
    }

 //remove particle animation
    for (ctr= 0; ctr < particleManager.particleAnimationFrames.length; ctr++) {
        particleManager.particleAnimationFrames[ctr].dispose();
    }

    particleManager.particleAnimationFrames = null;
    particleManager.particleBitmapData = null;
    particleManager.particlePool = null;
    trace("disposed");


//remove mines

    for (ctr= 0; ctr < mineManager.mineAnimationFrames.length; ctr++) {
        mineManager.mineAnimationFrames[ctr].dispose();
    }

    mineManager.mineAnimationFrames = null;
    mineManager.mines = null;
    mineManager.mineBitmapData = null;


    if (gameOver) {
        playerExplosionParticles = null;
    }
}
```

The disposeAll function up the objects between levels and at the end of each game. This saves memory by freeing them up for the garbage collection process.

The full GameFrameWork class

For reference, we have included the entire new com.efg.framework.GameFrameWork.as file in this section. Many changes have been made to this file in this chapter. We recommend that you replace the current GameFrameWork.as file with this one. We did not cover every line of each change in the earlier sections. Pay close attention to the comments that that show the changes in chapter 11.

```
package com.efg.framework
{

    import flash.display.Bitmap;
    import flash.display.BitmapData;
    import flash.display.MovieClip;
    import flash.events.Event;
    import flash.events.KeyboardEvent;
    import flash.geom.Point;
    import flash.text.TextFormat;
    import flash.utils.getTimer;
    import flash.utils.Timer;
    import flash.events.TimerEvent;

    public class GameFrameWork extends MovieClip {

        public static const EVENT_WAIT_COMPLETE:String = "wait complete";

        //added in chapter 11
        public static const KEY_MUTE:int = 77;   // added chapter 11
        public static const KEY_PAUSE:int = 80; //added chapter 11
        public var paused:Boolean = false;
        public var pausedScreen:BasicScreen;

        public var systemFunction:Function;
        public var currentSystemState:int;
        public var nextSystemState:int;
        public var lastSystemState:int;

        public var appBackBitmapData:BitmapData;
        public var appBackBitmap:Bitmap; ;

        public var frameRate:int;
        public var timerPeriod:Number;
        public var gameTimer:Timer;

        public var titleScreen:BasicScreen;
        public var gameOverScreen:BasicScreen;
        public var instructionsScreen:BasicScreen;
        public var levelInScreen:BasicScreen;
        public var scoreBoard:ScoreBoard;

        public var scoreBoardTextFormat:TextFormat;
        public var screenTextFormat:TextFormat;
        public var screenButtonFormat:TextFormat;

        public var levelInText:String;

        public var soundManager:SoundManager;

        //chapter 11 added
        public var frameCounter:FrameCounter = new FrameCounter();
        public var lastTime:Number;
        public var timeDifference:Number
```

```
        //Game is our custom class to hold all logic for the game.
        public var game:Game;

        //waitTime is used in conjunction with the STATE_SYSTEM_WAIT state
        // it suspends the game and allows animation or other processing to finish
        public var waitTime:int;
        public var waitCount:int = 0;

        //added chapter 11

        public var frameRateProfiler:FrameRateProfiler;

        public function GameFrameWork() {
            soundManager = new SoundManager(); // moved;
        }

        //function added in chapter 11
        public function addedToStage(e:Event = null):void {

            stage.addEventListener(KeyboardEvent.KEY_DOWN,keyDownListener);
            this.focusRect=false; // added chapter 11
            stage.focus = stage; // added chapter 11
            trace("gamFrameWork added to stage");

        }

         public function init():void {
           trace("inner init stub");
         }

         public function frameRateProfileComplete(e:Event):void {
          // stub
         }

       public function setApplicationBackGround(width:Number, height:Number, ⏎
           isTransparent:Boolean = false, color:uint = 0x000000):void {

           appBackBitmapData = new BitmapData(width, height, isTransparent, color);
           appBackBitmap = new Bitmap(appBackBitmapData);
           addChild(appBackBitmap);
       }
          //changed for chapter 11
       public function startTimer(timeBasedAnimation:Boolean=false):void {

           stage.frameRate = frameRate;
                            if (timeBasedAnimation) {
             lastTime = getTimer();
             addEventListener(Event.ENTER_FRAME, runGameEnterFrame);
           }else{
             timerPeriod = 1000 / frameRate;
             gameTimer=new Timer(timerPeriod);
             gameTimer.addEventListener(TimerEvent.TIMER, runGame);
             gameTimer.start();
           }
       }
```

```
public function runGame(e:TimerEvent):void {

    systemFunction();
    frameCounter.countFrames();
}
public function runGameEnterFrame(e:Event):void {

    timeDifference = getTimer() - lastTime
    lastTime = getTimer();
    systemFunction();
    frameCounter.countFrames();
}


public function switchSystemState(stateval:int):void {
    lastSystemState = currentSystemState;
    currentSystemState = stateval;

    trace("currentSystemState=" + currentSystemState)
    switch(stateval) {

        case FrameWorkStates.STATE_SYSTEM_WAIT:
            systemFunction = systemWait;
            break;

        case FrameWorkStates.STATE_SYSTEM_WAIT_FOR_CLOSE:
            systemFunction = systemWaitForClose;
            break;

        case FrameWorkStates.STATE_SYSTEM_TITLE:
            systemFunction = systemTitle;
            break;

        case FrameWorkStates.STATE_SYSTEM_INSTRUCTIONS:
            systemFunction = systemInstructions;
            break;

        case FrameWorkStates.STATE_SYSTEM_NEW_GAME:
            systemFunction = systemNewGame;
            break;

        case FrameWorkStates.STATE_SYSTEM_NEW_LEVEL:
            systemFunction = systemNewLevel;
            break;

        case FrameWorkStates.STATE_SYSTEM_LEVEL_IN:
            systemFunction = systemLevelIn;
            break;

        case FrameWorkStates.STATE_SYSTEM_GAME_PLAY:
            systemFunction = systemGamePlay;
            break

        case FrameWorkStates.STATE_SYSTEM_GAME_OVER:
            systemFunction = systemGameOver;
```

```
                break;
        }
}


public function systemTitle():void {
    addChild(titleScreen);

    titleScreen.addEventListener(CustomEventButtonId.BUTTON_ID, ↵
        okButtonClickListener, false, 0, true);

    switchSystemState(FrameWorkStates.STATE_SYSTEM_WAIT_FOR_CLOSE);
    nextSystemState = FrameWorkStates.STATE_SYSTEM_INSTRUCTIONS;
}


public function systemInstructions():void {

    //trace("system instructions");
    addChild(instructionsScreen);

    instructionsScreen.addEventListener(CustomEventButtonId.BUTTON_ID, ↵
        okButtonClickListener, false, 0, true);

    switchSystemState(FrameWorkStates.STATE_SYSTEM_WAIT_FOR_CLOSE);
    nextSystemState = FrameWorkStates.STATE_SYSTEM_NEW_GAME;
}

public function systemNewGame():void {
    addChild(game);

    game.addEventListener(CustomEventScoreBoardUpdate.UPDATE_TEXT, ↵
        scoreBoardUpdateListener, false, 0, true);

    game.addEventListener(CustomEventLevelScreenUpdate.UPDATE_TEXT, ↵
        levelScreenUpdateListener, false, 0, true);

    game.addEventListener(CustomEventSound.PLAY_SOUND, soundEventListener, ↵
        false, 0, true);

    game.addEventListener(Game.GAME_OVER, gameOverListener, false, 0, true);
    game.addEventListener(Game.NEW_LEVEL, newLevelListener, false, 0, true);

    game.newGame();
    switchSystemState(FrameWorkStates.STATE_SYSTEM_NEW_LEVEL);
}

public function systemNewLevel():void {
    game.newLevel();
    switchSystemState(FrameWorkStates.STATE_SYSTEM_LEVEL_IN);
}

public function systemLevelIn():void {
    addChild(levelInScreen);
    waitTime = 30;
```

```
    switchSystemState(FrameWorkStates.STATE_SYSTEM_WAIT);
    nextSystemState = FrameWorkStates.STATE_SYSTEM_GAME_PLAY;

    addEventListener(EVENT_WAIT_COMPLETE, waitCompleteListener, false, 0, true);

}

public function systemGameOver():void {
    removeChild(game);
    addChild(gameOverScreen);

    gameOverScreen.addEventListener(CustomEventButtonId.BUTTON_ID, ↵
       okButtonClickListener, false, 0, true);

    switchSystemState(FrameWorkStates.STATE_SYSTEM_WAIT_FOR_CLOSE);
    nextSystemState = FrameWorkStates.STATE_SYSTEM_TITLE;
}

public function systemGamePlay():void {
    game.runGame();
}

public function systemWaitForClose():void {
                   //do nothing
}

public function systemWait():void {
    waitCount++;
    if (waitCount > waitTime) {
       waitCount = 0;
       dispatchEvent(new Event(EVENT_WAIT_COMPLETE));
    }
}


public function okButtonClickListener(e:CustomEventButtonId):void {

    switch(e.id) {

       case FrameWorkStates.STATE_SYSTEM_TITLE:
          removeChild(titleScreen);
          titleScreen.removeEventListener(CustomEventButtonId.BUTTON_ID, ↵
            okButtonClickListener);

       break;

       case FrameWorkStates.STATE_SYSTEM_INSTRUCTIONS:
          removeChild(instructionsScreen);

          instructionsScreen.removeEventListener(CustomEventButtonId.BUTTON_ID, ↵
             okButtonClickListener);
```

567

```
                        break;

                case FrameWorkStates.STATE_SYSTEM_GAME_OVER:
                    removeChild(gameOverScreen);

                    gameOverScreen.removeEventListener(CustomEventButtonId.BUTTON_ID, ↵
                        okButtonClickListener);
                    break;

            }
            trace("next system state=" + nextSystemState);
            switchSystemState(nextSystemState);
    }


    public function scoreBoardUpdateListener(e:CustomEventScoreBoardUpdate):void {
        scoreBoard.update(e.element, e.value);
    }

    public function levelScreenUpdateListener(e:CustomEventLevelScreenUpdate):void {
        levelInScreen.setDisplayText(levelInText + e.text);
    }

    public function gameOverListener(e:Event):void {

        switchSystemState(FrameWorkStates.STATE_SYSTEM_GAME_OVER);

        game.removeEventListener(CustomEventScoreBoardUpdate.UPDATE_TEXT, ↵
            scoreBoardUpdateListener);

        game.removeEventListener(CustomEventLevelScreenUpdate.UPDATE_TEXT, ↵
            levelScreenUpdateListener);

        game.removeEventListener(CustomEventSound.PLAY_SOUND, soundEventListener);
        game.removeEventListener(Game.GAME_OVER, gameOverListener);
        game.removeEventListener(Game.NEW_LEVEL, newLevelListener);
    }

    public function newLevelListener(e:Event):void {
        switchSystemState(FrameWorkStates.STATE_SYSTEM_NEW_LEVEL);
    }

    public function waitCompleteListener(e:Event):void {

        switch(lastSystemState) {
            case FrameWorkStates.STATE_SYSTEM_LEVEL_IN:
                removeChild(levelInScreen);
                break
        }

        removeEventListener(EVENT_WAIT_COMPLETE, waitCompleteListener);
        switchSystemState(nextSystemState);
    }
```

```actionscript
        public function soundEventListener(e:CustomEventSound):void {
            if (e.type == CustomEventSound.PLAY_SOUND) {
                //trace("play sound");
                soundManager.playSound(e.name, e.isSoundTrack, e.loops, e.offset, e.volume );
            }else {
                soundManager.stopSound(e.name, e.isSoundTrack);
            }
        }

        public  function keyDownListener(e:KeyboardEvent):void {

            trace("key down: " + e.keyCode);
            switch(e.keyCode) {

              case KEY_PAUSE:
                  //pause key pressed
                  pausedKeyPressedHandler();
                  break;

              case KEY_MUTE:
                  muteKeyPressedHandler();
                  break;
            }
        }


        public function pausedScreenClickListener(e:Event):void {
            removeChild(pausedScreen);

            pausedScreen.removeEventListener(CustomEventButtonId.BUTTON_ID, ⏎
                okButtonClickListener);

            trace("clicked");
            paused - false;
            stage.focus = game;
        }

        public  function pausedKeyPressedHandler():void {
            trace("handle pause");
            addChild(pausedScreen);

            pausedScreen.addEventListener(CustomEventButtonId.BUTTON_ID , ⏎
                pausedScreenClickListener, false, 0, true);

            paused = true;
        }

        public  function muteKeyPressedHandler():void {
            soundManager.muteSound();
        }
    }
}
```

That is the complete GameFrameWork.as file as it stands in this chapter. We will make many additions to it when we cover preloading and Mochi integration in Chapter 12.

Test it!

If you have made it this far you, should have a ten-level post-retro blaster game. Test the build in your publishing system of choice. The `FrameRateProfiler` should start up right away, and when it is complete, you will be dropped into the simple title screen with the scoreboard off to the right. Once you click through the screen buttons, the game will begin. Use the mouse to move. Your ship will follow the mouse and automatically fire.

How is the frame rate running in the `frameCounter` under the scoreboard? Is the game running sluggishly on your machine? You can go back to the `FrameRateProfiler` settings in `Main.as` and adjust the profiler to test with more objects if the game is running too slowly. Adjusting the profiler will help the game set the `stage.quality` and `frameRateMultiplier` to a lower setting. Remember, you want to calibrate the profiled rate to the frame rate the game runs at on your machine so that they match. This will ensure that the profiler will work on other's users' machines.

Summary

We have covered a lot of ground at a rapid pace in this chapter. We covered many optimizations for blitted games that can also be applied to most other Flash games. We also created a new time-based step timer, added pause and mute functionality to the framework, and finished yet another complete game.

You should pat yourself on the back after this marathon session, but don't quit just yet. In Chapter 12, we will complete the framework by adding a preloader to both the Flex SDK and Flash IDE versions of the `Main.as` class. We will also cover how to create and promote a viral Flash game. Finally, we will explore adding Mochi Ads and Mochi high scores to your newly completed creation.

Chapter 12

Creating a Viral Game: Tunnel Panic

Throughout the first eleven chapters, we have explored nine different games and multiple updates to the framework presented in the Part 1. In this chapter, we are going start by discussing what it means to create a viral web game. Next, we will apply the game framework to one more simple game in the context of making a game for viral consumption. We will also explore how to add a preloader to in both the Flex SDK–based AS3 and the Flash IDE versions of the game. To finish up the framework, we will explore how to add in the Mochi Media Services framework to show advertisements and display high scores.

Tunnel Panic, the game we are going to create, was put together using our game framework in under two days. This mimics a possible viral game creation scenario that many readers might undertake. There are many possible methods for a viral game developer to earn money from games. We will discuss a few of these, such as licensing (with the help of FlashGameLicense.com) and self-hosting, but we will explore one of the most common methods: Using Mochi Media Services. Mochi offers a wealth of features for viral game developers. Our game will make use of the basic preloader ad and high score (leader board) functions.

Defining viral web games

Viral web games? They sound dangerous. In a way, they are. Viral web games have been devastating to parts of the traditional game industry for the past few years. In fact, some people point to the rise in viral web games as one of the contributing factors to the slow demise of the traditional PC game industry.

So what defines a **viral web** game? Here are some common traits that most viral web games share:

- These games play directly in a web browser using a plug-in that allows the game to work independently of the web page it sits on.
- They are written in Flash, Shockwave, Java, or more recently, Silverlight, HTML 5, and Unity.

- Games are designed so they can be passed around and embedded easily into other sites and portals. This can mean creating the entire game in a single file or distributing it in a way that can be easily embedded in any web site.
- Viral games can be played in online game portals and syndicated to other game portals.
- Finally, the games are sponsored, include in-game ads, and utilize a global high-score table and/or other distributed services such as micro transactions.

However, just knowing what a viral web game is does not tell you how to be successful at making them. The rest of this chapter will inform you on some ways to create, maintain, and make a make a little money from a viral web game.

Distributing a viral web game

After you have created a viral web game, the next thing you need to do is tell people about it. Your first inclination might be to announce it to the world immediately. While we will advise a bit later on why this might not be the best idea, here are some common ways to do just that.

Using your own web site

The quickest and easiest way to distribute your viral web game on the Internet is to set up your own web site to host your game. Hosting your own game also happens to be the most flexible way to go about it. After you have created a web site and embedded your SWF, there are a few more things you can do to help get the word out about your game

Using social news sites

Social news sites like Digg.com are a great way to start promoting your game. Digging a game is very easy. Just go to `http://digg.com`, create an account, and submit a new link. However, Digg.com is inundated with links on an hourly basis, so you might not see much of a response unless you can muster dozens of friends to digg your link and get it moved up the charts. However, even if you can make this happen, it will only work for a very short time. Other social news sites like Yahoo Buzz (`http://buzz.yahoo.com`) and Gamer Blips (`http://gamerblips.com`) are also useful for posting links but suffer from the same drawbacks as Digg.com. However, if your link gets picked up by a gaming news site and subsequently added to other sites, this technique can still be a very effective.

Twitter

Twitter can be another useful tool for informing the world of your new game. Creating a Twitter account is very easy, and there are some very useful widgets and tools, such as RSS feeds of your tweets (postings) available to every user. To use Twitter effectively though, you need to do two things:

- Get people to subscribe to your tweets. Just like with social news sites, you will need to start your Twitter promotions with any friends or colleagues that you can muster to help spread the word about your game. Gaining valuable subscribers that care about your games can take time and energy. Spamming and faking those valuable connections is not a real-world answer. The best way to gain a Twitter following for your games is to start by making something good, get people to your site using some of the other means described here, and offer the ability for people to sign-up for your tweets on your site (www.twitter.com offers many useful tools and APIs for doing this). However, once you get some quality subscribers, Twitter might just become one of the best ways for you to announce your new projects. Also, using a service such as Tweetmeme.com can help you keep track of how many people have tweeted about your game.

- Using the channels on Twitter is a very useful way to get your tweets into streams where they would otherwise not be seen (channels are indicated with a hash symbol, #). Many people on Twitter search for their favorite topics, and Twitter keeps a running tally of the most popular channels. To get your tweet into a channel, simply add something like #flashgame or #game to the end of your tweet. These types of channels are used by people who play and make Flash games—just the audience you want to see your game.

Facebook

Ways of integrating your game onto Facebook comes in several flavors, which range from very easy to very difficult.

The easiest way to go about integrating with Facebook is to post a link to your profile; just submit a link to www.facebook.com that looks like this:

http://www.facebook.com/share.php?u=[url]&t=[title]

where [url] is the URL of your game and [title] is an HTML-encoded string that represents the title of your message. Even though this method is very easy, it's also not very useful. Only your friends on Facebook will see your game, and they are probably already sick of hearing about it from all those tweets you've been sending out.

A better way to distribute your game through Facebook is to integrate with the Facebook APIs. However, those API are beyond the scope of this chapter. You can learn more about integrating with Facebook at the Facebook development web site, located at http://developers.facebook.com/.

Uploading to portals

Another way to distribute your Flash games is to contact game portals and directly upload your games there. If you have a game that stands out, this can be an effective way to get your games seen quickly. However, the effect still might not last as long as you would like. There are two basic types of portals to which you can upload your games: social gaming sites and selective portals.

Social gaming sites

Social gaming sites such as Kongregate and Newgrounds allow you to upload your games and have them instantly playable by anyone else using the portal. Using these sites is a great way to get instant feedback for your games and to get a few residual links back to your own web site. A great advantage to these sites is that, with rare exceptions because of improper content, they accept almost every game submitted.

However, there are some drawbacks to social gaming sites. First, sites like these contain rating systems that will probably not be kind to your game, no matter how good it might be. The communities on these sites are very opinionated and are looking for very specific games and genres (e.g., ultra professional-looking zombie defense games) that might not jibe with your creation. For this reason, the comments and ratings might not be as helpful as the exposure to your game gets in general. If you can stomach the ratings (and by the way, they could be very positive, especially if you hit with the right game at the right time), these sites can be a great way to find out how your game will play with a general audience. Some portals also have periodic contests that award developers cash for the best-rated and most-played games over a certain time period. However, there are pitfalls to contests. We will discuss some of them in the next section.

Selective portals

Many commercial portals, such as MindJolt.com and AddictingGames.com allow developers to upload their games for approval and publication. Some of these portals are very popular but also very selective about the games they publish. This is both an advantage and disadvantage for developers. It's an advantage because if your game is published, it can be played thousands or even hundreds of thousands of times. For sites that allow in-game ads (e.g., mindjolt.com), this can mean some significant ad revenue for a short time. For sites that don't allow ads, such as addictinggames.com, it means many plays, notoriety, and links back to your web site but no money (unless you get sponsorship, which is explained in the next section). The disadvantage, of course, is frustration. It can be very frustrating to have your games rejected by these portals. Portals reject games for many reasons, which don't always have to do with quality. Selective portals try to add games that fit certain categories and try not to dilute their offerings with too many of the same title. Also, these portals are in the business to keep players coming back as often as possible to play as long as possible. Because of this, games in popular genres will get picked up faster than other games. However, there are also many games being produced in those genres. Generally, to get your game one of these portals, you need a great game, a lot of skill, and a little luck.

Before uploading your games to a portal, be sure to read the fine legal print posted on the site so you know what you are getting into. Many commercial portals claim legal rights to your submissions as soon as you click the upload button. Be aware of the following words in terms of service agreements, and make sure they fit the site to which you are submitting your game:

- Irrevocable
- Perpetual
- Exclusive
- Royalty-free
- Fully paid
- Sublicenseable and transferable license to use
- Ability to modify
- Prepare derivative works of

We are not saying that you should not submit your games to portals; just be sure to read the legal terms and know what you might be doing when you submit your game.

Making money from your viral game

The "Distributing a viral web game" section was really just a way to show you that doing things on your own can be very difficult. There are, in fact, a couple other good ways to get your games distributed and a couple good reasons why you might not want to distribute your game at all—well, not at first anyway.

Using in-page ads

One very common method to make money with your game is to embed it in a web page and add Google Ad Sense advertising to the same page to make a few hundredths of a penny (or so) per play every time the page loads. In-page ads are very easy to set up through Google. Create an account at Google (https://www.google.com/adsense/), get a JavaScript ad tag, and add it to your page. Ads come is all shapes and sizes and can be customized to fit almost any space you might want to put an ad. In-page display ads can be an easy way to augment your income from a game. In fact, some developers find this to be the only way to make any real money. However, to make *a lot* of money with in-page ads you need a lot of visits, which is a very tough thing to make happen. And there are other pitfalls with in-page ads. You might be inclined, for instance, to surround every available space with advertisements around your games. This might work for a little while, but viral game players get tired or advertisements very quickly. Instead, choose a few strategic places for in-page ads and realize that, unless your game is a massive hit and the only place it is hosted is your site, these ads will make you only a small fraction of what some other methods might make.

Entering contests

You will see Flash game contests on many portals and even on gaming news and lifestyle sites across the Internet. Game contests are great way for web sites and portals to gather (mostly) free content from unsuspecting and sometimes desperate game developers. OK, that's not the case all the time, but many contests do seem to be set up to benefit only the owners of the contest.

Contests are good when they seem fair and don't ask developers to give up too much when they enter. You need to read the fine print of the legal documents. Remember the words in the terms and conditions that we told you about when discussing portals? Many of those same words apply here. Most contests are legitimate in that they do have prizes, and people (even people you might already know or one day will meet) win those contests. However, the chance of winning the contest might not be worth what you give away (in some cases your game and source code) for entering. Be careful, and read the fine print.

Inserting in-game ads with Mochi Media

The most common way to make money with your viral Flash game is to insert advertisements directly into your game. The key term to know when trying to make money from in-game ads (and in-page ads for that matter) is **eCPM**, which stands for "effective Cost Per Mille" (that is, cost per 1,000). eCPM doesn't show the total amount you've earned; it shows what you've earned per thousand views. It's calculated by dividing your earnings by the number of page impressions and multiplying by 1,000. Because of this calculation method, your eCPM will actually change over time depending on what kind of ads you're showing (different ads pay different rates) and how many page impressions you've had. The CPM is what the advertiser is paying for 1,000 clicks, views, or impressions, and the eCPM shows what that means in terms of your earnings. The eCPM basically shows how well you're doing, rather than how much you've earned.

Viral Flash game developers learn very quickly the meaning of eCPM because the rates change dramatically by region. For example, a viral game that is posted on a portal in the USA might get a \$.50 eCPM (that's 50 cents per mille), while the same game posted on a Chinese or South American portal might get a \$.01 eCPM. This is because the advertisers help set the eCPM rates, and advertisers like to pay for the eyeballs that might buy their products. Since most of the advertisers are in Western countries, Western portals will make you the best eCPM (at this point). However, don't discount those other, non-Western portals. Players love games just as much on those portals, and they are also more apt to pass around a viral game than some portals that give you a better eCPM. Furthermore, some non-Western portals are accepting of game styles that might not make it to the front pages of portals that pay high eCPM rates. For example, we have found that very well made retro style shooters seem to be very popular in Asian countries, while in some cases, racing games are all the rage in Eastern Europe. At the same time, zombie games seem to be popular in North America. However, these are not rules, only guidelines. The best idea is to look at any particular portal to see what types of games are popular so you will know how it should be targeted.

The best and most universal system available for in-game ads in Flash games is Mochiads created by Mochi Media (http://www.mochiads.com). Others, like CPMStar, exist as well, but we will focus on Mochi for this discussion. These days, Mochiads are nearly as ubiquitous in viral Flash games as Flash itself. It is also pretty well known that you don't necessarily make a ton of money from in-game ads, as showed in our eCPM discussion. However, in some cases, the money from ads is not the only reason for using them. Mochi Media offers many other services such as usage tracking, high scores, encryption, distribution, versioning, and even micro transactions using their Mochicoins system. We will touch on a few of these a bit later. Along with Flash Game License (discussed in the next section, www.mochiads.com should be one of your first stops when starting out in your viral Flash game career.

The best way to get started with Mochiads is to go to the site and create a developer account. With your developer account, you add a game and get the specific code you need to insert an in-game ad. In most cases, the code required is little more than a couple lines. We will demonstrate Mochi ad integration a bit later in this chapter.

Along with in-game ads, Mochi Media offers a plethora of other services for Flash game developers. Mochi High Scores allow you to add a robust, distributed high score system into your games. Mochi Distribution will allow you to distribute your games through the Mochi Network of portal partners, allows you to update your game on-the-fly without the need to send new versions of the game to portals, and will also allow you encrypt your game while it is in their system.

Finally, Mochi Media has recently created Mochicoins their in-game microtransactions system. **Microtransactions** are a way to make money by charging players for things in your game (new levels, new weapons, etc.). While Mochiads will take nearly any game submitted, Mochi Coins is much more selective. However, if you do make a game that is good and lucky enough to be included on Mochicoins, Mochi Media will prominently market it for you.

Obtaining licenses and sponsorships

We've been spending a lot of time telling you ways to get your game onto the screens of players by using portals and ads both on the page and in the game, but there might be some very good reasons why you do not want to do so right away. Why? Well, *unique* and *good* games are in high demand. At the same time, *new* games are the key for viral game portals. They need new games that do not exist on other sites so players will keep coming back.

When you have a new, good-playing, good-looking game, you have the power in your hands. If you put it on your own site or upload it to a social portal or to Mochiads too quickly, you lose that advantage. If you think your game has what it takes to make it big, the first thing you might want to try is getting it licensed or sponsored. However, exposure (any distribution at all) is the death knell for sponsorships and licenses. Well-paying portals want to know that they have something special on their hands, and they are willing to pay for that privilege. This means that, to make the most money, you will want to *disregard* most of what you have read already in this chapter and focus on the next section. However, if gaining licenses and sponsorships was easy, you would not need any other methods listed here, and you'd already be rich. In fact, attaining licenses and sponsorships is an uphill battle that gets harder every day. More and better games are released daily and all are trying to tap into the same sponsors, so your best chance is to make a great game that catches the eye of a sponsor.

There are several types of licenses and sponsorships that you can try to obtain.

Exclusive Licenses

Exclusive licenses refer to the situation when an entity buys the rights to display your game outright. These licenses can be with or without source code, but the intention is that the game will show up only on a single portal or web site either indefinitely or for a specified amount of time. In most cases, this is the most lucrative way for a developer to make money with a Flash game.

Sponsorships

Sponsorships mean that portals (or other sponsors) will pay you to put an advertisement of their own in your game (in lieu of Mochiads for instance) and then attempt to get that game placed in as many places as possible. In some cases, bonuses are given for the number of plays a game receives. In general, a developer can make almost as much, and maybe even more, from sponsorship than an exclusive license.

Nonexclusive licenses

Nonexclusive licenses (in general) do not pay as much as exclusive licenses, or sponsorships, but they offer the developer a lot more freedom. **Nonexclusive** means that a sponsor or licensor pays the developer to put an ad in the game or display it on their portal with the understanding that the game can be distributed on other portals with other advertisements as well. This means that a developer might not make a big sum from one portal or site but can make a good amount from multiple sites and portals.

API licenses

API licenses are the usually very easy to obtain but do not pay very much. Some portals will pay a developers small sum (e.g., $50) to insert high-score or achievement integration into their games. The code for these APIs is usually fairly easy to integrate, and some quick but limited money can be made this way.

Getting a game sponsored

Right now, there are two basic ways to try to get your game licensed or sponsored. The first is to find a portal that you are interested in and send that site a personalized message about your game. This technique is much easier if you already have some contact with portal owners or a history of making good games, but there are stories of first timers contacting portals directly and gaining good sponsorships or licenses. However, first impressions count. If you are going to contact these very busy portal owners, make sure you have the goods to show them—that means a good, unique game that plays well.

Using FlashGameLicense.com

The second most common way to gain a sponsorship or license is to use `FlashGameLicense.com`, which offers supplementary services to Mochi Media for Flash game developers. The site started in 2007 as a place for developers to post games before they were public, so sponsors and portal owners could view and bid on them. It quickly added forums for developers, a way to get feedback on games, and a game shop to sell games instead of getting them sponsored. More recently, the site added FlashGameDistribution.com (`http://flashgamedistribution.com/`) as a way to get your games seen by many different portals and sponsors, and GamerSafe.com (`https://www.gamersafe.com/`) is a service for developers to allow for a game to be saved and replayed from any web site that hosts it and for microtransactions.

Adding a game to `www.flashgamelicense.com` is very simple: create a developer account; upload your game, and you are done. The difference between FlashGameLicense.com and Mochi Media is that FlashGameLicense.com is a private site. All the games posted there for license are site locked to `www.flashgamelicense.com` and encrypted. This creates a welcome place for developers to show their games and for sponsors to see them, with little chance that games will leak out before their time. As a developer, you can choose the types of licenses you will accept and what prices you'd like to see for your games. FlashGameLicense.com requests a 10 percent fee for its service, but if you get a good sponsorship, it is well worth the price.

Using FlashGameDistribution and GamerSafe

In the event that your game does not get a license or sponsorship, FlashGameLicense.com has created FlashGameDistribution.com, a way to instantly send out your FlashGameLicense.com games to their viral partners. While this is nice addition to their suite of services, they have another offering that is even more interesting—GamerSafe.com.

GamerSafe.com offers three very useful services for Flash game developers. First, it offers a distributed Save Game feature. This allows users to play your game on any portal and save their state, so they can return any place and restart the game. For games that require play beyond a single session, this tool is invaluable. For years, Flash shared objects have been available to save game data locally, but storing the state has only been useful for games that are played on the same computer by a player. GamerSafe.com's implementation (and an implementation now available from Mochi Media through its services) opens up your game development to genres that so far have not been playable virally in any real way: RPGs, long-term adventure games, in-depth war games, and so on. GamerSafe.com also offers an in-game awards API, and like Mochi Media, a system for in-game microtransactions. It should be noted that MochiMedia has started to add "save game" features to match those of GamerSafe, and another service named HeyZap (heyzap.com) is quickly following suit too. HeyZap just added in-game advertisement functionality as this book went to press. As you might have surmised, this is an ever changing and competitive field, so it's a good idea to stay current on these services, and read-up on as much latest news and trends as possible.

Working with Adobe Flash Platform Services

Late in 2009, Adobe announced that it was getting into the business of distributing Flash-based applications. It offers three very interesting services that Flash game developers might find useful: Distribution, Social, and Shibuya.

Distribution appears to be Adobe's answer to Mochi Media. In a partnership with Gigya, Adobe has created a **Share** menu that you can include in your applications. This **Share** menu opens up the ad serving, tracking and promotion capabilities of Adobe's service. Promotion appears to be a paid service, although ad serving is opt-in and can be used to with services like Mochi. Tracking capabilities are similar to Mochi's offerings but are most likely powered by Adobe's acquisition of Omniture, one of the world's leading web analytics providers. You can find out more about Adobe's Distribution service here:

http://www.adobe.com/devnet/flashplatform/services/distribution/

Social is an API that opens up authentication and profile-data sharing through multiple social networks. Currently, Facebook, MySpace, Twitter, Yahoo, Google, and AOL are supported through this API. You can download Adobe's Social service library here:

http://labs.adobe.com/downloads/social.html

Shibuya is Adobe's system (in beta) for distributing and monetizing AIR-based applications. Adobe AIR is a technology that allows Flash applications to be converted into desktop applications for popular platforms such as Windows and Mac OS. Shibuya allows for try and buy licensing model for these AIR applications. You can find more information about Adobe Flash Platform Services here:

http://www.adobe.com/devnet/flashplatform/services/

Securing your viral games

Before we leave the topic of general viral Flash games and get into some hard core code, there are a couple more topics we need to cover: site locking and encryption.

Using site locking

As we said previously, site locking is a way for game developers to make sure a game can only be played on certain web sites. While we don't have any site-locking code in our game framework, here is some sample code that will site lock a game for you. Here is an example of how such code might be implemented:

```
var validDomainString:String="8bitrocket.com";
var isValidDomain:Boolean=false;

var currentDomain:String = this.root.loaderInfo.url.split("/")[2];
trace("currentDomain=" + currentDomain);

 if (currentDomain.indexOf(validDomainString) == (currentDomain.length - ↵
     validDomainString.length)) {
   isValidDomain=true;
}else{
 isValidDomain=false;
```

```
    systemInvalidDomain();
}

private function systemInvalidDomain():void {
    navigateToURL(new URLRequest("http://www.8bitrocket.com"), 'newwindow');
}
```

The basic idea is that we search for the valid domain ("8bitrocket.com"), using `this.loaderInfo.url.toLowerCase`. If we don't find it, we call the `systemInvalidDomain` function, which then redirects to a web site. If a portal or web site tries to embed this game, it will redirect to your site as soon as someone visits the page it sits on.

Encrypting your game

While both Mochi Distribution and FlashGameLicense.com offer limited encryption for your Flash games, to be very safe, you should use your own SWF encryption as well. Why encryption? Well, there are some people out there that steal code and games or take out ads, sponsorships, preloaders, and credit screens and try to pass the games off as their own work.

We have found that best solution for SWF encryption is Amayeta SWF Encrypt (`http://www.amayeta.com/`). This application will take a SWF file and render it unreadable with **obfuscation**. As well, it adds hooks to kill common SWF decompilers. The drawback is that that it will increase the size of the SWF, sometimes as much as twofold or more, depending on the strength of the encryption you choose in the utility. While SWF Encrypt is not free, the price (roughly $150) is worth every penny, especially after you discover some script kiddies have stolen your game and put their names on it. One more note. If you use Mochi Media Distribution services, you get a medium amount of encryption out of the box, just by loading your game into their system. However, even Mochi suggests you use an obfuscator along with their service.

Marketing viral Flash games

Your marketing strategy with a viral Flash game will depend on what goals you set for yourself. The two most common goals are to make the most money and get the most exposure. Let's discuss those goals and sample strategies for how to achieve them.

If you want to make the most money possible from your viral game, you might want to follow these steps:

1. Site lock your game in a hidden directory on your web site. Do not put in any in-game ads.

2. Submit games personally to premium portals (Addicting Games, Big Fish, etc.) that sponsor games. For sites that do not allow uploads, send them a personal e-mail with a link to the site-locked version.

3. Wait.

4. If you do not get any acceptable offers, submit your game to FlashGameLicense.com. Make it known that the game has not been in distribution and has only been offered up for potential sponsors.

5. Wait. Wait at least 3 weeks, unless you get an offer you can't refuse.

6. See the steps for getting the most exposure.

To get the most exposure for your game, try these steps:

1. Create a page for your game on your personal site.

2. Add your game to Mochiads.com. Insert ads and turn on Mochi Distribution.

3. Submit your game to a large commercial portal that does not allow ads (e.g., AddictingGames.com). You will not make money, but you will get links back to your site if the game is posted. Make sure this version does not have ads included. Use Mochiads filtering to exclude the domains of these portals so ads will not show up, but what will show up is other sites' that pick up the game and put it on their portals.

4. Create a landing page on your site for portals that link back to your game. Be sure to include the Mochiads <embed> code here, so if portals pick up the game virally, they will display the ad-enabled version.

5. Submit the game to any and all social and selective portals as you can find. Be sure to submit your game to FlashGameDistribution.com.

Some Other Great Web Resources

It's always a good idea to keep-up on the latest news and information about the viral Flash game industry. Here are some good sites to check out on a regular basis:

- **Games**

  - **Adobe Flash Game Technology Center**: http://adobe.com/devnet/games/
  - **Gaming Your Way**: www.gamingyourway.com
  - **Flash Game Blogs**: www.flashgameblogs.com
  - **Photon Storm**: www.photonstorm.com
  - **Ickydime**: blog.ickydime.com
  - **Game Poetry**: www.gamepoetry.com/blog/
  - **Blog.sokay.net**: blog.sokay.net
  - **Jobe Maker**: jobemakar.blogspot.com/
  - **Urban Squall**: www.urbansquall.com/blog/
  - **Michael J. Williams**: gamedev.michaeljameswilliams.com
  - **Freelance Flash Games**: www.freelanceflashgames.com
  - **Iain Lobb**: blog.iainlobb.com/ (site belongs to the technical editor of this book)
  - **8-bit Rocket**: www.8bitrocket.com (our site)

- **Commercial blogs**

  - **Mochiland**: mochiland.com

- **General Flash**

  - **Flash Enabled**: www.flashenabledblog.com
  - **ActionScript.org**: www.actionscript.org/
  - **Flash Kit**: www.flashkit.com/
  - **Scott Jeppesen**: scottjeppesen.blogspot.com/
  - **Flash Focus**: www.flashfocus.nl/
  - **Kirupa**: www.kirupa.com

Preparing to create our Tunnel Panic game

Our game will make use of the game com.efg.framework package along with some additions for preloading and using Mochi Media services.

No matter if you are using Flex, Flash Develop, Flash Builder, or the Flash IDE, you should create a new project folder to hold all of the code for this game.

Like all of the games in the book, Tunnel Panic will use the framework package structure we created in Chapter 2 (and have evolved over the last 10 chapters). Let's begin by creating the package necessary for our game in both the Flash IDE and Flash Develop (for use with the Flex SDK).

Creating the game project in the Flash IDE

By now, these steps to create the project in the Flash IDE should look very familiar to you:

1. Start up your version of Flash. We are using CS3, but this should work exactly the same in CS4 and CS5.

2. Create a .fla file in the /source/projects/tunnelpanic/flashIDE/ folder called tunnelpanic.

3. In the /source/projects/tunnelpanic/flashIDE folder, create the package structure for your game: com/efg/games/tunnelpanic/.

4. Set the frame rate of the Flash movie to **30 FPS**. Set the width to **600** and the height to **400**.

5. Set the document class to com.efg.games.tunnelpanic.Main.

6. We have not yet created the Main.as class, so you will see a warning. We are going to create this later in this chapter.

7. Now, we need to add the framework reusable class package to the class path for the FLA file. In the **Publish** settings, select **Flash** ➤ **ActionScript 3 Setting**.

8. Click the **Browse to Path** button, and find the /source folder we created in Chapter 2 for the package structure.

9. Select the classes folder and click the **Choose** button. Now the com.efg.framework package will be available for use when we begin to create our game.

Creating the game project in the Flash Develop

Here are the steps for creating the project in Flash Develop:

1. Create a folder inside the /source/projects/tunnelpanic/ folder called /flexSDK (if you have not already done so).

2. Start Flash Develop and create a new project; select **Flex 3 Project**, and give it the name tunnelpanic. The location should be the /source/projects/tunnelpanic/flexSDK folder, and the package should be com.efg.games.tunnelpanic.

    Do not have Flash Develop create a project folder automatically. Make sure the **Create Folder For Project** is *unchecked*. Click the **OK** button to create the project.

3. Now, we need to add the class path to the framework to the project. Go to the **Project ➤ Properties ➤ Classpaths** menu item.

4. Click the **Add Class Path** button. Find the /source folder we created earlier, and select the classes subfolder.

5. Click the **OK** button and then the **Apply** button.

6. Next, change the size of the output and frame rate. Go to the **Project ➤ Properties ➤ Classpaths** menu item again, and set the frame rate to 30, the width to 600, and the height to 400.

You now have the basic structure to start creating projects inside the framework. We are now going to discuss a few topics concerning the structure of the framework classes and then move into building the reusable framework code.

> For Flex Builder, Flash Builder, or another IDE, please refer to the documentation provided for that product to create a new project and set the default compile class.
>
> In a Flash Develop / Flash IDE workflow, a common method of Flash development is to use the Flash IDE for assets and organization and Flash Develop for code editing. If this is your workflow of choice, you will want to follow the Flash IDE folder and package structure rather than the Flex SDK folder structure.

This is the folder structure for the Flash IDE:

/source/projects/tunnelpanic/flashIDE/com/efg/games/tunnelpanic/

and for the Flex SDK (using Flash Develop):

/source/projects/tunnelpanic/flexSDK/

```
assets/
bin/
obj/
lib/
src/com/efg/games/tunnelpanic/
```

Preloading in the Flex SDK

Preloading using the Flex SDK and Flash develop is a relatively painless process, but it requires a fundamental change to the application structure. A Flex SDK application doesn't have a normal Flash timeline, so every asset and all code is always loaded before the application starts to run. This is in contrast to the Flash IDE applications, where the timeline gives us the advantage of moving assets off of the first frame to allow a very smooth and straightforward loading process.

With the Flex SDK, we will need to create a new class called `Preloader.as` that will sit in our project folder alongside `Main.as` and other game-specific classes. We have designed our preloader using the basic model for preloading that is created by Flash Develop if you choose the **New Project** ➤ **AS3 Project With Preloader** option. For this example though, we have made the changes manually to demonstrate exactly what is going on rather than simply use the preexisting Flash Develop code in its entirety.

Adding the compiler directive

To preload the Flex SDK version of our Tunnel Panic `Main.as` properly, we will have to make a change to how the compiler treats the `Main.as` class. First off, it will no longer be the document class (or the always-compile class in Flash Develop). The new `Preloader` class will now be the document or always-compile class. We do this because we want to be able to load the `Main` class in with our `Preloader`. The only way to do this is to trick the compiler into thinking that `Main.as` actually starts on frame 2 of our Flash SWF even though there really isn't a frame 2. How do we do this?

In Flash Develop you must have your project open and go to the **Project** ➤ **Properties** ➤ **Compiler Options** menu item.

In the **Compiler Options**, you must add in a new **Additional Compiler Option** as follows:

```
-frame start com.efg.games.tunnelpanic.Main
```

This tells the compiler that a class called Main will begin on frame 2; see Figure 12-1 for an illustration of this example.

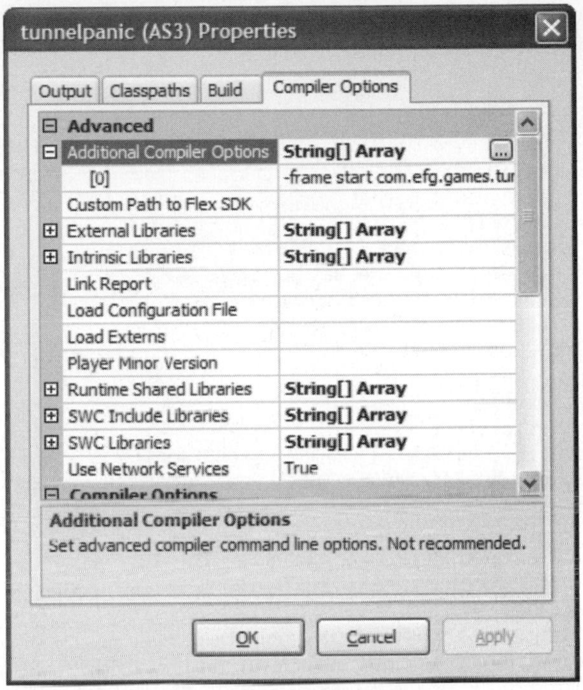

Figure 12-1. The Flash Develop Compiler Options screen

Adding the Preloader class code

Next, we need to create a new class called `Preloader.as`:

```
package com.efg.games.tunnelpanic
{
    //Must set compiler option of "-frame start Main" in Additional compiler options
    //for this to work.
    //not needed with Mochi pre-loader ad

    import flash.display.Bitmap;
    import flash.display.BitmapData;
    import flash.display.DisplayObject;
    import flash.display.MovieClip;
    import flash.events.Event;
    import flash.events.ProgressEvent;
    import flash.text.TextField;
    import flash.text.TextFormat;
    import flash.utils.getDefinitionByName;


    public class Preloader extends MovieClip
    {
        private var appBackBD:BitmapData = new BitmapData(600, 400, false, 0x000000);
        private var appBackBitmap:Bitmap = new Bitmap(appBackBD);
```

```
        private var textfield:TextField = new TextField();
        private var headerTextfield:TextField = new TextField();
        private var textFormat:TextFormat = new TextFormat("_sans", "11", "0xffffff",↵
            "true");
        private var loadingString:String;

        public function Preloader()
        {
            trace("pre loader");
            textfield.defaultTextFormat = textFormat;
            headerTextfield.defaultTextFormat = textFormat;
            headerTextfield.text = "loader on screen";
            textfield.x = 280;
            textfield.y = 200;
            addChild(appBackBitmap);
            addChild(textfield);
            addChild(headerTextfield);
            addEventListener(Event.ENTER_FRAME, checkFrame);
            loaderInfo.addEventListener(ProgressEvent.PROGRESS, progress);
        }

        private function progress(e:ProgressEvent):void
        {
             // update loader
            trace("loader");
            trace(e.bytesLoaded + "/" + e.bytesTotal);
            var loadingInt:int = (e.bytesLoaded / e.bytesTotal) * 100;
            loadingString = "Loading: " + loadingInt + "%";
            textfield.text = loadingString;
        }

        private function checkFrame(e:Event):void
        {
            if (currentFrame == totalFrames)
            {
                removeEventListener(Event.ENTER_FRAME, checkFrame);
                startup();
            }
        }

        private function startup():void
        {
            // hide loader
            removeChild(appBackBitmap);
            removeChild(textfield);
            stop();
            loaderInfo.removeEventListener(ProgressEvent.PROGRESS, progress);
            var mainClass:Class = getDefinitionByName("com.efg.games.tunnelpanic.Main")↵
                as Class;
            addChild(new mainClass() as DisplayObject);
        }

    }
}
```

The actual preloading is handled in a very simple, straightforward manner. We add a `BitmapData` background (appBackBD inside appBackBitmap) and a `TextField` (textfield) to display a status to the user. We also create two event listener functions: `checkFrame` listens for the `Event.EnterFrame` event and `progress` listens for the `ProgressEvent.PROGRESS` of the `LoaderInfo` class.

The `progress` function simply updates the `textField` with the current percentage loaded for the `Main` class, and the `checkFrame` function waits until the first frame has been loaded and the play head has moved to the fake frame 2 created with the compiler directive described earlier. When `checkFrame` detects that the movie is on frame 2 (currentFrame == totalFrames), the `startup` function is called.

The `startup` function removes the `appBackBitmap` and `textField` from the display list and adds an instance of the `Main` class to the display list. We must make some changes to the constructor and the init functions in `Main` for this to work properly.

Finally, we glue this to our old code by creating an instance of `Main` and add it to the display list of the stage. Here is the code that does that magic:

```
var mainClass:Class = getDefinitionByName("com.efg.games.tunnelpanic.Main") as Class;
addChild(new mainClass() as DisplayObject);
```

So now, you see that preloading with the Flex SDK actually requires a second class (Preloader) and a special compiler directive "-frame start com.cfg.games.tunnlepanic.Main) to effectively preload the Main and all the embedded assets.

Preloading in the Flash IDE

Preloading our game in the Flash IDE is different than doing it with the Flex SDK. The primary differences are in how the timeline and library assets interact with the preload process. For this example, we are going to use the assets needed for this chapter's game, Tunnel Panic. We need to import three sounds into our library for the game. We have created our own sounds and music specifically for this game. If you have the game assets from this book's web site, you can use those. If not, you will have to supply three sounds: a title screen music clip, a music clip to play during game play, and a sound for when the player ship is destroyed.

Adding files to the library

You will want to add your three sounds to the library, as shown in Figure 12-2. You will see that there is also a `MovieClip` called SoundHolder in the library; we'll discuss that one in a bit.

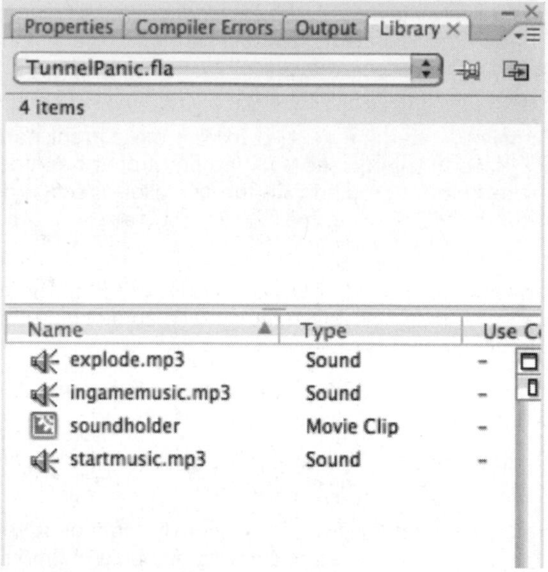

Figure 12-2. The library for Tunnel Panic and its preloader

Creating the timeline

The timeline for our FLA file will consist of three frames and two layers. The first frame will contain nothing other than a stop(); command in the **Actions** panel. The second frame will contain an instance of the soundHolder clip that we will create in the next section. The third frame, much like the first, will contain a stop(); command in the **Actions** panel. Figure 12-3 is an example of this structure.

There are also two layers: code and assets. The code layer will contain the stop commands for frames 1 and 3. The assets layer will contain a MovieClip with all of the assets for the game on frame 2. Figure 12-3 shows our timeline.

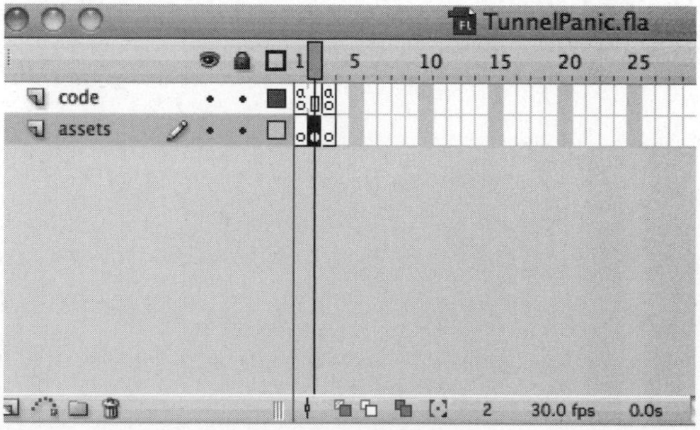

Figure 12-3. The timeline for Tunnel Panic and its preloader

Creating an asset holder MovieClip

We will need a movie clip to hold all of the game's library assets on frame 2 of our timeline. We call this an **asset holder clip**. We add this clip so the preloader can accurately load all of the bytes needed for the game's entire library without overloading frame 1. If assets are exported in the first frame, they cannot be preloaded properly, because the Main.as class will not start to run until all of the assets are loaded. This defeats the purpose of having a preloader message to the user, because the message will not show up until the frame 1 assets have been loaded. Loading everything before Main runs would cause a long delay and a blank screen for the user.

The soundHolder that you saw in the library previously will contain all of our sound assets for the game. If we had graphical assets, we could either create a graphicsHolder clip or just add them to the soundHolder clip. If you do have a combined assets clip, you might want to rename it assetsHolder instead of soundHolder. The name will not be used in code, so it is up to you how you name the clip.

The asset holder clip (SoundHolder in this example) will contain all of the assets for the game that are instantiated from the library in code. If assets are on the main timeline of your movie, or inside another clip on main timeline, then you will not need to put them inside the soundHolder (or assetsHolder) clip. None of the games in this book make use of too many (if any) timeline-based assets, so all of your assets for the games so far would need to be inside an assetsHolder clip for preloading purposes.

Linking the assets

There are three sounds in our library, and they should all have linkage names but will not be exported on the first frame. The linkage names will mirror the object instantiation names we will use in the Main.as class. Figure 12-4 shows an example for the explode.mp3 library asset. Notice that the linkage (SoundExplode) name and the library asset name (explode.mp3) are not the same. You can change these to be the same by renaming the library asset after import.

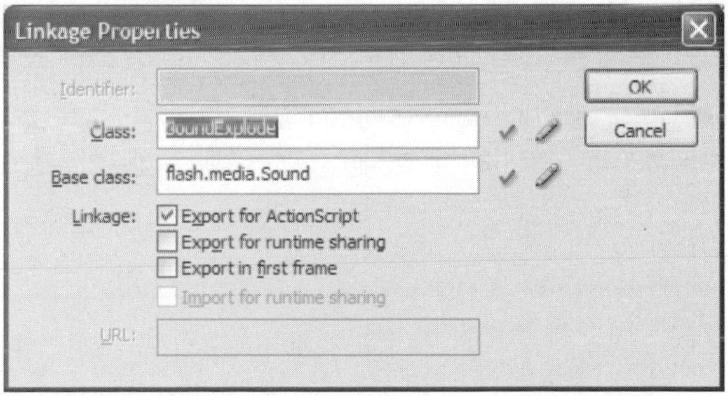

Figure 12-4. The linkage properties for explode.mp3

Table 12-1 shows the class names and corresponding library assets.

Table 12-1. Library asset names and their classes

Library	Class
explode.mp3	SoundExplode
ingamemusic.mp3	SoundMusicInGame
startmusic.mp3	SoundMusicTitle

Figure 12-5 shows the entire library.

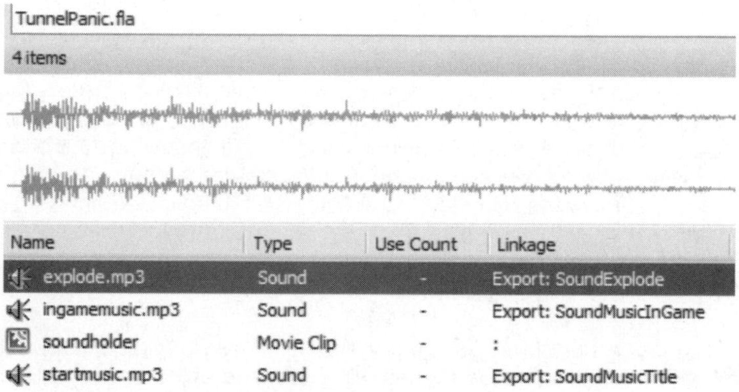

Figure 12-5. The linkage properties for all library assets

Putting the assets into the asset holder

We will next need to create the asset holder clip. Since we only have sound assets in our game, we have named it soundHolder. You are free to name it whatever you choose. You will want to create a timeline inside the clip that mirrors Figure 12-6.

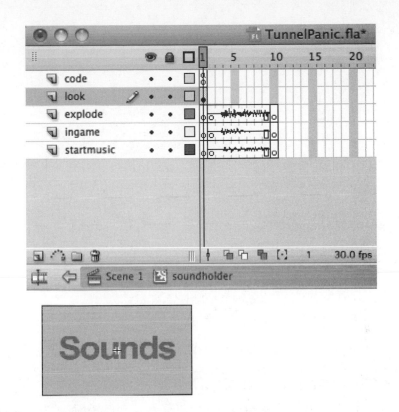

Figure 12-6. The soundHolder clip

The soundHolder clip contains ten frames, but only two of them are absolutely necessary. The extra frames are for visual purposes only. We also have five layers. Frame 1 of layer one (the code layer) contains just a stop command in the actions panel. Frame 1 of layer 2 (the look layer) can contain anything you want. We have placed a gray box with red text that says sounds. We have only done this so we will have a visual for the holder when it is placed on the screen. All of the assets in the holder will start on frame 2, so frame 1 will be a blank clip unless you add something into the look layer.

All of the sound assets are placed on frame 2, each in its own layer. This is a necessity for sounds as only a single sound can be on each layer of a MovieClip timeline. The sounds all begin on frame 2 for a very important reason. If they were all on frame 1, you would hear them all play as the play head on the main timeline passed over frame 2. If we were to have visual assets to preload, each asset could be placed on a single layer, but it is better organizationally to have a layer for each like the sounds. This structure makes it much easier to add and delete assets as needed.

Placing the asset holder on the main time line

The final thing we need to do to set up our FLA file for preloading is to place the soundHolder clip on (or off) the stage on frame 2 of the main time line, in the assets layer; see Figure 12-7.

Figure 12-7. Placement of the soundHolder clip on the main time line

Framework Changes for Flash IDE preloading

We will be making some significant changes to the com.efg.framework and Main.as class structure to add preloading to the IDE-based Main.as document class. Unlike the Flex SDK preloader, the Flash IDE-based preloader will not require a separate Preloader class. We will need to add in a new state to the Main.as state machine though. We did not need to do this for the Flex SDK preloader.

> Note: We will cover the entire Tunnel Panic Main.as code listing in the section called "Creating the Main.as for Tunnel Panic". What follows are just the additions to the Chapter 11 Main.as and the com.efg.framework classes to support the new preload and Mochi functions.

Adding in the new Flash IDE preloader state to the framework

We need to make some changes to com.efg.framework classes to support preloading with the Flash IDE. Flex SDK users should also follow along as some of the changes will also be needed to support that development environment.

First, we need to add some states. In the variable definition section of the FrameWorkStates.as class, we will need to add new constants for the preloading. We have also added constants for Mochi ads and leader boards that will be covered in the next section. Add the following lines to the constants definition section. Note that Flex SDK users do not need the STATE_SYSTEM_PRELOAD state, but they should add it to the FrameWorkStates.as in case they will use the framework with the IDE at a later date.

```
public static const STATE_SYSTEM_PRELOAD:int = 11;
public static const STATE_SYSTEM_MOCHI_HIGHSCORES:int = 12;
public static const STATE_SYSTEM_PAUSE:int = 99;
```

Adding new variables for the preloader state

Now, we need to add support in com.efg.framework.GameFrameWork.as file for the Flash IDE preloader. You need to add in a Boolean (preloaderStarted) and a String (preloadString). These will be used inside the preloader state function to control preloading status and display text to the user.

```
public var preloaderStarted:Boolean=false;
public var preloadString:String=new String();
```

Defining the preloadScreen instance

The preload screen will be an instance of the BasicScreen class. We will create an instance of the screen when we discuss the Tunnel Panic game later in this chapter. Add this line to the com.efg.framework.GameFrameWork.as file's variable definition section.

```
public var preloadScreen:BasicScreen;
```

Setting the preloader to be the first state in Main

At some point, you will want to display the preloader. It is necessary to always use the preloading state even if you are using another preloader (such as the Mochi Ads preloader discussed in the next section). You must do this to ensure all of the library assets will be available to your code when needed.

If STATE_SYSTEM_PRELOAD is the only preloader in your game (that is, if you are not using a Mochiad or other preloaded ad), you will need to set the first game state to be this state. This is done in the init function of the Main.as class. Again, you will see this in use shortly when we discuss Tunnel Panic. For now, you need not make any changes to GameFrameWork.as for this, but here's the how we will set the preloader state for reference:

```
switchSystemState(FrameWorkStates.STATE_SYSTEM_PRELOAD);
```

Adding to the switchSystemState function

We do need to make changes to the switchSystemState function in GameFrameWork.as to support preloading. It must be modified to include a way to change the state machine to the FrameWorkStates.STATE_SYSTEM_PRELOAD state. Add the following code to the switch statement in the switchSystemState function:

```
//*** add these lines
 case FrameWorkStates.STATE_SYSTEM_PRELOAD:
    systemFunction = systemPreload;
    break;
//*** end add these lines
```

Adding the new systemPreload and addSounds functions

The `systemPreload` function makes sure the entire SWF file has been loaded before the play head moves to frame 3 of the timeline. By moving to frame 3, the play head passes over frame 2 and allows code-level access to all of the assets contain inside the asset holder located on that frame.

```
private function systemPreload():void {
   if (!preloaderStarted) {
      trace("preload started");
      preloadScreen.setDisplayText("Loading: 0%"); //Changed chapter 12
      addChild(preloadScreen)
      preloaderStarted=true;
   }else{
      var percentLoaded:int=(this.loaderInfo.bytesLoaded/↵
       this.loaderInfo.bytesTotal)*100;
      trace(percentLoaded);
      preloadString="Loading: "+percentLoaded+"%";
      preloadScreen.setDisplayText(preloadString);
      if (percentLoaded >99) {
         trace(">99");
         this.play();
      }
      if (currentFrame==3) {
         trace("frame == 3")
         addSounds();
         removeChild(preloadScreen);
         nextSystemState = FrameWorkStates.STATE_SYSTEM_TITLE;
         switchSystemState(nextSystemState);
      }
   }
}
```

This function begins by checking the preloaderStarted Boolean variable. If that's false, it sets up the preloadScreen instance and places it on the screen. If the Boolean is true, it jumps down and monitors the preload of the SWF file.

The monitoring is a very simple process. The percentLoaded local variable is calculated and used to display text back to the user on the preloadScreen. The percentLoaded variable is also used to determine how much of the SWF file has been loaded. If more than 99 percent of the file has been loaded, the state is changed to the `FrameWorkStates.STATE_SYSTEM_TITLE` state. The play function is called to move the play head from frame 1 to frame 2 (and beyond).

Why 99 percent? In some rare occasions, Flash does not register that a file has loaded exactly 100 percent. In our experience, testing to make sure that more than 99 percent is loaded often helps resolve this issue. If you are uncomfortable with this, change the code to `if (percentLoaded >=100)`.

Once the play function has been called, we wait for the currentFrame property of the SWF to be equal to 3 before we can move forward with our game. The call to the `SoundManager.addSound` that instantiates the sounds in the library can all be triggered now. This will be part of the addSounds function. Also, we can switch the state machine to the next state.

The addSounds function is included here because it is called by systemPreload. However, to actually add sounds to the game, this function needs to be overridden by the Main class of the game. We will demonstrate this in Tunnel Panic.

```
public function addSounds():void {
    //stub only needed in IDE preloading
}
```

Adding Mochi preloader ads and leader boards

The changes to com.efg.framework.GameFrameWork.as to add basic Mochi preloader ads and leader boards are the same for both Flex SDK and Flash IDE based games. You will need to have created an account at www.mochimedia.com, added a game to your account, and created a leader board for the game before you can place your own ads and leader boards to your game. The game and board IDs shown in the next examples are real, live working ads. They work only for our test account though, and any money earned with those codes will go into that account. So be sure to *change the game and board IDs*. You have been warned!

The Mochi functionality will add new states in our state machine. If you are using the Flash IDE and have already read through the section on the preloader code, you will have seen the states added for the Mochi ads and leader boards. If you have not read that section but are using the Flash IDE, it is very important that you do so.

Importing the Mochi package

Once you have signed up for a Mochi account, you will be able to download the latest code API library.zip file. Inside the file, you will find a folder called Mochi. Place this folder inside your project. If you are using the Flex SDK, it can be inside your /src folder. For the Flash IDE, it can be in the same folder as your FLA. Alternatively, you can add it to the classes folder (as we have done for our code for this book) or anywhere else, as long as you as you add the reference directly to the class path of your development tool.

In the class import section of the com.efg.framework.GameFrameWork.as and Main.as class, add this line:

```
import mochi.as3.*;
```

Changing the Main.as object type

The Main.as class that extends com.efg.framework.GameFrameWork must be a specific type for it to work with the Mochi API. It must be a MovieClip, not a Sprite, and it must be declared Dynamic. For your game, change the Main.as class construction line to this:

```
dynamic public class Main extends MovieClip {
```

We will demonstrate this shortly with the Tunnel Panic game.

Adding Mochi-related variables to the framework

Just like we did with preloading, we need to add some states to com.efg.framework. FrameWorkStates.as to support the Mochi services. These are the lines we need to add to the class (you may have added these lines previously when you added the STATE_SYSTEM_PRELOAD for the Flash IDE):

```
public static const STATE_SYSTEM_MOCHI_AD:int = 10;
public static const STATE_SYSTEM_MOCHI_HIGHSCORES:int = 12;
```

We also need to add some new variables to GameFrameWork.as to support the Mochi services. mochiGameID is the Mochi supplied ID that Mochi uses to reference this game. mochiBoardId is the Mochi supplied ID used to reference the leader board for this game. lastScore is a variable we will create that will hold the last score a player received for a game. We will use this variable to send to the score to the Mochi leader board.

```
//*** added chapter 12 for Mochi Ads and Highscores
public var mochiGameId:String;
public var mochiBoardId:String;
public var lastScore:Number;
```

Changing switchSystemState

The changes to the GameFrameWork.as switchSystemState function are similar to the ones we presented earlier in the Flash IDE preloader section.

You will need to make sure that the following two additional states are added to the switchSystemState function:

```
case FrameWorkStates.STATE_SYSTEM_MOCHI_AD:
    systemFunction = systemMochiAd;
    break;

case FrameWorkStates.STATE_SYSTEM_MOCHI_HIGHSCORES:
    systemFunction = systemMochiHighscores;
    break;
```

Making Mochi ad-specific changes

The systemMochiAd function must be added to GameFrameWork.as. It calls the Mochi class and requests an ad to be displayed dynamically. We pass in the resolution (example: res:600x400) and a function (mochiAdComplete) to be called if the ad completes or is skipped, or if an error occurs. More options for the ads are described in the latest Mochi documentation, and new features are also being added all the time. This is a basic implementation of the Mochi ad functionality:

```
public function systemMochiAd():void {

    //format resolotion as string example: 600x400
    var resolution:String = stage.width + "x" + stage.height;
    MochiAd.showPreGameAd({clip:this, id:mochiGameId, res:resolution,⏎
        ad_finished:mochiAdComplete, ad_failed:mochiAdComplete,⏎
 ad_skipped:mochiAdComplete});
    switchSystemState(FrameWorkStates.STATE_SYSTEM_WAIT_FOR_CLOSE);
    nextSystemState = FrameWorkStates.STATE_SYSTEM_TITLE;
}

//*** new Function for Mochi ads chapter 12
public  function mochiAdComplete():void {
```

```
    switchSystemState(nextSystemState);
}
```

Once the showPreGameAd function call is made, the state machine moves into the standard FrameWorkStates.STATE_SYSTEM_WAIT_FOR_CLOSE state. When the ad is complete or skipped, or if an error occurs, the mochiAdComplete function is called. You can change these to individual functions if you have the need or desire to do so. For instance, you might want to sneak in an advertisement or your own web site in the event that the ad is skipped by the user.

In the Main.as for your specific game, you will need to add the following code:

```
mochiGameId = "81e8cd4f0999371e";
```

First, you set the mochiGameId to a specific ID for the game you are making. Again, this ID will be provided by Mochi when you create a new game for the system. You also need to set the proper state in Main.as so that the Mochi ad support will fire in the framework. The following line of code from the previous Main.as classes

```
switchSystemState(FrameWorkStates.STATE_SYSTEM_TITLE);
```

needs to change to this new line of code:

```
switchSystemState(FrameWorkStates.STATE_SYSTEM_MOCHI_AD);
```

Mochi preloads your game for you as the advertisement plays. However, if you still want to show your own preloader, you need to override the systemMochiAd function like this.

> Note: We have split this Flex SDK and Flash IDE versions. The Flex version will not need to call the preload sequence after the ad is shown because preloading is completed before the Main.as is loaded. The Flash IDE version might need preloading after the ad is shown. In any case, once the ad is shown we can set the framework to jump to the next desired state by overriding the systemMochiAd function like below.

```
override public function systemMochiAd():void {
    super.systemMochiAd();
    //*** flex sdk version
    nextSystemState = FrameWorkStates.STATE_SYSTEM_TITLE;
    //flash IDE version
    //nextSystemState = FrameWorkStates.STATE_SYSTEM_PRELOAD;
}
```

This function still operates the same as the preceding one, by calling super.systemMochiAd. The big change is that it changes the systemState to FrameWorkStates.STATE_SYSTEM_PRELOAD so that preloading will occur. This is only necessary when preloading with the Flash IDE.

Making the leader-board–specific changes

In the init function of Main.as, you will want to add in the following lines to specifically support a particular game with Mochi services. We have provided only the general code in GameFrameWork, so it can be used with any game that needs Mochi services. Some games do not use Mochi services, so you can manually turn on the service by changing Main.as with the following code (since we have not created out Main.as class file these are just for example purposes).

```
mochiBoardId = "ffe2de0ae221a7f4";
MochiServices.connect(mochiGameId, this);
```

We also need to override the systemGameOver function of Main.as to support Mochi leader boards. This is where we will use the lastScore variable we created in GameFrameWork. To make the leader boards work, we need to create and set a variable named lastScore in the game class that we can reference from Main (you will see this used in Tunnel Panic a bit later). We then set nextSystemState to FrameWorkStates.STATE_SYSTEM_MOCHI_HIGHSCORES, so that the function described next will be called. We will implement the following code when we create the Main.as for Tunnel Panic.

```
override public function systemGameOver():void {
    super.systemGameOver();
    lastScore = game.lastScore;
    nextSystemState = FrameWorkStates.STATE_SYSTEM_MOCHI_HIGHSCORES;
}
```

Finally, we will need to add in the systemMochiHighscores and mochiHighscores functions. The heart of these is the call to MochiScore.showLeaderBoard. This call is standard function call that Mochi provides. There are many other functions in the Mochi Services API, but this is the most basic way to support a leader board. Add these lines to the GameFrameWork.as file in the com.efg.framework package.

```
public  function systemMochiHighscores():void {
    var resolution:String = stage.width + "x" + stage.height;
    var o:Object = { n: [15, 15, 14, 2, 13, 14, 0, 10, 14, 2, 2, 1, 10, 7, 15, 4],↵
        f: function (i:Number,s:String):String { if (s.length == 16) return s;↵
        return this.f(i+1,s + this.n[i].toString(16));}};
    MochiScores.showLeaderboard({boardID: mochiBoardId, score: lastScore,↵
        onClose:mochiHighscoresComplete, res:resolution });

    switchSystemState(FrameWorkStates.STATE_SYSTEM_WAIT_FOR_CLOSE);
    nextSystemState = FrameWorkStates.STATE_SYSTEM_TITLE;
}

//*** new Function for Mochi ads chapter 12
public  function mochiHighscoresComplete():void {
    switchSystemState(nextSystemState);
}
```

When the user has finished submitting a score or closes the leader board without submitting, the mochiHighscoresComplete function is called. This function simply sets the state machine back to the FrameWorkStates.STATE_SYSTEM_TITLE state.

Creating our own viral game

Let's take a closer look at a real-world scenario that might actually occur in the viral Flash game industry. We are going to assume that you have made some other games and have created your own framework and reusable class structure similar to the one presented in the first 11 chapters of this book (and the first section of this chapter).

A client e-mail arrives on a Sunday evening at about 6:00 PM. In the e-mail is an urgent request for a simple game engine and a 48-hour deadline. The client wants an arcade-style game with no shooting and the game play time should last no more than about 60 seconds for each session. You are also told that the controls must be very easy and simple. You are given nothing else on the game content description, but you are also told that the game must use Mochi ads and leader boards.

The client also had no assets to provide but would like the game to have a very basic, 8-bit look and feel. Figure 12-8 offers a look at the game we will create.

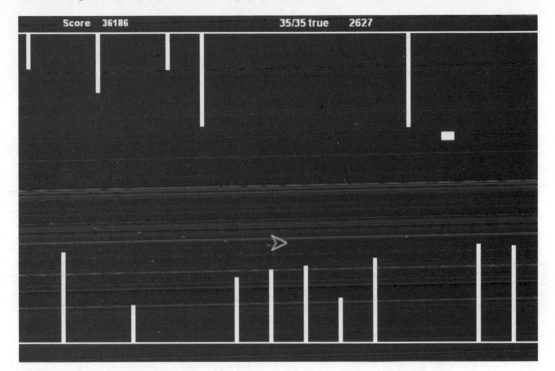

Figure 12-8. The Tunnel Panic game screen

Designing the Tunnel Panic game

Here's the basic design documentation for our Tunnel Panic game:

- **Game name**: Tunnel Panic
- **Game inspiration**: A classic Flash-style game that has been popping up more and more over the years is a skill based scrolling arcade game where the player uses a single key to control the on-screen avatar. In some of these types of games, the player needs to jump over obstacles, and in others, the player flies a space ship through caverns. We are going to make a game similar to the latter. The idea is for the game to end quickly and for the users to post high scores for the world to see.
- **Game objective**: Fly through a scrolling tunnel dodging obstacles for as long as you can. Obstacles come in three types: stalactites extending down from the top of the tunnel, stalagmites extending up from the bottom of the tunnel, and rocks in the center of the tunnel.

- **Game controls**: The spacebar moves the player's space ship up. There are no other controls. Gravity will be constantly pulling the ship down to the bottom on the screen.
- **Game level advancement**: There are no distinct game levels, but after each 10 seconds the obstacles become more plentiful (and longer), change color, and the speed of the game will increase.
- **Game end**: When the player hits an obstacle, the game is over.
- **Game scoring**: The player will receive points for each second in flight.

Let's talk now about the basic technical design information.

We now know the type of game that we want to create, and we have 48 hours to do it. With this limited time frame, we will need to make some vital decisions on how to proceed with the technical design. First, let's discuss the scrolling. We could employ a tile-based scrolling engine (see Chapter 10), or we could go with the screen-based engine presented in Chapter 11. Even though both of these engines have been created and the necessary classes are already part of the package structure, we might not even need to use them.

The only vital items that move in the game are the obstacles, and the world really is just a series of obstacles that scroll toward and passed the player from right to left. If done properly, we only need to make it appear that the player is moving from left to right, when in actuality, the player stays in the middle of the screen. We will add some extra hints at the player movement by adding some exhaust particles that move and fade out behind the player.

> Note: We will be showing a lot of code in the next sections as a demonstration of how functions will work. The entire set of code for Tunnel Panic is in the section called "Coding the TunnelPanic.as Class."

Creating the PlayerSprite object

For our player, we'll create a 32 × 32–pixel sprite using a standard Flash Sprite instance. The sprite will be drawn using a vector drawing canvas. The player ship will remain in the middle of the screen and will be pulled down by gravity each frame tick. The space bar will be used to move the object up. The variables needed for the player are as follows:

```
private var playerSprite:Sprite = new Sprite();
private var playerShape:Shape = new Shape();
private var playerSpeed:Number = 4;
private var playerStarted:Boolean = false;
private var gravity:Number = 1;
```

The playerShape variable will be the vector canvas that holds the shape we will draw for the player. playerSpeed represents how many pixels the ship will move up when the space bar is pressed by the game player. And the playerStarted variable will be used to stop player input when before a new the game play has begun.

The gravity value will be added to the y attribute of playerSprite on each frame tick, and playerSpeed will counteract this gravity when the player presses the space bar.

Creating the play field

The play field will be a very simple design consisting of a horizontal white line at the top and bottom of the screen. There will be a roughly 20-pixel buffer between the top and bottom of the screen and the play field lines. The playfieldSprite will be added to the display list and contain the playfieldShape (the white horizontal lines).

```
private var playfieldSprite:Sprite = new Sprite();
private var playfieldShape:Shape = new Shape();
private var playfieldminX:int = 0;
private var playfieldmaxX:int = 599;
private var playfieldminY:int = 21;
private var playfieldmaxY:int = 378;
```

Adding the obstacles

A pool of 1 × 1–pixel BitmapData objects will be created. Each will be housed inside a Bitmap object. The obstacles will start on the right-hand side of the screen and move to the left. This will simulate scrolling. When an obstacle is pulled from the inactive pool, it will be colored and resized before it is placed on the screen.

```
private var obstaclePool:Array = [];
private var obstacles:Array = [];
private var tempObstacle:Bitmap;
private var obstaclePoolLength:int = 200;
```

Animating the player ship's exhaust

The player's ship will emit exhaust from the rear. The effect has not game-play value and is just a decoration. These exhaust particles will be created using the BlitArrayAsset class from Chapter 11 (and the framework package structure presented earlier). They will be instances of the BasicBlitArrayParticle class, also from the package structure. These particles will be in a pool and will be blitted to a separate canvas than the rest of the game objects. This canvas will employ a new technique (for this book) called a "dirt rectangle" or "dirty rect erase," which is explained in the next section.

These variables create the background and canvas for our exhaust particles:

```
private var backgroundBitmapData:BitmapData = new BitmapData(580, 400, false, 0x000000);
private var canvasBitmapData:BitmapData = new BitmapData(580, 400, false, 0x000000);
private var canvasBitmap:Bitmap = new Bitmap(canvasBitmapData);
private var blitPoint:Point = new Point(0, 0);
```

The following are used for the exhaust pool (active and inactive):

```
private var exhaustPool:Array = [];
private var exhaustParticles:Array = [];
private var tempExhaustParticle:BasicBiltArrayParticle;
private var exhaustPoolLength:int = 30;
private var exhaustLength:int;
```

The exhaustAnimationList array holds the 10-frame fade of the exhaust particles as an array of BitmapData objects.

```
private var exhaustAnimationList:Array = [];
private var lastExhaustTime:int = 0;
private var exhaustDelay:int = 100+((obstacleSpeedMax * 10) - (10 * obstacleSpeed));
```

Figure 12-9 is another look at the Tunnel Panic game screen. This version now has the game elements annotated.

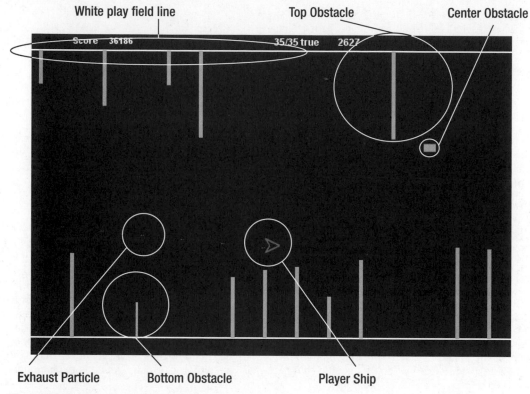

Figure 12-9. The annotatedTunnel Panic game screen

Using dirty rect erase

A **dirty rect erase** is a technique used to update only the parts of a blit canvas that have changed, as opposed to always clearing the entire canvas between each frame update. This can be a powerful tool, but its use necessitates the blurring of the update and render functions for the particles.

We will have to do the erase of the particle's original location in the update function, but the blit of the new location in the render function. Here is the update function code:

```
exhaustLength = exhaustParticles.length - 1;
canvasBitmapData.lock();
for (ctr = exhaustLength; ctr >= 0; ctr--) {
    tempExhaustParticle = exhaustParticles[ctr];
    //dirty rect blit erase
    blitPoint.x = tempExhaustParticle.x;
    blitPoint.y = tempExhaustParticle.y;
```

```
    canvasBitmapData.copyPixels(backgroundBitmapData,↩
        tempExhaustParticle.bitmapData.rect,↩
        blitPoint);
    if (tempExhaustParticle.update(timeBasedModifier)) {
        //return true if particle is to be removed
        tempExhaustParticle.frame = 0;
        exhaustPool.push(tempExhaustParticle);
        exhaustParticles.splice(ctr,1);
    }
}
canvasBitmapData.unlock();
```

You will notice that this blit is very similar to the blits in previous chapters. We simply need blitPoint to be the current location (x and y) of the particle. It is then erased by copying that background Rectangle from the same starting location to the canvasBitmapData. This effectively erases only the portion of the canvasBitmapData that needs to be updated and not the entire canvasBitmapData.

Increasing the game difficulty

As the game plays, we will increase its difficulty every 10 seconds (obstacleUpgradeWait value). Specifically, we will change the color, frequency, and speed of the obstacles. The lastObstacleUpgrade variable will hold the return value of a getTimer function call from the last difficulty increase.

```
private var obstacleUpgradeWait:int = 10000;
private var lastObstacleUpgrade:int;
```

Obstacles will be pulled from the pool and placed to start at the right-hand side of the play field based on the obstacleDelay value. This is the number of milliseconds to wait between obstacles. Every 10 seconds, along with the rest of the obstacle upgrades, this obstacleDelay will decrease by obstacleDelayDecrease until it reaches obstacleDelayMin.

```
private var lastObstacleTime:int;
private var obstacleDelay:int = 800;
private var obstacleDelayMin:int = 50;
private var obstacleDelayDecrease:int = 150;
```

When an obstacle is to be created, it will either be a top, bottom, or center obstacle. The centerFrequency value is the percentage chance that a center obstacle will be created. The centerWidth and centerHeight control the dimensions of all center obstacles.

```
private var centerFrequency:int = 15;
private var centerHeight:int = 10;
private var centerWidth:int = 15;
```

If a center obstacle is not going to be created, either a top or bottom obstacle will be created. The height of the obstacle is governed by a random value between obstacleHeightMin and obstacleHeightMax. When obstacles are upgraded after 10 seconds, the height is increased by obstcaleHeightIncrease until the height reaches obstcaleHeightLimit.

```
private var obstacleHeightMin:int = 40;
private var obstacleHeightMax:int = 60;
private var obstacleHeightLimit:int = 120;
private var obstacleHeightIncrease:int = 20;
```

All obstacles move from right to left at the same speed (obstacleSpeed) to create the illusion that the player is scrolling from left to right. Every 10 seconds the speed is increased by 1 until it reaches obstacleSpeedMax.

```
private var obstacleSpeed:int = 6;
private var obstacleSpeedMax:int = 12;
```

Every 10 seconds the obstacleColorIndex will increase by 1. This will change the color of the obstacles created from the pool to coincide with the color value in the aObstacleColor array.

```
private var obstacleColors:Array = [0xffffff, 0xff0000, 0x00ff00, 0x0000ff, 0x00ffff, ⏎
    0xffff00, 0xffaaff, 0xaaff99, 0xcc6600];
private var obstacleColorIndex:int = 0;
```

Ending the game

The game is over then the player hits an obstacle object. We will use standard hitTestObject collision detection for this because of the nature of the obstacles. Each obstacle is only a 1 × 1–pixel BitmapData element that we have scaled in code to create various objects. If we tried to use BitmapData.hitTest, we would find that the collisions would not be detected properly because BitmapData.hitTest works only with the pixels in the original BitmapData, not the stretched version we created by simply setting he scaleX and scaleY of the Bitmap holder for the BitmapData object.

When the game is over we want to set the lastScore variable for Main.as to submit to the Mochi leader board for the game. When the checkForEndGame function detects that the game is over (gameOver == true), it calls switchSystemState setting the new state to STATE_SYSTEM_PLAYER_EXPLODE. The playerExplodeComplete function actually sets the lastScore variable.

```
public function checkforEndGame():void {
    if (gameOver ) {
        playerStarted = false;
        switchSystemState(STATE_SYSTEM_PLAYER_EXPLODE);
        dispatchEvent(new CustomEventSound(CustomEventSound.PLAY_SOUND, ⏎
            Main.SOUND_EXPLODE,false, 1, 8, 1));
    }
}
```

The playerExplode function is called until the the player object has faded out.

```
private function systemPlayerExplode(timeDifference:Number=0):void {
    playerSprite.alpha -=.005;
    if (playerSprite.alpha <= 0) {
    playerExplodeComplete();
    }
}
```

This function, in turn, calls playerExplodeComplete function when the fade out is finished. This sets the lastScore variable (inherited by TunnelPanic from Game as you will see in the next section). This is the same variable that Main will use to set the score in the Mochi leader board.

```
private function playerExplodeComplete():void {
    dispatchEvent(new Event(GAME_OVER) );
    lastScore = score;
    trace("lastScore=" + lastScore);
    disposeAll();
}
```

Creating the Main.as for Tunnel Panic

Some of the changes to Main necessary for this game have already been presented in the earlier sections where we covered preloading and Mochi services integration. We will need to make a change to the com.efg.framework.Game.as class to support the lastScore variable. Let's look at that change first.

Changing Game.as for Tunnel Panic

To support the use of a high score system (in this case the Mochi leader board) we need to make one small change to com.efg.framework.Game. We need to add the lastScore property to the variable definition section of that class.

```
public var lastScore:Number = 0;
```

Changing Main.as for Tunnel Panic

We've already discussed the changes to the Main.as class for the game, Mochi ads, preloaders, and high scores. Follow along as we iterate through all rest of the changes necessary for both the Flex SDK and the Flash IDE version of the Main.as file. The major changes to this class are in bold to highlight the code necessary for preloading and adding Mochi services.

Note that there are also some code changes to facilitate the screens and sounds for Tunnel Panic. Since we have discussed these many times already, we will leave those changes for you to discover on your own.

However, we should note a few interesting things. This game uses the time-based step timer and frame-rate profiler from Chapter 11. Please refer to that chapter for an in-depth discussion of that code. Also, the systemWait and systemLevelIn functions are overridden to add a simple alpha tween for level transition similar to what we created for Chapter 11.

```
package com.efg.games.tunnelpanic
{

    import com.efg.framework.FrameCounter;
    import com.efg.framework.FrameRateProfiler;
    import flash.text.TextFormat;
    import flash.text.TextField;
    import flash.text.TextFormatAlign;
    import flash.geom.Point;
    import flash.events.Event;

    import com.efg.framework.FrameWorkStates;
    import com.efg.framework.GameFrameWork;
    import com.efg.framework.BasicScreen;
    import com.efg.framework.ScoreBoard;
    import com.efg.framework.SideBySideScoreElement;
    import com.efg.framework.SoundManager;
    import mochi.as3.*;

    dynamic public class Main extends GameFrameWork {

    //custom sccore board elements
```

```
public static const SCORE_BOARD_SCORE:String = "score";
public static var SOUND_TITLE_MUSIC:String = "titlemusic";
public static var SOUND_IN_GAME_MUSIC:String = "ingamemusic";
public static var SOUND_EXPLODE:String = "explode";

public function Main() {
   if (stage)
      addedToStage();
   else
      addEventListener(Event.ADDED_TO_STAGE, addedToStage,false,0,true);
}

override public function addedToStage(e:Event = null):void {
   if (e != null) {
     removeEventListener(Event.ADDED_TO_STAGE, addedToStage);
   }
   super.addedToStage();
   trace("in tunnel panic added to stage");
  init();
}

override public function init():void {
   trace("init");
   game= new TunnelPanic();
   setApplicationBackGround(600, 400, false, 0x000000);

   //add score board to the screen as the seconf layer
   scoreBoard = new ScoreBoard();
   addChild(scoreBoard);
   scoreBoardTextFormat = new TextFormat("_sans", "11", "0xffffff", "true");
   scoreBoard.createTextElement(SCORE_BOARD_SCORE, new ↵
      SideBySideScoreElement(200, 0, 20, "Score", ↵
      scoreBoardTextFormat, 25, "0", scoreBoardTextFormat));

   screenTextFormat = new TextFormat("_sans", "16", "0xffffff", "false");
   screenTextFormat.align = flash.text.TextFormatAlign.CENTER;
   screenButtonFormat = new TextFormat("_sans", "12", "0x000000", "false");

   titleScreen = new BasicScreen(FrameWorkStates.STATE_SYSTEM_TITLE,↵
      600,400,false,0x000000 );
   titleScreen.createOkButton("Play", new Point(250, 250), 100, 20, ↵
      screenButtonFormat, 0x000000, 0xff0000,2);
   titleScreen.createDisplayText("Tunnel Panic", 200, new Point(200, 150),↵
       screenTextFormat);

   instructionsScreen = new BasicScreen(FrameWorkStates.STATE_SYSTEM_INSTRUCTIONS,↵
      600,400,false,0x000000);
   instructionsScreen.createOkButton("Start", new Point(250, 250),↵
      100, 20,screenButtonFormat, 0x000000, 0xff0000,2);
   instructionsScreen.createDisplayText("Dodge everything\nCan you go far?.",300,↵
      new Point(150,150),screenTextFormat);

   gameOverScreen = new BasicScreen(FrameWorkStates.STATE_SYSTEM_GAME_OVER,↵
      600,400,false,0x0000dd);
```

606

```
    gameOverScreen.createOkButton("Game Over", new Point(250, 250), 100, 20,↵
        screenButtonFormat, 0x000000, 0xff0000,2);
    gameOverScreen.createDisplayText("Submit",100,new Point(250,150),screenTextFormat);

    levelInScreen = new BasicScreen(FrameWorkStates.STATE_SYSTEM_LEVEL_IN,↵
        600, 400, true, 0xbbff0000);
    levelInText = "GO!";
    levelInScreen.createDisplayText(levelInText,100,new↵
        Point(250,150),screenTextFormat);

    pausedScreen = new BasicScreen(FrameWorkStates.STATE_SYSTEM_PAUSE,↵
        400,400,false,0xff000000 );
    pausedScreen.createOkButton("UNPAUSE", new Point(250, 250), 100, 20,↵
        screenButtonFormat, 0x000000, 0xff0000,2);
    pausedScreen.createDisplayText("Puased", 100, new Point(250, 150),↵
        screenTextFormat);
    preloadScreen = new BasicScreen(FrameWorkStates.STATE_SYSTEM_PRELOAD,↵
        600, 400, true, 0xff0000ff);
    //*** Flex SDK Only. Comment out these lines if using the IDE.
    soundManager.addSound(SOUND_IN_GAME_MUSIC, new Library.SoundMusicInGame);
    soundManager.addSound(SOUND_TITLE_MUSIC,new Library.SoundMusicTitle);
    soundManager.addSound(SOUND_EXPLODE,new Library.SoundExplode);

//preloadScreen not needed for Flex SDK projects
    preloadScreen.createDisplayText("Loading...",150,new↵
        Point(250,150),screenTextFormat);

    //set initial game state

    switchSystemState(FrameWorkStates.STATE_SYSTEM_MOCHI_AD);

    //sounds added after pre-load in the addSounds() function

    //mochi
    mochiGameId = "81e8cd4f0999371e";
    mochiBoardId = "ffe2de0ae221a7f4";
    MochiServices.connect(mochiGameId, this);
    //framerate profiler

    frameRate = 40;

    frameRateProfiler = new FrameRateProfiler();
    frameRateProfiler.profilerRenderObjects = 4000;
    frameRateProfiler.profilerRenderLoops = 7;
    frameRateProfiler.profilerDisplayOnScreen= true;
    frameRateProfiler.profilerXLocation = 0;
    frameRateProfiler.profilerYLocation = 0;
    addChild(frameRateProfiler);
    frameRateProfiler.startProfile(frameRate);
    frameRateProfiler.addEventListener(FrameRateProfiler.EVENT_COMPLETE, ↵
    frameRateProfileComplete, false, 0, true);
}
```

```
override public function addSounds():void {
    //flash IDE only (uncomment these lines if using the IDE)
    //soundManager.addSound(SOUND_IN_GAME_MUSIC, new SoundMusicInGame);
    //soundManager.addSound(SOUND_TITLE_MUSIC,new SoundMusicTitle);
    //soundManager.addSound(SOUND_EXPLODE,new SoundExplode);
}

override public function frameRateProfileComplete(e:Event):void {
    //advanced timer
    trace("profiledFrameRate=" + frameRateProfiler.profilerFrameRateAverage);
    game.setRendering(frameRateProfiler.profilerFrameRateAverage, frameRate);
    game.timeBasedUpdateModifier = frameRate;
    removeEventListener(FrameRateProfiler.EVENT_COMPLETE, frameRateProfileComplete) ;
    removeChild(frameRateProfiler);

    //frame counter
    frameCounter.x = 400;
    frameCounter.y = 0;
    frameCounter.profiledRate = frameRateProfiler.profilerFrameRateAverage;
    frameCounter.showProfiledRate = true;
    addChild(frameCounter);
    startTimer(true);
}

override public function systemMochiAd():void {
    super.systemMochiAd();
    //*** flex sdk version
    nextSystemState = FrameWorkStates.STATE_SYSTEM_TITLE;
    //flash IDE version
    //nextSystemState =   FrameWorkStates.STATE_SYSTEM_PRELOAD;
}

override public function systemGameOver():void {
    super.systemGameOver();
    lastScore = game.lastScore;
    nextSystemState = FrameWorkStates.STATE_SYSTEM_MOCHI_HIGHSCORES;
}

override public function systemGamePlay():void {
    game.runGameTimeBased(paused,timeDifference);
    }

override public function systemTitle():void {
    soundManager.playSound(SOUND_TITLE_MUSIC, true,999, 20, 1);
    super.systemTitle();
}

override public function systemNewGame():void {
    trace("new game");
    soundManager.stopSound(SOUND_TITLE_MUSIC,true);
    super.systemNewGame();
}
```

```
override public function systemLevelIn():void {
    levelInScreen.alpha = 1;
    super.systemLevelIn();
}

override public function systemWait():void {
    //trace("system Level In");
    if (lastSystemState == FrameWorkStates.STATE_SYSTEM_LEVEL_IN) {
        levelInScreen.alpha -= .01;
        if (levelInScreen.alpha < 0 ) {
            dispatchEvent(new Event(EVENT_WAIT_COMPLETE));
            levelInScreen.alpha = 0;
        }
    }
}
}
}
}
```

Creating the Library.as class for Flex SDK only

Now, just add in the three sounds we will need. There are two music loops and a single sound effect for when the player's ship hits an obstacle. You will not need this class if you are using the Flash IDE.

```
package com.efg.games.tunnelpanic
{
    public class Library {

    [Embed(source = '../../../../../assets/startmusic.mp3')]
    public static const SoundMusicInGame:Class;

    [Embed(source = '../../../../../assets/ingamemusic.mp3')]
    public static const SoundMusicTitle:Class;

    [Embed(source-'../../../../../assets/explode.mp3')]
    public static const SoundExplode:Class;
    }

}
```

Adding to the Flash IDE Library

The previous section in the chapter on preloading has covered adding these same assets to the library and then placing them in an assets clip for preloading. If you have not read that section, you should go back and do so now.

> Note: In Main.as you only need to addSounds function if you are using the Flash IDE. If you are using the IDE, be sure to comment out the soundManager.addSound function calls in the init function.

Coding the TunnelPanic.as class

This section shows the complete code for the Game.as class and subclasses. As you will see, we have discussed much of the code and algorithms already.

The *class shell* includes the class import section, the variable definition section and the class constructor: We have taken a look at most of the variables already, and the rest of the shell consists of the constructor that calls the init function and the closing brackets for the class and package.

```
package com.efg.games.tunnelpanic
{

    import flash.display.*
    import flash.events.*;
    import flash.geom.Point;
    import flash.geom.Rectangle;
    import flash.utils.getTimer;

    import com.efg.framework.BasicBlitArrayObject;
    import com.efg.framework.BlitArrayAsset;
    import com.efg.framework.BasicBiltArrayParticle;
    import com.efg.framework.CustomEventLevelScreenUpdate;
    import com.efg.framework.CustomEventScoreBoardUpdate;
    import com.efg.framework.CustomEventSound;
    import com.efg.framework.Game;

    public class TunnelPanic extends com.efg.framework.Game
    {


    public static const STATE_SYSTEM_GAME_PLAY:int = 0;
    public static const STATE_SYSTEM_PLAYER_EXPLODE:int = 1;

    private var systemFunction:Function;
    private var currentSystemState:int;
    private var nextSystemState:int;
    private var lastSystemState:int;

    private var customerScoreBoardEventScore:CustomEventScoreBoardUpdate ⏎
        = new CustomEventScoreBoardUpdate(CustomEventScoreBoardUpdate.UPDATE_TEXT,⏎
        Main.SCORE_BOARD_SCORE, "");

    //Tunnel Panic game specific
    private var keyPressList:Array = [];
    private var keyListenersInit:Boolean = false;

    //player ship
    private var playerSprite:Sprite = new Sprite();
    private var playerShape:Shape = new Shape();
    private var playerSpeed:Number = 4;
    private var playerStarted:Boolean = false;

    //playfield
    private var playfieldSprite:Sprite = new Sprite();
    private var playfieldShape:Shape = new Shape();
```

```
private var playfieldminX:int = 0;
private var playfieldmaxX:int = 599;
private var playfieldminY:int = 21;
private var playfieldmaxY:int = 378;

//obstacles
private var obstaclePool:Array = [];
private var obstacles:Array = [];
private var tempObstacle:Bitmap;
private var obstaclePoolLength:int = 200;

//game play
//how long to wait before increasing obstacle difficulty
private var obstacleUpgradeWait:int = 10000;
private var lastObstacleUpgrade:int;

//obstacle frequency
private var lastObstacleTime:int;
private var obstacleDelay:int = 800;
private var obstacleDelayMin:int = 50;
private var obstacleDelayDecrease:int = 150;

//center obstacles
private var centerFrequency:int = 15;
private var centerHeight:int = 10;
private var centerWidth:int = 15;

//obstacle height
private var obstacleHeightMin:int = 40;
private var obstacleHeightMax:int = 60;
private var obstacleHeightLimit:int = 120;
private var obstacleHeightIncrease:int = 20;

//obstacleSpeed
private var obstacleSpeed:int = 6;
private var obstacleSpeedMax:int = 12;

//obstacleColors
private var obstacleColors:Array = [0xffffff, 0xff0000, 0x00ff00, 0x0000ff, 0x00ffff, ↵
    0xffff00, 0xffaaff, 0xaaff99, 0xcc6600];
private var obstacleColorIndex:int = 0;

private var gravity:Number = 1;

//exhaust blit canvas
private var backgroundBitmapData:BitmapData = new BitmapData(580, 400, false, 0x000000);
private var canvasBitmapData:BitmapData = new BitmapData(580, 400, false, 0x000000);
private var canvasBitmap:Bitmap = new Bitmap(canvasBitmapData);
private var blitPoint:Point = new Point(0, 0);

private var exhaustPool:Array = [];
private var exhaustParticles:Array = [];
private var tempExhaustParticle:BasicBiltArrayParticle;
private var exhaustPoolLength:int = 30;
private var exhaustLength:int;
```

```
private var exhaustAnimationList:Array = [];
private var lastExhaustTime:int = 0;

private var exhaustDelay:int = 100+((obstacleSpeedMax * 10) - (10 * obstacleSpeed));

//score
public var score:int = 0;
private var lastScoreEvent:int = 0;
private var scoreDelay:int = 1000;
private var gameOver:Boolean = false;

    public function TunnelPanic() {
        init();
    }
// end class
// end package
```

The init *functions* follow. The init functions for Tunnel Panic are the one-time setup functions for the player's ship, the drawing of the play field, the creation of the obstacle and exhaust pools and the creation and initialization of the canvas for the exhaust particles.

Note: Please make sure to add these new functions inside the class, after the constructor.

```
public function init():void {

    this.focusRect = false;

    createPlayerShip();
    createPlayfield();
    createObstaclePool();
    createExhaustPool();
    setUpCanvas();
    canvasBitmap.y = 20;
    addChild(canvasBitmap);
    addChild(playfieldSprite);

}

private function createPlayerShip():void {
    //draw vector ship and place it into a Sprite instance
    playerShape.graphics.clear();
    playerShape.graphics.lineStyle(2, 0xff00ff);
    playerShape.graphics.moveTo(15, 7);
    playerShape.graphics.lineTo(7, 24);
    playerShape.graphics.lineTo(15, 19);
    playerShape.graphics.moveTo(16, 19);
    playerShape.graphics.lineTo(24, 24);
    playerShape.graphics.lineTo(16, 7);

    playerShape.x = -16;
    playerShape.y = -16;
    playerSprite.addChild(playerShape);
}

private function createPlayfield():void {
```

```
    //draw playfield as two simple lines at top and bottom of screen

    playfieldShape.graphics.clear();
    playfieldShape.graphics.lineStyle(2, 0xffffff);
    playfieldShape.graphics.moveTo(playfieldminX, playfieldminY);
    playfieldShape.graphics.lineTo(playfieldmaxX, playfieldminY);
    playfieldShape.graphics.moveTo(playfieldminX, playfieldmaxY);
    playfieldShape.graphics.lineTo(playfieldmaxX, playfieldmaxY);

    playfieldSprite.addChild(playfieldShape);
}

private function createObstaclePool():void {
    for (var ctr:int = 0; ctr < obstaclePoolLength; ctr++) {
        var tempBitmapData:BitmapData = ↩
            new BitmapData(1, 1, false, obstacleColors[obstacleColorIndex]);
        var tempObstacle:Bitmap = new Bitmap(tempBitmapData)
        obstaclePool.push(tempObstacle);
    }
}

private function createExhaustPool():void {
    //create look for exhaust
    var tempBD:BitmapData = new BitmapData(32, 32, true, 0x00000000);
    tempBD.setPixel32(30, 15, 0xffff00ff);
    tempBD.setPixel32(28, 15, 0xffff00ff);
    tempBD.setPixel32(27, 15, 0xffff00ff);
    var tempBlitArrayAsset:BlitArrayAsset= new BlitArrayAsset();
    tempBlitArrayAsset.createFadeOutBlitArrayFromBD(tempBD, 20);
    exhaustAnimationList = tempBlitArrayAsset.tileList;

    for (var ctr:int = 0; ctr < exhaustPoolLength; ctr++) {
        var tempExhaustParticle:BasicBiltArrayParticle = ↩
            new BasicBiltArrayParticle(playfieldminX, playfieldmaxY, ↩
            playfieldminY, playfieldmaxY);
        exhaustPool.push(tempExhaustParticle);
    }
}

private function setUpCanvas():void {
    canvasBitmapData.lock();
    canvasBitmapData.copyPixels(backgroundBitmapData, backgroundBitmapData.rect, blitPoint);
    canvasBitmapData.unlock();
}
```

The following code sets up a *new game and level*. The newGame function resets all of the game variables such as those that define the size, and frequency of the obstacles. The newLevel function sets the player on the screen, starts up the in game music and resets the obstacle frequency counters. There is only one level in this version of the game, but if we wanted to add more levels this function affectively separates the newGame specific functions from the newLevel specific functions.

```
override public function newGame():void {
    score = 0;
    obstacleColorIndex = 0;
```

```
    lastObstacleTime = 0;
    lastExhaustTime = 0;
    lastScoreEvent = 0;
    obstacleDelay= 1000;
    obstacleHeightMax= 10;
    obstacleSpeed= 4;
    playerStarted = false;
    gameOver = false;
    playerSprite.alpha = 1;

    switchSystemState(STATE_SYSTEM_GAME_PLAY);
    //key listeners
    if (!keyListenersInit) {
        stage.addEventListener(KeyboardEvent.KEY_DOWN,keyDownListener);

        stage.addEventListener(KeyboardEvent.KEY_UP, keyUpListener);
        keyListenersInit = true;
        }

    updateScoreBoard();
    }

override public function newLevel():void {
    stage.focus = this;
    dispatchEvent(new CustomEventSound(CustomEventSound.PLAY_SOUND, ↵
        Main.SOUND_IN_GAME_MUSIC, true, 999, 8, 1));
    addChild(playerSprite);
    playerSprite.x = 300;
    playerSprite.y = 200;
    playerSprite.rotation = 90;
    playerStarted = true;
    lastObstacleUpgrade = getTimer();
    lastObstacleTime = getTimer();
}
```

This code creates *the game loop*. The game loop uses the time-based step timer introduced in Chapter 11. There are two values for the currentSystemState: SYSTEM_STATE_GAME_PLAY and SYSTEM_STATE_PLAYER_EXPLODE.

```
override public function runGameTimeBased(paused:Boolean=false, ↵
    timeDifference:Number=1):void {
    if (!paused) {
        systemFunction(timeDifference);
    }
}

public function switchSystemState(stateval:int):void {
    lastSystemState = currentSystemState;
    currentSystemState = stateval;

    switch(stateval) {
        case STATE_SYSTEM_GAME_PLAY:
            systemFunction = systemGamePlay;
            break;
```

```
            case STATE_SYSTEM_PLAYER_EXPLODE :
                systemFunction = systemPlayerExplode;
                break;

        }
    }

    private function systemGamePlay(timeDifference:Number=0):void {
        if (playerStarted) {
            checkInput();
        }
        update(timeDifference);
        checkCollisions();
        render();
        updateScoreBoard();
        checkforEndGame();
    }
    private function systemPlayerExplode(timeDifference:Number=0):void {
        playerSprite.alpha -=.005;
        if (playerSprite.alpha <- 0) {
            playerExplodeComplete();
        }
    }

    public function checkforEndGame():void {
        if (gameOver ) {
            playerStarted = false;
            switchSystemState(STATE_SYSTEM_PLAYER_EXPLODE);
            dispatchEvent(new CustomEventSound(CustomEventSound.PLAY_SOUND,↵
                Main.SOUND_EXPLODE, false, 1, 8, 1));
        }
    }

    private function playerExplodeComplete():void {
        dispatchEvent(new Event(GAME_OVER) );
        lastScore - score;
        trace("lastScore=" ı lastScore),
        disposeAll();
    }
```

This code allows *user input*. The only user input we need in Tunnel Panic is the space bar. When it is pressed, we decrease the y value of the playerSprite (moving it up the screen).

```
private function checkInput():void {
    if (keyPressList[32]) {
        playerSprite.y -= playerSpeed;
    }
}

private function keyDownListener(e:KeyboardEvent):void {
    keyPressList[e.keyCode] = true;
}

private function keyUpListener(e:KeyboardEvent):void {
    keyPressList[e.keyCode] = false;
}
```

The *update functions* come next. The update function upgrades the obstacle properties to increase game difficulty as the play progresses. It adds new obstacles based the lastObstacleTime value. Finally, it loops through the lists of obstacles and exhaustParicles, updating their positions on the game screen.

```
private function update(timeDifference:Number = 0):void {
    var timeBasedModifier:Number = (timeDifference / 1000)*timeBasedUpdateModifier;
    //score
    if (playerStarted && getTimer() > (lastScoreEvent + scoreDelay)) {
        score += (10 + obstacleSpeed);
    }
    //obstacles additions
    if (getTimer() > lastObstacleUpgrade +obstacleUpgradeWait) {
        lastObstacleUpgrade = getTimer();
        obstacleDelay -= obstacleDelayDecrease;
        if (obstacleDelay < obstacleDelayMin) {
            obstacleDelay = obstacleDelayMin;
        }
        trace("obstacleDelay=" + obstacleDelay);
        obstacleHeightMax += obstacleHeightIncrease;
        if (obstacleHeightMax > obstacleHeightLimit) {
            obstacleHeightMax = obstacleHeightLimit;
        }
        trace("obstacleHeightMax=" + obstacleHeightMax);
        obstacleSpeed++;
        if (obstacleSpeed > obstacleSpeedMax) {
            obstacleSpeed = obstacleSpeedMax;
        }
        trace("obstacleSpeed=" + obstacleSpeed);

        obstacleColorIndex++;
        if (obstacleColorIndex == obstacleColors.length) {
            obstacleColorIndex = obstacleColors.length - 1;
        }
        trace("obstacleColorIndex=" + obstacleColorIndex);

        exhaustDelay= 100+((obstacleSpeedMax * 10) - (10 * obstacleSpeed));
    }
    // add new obstacles
    var obstaclePoolCount:int = obstaclePool.length -1;
    if (getTimer() > (lastObstacleTime + obstacleDelay) && obstaclePoolCount>0) {
        //trace("creating an obstacle");
        lastObstacleTime = getTimer();
        tempObstacle = obstaclePool.pop();
        tempObstacle.bitmapData.setPixel(0, 0, obstacleColors[obstacleColorIndex]);

        //is it going to be in the center?
        if (int(Math.random() * 100) < centerFrequency) {
            tempObstacle.y = 120 + Math.random()*200;
            tempObstacle.scaleY = centerHeight;
            tempObstacle.scaleX = centerWidth;
        }else {
            tempObstacle.scaleY = randomNumberFromRange(obstacleHeightMin, obstacleHeightMax);
            tempObstacle.scaleX = 5;
```

```
        (int(Math.random() * 2) == 0)? tempObstacle.y = playfieldminY : tempObstacle.y =↵
            (playfieldmaxY - tempObstacle.height);
    }
    tempObstacle.x = playfieldmaxX;
    obstacles.push(tempObstacle);
    addChild(tempObstacle);
}
//update obstacles
var obstacleCount:int = obstacles.length - 1;
for (var ctr:int=obstacleCount;ctr>=0;ctr--) {
    tempObstacle= obstacles[ctr];
    tempObstacle.x -= obstacleSpeed*timeBasedModifier;
    if (tempObstacle.x < playfieldminX) {
        tempObstacle.scaleY = 1;
        tempObstacle.scaleX = 1;
        obstaclePool.push(tempObstacle);
        obstacles.splice(ctr, 1);
        removeChild(tempObstacle);
    }
}

var exhaustPoolCount:int = exhaustPool.length -1;

if (getTimer() > (lastExhaustTime + exhaustDelay) && exhaustPoolCount > 0 ) {
    lastExhaustTime = getTimer();
    tempExhaustParticle = exhaustPool.pop();
    tempExhaustParticle.lifeDelayCount=0;
    tempExhaustParticle.x=playerSprite.x-30;
    tempExhaustParticle.y = playerSprite.y-32;
    tempExhaustParticle.nextX=tempExhaustParticle.x;
    tempExhaustParticle.nextY=tempExhaustParticle.y;
    tempExhaustParticle.speed = obstacleSpeed;
    tempExhaustParticle.frame = 0;
    tempExhaustParticle.animationList =  exhaustAnimationList;
    tempExhaustParticle.bitmapData = ↵
    tempExhaustParticle.animationList[tempExhaustParticle.frame];
    tempExhaustParticle.dx = -1;
    tempExhaustParticle.dy = 0;
    tempExhaustParticle.lifeDelay = 3;
        exhaustParticles.push(tempExhaustParticle);
}
exhaustLength = exhaustParticles.length - 1;
canvasBitmapData.lock();
for (ctr = exhaustLength; ctr >= 0; ctr--) {
    tempExhaustParticle = exhaustParticles[ctr];
    //dirty rect blit erase
    blitPoint.x = tempExhaustParticle.x;
    blitPoint.y = tempExhaustParticle.y;
    canvasBitmapData.copyPixels(backgroundBitmapData, ↵
        tempExhaustParticle.bitmapData.rect, blitPoint);
    if (tempExhaustParticle.update(timeBasedModifier)) {
        tempExhaustParticle.frame = 0;
        exhaustPool.push(tempExhaustParticle);
```

```
            exhaustParticles.splice(ctr,1);
        }
    }
    canvasBitmapData.unlock();
    playerSprite.y += gravity;
}

private function randomNumberFromRange(min:int, max:int):int {
    return(int(Math.random() * (max - min)) + min);
}
```

As usual, after the update functions come the *collision checking and render functions*. The collision routines are very simple for Tunnel Panic. We have implemented the standard hitTestObject functions. We did this because the BitmapData that makes up our obstacles has been scaled for each obstacle. The BitmapData.hitTest functions will not work correctly on scaled or rotated objects.

```
private function checkCollisions():void {
    var playerHit:Boolean = false;
    if (playerSprite.y < playfieldminY+10 || playerSprite.y > playfieldmaxY-10) {
        trace("hit outside bounds");
        playerHit = true;
    }

    for each (tempObstacle in obstacles) {
        if (playerSprite.hitTestObject(tempObstacle)) {
            trace("hit obstacle");
            playerHit = true;
        }
    }
    if (playerHit) {
    gameOver = true;
    }
}

private function render():void {
    canvasBitmapData.lock();
    for each (tempExhaustParticle in exhaustParticles) {
        tempExhaustParticle.render(canvasBitmapData);
    }
    canvasBitmapData.unlock();
}
```

Finally, you have these remaining functions for clean up and similar operations:

```
private function updateScoreBoard():void {
    customerScoreBoardEventScore.value = score.toString();
    dispatchEvent(customerScoreBoardEventScore);
}

private function disposeAll():void {
    //move all obstacles left in active to pool
    var obstacleCount:int = obstacles.length - 1;
    for (var ctr:int = obstacleCount; ctr >= 0; ctr--) {
        tempObstacle = obstacles[ctr];
        removeChild(tempObstacle);
```

```
        obstaclePool.push(tempObstacle);
        obstacles.splice(ctr,1);
    }

    var exhaustCount:int = exhaustParticles.length - 1;
    for (ctr = exhaustCount; ctr >= 0; ctr--) {
        tempExhaustParticle = exhaustParticles[ctr];
        //dirty rect blit erase
        blitPoint.x = tempExhaustParticle.x;
        blitPoint.y = tempExhaustParticle.y;
        canvasBitmapData.copyPixels(backgroundBitmapData, ⤺
            tempExhaustParticle.bitmapData.rect, blitPoint);
        tempExhaustParticle.frame = 0;
        exhaustPool.push(tempExhaustParticle);
        exhaustParticles.splice(ctr,1);
    }
    trace("disposed");
}
```

We are not using the setRendering function in this game, so it is merely a placeholder in the preceding code.

Test it!

When you test this game, you will probably not see the preloader sequence, as the game does not have much content to preload. What you should see is a Mochi Services ad and the title screen for the game. The game play is very simple: simply press the space bar key to fly up, and avoid hitting anything, even the walls. When the game is complete, you should be able to submit your score to the Mochi Leader Board that we set up for this game.

Summary

Do you think that making viral Flash games is for you? It's a very competitive business, but the barriers to entry are low, so it's also accessible to almost anyone who wants to take a crack it. We've showed you many different ways to market and make money from your viral Flash games. We also showed you ways to take a game (Tunnel Panic) and prepare it for the viral Flash world with a preloader and Mochi services. The next step is up to you. Will you take what you have learned from this chapter, and by extension, the rest of this book and use it to make something you are proud of?

So now you have really been through it haven't you? If you have made it this far, you deserve to pat yourself on the back. Do you recall the first chapter, where we discussed our theory about making your second game? Does that make more sense now? Do you see that only by making games can you get good at making games? That's really what the second game theory is all about. In reality, the theory has little to do with what number your game is—second, third, fourth, thirtieth, or whatever. The ideas are still the same. Everything we tried to show you in this book boils down to two points:

- **Planning:** The best way that we have found to be successful when making games (or any kind of application) is planning. We are not talking about making flowcharts or reams of specifications and design documents; we are talking about creating a code base that can be used, reused, updated, and expanded upon as your development takes shape over the course of many projects. This book's game framework was a very good example of this. We were able to create code that could be reused for nearly every game in this book by laying down the framework first. However, that framework was not set in stone. We updated it, iterated it, and kept it relevant, even as the games expended and became more and more in-depth. At the same time, we made many different games, but all made use of the same framework. The planning that went into the game framework benefitted every project that came after it.

- **Practice**: We started the book by making some very simple games. The Balloon Saw game from Chapter 1 was really just a slight modification on the Atari arcade game Avalanche and the first catch games like Activision's Kaboom!. Those games were some of the very first arcade and video game contests. Over the course of 12 chapters, you iterated, practiced, refactored, and iterated some more until you were making games like the most modern arcade, casual, and web games around. We did this simply by making games. You can read all the game development books in the world that you want, but unless you actually put those words into practice, you still will never make a game.

You've finished this book, but we are not done with you. We encourage you to visit this book's web site at www.8bitrockert.com or www.friendsofed.com if you have not already done so. At these sites, you can get access to the code from this book, discuss games and development on the forums, and even read new Web-only tutorials and content about Flash games and the Flash game world. We'd love to meet you, play your games, and welcome you into the world of Flash game development. We hope to see you there.

In a sense, we now leave you with the eleventh game theory. We showed you how to make ten different games in this book and gave you the tools to make your eleventh game. What will that game be? We are anxious to find out.

Index

You Need the Companion eBook

Your purchase of this book entitles you to buy the companion PDF-version eBook for only $10. Take the weightless companion with you anywhere.

We believe this Apress title will prove so indispensable that you'll want to carry it with you everywhere, which is why we are offering the companion eBook (in PDF format) for $10 to customers who purchase this book now. Convenient and fully searchable, the PDF version of any content-rich, page-heavy Apress book makes a valuable addition to your programming library. You can easily find and copy code—or perform examples by quickly toggling between instructions and the application. Even simultaneously tackling a donut, diet soda, and complex code becomes simplified with hands-free eBooks!

Once you purchase your book, getting the $10 companion eBook is simple:

❶ Visit **www.apress.com/promo/tendollars/**.

❷ Complete a basic registration form to receive a randomly generated question about this title.

❸ Answer the question correctly in 60 seconds, and you will receive a promotional code to redeem for the $10.00 eBook.

233 Spring Street, New York, NY 10013

Offer valid through 8/10.